The Complete Works of John Owen

The Complete Works of John Owen

The Complete Works
of John Owen

THE CHURCH

VOLUME 28

The Church, the Scriptures, and the Sacraments

John Owen

INTRODUCED AND EDITED BY
Andrew M. Leslie

GENERAL EDITORS
Lee Gatiss and Shawn D. Wright

WHEATON, ILLINOIS

The Church, the Scriptures, and the Sacraments

© 2024 by Crossway

Published by Crossway
          1300 Crescent Street
          Wheaton, Illinois 60187

Cover design: Jordan Singer

Cover image: Marble Paper Artist: Vanessa Reynoso, Marble Paper Studio

First printing 2024

Printed in China

Hardcover ISBN: 978-1-4335-6037-8
ePub ISBN: 978-1-4335-8639-2
PDF ISBN: 978-1-4335-8637-8

Library of Congress Cataloging-in-Publication Data

Names: Owen, John, 1616–1683, author. | Leslie, Andrew M., editor.
Title: The church, the scriptures, and the sacraments / John Owen ; introduced and edited by Andrew M. Leslie ; general editors, Lee Gatiss and Shawn D. Wright.
Description: Wheaton, Illinois : Crossway, 2024. | Series: The complete works of John Owen; volume 28 | Includes bibliographical references and indexes.
Identifiers: LCCN 2022055011 (print) | LCCN 2022055012 (ebook) | ISBN 9781433560378 (hardcover) | ISBN 9781433586378 (pdf) | ISBN 9781433586392 (epub)
Subjects: LCSH: Bible—Criticism, interpretation, etc. | Sacraments. | Church.
Classification: LCC BS511.3 .O87 2024 (print) | LCC BS511.3 (ebook) | DDC 220.6—dc23/eng/20230419
LC record available at https://lccn.loc.gov/2022055011
LC ebook record available at https://lccn.loc.gov/2022055012

Crossway is a publishing ministry of Good News Publishers.

RRD			33	32	31	30	29	28	27	26	25	24
15	14	13	12	11	10	9	8	7	6	5	4	3	2	1

Volume 28

Contents

Works Preface

JOHN OWEN (1616–1683) is one of the most significant, influential, and prolific theologians that England has ever produced. His work is of such a high caliber that it is no surprise to find it still in demand more than four centuries after his birth. As a son of the Church of England, a Puritan preacher, a statesman, a Reformed theologian and Bible commentator, and later a prominent Nonconformist and advocate of toleration, he is widely read and appreciated by Christians of different types all over the globe, not only for the profundity of his thinking but also for the depth of his spiritual insight.

Owen was born in the year that William Shakespeare died, and in terms of his public influence, he was a rising star in the 1640s and at the height of his power in the 1650s. As chaplain to Oliver Cromwell, dean of Christ Church, and vice-chancellor of Oxford University, he wielded a substantial degree of power and influence within the short-lived English republic. Yet he eventually found himself on the losing side of the epic struggles of the seventeenth century and was ousted from his position of national preeminence. The Act of Uniformity in 1662 effectively barred him from any role in the established church, yet it was in the wilderness of those turbulent post-Restoration years that he wrote many of his most momentous contributions to the world of theological literature, despite being burdened by opposition, persecution, family tragedies, and illness.

There was an abortive endeavor to publish a uniform edition of Owen's works in the early eighteenth century, but this progressed no further than a single folio volume in 1721. A century later (1826), Thomas Russell met with much more success when he produced a collection in twenty-one volumes. The appetite for Owen only grew; more than three hundred people had subscribed to the 1721 and 1826 editions of his works, but almost three thousand subscribed to the twenty-four-volume set produced by William H. Goold from 1850 onward. That collection, with Goold's learned introductions and notes, became the standard edition. It was given a new lease on life when the Banner of Truth Trust reprinted it several times beginning in 1965, though without some of Owen's Latin works, which had appeared in Goold's edition, or his massive Hebrews commentary, which Banner did eventually reprint in 1991. Goold corrected various errors in the original seventeenth- and eighteenth-century publications, some of which Owen himself had complained of, as well as certain grammatical errors. He thoroughly revised the punctuation, numeration of points, and Scripture references in Owen and presented him in a way acceptable to nineteenth-century readers without taking liberties with the text.

Since the mid-nineteenth century, and especially since the reprinting of Goold's edition in the mid-twentieth century, there has been a great flowering of interest in seventeenth-century Puritanism and Reformed theology. The recent profusion of scholarship in this area has resulted in a huge increase of attention given to Owen and his contribution to these movements. The time has therefore come to attempt another presentation of Owen's body of work for a new century. This new edition is more than a reprint of earlier collections of Owen's writings. As useful as those have been to us and many others, they fail to meet the needs of modern readers who are often familiar with neither the theological context nor the syntax and rhetorical style of seventeenth-century English divinity.

For that reason, we have returned again to the original editions of Owen's texts to ensure the accuracy of their presentation here but have conformed the spelling to modern American standards, modernized older verb endings, reduced the use of italics where they do not clarify meaning, updated some hyphenation forms, modernized capitalization both for select terms in the text and for titles of Owen's works, refreshed the typesetting, set lengthy quotations in block format, and both checked and added Scripture references in a consistent format where necessary. Owen's quotations of others, however, including the various editions of the Bible he used or translated, are kept as they appear in his original. His marginal notes and footnotes have been clearly marked in footnotes as his (with "—Owen" appearing at the end of his content) to distinguish them from editorial comments. Foreign languages such as Greek, Hebrew, and Latin (which Owen knew and used extensively) have been translated into modern English, with the original languages retained in footnotes for scholarly reference (also followed by "—Owen"). If Goold omitted parts of the original text in his edition, we have restored them to their rightful place. Additionally, we have attempted to regularize the numbering system Owen employed, which was often imprecise and inconsistent; our order is 1, (1), [1], {1}, and 1st. We have also included various features to aid readers' comprehension of Owen's writings, including extensive introductions and outlines by established scholars in the field today, new paragraph breaks marked by a pilcrow (¶), chapter titles and appropriate headings (either entirely new or adapted from Goold), and explanatory footnotes that define archaic or obscure words and point out scriptural and other allusions in the text. When a contents page was not included in the original publication, we have provided one. On the rare occasions when we have added words to the text for readability, we have clearly marked them using square brackets. Having a team of experts involved, along with the benefit of modern online database technology, has also enabled us to make the prodigious effort to identify sources and citations in Owen that Russell and Goold deliberately avoided or were unable to locate for their editions.

Owen did not use only one English translation of the Bible. At various times, he employed the Great Bible, the Geneva Bible, or the Authorized Version (KJV), as well as his own paraphrases or translations from the original languages. We have not sought to harmonize his biblical quotations to any single version. Similarly, we have left his Hebrew and Greek quotations exactly as he recorded them, including the unpointed Hebrew text. When it appears that he has misspelled the Hebrew or Greek, we have acknowledged that in a footnote with reference to either *Biblia Hebraica Stuttgartensia* or *Novum Testamentum Graece.*

This new edition presents fresh translations of Owen's works that were originally published in Latin, such as his Θεολογούμενα Παντοδαπά (1661) and *A Dissertation on Divine Justice* (which Goold published in an amended eighteenth-century translation). It also includes certain shorter works that have never before been collected in one place, such as Owen's prefaces to other people's works and many of his letters, with an extensive index to the whole set.

Our hope and prayer in presenting this new edition of John Owen's complete works is that it will equip and enable new generations of readers to appreciate the spiritual insights he accumulated over the course of his remarkable life. Those with a merely historical interest will find here a testimony to the exceptional labors of one extraordinary figure from a tumultuous age, in a modern and usable critical edition. Those who seek to learn from Owen about the God he worshiped and served will, we trust, find even greater riches in his doctrine of salvation, his passion for evangelism and missions, his Christ-centered vision of all reality, his realistic pursuit of holiness, his belief that theology matters, his concern for right worship and religious freedom, and his careful exegetical engagement with the text of God's word. We echo the words of the apostle Paul that Owen inscribed on the title page of his book Χριστολογία (1679), "I count all things but loss for the excellency of the knowledge of Christ Jesus my Lord, for whom I have suffered the loss of all things, and do count them but dung that I may win Christ" (Phil. 3:8).

Lee Gatiss
CAMBRIDGE, ENGLAND

Shawn D. Wright
LOUISVILLE, KENTUCKY, UNITED STATES

Editor's Introduction

Andrew M. Leslie

GENERAL COMMENTS ON THE ORIGIN OF
THE CONTENTS IN THIS PRESENT VOLUME

The two major treatises in this volume, *Of the Divine Original, with the Authority, Self-Evidencing Power, and Light of the Scriptures* and *Of the Integrity and Purity of the Hebrew and Greek Text of the Scripture*, were two of three treatises by Owen on Holy Scripture that were published in 1659. While *Of the Divine Original* and *Of the Integrity* were published together with a single "Dedicatory Epistle,"[1] the third treatise was published separately in Latin, *Pro Sacris Scripturis adversus Huius Temporis Fanaticos Exercitationes Apologeticae Quatuor.*[2]

The remaining content of the present volume consists largely of posthumous collections of sermons that were arranged and published according to a particular theme, as well as several short letters and tracts. As Crawford Gribben notes, the 1721, 1756, and 1760 collections of sermons reproduce material that was initially transcribed in shorthand by John Hartopp and then expanded into a longhand form that is recorded in his notebooks.[3] The

---

1 John Owen, *Of the Divine Originall, Authority, Self-Evidencing Light, and Power of the Scriptures. With an Answer to That Enquiry, How We Know the Scriptures to Be the Word of God. Also a Vindication of the Purity and Integrity of the Hebrew and Greek Texts of the Old and New Testament; in Some Considerations on the Prolegomena, and Appendix to the Late "Biblia Polyglotta"* (London: Henry Hall for Tho: Robinson, 1659). Note that the title of the published collection as a whole differs slightly from the title of each treatise itself, as drawn from each individual title page within the collection.

2 In *Complete Works of John Owen*, vol. 38.

3 John Owen, *A Complete Collection of the Sermons of the Reverend and Learned John Owen, D.D. Formerly Published: With an Addition of Many Others Never before Printed. Also Several Valuable Tracts, Now First Published from Manuscripts: And Some Others, Which Were Very Scarce.*

Hartopp family was connected to Owen via his friend Charles Fleetwood and Fleetwood's third wife, Mary Hartopp. John Hartopp was Mary's son from her first marriage, and together they formed part of Owen's post-Restoration congregation that met initially in Fleetwood's home.[4] According to Gribben, the material contained in Hartopp's extant notebooks is "detailed and convincing" in its attempt to represent Owen accurately and honest about its limitations where need be.[5]

Two tracts in the present volume, *An Answer unto Two Questions* with its sequel, *Twelve Arguments, against Any Conformity of Members of Separate Churches, to the National Church,* were published by William and Joseph Marshall in 1720.[6] According to the "Booksellers Advertisement" of the two-volume collection in which these two tracts are contained, the collection consisted of material that had been under the possession of the Marshalls and was reprinted for posterity because it had become "very scarce and out of print."[7] Whatever points of correspondence we can identify with Owen's output published within his own lifetime, a question mark is likely to remain over the provenance of some of this posthumous material, despite protestations to the contrary by the respective publishers.

INTRODUCTION TO *OF THE DIVINE ORIGINAL* (1659)

Gribben overviews the historical circumstances that led Owen to turn his hand to the subject of biblical authority, not least of which was the gradual appearance of Brian Walton's monumental *Biblia sacra polyglotta* from 1653,

---

To Which Are Added His Latin Orations, Whilst Vicechancellor of Oxford, Taken from His Own Copies. And to the Whole Are Prefix'd Memoirs of His Life: Some Letters Written by Him upon Special Occasions: And His Funeral Sermon, Preach'd by Mr. David Clarkson (London: John Clark, 1721); John Owen, *Thirteen Sermons Preached on Various Occasions. By the Reverend and Learned John Owen, D.D. Of the Last Age. Never before Printed* (London: For J. Buckland, fold by E. Dilly, 1756); John Owen, *Twenty-Five Discourses Suitable to the Lord's Supper, Delivered Just before the Administration of That Sacred Ordinance* (London: J. Buckland, 1760).

4 Crawford Gribben, *John Owen and English Puritanism: Experiences of Defeat* (Oxford: Oxford University Press, 2016), 227.

5 Gribben, *John Owen and English Puritanism,* 239.

6 John Owen, *Seventeen Sermons Preach'd by the Reverend Dr. John Owen: With the Dedications at Large. Together with the Doctor's Life. In Two Volumes* (London: for William and Joseph Marshall, 1720), 2:377–400. Evidently, an identical version of the tracts was published together separately. See John Owen, *An Answer unto Two Questions: By the Late Judicious John Owen, D.D. With Twelve Arguments, against Any Conformity to Worship, Not of Divine Institution* (London: Joseph Marshall, 1720).

7 Owen, *Seventeen Sermons* (1720), I:*1 (page numbers with an asterisk refer to unnumbered pages in the original).

and especially the publication of its *Prolegomena* and *Appendix* in 1657.[8] But while Owen makes the odd oblique reference to the London Polyglot Bible in *Of the Divine Original*, there is every reason to believe the decision to publish both treatises together with a single "Dedicatory Epistle" was an alteration to an earlier intention to publish *Of the Divine Original* separately. Indeed, Owen begins to give focused attention to Walton's production only in the "Dedicatory Epistle" and *Of the Integrity*.

By comparison to *Of the Integrity*, Owen's tone in *Of the Divine Original* is far more irenic and constructive. Certainly, there is the occasional hint at the contextual forces that will become much more explicit in its sequel. The most notable of these is taken up in chapter 1, where Owen engages with the Salmurian theologian Louis Cappel (1585–1658) and his controversial opinions regarding emendations to the original Hebrew text of the Old Testament. As we shall see further below in this introduction, Owen is undoubtedly keen to defend the integrity of the extant original copies of Scripture, as a direct corollary of God's ongoing providential care for his church.[9] Aside from this, however, Owen's immediate polemical concerns in *Of the Divine Original* are rather muted. As Gribben mentions, it is possible that he is troubled by the proliferation of poor and inadequate translations that had been published of late, and the doubts this might sow in a believer's mind about the authority and reliability of Scripture.[10] Indeed, the major constructive theme in *Of the Divine Original* is Scripture's self-authentication, or the way in which it continues to manifest its divine authority to the faithful. Moreover, there are certainly suggestions that Owen is particularly alarmed by the way the Catholics had capitalized on any doubts about the authority of Scripture. He explicitly responds to the claim that Scripture's authority as the word of God is restricted to itself but does not extend to us (*quoad nos*), therein requiring the authentication of the Roman magisterium and its now officially authorized Vulgate translation. Owen's own recognizably Protestant account of Scripture's self-authentication, with its customary appeal to the internal work of the Spirit, betrays a marked sensitivity to the typical Catholic charges against it.[11] Appeals to the Spirit had become especially fraught with the rise of sectarianism during the Interregnum.

---

8   Brian Walton, *Biblia sacra polyglotta*, 6 vols. (London: Thomas Roycroft, 1653–1657). The *Prolegomena* and *Appendix* are in vols. 1 and 6, respectively, of that collection. See Gribben, *John Owen and English Puritanism*, 182–87.

9   Owen takes up this concern in *Of the Divine Original*, chap. 1.

10 Gribben, *John Owen and English Puritanism*, 182–87.

11 For a classic statement of this appeal, see John Calvin, *Institutes of the Christian Religion*, 2 vols., ed. John T. McNeill, trans. Ford Lewis Battles (Philadelphia: Westminster, 1960), 1.1.7.

In 1654, while vice-chancellor of Oxford University, Owen famously expelled two Quaker prophets for their displays of religious fanaticism. He was obviously sufficiently haunted by this experience over the immediately subsequent years that he explicitly set out to refute their notorious appeals to the Spirit's "inner light" in the third treatise of 1658, *Pro Sacris Scripturis*.[12] That Owen was looking over his shoulder in expectation that any Protestant reliance on the Spirit's internal testimony would be tarred with the brush of "vain enthusiasm" is abundantly clear throughout this treatise, as Gribben readily observes.[13]

There are a couple of features in *Of the Divine Original* that are worthy of our attention. The first is its defense of the so-called plenary inspiration of Scripture. A much more developed and sophisticated account of inspiration may be found in Owen's later *Πνευματολογια: Or, A Discourse concerning the Holy Spirit* of 1674;[14] nonetheless an outline of it is already evident in *Of the Divine Original*, where his position on the matter unfolds from what he perceives to be a straightforward exposition of 1 Peter 1:10–12 and various related claims in the New Testament such as Hebrews 1:1 and 2 Timothy 3:16. In particular, where God is said to have spoken "in the prophets" (ἐν τοῖς προφήταις) of old (Heb. 1:1), Owen draws two closely related inferences. The first is that every detail of what they recorded was revealed to them immediately by God so that no detail was left to their independent rational formulation or memory of events. A second inference follows: "They were not themselves enabled by any habitual light, knowledge or conviction of truth, to declare his mind and will, but only acted, as they were immediately moved by him."[15] It is true that Owen presents here a slightly stricter account of inspiration than some of his Protestant brethren.[16] As Richard Muller points out, some early modern Reformed theologians were willing to concede that no special revelation of the Spirit was necessary for matters a writer already knew or could discover from other sources, even if the Spirit still superintended and inspired the actual process of writing to prevent the possibility of error creeping into the text.[17]

---

12 See *Complete Works of John Owen*, vol. 38.

13 Gribben, *John Owen and English Puritanism*, 194.

14 See *Complete Works of John Owen*, vols. 5–6.

15 Owen, *Of the Divine Original*, chap. 1.

16 Such a stance was by no means unique. Cf., e.g., the similar statement of the early modern Lutheran Johann Quenstedt in *Theologia didactico-polemica* (Leipzig: Fritsch, 1715), pt. 1, chap. 4, sec. 2, q. 3 (I cc.100–101). Here and in the following, I am repeating my observations in Andrew M. Leslie, *The Light of Grace: John Owen on the Authority of Scripture and Christian Faith* (Göttingen: Vandenhoeck & Ruprecht, 2015), 209–12.

17 E.g., John Weemse, *Exercitations Divine: Containing Diverse Questions and Solutions for the Right Understanding of the Scriptures* (London: T. Cotes, 1632), 72–73. Cf., Richard A. Muller,

In making the stronger affirmation, Owen may well have been conscious of the way certain Catholic polemicists had adopted the looser approach with undesirable consequences.[18] Moreover, the divine inspiration of the writer did not stop with a mental illumination of content, Owen insists, but extended as far as the words chosen, right down to the last "tittle," so as to ensure that the original autograph of Scripture was infallible and "entirely" from God. Owen should not be caricatured as advancing a highly mechanistic account of inspiration that crudely bypasses the rational processes of the writer. He insists the writers not only made a "diligent inquiry" into what they received (1 Pet. 1:10) but also consciously concurred with the words that were chosen.[19] Once again, it is certainly true that Owen's commitment to the divine illumination of particular words is stronger than some,[20] but his general account stands in continuity with a broad doctrine of prophetic and biblical inspiration, which, as Muller notes, is ubiquitous in earlier medieval thought and passes over "virtually untouched by revision, into the sixteenth and seventeenth centuries."[21] In other words, Owen's account of inspiration is unlikely to have been particularly controversial in his day.

What was more controversial, at least from a Catholic perspective, was the appeal to the Spirit's internal testimony as the means by which the divine authority of Scripture authenticates itself to a believer. Having dismantled the Catholic reliance on ecclesiastical authority and replaced it with an exclusive dependence on the supremacy of Scripture, Protestants quickly found themselves charged with undermining religious certainty and promoting a dangerous individualism in biblical interpretation that had opened the floodgates to the sort of religious fanaticism that was beginning to tear

---

Post-Reformation Reformed Dogmatics: The Rise and Development of Reformed Orthodoxy, ca. 1520 to ca. 1725, 4 vols. (Grand Rapids, MI: Baker Academic, 2003), 2:248–50; noting Johannes Cocceius, *Opera omnia theologica, exegetica, didactica, polemica, philologica; divisa in decem volumina*, 3rd ed. (Amsterdam: P and J Blaev, 1701), 7:146a; Bénédict Pictet, *Theologia Christiana* (Edinburgh: T. Inkersley, 1820), 1.8.3 (24).

18 Robert Bellarmine (1542–1621) uses the argument that a writer's historical recollection may not be inspired (even if the actual writing of their thoughts was) to defend the canonical status of 2 Maccabees, where the author explicitly seeks a "pardon" (*veniam*) for any error in his recollection of events (2 Macc. 15:39 [38]). See Robert Bellarmine, *Opera omnia*, 6 vols. (Naples: Josephum Giuliano, 1856–1862), 1:47a–b.

19 Owen, *Of the Divine Original*, chap. 1.

20 E.g., as Muller notes, the Renaissance Spanish exegete Alfonso Tostatus (ca. 1410–1455) would argue that it was enough to insist the Spirit preserves the writer from error without having to claim that the Spirit actively furnishes the writer with particular words. See Alfonso Tostatus, *Opera omnia*, 27 vols. (Venetiis: ex Typographica Balleoniana, 1728), 20:411b. Cf., 18:3a; Muller, *Post-Reformation Reformed Dogmatics*, 2:46–47.

21 Muller, *Post-Reformation Reformed Dogmatics*, 2:61.

Europe apart. In this context, the standard Protestant appeal to the internal testimony of the Spirit as the guarantor of biblical authority only made matters worse—so much so that by the second half of the seventeenth century, it was no longer considered doctrinally viable, even among some Protestants.[22]

We have already noted Owen's alertness to a Catholic method of resolving the dilemma of religious certainty that distinguishes between Scripture's authority in itself as the word of God and its authentication "in respect of us" (*quoad nos*) through the testimony of the church.[23] This sort of distinction surfaced in the polemics between Catholics and Protestants in the latter half of the sixteenth century. As someone like Thomas Stapleton (1535–1598) maintained, the appeal to the public testimony of the church was considered the only viable way of sidestepping the specter of "spiritualism" or "enthusiasm," or even some Satanic delusion, which would accompany a "private" spiritual testimony to biblical authority.[24] In responding to this, Protestants were increasingly inclined to accentuate a public dimension to this spiritual testimony through objective evidence or marks that could be formulated into an argument supporting the Bible's authority as the inspired word of God. That way, an ongoing orthodox conviction of the Spirit's necessary internal work at the foundation of Christian faith could be framed in a way that explicitly avoided any suggestion that it amounted to an afflatus or private word from God to every individual believer. For however much the Spirit communicates the power and authority of God through Scripture to a believer, he does so in a way that radiates the objective and rational credibility of these marks.[25]

By the time Owen came to write his mature exposition of biblical authority, *The Reason of Faith, or An Answer unto That Enquiry, Wherefore We Believe*

---

22 For a comprehensive account of the initial polemical developments in the sixteenth century, see Susan E. Schreiner, *Are You Alone Wise? The Search for Certainty in the Early Modern Era* (Oxford: Oxford University Press, 2011). I have discussed some of the seventeenth-century developments in Andrew M. Leslie, "The Reformation a Century Later: Did the Reformation Get Lost Two Generations Later?," in *Celebrating the Reformation: Its Legacy and Continuing Relevance*, ed. Mark D. Thompson, Colin Bale, and Edward Loane (London: Apollos, 2017), 286–97.

23 Owen, *Of the Divine Original*, chap. 1.

24 Thomas Stapleton, *Principiorum fidei doctrinalium demonstratio methodica* (Paris: Michaelis Sonnius, 1579), 336; cf., 329–57.

25 For instance, in his exchange with Stapleton and Bellarmine, the Elizabethan divine William Whitaker would readily acknowledge that the arguments or evidences are incapable of inducing faith on their own, but when the Holy Spirit's internal testimony is "added" to them, the Spirit's testimony "fills our minds with a wonderful plenitude of assurance, confirms them [the arguments], and causes us most gladly to embrace the Scriptures, giving force to the preceding arguments." William Whitaker, *A Disputation on Holy Scripture: Against the Papists, Especially Bellarmine and Stapleton*, trans. William Fitzgerald (Cambridge: University Press, 1849), 295.

the Scripture to Be the Word of God in 1677, Protestant convictions about the necessity of the Spirit's internal work had begun to collapse. And here he would explicitly lock horns with some of his post-Restoration contemporaries who had gone as far as to rely almost entirely on the rational credibility of various arguments to defend the authority of Scripture. Owen was resolutely orthodox on this score and believed that without the Spirit's internal work at the foundation of Christian faith, all is lost. Yet *The Reason of Faith* offers what is easily one of the most sophisticated early modern Reformed defenses of the Bible's self-authenticating divine authority, responding to the anxieties of his contemporaries without in any way capitulating to a destructive rationalism.

This polemical context is not yet on the horizon in *Of the Divine Original*; nonetheless, many of the dogmatic foundations for Owen's later response certainly are. Like his orthodox Reformed brethren, Owen sought to articulate the spiritual authority of Scripture in a way that brought together the necessary internal or subjective work within a believer's faculties and its objective or public foundations in Scripture itself. Whatever it is that needs to happen within a believer in bringing them to faith in the authority of Scripture, it is only something the Spirit accomplishes "in and by" Scripture itself. On this score, Owen distinguished between the "subjective" and "objective" "testimony" of the Spirit. The objective testimony is what the Spirit communicates to a believer through Scripture itself. What is most distinctive about Owen's way of framing this objective testimony, however, is the way he disentangles from it any of the traditional marks or rational arguments. The Protestant habit of incorporating the traditional arguments into the Spirit's testimony, evident from as early on as William Whitaker's engagement with Stapleton and Robert Bellarmine, has been met with equivocal reception in secondary literature. Some regard it as a credible, thoroughly orthodox attempt to stave off any excessively fideistic subjectivism within confessional Protestantism, while others consider it to be an early capitulation, however partial, to a rationalizing trajectory that would become prominent within Protestantism by the eighteenth century.[26] Without delving into this debate here, at the very least it suggests a certain lack of dogmatic clarity in the later development, something that Owen successfully managed to circumvent.

---

26 For the former assessment see, e.g., Jeffrey Mallinson, *Faith, Reason, and Revelation in Theodore Beza, 1519–1605* (Oxford: Oxford University Press, 2003); for the latter, see, e.g., Henk van den Belt, *The Authority of Scripture in Reformed Theology* (Leiden: Brill, 2008). A more exaggerated form of the latter appraisal is found in Jack B. Rogers and Donald K. McKim, *The Authority and Interpretation of the Bible: An Historical Approach* (San Francisco: Harper and Row, 1979).

Owen agrees with his brethren that the traditional "artificial" arguments defending the authority of Scripture have a place, but they are subordinate to and, importantly, distinct from the objective and subjective testimony of the Spirit. Indeed, he explicitly walls them off from his discussion of the Spirit's testimony and mentions only those he considers credible as an afterword in the final chapter of the treatise (even here, Owen is doubtful that some are of much use, such as the traditional appeal to miracles).[27]

The two decisive dimensions of the Spirit's role in mediating the authority of Scripture to a believer are what Owen identifies as a communication of divine "light" and "power." These dimensions are "the formal reason of our faith," or the reason "why and wherefore we do receive and believe the Scripture to be the word of God."[28] In *Of the Divine Original*, Owen calls them "innate arguments" insofar as they are mediated through what the Spirit has inspired within the text of Scripture. But importantly, they are distinct from other "innate" arguments that have traditionally been used apologetically, like those "artificial arguments" he mentions in chapter 6, such as the nature of the doctrines contained in Scripture or Scripture's internal harmony and coherence. Rather, his account of Scripture's self-evidencing light and power gives them a unique theological status with a distinctly metaphysical hue that sets them apart from the other artificial, innate arguments.

In describing Scripture's self-evidencing light, he situates it within a more general context of what he calls "spiritual, moral, intellectual light, with all its mediums," a light that ultimately emanates from its origin in God himself through what he has communicated in all his external works. And it is by this light that God is "known." At a metaphysical level, Owen is clearly assuming the rudiments of the typical late medieval appropriation of the peripatetic cognitive tradition.[29] Here intellectual light is communicated from an object through a transparent medium via a multiplication of its form, or an intelligible species that would result in understanding of the object. Through the impression of an intelligible species of the object, the knower's mind is said to be formally "adequated" or conformed to the known object. Accordingly, with this metaphysical assumption in place, Owen is making the theological claim that God has communicated "self-evidencing" light, or his own formal likeness in all his external works (obviously in an accommodated

---

27 Owen evinces a certain skepticism toward the usefulness of miracles as a testimony at various points. E.g., *Of the Divine Original*, chaps. 3, 5.

28 Owen, *Of the Divine Original*, chap. 4.

29 For an extended summary of Owen's appropriation of this tradition, see Leslie, *Light of Grace*, 257–64.

or analogical fashion), thereby enabling him to be known by the human knower. And within God's economy, Scripture has a special place among all his works, having been inspired to be the unique medium for communicating the divine "light of the [glorious] gospel of Christ," words of the apostle Paul in 2 Corinthians that Owen quotes so frequently throughout his corpus, indicating that he clearly cherishes their profound significance (2 Cor. 4:4). Of course, as Paul indicates in this passage of his letter, and as Owen is quick to add, Scripture might well contain an objective impression of divine light, but sinners are naturally blind to it and therefore unable to recognize it as such. "Light is not eyes," he says, and cannot itself "remove the defect of the visive faculty." But in the case of a spiritually regenerated believer, this light is apprehended as "nothing but the beaming of the majesty, truth, holiness, and authority of God, given unto it, and left upon it, by its author the Holy Ghost." In other words, a believer recognizes the divine authority of Scripture through its self-evidencing reflection of divine light, with its capacity to dive "into the consciences of men, into all the secret recesses of their hearts" (alluding to Heb. 4:12–13).[30]

The question this begs about the authority of Scripture over the resistance of unbelief is resolved by the second dimension of Scripture's self-evidencing authority—namely, its "power." Here Owen cites a plethora of New Testament texts that attest to the sovereign power of God's word, something that is accompanied with "all manner of assurance and full persuasion of itself" (with specific allusions to 1 Cor. 2:4 and 1 Thess. 1:5). Owen is clear that this power is not somehow enclosed within Scripture itself but is always relative to God's creatures as an instrument of his authority. Again, alluding to texts such as John 6:68–69, Acts 20:32, 1 Corinthians 6:15, 15:57, Colossians 1:6, 2 Timothy 3:15, Hebrews 4:12, James 1:21, and so on, it is a power that is capable of conquering rebellion and bringing salvation, "causing men of all sorts, in all times and places, so to fall down before its divine authority, as immediately to renounce all that was dear to them in the world, and to undergo whatever was dreadful, terrible and destructive to nature in all its dearest concernments."[31]

Owen summarizes his discussion of these two "innate," "self-evidencing" "arguments" by concluding that the Scriptures "have that glory of light and power accompanying of them, as wholly distinguishes them by infallible signs and evidences from all words and writings not divine, conveying their

---

30 Owen, *Of the Divine Original*, chap. 4.
31 Owen, *Of the Divine Original*, chap. 4.

truth and power, into the souls and consciences of men, with an infallible certainty."[32] While he does not arrive at the distinction between the "objective" and "subjective" dimensions of the Spirit's "testimony" until chapter 5, it is clear that these two innate self-evidencing arguments exactly correspond to the "testimony of the Spirit, that respects the object, or the word itself."[33] Against Roman Catholic complaints about the Protestant appeal to the Spirit's self-authentication of Scripture, Owen will simply respond that the Spirit's authentication of Scripture is always "in and by" Scripture itself, and therefore thoroughly "public" in nature: "it is the public testimony of the Holy Ghost given unto all, of the word, by and in the word, and its own divine light, efficacy, and power."[34]

In *Of the Divine Original*, Owen has therefore managed to furnish a theological account of Scripture's authority that not only vindicates it as the sole, public, and objective medium of divine authority but also is uncompromisingly supernatural and spiritual in its character. The genius of his argument is the way he situates Scripture within the broader divine economy, in which every created element to varying degrees objectively communicates the truth and authority of God through a kind of analogical participation. At the same time, the uniqueness of Scripture among all God's works, and its distinctive role in the supernatural or salvific economy, remains intact in Owen's account. For now, at least, Scripture's divine authority is properly recognized only among the regenerate, or among those who actually encounter its saving power. Indeed, as an index of Scripture's peculiar role within the redemptive economy, Owen maintains there is still a necessary "subjective" dimension to the Spirit's attestation of its authority, a dimension that is clearly bound up with a believer's spiritual regeneration. First, "illumination," or an effectual communication of Scripture's saving light to overcome our natural, sinful blindness, is required. Second, the Spirit communicates an "effectual persuasion" of the mind, through the provision of spiritual wisdom and understanding, and renewed sensibility to spiritual things (alluding to Heb. 5:14). None of this amounts to some afflatus or "internal word." In a sense,

32 Owen, *Of the Divine Original*, chap. 4.
33 Owen, *Of the Divine Original*, chap. 5. As he explains, "The Holy Ghost speaking in and by the word, imparting to it virtue, power, efficacy, majesty and authority, affords us the witness, that our faith is resolved unto. And thus whereas there are but two heads, whereunto all grounds of assent do belong, namely authority of testimony, and the self-evidence of truth, they do here both concur in one. In the same word we have both the authority of the testimony of the Spirit, and the self-evidence of the truth spoken by him; yea so, that both these are materially one and the same, though distinguished in their formal conceptions."
34 Owen, *Of the Divine Original*, chap. 5.

it should be understood as the impact of the powerful word itself within the subjective domain of the individual's soul, providing the newly regenerate believer with the capacity to discern the divine power and wisdom spiritually at work "in and by" the word itself.

Thematic Outline

The primary question Owen proposes to address in *Of the Divine Original* is "how we may know assuredly the Scripture to be the word of God," which frames the bulk of the treatise proceeding from where he first poses it at the beginning of chapter 2.

Chapter 1 contains some preliminary observations regarding the divine inspiration of the Old and New Testaments, which he regards as foundational to the constructive discussion that will follow. He begins this by drawing attention to biblical texts that attest to the Holy Spirit's inspiration of Old Testament prophets (e.g., Heb. 1:1; 1 Pet. 1:10–11), followed by the inspiration of the written word (2 Pet. 1:20–21; 2 Tim. 3:16).[35] Something Owen particularly wishes to infer from these scriptural claims is that the original biblical autographs had to have been providentially superintended by the Spirit right down to the very "tittle," not just in their doctrinal content but even in their precise verbal form.[36] In his later treatise, Πνευματολογια (1674),[37] Owen discusses the manner of prophetic inspiration more comprehensively. Here he is simply content to insist that however much the prophet's "mind and understanding were used in the choice of words," the words they chose were nonetheless "not their own, but immediately supplied unto them [. . .] from God himself."[38] The significance of this claim extends to not only the inspiration of the original autographs but also the providential preservation of their substance in subsequent copies and translations. Herein lies the reason for Owen's acute concern regarding any critical emendation of the copies, which became a flashpoint within English Protestantism when Walton's London Polyglot began to appear in 1653. Owen flags his concerns about this practice here, and he will take them up more fully in *Of the Integrity*.[39] Having spoken to these issues, he concludes this chapter with a brief statement extending the same principle of divine inspiration to the New as well as Old Testaments.

35 Owen, *Of the Divine Original*, chap. 1.
36 Owen, *Of the Divine Original*, chap. 1.
37 *Complete Works of John Owen*, vols. 5–6.
38 Owen, *Of the Divine Original*, chap. 1.
39 Owen, *Of the Divine Original*, chap. 1.

With this preliminary claim in place, the question that naturally ensues is the basis upon which we can have confidence in its veracity—namely, that the Scriptures are truly the inspired word of God. Chapter 2 begins by outlining this question and stating the answer in summary form. The ultimate foundation or "formal reason" for confidence in the divine origin of Scripture, Owen believes, is no less than the authority of God himself. But a distinctive feature of his approach to this question is his sensitivity to the way this authority is mediated and evidenced directly to a believer through Scripture itself, hence his objection to the typical Catholic claim that Scripture's authority is self-contained in a way that it has no authority *quoad nos*, "in respect of us."[40]

Having outlined his answer in summary form, he proceeds to confirm it in the remainder of the treatise under three headings that stretch across the subsequent chapters.[41]

The first of these concludes chapter 2, where Owen defends the claim that each mode of divine revelation—his external "works," the internal "light of nature," and especially the "word"—each carry within them sufficient evidence to demonstrate their divine origin.[42]

In chapters 3–5, Owen outlines his second point, which drills down on the precise manner in which that evidence is conveyed in the scriptural word. Chapter 3 begins by observing that there are in general two kinds of arguments or testimonies that confirm the veracity of a thing: "inartificial" and "artificial." "Inartificial" arguments are immediately conveyed by the thing itself, whereas "artificial" arguments are rational inferences we may legitimately draw about the thing, to corroborate any inartificial testimony it makes about itself. When it comes to Scripture, Owen is particularly concerned with the inartificial testimony it communicates to authenticate its divine origin, and this is the subject of his second major point. People of faith not only are obliged to stand by this testimony, he says, but also will find rest in it alone against the objection of others. By contrast, artificial arguments—as true and valuable as they may be—have the more limited role of responding rationally to opponents of Scripture but do not form the foundation of a believer's faith.[43]

Owen proceeds by referring to two dimensions of an inartificial testimony to Scripture's divine origin. There is its own self-declaration as something that is θεόπνευστος or "divinely inspired" (2 Tim. 3:16), which is also accompanied

---

40 Owen, *Of the Divine Original*, chap. 2.
41 Owen, *Of the Divine Original*, chap. 2.
42 Owen, *Of the Divine Original*, chap. 2.
43 Owen, *Of the Divine Original*, chap. 3.

by evidence "ingrafted" within or "innate" to Scripture itself. As he explains at chapter 3, sections 9–11, God does not make any self-declaration of his authority that must be received upon threat of eternal damnation without providing "infallible tokens" (τεκμήρια) or a communication of "divine power" (θεῖον) to accompany and validate the declaration (cf. Jer. 23:29). By the "infallible tokens," Owen does not intend any miracles that might have accompanied the delivery of the divine word, which do not have the capacity to induce Christian faith, he insists.[44] Rather, he has in mind the kind of evidence "ingrafted" within Scripture itself, which he further outlines in chapter 4. This dimension of Scripture's inartificial testimony is of particular interest and concern to Owen, as it is by this evidence that the very authority of God is conveyed to provide the "formal reason of our faith." He breaks this ingrafted and innate evidence up into two categories—namely, God's very "light" and "power" that he communicates through Scripture as the basis of its authentication.[45]

In chapter 5, Owen seeks to clarify how this inartificial testimony relates to what is commonly referred to as the "testimony of the Spirit" regarding Scripture's divine authority. Here it is apparent that Owen thinks this inartificial self-testimony makes up the "objective" or "public" dimension of the Spirit's testimony "in and by" Scripture itself.[46] Against the typical accusation that any talk of the Spirit's testimony amounts to an appeal to some private afflatus, Owen seeks to differentiate the "subjective" or internal work of the Spirit in restoring the sinner's faculties from the external or public testimony within Scripture itself. However necessary the subjective dimension is to grasping the authority of Scripture, a Christian's faith in its divine origin is grounded exclusively in the public dimension of the testimony. Finally, he draws his extended discussion of this point to a close by highlighting the folly of grounding the authority of Scripture in tradition and miracles, concluding that it is simply inconceivable that God would fail to self-authenticate his word, let alone make its authenticity depend on human judgment.[47]

In chapter 6, Owen turns to his third confirmation of the claim by briefly outlining some "artificial" arguments or testimonies. Though falling short

---

44 Owen, *Of the Divine Original*, chap. 3.

45 Owen, *Of the Divine Original*, chap. 4.

46 Owen, *Of the Divine Original*, chap. 5. He writes, "And thus whereas there are but two heads, whereunto all grounds of assent do belong, namely, authority of testimony and the self-evidence of truth, they do here both concur in one. In the same word we have both the authority of the testimony of the Spirit and the self-evidence of the truth spoken by him; yea so, that both these are materially one and the same, though distinguished in their formal conceptions."

47 Owen, *Of the Divine Original*, chap. 5.

of inducing Christian faith, they are nonetheless of "great use," capable of convincing to the level of "undeniable probability," and prevailing "irresistibly on the understanding of unprejudiced men." Without intending to provide a comprehensive list, he expands on two he finds particularly persuasive— namely, the character of various doctrines in Scripture (referring to the atonement, worship, and the Trinity) and Scripture's overall design. At the beginning of chapter 3, Owen suggested that these arguments may be used against those who oppose the authority of Scripture, and here at the end of chapter 6 he adds that they may be of use in supporting a believer "in trials and temptations, and the like seasons of difficulty."[48]

INTRODUCTION TO *OF THE INTEGRITY* (1659)

In the opening paragraph of *Of the Integrity*, Owen indicates that he set out to write this treatise upon receipt of the recently published *Prolegomena* and *Appendix* to Walton's London Polyglot. As we noted earlier, Owen quite likely delayed the publication of *Of the Divine Original* until he had completed his response to Walton in *Of the Integrity*. Alarmed by what he now saw in Walton's *Prolegomena* and *Appendix*, Owen feared they rendered his earlier attempt at defending the integrity of the original biblical autographs somewhat incomplete.[49] *Of the Integrity* is an attempt to settle the score with a detailed response to what he considers the most problematic aspects of Walton's work.

One chief concern stands out among the "sundry principles" in the *Prolegomena* that Owen regards as "prejudicial to the truth." Fundamentally, it is the assumption that the extant Hebrew and Greek versions of the Old and New Testaments do not exactly correspond to the inspired original autographs, something that Walton believes licenses careful emendation of the extant texts through comparison with variant readings in other ancient translations. So deleterious is this assumption that Owen considers it to be "the foundation of Mohammedanism, [. . .] the chiefest and principal prop of

---

48 Owen, *Of the Divine Original*, chap. 6.

49 "Afterward, considering what I had written, about the providence of God in the preservation of the original copies of the Scripture in the foregoing discourse, fearing least from that great appearance of variations in the original copies, and those of all the translations published with so great care and diligence, there might some unconquerable objections against the truth of what I had asserted, be educed; I judged it necessary to stop the progress of those thoughts, until I could get time to look through the *Appendix*, and the various lections in that great volume exhibited unto us, with the grounds and reasons of them in the *Prolegomena*." Owen, *Of the Integrity*, chap. 1.

popery, the only pretense of fanatical antiscripturists, and the root of much hidden atheism in the world."[50]

The magnitude of Owen's worry requires some appreciation of the wider context. In the "Dedicatory Epistle" Owen refers to the gradual evolution of a controversy between Protestants and Catholics concerning the authenticity of the Hebrew Old Testament text that came to a head in the first half of the seventeenth century, culminating in the publication of the "Paris Polyglot" in 1645.

The first of the four great polyglot Bibles, the so-called Complutensian Polyglot, was published under the patronage of the Spanish Cardinal Francisco Jiménez de Cisneros (known as "Ximenes," 1436–1517) as early as 1514–1517. A remarkable achievement, the Complutensian set out the Hebrew text alongside the Greek Septuagint with the Latin Vulgate in between, and the Aramaic Targum Onkelos printed at the bottom of the pages of the Pentateuch. In his introduction, Ximenes famously compared this arrangement to the crucifixion of Christ between the two thieves, with the Vulgate placed, as it were, "between the Synagogue and the Eastern Church."[51] Even still, as Eveline van Staalduine-Sulman points out, this remark was not so much a reference to the versions themselves but to the interpretive voices associated with the respective texts. Indeed, the Complutensian retains a relatively high view of the Hebrew version, something with which Owen himself readily concurred.[52] While Ximenes regarded the extant Vulgate as the final authority for church doctrine, he nonetheless acknowledged the value of the Hebrew and Aramaic versions for correcting any corruptions that had entered various manuscripts of the Vulgate.[53]

As Owen alludes, however, the relatively sober assessment of the "Hebrew verity" found in the Complutensian, and in other Catholic writings before and after the Council of Trent such as in the noteworthy contributions of Arias Montanus (1527–1598),[54] eventually gave way to the much more negative appraisal exemplified in the Paris Polyglot. Michel Lejay's (1588–1674) Parisian production was championed by a Huguenot convert

50 Owen, *Of the Integrity*, chap. 1.

51 Quotation in Eveline van Staalduine-Sulman, *Justifying Christian Aramaism: Editions and Latin Translations of the Targums from the Complutensian to the London Polyglot Bible (1517–1657)* (Leiden: Brill, 2017), 20, 22.

52 Van Staalduine-Sulman, *Justifying Christian Aramaism*, 22. Cf., "Dedicatory Epistle."

53 Van Staalduine-Sulman, *Justifying Christian Aramaism*, 22, 35–36.

54 The Spanish theologian Arias Montanus was most famous for his involvement in the publication of the "Plantin" or "Antwerp Polyglot." See Arius Montanus, *Biblia sacra Hebraice, Chaldaice, Graece, et Latine* (Antwerp: Christoph. Plantinus, 1569–1572).

to Catholicism, Jean Morin (1591–1659), whose own Samaritan Pentateuch was included within it. In the preface to a new edition of the Septuagint in 1628, Morin had already argued that the Greek and Latin versions of the Bible had equal canonical status and were less susceptible to corruption than the Hebrew text, arguments that he extended in the first part of his famous *Exercitationes biblicae*, published in 1633.[55] And as Peter N. Miller points out, these arguments were essentially reproduced in the anonymous preface to the Paris Polyglot, which Owen believes is likely to have been the work of Morin.[56]

By the first half of the seventeenth century, this polemicizing of the Hebrew text's veracity essentially bound the remarkable flowering in humanist biblical scholarship represented by the polyglots to the ecclesiastical politics between Protestants and Catholics concerning the papacy and its authorized Vulgate edition of the Scriptures.

As one might expect, Owen reserves fairly savage criticism for Morin's agenda, but amid his general cynicism, one issue of particular concern surfaces—namely, the dating of the vowel points in the extant Hebrew text. As Muller points out, there was no particular controversy surrounding the vowel points in the early sixteenth century, with a range of viewpoints among Catholics and Protestants regarding their origin, from the moment Moses received the Law on Sinai through to a much later Masoretic origin.[57] In 1538, the Jewish grammarian Elias Levita (1469–1549) published his commentary on the *Masora* in which he carefully argued that the insertion of the vowel points was the meticulous work of the Masoretes. Levita was well known among the Protestant community, and his work was generally greeted with enthusiasm. By the second half of the sixteenth century, however, influential Catholic polemicists like Robert Bellarmine, and numerous others, were increasingly leveraging the late dating of the vowel points to insist that the

---

55 See discussion in Nicholas Hardy, *Criticism and Confession: The Bible in the Seventeenth Century Republic of Letters* (Oxford: Oxford University Press, 2017), 257–74. For the first part of this treatise, see Jean Morin, *Exercitationes biblicae de Hebraei Graecique textus sinceritate: Pars prior* (Paris: Antonius Vitray, 1633). The second edition, which included the second part, was published posthumously in 1660, after the appearance of the Paris Polyglot and the completion of Owen's *Of the Integrity*. See Jean Morin, *Exercitationum biblicarum de Hebraei Graecique textus sinceritate, libri duo* (Paris: Gasparus Meturas, 1660).

56 Peter N. Miller, "Making the Paris Polyglot Bible: Humanism and Orientalism in the Early Seventeenth Century," in *Die europäische Gelehrtenrepublik im Zeitalter des Konfessionalismus / The European Republic of Letters in the Age of Confessionalism*, ed. Herbert Jaumann (Wiesbaden: Harrassowitz 2001), 77. See "Dedicatory Epistle."

57 For this and the following, I have drawn on Richard A. Muller, *After Calvin: Studies in the Development of a Theological Tradition* (New York: Oxford University Press, 2003), 146–51.

Hebrew Old Testament had been subject to Jewish corruption, necessitating reliance on the papally authorized Vulgate to emend the corrupted text.

Naturally enough, Morin put this polemic to full effect in his advocacy for the Paris Polyglot in the first half of the seventeenth century. By this stage, numerous Protestants had locked horns with their Catholic opponents, and Levita's contribution was no longer met with the enthusiasm it once had received. Most significant among these Protestant voices was the remarkable work of the father and son duo Johann Buxtorf Sr. (1564–1629) and Johann Buxtorf Jr. (1599–1664). In his *Tiberias, sive Commentarius Masorethicus*, published in 1620, Buxtorf Sr. argued that the vowel points were the work of the great synagogue called by Ben Ezra, the so-called Men of the Great Assembly, which is thought to have been held from about 516 to 332 BC.[58] In Buxtorf Sr.'s mind, an early date for the vowel points was considered critical for guarding the spiritual inspiration of an originally perspicuous Old Testament text. For the "vowel points are the souls of the expressions and words, which enliven them. . . . Whence the word written with naked consonants, without the vowel points cannot be read and understood."[59]

For those inclined to sympathize with Buxtorf Sr.'s doctrinal concerns, matters were made worse by the Protestant contribution of Louis Cappel to the debate in 1624, *Arcanum punctationis revelatum*.[60] Cappel carefully revived Levita's argument concerning the Masoretic origin of the vowel points. Cappel was initially optimistic about the accuracy of the oral tradition in preserving the vocalization of the consonants. However, by the time he published his *Critica sacra* in 1650,[61] he had come to assume that corruption had entered the transmission and that the extant Textus Receptus ought to be amended through comparison to ancient translations such as the Chaldee, Syriac, and the Septuagint. As noted already, the immediate trigger for Owen's *Of the Integrity* was the publication of Walton's London Polyglot. But in many ways, it was Cappel's contribution that proved to be the thin end of the wedge. For the first time, a significant Protestant voice was now arguing in favor of making critical amendments to an allegedly corrupted Hebrew original.

---

58 Johann Buxtorf Sr., *Tiberias, sive Commentarius Masorethicus triplex* (Basel: J. J. Deckeri, 1665), 109–10; cf. 86–88, 96–116.

59 *Vocales sunt animae dictionum & vocum, quae eas vivificant. . . . Unde vox nudis consonis scripta, sine vocalib. legi & intelligi nequit.* Buxtorf Sr., *Tiberias*, 86–87.

60 Louis Cappel [s.n.], *Sôd han-nîqqûd han-nigle, hoc est arcanum punctationis revelatum* [. . .] *edita a Thoma Erpenio* (Leiden: Johannes Maire, 1624).

61 Louis Cappel, *Critica sacra, sive De variis quae in sacris Veteris Testamenti libris occurrunt lectionibus* (Paris: S&G Cramoisy, 1650).

The London cleric and later Bishop Brian Walton (1600–1661) hatched the idea of an English polyglot Bible under the patronage of Archbishop William Laud (1573–1645).[62] With the execution of Laud in 1645, the project did not actually begin to materialize until 1652, when the Council of State agreed to endorse it with the support of prominent figures such as Archbishop James Ussher (1581–1656) and the parliamentarian John Selden (1584–1654). Walton then collaborated with several of the most significant Hebraists in England to produce the Polyglot, which gradually appeared from 1653 to 1657.[63] Eventually, six volumes were produced. Four of these contain the various versions set out across the page in up to nine different languages. These core volumes are bookended by Walton's *Prolegomena* and an *Appendix*, the latter of which gathers together a number of collections of variant readings.

Undoubtedly the pinnacle of the four polyglot editions, the London Polyglot remained highly influential till the nineteenth century. In comparison to the Paris Polyglot, or even Cappel's later work, its critical stance is relatively conservative. As Miller points out, Walton generally had a high view of the inspired Hebrew original and its priority over the translations.[64] He rejected any conspiracies about a Jewish corruption of the text and was confident of God's providential preservation of its authenticity over successive generations.[65]

A commitment to the divine providential preservation of the inspired texts was also a central concern of Owen's, a point Owen reiterates in *Of the Divine Original* and *Of the Integrity*.[66] As he puts it in his later *Causes, Ways, and Means of Understanding the Mind of God as Revealed in his Word* (1678), Owen is adamant that the protection of the text from any material corruption is a direct function of Christ's spiritual care for his church. To suggest otherwise is "to countenance the atheistical notion that God has no especial regard to his word and worship in the world."[67] In large measure, Walton would agree. Indeed, at times, one may be forgiven for wondering whether

---

62 For these background historical details, I have drawn on Gribben, *John Owen and English Puritanism*, 187–95; and Peter N. Miller, "The 'Antiquarianization' of Biblical Scholarship and the London Polyglot Bible (1653–1657)," *Journal of the History of Ideas* 62 (2001): 463–82.

63 As Gribben notes, from comments he makes in his "Dedicatory Epistle," Owen may have been overly hasty in failing to realize that the likes of Ussher, Edward Pococke (1604–1691), and Seth Ward (1617–1689) were in fact eminent royalist collaborators in Walton's project. See Gribben, *John Owen and English Puritanism*, 189.

64 Miller, "London Polyglot," 477.

65 See, e.g., the quotation in Theodore Letis, "John Owen Versus Brian Walton: A Reformed Response to the Birth of Text Criticism," in *The Majority Text: Essays and Reviews in the Continuing Debate*, ed. Theodore P. Letis (Grand Rapids, MI: The Institute for Biblical Textual Studies, 1987), 158.

66 Owen, *Of the Divine Original*, chaps. 1, 5; Owen, *Of the Integrity*, chaps. 1, 2.

67 See *Complete Works of John Owen*, 7:348.

the substance of any disagreement between Owen and Walton is considerably less significant than the polemical tone that Owen's treatise might otherwise suggest.[68] Certainly, in his rejoinder to Owen, Walton strenuously reiterates his commitment to the divine preservation of the originals and takes great exception to any insinuation to the contrary.[69] It is true that Walton had conceded that "casual" and "involuntary" scribal errors are likely to have touched matters of relative insignificance in the extant copies,[70] even while insisting that anything pertaining to "faith," "obedience," "life," or "salvation" was untouched and remained intact.[71] Perhaps this admission was a step too far for Owen, although even he would agree that in some ancient copies of the New Testament, "diverse readings, in things or words of less importance" do readily exist.[72] And like Walton, Owen believes that differences like this, along with the various scribal marginalia in the Masoretic Text, or the *Qere* and *Ketiv*, can easily be harmonized through appeal to the analogy of faith.[73]

Yet for all Walton and Owen share in common in their attitude to the originals, Owen has a couple of lingering concerns. And to his mind, they are far from insignificant. The first is a question of degree. For all Walton's protestations about the integrity of the originals, Owen is clearly troubled by a contrary impression created by the enormous bulk of "lections" (variant readings) from various ancient copies and translations indiscriminately presented in the *Appendix* to the Polyglot. Here, Owen believes, one will find unnecessary duplication (e.g., of the *Qere* and *Ketiv*), many instances that are too conjectural or insignificant to be considered genuine lections, not to mention supposed variants that arise from translations whose authenticity

68 In this sense, perhaps Letis is right to say that "Walton's formal positions" do in fact "differ little from Owen's." Letis, "John Owen Versus Brian Walton," 157.
69 Brian Walton, *The Considerator Considered: Or, a Brief View of Certain Considerations upon the "Biblia polyglotta," the "Prolegomena" and "Appendix" Thereof* (London: Thomas Roycroft, 1659), 14, 48. Cf., Brian Walton, *In Biblia polyglotta prolegomena*, 2 vols. (Cambridge: J. Smith, 1827–1828), prolegom. 7 (1:358–412). The *Prolegomena* has been published numerous times independently of the London Polyglot, including the nineteenth-century critical edition cited here.
70 E.g., Walton, *The Considerator Considered*, 49.
71 Walton, *The Considerator Considered*, 40–41, 49, 66, 77–78, 95, 127, 52, 66, 266. Cf. Walton, *Prolegomena*, prolegom. 6, sec. 1 (1:321), where he writes, *Ita tamen invigilavit Providentia Divina Ecclesiaeque diligentia, ut in iis quae ad salutem necessaria sunt, et ad fidem et mores spectant, omnia pura et integra sint* ("Divine Providence and the diligent care of the Church so watched over [the texts] that everything in them that is necessary for salvation and has regard to faith and morals is pure and complete").
72 Owen, *Of the Integrity*, chap. 3. Likewise, Owen, *Of the Divine Original*, chap. 1.
73 Owen, *Of the Integrity*, chap. 7. Cf., e.g., Walton, *Prolegomena*, prolegom. 6, sec. 6 (1:332–33); Walton, *The Considerator Considered*, 50.

can easily be set aside. Owen fears that to the unwary eye, such a "bulky collection" all too readily suggests that "gross corruptions" have indeed entered the extant copies of the originals after all.[74] Even he was "startled" at first sight of the volume. In other words, there was enough smoke in Walton's production to suspect a fire!

A similar concern stems from Walton's commitment to the late dating of the Hebrew vowel points. In Owen's mind, the absence of the points clearly casts a shadow over the perspicuity of the text: "vowels are the life of words," he remarks; "consonants without them are dead and immovable."[75] Once again, there is a sense in which Walton would readily agree,[76] insisting that under the care of the Holy Spirit, the Masoretic pointing merely made explicit what was already implied in the divinely inspired arrangement of the consonants.[77] Walton insists there is nothing remarkable in this claim: a claim that is furnished with good Protestant pedigree.[78] Even though Owen undoubtedly ties the perspicuity of the Hebrew text more closely to the presence of

---

[74] E.g., Owen, *Of the Integrity*, chaps. 1, 2, 3, 4, 7, 8.

[75] Owen, *Of the Integrity*, chap. 5.

[76] *Respondemus, verissimum esse nullam linguam vocalibus carere posse, nec vocem ullam sine vocalibus pronunciari* ("We respond that it is certainly true that no language can lack vowels, and that no word can be pronounced without vowels"). Walton, *Prolegomena*, prolegom. 3, sec. 49 (1:223).

[77] *Tandem et hoc est notandum Masorethas, dum puncta invenerunt, non novos vocalium sonos vel pronunciationem novam induxisse, sed juxta consuetudinem ipsis traditam Libros Sacros punctasse: ideoque lectionem non ab ipsis pendere, licet ipsi apices excogitarunt, nec ideo veram esse lectionem quia est a Masorethis; sed quia verum Spiritus Sancti sensum exprimit, quem Scriptoribus Sacris dictavit et per eos litteris consignavit, quemque tum Judaei tum Christiani conservarunt. Non enim punctarunt Masorethae Sacros Codices pro arbitrio; sed secundum veram et receptam lectionem, quam diligenter poterant, puncta apposuere* ("Finally, this must also be noted: The Masoretes, when they invented the points, did not bring in new vowel sounds or a new punctuation, but they punctuated the Sacred Books according to the custom handed down to them; so the reading does not depend upon them as if they thought up the points themselves; nor indeed is it the true reading because it comes from the Masoretes but because it expresses the true sense of the Holy Spirit that he dictated to the Holy Writers and recorded through them in the letters, and that both Jews and Christians have preserved. For the Masoretes did not punctuate the Holy Texts at will, but they added the points according to the true and received reading as carefully as they could"). Walton, *Prolegomena*, prolegom. 3, sec. 51 (1:235). Cf., Walton, *The Considerator Considered*, 201–9.

[78] "One would think . . . that the *Prolegomena* had delivered some strange and dangerous opinion, never heard of before, which overthrows all certainty, and by consequence all authority of Scripture, whereas it is there proved, and shall now be made appear, that the same doctrine of the original points was delivered by the greatest Reformers, the most eminent Protestant divines, both at the beginning of the Reformation, and since, and the best skilled in Eastern learning, which then were, or at this day are in the Christian world, and the greatest patrons of the integrity of the Hebrew text." Walton, *The Considerator Considered*, 199–200.

vowel points than Walton, he too is alert to the distinction that is implied in Walton's position between the spiritual sense of the text and the outward signs through which that sense is represented. With the Buxtorfs, Owen traces the origin of the points to the Men of the Great Assembly rather than the first inspiration of the Hebrew text.[79] Yet to make such an admission, Owen clearly has to commit himself to distinguishing between the initial inspiration of the vowels, as they were implied in the arrangement of the original script, and the later addition of the points that make those vowels outwardly explicit. And sure enough, Owen cites the Italian Jewish Hebraist Azariah de' Rossi (1511–1578) in precise acknowledgement of this fact: "And the same Azarias shows the consistency of the various opinions that were among the Jews about the vowels, ascribing them as to their virtue and force, to Moses, or God on Mount Sinai; as to their figure and character to Ezra; as to the restoration of their use, unto the Masoretes."[80] So once again, one might wonder whether there is anything of substance separating the two on this score, for whatever differences they might have about the exact dating of the points.

For Owen, however, the bigger issue with the late dating of the points is the implication he sees in surrendering responsibility for the text's final form to the work of the non-Christian Masoretes, the "foundation of whose religion," he says, "was infidelity, and . . . an opposition to the gospel."[81] Aside from his incredulity that the vowel sounds could have been preserved through oral tradition when the Hebrew tongue had not been the vulgar tongue for a thousand years,[82] Owen thought it was simply "not tolerable" to countenance that God would have deployed these men as his chosen instrument to inspire the points. Indeed, Owen is so appalled by the prospect that should it be conclusively proven that the punctuation was their work, he would "labor to the utmost to have it utterly taken away out of the Bible."[83] In other words, the intolerable consequence Owen sees lurking beneath the surface here is yet again the possible corruption of the text, this time at the hands of men who simply could not be entrusted with the addition of something as important as the vowel points. It should be noted, of course, that Owen would not see the same difficulty in tracing the punctuation to the Men of the Great Assembly. Unlike the Masoretes, those men actually belonged to the church under its Old

---

79 Owen, *Of the Integrity*, chap. 5.
80 Owen, *Of the Integrity*, chap. 6.
81 Owen, *Of the Integrity*, chap. 5.
82 Owen, *Of the Integrity*, chap. 6.
83 Owen, *Of the Integrity*, chap. 5.

Testament Jewish administration, which, at least as tradition has it, included the postexilic prophets, Haggai, Zechariah, and Malachi.

If Owen's first major concern with Walton's Polyglot consists in the shadow it might cast over the integrity of the originals, the second concern is with Walton's approval of the practice of textual emendation. Here too Walton's proposal is relatively modest. Having ruled out the possibility of any substantial doctrinal error in the extant originals, only minor corrections are in view. And with an application of the analogy of faith, the analogy of Scripture, together with a sober preference for the most ancient, and more widely accepted lection in the instance of some variant, he is confident that the text can be improved by the practice.[84] As Miller puts it, "Walton saw the glass as half-full: comparison did not threaten the text but rather allowed for its repair."[85] Owen is most troubled by the appeal to differing ancient translations as arbiters for amending the original. It is "to set up an altar of our own by the altar of God, and to make equal the wisdom, care, skill, and diligence of men, with the wisdom, care, and providence of God himself."[86] Morin's advocacy for the Vulgate is clearly the most flagrant example of this practice, as Owen readily acknowledges. But he also singles out Cappel, and especially his deference to the Septuagint, as a worrying Protestant precedent and wonders whether Walton's proposal is really any different.[87] Walton denies that he ever advocated the use of translations to "correct the original"—explicitly distancing himself from the likes of Morin—so much as an aid to discern whether an error has crept into the original.[88] But for Owen, even this seems to be a step too far. In his mind, the only valid use of translations is as an aid to the exposition of Scripture, and nothing more.[89]

Miller draws attention to what he calls an "antiquarianization" of biblical scholarship in Walton's project. For all of Walton's affirmations concerning the integrity of the originals, there is nonetheless a subtle tendency to elevate

---

84 E.g., Walton, *Prolegomena*, prolegom. 6, sec. 6 (1:332–36). Here Walton provides a number of rules for deciding between variants.

85 Miller, "London Polyglot," 474. Or as Walton himself insists, "To correct an error crept into the original, is not properly to correct the original, but to restore the original to the true reading, for no error is part of the original text." Walton, *The Considerator Considered*, 92.

86 Owen, *Of the Integrity*, chap. 2.

87 Owen gives his own account of this development in the "Dedicatory Epistle." See also Owen, *Of the Integrity*, chap. 8.

88 Walton, *The Considerator Considered*, 84–106. As Hardy argues, Walton's stance towards the use of translations and conjectural emendation was generally more circumspect than Cappel's. His most contentious statements were those concerning the accuracy of the *Septuagint*. See Hardy, *Criticism and Confession*, 365–67.

89 Owen, *Of the Integrity*, chap. 8.

the significance of tradition and the judgment of the church in deciding upon the final form of the text. Miller also speaks of a "mitigated skepticism" in Walton's posture of assuming that minor scribal errors crept into the copies, which at least echoes the much more exaggerated skeptical tone of those advocating for the supremacy of the Vulgate.[90] Nicholas Hardy may be right in questioning whether Walton's project was as ideologically driven or consciously coherent as this. In reality, it looks more like a hotchpotch, or a "messy and contentious accommodation of different Protestant and Catholic positions."[91] Even so, couple Walton's mitigated skepticism about the text with a deference to ancient translations and the consensus of the church in detecting scribal error, and it is perhaps no wonder that a "hotter sort of Protestant" like Owen is rather alarmed by what he sees.

Posterity has not looked favorably on Owen's argument, especially in regard to the dating of the vowel points.[92] And one may justifiably question Owen's concern to tie the inherent perspicuity of the Hebrew original closely to the presence of the vowel points, even by the yardstick of classical Protestant precedent. But in assessing Owen's position by modern standards, the polemics of his own context need to be remembered. Underneath Owen's position lay an orthodox Protestant devotion to the inherent perspicuity of Scripture, both in the original and in its extant copies, reflecting God's faithfulness and providential care of his church. And in his mind, the emerging doubts about the integrity of the originals, together with an evolving permissiveness toward critical emendations of the text simply clashed with this commitment and could not be tolerated any more than the Catholic elevation of the Vulgate. Indeed, in some ways Owen's fears were prescient, at least in regard to the eventual collapse in confidence regarding the integrity and perspicuity of the original biblical text. And in this respect, hindsight also allows one to see that Walton's convictions regarding the stability of the church's tradition

90 Miller, "London Polyglot," 478. The classic study for the impact of a revived ancient skepticism on early modern debates is Richard Popkin's *The History of Scepticism: From Savonarola to Bayle* (Oxford: Oxford University Press, 2003). See his commentary in relation to the Catholic appeal to the supremacy of the Vulgate in the context of a wider skepticism that was emerging in early modern biblical scholarship. Popkin, *The History of Scepticism*, 219–38. Gribben and Van Staalduine-Sulman also speak of a distinct "Laudian" or "high church" agenda in Walton's project. See Crawford Gribben, "The Commodification of Scripture, 1640–1660: Politics, Ecclesiology, and the Cultures of Print," in *The Oxford Handbook of the Bible in Early Modern England, c. 1530–1700*, ed. Kevin Killeen, Helen Smith, and Rachel Willie (Oxford: Oxford University Press, 2015), 233; Van Staalduine-Sulman, *Justifying Christian Aramaism*, 206–9, 228–29.

91 Hardy, *Criticism and Confession*, 368.

92 In this and the following paragraph, I at points repeat and closely follow my own conclusions elsewhere. See Leslie, *Light of Grace*, 216–17.

and judgment would quickly prove to be rather naive. As Miller puts it, "The collapse of *historica critica* in turn undermined the philology represented in the Polyglot Bibles."[93]

Owen's *Of the Integrity* should be recognized as a sophisticated and scholarly attempt to defend the veracity of Scripture in an increasingly complex intellectual environment, proceeding from a settled conviction that God has revealed himself clearly and authoritatively in this text. It is an attempt; and like all attempts, it will be open to objection and disagreement at points. But if the primary intention is to cast judgment, one may fail to see it for what it is on its own terms as it is situated within its own historical context.[94]

Thematic Outline

Owen begins this treatise with an explanation of its occasion—namely, his receipt of Walton's *Prolegomena* and *Appendix* to the London Polyglot Bible. As Owen explains, the manuscript of his treatise *Of the Divine Original* was already complete when he received the *Prolegomena* and *Appendix*, but having now engaged with the latter, he feels compelled to compose this treatise as a supplement to *Of the Divine Original*, lest Walton's work threaten his earlier conclusions about God's providential preservation of the authentic scriptural text.[95] Indeed, right at the outset, Owen flags his primary concern with what seems to be an underlying presupposition of Walton's work—namely, that the original text of Scripture has been corrupted, leading to a proliferation of variant readings, and permitting the practice of textual emendation according to the best evidence available. In his mind, this underlying assumption cannot but erode our confidence in Scripture's divine authority, and is no less than "the foundation of Mohammedanism, . . . the chiefest and principal prop of popery, the only pretense of fanatical antiscripturalists, and the root of much hidden

---

93 Miller, "London Polyglot," 472.

94 It is worth quoting Hardy's sagacious assessment: "It may now be possible to reconsider the famous quarrel between Walton and John Owen, which it has been tempting to regard as a moment of clear opposition between a progressive 'critical' and a reactionary 'Reformed' or 'scholastic' view of biblical authority. In fact, Owen was quite up to speed with contemporary biblical scholarship, and not all of his arguments were nakedly theological ones. However credulous Owen's strong faith in the reliability of the Masoretic vocalization may seem, Owen had coherent scholarly reasons not to take the alternatives presented by Cappel, Morin, and Walton any more seriously—and that was before he contemplated their ecclesiological and confessional consequences." Hardy, *Criticism and Confession*, 369–70.

95 Owen, *Of the Integrity*, chap. 1.

atheism." By contrast, Owen restates the basic assertion he outlined in *Of the Divine Original* concerning the divinely preserved integrity of the extant scriptural text, which self-evidently manifests its inspired authority right down to "the least iota or syllable." Lest his criticism of the London Polyglot be misunderstood, however, Owen is keen to express his great esteem for the work and acknowledge its considerable value,[96] even if he will take issue with the points he enumerates later in the chapter.

Before outlining his objections to these points in detail, chapter two expands on his key convictions regarding the "purity" of the extant Scriptural text. At the outset Owen readily acknowledges that the inspired autographs are no longer in existence and that the remaining copies are neither inspired nor infallible. Evidently both the Catholic Morin and the Protestant Cappel had caricatured their opponents as maintaining that the extant copies of the Scriptures must be as divinely inspired and infallible as the originals. Even still, Owen remains convinced that the copies preserve the "whole Scripture entire, as given out from God, without any loss." And later in chapter 2, he outlines twelve arguments for this assertion, which include the fundamental theological conviction already mentioned—namely, God's providential care of his word—but which also extend to the great concern demonstrated in the scribal duplication of the text, and the watchful maintenance of the copies by Jews and Christians alike. Accordingly, any variations that do exist in the copies are manifestly of little doctrinal significance.[97]

Subsequent chapters then take up Owen's objections to Walton's *Prolegomena* and *Appendix* in more detail. Although the bulk of his concerns naturally pertain to the Old Testament, Owen is even alarmed at the way the *Appendix* has needlessly "swelled" the number of variant readings for the New Testament. So in chapter 3, he castigates Walton for presenting what are plainly copying errors and the like as alternative readings, concluding with several suggestions for the way this number of variants might be reduced.[98]

Chapter 4 turns to the chief assertions of the *Prolegomena* and *Appendix* concerning the Old Testament. Owen outlines them briefly in chapter 4. Among other things, they include the claims that the present Hebrew characters are Chaldean and not original; that the vowel points are of late origin; that the *Qere* and *Ketiv*, or *Keri* and *Ketib*, as Owen calls them, are late variant

96 Owen, *Of the Integrity*, chap. 1.
97 Owen, *Of the Integrity*, chap. 2.
98 Owen, *Of the Integrity*, chap. 3.

readings of the Masoretes and Rabbins; and that early translations may be used to emend the extant Hebrew text.[99] Alarmed that these claims are now being readily accepted by fellow Protestants, Owen is keen to point out that they have already been seized upon by the Catholics to undermine confidence in Scripture and galvanize dependence on an infallible Papacy together with its authorized Vulgate translation.[100]

In Chapters 5 and 6, Owen extensively engages with the argument concerning the late origin of the Hebrew vowel points. Here Walton follows Cappel, who advocated for their addition by the Tiberian Masoretes and Rabbins at least as late as the sixth or seventh century AD. Owen's general response begins by noting the critical importance of the vowel points to the perspicuity of the text, an observation with which various Catholic apologists for the Vulgate were, unsurprisingly, keen to agree. He then turns to the argument itself. The first prong of his response largely seeks to discredit the integrity and, therefore, reliability of the Jewish rabbinical tradition after the destruction of Jerusalem. Whereas the Jewish church faithfully preserved the Scriptures until the coming of Christ, Owen believes the later apostasy of the Jewish community renders them unfit custodians of God's word. At any rate, Owen is keen to note that most Jews hold to the antiquity of the points, and even where they do not (e.g., Levita), they still revere the points as if they were the ancient work of Ezra.[101] As for a more detailed defense of the antiquity of the points, Owen believes the recent work of Buxtorf Jr. remains as yet unanswered,[102] and thus he is content to leave it there. Even still, he finishes the chapter with two additional considerations of his own for their antiquity.[103]

Owen's response to the arguments for the novelty of the vowel points continues in chapter 6. Here he responds to some of the specific arguments for their late addition:

1. He judges the conjecture that the unpointed Samaritan Hebrew characters correspond to the original—rather than the extant, supposedly Chaldean characters—to be highly speculative.

---

99 For consistency, I have retained Owen's usual transliteration, *Keri* and *Ketib*, in the headings of chapters but have used the modern convention in transliterating Owen's Hebrew references to the marginalia.

100 Owen, *Of the Integrity*, chap. 4.

101 Owen, *Of the Integrity*, chap. 5.

102 Cf., Johann Buxtorf Jr., *Tractatus de punctorum vocalium et accentum, in libris Veteris Testamenti Hebraicis, origine, antiquitate, et authoritate* (Basel: L. König, 1648).

103 Owen, *Of the Integrity*, chap. 5.

2. He responds to the practice of preserving unpointed copies of the Law in the synagogue by noting again that most Jewish scholars still uphold the divine inspiration of the points.

3. He questions the testimony of Levita, noting that there are other ways of accounting for the reception of the vowel points from the Tiberian Masoretes than to suppose they were responsible for their composition.

4. He notes that despite the silence of the Mishnah, Talmud, and Gemara concerning the points, the sense implied in their quotation of Scripture presumes the presence of the points.

5. He contends that the *Qere* and *Ketiv* pertain to the consonants of the text and have no bearing on the antiquity of the points.

6. He rejects the suggestion that the large number of Hebrew vowels necessarily suggests their arbitrary human invention.

7. He similarly denies that the variety in the various ancient translations necessarily suggests the absence of points in the originals.

8. He maintains that Jerome's failure to discuss the points is essentially an argument from silence.

9. Finally, he dismisses as fanciful and mistaken an inference Morin makes from a discourse by Aben Ezra (Abraham ibn Ezra) that the vowel points were the invention of the Jewish grammarians.[104]

In his conclusion to the chapter, Owen is simply incredulous when it comes to Cappel's belief that an oral tradition could maintain the precise pronunciation over a millennium stretching from the time the Hebrew language ceased to be spoken up to that of the Tiberian Masoretes.

In chapter 7, Owen seeks to refute any claim that the *Qere* and *Ketiv* might represent a corruption of the original text. While Owen is somewhat hesitant about their origin, he believes their antiquity is indisputable, mitigating against any suggestion that they might represent later critical amendments to the text. In this respect, he applauds the generally conservative approach of the Polyglot Bible, as compared to Cappel's more radical insinuations regarding their origin. At any rate, the differences they make to the meaning of the original text is immaterial.[105]

The final chapter seeks to address the use of ancient translations vis-à-vis the Hebrew text. In Owen's mind, an appropriate use of translations can aid the exposition of Scripture by providing a kind of commentary on the sense of the

---

104 Owen, *Of the Integrity*, chap. 6.
105 Owen, *Of the Integrity*, chap. 7.

original. In this respect, he welcomes the accessibility of these translations in the new Polyglot Bible. But he strongly objects to the practice suggested by the *Prolegomena* of using ancient translations to correct any alleged corruptions in the copies of the original. As Owen notes, it is the undeniable variations in the most famous of these, the Septuagint, that is typically advanced as grounds for corruptions within the extant Hebrew text. While he clearly believes this is unwarranted, given the lack of ancient testimony to this effect, and not least the witness of Christ himself to the integrity and authority of the Hebrew text, Owen proceeds to weigh the reliability of the most prominent translations, case by case. While each of those he evaluates—the Arabic, Syriac, Samaritan Pentateuch, Chaldee Paraphrase, Vulgate, and Septuagint—offer varying degrees of utility to the biblical expositor, all of them fall manifestly well short of meeting the standard of guaranteed correspondence to the original that might warrant their deployment in amending the extant Hebrew copies. Much the same can be said for corresponding translations of the New Testament. Owen concludes the chapter with a brief statement rejecting the premise of a corrupted original. Naturally enough, then, he finds the proliferation of variants in the *Appendix*, which include those gathered from other places like Grotius's *Annotations*, redundant, to say the least.[106]

INTRODUCTION AND THEMATIC OUTLINE FOR *TWENTY-FIVE DISCOURSES SUITABLE TO THE LORD'S SUPPER* (1760) AND *THREE DISCOURSES DELIVERED AT THE LORD'S TABLE* (1750)

The first of the posthumous collection, and the third major treatise, in this present volume is *Twenty-Five Discourses Suitable to the Lord's Supper, Delivered Just before the Administration of That Sacred Ordinance*. As the published title suggests, this "treatise" consists, in fact, of twenty-five sermons that were delivered between 1669 and 1682 in preparation for the sacrament itself, most likely delivered just before the ordinance in addition to a separate sermon.[107] They were published together in 1760 under the supervision of Richard Winter, an Independent church pastor in London.[108] As Winter's introduction indicates, the sermons were reproduced from one of John Hartopp's notebooks that had been preserved by his granddaughter, a certain Mrs. Cooke of Stoke Newington.

106 Owen, *Of the Integrity*, chap. 8.
107 Note too the opening remarks by Owen, *Twenty-Five Discourses*, discourses 8, 12, 18, 22, 24.
108 Owen, *Twenty-Five Discourses*.

The three separate discourses on the Lord's Supper, *Three Discourses Delivered at the Lord's Table*, dated originally to 1673, are brief shorthand reproductions from sermons containing themes that are readily apparent in the larger collection. Evidently, these first appeared in 1750 as a prefix to a tract by John Greene of Chipping Onger with the title *The Lord's Supper Fully Considered, in a Review of the History of Its Institution*.[109] As with the larger collection, Greene's prefatory comments indicate that the discourses were "taken from Dr. Owen's mouth by one who was a member of the church of which he was a pastor,"[110] most likely referring again to one of Hartopp's notebooks.

Jon D. Payne has provided an extended outline of the development in Owen's thought on the Lord's Supper as an introduction to his own edition of the twenty-five discourses.[111] With an eye to the record of Owen's personal library collection, Payne notices likely points of connection to the sacramentology of magisterial Reformers like John Calvin and Peter Martyr Vermigli, as well as his own contemporaries like Samuel Bolton, Richard Vines, Edward Reynolds, and Philip Goodwin.

Thematic Outline

The twenty-five discourses, as published, are arranged chronologically[112] and not in a strictly methodical fashion. Even so, it is possible to categorize them thematically. While there are several discourses that give more focused attention to the nature, purpose, and administration of the ordinance itself,[113] the vast majority are devoted to the participants themselves and the way their relationship with God is uniquely enriched through engaging in the ordinance. Throughout the collection, Owen's abiding interest concerns the way the Lord's Supper conveys to the believer a peculiar communion with God that extends beyond what arises from the ministry of the word alone. In this vein, Owen sets out the duties that are necessary to prepare for the Supper,[114] various directions for rightly approaching the Lord's Table and receiving the

---

109 John Greene and John Owen, *The Lord's Supper Fully Considered, in a Review of the History of Its Institution. With Meditations and Ejaculations Suited to the Several Parts of the Ordinance. To Which Are Prefixed Three Discourses Delivered at the Lord's Table, by the Reverend and Learned John Owen, D.D. Never before Published: And Some Remarks on the Plain Account of the Sacrament* (London: J. Buckland, 1750).

110 J. Green, advertisement to the 1750 edition of Owen, *Three Discourses*.

111 Jon D. Payne, *John Owen on the Lord's Supper* (Edinburgh: Banner of Truth, 2004), 1–75.

112 A small number of discourses in the collection are undated.

113 Owen, *Twenty-Five Discourses*, discourses 2, 3, 4, 7, 10, 13, 14 17.

114 Owen, *Twenty-Five Discourses*, discourses 5, 6.

sacrament,[115] with a particular accent on the special act and object of faith's exercise in the ordinance,[116] and, finally, the benefits and duties that ensue from participating in the Supper.[117]

Four Fundamental Convictions concerning the Supper Itself

In terms of the ordinance itself, Owen summarizes four fundamental convictions concerning its nature in discourse 2, and develops them further in other discourses.

1. IT IS COMMEMORATIVE OF CHRIST'S ATONING DEATH

In accord with Christ's own institution (Luke 22:19) and Paul's directions in 1 Corinthians 11:24–25, the ordinance is first of all "commemorative" of Christ's atoning sufferings and death. Discourse 13 expands on this by noting how the Supper recalls the "grace and love of God" in the Father's gift of the Son to die as a sacrifice for sin, as well as the love of Christ himself, who willingly gave himself for our salvation. Behind this gift is its foundation in the eternal, intra-Trinitarian "counsel of peace" or so-called *pactum salutis*, wherein the Son freely consented to "undertake and answer for what we had done," and the Father agreed to grant "righteousness, life and salvation" to sinners as a result.[118] Most importantly, however, the Supper recalls the suffering of Christ itself. Owen draws attention to the sufferings of Christ's human soul in its privative loss of divine fellowship and its positive infliction with the curse of God's wrath directed against sinners. As he explains in discourse 17, this suffering ensues from the "imputation" of iniquity and guilt to him, fulfilling its typological representation in the Old Testament sacrificial rituals. Alongside this anguish of soul, Christ's bodily suffering is neither to be forgotten nor disproportionally overemphasized, and in passing Owen also mentions the peculiar suffering that resulted from the punitive dissolution of Christ's body and soul in death.

2. IT ENTAILS A PECULIAR PROFESSION OF CHRIST

There is a "peculiar profession" that accompanies the Supper (see 1 Cor. 11:26). Owen develops this in discourse 4. There he speaks of the way Christ's death is represented to the believer in the Supper, in its vivid exhibition of his sufferings, in the promissory offer that accompanies the elements, and

115 Owen, *Twenty-Five Discourses*, discourses 4, 8, 9, 10, 11, 14, 20, 21, 22, 24.
116 Owen, *Twenty-Five Discourses*, discourses 1, 2, 3, 15, 16, 18, 19. Cf. the separate *Three Discourses*.
117 Owen, *Twenty-Five Discourses*, discourses 12, 16, 25.
118 Owen, *Twenty-Five Discourses*, discourse 13.

in its reception and incorporation within the believer. Owen is of course keen to distinguish this spiritual representation from a merely physical impression upon the "fancy" or "imagination," a tendency he condemns in the proliferation of "pictures and images" of Christ among his Catholic adversaries. Such a practice, he adds, epitomizes a decline in faith and a loss of contact with the spiritual reality.[119] Unsurprisingly, then, Owen excludes the "carnal" representation of Christ that he believes is enshrined in the doctrine of transubstantiation. The elements of the Supper cannot in themselves convey the spiritual representation but are arbitrarily instituted by God to express a reality that is received by faith alone. Even so, the Supper also serves to strengthen that spiritual reality in a way that the ministry of the word cannot accomplish on its own. Discourse 14 further explains what Owen means. Through participating in the Supper, faith "rises up" or comes closest to what he calls a "spiritual, sensible experience," drawing nearest to its object. In other words, the divine institution of the physical elements—bread and wine—is a deliberate and particularly fitting representation of Christ, insofar as "things of sense are chosen to express faith wrought up to an experience."[120]

There are two dimensions to this spiritual experience, Owen suggests. First, the tangible offer of the elements to be consumed by the believer aligns with a spiritual reality wherein Christ is "more present to the soul" than he would be if were simply "visible" before our bodily eyes.[121] When speaking of the spiritual representation of Christ in his ordinances, one of Owen's favorite refrains is Paul's admonishment of the Galatians: "It was before your eyes that Jesus Christ was publicly portrayed as crucified" (Gal. 3:1 ESV; with Rom. 3:25). And what the Supper offers a believer is a vivid exhibition of Christ's suffering that is perhaps the nearest and most evident of all.[122] As he notes on several occasions, whereas the Father offers Christ to the believer in the gospel, there is a sense in which Christ immediately and directly offers himself in the institution of the Supper.[123] Equally as significant as the spiritual offer of Christ in the Supper is, secondly, the tangible receipt of him by the communicant, as represented by the acts of eating and drinking the elements. Through the believer's active participation in the Supper, "the flesh and blood

---

119 Owen, *Twenty-Five Discourses*, discourse 4.

120 Owen, *Twenty-Five Discourses*, discourse 14.

121 Owen, *Twenty-Five Discourses*, discourse 14.

122 "But of all things that belong unto the gospel, he is most evidently crucified before our eyes in this ordinance." Owen, *Twenty-Five Discourses*, discourse 10.

123 E.g., Owen, *Twenty-Five Discourses*, discourse 10.

of Christ as communicated in this ordinance through faith" is "turned and changed . . . into spiritual vital principles," bringing growth, satisfaction, and nourishment to the soul.[124]

Behind these statements is a particular perspective on the sacramental presence of Christ in the ordinance. We have already noted Owen's dismissal of a crudely carnal form of Christ's presence. Aside from the usual complaint that transubstantiation chafes against "every thing that is in sense, reason, and the faith of a man,"[125] Kelly Kapic also draws attention to an interesting pneumatological objection Owen makes. In Owen's mind, a literal transubstantiation of the elements inevitably sidelines Christ's promises concerning the Spirit's distinctive ministry after his bodily ascension (see John 16:7).[126] On the other hand, Owen also resists reducing the Supper to a mere "naked representation" or a purely symbolic remembrance of Christ's passion.[127] It is not some "empty, painted feast," he says: it involves a real, albeit spiritual, exhibition and communication of Christ's body and blood "to feed our souls." In other words, there is a genuine "sacramental relation . . . between the outward elements and the thing signified" that ensures there is no pretense in the Supper's invitation to feast on the body and blood of Christ, together with all its spiritual benefits.[128] Consequently, Owen is able to speak of a "mysterious reception of Christ in this peculiar way of exhibition . . . so as to come to a real substantial incorporation in our souls."[129] While it is a fraught business attempting to categorize various early modern Protestant perspectives on Christ's sacramental presence in the Supper, Kapic, like Payne, is right to identify here substantial continuity between Owen's understanding and the sort of "mediated position" typically associated with Calvin, Vermigli, and the Reformed Confessions.[130]

There is a further sense in which the Supper makes a more public "profession" of Christ, beyond that which is tendered to the individual believer's soul. Every time the ordinance is celebrated, Owen maintains, there is a profession of Christ's shameful death before the open contempt of the world, in opposition to the curse, and in triumph over the power of Satan.

124 Owen, *Twenty-Five Discourses*, discourse 14.
125 Owen, *Twenty-Five Discourses*, discourse 10.
126 Owen, *Twenty-Five Discourses*, discourse 10. Kelly M. Kapic, *Communion with God: The Divine and the Human in the Theology of John Owen* (Grand Rapids, MI: Baker Academic, 2007), 224.
127 Owen, *Twenty-Five Discourses*, discourse 7; cf. Owen, *Three Discourses*, discourse 1.
128 Owen, *Twenty-Five Discourses*, discourse 23.
129 Owen, *Twenty-Five Discourses*, discourse 25.
130 Kapic, *Communion*, 224–25. Cf. Jan Rohls, *Reformed Confessions: Theology from Zurich to Barmen* (Louisville: Westminster John Knox, 1998), 177–88; 219–37.

3. IT IS PECULIARLY EUCHARISTICAL

Owen's third fundamental conviction about the Supper is that it is "peculiarly eucharistical." Paul speaks of the "cup of blessing" or "thanksgiving" (1 Cor. 10:16). In Owen's words, "It is called 'The cup of blessing,' because of the institution, and prayer for the blessing of God upon it; and it is called 'The cup of thanksgiving,' because we do in a peculiar manner give thanks to God for Christ, and for his love in him."[131]

4. IT IS A FEDERAL ORDINANCE CONFIRMING THE COVENANT

Finally, following Christ's own cue in Matthew 26:28, Owen speaks of the Supper as a "federal ordinance, wherein God confirms the covenant unto us, and wherein he calls us to make a recognition of the covenant unto God."[132] Of course, God has no need to renew his gracious covenant every time the ordinance is celebrated: it was sealed once and for all by blood of Christ's sacrifice. But there is a sense in which the ordinance repeatedly testifies to this covenant, and each time it is celebrated, it provides the believer an opportunity to renew their commitment as beneficiaries of this covenant "by a universal giving up ourselves unto God."[133]

Instructions in Preparation for the Ordinance

Given Owen's emphasis on the Supper as a means of grace that engages a person's faith to the fullest extent, it is not surprising that he devotes a considerable amount of time to instructing believers in preparation for the ordinance, and in the right posture for approaching the Table and receiving the sacrament.

In one respect, preparation for the Supper is no different from what is commonly necessary for any divine ordinance.[134] Here Owen identifies a preparation that has reference to God. This involves a careful consideration of his authority in the ordinance's institution and his holy and gracious presence in it as the object of worship. It will also attend to him as the end of the ordinance, both in terms of his glorification by it and in terms of the acceptance and blessing he bestows on the worshiper in Christ. There is also a preparation that respects the believer himself, which involves an appropriately remorseful regard to their own iniquity, an appropriate self-abasement, and the cultivation of "a habitual frame of love in the heart" for the ordinance.

131 Owen, *Twenty-Five Discourses*, discourse 2.
132 Owen, *Twenty-Five Discourses*, discourse 2.
133 Owen, *Twenty-Five Discourses*, discourse 10.
134 For the following, see Owen, *Twenty-Five Discourses*, discourse 5.

Owen also refers to a kind of preparation that is attentive to the proper, divinely authorized instructions for the administration of the ordinance, lest a person risk the kind of disapproval that greeted Uzzah's infamous grasping of the ark in 1 Chronicles 13.

In terms of the Supper itself, Owen suggests that suitable time needs to be set aside to prepare for the ordinance.[135] Scripture clearly allows for considerable liberty on this score, but Owen exhorts believers to be alert to fitting opportunities and circumstances that will enable them to perform the duty effectually.

The preparation itself should entail meditation on a number of "special objects," all centering on Christ's suffering. To begin with, such meditation ought to consider the "horrible guilt and provocation" of sin that is represented in the cross. Second, there is the "purity, the holiness, and the severity of God, that would not pass by sin, when it was charged upon his Son." There is also the "infinite wisdom" and "love of God that found out this way of glorifying his holiness and justice, and dealing with sin according to its demerit." Then there is the "infinite love of Jesus Christ himself," who gave himself that sinners might have their sins washed away in his blood. Finally, a believer should be attentive to the end of Christ's suffering in making "peace and reconciliation." Owen directs believers to be mindful of their own spiritual state as they meditate on these realities, and to be attentive to anything that aids their spirits in this duty, conscious that "most Christians are poor in experience." Beyond meditation, preparation for the Supper should also involve honest self-examination and repentance in light of Christ's cross, supplication, and expectation that God will graciously answer the longings of our hearts.

The Exercise of Faith in Approaching the Table Itself

When it comes to approaching the Table itself, Owen is particularly concerned to direct communicants' attention to the ways in which the ordinance kindles their faith and love for Christ. To a large degree, these directions correspond to the nature of the ordinance itself in its special representation and exhibition of Christ's death to the sinner. But of particular importance to Owen is having clarity about the "special object of faith" in this ordinance. It was commonplace among Reformed orthodox theologians to distinguish between the formal object of faith, in its most general sense as the veracity and authority of God, and the special, material object of justifying faith, which is the particular promise of forgiveness through Christ held out in the gospel

---

135 For this and the following, see Owen, *Twenty-Five Discourses*, discourse 6.

offer. These two aspects of faith are obviously presupposed in a believer's participation in the Supper. But Owen also refers to a more particular and immediate "special object" of faith in this ordinance.

As he outlines it in discourse 2, this special object is in its fullest respect the "human nature of Christ, as the subject wherein mediation and redemption was wrought."[136] Therefore, faith will in an "especial manner" consider the body God prepared for that end (cf. Heb 10:5). Faith then goes further to consider the constituent parts of Christ's human nature: his body and blood, in union to his soul, from whence is "its value and excellency." Faith will also consider the way these parts are distinguished in the Supper, one element representing the body and another the blood. And finally, faith will consider the way in which these parts are violently separated in his suffering: his body bruised and broken, and his blood shed, both represented in the breaking of the bread and the pouring of the cup.

From here, faith should move on to reflect upon the causes that led to the separation of Christ's body and blood. First, there is a "moving cause"—namely, "the eternal love of God in giving Christ in this manner, to have his body bruised, and his blood shed." It is one thing that God sent his Son, Owen says, but it is another that he "spared not his own Son" (Rom. 8:32). When discussing the special object of faith in discourse 18, Owen also refers distinctly to the love of Christ himself, who voluntarily "gave himself" for sinners (cf. Gal. 2:20). Second, there is a "procuring cause"—namely, the sin for which Christ died "to make reconciliation and atonement." Then there is the "efficient cause." The "principal" efficient cause is the justice and righteousness of God wherein Christ was set forth "to be a propitiation" to "declare his righteousness" (Rom. 3:25). The "instrumental" efficient cause is the law of God that pronounced its curse so that Christ was hung "upon the tree" (Gal. 3:13). The "adjuvant" (assisting) efficient cause was "the wrath and malice of men" who conspired in his death. And ultimately faith should consider the "final" cause, which is the glorification of God in Christ's suffering.[137]

Much of Owen's instruction for approaching the Table expands on that which will encourage faith's regard for Christ as he is "lifted up" in this ordinance. We have already made reference to Owen's reflections on the way in which Christ's death for sinners is "exhibited" or "set forth" in the ordinance. But in addition to this, the discourses contain rich meditations on the intra-Trinitarian love of God and the particular love of Christ

136 Owen, *Twenty-Five Discourses*, discourse 2.
137 Owen, *Twenty-Five Discourses*, discourse 2.

toward sinners,[138] the faith and obedience of Christ in his sufferings,[139] the imputation of sin and guilt to Christ,[140] short expositions of pertinent scriptural texts that speak to his suffering,[141] specific directions for recalling Christ's sufferings and exercising faith when approaching the Table,[142] as well as pastoral advice targeted at the various spiritual conditions of communicants.[143]

As noted above, communion with Christ in this ordinance will not result without faith actively engaging in the sacrament to receive and appropriate its spiritual object personally, and in a way that will "set love at work."[144] The resulting communion stems from a real incorporation of Christ within the believer that occurs through the sacrament. Owen clearly does not intend to suggest that the ordinance somehow supplants spiritual regeneration as the means by which Christ is initially formed within a believer, so much as it results in "a farther incorporation of Christ in our souls."[145] He speaks of it increasing and "quickening" "vital principles," bringing spiritual growth and satisfaction through "receiving suitable food and nourishment."[146] In particular, when individuals exercise their faith through participating in the ordinance, Owen anticipates that their affections will be kindled by the love of Christ, which has a peculiarly conforming or "constraining" power on the soul (cf., 2 Cor. 5:14).[147] Unremarkably for an early modern Protestant, Owen does not consider love to be the "form" of faith so much as he expects that authentic Christian faith will be the root or foundation of a transformative love and obedience to Christ. In other words, while there are certainly duties that Owen outlines for the Christian to engage their affections through participation in the sacrament,[148] the spiritual strength for this conformity stems from Christ alone. It is only as faith takes in a "view" of Christ "as lifted up," with the "transforming power, property, and efficacy" of his love,[149] that the soul will find itself conformed into his

---

138 Owen, *Twenty-Five Discourses*, discourses 20, 21, 22.
139 Owen, *Twenty-Five Discourses*, discourse 3.
140 Owen, *Twenty-Five Discourses*, discourse 17.
141 Owen, *Twenty-Five Discourses*, discourse 11.
142 Owen, *Twenty-Five Discourses*, discourses 1, 8, 13, 14, 15, 18, 19, 25.
143 Owen, *Twenty-Five Discourses*, discourse 9.
144 Owen, *Twenty-Five Discourses*, discourse 16.
145 Owen, *Twenty-Five Discourses*, discourse 18.
146 Owen, *Twenty-Five Discourses*, discourse 14.
147 Owen, *Twenty-Five Discourses*, discourse 20.
148 Owen, *Twenty-Five Discourses*, discourses 12, 16, 21, 24.
149 Owen, *Twenty-Five Discourses*, discourse 20.

image and likeness. Given the specific attention this sacrament gives to the sufferings of Christ, there is a peculiar conformity to Christ's death that ought to ensue, touching a believer's thoughts, conversation, desires, and, not least, attitude toward sin.[150]

INTRODUCTION TO THE REMAINING CONTENTS OF THE PRESENT VOLUME

Several Practical Cases of Conscience Resolved (1721)

The collection of sermons, dated between 1672–1680[151] and gathered together in 1721 under the title *Several Practical Cases of Conscience Resolved: Delivered in Some Short Discourses at Church Meetings*,[152] evinces the sort of pastoral casuistry that was typical among many Puritan authors. If the dates that are occasionally cited for the *Discourses* in the collection are anything to go by, it appears they may have been delivered at special meetings "for conference," as Owen puts it in discourse 14, outside the usual gathering on the Lord's Day.

Here we are given an insight into Owen's deep concerns about the religious climate in post-Restoration England. In the third discourse, for instance, Owen decries an "irreligion" and "atheism" among his countryfolk that he believes is virtually unparalleled in any age. In spite of recent providential warnings—"the pestilence, the fire, the sword," undoubtedly an allusion to the Great Plague and subsequent Great Fire of London, along with other tumultuous events only a few years earlier[153]—the complacent godlessness of the nation had reached giddy heights. Among a number of deplorable sins that deeply trouble him, Owen singles out a general reproach of the Spirit as being perhaps "the peculiar sin of the nation at this day, and that the like has not been known, or heard of, in any nation under the sun."[154] Indeed, so alarmed by this disdain for the supernatural work of the Spirit, Owen was compelled to write his major contemporaneous treatise, Πνευματολογια in 1674, a labor that would extend into several sequel volumes.[155]

Surrounded by a dramatic loss of religious zeal, together with the prospect of a heavy hand of divine providential judgment, Owen's concern throughout this collection of sermons is chiefly pastoral and practical rather

---

150 Owen, *Twenty-Five Discourses*, discourse 24; cf. discourse 12.
151 Not all the sermons are published with dates.
152 Owen, *Complete Collection of Sermons etc.* (1721), 539–71.
153 Cf. Gribben, *John Owen and English Puritanism*, 257.
154 Owen, *Cases of Conscience*, discourse 3.
155 *Complete Works of John Owen*, vols. 5–8.

than polemical or even theological, at least in any technical or constructive sense. There is a notable tone of urgency in the sermons. As he exhorts his hearers, "There is more than an ordinary earnestness and fervency of spirit, and wrestling with God required of us at this day, for the cause of Zion, the interest of Christ, and defeating of his adversaries."[156]

In keeping with Owen's convictions about the gracious, Christological foundation of the Christian life, a large proportion of the collection offers practical instructions for a believer to kindle his or her trust in Christ.[157] "The whole of our fruitfulness," he insists, "depends upon our abiding in Christ."[158] Here Owen points his hearers to the usual means of grace, with specific directions for applying our minds, wills, and affections to the contemplation of Christ, as well as exhortations to engage in regular fellowship that intentionally focusses on one another's spiritual state, alongside the ordinances of public worship and, of course, prayer.

A number of sermons address a believer's decays in grace and the case of besetting sin.[159] While Owen is clearly attentive to the dilemma that habitual sin poses for a person's assurance of salvation, here he is more immediately interested in outlining the circumstances that might enflame it, and the ways in which it can be diagnosed and remedied. Owen is confident that the warnings of Scripture and the exhortations to seek relief from Christ will in due course function as means of grace to restore those who are genuinely regenerate from the snare in which they have been caught.

Reflections on a Slanderous Libel (1671, 1721)

Some of the material contained in these posthumous collections was of a more controversial nature, stemming from Owen's sustained advocacy for the Independent cause after the Restoration. One such item of correspondence contained in the present volume was a letter originally published in 1671, in a tract with the title *An Expostulatory Letter to the Author of the Slanderous Libel against Dr. O. With Some Short Reflections Thereon.*[160] In the 1721 collection, it was reprinted with the title, *Reflections on a Slanderous Libel against Dr. Owen, in a Letter to Sir Thomas Overbury.*[161] Here Owen is responding to

---

156 Owen, *Cases of Conscience*, discourse 13.
157 Owen, *Cases of Conscience*, discourses 1, 2, 4, 5, 6, 10.
158 Owen, *Cases of Conscience*, discourse 6.
159 Owen, *Cases of Conscience*, discourses 4, 6, 7, 8, 9, 10.
160 John Owen, "[Reflections]," in *An Expostulatory Letter to the Author of the Slanderous Libel against Dr. O. With Some Short Reflections Thereon* (London: n.p., 1671).
161 Owen, *Complete Collection of Sermons etc.* (1721), 615–21.

Gloucestershire parson George Vernon, who anonymously leveled a number of serious accusations, including sedition, the violation of lawful promises and oaths, theological heterodoxy, and moral duplicity. Vernon clearly intends to portray Owen as a ringleader of Nonconformist mischief-making. Owen, of course, vehemently denies the charges and seeks to defend his integrity.

A Letter concerning the Matter of the Present Excommunications (1683, 1721)

Another letter of polemical tone and also contained in the present volume was first published in 1683, Owen's final year, with the title *A Letter concerning the Matter of the Present Excommunications*.[162] This too is reproduced in the 1721 collection.[163] Little is known about the specific occasion of this letter or its intended recipient, although Owen remarks with some surprise that he had been requested to comment on the effect that the prosecution of the Dissenters might have on their consciences. At any rate, the general circumstances of the letter are readily apparent. Having retired from the Leadenhall Street congregation in 1681, Owen and his fellow Dissenters would continue to chafe against the establishment authorities throughout his final years—encounters that were no doubt exacerbated by the political volatility that lingered after the alleged Popish Plot of 1678–1681.[164]

Throughout this letter, Owen objects to what he believes is an entirely illegitimate abuse of authority in the excommunication of Nonconformists by the Crown's civil prosecutors at Doctors' Commons. It is one thing to render public gatherings illegal, as the 1670 reiteration of the Conventicles Act had done, and to prosecute offenders accordingly. However abhorrent the practice, Owen readily acknowledges that civil and penal statutes can legitimately execute this outcome. But it is an entirely different matter for the Crown, through its lawyers and ecclesiastical officers, to presume for itself what is strictly a spiritual ordinance of Christ.[165] In short, Owen answers

---

162 John Owen, *A Letter concerning the Matter of the Present Excommunications* (London: for Benjamin Alsop, 1683).

163 Owen, *Complete Collection of Sermons etc.* (1721), 597–604.

164 Gribben, *John Owen and English Puritanism*, 257–61.

165 Speaking of "chancellors, archdeacons, commissaries, officials, with their court attendants," Owen tartly remarks, "these horrid names, with the reports concerning them, and their power, are enough to terrify poor harmless men, and make them fear some evil from them. But excommunication is that which no man knows on what grounds to fear, from these names, titles, and offices: for that is the name of a divine ordinance instituted by Christ in the gospel, to be administered according to the rule and law thereof; but these names, and those unto whom they do belong, are utterly foreign unto the Scriptures, and as unto this work, to the practice of the

his correspondent's query by insisting that any public writ of excommunication issued outside the lawful bounds of Christ's spiritual order as set out in Scripture has no power to bind the conscience of any individual in question, regardless of the impact it might have on their outward circumstances.

A Discourse concerning the Administration of Church Censures (1721)

Alongside this letter, and also in the posthumous 1721 collection, are Owen's more constructive observations on the practice of church discipline and excommunication, published under the title *A Discourse concerning the Administration of Church Censures.*[166] Whether or not this had already been published, as Goold postulates, or was first compiled for the 1721 collection from the notebooks of Hartopp, is difficult to know.[167] The tract itself explores the complicated situation where the discipline of a particular congregation might need to be evaluated or vindicated in the face of objection. Consistent with his mature ecclesiological convictions, Owen is adamant that each congregation retains a liberty to govern its own affairs according to the immediate authority of Christ and his word. Accordingly, an individual congregation possesses the right to excommunicate a member according to such Christ-ordained jurisdiction without any external interference. Yet, on the assumption that congregations may occasionally err and make false judgments, Owen appeals to principles of natural justice that impel cases to be weighed by other congregations in a collaborative fashion, according to general biblical guidelines about the way disputes should be resolved.

An Answer unto Two Questions, and *Twelve Arguments, against Any Conformity of Members of Separate Churches, to the National Church* (1720)

Owen's ecclesiological convictions are also clearly on display in *An Answer unto Two Questions,* with its sequel, *Twelve Arguments, against Any Conformity of Members of Separate Churches, to the National Church,* published by William and Joseph Marshall in 1720.[168] Owen's nineteenth-century biographer William Orme indicates that this tract appeared around the time of Owen's death and

church for a thousand years; what therefore is done by them of this kind, must of necessity be utterly null, seeing that as such, they have no place in the church themselves by the authority of Christ." Owen, *Letter concerning Excommunications.*

166 Owen, *Complete Collection of Sermons etc.* (1721), 605–14.
167 John Owen, *The Works of John Owen,* ed. William H. Goold, 24 vols. (Edinburgh: Johnstone and Hunter, 1850–1855), 16:222 (hereafter cited as *Works*).
168 Owen, *Seventeen Sermons* (1720), 379–400.

was quickly refuted by his longtime sparring partner, Richard Baxter.[169] As Owen had maintained elsewhere, his chief contention with the public worship of the established church did not so much concern the theological content of its liturgy, as contained in the Book of Common Prayer, or even in the use of set liturgical forms per se, but with its enforced imposition in public worship. To his mind, such an imposition entailed an illegitimate encroachment upon Christ's immediate authority over the affairs of the church and its public worship, as reflected in the explicit directions of Scripture. Owen's adherence to something like the so-called regulative principle was always driven more by Christological convictions than anything else.[170] And in these two tracts, he insists that it is as illegitimate to participate in the public worship of the established church after having once dissented from it, as it is to impose the liturgy in the first place. Owen readily concedes that a person may freely use set forms of prayer as an aid in personal devotion or even public worship, although he is circumspect about such a prospect, no doubt. But that is not his chief concern here. Rather, what cannot be sanctioned is a Dissenter participating in the public worship of the established church, for that amounts to no less than a tacit and ultimately disingenuous approval of what the individual once denounced.

Of Infant Baptism, and Dipping (1721)

Of Infant Baptism, and Dipping, published in the 1721 collection, is actually an assemblage of three shorter tracts, one defending the practice of infant baptism, followed by a refutation of "Mr. Tombs," a cleric known for his opposition to infant baptism, who in doing so appealed to two passages from Irenaeus's *Adversus haereses*. The final tract contains some exegetical notes questioning the biblical precedent typically cited for insisting that baptism must always entail full immersion.[171]

As Gribben notes, the provenance of the collection is uncertain.[172] It is hard to know whether the three tracts were written at the same time, although Lee

---

169 John Owen, *The Works of John Owen*, ed. Thomas Russell (London: Richard Baynes, 1826), 384. Cf. Richard Baxter, *Catholick Communion Defended against Both Extremes: and Unnecessary Division Confuted, by Reasons against Both the Active and Passive Ways of Separation* (London: Tho. Parkhurst, 1684).

170 I have argued this claim more fully elsewhere. See Andrew M. Leslie, "John Owen and the Immediacy of Christ's Authority Over Christian Worship," *Westminster Theological Journal* 80, no. 1 (2018): 25–50.

171 Owen, *Complete Collection of Sermons etc.* (1721), 575–82.

172 Crawford Gribben, "John Owen, Baptism, and the Baptists," in *By Common Confession: Essays in Honor of James M. Renihan*, ed. Ronald S. Baines, Richard C. Barcellos, and James P. Butler (Palmdale, CA: Reformed Baptist Academic Press, 2015), 53–71.

Gatiss provides a possible reconstruction of the circumstances that date at least the first two tracts soon after the appearance of the third part of John Tombes's *Anti-Paedobaptism* in 1657, which includes his appeal to Irenaeus.[173] Even so, it has been questioned whether the tracts were ever intended to be published or whether the argument contained therein represents Owen's mature thinking on the matter, or whether Owen was indeed their author. Certainly, Owen's views on baptism do show signs of evolution across his corpus,[174] and his distinctive model of the biblical covenants, as outlined in his famous commentary on the book of Hebrews, has captured the attention of particular Baptists from figures as early as Edward Hutchinson, Thomas Delaune, and Nehemiah Coxe.[175] There it is true that Owen occasionally hints at a distinction between the covenant of grace and a "carnal" covenant with Abraham in a way that he does not in this tract.[176] Leaving aside questions of provenance, it is possible to overstate the difference, however. As Samuel Renihan rightly observes, Owen's mature position on the Abrahamic covenant does not neatly separate its carnal and spiritual dimensions, something that is most evident in the fact that he clearly regards circumcision to be a sacrament of the covenant of grace.[177] And aside from this, the arguments in this tract are otherwise consistent with Owen's mature view of infant baptism in the Hebrews commentary.[178] What is noteworthy is the way the tract grounds the practice of infant baptism not only in a continuity within the covenant

---

173 Lee Gatiss, *Cornerstones of Salvation: Foundations and Debates in the Reformed Tradition* (Welwyn Garden City, UK: Evangelical Press, 2017), 161n7. Cf. John Tombes, *Anti-Paedobaptism: Or the Third Part* (London: E. Alsop, 1657), 760–62.

174 See Gribben, "Baptism."

175 See, e.g., Pascal Denault, *The Distinctiveness of Baptist Covenant Theology: A Comparison between Seventeenth-Century Particular Baptist and Paedobaptist Federalism* (Vestavia Hills, AL: Solid Ground Christian Books, 2013); Samuel D. Renihan, *From Shadow to Substance: The Federal Theology of the English Particular Baptists (1642–1704)* (Oxford: Regent's Park College, 2018).

176 Part of the issue might be that Owen is not speaking of a "covenant" with Abraham univocally in every instance. On occasion, he seems to deploy the concept in terms broadly equivalent to the covenant of grace, loosely speaking, of course, since strictly speaking, he believes this covenant existed only in the Old Testament in promissory form before was formally ratified as such by Christ's death. E.g., Owen, *Works*, 18:120; 23:62–63. At other times, Owen suggests an Abrahamic covenant that has a discrete temporal purpose sitting alongside the gracious promise, much as he thinks the Mosaic covenant does. E.g., Owen, *Works*, 23:74.

177 In the Hebrews commentary, Owen is explicit that circumcision functioned as a sacrament of initiation into Christ just as baptism does. Owen, *Works*, 21:155. Cf. Renihan, *From Shadow to Substance*, 214.

178 I will leave aside the arguments particular Baptists have made for a compatibility between Owen's model of the covenants in the Hebrews commentary and their own "anti-paedobaptist" position.

of grace but also in a principle of the natural law and justice, or what it calls the "law of the creation of humankind" that binds children to the rights and privileges of their parents.[179]

Of Marrying after Divorce in Case of Adultery (1721)

The final short tract in this present volume, also published in 1721, and of unknown origin, is an essay on the question of remarriage after divorce.[180] Here Owen disputes with what he labels a Catholic indissolublist position on divorce and argues that divorce stemming from adultery, malicious desertion, or a renunciation of the Christian faith results in a dissolution of the marriage contract and must result in freedom for the innocent party to remarry. In support of his case, Owen appeals to the famous "Matthean exception" (Matt. 19:9), the apostle Paul's remarks in 1 Corinthians 7:15, as well as the law of nature with the consent of the nations more generally.

Leaving aside the provenance of this tract, Owen's position here is consistent with the sixteenth-century Protestant attempt to codify divorce parameters within Church of England canon law in the proposed *Reformatio legum ecclesiasticarum* of 1552.[181] This codification was never passed, however, and in the eventual appearance of canon law in 1604, the laws permitting divorce were much more restrictive; and so while marriage was no longer regarded as a sacrament, it remained virtually indissoluble in practice until the nineteenth century.[182]

---

179 Owen, *Of Infant Baptism, and Dipping*. Cf., Owen, *Works*, 23:354.

180 Owen, *Complete Collection of Sermons etc.* (1721), 572–74.

181 A manuscript copy survives in the British Museum. A published version is dated to 1571, and in subsequent English translations. See James C. Spalding, "The Reformatio Legum Ecclesiasticarum of 1552 and the Furthering of Discipline in England," *Church History* 39, no. 2 (June 1970): 167.

182 Cf. Diarmaid MacCulloch, *Reformation: Europe's House Divided* (London: Penguin, 2004), 660–61.

PART 1

WORKS ON SCRIPTURE

OF THE DIVINE ORIGINAL, AUTHORITY, SELF-EVIDENCING LIGHT, AND POWER OF THE SCRIPTURES.

With an Answer to That Enquiry, *How We Know the Scriptures to Be the Word of God.*

———

Also
A Vindication of the Purity and Integrity of the Hebrew and Greek Texts of the Old and New Testament; in some Considerations on the *Prolegomena, and Appendix to the late Biblia Polyglotta.*

———

Whereunto Are Subjoined Some Exercitations about the Nature and Perfection of the Scripture, the Right of Interpretation, Internal Light, Revelation, Etc.

———

By John Owen: D.D.

———

Ἐραυνᾶτε τὰς γραφάς. Joh. 5.39.

———

Oxford,
Printed by Henry Hall, Printer
to the University,
for Tho: Robinson. 1659.

Of the Divine Original
Contents

The third tract mentioned on the title page above was published separately in Latin in 1658; namely, *Pro Sacris Scripturis*. Chapter titles for this treatise have been added by the volume editor.

The Dedicatory Epistle

To My Reverend and Worthy Friends
The Prebends of Christ Church College in Oxford
With All the Students in Divinity in That Society

THE REASON OF MY INSCRIBING the ensuing pleas for the authority, purity, and perfection of the Scripture, against the pretenses of some to the contrary, in these days, unto you, is because some of you value and study the Scripture as much as any I know, and it is the earnest desire of my heart, that all of you would so do. Now whereas two things offer themselves unto me, to discourse with you by the way of preface, namely the commendation of the Scripture, and an exhortation to the study of it on the one hand, and a discovery of the reproach that is cast upon it, with the various ways and means that are used by some for the lessening and depressing of its authority and excellency on the other; the former being to good purpose, by one or other almost every day performed; I shall insist at present on the latter only; which also is more suited to discover my aim and intention in the ensuing discourses. Now herein as I shall, it may be, seem to exceed that proportion which is due unto a preface to such short discourses as these following; yet I know, I shall be more brief than the nature of so great a matter as that proposed to consideration does require. And therefore ἄνευ προοιμίων καὶ παθῶν,[1] I shall fall upon the subject that now lies before me.

Many there have been and are, who, through the craft of Satan, and the prejudice of their own hearts, lying under the power of corrupt and carnal interest, have engaged themselves to decry, and disparage, that excellency of the Scripture which is proper and peculiar unto it. The several sorts of them are too many particularly to be considered, I shall only pass through them in general, and fix upon such instances by the way as may give evidence to the things insisted on.

---

1 Gk. "without introduction and solemnity."

Those who in this business are first to be called to an account, whose filth and abominations given out in gross, others have but parceled among themselves, are they of the synagogue of Rome. These pretend themselves to be the only keepers and preservers of the word of God in the world; the only "ground and pillar of truth."[2] Let us then a little consider in the first place, how it has discharged this trust; for it is but equal that men should be called to an account upon their own principles; and those who supposing themselves to have a trust reposed in them, do manifest a treacherous mind, would not be one whit[3] better if they had so indeed.

What then have these men done in the discharge of their pretended trust? Nay what has that synagogue left unattempted? Yea what has it left unfinished, that may be needful to convince it of perfidiousness?[4] that says the Scripture was committed to it alone, and would, if it were able, deprive all others of the possession of it or of their lives; what Scripture then was this, or when was this deed of trust made unto them? The oracles of God, they tell us, committed to the Jews under the Old Testament, and all the writings of the New; and that this was done from the first foundation of the church by Peter, and so on to the finishing of the whole canon. What now have they not done in adding, detracting, corrupting, forging, aspersing those Scriptures to falsify their pretended trust? They add more books to them, never indited by the Holy Ghost, as remote from being θεόπνευστα, ὡς οὐρανὸς ἐστ᾽ ἀπὸ γαίης:[5] so denying the self-evidencing power of that word, which is truly ἐξ οὐρανοῦ,[6] by mixing it with things ἐξ ἀνθρώπων,[7] of a human rise and spring; manifesting themselves to have lost the Spirit of discerning, promised with the word, to abide with the true church of God forever (Isa. 59:21). They have taken from its fullness and perfection, its sufficiency and excellency, by their Masora,[8] their oral law or *verbum* ἄγραφον,[9] their unknown, endless, bottomless, boundless treasure of traditions; that πάνσοφον φάρμακον[10] for

---

2 1 Tim. 3:15.

3 I.e., a very small part or particle.

4 I.e., the quality of disloyalty or unfaithfulness.

5 Gk. "divinely inspired, 'as heaven is from earth.'" Owen is alluding to Hesiod's *Theogony*, line 720. For the original Greek text and an English translation, see Hesiod, *Theogony. Works and Days. Testimonia*, trans. Glenn W. Most, Loeb Classical Library 57 (Cambridge, MA: Harvard University Press, 2018), 60–61.

6 Gk. "from heaven."

7 Gk. "of human origin."

8 I.e., the body of scribal annotations on the text of the Hebrew Bible compiled during the first millennium AD.

9 Lat., Gk. "unwritten word" (i.e., oral tradition).

10 Gk. "learned potion."

all their abominations. The Scripture itself; as they say, committed to them, they plead, to their eternal shame, to be in the original languages corrupted, vitiated, interpolated,[11] so that it is no stable rule to guide us throughout in the knowledge of the will of God. The Jews, they say, did it while they were busy in burning of Christians. Therefore in the room of the originals, they have enthroned a translation that was never committed to them, that came into the world they know neither how, nor when, nor by whom. So that one says of its author, "If anyone were to inquire whether he was a Gaul or Sarmatian, a Jew or Christian, a man or woman, his advocates would find no easy answer."[12] All this to place themselves in the throne of God, and to make the words of a translation authentic from their stamp upon them, and not from their relation unto, and agreement with, the words spoken by God himself. And yet further, as if all this were not enough to manifest what trustees they have been, they have cast off all subjection to the authority of God in his word, unless it be resolved into their own; denying that any man in the world can know it to be the word of God, unless they tell him so; it is but ink and paper, skin of parchment, a dead letter, a nose of wax, a Lesbian rule,[13] of no authority unto us at all. O faithful trustees! Holy mother church! Infallible chair! Can wickedness yet make any farther progress? Was it ever heard of from the foundation of the world, that men should take so much pains, as these men have done, to prove themselves faithless, and treacherous in a trust committed to them? Is not this the sum and substance of volumes that have even filled the world; the word of God was committed to us alone, and no others; under our keeping it is corrupted, depraved, vitiated; the copies delivered unto us we have rejected, and taken up one of our own choice; nor let any complain of us, it was in our power to do worse. This sacred *depositum*[14] had no κριτήρια,[15] whereby it might be known to be the word of God; but it

---

11 I.e., corrupted with the insertion of additional material.

12 In the text: *Si quis percontetur Gallus fuerit an Sarmata, Judaeus an Christianus, vir an mulier, nihil habituri sint ejus patroni quod expedite respondeant.*—Owen. Editor's translation. Owen footnotes the quotation with "Erasmus." Desiderius Erasmus (1466–1536) was a Dutch Catholic priest and humanist who is most famous for his Latin and Greek editions of the New Testament, and for his disputations with Martin Luther on the liberty of the human will. The quotation comes from Erasmus's preface to the fourth and fifth editions of his Greek New Testament, "De duabus postremis aeditionibus quarta et quinta," in *Novum Testamentum, iam quintum accuratissima cura recognitum à Des. Erasmo Roter* (Basel: Frobenius, 1535), *4 (page numbers with an asterisk refer to unnumbered pages in the original). Owen has added "*ejus patroni*" to the original quotation.

13 I.e., a lead mason's tool that was flexible and used for measuring and marking out curves.

14 Lat. "deposit."

15 Gk. "criteria."

is upon our credit alone, that it passes in the world, or is believed; we have added to it many books upon our own judgment, and yet think it not sufficient for the guidance of men, in the worship of God, and the obedience they owe unto him: yet do they blush? Are they ashamed as a thief when he is taken? Nay do they not boast themselves in their iniquity? and say, they are sold to work all these abominations? The time is coming, yea it is at hand, wherein it shall repent them forever, that they have lifted up themselves against this sacred grant of the wisdom, care, love, and goodness of God.

Sundry other branches there are of the abominations of these men, besides those enumerated; all which may be reduced to these three corrupt and bloody fountains.

1. That the Scripture at best, as given out from God, and as it is to us continued, was, and is, but a partial revelation of the will of God: the other part of it, which how vast and extensive it is no man knows (for the Jews have given us their δευτερώσεις[16] in their Mishnah[17] and Gemara; these kept them locked up in the breast, or chair of their holy Father), being reserved in their magazine of traditions.

2. That the Scripture is not able to evince or manifest itself to be the word of God, so as to enjoy and exercise any authority in his name, over the souls and consciences of men; without an accession of testimony, from that combination of politic, worldly minded men, that call themselves the Church of Rome.

3. That the original copies of the Old and New Testaments are so corrupted (*ex ore tuo, serve nequam*)[18] that they are not a certain standard and measure of all doctrines, or the touchstone of all translations.

Now concerning these things you will find somewhat offered unto your consideration in the ensuing discourses; wherein, I hope, without any great altercation or disputes, to lay down such principles of truth, as that their idol imaginations will be found cast to the ground before the sacred ark of the word of God, and to lie naked without wisdom or power.

It is concerning the last of these only, that at present I shall deliver my thoughts unto you; and that because we begin to have a new concernment therein, wherewith I shall afterward acquaint you. Of all the inventions of Satan to draw off the minds of men from the word of God, this of decrying the authority of the originals seems to me the most pernicious. At the beginning of the Reformation, before the Council of Trent, the Papists did but faintly,

16 Gk. "second rank." This is a reference to the Jewish "secondary" literature, or the inscribed oral tradition known as the Mishnah.
17 "Mishna" in original, updated to modern spelling convention.
18 Lat. "from your own mouth, O wicked servant" (an allusion to Luke 19:22).

and not without some blushing, defend their Vulgar Latin translation. Some openly preferred the original before it, as Cajetan,[19] Erasmus, Vives,[20] and others. Yea, and after the council also, the same was done by Andradius,[21] Ferrarius,[22] Arias Montanus,[23] Masius,[24] and others. For those who understood nothing but Latin among them, and scarcely that, whose ignorance was provided for in the Council, I suppose it will not be thought meet that in this case we should make any account of them. But the state of things is now altered in the world, and the iniquity, which first wrought in a mystery, being now discovered, casts off its vizard[25] and grows bold; *nihil est audacius istis deprensis.*[26] At first the design was managed in private writings, Melchior Canus,[27] Gulielmus

19 In the margin: Praef. In 5. Lib. Mos.—Owen. See "Praefatio Thomae de Vio Caietani Cardinalis S. Xysti, in Quinque Mosaicos Libros," in Thomas Cajetan, *Opera omnia quotquot in sacrae Scripturae expositionem reperiuntur* [*tomus primus*] (Lyon: Iacobus et Petrus Prost, 1639). Thomas Cajetan (1469–1534) was an Italian Dominican Cardinal who is most famous for his highly influential commentary on Thomas Aquinas's *Summa theologiae*, and his polemical engagement with Martin Luther.

20 In the margin: In August. De Civitis Dei lib. 15. Cap. 13.—Owen. Juan Luis Vives (1493–1540) was a Spanish humanist who had a high regard for the original Hebrew text of the Old Testament. Owen is here referring to Juan Luis Vives's edition of Augustine's *De civitate Dei*, with Vives's own commentary on Augustine's text. See Augustine, *De civitate Dei* [. . .]; *insuper commentariis per undeque doctiss. virum Ioann. Lodovicum vivem illustrati et recogniti* (Basil: Frobenius, 1555), 830.

21 In the margin: *Defens. Conc. Trid*: lib. 4.—Owen. See Diogo de Paiva de Andrade, *Defensio Tridentinae fidei catholicae et integerrimae quinque libris compraehensa* (Lisbon: Antonius Riberius, 1578), 238r–295v. Diogo de Paiva de Andrade (1528–1575) was a Portuguese theologian most famous for his *Defensio Tridentinae fidei Catholicae* and his contributions to the Council of Trent.

22 In the margin: *Proleg. Biblica.*—Owen. See Nikolaus Serarius, *Prolegomena biblica, et commentaria in omnes epistolas canonicas* (Mainz: Balthasar Lippius, 1612). Nikolaus Serarius (1555–1609) was a French Jesuit biblical commentator who taught ethics, philosophy, and theology in Germany.

23 In the margin: *Praef. In Bibl: in Lat: & passim.*—Owen. See Arius Montanus, *Biblia sacra Hebraice, Chaldaice, Graece, et Latine* (Antwerp: Christoph. Plantinus, 1569–1572). Benedictus Arias Montanus (1527–1598), a Spanish Catholic priest and scholar, is particularly known for his work on the so-called Antwerp Polyglot Bible.

24 In the margin: *Praef. In Comment. In Josh.*—Owen. See Andreas Masius, *Iosuae imperatoris historia* (Antwerp: Christophorus Plantinus, 1574). Andreas Masius (1514–1573) was a Flemish Syriacist who was involved in the production of the Antwerp Polyglot Bible.

25 I.e., a mask.

26 Lat. "nothing is more audacious than those who have been caught in the act." Owen is alluding to Juvenal's *Satires* 6, lines 284–85. For the original Latin text and an English translation, see Juvenal, Persius, *Juvenal and Persius*, trans. Susanna Morton Braund, Loeb Classical Library 91 (Cambridge, MA: Harvard University Press, 2004), 258–59.

27 In the margin: *Loc. Com. Lib. 1. Cap. 13.*—Owen. See Melchior Cano, *Opera: In duo volumina distributa* (Madrid: Raymundus Ruiz, 1791–1792), 1:116–30. Owen's original has "lib. 1," which

Lindanus,[28] Bellarminus,[29] Gregorius de Valentia,[30] Leo Castrius,[31] Huntlaeus,[32] Hanstelius [*sic*],[33] with innumerable others, some on one account, some on another, have pleaded that the originals were corrupted; some of them with more impudence than others. Leo Castrius, as Pineda observes, raves almost, wherever he falls on the mention of the Hebrew text. "But that author is," says he, "barely in control of himself when he comes upon such Hebraisms; and although with good intention, nevertheless is carried away beyond the limits of truth and modesty either out of ignorance of certain things or from some more ardent desire; and if we were to appraise that man Leo only from the claws he has shown here, we would not judge him, even on the basis of his other outstanding efforts, to be a mouse, a fox, or a dog, or some other more worthless creature."[34] Yea, Morinus, who seems to be ashamed of nothing, yet

---

appears to be an error. Melchior Cano (1509–1560) was a Spanish Dominican most famous for his posthumously published *De locis theologicis.*

28 In the margin: *De opt. Gen. Interpr.* Lib.1.—Owen. See Willem van der Lindt, *De optimo Scripturas interpretandi genere libri iii* (Cologne: Maternus Cholinus, 1558), 15r–60r. Willem van der Lindt (1525–1588) was a Dutch Bishop and Catholic apologist.

29 In the margin: Lib. 2. *De verb. Dei.*—Owen. See Robert Bellarmine, *Opera omnia*, 6 vols. (Naples: Josephum Giuliano, 1856–1862), 1:61–95. Robert Bellarmine (1542–1621) was an Italian Jesuit Cardinal and polemicist prominent for his contribution to the Counter-Reformation.

30 In the margin: Tom. 1. D. 5 Q. 3.—Owen. See Gregorio de Valentia, *Commentariorum theologicorum* (Lyon: Horatio Cardon, 1609), 1:1057–74. Gregorio de Valentia (1550–1603) was a Spanish Jesuit most famous for his *Commentariorum theologicorum* on Thomas Aquinas's *Summa theologiae.*

31 In the margin: *De Translat. Srae. Cum Comment. In Isa.*—Owen. See León de Castro, *Commentaria in Esaiam prophetam, ex sacris Scriptoribus Graecis, et Latinis confecta* (Salamanca: Mathias Gastius, 1570). León de Castro (ca. 1505–1585) was a Spanish Professor of theology at Salamanca, famous for his polemical interaction with Arias Montanus's use of the Hebrew and Chaldean text in the Antwerp Polyglot Bible.

32 In the footnote: *Epito. Controv. Contr.* 1. C. 8.—Owen. See James Gordon, *Controversiarum epitomes [tomus primus]* (Poitiers: Ex praelo Antonii Mesnerii, 1612), 19–25. James Gordon (1543–1620), referred to by Owen as Huntley the Jesuit, was a Scottish-born Jesuit scholar of Hebrew and theology, and also known as a zealous apologist for the Catholic cause.

33 In the margin: *Dispunctio Calum. Casaub.*—Owen. See Pierre Lanssel, "Brevis omnium qua notarum, qua calumniarum quae ab Isaaco Casaubono in Exercitationibus suis adversus Illustr. Cardin. Baronium Iustino Martyri inuruntur, dispunctio," in *Sancti Iustini philosophi et martiris opera* (Paris: Sébastien Cramoisy, 1636), 517–39. The published edition incorrectly reads "Hanstelius" in reference to Pierre Lanssel (1579–1632), who was a Jesuit priest, most famous for his edition of the works of Dionysius the Areopagite.

34 In the text: *Sed is est author* [...] *dum in hujusmodi Ebraizationes incidit, vix sui compos; & bono licet zelo, tamen vel ignoratione rerum quarundam, vel vehementiori aliqua affectione, extra fines veritatis & modestiae rapitur:& si ex hujusmodi tantum unguibus Leonem illum estimaremus, non etiam ex aliis praeclaris conatibus, aut murem aut vulpem censeremus, aut canem aut quiddam aliud ignobilius.*—Owen. Editor's translation. In the footnote: *Pined. Lib.* 5. *De Reb. Solom.* C. 4. S.1.—Owen. See John de Pineda, *De rebus Salomonis Regis libri octo* (Mainz: Antonius Hieratus,

shrinks a little at this man's impudence and folly. "He wrote" says he, "six very long books, in which he seeks to demonstrate nothing other than the malicious and willful corruptions of the Jews; Castrius indeed wrote with holy zeal, but for such a great task as he has undertaken regarding the Hebrew text, he has been inadequately equipped."[35] In the steps of this Castrius walks Huntley, a subtle Jesuit, who in the treatise above cited,[36] ascribes the corruption of the Hebrew Bible to the good providence of God, for the honor of the Vulgar Latin. But these with their companions have had their mouths stopped by Reynolds,[37] Whitaker,[38] Junius,[39] Lubbertus,[40] Rivetus,[41] Chamierus,[42] Gerardus,[43] Amesius,[44]

1613), 352. John de Pineda (1558–1637) was a Spanish Jesuit scholar. He was distinguished for his engagement with biblical textual criticism, among other areas.

35 In the text: *Apologetici libros* [. . .] *sex bene longos scripsit, quibus nihil quam Judaeorum voluntarias & malignas depravationes demonstrare nititur; zelo sanè pio scripsit Castrius, sed libris Hebraicis ad tantum opus quod moliebatur parum erat instructus.*—Owen. In the margin: *Morin. Exercit. De Sincerit. Exerc. 1. C. 2.*—Owen. Editor's translation. See Jean Morin, *Exercitationes biblicae de Hebraei Graecique textus sinceritate: Pars prior* (Paris: Antonius Vitray, 1633), 22. Jean Morin (1591–1659) was a French Catholic priest and scholar most famous for his work on the Samaritan Pentateuch in the Paris Polyglot Bible, and for advocating the theory that the Masoretic Text had been corrupted.

36 In the margin: *cap. 10. Lib. 1.*—Owen. Cf., e.g., *Divina providentia factum esse ut haberemus vulgatam editionem ex Hebraeo textu, ante quam ille depravaretur.* Editor's translation: "Divine providence has enabled us to have the Vulgate edition of the Hebrew text as it was before it was corrupted." See Gordon, *Controversiarum epitomes* 1:46; cf. 35–46.

37 John Rainolds (1549–1607) was an English Puritan scholar, well respected in his time as an advocate of English Protestantism against the Counter-Reformation. He is also particularly remembered for his key role in presenting the need for a new English Bible translation, which resulted in the King James Bible.

38 William Whitaker (1548–1595) was an Elizabethan Protestant scholar and Master of St. John's College, Cambridge, who was well known for his Reformed convictions and as an active opponent of Catholic doctrine.

39 Franciscus Junius, the elder (1545–1602), a student of John Calvin, was a widely influential theologian, pastor, and biblical scholar throughout Europe. His contributions to Reformed theology include work on the Belgic Confession, the Tremellius-Junius Bible translation, and his *De vera theologia.*

40 Sibrand Lubbert (ca. 1555–1625) was a Dutch Reformed theologian, known for his polemical engagement with Hugo Grotius and Robert Bellarmine, and for his opposition to the Remonstrants and Socinians.

41 André Rivet (1572–1651) was a French Huguenot theologian, known for his opposition to Roman Catholicism and his contribution to the *Synopsis purioris theologiae.*

42 Daniel Chamier (1564–1621) was a French Huguenot theologian who established the Academy of Montpellier and was known for his polemical engagement with Roman Catholicism.

43 Johann Gerhard Sr. (1582–1637) was a German Lutheran theologian, famous for his opposition to Roman Catholicism and his *Loci theologici.*

44 William Ames (1576–1633) was an English Puritan clergyman and scholar, a student of William Perkins, and most famous for his polemical engagement with the Remonstrants as well as his *Medulla theologiae* (or *The Marrow of Theology*).

Glassius,[45] Alstedius,[46] Amama,[47] and others. So that a man would have thought this fire put to the house of God had been sufficiently quenched. But after all the endeavors hitherto used, in the days wherein we live, it breaks out in a greater flame; they now print the original itself and defame it; gathering up translations of all sorts, and setting them up in competition with it. When Ximenes put forth the Complutensian Bible,[48] Vatablus his,[49] and Arias Montanus those of the king of Spain, this cockatrice[50] was not hatched, whose fruit is now growing to a fiery flying serpent. It is now but saying the ancient Hebrew letters are changed from the Samaritan to the Chaldean; the points or vowels, and accents, are but lately invented, of no authority; without their guidance and direction nothing is certain in the knowledge of that tongue; all that we know of it comes from the translation of the LXX;[51] the Jews have corrupted the Old Testament; there are innumerable various lections both of the Old and New; there are other copies differing from those we now enjoy that are utterly lost. So that upon the matter there is nothing left unto men but to choose whether they will be Papists or atheists.

Here that most stupendous fabric that was ever raised by ink and paper, termed well by a learned man, "that most magnificent biblical work (which was ever brought to light since men have arisen),"[52] I mean the Parisian

---

45 Salomon Glass (1593–1656) was a German Hebraist and theologian. Inhabiting various chairs at universities throughout his career, his most famous work is his *Philologiae sacrae*, through which he made a significant contribution to contemporary biblical criticism.

46 Johann Heinrich Alsted (1588–1638) was a German-born Reformed theologian, most famous as an encyclopedist, for his contributions to Ramist logic, and for his theological opposition to Socinianism.

47 Sixtinus Amama (1593–1629) was a Dutch Reformed scholar who promoted knowledge of the biblical languages as an essential skill for theology.

48 I.e., the so-called Complutensian Polyglot Bible (1587). This was the first of the major Polyglot Bibles of the early modern period, patronized by Francisco Jiménez de Cisneros and published by the Complutense University in the Spanish city Alcalá de Henares. See *Vetus Testamentum multiplici lingua nunc primo impressum*, (Alcalá de Henares: Arnao Guillén de Brocar, 1514–1517). Francisco Jiménez de Cisneros was a Spanish Cardinal and statesman, regent of Spain on two occasions, and most famous for his involvement in the Grand Inquisition, his promotion of the Crusades, and his patronage of the Complutensian Polyglot.

49 Francis Vatablus, or François Vatable (late 1400s–1547) was a French humanist and linguist with notable skill in Hebrew and Greek.

50 I.e., a basilisk, a winged mythical beast that had the power of destroying animals and plants by its gaze or breath.

51 I.e., the Septuagint, the Greek translation of the Old Testament produced in the second and third centuries BC, and which is attributed in legend to seventy representatives of the twelve tribes of Israel, who independently were said to have produced an identical translation of the Hebrew Bible.

52 In the margin: *Edm. Castel. Praef. Ad Animad: Samar. In Bib. Poly.*—Owen. In the text: *Magnificentissimum illud (quod post homines natos in lucem prodiit unquam) opus biblicum.*—Owen.

Bibles,[53] is prefaced by a discourse of its erector, Michael Le Jay, wherein he denies the Hebrew text, prefers the Vulgar Latin[54] before it, and resolves that we are not left to the word for our rule, but to the Spirit that rules in their church:

> Therefore, for certain and without any doubt, the Vulgate edition ought to be before us, as that which contains the true and authentic origin of Holy Scripture in the universal tongue of the Catholic Church; this always ought to be consulted whenever the teachings of the faith are to be recalled; [...] moreover, it is reasonable to conclude from this that the true and most certain originals of the Christian faith reside in the Spirit of the church, and are not to be attacked again by the hands of her enemies.
>
> And certainly, whatever kind of holiness they pretend unto, they do not come to Holy Scripture with any piety or sincere veneration when they talk of it [Scripture] alone as the inescapable rule of salvation. Whether it be the chief enemies of the faith, or those less than well disposed toward the church, they have not resolved to search after the true Spirit of the Gospel when they consider the interpretation of contexts and the original sense of the holy books. They rush back with inordinate curiosity to the original autographs from which scarcely anything remains apart from certain things that are exceedingly obscure. That is to say, there is no more convenient way to stray from its [the Vulgate's] royal road, nor can they rest more pleasantly than in the theories of their private opinions, which they have typically determined to chase after as the only rule of their doctrine.

Editor's translation. Owen is quoting here, with slight alteration, from Edmund Castell's introduction to the collection of variant lections drawn from the *Samaritan Penteteuch* in the *Appendix* to Walton's London Polyglot Bible. See "Praefatio, de animadversionum Samariticarum in totum pentateuchum," in Brian Walton, *Biblia sacra polyglotta*, 6 vols. (London: Thomas Roycroft, 1653–1657), vol. 6, chap. 4, p. 1. Edmund Castell (1606–1685) was an English scholar of Semitic languages, he assisted Brian Walton in the production of the London Polyglot Bible before going on to produce his life's work, the *Lexicon heptaglotton* of 1669, a landmark publication of significant length and scholarship.

53 I.e., the so-called Paris Polyglot Bible (1645). This is the second to last of the major early modern polyglot Bibles, produced under the supervision of Guy-Michel Lejay. See *Biblia: 1. Hebraica, 2. Samaritana, 3. Chaldaica, 4. Graeca, 5. Syriaca, 6. Latina, 7. Arabica: Quibus textus originales totius scripturae sacrae, quorum pars in editione complutensi* (Paris: Antonius Vitray, 1645). Guy-Michel Lejay was an advocate at the French Parliament and is most famous for his patronage of the Paris Polyglot Bible.

54 I.e., the Vulgate, Jerome's fourth-century Latin translation of the Bible, which was recognized as the authoritative Latin text by the Catholic Church at the Council of Trent.

Banish the blind fancy of their souls! The letter no longer abides in our instruction but the Spirit of the church; nor should anything be drawn from the sacred texts except what it [the church] desires to be communicated with us.[55]

So he, or Morinus in his name; and if this be indeed the true state of things, I suppose he will very hardly convince men of the least usefulness of this great work and undertaking. To usher those Bibles into the world, Morinus puts forth his Exercitations,[56] entitled *Of the Sincerity of the Hebrew and Greek Texts*,[57] indeed to prove them corrupt and useless. He is now the man among them that undertakes to defend this cause: in whose writings whether there be more of Pyrgopolynices,[58] or Rabshakeh,[59] is uncertain. But dogs that bark

---

55 In the margin: *Mich. Le Jay Praefat. Ad opus Bibl.*—Owen. In the text: *pro certo igitur atque indubitato apud nos esse debet, vulgatam editionem, quae communi catholicae ecclesiae lingua circumfertur verum esse & genuinum sacrae Scripturae fontem; hanc consulendam ubiq;, inde fidei dogmata repetenda; [. . .] ex quo insuper consentaneum est, vera ac certissima fidei Christianae autographa in Spiritu ecclesiae residere, neque ab ejus hostium manibus repetenda. [. . .]*

    Et certe quamcunque pietatis speciem praetexunt, non religione quapiam, aut sincera in Scripturam sacram veneratione aguntur, dum eam unicam, quasi ineluctabilem salutis regulam, usurpant, neque spiritûs evangelici veritatem investigare decreverunt; dum ad autographa curiosius recurrentes, ex quibus, praeter perplexa quaedam vestigia, vix aliquid superest, vel capitales fidei hostes, vel eos qui ecclesiae minus faverint, de contextuum interpretatione [sic; original has integritate] ac germano sacrorum codicum sensu consulunt. Scilicet non alia est opportunior via a regio illius itinere secedendi, neque in privatarum opinionum placitis blandius possunt acquiescere [sic; original has conquiescere], quas velut unicas doctrinae suae regulas sectari plerumque censuerunt [sic; original has consueuerunt].

    Apage caecam animorum libidinem, non jam in institutionem nostram subsistit litera, sed ecclesiae spiritus; neque e sacris codicibus hauriendum quidquam, nisi quod illa communicatum esse nobiscum voluerit.—Owen. Editor's translation. Owen is quoting here, with slight alteration, from Guy-Michel Lejay's introduction to the so-called Paris Polyglot Bible, "Instituti operis ratio," in *Biblia* [Paris Polyglot], 1:*11–12. More material alterations are noted. While the introduction is written under Lejay's name, Owen suspects it was actually written by Jean Morin, whose own translation of the Samaritan Pentateuch is published in the collection.

56 I.e., technical explorations of a matter in the form of a discourse.

57 See Morin, *Exercitationes pars prior*. This first edition contains the first part of the *Exercitationes*. The second part is only sketched in outline form at the end of this edition. The two parts were eventually published posthumously in 1660. See Jean Morin, *Exercitationum biblicarum de Hebraei Graecique textus sinceritate, libri duo* (Paris: Gasparus Meturas, 1660).

58 I.e., a soldier in a second-century BC Roman play who had an enormous ego and little intellect. For Owen to refer to this character is effectively to describe his target as a loud and proud fool with no real substance.

59 I.e., a title referring to a high official in the Assyrian army. The Rabshakeh was sent by Sennacherib to King Hezekiah in 2 Kings 18:17–37 (cf. Isa. 36:1–22). Owen may be referring to him here as a type of someone whose words are lofty and threatening but will ultimately amount to nothing.

loud, seldom bite deep; nor do I think many ages have produced a man of more confidence and less judgment; a prudent reader cannot but nauseate at all his leaves, and the man is well laid open by a learned person of his own party.[60] By the way, I cannot but observe, that in the height of his boasting, he falls upon his mother church, and embraces her to death,[61] that he might vaunt himself to be the first and only discoverer of corruptions in the original of the Old Testament, with the causes of them, he falls into a profound contemplation of the guidance of his church, which being ignorant of any such cause of rejecting the originals, as he has now informed her of, yet continued to reject them, and prefer the Vulgar Latin before them. "Here admire, reader," says he, "the Spirit of God who is closely present to the church, leading it with unhindered foot through matters which are obscure, mysterious and impenetrable; although the wanton neglect of the Rabbis, the monstrous ignorance and filthy corruptions of the Jewish books were unknown, and although heretics were audaciously hurling their opposition to these in a great procession of words, even so, it was not possible for the church to be moved to print again according to the norm and rule of Hebrew text the version that alone had been used for almost eleven hundred years."[62] But is it so indeed, that their church receives its guidance in a stupid, brutish manner, so as to be fixed obstinately on conclusions, without the least acquaintance with the premises? It seems she loved not the originals, but she knew not why; only she was obstinate in this, that she loved them not. If this be the state with their church, that when she has neither Scripture, nor tradition, nor reason, nor new revelation, she is guided she knows not how, as Socrates was by his demon,[63] or by secret and inexpressible species of pertinacity[64] and stubbornness falling upon her

---

60 In the margin: *Simeon de Muys. De sens. Sinc. Text. Heb.*—Owen. See Siméon Marotte de Muis, *Assertio hebraicae veritatis altera* (Paris: Ionannes Libert, 1634). Siméon Marotte de Muis (1587–1644) was a French Hebraist who objected to Morin's preference for the Samaritan Pentateuch over the Masoretic Text and is best known for his defenses of the Hebrew text.

61 In the text: *Exercit.* 1, cap. 1. Pag. 11.—Owen. See Morin, *Exercitationes pars prior*, 11.

62 In the text: *Hic admirare lector* [. . .] *Dei Spiritum ecclesiae praesentissimum, illam per obscura, perplexa, & invia quaeque, inoffenso pede agentem: quanquam incognita esset Rabbinorum supina negligentia, portentosa ignorantia, foedaque librorum Judaicorum corruptela, & Haeretici contraria his magna verborum pompa audacter jactarent; adduci tamen non potuit ecclesia, ut versio, qua sola per mille fere & centum annos usa fuerit, ad normam & amussim Hebraei textus iterum recuderetur.*—Owen. Editor's translation. See Morin, *Exercitationes pars prior*, 11.

63 Socrates (ca. 470–399 BC) was a Greek philosopher whose words and life have, via his famous student Plato, exercised great influence on philosophical thought from his time to today. His "demon" is a reference to something intangible that prevented him from acting in ways that would be harmful to himself.

64 I.e., a resolute adherence to a particular opinion or intention.

imagination; I suppose it will be in vain to contend with her any longer. For my own part I must confess, that I shall as soon believe a poor deluded fanatical Quaker, pretending to be guided by an infallible Spirit, as their pope with his whole conclave of cardinals, upon the terms here laid down by Morinus.

But to let these men pass for a season; had this leprosy kept itself within that house which is thoroughly infected, it had been of less importance: it is but a farther preparation of it for the fire. But it is now broken forth among Protestants also; with what designs, to what end or purpose, I know not, θεὸς οἶδε,[65] God knows, and the day will manifest. To declare at large how this is come about, *longa esset historia;*[66] too long for me to dwell upon; some heads of things I shall briefly touch at. It is known to all, that the reformation of religion, and restoration of good learning were begun, and carried on at the same time, and mostly by the same persons. There was indeed a triumvirate among the Papists of men excellently skilled in rabbinical learning before the Reformation. Raymundus Martinus,[67] Porchetus de Sylvaticis,[68] and Petrus Galatinus,[69] are the men; of the which, the last dedicated his book to Maximilian the emperor,[70] after that Zuinglius[71] and Luther[72] had begun to preach.

65 Gk. "God knows." This is a classical tag found, for instance, in Plato's *Phaedrus*, sec. 266b. See Plato, *Lysis. Symposium. Phaedrus*, ed. and trans. Chris Emlyn-Jones and William Preddy, Loeb Classical Library 166 (Cambridge, MA: Harvard University Press, 2022), 482–83.

66 Lat. "it would be a long story." This is a natural Latin phrase in the context and could be simply Owen's own comment. However, it may be a quotation from Petrarch, who uses this phrase on a couple of occasions, including in his *Epistolae de rebus familiaribus*, bk. 16, ep. 9. *Bibliotheca Oweniana* i.29.157 lists *Fr. Petrarchae Epistolae Familiares, Lugdb. 1601*, which Owen may therefore have had in his possession. For Latin text, see *Francisci Petrarcae epistolae de rebus familiaribus*, ed. Joseph Fracassetti, 3 vols. (Florence: Le Monnier, 1859–1863), 2:392.

67 Raimund Martini (ca. 1220–1284) was Spanish Dominican polemicist who engaged in missionary activity to Jews and Muslims. He was highly competent in Eastern languages and Rabbinic writings and is best known for his anti-Jewish polemic *Pugio fidei*.

68 Porchetus de Salvaticis (d. 1315) was an Italian Carthusian polemicist, whose chief anti-Semitic publication, *Victoria Porcheti adversus impios Hebraeos* (Paris: G. Desplains, 1520), closely followed Martini's arguments in *Pugio fidei*.

69 Pietro Colonna Galatino (1460–1540) was an Italian theologian and anti-Semitic polemicist who had a thorough knowledge of biblical languages. Like Porchetus de Salvaticis, his main polemical work borrowed significantly from that of Raimund Martini, though with more adjustments of his own.

70 Pietro Colonna Galatino, *De arcanis Catholicae veritatis* (Basel: Ioannes Hervagius, 1561). Maximilian I (1459–1519) was the Holy Roman Emperor and member of the Habsburg family. He was a powerful political figure in Europe.

71 Huldrych Zwingli (1484–1531), formerly a priest and later a Zürich pastor, was responsible for leading the Protestant Reformation in Switzerland.

72 Martin Luther (1483–1546), formerly an Augustinian friar and priest, initiated the Protestant Reformation in Germany. His work has been of foundational significance for the Protestant movement as a whole.

Upon the matter these three are but one: great are the disputes whether Galatinus stole his book from Raymundus or Porchetus; says Morinus, and calls his work "a monstrous theft, nothing comparable to which has ever been done":[73] from Raymundus, says Scaliger,[74] mistaking Raymundus Martinus for Raymundus Sebon; but giving the first tidings to the world of that book.[75] From Raymundus also, says Josephus de Voysin in his *Prolegomena* to the *Pugio fidei*,[76] and from him Hornbeck in his *Proleg. ad Jud.*[77] I shall not interpose in this matter, the method of Galatinus and his style are peculiar to him, but the coincidences of his quotations too many to be ascribed to common

73 In the text: *Plagium portentosum, cui vix simile unquam factum est: Exerc*: 1. Cap. 2.—Owen. Editor's translation. See Morin, *Exercitationes pars prior*, 16.

74 In the text: Epist. 2.41 [*sic*: 241].—Owen.

75 Joseph Scaliger (1540–1609) was a French classicist and Protestant convert. He was skilled in numerous languages and is noted for his contribution to the study of chronology. Scaliger discovered the lost *Pugio fidei*, suggesting that it should be attributed to the later Catalan theologian "Raimund Sebon" (confusing him with the earlier Catalan Dominican divine Raimund Martini), and that Pietro Colonna Galatino plagiarized portions of this work in his own *De arcanis Catholicae veritatis* (1561). Here Owen appears to be referring to a letter by Scaliger to Richard Thomson, where he remarks, *Perplurima inepta, futilia & sublesta eiusmodi in illo opera sunt, alioquin in quibusdam utili, addo etiam necessario; sed quod non temere, nec sine delectu tractandum. Est epitome ingentis operis, cui nomen, Pugio fidei adversus Iudaeos, auctore Raimundo Sebon Dominicano [. . .]. Quare ingratus fuit Galatinus iste Franciscanus, qui ne semel quidem nomen Raimundi Sebon memoravit.* Editor's translation: "There are a great many inept, pointless, and trifling comments of this kind in that work; otherwise it is in certain respects useful and, I would even add, necessary; but it needs to be handled with care and discrimination. It is an abridgement of that remarkable work called *Pugio fidei adversus Iudaeos*, by the Dominican author Raimund Sebon. Wherefore Galantino, that Franciscan, was ungrateful in that he did not once acknowledge the name of Raimund Sebon." It is likely that Owen is citing from this edition of Scaliger's letters, where it is numbered "241" (in bk. 3). See Joseph Scaliger, *Epistolae omnes quae reperiri potuerunt, nunc primum collectae ac editae* (Frankfurt: Aubriorus et Clemens Schleichius, 1628), 474.

76 Joseph de Voisin (1610–1685) was a French Hebraist most famous for his *Theologia Iudaeorum*. De Voisin contributed annotations to an edition of the *Pugio fidei*, which also attributes the work to Raimund Martini. Owen may be referring to comments in the *Prolegomena in pugionem fidei* (in this edition), which is attributed to Philippe Jacques de Maussac (Philippus Jacobus Maussacus). E.g., *Raymundum autem Martini verum auctorem. Eumque primum Iudaeos propriis armis confodisse. Galatinum vero quae habet bona, & utilia in Arcanis Catholicae veritatis, deinde ab ipso fuisse suffuratum.* Editor's translation: "The true author, however, is Raimund Martini. And he was the first to have struck down the Jews with his own weapons. In truth, that which has value and usefulness in *De arcanis Catholicae veritatis*, Galatino afterward stole from him." See Raimund Martini, *Pugio fidei* [. . .] *adversus Mauros, et Iudaeos* (Paris: Mathurinus Henault).

77 Cf., Johannes Hoornbeeck, *Tešuvah Jehuda, sive, Pro convincendis, et convertendis Judaeis* (Leiden: Petrus Leffen, 1655), 8–9. Johannes Hoornbeeck (1617–1666) was a Dutch Reformed theologian, a student of Gisbertus Voetius (1589–1676), and later professor of theology at Utrecht and Leiden.

accident. That Porchetus took his *Victoria adversus impios Judaeos* for the most part from Raymundus, himself confesses in his preface.[78] However certain it is, Galatinus had no small opinion of his own skill, and therefore, according to the usual way of men, who have attained, as they think, to some eminency in any one kind of learning, laying more weight upon it than it is able to bear, he boldly affirms, that the original of the Scripture is corrupted, and not to be restored but by the Talmud; in which one concession he more injures the cause he pleads for against the Jews, than he advantages it by all his books beside. Of his גלי רזייא of Rabbi Hakkadosh there is no more news as yet in the world, than what he is pleased to acquaint us withal.[79] At the same time Erasmus, Reuchlin,[80] Vives, Xantes Pagninus,[81] and others, moved effectually for the restoration of the Hebrew, Greek, and Latin. But the work principally prospered in the hands of the first Reformers, as they were all of them generally skilled in the Hebrew, so some of them as Capito,[82] Bibliander,[83] Fagius,[84] Munster[85] to that height and usefulness, that they may well be reckoned as the fathers and patriarchs of that learning. At that time lived Elias

78   See Porchetus de Salvaticis, *Victoria Porcheti adversus impios Hebraeos* (Paris: G. Desplains, 1520).

79   In his *De arcanis Catholicae veritatis*, Galatino refers to a Christian Kabbalistic apologetic text, גלי רזייא ("*Gale Razeya*," as per Galatino's Latin translation), which he alleges to be the work of Rabbi Hakkadosh or Judah Ha-Nasi (ca. AD 135–217), who is famous for compiling the Mishnah. The text does not actually exist and is likely to be a forgery, a charge which Galatino would emphatically deny. Owen, like others, is clearly doubtful of its authenticity, and in *Of the Integrity* remarks that it should be ignored. Cf. de Maussac's remarks about it in the *Prolegomena* to de Voisin's annotated edition of the *Pugio fidei*: *soli quoque Galatino valde familiarem; credendum est firmiter spurium eum esse, & supposititium nec a vero forte aberrabitur si ab eius inscriptione Arcana fuisse formata dicatur; Gale Razaija, namque revelans Arcana denotat.* Editor's translation: "It is also intimately known to Galatino alone; [and] it should be firmly judged as spurious and a forgery. Nor would it be wandering far from the truth if it is said to have been inspired from the title of his *Arcana*, i.e., *Gale Razaija*, for it denotes the revealing of a secret." See Martini, *Pugio fidei* [. . .] *adversus Mauros, et Iudaeos*, *7.

80   Johann Reuchlin (1455–1522) was a German humanist and Hebraist who was a notable Catholic advocate for the authenticity of the Hebrew text of the Old Testament.

81   Santes Pagnino (1470–1541) was an Italian Dominican friar who was a leading philologist, notable for his translation of the Scriptures and his lexical work on the Hebrew text of the Old Testament.

82   Wolfgang Capito (1478–1541) was an early German Protestant Reformer who settled in Strasbourg.

83   Theodore Bibliander (1509–1564) was a Swiss Reformer and Professor of theology at Basel, most notable for his biblical exegesis and Hebrew grammars.

84   Paul Fagius (1504–1549) was a German Protestant Hebraist who taught Old Testament at Strasbourg and later at Cambridge.

85   Sebastian Münster (1488–1552), a student of Elias Levita, was a German Protestant Hebraist who published an influential edition of the Hebrew Bible with a Latin translation.

Levita,[86] the most learned of the Jews of that age, whose grammatical writings were of huge importance in the studying of that tongue. This man, as he was acquainted with many of the first reformers, so he lived particularly with Paulus Fagius, as I have elsewhere declared.[87] Now in one book, which in those days he published, called *Masoreth Hammasoreth*, he broached a new opinion, not much heard of, at least not at all received among the Jews, nor for aught that yet appears, once mentioned by Christians before, namely that the points or vowels, and accents used in the Hebrew Bible, were invented by some critical Jew or Masorete,[88] living at Tiberias about five or six hundred years after Christ:[89] no doubt the man's aim was to reduce the world of Christians to a dependence on the ancient Rabbins, for the whole sense of the Scripture; *Hinc prima mali labes*,[90] here lies the first breach in this matter. The fraud being not discovered, and this opinion being broached and confirmed by the great and almost only master of the language of that age, some even of the first Reformers embraced his fancy.[91] Perhaps Zuinglius had spoken to it before:

86 Elias Levita (1469–1549) was a famous German Jewish Hebraist. He is known for his commentary on the Masoretic annotations on the Hebrew Bible, the *Massoreth Ha-Massoreth* or, as Owen refers to it here, the *Masoreth Hammasoreth*. Levita had a particular influence on a number of early Protestants, including his student Sebastian Münster, who translated Levita's works into Latin. As Owen goes on to allude, Levita also spent 1540–1542 with Paul Fagius, overseeing the Hebrew printing press at Isny.

87 Owen appears to be referring to his remarks in *Of the Integrity*, chap. 5.

88 The Masoretes (ca. 500–ca. 1000) were a community of Jewish scholars dedicated to meticulously preserving and transmitting both the consonantal text of the Hebrew Old Testament and the Jewish oral tradition of vocalization. The Tiberian Masoretes (ca. 600 onward) were a prominent branch of this movement based in the city of Tiberias, next to the sea of Galilee.

89 A parallel Hebrew and English edition of this work was published in the nineteenth century: Elias Levita, *The Massoreth Ha-Massoreth of Elias Levita*, ed. Christian D. Ginsburg (London: Longmans, Green, Reader, and Dyer, 1867).

90 Lat. "From this comes the first slide toward misfortune." Owen is quoting Virgil's *Aeneid*, bk. 2, line 97. For Latin text and an English translation, see Virgil, *Eclogues. Georgics. Aeneid: Books 1–6*, trans. H. Rushton Fairclough, rev. G. P. Goold, Loeb Classical Library 63 (Cambridge, MA: Harvard University Press, 1999), 322–33.

91 As Richard Muller observes, early Reformers such as Luther and Calvin saw no difficulty in affirming the late origin of the vowel points, without mentioning Levita's commentary on the Massora, which was published in 1538. Once published, Levita's theory was quickly disseminated by early Protestant Hebraists like Münster, who was responsible for reprinting his commentary in Basel. One of the first suggestions of controversy over the origin of the points arose in a debate between Bishop John Jewel and the Catholic polemicist Thomas Harding (see his *Answer to M. Harding's Answer*, first published in 1565: John Jewel, *The Works*, 4 vols., ed. John Ayre [Cambridge: The University Press, 1845–1850], 2:678–79), who leveraged their late origin in service of arguing that "the vulgar people" should be prevented from reading Scripture. See Richard A. Muller, *After Calvin: Studies in the Development of a Theological Tradition* (New York: Oxford University Press, 2003), 146–47.

justly I know not. After a while the poison of this error beginning to operate, the Papists waiting on the mouths of the Reformers, like the servants of Benhadad on Ahab,[92] to catch at every word that might fall from them to their advantage, began to make use of it. Hence Cochlaeus[93] applauds Luther, for saying the Jews had corrupted the Bible with points and distinctions, as well he might, for nothing could be spoken more to the advantage of his cause against him. Wherefore other learned men began to give opposition to this error; so did Munster, Junius, and others, as will be shown in the ensuing discourse. Thus this matter rested for a season. The study of the Hebrew tongue and learning being carried on, it fell at length on him, who undoubtedly has done more real service for the promotion of it, than any one man whatever, Jew or Christian. I mean Buxtorfius the elder;[94] his *Thesaurus grammaticus*,[95] his *Tiberias*, or *Commentarius Masorethicus*,[96] his Lexicons and Concordances,[97] and many other treatises, whereof some are not yet published,[98] evince this to all the world. Even Morinus says that he is the only man among Christians, that ever thoroughly understood the Masora; and Simeon de Muis acknowledges his profiting by him, and learning from him; other Jews who undertake to be teachers, know nothing but what they learn of him. To omit the testimony of all sorts of learned men, giving him the preeminence in this learning, it may suffice that his works praise him. Now this man in his *Tiberias* or

92   Owen is referring to the Syrian king Benhadad's war with the Israelite king Ahab (1 Kings 20) and may have in mind the way the servants of Benhadad sought to take advantage of Ahab's leniency by dressing in rough cloths and placing ropes on their heads.

93   In the text: *lib. De Auth. Scripturae, cap.* 5.—Owen. See Johannes Cochlaeus, *De canonicae Scripturae, et Catholicae Ecclesiae authoritate* (Rome: D. Hieronymam de Cartulariis, 1543), 32r–v. Johann Cochlaeus (1479–1552) was a German humanist and anti-Lutheran polemicist.

94   Johann Buxtorf Sr. (1564–1629) was a notable German Protestant Hebraist who was famous for his posthumously published *Lexicon Chaldaicum, Talmadicum et rabbinicum* and his *Tiberius, sive Commentarius Masoreticus triplex*, which disputes Levita's late dating on the origin of the Hebrew vowel points in the Old Testament. Buxtorf Sr.'s legacy was continued by his son, Buxtorf Jr.

95   See Johann Buxtorf Sr., *Thesaurus grammaticus linguae sanctae Hebraeae: Duobus libris methodice propositus* (Basel: Conradus Waldkirchus, 1609).

96   See Johann Buxtorf Sr., *Tiberias, sive Commentarius Masorethicus triplex* (Basel: J. J. Deckeri, 1665); first published in 1620.

97   See Johann Buxtorf Sr., *Lexicon Hebraicum et Chaldaicum* (Basel: n.p., 1607); Buxtorf Sr., *Lexicon Chaldaicum, Talmudicum et rabbinicum* (Basel: Ludovicus König, 1639) (incomplete and edited by his son, Buxtorf Jr.); Buxtorf Sr., *Concordantiae Bibliorum Hebraicae* (Basel: Ludovicus König, 1632) (also incomplete and edited by his son, Buxtorf Jr.).

98   In *Of the Integrity*, Owen makes reference to Buxtorf Jr.'s note concerning his father's forthcoming treatise, *Babylonia, sive Commentarius criticus in universum Targum, sive paraphrasin bibliorum Chaldaicum* (Universitätsbibliothek Basel, MS F IX 41), which was never published but used by Brian Walton in his comments on the Targums in the London Polyglot Bible.

Commentarius Masorethicus,[99] printed with the great Rabbinical Bible of his own correct setting forth at Basil, *anno* 1620,[100] considers at large this whole matter of the points, and discovers the vanity of Elias' pretension about the Tiberian Masoretes. But we must not it seems rest here: within a few years after, to make way for another design, which then he had conceived; Ludovicus Cappellus published a discourse in the defense of the opinion of Elias (at least so far as concerned the rise of the punctuation), under the title of *Arcanum punctationis revelatum*. The book was published by Erpenius without the name of the author.[101] But the person was sufficiently known; and Rivetus not long after took notice of him, and says he was his friend, but concealed his name.[102] This new attempt immediately pleases some. Among others, our learned professor Dr. Prideaux reads a public lecture on the vespers of our Comitia on that subject; wherein though he prefaces his discourse with an observation of the advantage the Papists make of that opinion of the novelty of the points, and the danger of it, yet upon the matter he falls in wholly with Cappellus, though he names him not.[103] Among the large encomiums[104] of himself, and his work, printed by Cappellus in the close of his *Critica sacra*, there are two letters from one Mr. Eyre here in England, in one whereof he tells him, that without doubt the Doctor read on that subject by the help of

---

99 See Buxtorf Sr., *Tiberias*.

100 Buxtorf Sr.'s Rabbinical Bible actually appeared two years prior to his *Tiberias*, in 1618. See Johann Buxtorf Sr., *Biblia sacra Hebraica et Chaldaica* (Basel: Ludovicus König, 1618).

101 Louis Cappel [s.n.], *Sôd han-niqqûd han-nigle, hoc est arcanum punctationis revelatum* [. . .] *edita a Thoma Erpenio* (Leiden: Johannes Maire, 1624). Louis Cappel (1585–1658) was a Huguenot and Hebraist at the Academy of Saumur, most controversial for his late dating of Hebrew vowel points and his *Critica sacra*, which promoted the practice of critical emendation of the Hebrew text, among other things.

102 In the text: *Isag. Ad Scr. 1. Cap. 8.*—Owen. See André Rivet, *Isagoge, seu introductio generalis, ad Scripturam sacram Veteris et Novi Testamenti* (Leiden: I. Commelinus, 1627), 103–4.

103 See "De Punctorum Hebraicorum origine: In Vesperiis Comitiorum habita Oxon" (Lectio XII), in John Prideaux, *Opera theologica* (Zurich: Davidis Gesseneri, 1672), 160–76. John Prideaux (1578–1650) was vice-chancellor of Oxford (on several occasions, in fact, prior to Owen), Regius Professor of Divinity, and later bishop of Worcester. Note, for instance, Prideaux's caveat against Bellarmine's agenda in advocating the novelty of the points: *Quicquid sit, ferendum non est, ut Jesuitae insultent nostris litigiis, aut urgeant tandem aliquid, quo deprimatur fons Hebraicus infra Tridentinam vulgaris Editionis authentiam; aut Papae authoritas tam in corruptis versionibus, quam in Sanctis suis canonizandis postliminio aliquid obtineat.* Editor's translation: "Whatever the case, the Jesuit exploitation of our dispute is not to be tolerated, whether it is in pressing upon us anything by which the original Hebrew might be suppressed beneath the Tridentine authenticity of the Vulgate edition, or that the authority of the pope should gain the right of judgment as much in this matter of allegedly corrupt versions as it has in canonizing their saints." See Prideaux, *Opera theologica*, 162.

104 I.e., expressions of praise.

his book; as indeed he uses his arguments, and quotes his treatise, under the name of *Sud Hanisebhoth Hanaegalah* [*sic*].[105] But that (I say) which seems to me most admirable in the Doctor's discourse is, that whereas he had prefaced it with the weight of the controversy he had in hand, by the advantage the Papists make of the opinion of the novelty of the points, citing their words to that purpose, himself in the body of his *Exercitations* falls in with them, and speaks the very things which he seemed before to have blamed. And by this means this opinion tending so greatly to the disparagement of the authority of the originals, is crept in among Protestants also. Of the stop put unto its progress by the full and learned answer of Buxtorfius the younger (who alone in this learning, in this age, seems to answer his father's worth) unto Cappellus, in his discourse *De origine et antiquitate punctorum*,[106] I shall speak more afterward. However it is not amiss fallen out that the masters of this new persuasion are not at all agreed among themselves. Cappellus would have it easy to understand the Hebrew text, and every word, though not absolutely by itself, yet as it lies in its contexture, though there were no points at all. Morinus would make the language altogether unintelligible on that account; the one says, that the points are a late invention of the Rabbins, and the other, that without them, the understanding of the Hebrew is ἐκ τῶν ἀδυνάτων,[107] yet though they look diverse ways, there is a firebrand between them. But we have this brand brought yet nearer to the church's bread-corn, in the *Prolegomena* to the *Biblia polyglotta*, lately printed at London.[108] The solemn

---

105 Cappel refers to and quotes several letters to him from the English Protestant divine William Eyre (1612–1670). Eyre clearly believes that Cappel is the author of the "Diatribe" edited by Erpenius, which he identifies by the title סוד הניקוד הנגלה (incorrectly transliterated here as *Sud Hanisebhoth Hanaegalah*). In the second letter (dated 1635), Eyre refers to Prideaux's dependence on Cappel's Diatribe. See Louis Cappel, *Critica sacra, sive De variis quae in sacris Veteris Testamenti libris occurrunt lectionibus* (Paris: S&G Cramoisy, 1650), 630; cf. 29–32.

106 See Johann Buxtorf Jr., *Tractatus de punctorum vocalium et accentum, in libris Veteris Testamenti Hebraicis, origine, antiquitate, et authoritate* (Basel: L. König, 1648). Johann Buxtorf Jr. (1599–1664) was a Protestant Hebraist and son of Johann Buxtorf Sr. He was involved in the eventual publication of his father's *Concordantiae Bibliorum Hebraicae* and *Lexicon Chaldaicum, Talmudicum et Rabbinicum*. He is well known for his polemical engagement with Louis Cappel over the origin of the Hebrew vowel points, arguing with his father for an early dating that traces their origin to the great synagogue called by Ezra (the so-called Men of the Great Assembly) in the period from around 516 to 332 BC.

107 Gk. "one of those things that is impossible."

108 The *Prolegomena* to the so-called London Polyglot Bible (1657), edited by Brian Walton. See Walton, *Biblia sacra polyglotta*. The London Polyglot Bible is the last and greatest of the early modern polyglot bibles that remained a landmark in biblical criticism for several centuries. It is Owen's receipt of Walton's *Prolegomena* and *Appendix* that is the occasion of his *Of the Integrity*. In *Of the Integrity*, Owen does not question the immense learning and contribution of

espousal of this opinion of the Hebrew punctuation, in that great work, was one chief occasion of the second discourse,[109] as you will find it at large declared in the entrance of it. I dare not mention the desperate consequences that attend this imagination, being affrighted among other things, by a little treatise lately sent me (upon the occasion of a discourse on this subject) by my worthy and learned friend Dr. Ward, entitled *Fides divina*, wherein its author, whoever he be, from some principles of this nature, and unwary expressions of some learned men among us, labors to eject and cast out as useless the whole Scripture or word of God.[110] I should have immediately returned an answer to that pestilent discourse, but that upon consideration, I found all his objections obviated or answered in the ensuing treatises, which were then wholly finished. And this, as I said, was the first way whereby the poison of undervaluing the originals crept in among Protestants themselves.

Now together with the knowledge of the tongues, the use of that knowledge in critical observations, did also increase. The excellent use of this study and employment, with the fruits of it in the explanation of sundry difficulties, with many other advantages, cannot be easily expressed. But as the best things are apt to be most abused, so in particular it has fallen out with this kind of learning and study. Protestants here also have chiefly managed the business. Beza,[111] Camerarius,[112] Scaliger, Casaubon,[113] Drusius,[114] Gomarus,[115]

---

this publication but is chiefly concerned with its advocacy for a late dating of the Hebrew vowel points, and its promotion of a modest critical emendation of the Hebrew text in light of other ancient editions. The *Prolegomena* to the London Polyglot Bible is published in vol. 1 of the collection, and was subsequently published separately in numerous editions (cf. the nineteenth-century edition, Brian Walton, *In Biblia polyglotta prolegomena*, 2 vols. [Cambridge: J. Smith, 1827–1828]). The *Appendix* is a collection of variant readings and is published in vol. 6.

109 *Of the Integrity*.

110 Owen is referring to Seth Ward (1617–1689), the Savilian Professor of Astronomy at Oxford and later bishop of Exeter, then Salisbury. The anonymous treatise he mentions here is *Fides divina: The Ground of True Faith Asserted* (London: n.p., 1657). Some of the names associated with these "unwary expressions" include John Goodwin, Daniel Featley, and Richard Baxter.

111 Theodore Beza (1519–1605) was a French Reformed theologian who famously succeeded John Calvin in Geneva.

112 Joachim Camerarius (1500–1574) was a German Lutheran and classicist who was involved in seeking reconciliation between Protestant and Catholics.

113 Isaac Casaubon (1559–1614) was a Huguenot classicist and philologist who was consulted during the production of the translation for the King James Version of the Bible.

114 Johannes van den Driesche (1550–1616) was a Flemish Protestant Hebraist who taught in Oxford, Leiden, and Franeker. Many of his exegetical contributions were included in the famous compilation of Latin biblical commentaries, *Critici sacri, sive Doctissimorum vivorum in ss. Biblia annotationes et tractatus*.

115 Franciscus Gomarus (1563–1641) was a Dutch Reformed theologian, famous for his polemical engagement with Jacobus Arminius and his contribution to the Synod of Dort. His last position was professor of Hebrew at Groningen.

Ussher,[116] Grotius,[117] Heinsius,[118] Fuller,[119] Dieu,[120] Mede,[121] Cameron,[122] Glassius, Cappellus, Amama, with innumerable others, have excelled in this kind. But the mind of man being exceedingly vainglorious,[123] curious, uncertain, after a door to reputation and renown, by this kind of learning was opened in the world, it quickly spread itself over all bounds and limits of sobriety. The manifold inconveniences, if not mischiefs, that have ensued on the boldness and curiosity of some in criticizing the Scripture, I shall not now insist upon; and what it might yet grow unto, I have often heard the great Ussher, expressing his fear. Of the success of Grotius in this way we have a solid account weekly in the lectures of our learned professor, which I hope, he will in due time benefit the public withal. But it is only one or two things that my present design calls upon me to remark.

Among other ways that sundry men have fixed on to exercise their critical abilities, one has been the collecting of various lections both in the Old Testament and New. The first and most honest course fixed on to this purpose, was that of consulting various copies, and comparing them among themselves; wherein yet there were sundry miscarriages, as I shall show in the second treatise. This was the work of Erasmus, Stephen,[124] Beza, Arias Montanus, and some others; some that came after them finding this province possessed, and no other world of the like nature remaining for them to conquer, fixed upon another way,

116 James Ussher (1581–1656) is most famous for his position as Archbishop of Armagh and Primate of All Ireland, but aside from his theological contributions, he was a well-known chronologist, and he also sought to defend the veracity of the Hebrew text of the Old Testament.

117 Hugo Grotius (1583–1645) was a Dutch statesman, lawyer, and humanist who wrote most influentially on natural law. His other works include his *Annotationes in Vetus Testamentum* (included in the *Appendix* of the London Polyglot Bible) and his defense of the satisfaction of Christ against Faustus Socinus.

118 Daniël Heinsius (1580–1655) was a Dutch classicist and one-time professor of Greek at Leiden.

119 Nicholas Fuller (ca. 1557–1626) was an English Hebraist and philologist most noted for his *Miscellaneorum theologicorum*.

120 Lodewijk de Dieu (1590–1642) was a Dutch Hebraist, biblical exegete, and chronologist who was governor of Walloon College, Leiden.

121 Joseph Mede (1586–1638) was an English Hebraist and biblical exegete, and was a fellow of Christ's College, Cambridge.

122 John Cameron (ca. 1579–1625) was a Scottish theologian most famous for his association with the Academy of Saumur and is known for his biblical annotations published as *Myrothecium evangelicum, hoc est, Novi Testamenti loca quamplurima ab eo.*

123 I.e., boastful of one's accomplishments.

124 Robert Estienne (1503–1559), also known as Robertus Stephanus, was a French Protestant classicist and printer who produced editions of the Greek New Testament, including the Textus Receptus (1550), the Vulgate and Erasmus's Latin translation of the New Testament, Pagninus's translation of the Old Testament, and Beza's Latin translation of the New Testament.

substituting to the service of their design, as pernicious a principle, as ever I think
was fixed on by any learned man since the foundation of the church of Christ,
excepting only those of Rome. Now this principle is that upon many grounds,
which some of them are long in recounting: there are sundry corruptions crept
into the originals, which by their critical faculty, with the use of sundry engines,
those especially of the old translations, are to be discovered and removed. And
this also receives countenance from those *Prolegomena* to the *Biblia polyglotta*,
as will afterward be shown and discussed. Now this principle being once fixed,
and a liberty of criticizing on the Scripture, yea a necessity of it thence evinced,
it is inconceivable what springs of corrections and amendments rise up under
their hands. Let me not be thought tedious if I recount some of them to you.

1. It is known that there is a double consonancy in the Hebrew consonants
among themselves; of some in figure that are unlike in sound, of some in
sound that are unlike in figure, of the first sort are ב and כ, ג and נ, י and ו, ו and
ז, ז and ן, ד and ר, מ and ס,[125] מ and ט, ה and ח, ח and ת, ע and צ; of the latter
are כ and ק, א and ע, ס and שׂ, ו and ב, צ and ז. Now this is one principle of
our new critics, that the scribes of the Bible were sometimes mistaken by
the likeness of the letters, in respect of figure, sometimes by their likeness in
respect of sound; and so remembering the words they wrote, oftentimes put
one for another; so that whether they used their eyes, or their memories, they
failed on one hand or another; though the Jews deny any copy among them
to be written but exactly by pattern, or that it is lawful for a man to write
one word in a copy, but by pattern, though he could remember the words of
the whole Bible: now whereas the signification of every word is regulated by
its radix, it often falls out, that in the formation and inflection of words, by
reason of letters that are defective, there remains but one letter of the radix in
them, at least that is pronounced: how frequent this is in this tongue, those
who have very little skill in it, may guess by only taking a view of Frobenius
[in] his Bible, wherein the radical letters are printed in a distinct character,
from all the prefixes and affixes in their variations. Now if a man has a mind
to criticize and mend the Bible, it is but taking his word, or words, that he
will fix upon, and try what they will make by the commutation of the letters
that are alike in figure and sound. Let him try what ב will do in the place of
כ or on the contrary; which as they are radical, or as they are prefixed, will
sufficiently alter the sense; and so of all the rest mentioned. If by this means
any new sense that is tolerable, and pleases the critic, does emerge, it is but
saying the scribe was mistaken in the likeness of the letters, or in the affinity

125 The correct Hebrew is "ם and ס." As per Goold.

of the sound, and then it is no matter, though all the copies in the world agree to the contrary, without the least variation. It is evident that this course has stood Cappellus and Grotius in very good stead. And Simeon de Muis tells us a pretty story of himself to this purpose.[126] Yea this is the most eminent spring of the criticisms on the Old Testament, that these times afford: a thousand instances might be given to this purpose.

2. But in case this course fail, and no relief be afforded this way, then the transposition of letters offers its assistance; those who know anything of this language, know what alteration in the sense of words may be made by such a way of procedure, frequently words of contrary senses, directly opposite consist only of the same letters diversely placed. Every lexicon will supply men with instances, that need not to be here repeated.

3. The points are taken into consideration; and here bold men may even satisfy their curiosity. That word, or those three letters דבר are instanced by Jerome to this purpose:[127] as it may be pointed it will afford eight several senses דָּבָר is *verbum*[128] and דֶּבֶר is *pestis*[129] as far distant from one another as life and death; those letters in that order may be read with ָ ֱ and ֵ ֶ and ֻ and ֺ and ֽ ֗ , the Jews give instances how by this means, men may destroy the world.[130] But

4. Suppose that this ground proves barren also, it is but going to an old translation, the LXX, or Vulgar Latin, and where any word likes us, to consider

126 In the text: *de Heb. Edit. Antiq. & Verit. S. S.*—Owen. Owen is likely referring to the first of the three polemical treatises de Muis composed against Jean Morin. While originally published separately, the three treatises are published under the title *Triplex assertio Hebraicae veritatis adversus exercitationes Ionnis Morini*, in de Muis, *Assertio*, tome II, 129–258.

127 In the text: Hom. 9. 12.—Owen. It is difficult to know precisely what Owen is citing here, although Jerome's comments to this effect may be found, for instance, in his commentary on Hab. 3:5: "What we translated as *death*, in Hebrew three letters are recorded: *dalet* [ד], *bet* [ב], *resh* [ר] with no vowels. If these are read as *dabar* [דָּבָר], they mean 'word' (*verbum*). If they are read as *deber* [דֶּבֶר], they mean 'plague' [*pestem*]." See Jerome, *Commentaries on the Twelve Prophets*, 2 vols., ed. Thomas P. Scheck, Ancient Christian Texts (Downers Grove, IL: IVP Academic, 2016), 1:222. For Latin text, see Jerome, *Commentarii in Prophetas Minores*, ed. Sincero Mantelli, Corpus Christianorum: Series Latina 76–76a (Turnhout: Brepolis, 2018), 65. Jerome (347–420) was a Latin priest, biblical scholar, and historian. Aside from his biblical commentaries, he is known best for his translation of the Bible into Latin (the Vulgate) from the original Greek and Hebrew, which was used as the main translation in the West for the subsequent millennium. In the sixteenth century, the Vulgate became the official authoritative translation for the Catholic Church.

128 Lat. "word."

129 Lat. "plague."

130 Owen's point here is that some arrangements of Hebrew consonants, such as דבר, have a wide semantic range, depending on the vowels.

what Hebrew word answers unto it, and if it discover an agreement in any one letter, in figure or sound, with the word in that text, then to say that so they read in that copy; yea rather than fail, be the word as far different from what is read in the Bible as can be imagined, aver it to yield the more convenient sense, and a various lection is found out.

And these are the chief heads and springs of the criticisms on the Old Testament, which with so great a reputation of learning men have boldly obtruded[131] on us of late days. It is not imaginable what prejudice the sacred truth of the Scripture, preserved by the infinite love and care of God, has already suffered hereby, and what it may further suffer, for my part, I cannot but tremble to think. Lay but these two principles together, namely that the points are a late invention of some Judaical Rabbins (on which account there is no reason in the world that we should be bound unto them) and that it is lawful to gather various lections by the help of translations, where there are no diversities in our present copies, which are owned in the *Prolegomena* to the *Biblia polyglotta*, and for my part I must needs cry out δὸς ποῦ στῶ,[132] as not seeing any means of being delivered from utter uncertainty in and about all sacred truth. Those who have more wisdom and learning, and are able to look through all the digladiations[133] that are likely to ensue on these principles, I hope will rather take pains to instruct me, and such as I am, then be angry or offended with us, that we are not so wise or learned as themselves. In the meantime I desire those who are shaken in mind by any of the specious pretenses of Cappellus and others, to consider the specimen, given us, of reconciling the difficulties, that they lay as the ground of their conjectures in the miscellany notes, or exercitations of the learned Mr. Pococke;[134] as useful and learned a work as is extant in that kind, in so few sheets of paper. The dangerous and causeless attempts of men, to rectify our present copies of the Bible, the reader may there also find discovered and confuted.

---

131 I.e., imposed unwelcomely.

132 Gk. "give [me] a place to stand." This is a quotation of the saying attributed to Archimedes: "Give me a place to stand and with a lever I will move the whole world." The words Owen gives can be found in Pappus of Alexandria, *Synagoge*, bk. 8, sec. 19. For the Greek text, see *Pappi Alexandrini collectio*, vol. 3, ed. Fridericus Hultsch (Berolini: apud Weidmannos, 1878), 1060.

133 I.e., violent combats.

134 "Appendix Notarum Miscellanea," in Maimonides, *Porta Mosis, sive, Dissertationes aliquot a R. Mose Maimonide, suis in varias Mishnaioth*, ed. Edward Pococke (Oxford: H. Hall, 1655). Edward Pococke (1604–1691) was an English biblical scholar and orientalist who specialized in Arabic texts. He was a friend of Owen's.

But we have not as yet done; there is a new invention of Cappellus, greatly applauded among the men of these opinions. He tells us: "It is clear that all knowledge of the Hebrew language in the world today is ultimately to be preserved by and to be attributed to the Greek translation of the Holy Bible of the LXX."[135] This is greedily taken up by Morinus (as nothing could be spoken more to his purpose), who also tells us, that the learned prefacer to these *Biblia polyglotta* is of the same judgment.[136] Hereupon he informs us, that in the translation of the Pentateuch he went for the meaning of sundry words unto Jerome, and the translation of the LXX. But it is not unknown to these learned persons, that Jerome, whom one of them makes his rule; tells us over and over, that notwithstanding the translation of the LXX he had his knowledge of the Hebrew tongue, from the Hebrew itself; and the help of such Hebrews as he hired to his assistance. And [as] for Cappellus, is not that the Helena for which he contends, and upon the matter the only foundation of his sacred work of criticizing on the Scripture, that there was a succession of learned men of the Jews at Tiberias until a hundred years after Jerome, who invented the points of the Hebrew Bible, and that not in an arbitrary manner, but according to the tradition they had received from them who spoke that language in its purity? Shall these men be thought to have had the knowledge of the Hebrew tongue from the translation of the LXX; certainly they would not then have hated it so, as he informs us they did. But this thing is plainly ridiculous. The language gives us the knowledge of itself. Considering the helps that by providence have been in all ages, and at all times afforded thereunto, ever since the time wherein Cappellus says, some knew it so well, as to invent and affix the present punctuation, there has been a succession of living or dead masters to further the knowledge of it. And this will not seem strange to them who have given us exact translations of the Persian, and Ethiopic

---

135   In the text: lib. 6. c. 10. *Crit. Sacr: Planum est omnem quae hodie est in terrarum orbe linguae Hebraicae cognitionem servandam* [sic: *revocandum* in original] *tandem esse & ascribendam Graecae* τῶν LXX. *Sacrorum Bibliorum translationi.*—Owen. Editor's translation. See Cappel, *Critica sacra,* 432.

136   In the text: Morin: *Praefat: ad opusc. Haebr: Samarit.*—Owen. Morin quotes Cappel's statement above, then adds, *Quam eius sententiam amplectitur & laudat Brianus Valton istarum quoque rerum peritissimus in erudita Praefatione* προδρόμῳ *ad editionem Bibliorum* πολλαπλων, *quae Londini magno cum variarum Linguarum apparatu continenter, & festinanter admodum cuduntur.* Editor's translation: "Brian Walton, who is also most expert in these matters, embraces and praises his opinion in the erudite prolegomenous introduction to the polyglot edition of the Bible, which is very speedily being published in London, bound replete with the apparatus of various languages." See "Praefatio" in Jean Morin, *Opuscula Hebraeo-Samaritica* (Paris: Gaspardus Metras, 1657), *7–8.

pieces of Scripture. In the ἅπαξ λεγόμενα[137] we are a little assisted by the LXX. The chiefest seeming help unto this tongue is from the Arabic.¶[138]

And thus have I given you a brief account how, by the subtlety of Satan, there are principles crept in, even among Protestants, undermining the authority of the "Hebrew verity," as it was called of old; wherein Jerusalem has justified Samaria, and cleared the Papists in their reproaching of the word of God. Of the New Testament I shall speak particularly in the second discourse ensuing. Morinus indeed tells us,[139] it is a jocular thing that the heretics in their disputations do grant, that there are corruptions, and various lections in the Greek and Latin copies of the Scripture, but deny it as to the Hebrew: but why, I pray, is this so ridiculous? It is founded on no less stable bottom than this experience, that whereas we evidently find various lections in the Greek copies which we enjoy, and so grant that which ocular inspection evinces to be true; yet although men discover such virulent and bitter spirits against the Hebrew text, as this Morinus does, calling all men fools or knaves that contend for its purity, yet they are none of them able to show out of any copies yet extant in the world, or that they can make appear ever to have been extant, that ever there were any such various lections in the originals of the Old Testament. And is there any reason that we should be esteemed ridiculous, because believing our own eyes, we will not also believe the testimony of some few men of no credit with us, asserting that for truth, which we have abundant cause to believe to be utterly false; but of these men so far.

I thought at the entrance of my discourse to have also insisted on some other ways, whereby Satan in these days assaults the sacred truth of the word of God in its authority, purity, integrity, or perfection; especially in the poor, deluded, fanatical souls among us, commonly called Quakers. For the instruction of the younger sort, against whose abominations I have subjoined the theses in the close of the other treatises. But I am sensible how far I have already exceeded the bounds of a preface unto so small treatises as these ensuing; and therefore giving a brief account of my undertaking in this cause of God and his word, for the vindication of the authority and integrity of it, I shall put a close to this discourse.

It may be some of you have heard me professing my unwillingness to appear any more in the world this way. I have not in some things met with such

---

137 Gk. "once said"; i.e., words only appearing once.

138 The ¶ symbol indicates that a paragraph break has been added to Owen's original text.

139 In the text: *de Heb: & Graec: Tex: Sincerit. Exercitat*: 1. cap: 1. p. 5.—Owen. See Morin, *Exercitationes pars prior*, 5.

pleasing entertainment, as to encourage me unto it: where I have been for peace, others have made themselves ready for war. Some of them, especially one[140] of late, neither understanding me, nor the things that he writes about, but his mind for opposition was to be satisfied. This is the manner of not a few in their writings; they measure other men by their own ignorance, and what they know not themselves, they think is hid to others also; hence when any thing presents itself new to their minds; as though they were the first that knew, what they then first know, and which they have only an obscure glimpse of, they rest not until they have published it to their praise. Such are the discourses of that person, partly trivial, partly obviated and rendered utterly useless to his purpose by that treatise, which he ventured weakly to oppose. I wish I could prevail with those, whose interest compels them to choose rather to be ignorant, than to be taught by me, to let my books alone. Another[141] after two or three years' consideration, in answer to a book of near a hundred and forty sheets of paper, returns a scoffing reply to so much of it, as was written in a quarter of an hour. I am therefore still minded to abstain from such engagements. And I think I may say if there were less writing by some, there would be more reading by others, at least to more purpose. Many books full of profound learning lie neglected, while men spend their time on trifles; and many things of great worth are suppressed by their authors, while things of no value are poured out, one on the neck of another. One of yourselves[142] I have often solicited for the publishing of some divinity lectures read at solemn times in the university, which, if I know ought, are, to say no more, worthy of public view. I yet hope a short time will answer my desire and expectation. Of my present undertaking there are three parts. The first is a subject that having preached on, I was by many urged to publish my thoughts upon it, judging it might be useful: I have answered their requests;

---

140 The original margin note has initials "M.G.F.," referring to Giles Firmin (1614–1697), who, as Goold observes, replied to Owen's treatise *Of Schism: The True Nature of it Discovered and Considered with Reference to the Present Differences in Religion* (1657), with his own *Of Schism, Parochial Congregations, and Ordination by Imposition of Hands; Wherein Dr Owen's Discovery of the True Nature of Schism Is Briefly and Friendly Examined* (1658). Firmin was an advocate of a reformed form of episcopacy, and with Richard Baxter was an opponent of Independents like Owen, regarding them as schismatic.

141 The original margin note has "Mr. I.G.," referring to John Goodwin, who responded to Owen's treatise, *The Doctrine of the Saints' Perseverance Explained and Confirmed* (1654). John Goodwin (1594–1665) was a Nonconformist with Arminian sympathies whose views Owen sought to refute extensively in his *The Doctrine of the Saints' Perseverance*.

142 In the margin: Dr Henry Wilkinson, Public Reader of Divinity in the University.—Owen. Wilkinson (1616–1690) was principal of Magdalen Hall, Oxford, and professor of moral philosophy, and was later ejected from his post as a Nonconformist.

what I have performed through the grace of Christ in the work undertaken, is left to the judgment of the godly learned reader. The second concerns the *Prolegomena* and *Appendix* to the late *Biblia polyglotta*; of this I said often, "I would rather this had been done by anyone other than by me; even so, by me is better than by no one."[143] The reasons of my engaging in that work are declared at large in the entrance of it. The theses in the close were drawn in by their affinity in subject to the other discourses, and to complete the doctrine of the Scripture concerning the Scripture, I endeavored to comprise in them the whole truth about the word of God, as to name and thing opposed by the poor fanatical Quakers, as also to discover the principles they proceed upon in their confused opposition to that truth.

I have no more to add, but only begging I may have the continuance of your prayers, and assistance in your several stations, for the carrying on the work of our Lord and Master in this place committed unto us, that I may give in my account with joy and not with grief, to him that stands at the door, I commend you to the powerful word of his grace; and remain your fellow laborer and brother in our dear Lord Jesus.

J. O.

FROM MY STUDY,

SEPTEMBER 22, 1658

---

143 In the text: *Ab alio quovis hoc fieri mallem, quam a me, sed a me tamen potius quam a nemine.*— Owen. Editor's translation.

Of the Divine Original, with the
Authority, Self-Evidencing Power,
and the Light of the Holy Scriptures

1

The Divine Origin of the Scriptures the Only Foundation of Their Authority

[1.] The divine original of the Scripture, the sole foundation of its authority. [2–3.] The original of the Old Testament (Heb 1:11). [4.] Several ways of immediate revelation. [5–10.] The peculiar manner of the revelation of the word. Considerations thereon. [11–12.] Various expressions of that way (2 Pet 1:20–21). [13–14.] The written word, as written, preserved by the providence of God. [15–16.] Cappellus's opinion about various lections considered. [17–20.] The Scripture not ἰδίας ἐπιλύσεως. The true meaning of that expression. [21.] How the word came of old, and how it was received. [22.] Entirely from God to the least tittle. [23–25.] Of the Scriptures of the New Testament and their peculiar prerogative.

THE DIVINE ORIGINAL OF THE SCRIPTURE
THE SOLE FOUNDATION OF ITS AUTHORITY

1. That the whole authority of the Scripture in itself, depends solely on its divine original, is confessed by all who acknowledge its authority. The evincing and declaration of that authority, being the thing at present aimed at; the discovery of its divine spring and rise, is in the first place, necessarily to be premised thereunto. That foundation being once laid, we shall be able to educe our following reasonings and arguments, wherein we aim more at weight than number, from their own proper principles.

THE ORIGINAL OF THE OLD TESTAMENT

2. As to the original of the Scripture of the Old Testament, it is said, God spoke πάλαι ἐν τοῖς προφήταις (Heb. 1:1); "of old," or "formerly in the prophets." From the days of Moses the lawgiver, and downward, unto the consignation and bounding of the canon delivered to the Judaical Church, in the days of Ezra and his companions, אנשי כנסת הגדולה the "men of the great congregation," so God spoke. This being done only among the Jews, they as his church, ἐπιστεύθησαν τὰ λόγια τοῦ θεοῦ (Rom. 3:2; 9:4), were "entrusted with the oracles of God." God spoke, ἐν τοῖς προφήταις;[1] ἐν for διά[2] "in" for "by": διὰ τῶν προφητῶν, "by the prophets," as Luke 1:70, διὰ στόματος τῶν ἁγίων προφητῶν, "by the mouth of the holy prophets"; but there seems to be somewhat further intended in this expression.

3. In the exposition, or giving out the eternal counsel of the mind and will of God unto men, there is considerable[3] his speaking unto the prophets, and his speaking by them unto us. In this expression, it seems to be, that בת כיל[4] or *filia vocis*,[5] that voice from heaven that came to the prophets which is understood. So God spoke in the prophets, and in reference thereunto there is propriety in that expression, ἐν τοῖς προφήταις, "in the prophets." Thus the Psalms are many of them said to be, to this, or that man: מכתם לדוד "A golden psalm to David"; that is, from the Lord; and from thence their tongue was as the pen of a writer (Ps. 45:1). So God spoke in them, before he spoke by them.

Several Ways of Immediate Revelation

4. The various ways of special revelation, by dreams, visions, audible voices, inspirations, with that peculiar one of the lawgiver under the Old Testament, called פנים אל־פנים "face to face" (Ex. 33:11; Deut. 34:10): and פה אל־פה[6] (Num. 12:8); with that which is compared with it, and exalted above it (Heb. 1:1–3) in the New, by the Son, ἐκ κόλπου τοῦ πατρός, "from the bosom of

---

1   Gk. "in the prophets."
2   In the text: (Chrysostom, Theophylact).—Owen. Owen appears to be referring to the commentaries of John Chrysostom and Theophylact of Ohrid on Hebrews 1:1. See John Chrysostom, *Opera omnia*, t. 12, ed. J. P. Migne, Patrologia Graeca 63 (Paris: Migne, 1862), 13–14; Theophylact of Ohrid, *Opera*, t. 125, ed. J P. Migne, Patrologia Graeca 125 (Paris: Migne, 1864), 187–90.
3   Owen's expression means "there is to be considered."
4   As per original. It should read קול.
5   Heb., Lat. "the daughter of a voice." Owen is referring to a Jewish expression for the mode of revelation that was by direct address to a prophet from God without a mediator (e.g., an angel).
6   Heb. "mouth to mouth."

the Father" (John 1:17, 18),[7] are not of my present consideration, all of them belonging to the manner of the thing inquired after, not the thing itself.

The Peculiar Manner of the Revelation of the Word and Considerations Thereon

5. By the assertion then laid down of God "speaking in the prophets of old," from the beginning to the end of that long tract of time, consisting of one thousand years, wherein he gave out the writings of the Old Testament; two things are ascertained unto us, which are the foundation of our present discourse.

6. First,[8] that the laws they made known, the doctrines they delivered, the instructions they gave, the stories they recorded, the promises of Christ, the prophecies of gospel times they gave out, and revealed, were not their own, not conceived in their minds, not formed by their reasonings, not retained in their memories from what they heard not by any means beforehand comprehended by them (1 Pet. 1:10, 11), but were all of them immediately from God; there being only a passive concurrence of their rational faculties in their reception, without any such active obedience, as by any law they might be obliged unto. Hence,

7. Secondly, God was so with them, and by the Holy Ghost so spoke in them, as to their receiving of the word from him, and their delivering of it unto others by speaking or writing, as that they were not themselves enabled by any habitual light, knowledge or conviction of truth, to declare his mind and will, but only acted, as they were immediately moved by him. Their tongue in what they said, or their hand in what they wrote, was עט סופר[9] no more at their own disposal, than the pen is, in the hand of an expert writer.

8. Hence, as far as their own personal concernments, as saints, and believers did lie in them, they are said ἐρευνᾶν, to make a "diligent inquiry" into, and investigation of the things, which ἐδήλου τὸ ἐν αὐτοῖς πνεῦμα χριστοῦ, "the Spirit of Christ," that spoke "in themselves did signify" (1 Pet. 1:10, 11). Without this, though their visions were express, so that in them their eyes were said to be open (Num. 24:3, 4); yet they understood them not. Therefore also, they studied the writings and prophecies of one another (Dan. 9:2). Thus they attained a saving useful habitual knowledge of the truths delivered by

---

7   Owen's Greek citation varies slightly from the text of John 1:18 in *Novum Testamentum Graece*, which has εἰς τὸν κόλπον ("in the bosom"). *Novum Testamentum Graece*, ed. B. Aland et al., 28th rev. ed. (Stuttgart: Deutsche Bibelgesellschaft, 2012). Hereafter cited as NA[28].

8   "1." in the original, but altered to be consistent with verbally numbered list that follows.

9   Heb. "the pen of a writer" (an allusion, perhaps, to Ps. 45:1).

themselves and others, by the illumination of the Holy Ghost, through the study of the word, even as we (Ps. 119:104). But as to the receiving of the word from God, as God spoke in them, they obtained nothing by study or meditation by inquiry or reading (Amos 7:15). Whether we consider the matter, or manner of what they received, and delivered, or their receiving and delivering of it, they were but as an instrument of music, giving a sound according to the hand, intention, and skill of him that strikes it.

9. This is variously expressed. Generally, it is said דבר היה "the word was" to this, or that prophet, which we have rendered, "the word came" unto them (Ezek. 1:3) היה היה דבר it "came expressly;" *essendo fuit;*[10] it had a subsistence given unto it, or an effectual in-being, by the Spirit's entering into him (verse 14).[11] Now this coming of the word unto them, had oftentimes such a greatness, and expression of the majesty of God upon it, as filled them with dread and reverence of him (Hab. 3:16), and also greatly affected even their outward man (Dan. 8:27). But this dread and terror (which Satan strove to imitate in his filthy tripods, and ἐγγαστρίμυθοι[12]) was peculiar to the Old Testament, and belonged to the pedagogy thereof (Heb. 12:18–21). The Spirit in the declaration of the New Testament, gave out his mind and will in a way of more liberty and glory (2 Cor. 3). The expressness and immediacy of revelation was the same; but the manner of it related more to that glorious liberty in fellowship and communion with the Father, whereunto believers had then an access provided them by Jesus Christ (Heb. 9:8; 10:19, 20; 12:23–24). So our Savior tells his apostles (Matt. 10:20) οὐχ ὑμεῖς ἐστε οἱ λαλοῦντες;[13] "you are not the speakers" of what you deliver, as other men are, the figment and imagination of whose hearts are the fountain of all that they speak; and he adds this reason τὸ γὰρ πνεῦμα τοῦ πατρὸς τὸ λαλοῦν ἐν ὑμῖν;[14] "the Spirit of the Father (is) he that speaketh in you." Thus the word that came unto them, was a book which they took in, and gave out without any alteration of one tittle or syllable (Ezek. 2:8–11; 3:3; Rev. 10:9–11).

10. Moreover, when the word was thus come to the prophets, and God had spoken in them, it was not in their power to conceal it, the hand of the Lord being strong upon them. They were not now only on a general account to utter the truth they were made acquainted withal, and to speak the things they had heard and seen, which was their common preaching work according

---

10 Lat. "it was in being"—that is, it (the word of the Lord) came to inhabit the prophet.
11 Owen is likely referring to Ezek. 1:12.
12 Gk. "ventriloquists."
13 With slight variation from the Greek original of Matt. 10:20. See NA[28].
14 With slight variation from the Greek original of Matt 10:20. See NA[28].

to the analogy of what they had received (Acts 4:20); but also the very individual words that they had received were to be declared. When the word was come to them, it was as a fire within them, that must be delivered, or it would consume them (Ps. 39:3; Jer. 20:9; Amos 3:8, 7:15, 16). So Jonah found his attempt to hide the word that he had received, to be altogether vain.

Various Expressions of That Way (2 Pet. 1:20–21)

11. Now because these things are of great importance and the foundation of all that does ensue; namely, the discovery that the word is come forth unto us from God, without the least mixture or intervenience[15] of any medium obnoxious to fallibility (as is the wisdom, truth, integrity, knowledge, and memory, of the best, of all men), I shall further consider it from one full and eminent declaration thereof, given unto us (2 Pet. 1:20–21). The words of the Holy Ghost are; τοῦτο πρῶτον γινώσκοντες, ὅτι πᾶσα προφητεία γραφῆς, ἰδίας ἐπιλύσεως οὐ γίνεται, οὐ γὰρ θελήματι ἀνθρώπου ἠνέχθη ποτὲ προφητεία, ἀλλ᾽ ὑπὸ πνεύματος ἁγίου φερόμενοι ἐλάλησαν οἱ ἅγιοι θεοῦ ἄνθρωποι, "Knowing this first, that no prophecy of Scripture is of any private interpretation; for the prophecy came not in old time by the will of man, but holy men of God spoke, as they were moved by the Holy Ghost."

12. That which he speaks of is, προφητεία γραφῆς; the prophecy of Scripture, or "written prophecy."

There were then traditions among the Jews, to whom Peter wrote, exalting themselves into competition with the written word, which not long after got the title of an oral law, pretending to have its original from God. These the apostle tacitly condemns; and also shows under what formality he considered that, which (2 Pet. 1:19) he termed λόγος προφητικός, the "word of prophecy"; namely as written. The written word, as such, is that whereof he speaks. Above fifty times is ἡ γραφή, or αἱ γραφαί,[16] in the New Testament put absolutely for the word of God. And כתב[17] is so used in the Old for the word of prophecy (2 Chron. 21:12). It is the ἡ γραφή, that is θεόπνευστος (2 Tim. 3:16); "the writing," or "word written," is "by inspiration from God." Not only the doctrine in it, but the γραφή itself, or the doctrine as written, is so from him.

The Written Word, as Written, Preserved by the Providence of God

13. Hence the providence of God has manifested itself no less concerned in the preservation of the writings than of the doctrine contained in them. The

---

15 I.e., intervention.
16 Gk. "the writing"; "the writings."
17 As per original. Goold has מִכְתָּב.

writing itself being the product of his own eternal counsel for the preservation of the doctrine, after a sufficient discovery of the insufficiency of all other means for that end and purpose. And hence the malice of Satan has raged no less against the book, than [against] the truth contained in it. The dealings of Antiochus[18] under the Old Testament, and of sundry persecuting emperors under the New, evince no less. And it was no less crime of old to be *traditor libri*,[19] than to be *abnegator fidei*.[20] The reproach of *chartacea scripta*,[21] and *membranae*[22] reflects on its author.[23] It is true we have not the αὐτόγραφα[24] of Moses and the prophets, of the apostles and evangelists; but the ἀπόγραφα or "copies" which we have, contain every iota[25] that was in them.

14. It is no doubt but that in the copies we now enjoy of the Old Testament there are some diverse readings, or various lections. The קרי וכתיב [Heb. *Qere* and *Ketiv*],[26] the תקון סופרים,[27] the עטור סופרים,[28] (for the סבירין[29] are of another nature) the various lections of Ben-Asher, or Rabbi Aaron the son of Rabbi Moses of the tribe of Asher,[30] and Ben Naphtali, or R. Moses the son

---

18   I.e., Antiochus IV Epiphanes (ca. 215–164 BC), the Seleucid king whose harsh persecution of the Jews sparked the Maccabean revolt.

19   Lat. "a traitor to the book."

20   Lat. "a denier of the faith."

21   Lat. "papyrus script."

22   Lat. "parchments." In the text: (*Coster: Enchirid: Cap.* 1).—Owen. See Franciscus Coster, *Enchiridion controversiarum praecipuarum nostri temporis de religione* (Lyon: Guillaume Rouillé, 1604), 41–70.

23   In the margin: *Hebraea volumina nec in una dictione corrupta invenies. Sant. Pag.* ἰῶτα ἕν ἤ μία κεραία οὐ μὴ παρέλθῃ. Matt. 5.18.—Owen. Editor's translation: "You will not find the Hebrew volumes corrupted in one utterance." Owen has slightly amended the original, which reads, *Hebraea vero volumina nec una in dictione corrupta reperies.* See Santes Pagnino, *Hebraicarum institutionum libri iv* (Paris: Robertus Stephanus, 1549), ad Frederico Fregosio, *2. "Not an iota, not a dot, will pass" (Matt. 5:18 ESV).

24   Gk. "autographs"—that is, original manuscripts.

25   I.e., the ninth letter of the Greek alphabet, used figuratively to indicate a "single letter" (see Matt. 5:18).

26   In the margin: a Reading, in the margin, and writing, in the line.—Owen. I.e., the system of scribal marginalia in the Hebrew Bible noting the difference between how the Hebrew consonants are written (the *Ketiv*) and how they are to be pronounced (the *Qere*).

27   In the margin: *Correctio scribarum*, or the correction of the scribes, or the amendment of some small *apiculi* [points] in eighteen places.—Owen.

28   In the margin: *Ablatio scribarum* a removal by the scribes or a note of the redundancy of ו in five places. *Vid. Raymond: pugio fid. Petrus Galat. Lib:* 1: *cap:* 8.—Owen. See, respectively, Raimund Martini, *Pugio fidei* [. . .] *adversus Mauros, et Iudaeos* (Paris: Mathurinus Henault, 1651); Pietro Colonna Galatino, *De arcanis Catholicae veritatis* (Basel: Ioannes Hervagius, 1561), 19–27.

29   Heb., *Sebirin*, a technical term referring to a word with an unusual form, which the Masoretes marked to prevent it from being changed by future scribes who might have otherwise sought to "correct" an assumed error.

30   Aaron ben Moses ben Asher (d. 960) was a Tiberian Masorete who is credited with having preserved the most accurate version of the Masoretic Text of the Hebrew Bible, with its vocalization. He has exercised considerable influence on subsequent study of Hebrew grammar.

of David of the tribe of Naphtali;[31] of the East and Western Jews, which we have collected at the end of the great Bible with the Masora,[32] evince it.[33] But yet we affirm that the whole word of God, in every letter and tittle, as given from him by inspiration, is preserved without corruption. Where there is any variety it is always in things of less, indeed of no importance.[34] God by his providence preserving the whole entire, suffered this lesser variety to fall out, in or among the copies we have, for the quickening and exercising of our diligence in our search into his word.

Cappellus's Opinion about Various Lections Considered

15. It was an unhappy attempt (which must afterward be spoken unto) that a learned man has of late put himself upon,[35] namely, to prove variations in all the present Ἀπόγραφα[36] of the Old Testament in the Hebrew tongue from the copies used of old, merely upon uncertain conjectures, and the credit of corrupt translations. Whether that plea of his be more unreasonable in itself and devoid of any real ground of truth, or injurious to the love and care of God over his word and church, I know not: sure I am, it is both in a high degree. The translation especially insisted on by him, is that of the LXX. That

---

31 Ben Naphtali, or Moses ben David, (fl. 890–940) was a Tiberian Masorete who produced an alternative Hebrew text of the Old Testament to ben Asher's received Masoretic Text. Although it has not been preserved, his variations from the Masoretic Text have been, and largely pertain to, the placement of accents in the text.

32 I.e., the body of scribal annotations on the text of the Hebrew Bible compiled during the first millennium AD. By the "great Bible," Owen is likely referring to the Rabbinic Bible, the *Mikraot Gedolot*, published by the Venetian printer Daniel Bomberg in two editions (1516–1517 and 1525). These lections of the so-called Eastern and Western Jews were also published in the *Appendix* to Brian Walton's *Biblia sacra polyglotta*, or the London Polyglot Bible (1657), that Owen came upon just as this treatise was about to be printed, leading him to write its sequel, *Of the Integrity*. See Walton, *Biblia sacra polyglotta*, vol. 6, chap. 1, pp. 14–15.

33 Goold has "—the lections also of the eastern and western Jews, which we have collected at the end of the great Bible with the Masora—evince it." Emended as per original.

34 In the margin: *Hebraei V. T. Codices per universum terrarum orbem, per Europam, Asiam & Africam, ubique sibi sunt similes, eodemque modo ab omnibus scribuntur & leguntur; si forte exiguas quasdam apiculorum quorundam differentias excipias, quae ipsae tamen nullam varietatem efficiunt.* Buxtorf. Vindic. Ver. *Heb.* 2. *Cap.* 14.—Owen. Editor's translation: "The Old Testament Hebrew codices, throughout the whole world, throughout Europe, Asia, Africa, are alike in all things in themselves, and they have been copied and read in the same manner by everyone; if, perhaps, you exclude certain little differences of minute details, which nevertheless themselves make no difference." See Johann Buxtorf Jr., *Anticritica: Seu vindiciae veritatis Hebraicae* (Basel: Ludovicus Rex, 1653), 1024.

35 In the margin: Lud. Capell. Crit. Sac.—Owen. See Louis Cappel, *Critica sacra, sive De variis quae in sacris Veteris Testamenti libris occurrunt lectionibus* (Paris: S&G Cramoisy, 1650).

36 Gk. "official written copies."

this translation either from the mistakes of its first authors (if it be theirs, whose name and number it bears) or the carelessness or ignorance, or worse of its transcribers, is corrupted and gone off from the original in a thousand places twice told, is acknowledged by all who know ought of these things. Strange that so corrupt a stream should be judged a fit means to cleanse the fountain. That such a Lesbian rule[37] should be thought a fit measure to correct the original by; and yet on the account hereof, with some others not one whit better, or scarce so good, we have 1,826 various lections exhibited unto us, with frequent insinuations of an infinite number more yet to be collected. It were desirable that men would be content to show their learning, reading and diligence, about things where there is less danger in adventures.

Nor is the relief he provides against the charge of bringing things to an uncertainty in the Scripture, which he found himself obnoxious unto, less pernicious than the opinion he seeks to palliate[38] thereby; although it be since taken up and approved[39] by others. The saving doctrine of the Scripture, he tells us,[40] as to the matter and substance of it, in all things of moment, is preserved in the copies of the original and translations that do remain.

16.[41] It is indeed a great relief, against the inconvenience of corrupt translations, to consider that although some of them be bad enough, yet if all the errors and mistakes that are to be found in all the rest, should be added to

---

37 I.e., a lead mason's tool that was flexible and was used for measuring and marking out curves.
38 I.e., easing symptoms of a disease without curing it.
39 In the margin: *Proleg. ad Bibl. polyglot.*—Owen. Owen is referring to the *Prolegomena* of Walton's London Polyglot Bible. With the *Appendix*, the *Prolegomena* came into Owen's hands late in the process and delayed the publication of this treatise until he had completed its sequel, *Of the Integrity*. The *Prolegomena* and *Appendix* are published in vols. 1 and 6 of the Polyglot collection, respectively. The *Prolegomena* has been published separately in numerous editions. The edition cited here will be Brian Walton, *In Biblia polyglotta prolegomena*, 2 vols. (Cambridge: J. Smith, 1827–1828).
40 In the margin: *Satis ergo est quod eadem salutaris doctrina quae fuit à Mose, prophetis, apostolis et evangelistis in suis αὐτογράφοις primum literis consignata, eadem omnino pariter in textibus Graeco & Hebreao, & in translationibus cum veteribus, tum recentibus, clarè certò & sufficienter inveniatur. Pariter illae omnes unà cum textibus Graeco & Hebraeo sunt & dici possunt authenticae, sacrae, divinae, Θεόπνευστοι—respectu materiae, &c. Sunt in Scripturis multa alia non usque adeo scitu necessaria, &c. Capel. Critic. Sac. L. 6. Cap. 5. §. 10, 11.*—Owen. Editor's translation: "It is therefore sufficient that all the same saving doctrine that was first recorded by Moses, the prophets, the apostles, and evangelists in their original autographs may be clearly, certainly, and sufficiently found altogether equally the same in the Greek and Hebrew texts and in both ancient and recent translations. All those things are equally one with the Greek and Hebrew texts, and are able to be called authentic, sacred, divine, God-breathed—in respect of material teaching, etc. There are in the Scriptures many other things that are not necessary to know to the same degree, etc." Owen's quotation is slightly amended from the original Latin text. See Cappel, *Critica sacra*, 403.
41 Original has "17."

the worst of all, yet every necessary saving fundamental truth, would be found sufficiently testified unto therein. But to depress the sacred truth of the originals, into such a condition, as wherein it should stand in need of this apology, and that without any color or pretense from discrepancies in the copies themselves that are extant, or any tolerable evidence that there ever were any other, in the least differing from these extant in the world, will at length be found a work unbecoming a Christian Protestant divine. Besides the injury done hereby to the providence of God toward his church, and care of his word, it will not be found so easy a matter, upon a supposition of such corruption in the originals as is pleaded for, to evince unquestionably that the whole saving doctrine itself, at first given out from God, continues entire and incorrupt. The nature of this doctrine is such, that there is no other principle or means of its discovery, no other rule or measure of judging and determining any thing about or concerning it, but only the writing from whence it is taken: it being wholly of divine revelation, and that revelation being expressed only in that writing. Upon any corruption then supposed therein, there is no means of rectifying it. It were an easy thing to correct a mistake or corruption in the transcription of any problem or demonstration of Euclid, or any other ancient mathematician, from the consideration of the things themselves about which they treat, being always the same, and in their own nature equally exposed to the knowledge and understanding of men, in all ages. In things of pure revelation, whose knowledge depends solely on their revelation, it is not so. Nor is it enough to satisfy us, that the doctrines mentioned are preserved entire; every tittle and ἰῶτα[42] in the word of God, must come under our care and consideration, as being as such from God; but of these things we shall treat afterward at large; return we now to the apostle.

The Scripture Not ἰδίας ἐπιλύσεως ("of One's Own Interpretation") and the True Meaning of That Expression

17.[43] This προφητεία γραφῆς, this "written prophecy," this λόγος προφητικος;[44] says he ἰδίας ἐπιλύσεως οὐ γίνεται; "is not of any private interpretation."[45] Some think that ἐπιλύσεως[46] is put for ἐπηλύσεως[47] or ἐπελεύσεως,[48] which

---

42 Gk. "iota" (see Matt. 5:18).
43 As per original.
44 Gk. "prophetic word."
45 2 Pet. 1:20.
46 Gk. "of interpretation."
47 Gk. "of an approach."
48 Gk. "of an impulse."

according to Hesychius[49] denotes afflation, inspiration, conception within; so Calvin;[50] in this sense the importance of the words, is the same with what I have already mentioned; namely that the prophets had not their private conceptions, or self-fancied enthusiasms of the things they spoke. To this interpretation assents Grotius. And ἐπηλύσεως, for ἐπιλύσεως, is reckoned among the various lections that are gathered out of him, in the *Appendix* to the *Biblia polyglotta*. Thus ἰδίας ἐπιλύσεως οὐ γίνεται is the other side of that usual expression, ἐπῆλθεν ἐπ᾽ ἐμὲ ὁ λόγος,[51] or τὸ πνεῦμα.[52] Camero contends for the retaining of ἐπιλύσεως; and justly. We begin a little too late to see, whether men's bold conjectures in correcting the original text of the Scriptures are like to proceed. Here is no color for a various lection; one copy it seems by Stephen[53] read διαλύσεως;[54] without ground, by an evident error; and such mistakes are not to be allowed the name or place of various readings. But yet says Camero, ἐπίλυσις[55] is such a resolution and interpretation as is made by revelation. He adds that in that sense ἐπιλύειν[56] is used by the LXX, in the business of Joseph's interpretation of Pharaoh's dream (Gen. 40); which was by revelation. But indeed the word is not used in that chapter. However he falls in with this sense, (as do Calvin and Grotius) that ἰδίας ἐπιλύσεως,[57] is not to be referred to our interpretation of the prophets, but to the way and manner of their receiving the counsel and will of God.

18. And indeed, ἰδίας ἐπιλύσεως οὐ γίνεται; taking ἐπίλυσις, for an interpretation of the word of prophecy given out by writing, as our translation bears it, is an expression that can scarcely have any tolerable sense affixed unto it; γίνεται,[58] or οὐ γίνεται,[59] relates here, to προφητεία γραφῆς,[60] and denotes the first giving out of its word, not our after-consideration of its sense and meaning. And without this sense it stands in no coherence with,

49 Hesychius of Jerusalem was a Christian exegete who flourished around the first half of the fifth century.

50 John Calvin (1509–1564), one of the best known of the early Protestant Reformers, was a French theologian and pastor in Geneva, noted for his exegetical commentaries and the several editions of his *Institutio*, or *Institutes of the Christian Religion*.

51 Gk. "the word came upon me."

52 Gk. "the Spirit."

53 Robert Estienne, or Robertus Stephanus.

54 Gk. "of separation."

55 Gk. "an interpretation."

56 Gk. "to interpret."

57 Gk. "private interpretation."

58 Gk. "came about."

59 Gk. "did not come about."

60 Gk. "prophecy of Scripture."

nor opposition to, the following sentence, which, by its causal connection to this, manifests that it renders a reason of what is herein affirmed, in the first place; and in the latter, turning with the adversative ἀλλά,[61] an opposition unto it: οὐ γὰρ θελήματι ἀνθρώπου ἠνέχθη ποτὲ προφητεία, ἀλλ᾽ ὑπὸ πνεύματος ἁγίου φερόμενοι ἐλάλησαν ἅγιοι θεοῦ ἄνθρωποι; "For prophecy came not at anytime by the will of man, but holy men of God spake as they were moved by the Holy Ghost."[62] What reason is in the first part of this verse, why the Scripture is not of our private interpretation? Or what opposition in the latter to that assertion? Nay on that supposal, there is no tolerable, correspondency of discourse in the whole περιοχή.[63] But take the word to express the coming of the prophecy to the prophets themselves, and the sense is full and clear.

19. This then is the intention of the apostle; the prophecy which we have written, the Scripture, was not an issue of men's fancied enthusiasms;[64] not a product of their own minds and conceptions, not an interpretation of the will of God by the understanding of man, that is of the prophets themselves; neither their rational apprehensions, inquiries, conceptions of fancy, or imaginations of their hearts, had any place in this business; no self-afflation, no rational meditation managed at liberty by the understanding and will of men, had place herein.

20. Of this, says the apostle, τοῦτο πρῶτον γινώσκοντες; "knowing," "judging," and "determining" "this in the first place." This is a principle to be owned and acknowledged by everyone that will believe anything else. γινώσκω[65] is not only to know, to perceive to understand; but also to judge, own, and acknowledge. This then in our religion is to be owned, acknowledged, submitted unto, as a principle, without further dispute. To discover the grounds of this submission and acknowledgment, is the business of the ensuing discourse.

How the Word Came of Old and How It Was Received

21. That this is so indeed, as before asserted, and to give a reason why this is to be received as a principle, he adds, verse 21, οὐ γὰρ θελήματι ἀνθρώπου ἠνέχθη ποτὲ προφητεία.[66] That word of prophecy which we have written, is

---

61 Gk. "but."
62 2 Pet. 1:21.
63 Gk. "passage."
64 I.e., a common pejorative reference to private spiritual interpretations.
65 Gk. "I know."
66 Gk. "for it came not at any time by the will of man," per Owen's translation in the subsequent sentence.

not ἰδίας ἐπιλύσεως, "of private conception," for it came not at any time by the will of man. ἠνέχθη which is the passive conjugation of φέρω[67] from ἐνέγκω,[68] denotes at least to be "brought in"; more than merely it "came"; it was brought into them by the will of God. The affirmative, as to the will of God, is included in the negative, as to the will of man. Or it came as the voice from heaven to our Savior on the mount: verse 18; where the same word is used. So Ezek. 1:3 היה היה דבר[69] *essendo fuit verbum;*[70] it was brought into him, as was showed before. Thus God brought the word to them, and spoke in them, in order of nature, before he spoke by them. As ἠνέχθη, it was brought to them, it was קול יהוה "the voice of the Lord" (Gen. 3:8), or בת קול as the Jews call it; as spoken by them or written, it was properly דבר־יהוה *verbum Dei,* "the word of God"; which by his immediate voice he signified to the prophets. Thus some of them in visions, first eat a written book, and then prophesied, as was instanced before. And this is the first spring of the Scripture; the beginning of its emanation from the counsel and will of God. By the power of the Holy Ghost, it was brought into the organs or instruments, that he was pleased to use, for the revelation, and declaration of it unto others.

The Word, to the Least Tittle, Came Entirely from God

22. That which remains for the completing of this dispensation of the word of God unto us, is added by the apostle; ὑπὸ πνεύματος ἁγίου φερόμενοι ἐλάλησαν ἅγιοι θεοῦ ἄνθρωποι;[71] when the word was thus brought to them, it was not left to their understandings, wisdoms, minds, memories, to order, dispose, and give it out; but they were borne, acted, carried out by the Holy Ghost, to speak, deliver, and write all that, and nothing but that, to every tittle, that was so brought to them. They invented not words themselves, suited to the things they had learned; but only expressed the words, that they received. Though their mind and understanding were used in the choice of words, whence arise all the difference, that is in their manner of expression (for they did use דברי חפץ "words of will," or choice), yet they were so guided, that their words were not their own, but immediately supplied unto them; and so they gave out כתוב ישר the "writing of uprightness," and דברי אמת "words of truth," itself (Eccl. 12:10). Not only the doctrine they taught, was the word of truth, truth itself (John 17:17); but the words whereby they taught it, were

---

67   Gk. "I carry."
68   Gk. "I carry."
69   Heb. "the word [of the Lord] came expressly," or powerfully.
70   Lat. "the word was in being"—that is, it came to inhabit the prophet.
71   Gk. "carried by the Holy Spirit, holy men spoke from God" (2 Pet. 1:21).

words of truth from God himself. Thus allowing the contribution of passive instruments for the reception and representation of words, which answers the mind and tongue of the prophets, in the coming of the voice of God to them, every apex of the written word is equally divine, and as immediately from God as the voice wherewith, or whereby he spoke to, or in the prophets; and is therefore accompanied with the same authority, in itself, and unto us.

Of the Scriptures of the New Testament and Their Peculiar Prerogative

23. What has been thus spoken of the Scripture of the Old Testament, must be also affirmed of the New; with this addition of advantage and preeminence, that ἀρχὴν ἔλαβεν λαλεῖσθαι διὰ τοῦ κυρίου (Heb. 2:3),[72] it received its beginning of being spoken by the Lord himself, God spoke in these last days ἐν τῷ υἱῷ "in the Son" (Heb. 1:1).[73]

24. Thus God, who himself began the writing of the word with his own finger (Ex. 31:11);[74] after he had spoken it (Ex. 20); appointing or approving the writing of the rest that followed (Deut. 31:12; Josh. 23:6; 1 Kings 2:3; 2 Kings 14:6; 17:13; 1 Chron. 21:15;[75] 2 Chron. 25:4; Ezek. 2:9, 10;[76] Hab. 2:2; Luke 16:29; John 5:39; 20:31; Acts 17:11); does lastly command the close of the immediate revelation of his will, to be written in a book (Rev. 1:11); and so gives out the whole of his mind and counsel unto us in writing; as a merciful and steadfast relief, against all that confusion, darkness, and uncertainty, which the vanity, folly, and looseness of the minds of men, drawn out and heightened by the unspeakable alterations, that fall out among them, would otherwise have certainly run into.

25. Thus we have laid down the original of the Scriptures, from the Scripture itself; and this original is the basis and foundation of all its authority. Thus is it from God; entirely from him; as to the doctrine contained in it, and the words wherein that doctrine is delivered, it is wholly his; what that speaks, he speaks himself. He speaks in it and by it; and so it is vested with all the moral authority of God over his creatures.

72 Gk. "It was declared at first by the Lord" (Heb. 2:3 ESV).
73 Owen is referring to Heb. 1:2.
74 Owen is referring to Ex. 31:18.
75 Owen is referring to 1 Chron. 22:13.
76 Owen is referring to Ezek. 2:8–10.

2

The Authority of Scripture and Divine Faith

[1–2.] The main question proposed to consideration. How we may know assuredly the Scripture to be the word of God. The Scripture to be received by divine faith. The ground and foundation of that faith inquired after. [3.] The answer in the general thesis of this discourse. The authority of God the foundation. [4–5.] The way whereby that authority is evidenced or made known. [6.] What is meant by the authority of the Scriptures. [7–9.] Authority is in respect of others. [10–16.] First general evidence given to the thesis laid down. The various ways of God's revealing himself and his mind. 1. By his works: 2. By the light of nature; 3. By his word. Each of these evince themselves to be from him. His word especially.

THE MAIN QUESTION PROPOSED TO CONSIDERATION

1. Having laid, in the foregoing chapter the foundation that we are to build and proceed upon, I come now to lay down the inquiry, whose resolution must thence be educed. That then which we are seeking after is; how we, and the rest of men in the world, who through the merciful dispensation of God, have the book or books wherein the Scripture given out from him as above declared, is contained, or said to be contained, [and we]¹ who live so many ages from the last person who received any part of it immediately from God, or who have not received it immediately ourselves, may come to be ascertained,

1 Goold adds "we."

as to all ends and purposes wherein we may be concerned therein, that the whole and entire written word in that book, or those books, has the original and consequently the authority that it pleads and avows, namely that it is, ἐξ οὐρανοῦ[2] and not ἐξ ἀνθρώπων,[3] from God, in the way and manner laid down, and not the invention of men, attending σεσοφισμένοις μύθοις, (2 Pet. 1:26);[4] or to "cunningly devised fables."

2. Now seeing it is expected from us, and required of us by God himself, and that on the penalty of his eternal displeasure, if we fail in our duty (2 Thess. 1:8, 9, 10)[5] that we receive the Scripture not as we do other books in relation to their author, with a firm opinion, built on prevailing probable arguments, prevalent against any actual conclusions to the contrary; but with divine and supernatural faith, omitting all such inductions as serve only to ingenerate a persuasion, not to be cast out of the mind by contrary reasonings or objections; it is especially inquired, what is the foundation and formal reason of our doing so, if we so do. Whatever that be, it returns an answer to this important question; why, or on what account do you believe the Scriptures, or books of the Old and New Testament to be the word of God. Now the formal reason of things being but one, whatever consideration may be had of other inducements or arguments to beget in us a persuasion that the Scripture is the word of God, yet they have no influence on that divine faith wherewith we are bound to believe them. They may indeed be of some use, to repel the objections that are, or may, by any, be raised against the truth we believe; and so indirectly cherish, and further faith itself; but as to a concurrence unto the foundation, or formal reason of our believing, it is not capable of it.

The Answer in the General Thesis of This Discourse: The Authority of God the Foundation

3. Having then laid down the divine original of the Scriptures, and opened the manner of the word's coming forth from God, an answer shall now on that sole foundation be returned to the inquiry laid down. And this I shall do in the ensuing position.

The authority of God, the supreme Lord of all; the first and only absolute Truth whose word is truth, speaking in, and by the penmen of the Scriptures, evinced singly in, and by the Scripture itself, is the sole bottom and foundation, or formal reason, of our assenting to those Scriptures as his word, and of our

2 Gk. "from heaven."
3 Gk. "from men."
4 Owen is referring to 2 Pet. 1:16.
5 Owen is referring to 2 Thess. 1:7–10.

submitting our hearts and consciences unto them, with that faith and obedience, which morally respect him, and are due to him alone.

The Way Whereby That Authority Is Evidenced or Made Known

4. God speaking in the penmen of the Scripture (Heb. 1:1), his voice to them was accompanied with its own evidence, which gave assurance unto them; and God speaking by them, or their writings unto us, his word is accompanied with its own evidence, and gives assurance unto us. His authority and veracity did, and do in the one and the other sufficiently manifest themselves, that men may quietly repose their souls upon them, in believing and obedience. Thus are we built ἐπὶ τῷ θεμελίῳ τῶν ἀποστόλων καὶ προφητῶν (Eph. 2:20), "on the foundation of the apostles and prophets," in our believing.

5. That then which to the establishment of the souls of believers, I shall labor to prove and evince, is plainly this; namely, that the Scriptures of the Old and New Testament, do abundantly, and uncontrollably manifest themselves to be the word of the living God; so that merely on the account of their own proposal of themselves unto us, in the name and majesty of God, as such, without the contribution of help or assistance from tradition, church, or anything else without themselves, we are obliged upon the penalty of eternal damnation (as are all to whom by any means they come, or are brought) to receive them, with that subjection of soul which is due to the word of God. The authority of God shining in them, they afford unto us all the divine evidence of themselves, which God is willing to grant unto us, or can be granted us, or is any way needful for us. So then, the authority of the written word, in itself and unto us, is from itself, as the word of God, and the eviction of that authority unto us, is by itself.

What Is Meant By the Authority of the Scriptures

6. When the authority of the Scripture is inquired after, strictly its power to command, and require obedience in the name of God, is intended. To ask, then, whence it has its authority, is to ask, whence it has its power to command in the name of God. Surely men will not say, that the Scripture has its power to command in the name of God, from anything but itself. And it is indeed a contradiction for men to say, they give authority to the Scriptures. Why do they do so? Why do they give this authority to that book rather than another? They must say, because it is the word of God. So the reason why they give authority unto it, is the formal reason of all its authority, which it has antecedently to their charter and concession of power. ὁ λόγος ὁ σὸς ἀλήθειά ἐστι (John 17:17). "Thy word is truth."

Authority Is in Respect of Others

7. Some say indeed, that the Scripture has its authority in itself, and from itself, or its own divine original, but not *quoad nos* "in respect of us"; that it may reach us, that we may know, and understand, and submit to its authority, it must be testified unto *aliunde*, from some other person, or thing appointed thereunto: *Answer*

⁶But may not this be said of God himself, as well as of his word? If God reveal himself to us, it must be by means; and if those means may not be understood to reveal him, unless they are testified unto from somewhat else, God cannot reveal himself to us. *Si Deus hominibus non placuerit, utique Deus non erit.*⁷ If God and his word, will keep themselves, within themselves, to themselves, they may be God and his word still, and keep their authority; but if they will deal with us, and put forth their commands to us, let them look that they get the church's testimonials, or on this principle, they may be safely rejected; but,

8. Authority is a thing that no person or thing can have in him, or itself, that has it not in respect of others. In its very nature it relates to others, that are subject unto it. All authority arises from relation; and answers it throughout. The authority of God over his creatures, is from their relation to him as their Creator. A king's authority is in respect of his subjects. And he who has no subjects, has no kingly authority in himself, but is only a stoical king. The authority of a minister relates to his flock; and he who has no flock, has no authority of a minister; if he have not a ministerial authority, in reference to a flock, a people, a church; he has none, he can have none in himself. So is it in this case; if the Scripture has no authority from itself, in respect of us, it has none in itself, nor can have. If it has it in itself, it has it in respect of us. Such a respect, that is, a right to command and oblige to obedience, is as inseparable from authority, or a moral power, as heat is from fire. It is true: a man may have de jure, a lawful authority over them, whom de facto, he cannot force or compel to obedience. But want of force does not lessen authority. God loses not his authority over men, though he put not forth toward them, ὑπερβάλλον μέγεθος τῆς δυνάμεως, or ἐνέργειαν τοῦ κράτους τῆς ἰσχύος, "the greatness of his power," or "the efficacy of the might of his strength,"⁸

---

6   Original has "1." but is omitted here since the list does not appear to continue.
7   Lat. "If God will not please men, he certainly will not be God." This is a paraphrase of Tertullian's remark in his *Apology*, chap. 5, sec. 1. See Tertullian, *Apology. De spectaculis. Minucius Felix: Octavius*, trans. T. R. Glover and Gerald H. Rendall, Loeb Classical Library 250 (Cambridge, MA: Harvard University Press, 1966), 28–29.
8   Eph. 1:19. In the first Greek citation, Owen has omitted translating ὑπερβάλλον, as in "immeasurable" (ESV).

to cause them to obey. It is fond then to imagine, that a man, or any thing, should have an authority in himself, or itself, and yet not have that authority in respect of them who are to be subject thereunto. That is not a law properly at all, which is not a law to some. Besides, all the evil of disobedience relates to the authority of him that requires the obedience (James 2:10, 11). No action is disobedience, but from the subjection of him who performs it, unto him who requires obedience. And therefore if the Scripture has not an authority in itself, toward us, there is no evil in our disobedience unto its commands; or our not doing what it commands, and our doing what it forbids, is not disobedience, because it has not an authority over us; I speak of it as considered in itself, before the accession of the testimony pretended necessary to give it an authority over us. Hitherto then have we carried this objection; to disobey the commands of the Scripture before the communication of a testimony unto it by men, is no sin; *credat Apella.*[9]

9. The sense then of our position is evident and clear; and so our answer to the inquiry made. The Scripture has all its authority from its Author, both in itself, and in respect of us; that it has the Author and original pleaded for, it declares itself, without any other assistance by the ways and means, that shall afterward be insisted on: the truth whereof, I shall now confirm [first] by one general induction. Secondly, by testimonies. Thirdly, by arguments, expressing the ways and means of its revelation of itself.

FIRST GENERAL EVIDENCE GIVEN TO THE THESIS LAID DOWN

The Various Ways of God's Revealing Himself and His Mind

10. There are three ways, whereby God in several degrees reveals himself, his properties, his mind, and will, to the sons of men.

By His Works

First, he does it by his works, both of creation and providence. "All thy works praise thee" (Ps. 145:10, etc.). "The heavens declare the glory of God, and the firmament telleth the works of his hands. Day unto day uttereth speech, and night unto night declareth knowledge. There is no speech or

---

9 Lat. "Let Apella believe it." This is a figurative saying drawn from Horace indicating incredulity. Horace remarks, *credit Iudaeus Apella, non ego* (*Satires*, bk. 1, satire 5, line 100). "Apella, the Jew, may believe it, not I." For English translation, see Horace, *Satires. Epistles. The Art of Poetry*, trans. H. Rushton Fairclough, Loeb Classical Library 194 (Cambridge, MA: Harvard University Press, 1926), 73.

language where their voice is not heard. Their line is gone out throughout the earth, and their word to the end of the world" (Ps. 19:1–4, etc.). So Job 37, 38, 39; throughout. "God, who made heaven and earth, and the sea, and all things that are therein, suffered in times past all nations to walk in their own ways, yet he left not himself without witness in that he did good, and gave us rain from heaven and fruitful seasons, filling our hearts with food and gladness" (Acts 14:15–17). And, "God that made the world and all things therein, seeing he is the Lord of heaven and earth, dwelleth not in temples made with hands, neither is worshipped with men's hands, as though he needed any thing, seeing he giveth unto all life and breath, and all things, and has made of one blood all mankind to dwell on the face of the earth, and assigned the seasons which were ordained before, and the bounds of their habitations," ζητεῖν τὸν κύριον ἐι ἄραγε ψηλαφήσειαν αὐτὸν καὶ εὕροιεν, "that they should seek the Lord, if happily they might feel after him and find him" (Acts 17:24–27): for, "that which may be known of God is manifest in them, for God has showed it unto them; for the invisible things of him, from the creation of the world are clearly seen, being understood by the things that are made, even his eternal power and Godhead" (Rom. 1:18, 19, 20).[10] All which places God assisting shall be opened before long, in another treatise.[11] The sum of them amounts to what was before laid down; namely, that God reveals and declares himself unto us, by the works of his hands.

By the Light of Nature

11. Second,[12] God declares himself, his sovereign power and authority, his righteousness and holiness, by the innate (or engrafted) light of nature, and principles of the consciences of men. That indispensable moral obedience, which he requires of us, as his creatures subject to his law, is in general thus made known unto us. For "the Gentiles which have not the law, do by nature the things contained in the law; they having not the law, are a law unto themselves, showing the work of the law written in their hearts, their consciences also bearing witness, and their thoughts in the mean time excusing or accusing one another." (Rom. 2:14, 15). By the light that God has indelibly implanted in the minds of men, accompanied with a moral instinct of good and evil,

10 Owen's text quotes only Rom. 1:19–20.
11 In the margin: *De Natura & Studio Theologiae*—Owen. Owen is referring here to his Latin treatise, Θεολογούμενα Παντοδαπά. *Sive de Natura, Ortu, Progressu, et Studio, Verae Theologiae* (1661). See *Complete Works of John Owen*, vol. 38.
12 Absent in original but added to continue the list that began in the previous paragraph.

seconded by that self-judgment which he has placed in us, in reference to his own over us, does he reveal himself unto the sons of men.

By His Word

Thirdly, God reveals himself by his *word*, as is confessed.

Each of These Evince Themselves to Be from Him, His Word Especially

It remains then that we inquire, how we may know, and be ascertained that these things are not deceivable pretenses, but that God does indeed so reveal himself by them.

12. First; the works of God, as to what is his will to teach and reveal of himself by them, have that expression of God upon them; that stamp and character of his eternal power and Godhead, that evidence with them that they are his, that wherever they are seen and considered, they undeniably evince that they are so, and that what they teach concerning him, they do it in his name and authority. There is no need of traditions, no need of miracles, no need of the authority of any churches to convince a rational creature, that the works of God are his, and his only; and that he is eternal, and infinite in power that made them. They carry about with them their own authority. By being what they are, they declare whose they are. To reveal God by his works, there is need of nothing, but that they be by themselves represented, or objected to the consideration of rational creatures.

13. The voice of God in nature is in like manner effectual. It declares itself to be from God by its own light and authority. There is no need to convince a man by substantial witnesses, that what his conscience speaks, it speaks from God. Whether it bear testimony to the being, righteousness, power, omniscience, or holiness of God himself; or whether it call for that moral obedience which is eternally and indispensably due to him, and so shows forth the work of the law in the heart; it so speaks and declares itself, that without further evidence or reasoning, without the advantage of any considerations, but what are by itself supplied, it discovers its author from whom it is, and in whose name it speaks. Those κοιναὶ ἔννοιαι, καὶ προλήψεις, those "common notions, and general presumptions" of him and his authority, that are inlaid in the natures of rational creatures by the hand of God, to this end, that they might make a revelation of him as to the purposes mentioned, are able to plead their own divine original, without the least contribution of strength or assistance from without.

14. And thus is it with those things; now the psalmist says unto God, "Thou hast magnified" עַל־כָּל שִׁמְךָ אִמְרָתֶךָ "over all thy name the word thou has

spoken."[13] The name of God is all that whereby he makes himself known. Over all this, God magnifies his word. It lies all in a subserviency thereunto. The name of God, is not here God himself; but every thing whereby God makes himself known. Now it were very strange that those low, dark and obscure principles and means of the revelation of God and his will, which we have mentioned, should be able to evince themselves to be from him, without any external help, assistance, testimony, or authority, and that which is by God himself magnified above them, which is far more noble and excellent in itself, and in respect of its end and order, has far more divinely conspicuous and glorious impressions and characters of his goodness, holiness, power, grace, truth, than all the creation, should lie dead, obscure, and have nothing in itself to reveal its author, until this or that superadded testimony, be called in to its assistance. We esteem them to have done no service unto the truth, who among innumerable other bold denials, have insisted on this also; that there is no natural knowledge of God arising from the innate principles of reason, and the works of God proposing themselves to the consideration thereof; let now the way to the progress of supernatural revelation be obstructed, by denying, that it is able to evince itself to be from God, and we shall quickly see what banks are cut to let in a flood of atheism upon the face of the earth.

15. Let us consider the issue of this general induction. As God in the creation of the world, and all things therein contained, has so made and framed them, has left such characters of his eternal power and wisdom, in them, and upon them, filled them with such evidences of their author, suited to the apprehensions of rational creatures, that without any other testimony from himself, or any else, under the naked consideration and contemplation of what they are, they so far declare their Creator, that they are left wholly inexcusable, who will not learn, and know him from thence; so in the giving out of his word to be the foundation of that world, which he has set up in this world, as האופן בתוך האופן "a wheel within a wheel,"[14] his church, he has by his Spirit implanted in it, and impressed on it, such characters of his goodness, power, wisdom, holiness, love to mankind, truth, faithfulness, with all the rest of his glorious excellencies and perfections, that at all times, and in all places when הרקיע "the expansion" of it, is stretched over men by his providence, without any other witness or testimony given unto it, it declares itself to be his, and makes good its authority from him, so that the refusal of it upon its own evidence brings unavoidable condemnation on the souls of

---

13 Ps. 138:2.
14 Owen is alluding to Ezek. 1:16.

men. This comparison is insisted on by the psalmist, Psalm 19, where, as he ascribes קול and קו a "voice," and "line," to the creatures, so אור[15] etc. Light, power, stability, and permanency, like that of the heavens and sun, in commutation of properties to the word, and in an inexpressible exaltation of it above them; the light of one day of this sun, being unspeakably more, than that of seven others, as to the manifestation of the glory of God.

16. This then is fixed as a principle of truth; whatever God has appointed to reveal himself by, as to any special or general end, that those whom he intends to discover himself unto, may either be effectually instructed in his mind and will, according to the measure, degree, and means of the revelation afforded, or be left inexcusable for not receiving the testimony that he gives of himself, by any plea or pretense of want of clear, evident, manifest revelation; that, whatever it be has such an impression of his authority upon it, as undeniably to evince that it is from him. And this now concerning his word, comes further to be confirmed by testimonies and arguments.

15 Heb. "light."

3

Second Evidence of the Thesis

Arguments by Way of Testimony

[2–3.] Arguments of two sorts. [4–6.] Inartificial arguments, by
way of testimony to the truth. To whom these arguments are
valid. [7–8.] Of θεοπνευστία (Isa. 8:20; 2 Tim. 3:16). [9–11.]
The τὸ θεῖον that accompanies the voice of God (Jer. 23:26–29).
[12–13.] The rejection of a plea of θεοπνευστία, wherein it
consists (Luke 16:31). [14–16.] Of miracles, their efficacy to
beget faith, compared with the word (2 Pet. 1:16, 19, 20).

1. HAVING DECLARED the divine original, and authority of the Scripture,
and explained the position laid down as the foundation of our ensuing discourse, way is now made for us, to the consideration of those self-evidences
of its divine rise, and consequently authority that it is attended withal, upon
the account whereof we receive it, as, (believing it to be) the word of God.

ARGUMENTS OR TESTIMONIES OF TWO
SORTS: INARTIFICIAL AND ARTIFICIAL

2. The arguments whereby anything is confirmed are of two sorts; inartificial,
by the way of testimony; and artificial, by the way of deductions and inferences. Whatever is capable of contributing evidence unto truth, falls under
one of these two heads. Both these kinds of proofs we make use of, in the
business in hand. Some profess they own the authority of the Scriptures, and
also urge others so to do; but they will dispute on what grounds and accounts

they do so. With those we may deal, in the first way, by testimony from the Scriptures themselves, which upon their own principles they cannot refuse. When they shall be pleased to inform us that they have relinquished those principles, and do no longer own the Scripture to be the word of God, we will withdraw the witnesses, upon their exceptions, whom for the present we make use of. Testimonies that are innate and ingrafted in the word itself, used only as mediums of artificial arguments to be deduced from them, which are of the second sort, may be used toward them who at present own not the authority of the Scripture on any account whatever, or who are desirous to put on themselves the persons of such men, to try their skill and ability for the management of a controversy against the word of God.

3. In both these cases the testimony of the Scripture is pleaded, and is to be received, or cannot with any pretense of reason be refused; in the former, upon the account of the acknowledged authority and veracity of the witness though speaking in its own case; in the latter upon the account of that self-evidence which the testimony insisted on is accompanied withal, made out by such reasonings and arguments as for the kind of them, persons who own not its authority, cannot but admit. In human things; if a man of known integrity and unspotted reputation bear witness in any cause, and give uncontrollable evidence to his testimony, from the very nature and order of the things whereof he speaks, as it is expected that those who know and admit of his integrity and reputation do acquiesce in his assertion, so those to whom he is a stranger, who are not moved by his authority, will yet be overcome to assent to what is witnessed by him, from the nature of the things he asserts, especially if there be a coincidence of all such circumstances, as are any way needful to give evidence to the matter in hand.

INARTIFICIAL ARGUMENTS, BY WAY OF TESTIMONY TO THE TRUTH: TO WHOM THESE ARGUMENTS ARE VALID

4. Thus it is, in the case under consideration. For those who profess themselves to believe the Scriptures to be the word of God, and so own the credit and fidelity of the witness, it may reasonably be expected from them, yea in strict justice demanded of them, that they stand to the testimony, that they give to themselves, and their own divine original. By saying that the Scripture is the word of God, and then commanding us to prove it so to be, they render themselves obnoxious unto every testimony that we produce from it, that so it is; and that it is to be received on its own testimony. This witness they

cannot waive without disavowing their own professed principles; without which principles they have not the least color of imposing this task on us.

5. As for them, with whom we have not the present advantage of their own acknowledgment, it is not reasonable to impose upon them with the bare testimony of that witness concerning whom the question is, whether he be worthy the acceptation pleaded for; but yet arguments taken from the Scripture, from what it is, and does, its nature and operation, by which the causes and springs of all things are discovered, are not to be refused.

6. But it is neither of these, that principally I intend to deal withal; my present discourse is rather about the satisfaction of our own consciences, than the answering of others' objections. Only we must satisfy our consciences upon such principles as will stand against all men's objections. This then is chiefly inquired after; namely what it is that gives such an assurance of the Scriptures being the word of God, as that relying thereon we have a sure bottom and foundation for our receiving them as such; and from whence it is, that those who receive them not in that manner, are left inexcusable in their damnable unbelief. This we say, is in, and from the Scripture itself; so that there is no other need of any further witness or testimony, nor is any, in the same kind, to be admitted.

SCRIPTURE'S OWN SELF-TESTIMONY

Of θεοπνευστία, "Divinely Inspired" (Isa. 8:20; 2 Tim. 3:16)

7. It is not at all in my purpose to insist largely at present on this subject, and therefore I shall content myself with instancing some few testimonies and arguments, beginning with one or two of the first sort. "To the law and to the testimony, if they speak not according to this word, [. . .] there is no light in them." (Isa. 8:20). Whatever any one says be it what, or who it will, church, or person, if it be in or about the things of God, concerning his will or worship, with our obedience to him, it is to be tried by the law and testimony. Hither we are sent; this is asserted to be the rule and standard, the touchstone of all speakings whatever. Now that must speak alone for itself, which must try the speaking of all, but itself, yea its own also.

8. But what does this law and testimony, that is, this written word plead, on the account whereof, it should be thus attended unto? What does it urge for its acceptance? Tradition, authority of the church, miracles, consent of men? or does it speak αὐτοκρατορικῶς,[1] and stand only upon its own

---

1 Gk. "on its own supreme authority."

sovereignty? The apostle gives us his answer to this inquiry, πᾶσα γραφὴ θεόπνευστος (2 Tim. 3:16).[2] Its plea for reception in comparison with, and opposition unto all other ways of coming to the knowledge of God, his mind and will, founded whereon, it calls for attendance and submission with supreme, uncontrollable authority is its θεοπνευστία or "divine inspiration." It remains then only to be inquired, whether, when θεοπνευστία is pleaded, there be any middle way, but either that it be received with divine faith, or rejected as false.

The τὸ θεῖον, "The Divine Power," That Accompanies the Voice of God (Jer. 23:26–29)

9. Suppose a man were θεόπνευστος, "divinely inspired," and should so profess himself in the name of the Lord, as did the prophets of old (Amos 7), supposing I say he were so indeed; it will not be denied, but that his message were to be received and submitted unto on that account. The denial of it, would justify them, who rejected and slew those, that spoke unto them in the name of the Lord. And that is to say in plain terms, we may reject them whom God sends. Though miracles were given only with respect to persons, not things, yet most of the prophets, who wrought no miracles, insisted on this, that being θεόπνευστοι "divinely inspired," their doctrine was to be received, as from God. In their so doing, it was sin, even unbelief, and rebellion against God, not to submit to what they spoke in his name. And it always so fell out, to fix our faith on the right bottom, that scarce any prophet that spoke in the name of God, had any approbation from the church, in whose days he spoke (Matt. 5:12; 23:29; Luke 11:47, 48; Acts 7:52; Matt. 21:33–38). It is true! ἐγένοντο [. . .] ψευδοπροφῆται ἐν τῷ λαῷ (2 Pet. 2:1); "there were false prophets [among the people]," that spoke in the name of the Lord, when he sent them not (Jer. 23:21).[3] Yet were those whom he did send, to be received on pain of damnation: on the same penalty were the others to be refused (Jer. 23:28, 29). The foundation of this duty lies in the τὸ θεῖον[4] that accompanied the word that was ἐκ θεοπνευστίας;[5] of which afterward. And without a supposal hereof, it could not consist with the goodness and righteousness of God, to require of men, under the penalty of his eternal displeasure, to make such a discrimination, where he had not given them τεκμήρια, "infallible tokens," to enable them so to do.

---

2 Gk. "All Scripture is divinely inspired."
3 Original has "Jer. 23:22."
4 Gk. "the divinity or divine power."
5 Gk. "from divine inspiration."

10. But that he had, and has done so, he declares:

How long shall this be in the heart of the prophets that prophesy lies? that are prophets of the deceit of their own heart; which think to cause my people to forget my name by their dreams, which they tell every man to his neighbor, as their fathers have forgotten my name for Baal. The prophet that has a dream, let him tell a dream, and he that has my word, let him speak my word faithfully; what is the chaff to the wheat? saith the Lord; is not my word like a fire, saith the Lord, and like a hammer that breaketh the mountains in pieces. (Jer. 23)[6]

In the latter days of that church, when the people were most eminently perplexed with false prophets, both as to their number and subtlety, yet God lays their eternal and temporal safety, or ruin, on their discerning aright between his word and that which was only pretended so to be. And that they might not complain of this imposition, he tenders them security of its easiness of performance. Speaking of his own word comparatively, as to every thing that is not so, he says, it is as wheat to chaff, which may infallibly, by being what it is, be discerned from it; and then absolutely that it has such properties, as that it will discover itself; even light and heat, and power. A person then who was truly θεόπνευστος, was to be attended unto, because he was so.

11. As then was said before, the Scriptures being θεόπνευστοι, is not the case the same, as with a man that was so? Is there anything in the writing of it by God's command, that should impair its authority? Nay is it not freed from innumerable prejudices that attended it, in its first giving out by men; arising from the personal infirmities and supposed interests of them that delivered it? (Jer. 43:3; John 9:29; Acts 24:5).

The Rejection of a Plea of θεοπνευστία, "Divinely Inspired," Wherein It Consists (Luke 16:31)

12. This being pleaded by it, and insisted on, its testimony is received, or it is not. If it be received on this account, there is in it we say the proper basis and foundation of faith, whereon it has its ὑπόστασις or "subsistence." If it be rejected, it must be not only with a refusal of its witness, but also with a high detestation of its pretense to be from God. What ground or plea for such a refusal and detestation any one has, or can have, shall be afterward considered. If it be a sin to refuse it, it had been a duty to receive it: if a duty

---

6 Owen is quoting Jer. 23:26–29.

to receive it as the word of God, then was it sufficiently manifested so to be. Of the objection arising from them who pretend to this inspiration falsely, we have spoken before; and we are as yet dealing with them that own the book whereof we spoke to be the word of God, and only call in question the grounds on which they do so; or on which others ought so to do. As to these it may suffice, that in the strength of all the authority and truth they profess to own and acknowledge in it, it declares the foundation of its acceptance to be no other, but its own divine inspiration; hence it is λόγος [. . .] πάσης ἀποδοχῆς ἄξιος.[7]

13. Again in that dispute, that was between Abraham and the rich man (Luke 16:31), about the best and most effectual means of bringing men to repentance: the rich man in hell, speaking his own conception, fixes upon miracles; if one rise from the dead, and preach, the work will be done. Abraham is otherwise minded, that is, Christ was so, the author of that parable: he bids them attend to Moses and the prophets, the written word, as that which all faith and repentance was immediately to be grounded on. The inquiry being, how men might be best assured, that any message is from God, did not the word manifest itself to be from him, this direction had not been equal.

Of Miracles, Their Efficacy to Beget Faith Compared with the Word (2 Pet. 1:16, 19–20)

14. The ground of the request for the rising of one from the dead, is laid in the common apprehension of men not knowing the power of God in the Scriptures; who think, that if an evident miracle were wrought, all pretenses and pleas of unbelief would be excluded; who does not think so? Our Savior discovers that mistake, and lets men know, that those who will not own, or submit to the authority of God in the word, would not be moved by the most signal miracles imaginable. If a holy man, whom we had known assuredly to have been dead for some years, should rise out of his grave, and come unto us with a message from God; could any man doubt whether he were sent unto us of God or no? I suppose not. The rising of men from the dead was the greatest miracle that attended the resurrection of our Savior (Matt. 27:52, 53), yea greater than his own, if the Socinians[8] may be believed: namely; in that he raised not himself by his own power; yet the evidence of the mission

---

7   Gk. "The saying is [. . .] deserving of full acceptance" (1 Tim. 1:15 ESV).
8   Socinianism was an antitrinitarian movement, named after the Italian pair Faustus Socinus (1539–1604) and his uncle, Laelius Socinus (1525–1562). The movement emerged out of a minority within the Polish Reformed church, known as the Polish Brethren, and spread across Europe in the early seventeenth century. In England, it became particularly associated with

of such a one, and the authority of God speaking in him, our Savior being judge, is not of an efficacy to enforce belief beyond that which is in the written word, nor a surer foundation for faith to repose itself upon.

15. Could we hear a voice from heaven, accompanied with such a divine power, as to evidence itself to be from God, should we not rest in it as such? I suppose men think they would; can we think that any man should withdraw his assent, and say, yea but I must have some testimony that this is from God; all such evasions are precluded in the supposition, wherein a self-evidencing power is granted. What greater miracle did the apostles of Christ ever behold, or hear; than that voice that came ὑπὸ τῆς μεγαλοπρεποῦς δόξης, "from the most excellent glory";[9] "this is my beloved Son"; yet Peter who heard that voice tells us, that comparatively we have greater security from, and by the written word, than they had in, and by that miraculous voice: we have βεβαιότερον τὸν προφητικὸν λόγον;[10] we heard says he that voice indeed, but we have "a more sure word of prophecy" to attend unto. More sure! not in itself, but in its giving out its evidence unto us. And how does it appear so to be? The reason he alleges for it, was before insisted on (2 Pet. 1:18, 19, 21).

16. Yea suppose that God should speak to us from heaven, as he spoke to Moses; or as he spoke to Christ; or from some certain place, as Numbers 7:8, 9. How should we be able to know it to be the voice of God? Cannot Satan cause a voice to be heard in the air, and so deceive us? or, may not there be some way in this kind found out, whereby men might impose upon us with their delusions. Pope Celestine thought he heard a voice from heaven, when it was but the cheat of his successor. Must we not rest at last in that τὸ θεῖον, which accompanies the true voice of God, evidencing itself, and ascertaining the soul beyond all possibility of mistake. Now did not this τεκμήριον[11] accompany the written word at its first giving forth? If it did not, as was said, how could any man be obliged to discern it from all delusions; if it did, how came it to lose it? Did God appoint his word to be written, that so he might destroy its authority? If the question be whether the doctrines proposed to be believed, are truths of God, or "cunningly devised fables," we are sent to the Scripture itself, and that alone, to give the determination.

John Biddle (1615–1662), who was responsible for the highly controversial publication of the Polish Brethren's *Racovian Catechism* into English.

9 2 Pet. 1:17.

10 Gk. "a more sure word of prophecy," as per Owen's translation later in the sentence, quoting 2 Pet. 1:19.

11 Gk. "certain proof."

Second Evidence of the Thesis Continued

Innate Arguments

[1.] Innate arguments in the Scripture, of its divine original
and authority. These the formal reason of our believing.
[2–3.] Its self-evidencing efficacy. [4–5.] All light manifests itself.
[6–8.] The Scripture, light. [9–10.] What kind of light it is. Spiritual
light evidential. [11–13.] Consectaries[1] from the premises laid down.
[14–15.] What the self-evidencing light of the Scripture peculiarly
is. The proposition of the Scripture as an object of faith is from and
by this light. [16.] Power, self-evidencing. [17–18.] The Scripture
the power of God. [19.] And powerful. [20.] How this power
exerts itself. [21.] The whole question resolved.

THE INNATE TESTIMONY INGRAFTED IN SCRIPTURE ITSELF

1. Having given some few instances of those many testimonies, which the
Scripture in express terms bears to itself, and the spring, rise, and fountain
of all that authority, which it claims among and over the sons of men, which
all those who pretend on any account whatever, to own and acknowledge its
divinity, are bound to stand to, and are obliged by; the second thing proposed,
or the innate arguments that the word of God is furnished withal for its own

1 I.e., consequences.

manifestation, and whereby the authority of God is revealed for faith to repose itself upon, comes in the next place into consideration. Now these arguments contain the full and formal grounds of our answer, to that inquiry before laid down; namely, why and wherefore we do receive and believe the Scripture to be the word of God; it being the formal reason of our faith, that whereon it is built, and whereinto it is resolved that is inquired after, we answer as we said before; we do so receive, embrace, believe, and submit unto it, because of the authority of God who speaks it, or gave it forth as his mind and will, evidencing itself, by the Spirit, in, and with that word unto our minds and consciences; or because that the Scripture being brought unto us, by the good providence of God, in ways of his appointment and preservation, it does evidence itself infallibly unto our consciences to be the word of the living God.

2. The self-evidencing efficacy of the Scripture, and the grounds of it, which consist in common mediums, that have an extent and latitude answerable to the reasons of men, whether as yet they acknowledge it to be the word of God or no, is that then which in the remainder of this discourse I shall endeavor to clear and vindicate. This only I shall desire to premise, that whereas some grounds of this efficacy seem to be placed in the things themselves contained in the Scripture, I shall not consider them abstractedly as such, but under the formality of their being the Scripture or written word of God; without which consideration and resolution, the things mentioned would be left naked and utterly divested of their authority and efficacy pleaded for; and be of no other nature and importance, than the same things found in other books. It is the writing itself, that now supplies the place and room of the persons, in, and by whom God originally spoke to men. As were the persons speaking of old, so are the writings now: it was the word spoken, that was to be believed, yet as spoken by them from God; and it is now the word written, that is to be believed, yet as written by the command and appointment of God.

3. There are then two things, that are accompanied with a self-evidencing excellency; and every other thing does so, so far as it is partaker of their nature, and no otherwise; now these are (1) Light. (2) Power for, or in operation.

SCRIPTURE'S SELF-EVIDENCING LIGHT

All Light Manifests Itself

4. First,[2] light manifests itself. Whatever is light does so: that is, it does whatever is necessary on its own part for its manifestation and discovery. Of the

---

2   Original has "1." The second point begins on p. 119, sec. 16.

defects that are, or may be in them, to whom this discovery is made, we do not as yet speak: and "whatever manifests itself is light," πᾶν γὰρ τὸ φανερού-μενον φῶς ἐστι (Eph. 5:13). Light requires neither proof nor testimony for its evidence. Let the sun arise in the firmament, and there is no need of witnesses to prove and confirm unto a seeing man that it is day. A small candle will so do. Let the least child bring a candle into a room that before was dark, and it would be a madness to go about to prove by substantial witnesses, men of gravity and authority, that light is brought in. Does it not evince itself, with an assurance above all that can be obtained by any testimony whatever? Whatever is light, either naturally or morally so, is revealed by its being so. That which evidences not itself, is not light.

5. That the Scripture is a light, we shall see immediately. That it is so, or can be called so, unless it has this nature and property of light, to evidence itself, as well as to give light unto others, cannot in any tolerable correspondency of speech be allowed. Whether light spiritual and intellectual regarding the mind, or natural with respect to bodily sight, be firstly and properly light, from whence the other is by allusion denominated, I need not now inquire. Both have the same properties in their several kinds. φῶς ἀληθινὸν φαίνει: "True light shineth."[3] ὁ θεὸς φῶς ἐστι[4] (1 John 1:5): God himself is light; and he inhabits φῶς ἀπρόσιτον[5] (1 Tim. 6:16), not a shining glistering brightness, as some grossly imagine,[6] but the glorious unsearchable majesty of his own being, which is inaccessible to our understandings. So Isaiah (57:15), "[God] inhabiteth eternity." So עטה אור says the Psalmist, "thou [. . .] clothest thyself with light":[7] and Daniel 2:22 שרא ונהורא עמה[8] the "light remaineth with him"; God, he is light essentially, and is, therefore known by the beaming of his eternal properties, in all that outwardly is of him. And light abides with him, as the fountain of it; he communicating light to all others. This being the fountain of all light, the more it participates of the nature of the fountain, the more it is light; and the more properly, as the properties and qualities of it are considered. It is then spiritual, moral, intellectual light, with all its mediums, that has the preeminence, as to a participation of the nature and properties of light.

3 Owen is alluding to 1 John 2:8.
4 Gk. "God is light."
5 Gk. "light unapproachable."
6 In the margin: Biddle *Catech.*—Owen. See John Biddle, *Twofold Catechism* (London: J. Cottrel, 1654).
7 Ps. 104:2.
8 As per original. The order of the Hebrew text is ונהירא עמה שרא. See *Biblia Hebraica Stuttgartensia*, ed. Karl Elliger and Wilhelm Rudolph (Stuttgart: Deutsche Bibelgesellschaft, 1983).

The Scripture Is Light

6. Now the Scripture, the word of God, is light; those that reject it are called אור מרדי "light's rebels,"[9] men resisting the authority which they cannot but be convinced of (Ps. 19:9;[10] 43:3; 119:105, 130; Prov. 6:23; Isa. 9:2; Hos. 6:5; Matt. 4:16; 5:14; John 3:20, 21): it is a light so shining with the majesty of its author, as that it manifests itself to be his (2 Pet. 1:19). "A light shining in a dark place," with an eminent advantage for its own discovery, as well as unto the benefit of others.

7. Let a light be ever so mean and contemptible; yet if it shines, casts out beams and rays in a dark place, it will evidence itself. If other things be wanting in the faculty, the light as to its innate glory and beauty, is not to suffer prejudice. But the word is a glorious shining light, as has been showed; an illuminating light; compared to, and preferred above the light of the sun (Ps. 19:5–8; Rom. 10:18). Let not then a reproach be cast upon the most glorious light in the world, the most eminent reflection of uncreated light and excellencies, that will not be fastened on any thing, that on any account is so called (Matt. 5:19).[11]

8. Now as the Scripture is thus a light, we grant it to be the duty of the church, of any church, of every church, to hold it up, whereby it may become the more conspicuous. It is a ground, and pillar to set this light upon (1 Tim. 3:15). στύλος καὶ ἑδραίωμα τῆς ἀληθείας,[12] may refer to the mystery of godliness, in the next words following, in good coherence of speech, as well as to the church; but granting the usual reading, no more is affirmed, but that the light and truth of the Scripture is held up, and held out by the church. It is the duty of every church so to do: almost the whole of its duty. And this duty it performs ministerially, not authoritatively. A church may bear up the light, it is not the light. It bears witness to it, but kindles not one divine beam to further its discovery. All the preaching that is in any church, its administration of ordinances, all its walking in the truth, hold up this light.

What Kind of Light? Spiritual Light Evidential

9. Nor does it in the least impair this self-evidencing efficacy of the Scripture, that it is a moral and spiritual, not a natural light. The proposition is universal to all kinds of light; yea more fully applicable to the former, than the latter. Light I confess of itself will not remove the defect of the visive faculty.

---

9   Job 24:13.
10   Owen is referring to Ps. 19:8.
11   Owen is referring to Matt. 5:15–16.
12   Gk. "a pillar and buttress of the truth" (1 Tim. 3:15 ESV).

It is not given for that end; light is not eyes. It suffices that there is nothing wanting on its own part for its discovery and revelation. To argue that the sun, cannot be known to be the sun, or the great means of communicating external light unto the world, because blind men cannot see it, nor do know any more of it, than they are told will scarce be admitted; nor does it in the least impeach the efficacy of the light pleaded for, that men stupidly blind cannot comprehend it (John 1:5).

10. I do not assert from hence, that wherever the Scripture is brought, by what means soever (which indeed is all one), all that read it, or to whom it is read, must instantly, of necessity assent unto its divine original. Many men (who are not stark blind) may have yet so abused their eyes, that when a light is brought into a dark place, they may not be able to discern it. Men may be so prepossessed with innumerable prejudices, principles received by strong traditions, corrupt affections, making them hate the light, that they may not behold the glory of the word, when it is brought to them. But it is nothing to our present discourse, whether any man living be able by and of himself to discern this light, while the defect may be justly cast on his own blindness. "[B]y the manifestation of the truth we commend ourselves to every one's conscience in the sight of God; but if our gospel be hid, it is hid to them that are lost: in whom the god of this world has blinded the minds of them that believe not, lest the light of the [glorious] gospel of Christ who is the image of God, should shine unto them." (2 Cor. 4:2–4). There is in the dispensation of the word an evidence of truth commending itself to the consciences of men; some receive not this evidence; is it for want of light in the truth itself? No! that is a glorious light that shines into the hearts of men; is it for want of testimony to assert this light? No! but merely because the god of this world has blinded the eyes of men, that they should not behold it.

Two Consequences from the Premises Laid Down

11. From what then has been laid down, these two things may be inferred.

(1) That as the authority of God the first and only absolute truth, in the Scripture, is that alone which divine faith rests upon, and is the formal object of it; so wherever the word comes, by what means soever, it has in itself a sufficiency of light to evidence to all (and will do it eventually to all that are not blinded by the god of this world) that authority of God its author; and (2),[13] the only reason why it is not received by many in the world to whom it is come,

---

13 Absent in original but added as Owen begins the list with "1." and specifically mentions "two things" that are to be inferred.

is, the advantage that Satan has to keep them in ignorance and blindness, by the lusts, corruptions, prejudices, and hardness of their own hearts.

12. The word then makes a sufficient proposition of itself, wherever it is. And he to whom it shall come, who refuses it because it comes not so, or so testified, will give an account of his atheism and infidelity. He that has the witness of God, need not stay for the witness of men, for the witness of God is greater.

13. Wherever the word is received indeed, as it requires itself to be received, and is really assented unto as the word of God; it is so received upon the evidence of that light which it has in itself, manifestly declaring itself so to be. It is all one, by what means, by what hand, whether of a child or a church, by accident or traditions, by common consent of men, or peculiar providence, the Scripture comes unto us; come how it will, it has its authority in itself, and toward us, by being the word of God; and has its power of manifesting itself so to be, from its own innate light.

What the Self-Evidencing Light of the Scripture Peculiarly Is

14. Now this light in the Scripture for which we contend, is nothing but the beaming of the majesty, truth, holiness, and authority of God, given unto it, and left upon it, by its author the Holy Ghost; an impress it has, of God's excellency upon it, distinguishing it by infallible τεκμήρια,[14] from the product of any creature; by this it dives into the consciences of men, into all the secret recesses of their hearts; guides, teaches, directs, determines, and judges in them, upon them, in the name, majesty and authority of God. If men who are blinded by the god of this world, will yet deny this light, because they perceive it not, it shall not prejudice them who do. By this self-evidencing light, I say, does the Scripture make such a proposition of itself, as the word of God, that whoever rejects it, does it at the peril of his eternal ruin; and thereby a bottom or foundation is tendered for that faith which it requires, to repose itself upon.

15. For the proof then of the divine authority of the Scriptures, unto him or them, who as yet on no account whatever do acknowledge it, I shall only suppose, that by the providence of God, the book itself be so brought unto him or them, as that he, or they, be engaged to the consideration of it; or do attend to the reading of it. This is the work of God's providence in the government of the world; upon a supposal hereof, I leave the word with them; and if it evidence not itself unto their conscience, it is because they are blinded by the god of this world; which will be no plea for the refusal of it, at the last

14   Gk. "certain proofs."

day; and they who receive it not on this ground, will never receive it on any, as they ought.

SCRIPTURE'S SELF-EVIDENCING POWER

Power Is Self-Evidencing

16. The second sort of things that evidence themselves, are things of an effectual powerful operation in any kind. So does fire by heat, the wind by its noise and force; salt by its taste and savor, the sun by its light and heat; so do also moral principles that are effectually operative (Rom. 2:14, 15). Men in whom they are, ἐνδείκνυνται τὸ ἔργον, "do manifest the work" of them; or manifest them by their work and efficacy. Whatever it be that has an innate power in itself, that will effectually operate on a fit and proper subject, it is able to evidence itself, and its own nature and condition.

The Scripture Is the Power of God

17. To manifest the interest of the Scripture to be enrolled among things of this nature, yea under God himself, who is known by his great power and the effects of it, to have the preeminence, I shall observe only one or two things concerning it, the various improvement whereof, would take up more time, and greater space, than I have allotted to this discourse.

18. It is absolutely called the "power of God"; and that unto its proper end, which way lies the tendency of its efficacy in operation (Rom. 1:16). It is δύναμις θεοῦ, *vis*,[15] *virtus Dei*; the "power of God." ὁ λόγος ὁ τοῦ σταυροῦ, the "word concerning the cross," that is the gospel, is δύναμις θεοῦ (1 Cor. 1:18); the "power of God"; and faith which is built on that word, without other helps or advantages, is said to stand in the "power of God" (1 Cor. 2:5). That is, effectually working, in and by the word; it works, ἐν ἀποδείξει πνεύματος καὶ δυνάμεως; "in the demonstration of the Spirit and of power."[16] ἐν διὰ δυοῖν:[17] its spiritual power gives a demonstration of it. Thus it comes not as a naked word but in "power, and in the Holy Ghost" (1 Thess. 1:5), and ἐν πληροφορίᾳ πολλῇ;[18] giving all manner of assurance and full persuasion of itself, even by its power and efficacy. Hence it is termed מטה עז "the rod of

---

15 Lat. "power."
16 1 Cor. 2:4.
17 Gk. "hendiadys," or two words connected by "and" forming a single idea. In this case, Owen is referring to "in the demonstration of the Spirit *and* of power," as in a "spiritual power which gives a demonstration" of it.
18 Gk. "in full assurance."

power" or strength (Ps. 110:2); denoting both authority and efficacy; surely that which is thus the power and authority of God, is able to make itself known so to be.

And Powerful in Respect of Us

19. It is not only said to be δύναμις, "power," the power of God in itself, but also δυνάμενος, "able" and "powerful" in respect of us. "Thou hast learned" says Paul to Timothy τὰ ἱερὰ γράμματα, "the sacred letters" (the written word) τὰ δυνάμενά σε σοφίσαι εἰς σωτηρίαν, "which are able to make thee wise unto salvation."[19] They are powerful and effectual to that purpose. It is λόγος [. . .] δυνάμενος σῶσαι τὰς ψυχάς. "The word" that has "power" in it, "to save [souls]." (James 1:21). So Acts 20:32: "I commend you" λόγῳ τῷ δυναμένῳ, to the "able," "powerful word." And that we may know what kind of power it has, the apostle tells us, that it is ζῶν καὶ ἐνεργὴς, it is "living and effectual" (Heb. 4:12) and "sharper than any two-edged sword, piercing even to the dividing asunder of soul and spirit, and of the joints and marrow, and is a discerner of the thoughts and intents of the heart." It is designed of God to declare τὴν ἐνέργειαν τῆς δυνάμεως, "the effectual working of his power."[20] (See John 6:68, 69; 1 Cor. 6:41;[21] 15:58;[22] Gal. 2:8). By virtue of this power, it brought forth fruit in all the world (Col. 1:6). Without sword, without (for the most part) miracles, without human wisdom, or oratory, without any inducements or motives, but what were merely and solely taken from itself, consisting in things, that "eye had not seen, nor ear heard, nor could enter into the heart of man to conceive"; has it exerted this its power and efficacy, to the conquest of the world; causing men of all sorts, in all times and places, so to fall down before its divine authority, as immediately to renounce all that was dear to them in the world, and to undergo whatever was dreadful, terrible and destructive to nature in all its dearest concernments.

How This Power Exerts Itself

20. It has been the work of many to insist on the particulars, wherein this power exerts itself: so that I shall not enlarge upon them. In general they have this advantage, that as they are all spiritual, so they are such, as have their seat, dwelling and abode in the hearts and consciences of men, whereby they are not liable to any exception as though they were pretended. Men cannot

---

19 2 Tim. 3:15.
20 Eph. 3:7.
21 Owen is referring to 1 Cor. 6:14.
22 Owen is referring to 1 Cor. 15:57.

harden themselves in the rejection of the testimony they give, by sending for magicians to do the like; or by any pretense that it is a common thing, that is befallen them on whom the word puts forth its power. The seat or residence of these effects, is safeguarded against all power and authority but that of God. Its diving into the hearts, consciences and secret recesses of the minds of men, its judging and sentencing of them in themselves, its convictions, terrors, conquests, and killing of men; its converting, building up, making wise, holy, obedient, its administering consolations in every condition, and the like effects of its power, are usually spoken unto.

The Whole Question Resolved

21. These are briefly the foundations of the answer returned to the inquiry formerly laid down which might abundantly be enlarged. How know we that the Scripture is the word of God; how may others come to be assured thereof? The Scripture, say we, bears testimony to itself, that it is the word of God; that testimony is the witness of God himself, which who so does not accept and believe, he does what in him lies to make God a liar; to give us an infallible assurance that in receiving this testimony, we are not imposed upon by cunningly devised fables, the αἱ γραφαί,[23] the ἵερα γράμματα,[24] the Scriptures, have that glory of light and power accompanying of them, as wholly distinguishes them by infallible signs and evidences from all words and writings not divine, conveying their truth and power, into the souls and consciences of men, with an infallible certainty. On this account are they received, by all that receive them as from God; who have any real distinguishing foundation of their faith, which would not be, separated from these grounds, as effectual an expedient for the reception of the Alcoran.[25]

23 Gk. "the Scriptures."
24 Gk. "the Holy Scriptures."
25 I.e., the Qur'an.

Second Evidence of the
Thesis Concluded

[1–14.] Of the testimony of the Spirit. [15.]
Traditions. [16–18.] Miracles

OF THE TESTIMONY OF THE SPIRIT:
SUBJECTIVE AND OBJECTIVE

1. Before I proceed to the consideration of those other testimonies, which are as arguments drawn from those innate excellencies, and properties of the word which I have insisted on, some other things whose right understanding is of great importance in the cause under debate, must be laid down and stated. Some of these refer to that testimony of the Spirit, that is usually and truly pleaded, as the great ascertaining principle, or that on the account whereof, we receive the Scriptures to be the word of God. That it may be seen, in what sense, that is usually delivered by our divines, and how far there is a coincidence between that assertion, and what we have delivered, I shall lay down what that testimony is, wherein it consists, and what is the weight or stress that we lay upon it.

2. That the Scripture be received as the word of God, there is required a twofold efficacy of the Spirit. The first respects the subject or the mind of man that assents unto the authority of the Scripture; now concerning this act, or work of the Spirit, whereby we are enabled to believe the Scripture, on the account whereof we may say that we receive the Scripture to be the word of God, or upon the testimony of the Spirit, I shall a little inquire, what it is, and wherein it does consist.

3. First, then, it is not an outward or inward vocal testimony concerning the word, as the Papist would impose upon us to believe and assent. We do not affirm that the Spirit immediately, by himself, says unto every individual believer, this book is, or contains, the word of God; we say not that the Spirit ever spoke to us of the word, but by the word. Such an enthusiasm as they fancy is rarely pretended, and where it is so, it is for the most part quickly discovered to be a delusion. We plead not for the usefulness, much less the necessity of any such testimony. Yea the principles we have laid down, resolving all faith into the public testimony of the Scriptures themselves, do render all such private testimonies altogether needless.

4. Secondly, this testimony of the Spirit consists not in a persuasion that a man takes up, he knows not well how, or why; only this he knows, he will not depose it though it cost him his life. This would be like that, which by Morinus is ascribed to the Church of Rome, which though it knew no reason why it should prefer the Vulgar Latin translation before the original,[1] yet by the guidance of the Spirit would do so, that is unreasonably. But if a man should say, that he is persuaded that the Scripture is the word of God, and that he will die a thousand times to give testimony thereunto; and not knowing any real ground of this persuasion, that should bear him out in such a testimony, shall ascribe it to the Spirit of God, our concernment lies not in that persuasion. This may befall men by the advantage of traditions, whereof men are usually zealous; and obstinate in their defense. Education in some constitutions will give pertinacity in most vain and false persuasions. It is not then a resolution and persuasion induced into our minds we know not how, built we know not upon what foundation, that we intend in the assignation of our receiving the Scripture, to be the word of God, to the effectual work and witness of the Holy Ghost.

The Subjective Testimony of the Spirit: Two Principles

Illumination of the Mind

5. Two things then we intend by this work of the Spirit upon the mind of man. First, his communication of spiritual light; by an act of His power, enabling the mind to discern the saving truth, majesty, and authority of the word, πνευματικὰ πνευματικῶς.[2] There is a blindness, a darkness upon the minds of men, πνεῦμα μὴ ἐχόντων,[3] that not only disenables them from discerning

---

1   In the footnote: Morin. *Excerc. de Heb. Tex. sincer & excercit.* I. cap. i.—Owen. See Jean Morin, *Exercitationes biblicae de Hebraei Graecique textus sinceritate: Pars prior* (Paris: Antonius Vitray, 1633), 1–13.

2   Gk. "spiritual things, spiritually discerned."

3   Gk. "not having the Spirit."

the things of God, in their certainty, evidence, necessity, and beauty (for ψυχικὸς ἄνθρωπος οὐ δέχεται τὰ τοῦ θεοῦ[4]); but also causes them to judge amiss of them; as things weak and foolish, dark, unintelligible, not answering to any principle of wisdom whereby they are guided (1 Cor. 2). While this γλαύκωμα[5] abides on the minds of men, it is impossible that they should on any right abiding foundation assent to the word of God. They may have a prejudicate[6] opinion, they have no faith concerning it. This darkness then must be removed by the communication of light by the Holy Ghost, which work of his illumination is commonly by others spoken unto; and by me also in another place.

An Effectual Persuasion of the Mind

6. Second, the Holy Ghost together with, and by his work of illumination, taking off the perverse disposition of mind that is in us by nature, with our enmity to, and aversation[7] from the things of God, effectually also persuades the mind, to a receiving and admitting of the truth, wisdom, and authority of the word; now because this perverse disposition of mind, possessing the ἡγεμονικόν[8] of the soul, influences the will also into an aversation and dislike of that goodness, which is in the truth proposed to it; it is removed by a double act of the Holy Ghost.

7. (1) He gives us wisdom, understanding, a spiritual judgment, whereby we may be able to compare spiritual things with spiritual, in a spiritual manner, and to come thereby to a clear and full light of the heavenly excellency and majesty of the word; and so enables us to know of the doctrine, whether it be of God. Under the benefit of this assistance, all the parts of the Scripture in their harmony and correspondency, all the truths of it in their power and necessity, come in together to give evidence one to another, and all of them to the whole; I mean as the mind is enabled to make a spiritual judgment of them.

8. (2) He gives αἴσθησιν πνευματικήν,[9] a spiritual sense, a taste of the things themselves upon the mind, heart, and conscience; when we have αἰσθητήρια γεγυμνασμένα "senses exercised" to discern such things.[10] These

---

4   Gk. "the unspiritual man does not accept the things of God" (an almost verbatim quotation of 1 Cor. 2:14).
5   Gk. "blindness."
6   I.e., to decide beforehand.
7   I.e., an aversion.
8   Gk. "the ruling principle."
9   Gk. "a spiritual taste, or sense."
10   An allusion to Heb. 5:14.

things deserve a more full handling, and to be particularly exemplified from Scripture, if the nature of our present design would admit thereof.

9. As in our natural estate in respect of these things of God, the mind is full of vanity, darkness, blindness, yea is darkness itself, so that there is no correspondency between the faculty and the object; and the will lies in an utter unacquaintedness, yea impossibility of any acquaintance with the life, power, savor, sweetness, relish, and goodness, that is in the things proposed to be known and discerned, under the dark shades of a blind mind; so for a removal of both these, the Holy Ghost communicates light to the understanding, whence it is able to see and judge of the truth, as it is in Jesus, and the will being thereby delivered from the dungeon wherein it was, and quickened anew, performs its office, in embracing what is proper and suited unto it in the object proposed. The Spirit, indeed, discovers to everyone καθῶς βούλεται;[11] according to the counsel of his will; but yet in that way, in the general whereby the sun gives out his light and heat, the former making way for the latter: but these things must not now be insisted on.

10. Now by these works of the Spirit, he does, I say, persuade the mind concerning the truth and authority of the Scripture; and therein leave an impression of an effectual testimony within us: and this testimony of his, as it is authoritative, and infallible in itself, so [is it] of inconceivably more efficacy, power and certainty unto them that do receive it, than any voice, or internal word, boasted of by some, can be. But yet this is not the work of the Spirit at present inquired after.

The Objective Testimony of the Spirit

11.[12] There is a testimony of the Spirit, that respects the object, or the word itself; and this is a public testimony, which, as it satisfies our souls in particular, so it is, and may be pleaded, in reference unto the satisfaction of all others, to whom the word of God shall come. The Holy Ghost speaking in and by the word, imparting to it virtue, power, efficacy, majesty and authority, affords us the witness, that our faith is resolved unto. And thus whereas there are but two heads, whereunto all grounds of assent do belong, namely authority of testimony, and the self-evidence of truth, they do here both concur in one. In the same word we have both the authority of the testimony of the Spirit, and the self-evidence of the truth spoken by him; yea so, that both these are

---

11   Gk. "according to his will."

12   Original begins this section with "2." Owen is referring here to the objective testimony of the Spirit, having discussed the subjective testimony of the Spirit. Contra Goold, who begins this section with "3," this is not a continuation of the list of points immediately prior.

materially one and the same, though distinguished in their formal conceptions. I have been much affected with those verses of Dante the Italian poet,[13]
which somebody has thus word for word turned into Latin:

> *Larga pluvia*
> *Spiritus sancti quae est diffusa*
> *Super veteres, et super novas membranas,*
> *Est syllogismus qui eam mihi conclusit*
> *Acute adeo ut prae illa*
> *Omnis demonstratio mihi videatur obtusa.*[14]

The Spirit's communication of his own light, and authority to the Scripture,
as evidence of its original, is the testimony pleaded for.

12. When then we resolve our faith into the testimony of the Holy Ghost,
it is not any private whisper, word, or voice given to individual persons; it
is not the secret and effectual persuasion of the truth of the Scriptures, that
falls upon the minds of some men, from various involved considerations
of education, tradition, and the like, whereof they can give no particular
account: it is not the effectual work of the Holy Ghost upon the minds and
wills of men, enabling them savingly to believe, that is intended; the Papists
for the most part pleading about these things, do but show their ignorance
and malice. But it is the public testimony of the Holy Ghost given unto all,
of the word, by and in the word, and its own divine light, efficacy, and power.

13. Thus far then have we proceeded. The Scripture, the written word has
its infallible truth in itself; ὁ λόγος ὁ σὸς ἀλήθειά ἐστι (John 17:17),[15] from
whence it has its verity, thence it has its authority; for its whole authority is
founded in its truth. Its authority in itself, is its authority in respect of us; nor
has it any whit more in itself, than de jure it has towards and over all them to
whom it comes; that de facto some do not submit themselves unto it, is their
sin and rebellion. This truth and consequently this authority, is evidenced

---

13 Dante Alighieri (ca. 1265–1321) was an Italian poet who is most famous for his *Divina com-
media*, or *Divine Comedy.*

14 Latin translation of the quotation from Dante's *Paradiso* left in the text intentionally. English
translation (from the original Italian text): "The abundant dew / Of the Holy Spirit which is so
outpoured / Upon the ancient parchments and the new / Is argument compelling my accord /
With such precise proof that, compared with it, / All demonstration else appeareth blurred." For
English translation, see *The Divine Comedy* (*Paradiso*, Canto XXIV, 91–96), in Dante Alighieri,
The Portable Dante, ed. Paulo Milano, trans. Laurence Binyon and D. G. Rossetti (New York:
Penguin, 1977), 493.

15 Gk. "your word is truth."

and made known to us, by the public testimony which is given unto it by the Holy Ghost speaking in it, with divine light and power, to the minds, souls, and consciences of men: being therein by itself proposed unto us, we being enlightened by the Holy Ghost (which in the condition wherein we are, is necessary for the apprehension of any spiritual thing or truth in a spiritual manner), we receive it, and religiously subject our souls unto it, as the word and will of the ever-living, sovereign God, and Judge of all. And if this be not a bottom and foundation of faith, I here publicly profess, that for ought I know, I have no faith at all.

Some Pretenses Considered: Traditions and Miracles

14. Having laid this stable foundation; I shall with all possible brevity consider some pretenses, and allegations, for the confirmation of the authority of the Scripture, invented and made use of by some, to divert us from that foundation, the closing wherewith, will in this matter alone bring peace unto our souls; and so this chapter shall as it were, lay in the balance, and compare together, the testimony of the Spirit before mentioned and explained, and the other pretenses and pleas, that shall now be examined.

Traditions

15.[16] Some say, when on other accounts they are concerned so to say, that we have received the Scripture from the Church of Rome, who received it by tradition, and this gives a credibility unto it. Of tradition in general, without this limitation which destroys it, of the Church of Rome, I shall speak afterward. Credibility, either keeps within the bounds of probability, as that may be heightened to a manifest uncontrollableness, while yet its principles exceed not that sphere; in which sense it belongs not at all to our present discourse; or it includes a firm, suitable foundation, for faith supernatural and divine. Have we in this sense received the Scripture from that church, as it is called? Is that church able to give such a credibility to anything? Or does the Scripture stand in need of such a credibility to be given to it from that church? Are not the first most false, and is not the last blasphemous? To receive a thing from a church, as a church, is to receive it upon the authority of that church: if we receive anything from the authority of a church, we do it not because the thing itself is ἀποδοχῆς ἄξιος, "worthy of acceptation," but because of the authority alleged. If then we thus receive the Scriptures from the Church

---

16 Original begins this section with "1.," referring to the discussion of "tradition" over and against the discussion of "miracles" which follows.

of Rome, why (in particular) do we not receive the apocryphal books also, which she receives? How did the Church of Rome receive the Scriptures? Shall we say that she is authorized to give out what seems good to her, as the word of God? Not:[17] but she has received them by tradition; so she pleads, that she has received the apocryphal books also; we then receive the Scriptures from Rome; Rome by tradition; we make ourselves judges of that tradition; and yet Rome says, this is one thing, that she has by the same tradition, namely, that she alone is judge of what she has by tradition; but the common fate of liars is befallen that harlot: she has so long, so constantly, so desperately lied in many, the most things that she professes, pretending tradition for them, that indeed she deserves not to be believed, when she tells the truth. Besides, she pleads that she received the Scriptures from the beginning, when it is granted that the copies of the Hebrew of the Old, and the Greek of the New Testament were only authentic: these she pleads now under her keeping to be woefully corrupted, and yet is angry that we believe not her tradition.

Miracles

16. Some add that we receive the Scripture to be the word of God upon the account of the miracles that were wrought at the giving of the Law, and of the New Testament; which miracles we have received by universal tradition. But first I desire to know whence it comes to pass, that seeing our Savior Jesus Christ wrought many other miracles besides those that are written (John 20:30; 21:25), and the apostles likewise, they cannot by all their traditions help us to so much as an obscure report of any one, that is not written (I speak not of legends); which yet at their performance were no less known than those that are; nor were less useful for the end of miracles than they. Of tradition in general afterward. But is it not evident that the miracles whereof they speak, are preserved in the Scripture and no otherwise? And if so; can these miracles operate upon the understanding or judgment of any man, unless he first grant the Scripture to be the word of God, I mean to the begetting of a divine faith of them, even that there were ever any such miracles. Suppose these miracles alleged, as the ground of our believing of the word, had not been written, but like the sibyl's leaves[18] had been driven up and down, by the worst and fiercest wind that blows in this world, the breath of man; those who should keep them by tradition, that is men, are by nature so vain, foolish,

---

17 Owen is answering his rhetorical question, as in "No, [. . .]."
18 The Sibyls were ancient Greek oracles or prophecies that were said to be divinely inspired. Owen is alluding to the Cumaean Sibyl, where the virgin priestess would compose her prophesies on oak leaves and allow the wind to blow them out of order.

malicious, such liars, adders, detractors, have spirits and minds so unsuited
to spiritual things, so liable to alteration in themselves, and to contradiction
one to another, are so given to impostures, and are so apt to be imposed upon,
have been so shuffled and driven up and down the world in every generation,
have for the most part so utterly lost the remembrance of what themselves
are, whence they come, or whither they are to go, that I can give very little
credit to what I have nothing but their authority to rely upon for, without
any evidence from the nature of the thing itself.

17. Abstracting then from the testimony given in the Scriptures to the
miracles wrought by the prime revealers of the mind and will of God in the
word; and no tolerable assurance as to the business in hand, where a foundation for faith is inquired after, can be given that ever any such miracles
were wrought. If numbers of men may be allowed to speak, we may have
a traditional testimony given to the blasphemous figments of the Alcoran,
under the name of true miracles. But the constant tradition of more than a
thousand years, carried on by innumerable multitudes of men, great, wise, and
sober, from one generation to another, does but set open the gates of hell for
the Mohammedans;[19] yet setting aside the authority of God in his word, and
what is resolved thereinto, I know not why they may not vie traditions with
the rest of the world. The world indeed is full of traditions flowing from the
word; that is, a knowledge of the doctrines of the word in the minds of men;
but a tradition of the word, not resolved into the word, a tradition referred
to a fountain of sense in seeing, and hearing, preserved as an oral law, in a
distinct channel, and stream by itself, when it is evidenced, either by instance
in some particular preserved therein, or in a probability of securing it through
the generations past, by a comparison of some such effect in things of the
like kind, I shall be ready to receive it.

18. Give me then, as I said before, but the least obscure report, of any one
of those many miracles that were wrought by our Savior and the apostles,
which are not recorded in the Scriptures, and I shall put more valuation on the
pretended traditions, than I can as yet persuade myself unto. Besides! many
writers of the Scripture wrought no miracles, and by this rule their writings
are left to shift for themselves. Miracles indeed were necessary to take off all
prejudices from the persons, that brought any new doctrine from God; but
the doctrine still evidenced itself: the apostles converted many, where they
wrought no miracles (Acts 16–18); and where they did so work, yet they for

19 I.e., followers of Mohammed or Muslims. Owen tends to use a variety of spellings for this and
related names. Throughout this edition, his spelling has been adjusted according to the more
familiar modern convention.

their doctrine, and not the doctrine on their account was received. And the Scripture now has no less evidence and demonstration in itself of its divinity, than it had when by them it was preached.

FURTHER GENERAL REFLECTIONS ON THE PRETENSE OF TRADITION

19. But because this tradition is pretended with great confidence as a sure bottom and foundation for receiving of the Scriptures, I shall a little further inquire into it. That which in this case is intended, by this מסורה[20] or "tradition," is a report of men,[21] which those who are present have received from them that are gone before them. Now this may be either of all the men of the world, or only of some of them; if of all; either their suffrages must be taken in some convention, or gathered up from the individuals as we are able, and have opportunity. If the first way of receiving them were possible, which is the utmost improvement that imagination can give the authority inquired after, yet every individual of men being a liar, the whole convention must be of the same complexion, and so not be able to yield a sufficient basis to build a faith upon, *cui non potest subesse falsum*, that is infallible, and "that cannot possibly be deceived": much less is there any foundation for it, in such a report as is the emergency of the assertion of individuals.

21. But now if this tradition be alleged as preserved only by some in the world, not the half of rational creatures, I desire to know, what reason I have to believe those who have that tradition, or plead that they have it, before and against them who profess they have no such report delivered to them from their forefathers; is the reason hereof because I live among those who have this tradition, and they are my neighbors whom I know? By the same rule those who live among the other parts of men, are bound to receive what they deliver them upon tradition; and so men may be obliged to believe the Alcoran to be the word of God.

22. It is more probable it will be answered, that their testimony is to be received because they are the church of God; but it does not yet appear, that

---

20 Heb. "Masora."

21 In the margin: *Est* [*vel*] *rei de manu in manum, aut doctrinae ex animo in animum mediante docentis voce, qua seu* [*sic: ceu* in original] *manu doctrina alteri traditur.* Buxtor. *Comment. Mas.*—Owen. Editor's translation: "It [the Masora or Masoretic tradition] is either handed down as a physical object from hand to hand or as teaching from mind to mind by way of the mediating voice of the teacher that is as if the teaching is passed on to another by hand." The original begins with *"Hinc Masora sive Massoreth Traditio"* ("This Masora or Masoretic Tradition"), which Owen has abbreviated with the verb *"Est"* ("It is"). See Johann Buxtorf Sr., *Tiberias, sive Commentarius Masorethicus triplex* (Basel: J. J. Deckeri, 1665), chap. 1, p. 4.

I can any other way have any knowledge of them so to be, or of any authority that any number of men, more, or less, can have in this case, under that name or notion, unless by the Scripture itself; and if so, it will quickly appear what place is to be allotted to their testimony, who cannot be admitted as witnesses, unless the Scripture itself be owned and received; because they have neither plea nor claim to be so admitted, but only from the Scripture: if they shall aver, that they take this honor to themselves, and that without relation to the Scripture they claim a right of authoritative witness bearing in this case, I say again, upon the general grounds of natural reason, and equity, I have no more inducements to give credit to their assertions, than to an alike number of men holding out a tradition utterly to the contrary of what they assert.

23. But yet suppose, that this also were granted, and that men might be allowed to speak in their own name and authority, giving testimony to themselves, which upon the hypothesis under consideration, God himself is not allowed to do; I shall desire to know whether, when the church declares the Scriptures to be the word of God unto us, it does apprehend anything in the Scripture as the ground of that judgment and declaration or no? If it says no; but that it is proposed upon its sole authority; then surely if we think good to acquiesce in this decision of this doubt and inquiry, it is full time for us, to lay aside all our studies and inquiries after the mind of God, and seek only what that man, or those men say, who are entrusted with this authority, as they say, and as they would have us believe them, though we know not at all how or by what means they came by it; seeing they dare not pretend anything from the Scripture, lest thereby they direct us to that, in the first place.

24. If it be said, that they do upon other accounts judge and believe the Scripture to be true, and to be the word of God; I suppose it will not be thought unreasonable if we inquire after those grounds and accounts, seeing they are of so great concernment unto us; all truths in relations consisting, in their consonancy and agreement, to the nature of the things they deliver, I desire to know how they came to judge of the consonancy, between the nature of the things delivered in the Scripture, and the delivery of them therein? The things whereof we speak being heavenly, spiritual, mysterious, and supernatural, there cannot be any knowledge obtained of them but by the word itself. How then can they make any judgment of the truth of that Scripture in the relation of these things, which are nowhere to be known (I speak of many of them) in the least, but by that Scripture itself.

25. If they shall say, that they found their judgment and declaration upon some discovery, that the Scripture makes of itself unto them; they affirm

the same that we plead for: only they would very desirously appropriate to themselves the privilege of being able to discern that discovery so made in the Scripture. To make good this claim, they must either plead somewhat from themselves, or from the Scriptures: if from themselves, it can be nothing, but that they see, like the men of China, and all others are blind, or have but one eye at the best, being wiser than any others, and more able to discern than they. Now though I shall easily grant them to be very subtle and cunning, yet that they are so much wiser than all the world besides, that they are meet to impose upon their belief things that they neither do, nor can discern or know, I would not be thought to admit, until I can believe myself and all others not of their society or combination, to be beasts of the field, and they as the serpent among us.

26. If it be from the Scripture that they seek to make good this claim; then as we cause them there to make a stand, which is all we aim at, so their plea must be from the promise of some special assistance granted to them for that purpose; if their assistance be that of the Spirit, it is either of the Spirit that is promised to believers, to work in them as before described and related, or it is some private testimony that they pretend is afforded to them; if the former be affirmed, we are in a condition, wherein the necessity of devolving all on the Scripture itself, to decide and judge who are believers, lies in everyone's view; if the latter, who shall give me assurance, that when they pretend that witness and testimony, they do not lie and deceive; we must here certainly go either to the Scripture, or to some cunning man to be resolved (Isa. 8:19, 20).

27. I confess the argument which has not long since been singled out, and dexterously managed, by an able and learned pen,[22] namely; of proving the truth of the doctrine of the Scripture, from the truth of the story, and the truth of the story from the certainty there is that the writers of the books of the Bible, were those persons whose names and inscriptions they bear; so pursuing the evidence, that what they wrote was true and known to them so to be, from all *requisita*[23] that may possibly be sought after for the strengthening of such evidence. It is, I say, of great force and efficacy as to the end for which it is insisted on, that is, to satisfy men's rational inquiries, but as to a ground of faith, it has the same insufficiency with all other arguments of the like kind. Though I should grant that the apostles and penmen of the

---

22 In the margin: D. Ward. *Essay &c.*—Owen. Owen is likely to be referring to Seth Ward, *A Philosophicall Essay towards an Eviction of the Being and Attributes of God; Immortality of the Souls of Men; Truth and Authority of Scripture* (Oxford: Leonard Lichfield, 1652).

23 Lat. "things required."

Scripture were persons of the greatest industry, honesty, integrity, faithfulness, holiness, that ever lived in the world, as they were; and that they wrote
nothing but what themselves had as good assurance of as what men by their
senses of seeing and hearing are able to attain; yet such a knowledge or assurance is not a sufficient foundation for the faith of the church of God. If
they received not every word by inspiration, and that evidencing itself unto
us otherwise than by the authority of their integrity, it can be no foundation
for us to build our faith upon.

28. Before the committing of the Scriptures to writing, God had given
the world an experiment what keepers men were of this revelation by tradition; within some hundreds of years after the flood, all knowledge of him,
through the craft of Satan, and the vanity of the minds of men, which is
unspeakable was so lost, that nothing, but as it were the creation of a new
world, or the erection of a new church state by new revelations, could relieve it. After that great trial, what can be further pretended, on the behalf
of tradition I know not.

29. The sum of all is; the merciful good providence of God, having by
divers and various means; using therein among other things, the ministry
of men and churches, preserved the writings of the Old and New Testament
in the world; and by the same gracious disposal afforded them unto us, they
are received and submitted unto by us, upon the grounds and evidences of
their divine original before insisted on.

30. Upon the whole matter, then, I would know, whether if the Scripture
should be brought to any man, when, or where, he could not possibly have
it attested to be the word of God, by any public or private authority of man,
or church, tradition, or otherwise, he were bound to believe it or no, whether
he should obey God in believing, or sin in the rejecting of it. Suppose he do
but take it into consideration, do but give it the reading or hearing, seeing in
every place it avers itself to be the word of God, he must of necessity either
give credit unto it, or disbelieve it; to hang in suspense, which arises from
the imperfect actings of the faculties of the soul, is in itself a weakness, and
in this case being reckoned on the worst side, is interpretatively a rejection.
If you say it were the duty of such a one to believe it, you acknowledge in the
Scripture itself a sufficient evidence of its own original authority; without
which it can be no man's duty to believe it. If you say, it would not be his
sin to reject and refuse it, to disbelieve all that it speaks in the name of God;
then this is what you say; God may truly and really speak unto a man (as he
does by the Scripture), and yet that man not be bound to believe him. We
deal not thus with one another.

Second General Demonstration of the Thesis Laid
Down: Two Consequent Considerations

31. To wind up then the plea insisted on in the foregoing chapter, concerning the self-evidencing light and power of the Scripture, from which we have diverted, and to make way for some other considerations, that tend to the confirmation of their divine original, I shall close this discourse with the two general considerations following.

*The Moral Impossibility That Scripture Would
Not Manifest Its Divine Authority*

32.[24] Then laying aside these failing pleas, there seems to be a moral impossibility that the word of God, should not manifest its own original, and its authority from thence. *Quaelibet herba Deum.*[25] There is no work of God, as was showed, but reveals its author. A curious artificer imparts that of form, shape, proportion, and comeliness to the fruit of his invention, and work of his hands, that everyone that looks upon it, must conclude, that it comes from skill and ability. A man in the delivery of his mind in the writing of a book, will give it such an impression of reason, that though you cannot conclude that this, or that man wrote it, yet you must, that it was the product of a man, or rational creature: yea some individual men of excellency in some skill, are instantly known by them, that are able to judge in that art or skill, by the effects of their skill. This is the piece, this is the hand, the work of such a one. How easy is it for those who are conversant about ancient authors to discover an author by the spirit and style of his writings. Now certainly this is strange beyond all belief, that almost every agent should give an impress to his work, whereby it may be appropriated unto him, and only the word, wherein it was the design of the great and holy God to give us a portraiture as it were of his wisdom, holiness, and goodness, so far as we are capable of an acquaintance with him in this life, is not able to declare and evince its original. That God who is *prima veritas*,[26] the first and sovereign Truth, infinitely separated and distinguished from all creatures on all accounts whatever, should write a book, or at least immediately indite it, commanding us to receive it as his, under

---

24 Original begins this section with "1."
25 Lat. "any blade of grass points to God." This is an abbreviation of "*praesentemque refert quaelibet herba Deum*" ("any blade of grass shows that God is present"), a line by the sixteenth-century German poet and university teacher of rhetoric Johannes Stigelius (1515–1562) from his poem "*Ad Paulum Eberum*," line 10. See the Latin text, for example, in *Poematum Io. Stigelii Gothani ex recensione Adami Siberi volumen secundum* (Jena: Donat Richtzenhan, 1577), 476.
26 Lat. "the first truth."

the penalty of his eternal displeasure, and yet that book not make a sufficient discovery of itself to be his, to be from him, is past all belief. Let men that live on things received by tradition from their fathers, who perhaps never had sense of any real transaction between God and their souls, who scarce ever perused the word seriously in their lives, nor brought their consciences to it; please themselves in their own imaginations; the sure anchor of a soul that would draw nigh to God in and by his word, lies in the things laid down.

33. I suppose it will not be denied but that it was the mind and will of God, that those to whom his word should come, should own it and receive it as his; if not, it were no sin in them to reject it, unto whom it does so come; if it were, then either he has given those characters unto it, and left upon it that impression of his majesty whereby it might be known to be his, or he has not done so; and that either because he would not, or because he could not; to say the latter, is to make him more infirm than a man, or other worms of the earth, than any naturally effectual cause. He that says the former, must know, that it is incumbent on him, to yield a satisfactory account, why God would not do so, or else he will be thought blasphemously to impute a want of that goodness and love of mankind unto him, which he has in infinite grace manifested to be in himself. That no man is able to assign any such reason, I shall firmly believe, until I find some attempting so to do; which as yet none have arrived at that height of impudence and wickedness as to own.

The Absurdity That Scripture's Authority Would Depend on Human Judgment

34.[27] How horrible is it to the thoughts of any saint of God, that the Scripture should not have its authority from itself. Tertullian objects this to the Gentiles; "It bears also on our case, because among you a god's divinity depends on man's decision. Unless a god please man, he shall not be a god at all; in fact, man must be gracious to God!"[28] Would it be otherwise in this case if the Scripture must stand to the mercy of man for the reputation of its divinity? Nay of its verity; for whence it has its authority, thence it has its verity also, as was observed before; and many more words of this nature might be added.

---

27 Original begins this section with "2ly."

28 In the text: *Apol. Cap.* 5. *Facit et hoc ad causam nostram, quod apud vos de humano arbitratu divinitas pensitatur; nisi homini Deus placuerit, Deus non erit; homo jam Deo propitius esse debebit.*—Owen. For the Latin text and English translation, see Tertullian, *Apology. De spectaculis. Minucius Felix: Octavius*, trans. T. R. Glover and Gerald H. Rendall, Loeb Classical Library 250 (Cambridge, MA: Harvard University Press, 1966), 28–29.

6

Consequential Considerations for the Confirmation of the Divine Authority of the Scripture

THIRD DEMONSTRATION OF THE THESIS LAID DOWN: ARTIFICIAL ARGUMENTS

1. I said, in the former chapter, that I would not employ myself willingly, to enervate or weaken any of the reasons or arguments that are usually insisted on, to prove the divine authority of the Scripture. Though I confess, I like not to multiply arguments, that conclude to a probability only, and are suited to beget a firm opinion at best, where the principle intended to be evinced is *de fide*,[1] and must be believed with faith divine, and supernatural. Yet because some may happily be kept to some kind of adherence to the Scriptures; by mean grounds, that will not in their own strength abide, until they get footing in those that are more firm; I shall not make it my business to drive them from their present station; having persuaded them by that which is better.

2. Yea, because on supposition of the evidence formerly tended, there may be great use at several seasons, of some consequential considerations and arguments to the purpose in hand, I shall insist on two of that kind, which to me, who have the advantage of receiving the word on the aforementioned account, seem not only to persuade, and in a great measure to convince to undeniable probability, but also to prevail irresistibly on the understanding of unprejudiced men, to close with the divine truth of it.

---

1 Lat. "a matter of faith."

TWO CONSEQUENTIAL CONSIDERATIONS FOR THE CONFIRMATION OF THE DIVINE AUTHORITY OF THE SCRIPTURE

3. The first of these is taken from the nature of the doctrine itself, contained in the Scripture, the second from the management of the whole design therein; the first is innate, the other of a more external and rational consideration.

The Nature of the Doctrine Contained in Scripture

4. For the first of them, there are two things considerable in the doctrine of the Scripture, that are powerful, and if I may so say, uncontrollably prevalent as to this purpose.

5. First its universal suitableness upon its first clear discovery and revelation to all the entanglements and perplexities of the souls of men, in reference to their relation to, and dependence upon God. If all mankind have certain entanglements upon their hearts and spirits in reference unto God, which none of them that are not utterly brutish, do not wrestle withal, and which all of them are not able in the least to assoil[2] themselves in, and about, certainly that doctrine which is suited universally to satisfy all their perplexities, to calm and quiet their spirits in all their tumultuatings,[3] and does break in upon them with a glorious efficacy to that purpose in its discovery and revelation, must needs be from that God, with whom we have to do, and none else. From whom else I pray should it be. He that can give out such a word, *ille mihi semper erit Deus.*[4]

6. Now there are three general heads of things, that all and every one of mankind, not naturally brutish are perplexed withal, in reference, to their dependence on God, and relation to him.

(1) How they may worship him as they ought.
(2) How they may be reconciled, and at peace with him, or have an atonement for that guilt which naturally they are sensible of.
(3) What is the nature of true blessedness, and how they may attain it, or how they may come to the enjoyment of God.

2 I.e., acquit.
3 I.e., actions that cause a disturbance.
4 Lat. "he will always be God to me." Owen is quoting, with slight emendation, from Virgil's *Eclogues*, bk. 1, line 7. For the Latin text and an English translation, see Virgil, *Eclogues. Georgics. Aeneid: Books 1–6*, trans. H. Rushton Fairclough, rev. G. P. Goold, Loeb Classical Library 63 (Cambridge, MA: Harvard University Press, 1999), 24–25.

7. That all mankind are perplexed and entangled with, and about these considerations, that all men ever were so, without exception more or less, and continue so to be to this day; that of themselves, they miserably grope up and down in the dark, and are never able to come to any satisfaction, neither as to what is present, nor as to what is to come, I could manifest from the state, office, and condition of conscience, the indelible προλήψεις[5] and presumptions about them, that are in the hearts of all by nature. The whole history of all religion which has been in the world, with the design of all ancient and present philosophy, with innumerable other uncontrollable convictions (which also God assisting, I shall in another treatise declare[6]) do manifest this truth.

8. That, surely then which shall administer to all and every one of them, equally and universally, satisfaction as to all these things, to quiet and calm their spirits, to cut off all necessity of any further inquiries, give them that wherein they must acquiesce, and wherewith they will be satiated, unless they will cast off that relation, and dependence on God, which they seek to confirm and settle; surely I say, this must be from the all-seeing, all-satisfying Truth, and Being, and from none else. Now this is done by the doctrine of the Scripture, with such a glorious uncontrollable conviction, that everyone to whom it is revealed, the eyes of whose understanding are not blinded by the god of this world, must needs cry out Ἕυρηκα, "I have found" that which in vain I sought elsewhere, waxing foolish in my imaginations.

The Nature of the Atonement

9. It would be too long to insist on the several; take one instance in the business of atonement, reconciliation, and acceptance with God. What strange horrible fruits and effects have men's contrivances on this account produced? What have they not invented? What have they not done? What have they not suffered? and yet continued in dread and bondage all their days? Now with what a glorious, soul-appeasing light does the doctrine of satisfaction and atonement, by the blood of Christ the Son of God, come in upon such men? This first astonishes, then conquers, then ravishes, and satiates the soul. This is that they looked for, this they were sick for, and knew it not. This is the design of the apostle's discourse in the three first chapters of the epistle to the Romans. Let any man read that discourse from Romans 1:18,

---

5 Gk. "preconceptions."
6 In the margin: *de natura Theologiae*—Owen. Owen is referring here to his Latin treatise, Θεολογούμενα Παντοδαπά. *Sive de Natura, Ortu, Progressu, et Studio, Verae Theologiae* (1661), in *Complete Works of John Owen*, vol. 38.

and onward, and he will see with what glory and beauty, with what full and ample satisfaction this doctrine breaks out (Rom. 3:21–26).

The Nature of Present Worship and Future Blessedness

10. It is no otherwise as to the particulars of present worship, or future blessedness; this meets with men in all their wanderings, stops them in their disquisitions, convinces them of the darkness, folly, uncertainty, falseness of all their reasonings about these things; and that with such an evidence and light, as at once subdues them, captivates their understanding, and quiets their souls: so was that old Roman world conquered by it; so shall the Mohammedan be, in God's good and appointed time.

11. Of what has been spoken, this is the sum. All mankind that acknowledge their dependence upon God, and relation to him, are naturally (and cannot be otherwise) grievously involved and perplexed in their hearts, thoughts, and reasonings, about the worship of God, acceptation with him having sinned, and the future enjoyment of him; some with more clear and distinct apprehensions, of these things; some under more dark and general notions of them are thus exercised; to extricate themselves, and to come to some issue in and about these inquiries, has been the great design of their lives, the aim they had in all things they did, as they thought, well and laudably in this world. Notwithstanding all which, they were never able to deliver themselves, no not one of them, or attain satisfaction to their souls, but waxed vain in their imaginations, and their foolish hearts were more and more darkened; in this estate of things, the doctrine of the Scripture coming in with full, unquestionable satisfaction to all these, suited to the inquirings of every individual soul, with a largeness of wisdom, and depth of goodness, not to be fathomed, it must needs be from that God with whom we have to do. And those who are not persuaded hereby, that will not cast anchor in this harbor, let them put to sea once more, if they dare; turn themselves loose to other considerations, and try if all the aforementioned perplexities do not inevitably return.

The Nature of the Trinity

12. Another consideration of the doctrine of the Scripture to this purpose regards some particulars of it. There are some doctrines of the Scripture, some revelations in it, so sublimely glorious, of so profound and mysterious an excellency, that at the first proposal of them, nature startles, shrinks, and is taken with horror, meeting with that which is above it, too great and too excellent for it, which it could desirously avoid and decline; but yet gathering itself up to them, it yields, and finds, that unless they are accepted, and

submitted unto, though unsearchable, that not only all that has been received, must be rejected, but also the whole dependence of the creature on God be dissolved, or rendered only dreadful, terrible, and destructive to nature itself. Such are the doctrines of the Trinity, of the incarnation of the Son of God, of the resurrection of the dead, of the new birth, and the like. At the first revelation of these things, nature is amazed, cries, how can these things be? Or gathers up itself to opposition; this is "babbling," like the Athenians; "folly," as all the wise Greeks.[7] But when the eyes of reason are a little confirmed, though it can never clearly behold the glory of this sun, yet it confesses a glory to be in it, above all that it is able to apprehend. I could manifest in particular, that the doctrines before mentioned, and several others are of this importance; namely though great, above and beyond the reach of reason, yet upon search found to be such, as without submission to them, the whole comfortable relation between God and man must needs be dissolved.

13. Let us take a view in our way of one of the instances. What is there in the whole book of God, that nature at first sight does more recoil at, than the doctrine of the Trinity? How many do yet stumble and fall at it? I confess the doctrine itself is but sparingly, yet it is clearly and distinctly delivered unto us in the Scripture. The sum of it is; that God is one; his nature, or his being, one; that all the properties, or infinite essential excellencies of God, as God, do belong to that one nature and being. This God is infinitely good, holy, just, powerful, he is eternal, omnipotent, omnipresent; and these things belong to none, but him that is that one God. That this God is the Father, Son, and Holy Ghost; which are not diverse names of the same person, nor distinct attributes or properties of the same nature or being; but one, another, and a third, all equally that one God, yet really distinguished between themselves by such incommunicable properties, as constitute the one to be that one, and the other to be that other; and the third to be that third. Thus the Trinity is not the union, nor unity of three, but it is a trinity in unity, or the ternary number of persons in the same essence; nor does the Trinity in its formal conception denote the essence, as if the essence were comprehended in the Trinity, which is in each person; but it denotes only the distinction of the persons comprised in that number.

14. This I say is the sum of this doctrine, as it is delivered unto us in the Scripture. Here reason is entangled; yet after a while finds evidently, that unless this be embraced, all other things wherein it has to do with God, will not

---

7   Owen is making a parody of the Epicurean and Stoic philosophers' reaction to Paul in Athens (Acts 17:18) and of Paul's description of the Gentile Greeks' response to his preaching as "foolishness" (1 Cor. 1:25).

be of value to the soul; this will quickly be made to appear. Of all that communion which is here between God and man, founded on the revelation of his mind and will unto him, which makes way for his enjoyment in glory, there are these two parts. (1) God's gracious communication of his love, goodness etc., with the fruits of them unto man: (2) The obedience of man unto God in a way of gratitude for that love, according to the mind and will of God revealed to him. These two comprise the whole of the intercourse between God and man. Now when the mind of man is exercised about these things, he finds at last that they are so wrapped up in the doctrine of the Trinity, that without the belief, receiving, and acceptance of it, it is utterly impossible that any interest in them should be obtained or preserved.

15. For the first; or the communication of God unto us in a way of love and goodness, it is wholly founded upon, and enwrapped in this truth, both as to the eternal spring, and actual execution of it. A few instances will evince this assertion. The eternal fountain of all grace, flowing from love and goodness, lies in God's election, or predestination. This being an act of God's will, cannot be apprehended, but as an eternal act of his wisdom, or word also. All the eternal thoughts of its pursuit, lie in the covenant that was between the Father and the Son, as to the Son's undertaking to execute that purpose of his. This I have at large elsewhere declared.

Take away then the doctrine of the Trinity, and both these are gone; there can be no purpose of grace by the Father in the Son, no covenant for the putting of that purpose in execution; and so the foundation of all fruits of love and goodness, is lost to the soul.

16. As to the execution of this purpose, with the actual dispensation of the fruits of grace and goodness unto us, it lies wholly in the unspeakable condescension of the Son unto incarnation with what ensued thereon. The incarnation of the eternal Word, by the power of the Holy Ghost, is the bottom of our participation of grace. Without it, it was absolutely impossible that man should be made partaker of the favor of God. Now this enwraps the whole doctrine of the Trinity in its bosom; nor can once be apprehended, without its acknowledgment. Deny the Trinity, and all the means of the communication of grace, with the whole of the satisfaction, and righteousness of Christ fall to the ground. Every tittle of it speaks this truth: and they who deny the one, reject the other.

17. Our actual participation of the fruits of this grace, is by the Holy Ghost. We cannot ourselves seize on them, nor bring them home to our own souls. The impossibility hereof I cannot now stay to manifest. Now whence is this Holy Ghost? Is he not sent from the Father, by the Son? Can we entertain

any thought of his effectual working in us, and upon us, but it includes this whole doctrine? They therefore who deny the Trinity deny the efficacy of its operation also.

18. So it is, as to our obedience unto God, whereby the communion between God and man is completed. Although the formal object of divine worship be the nature of God; and the persons are not worshiped as persons distinct, but as they are each of them God; yet as God they are every one of them distinctly to be worshiped. So is it, as to our faith, our love our thanksgiving, all our obedience, as I have abundantly demonstrated in my treatise of distinct communion with the Father in love, the Son in grace, and the Holy Ghost in the privileges of the gospel.[8] Thus without the acknowledgment of this truth, none of that obedience which God requires at our hands, can in a due manner be performed.

19. Hence the Scripture speaks not of anything between God and us, but what is founded on this account. The Father works, the Son works, and the Holy Ghost works. The Father works not but by the Son and his Spirit; the Son and Spirit work not, but from the Father. The Father glorifies the Son; the Son glorifies the Father; and the Holy Ghost glorifies them both. Before the foundation of the world, the Son was with the Father, and rejoiced in his peculiar work for the redemption of mankind. At the creation, the Father made all things, but by the Son, and the power of the Spirit. In redemption the Father sends the Son; the Son by his own condescension undertakes the work, and is incarnate by the Holy Ghost. The Father as was said, communicates his love, and all the fruits of it unto us by the Son; as the Holy Ghost does the merits, and fruits of the mediation of the Son. The Father is not known nor worshiped, but by and in the Son; nor Father nor Son but by the Holy Ghost, etc.

20. Upon this discovery the soul that was before startled at the doctrine in the notion of it, is fully convinced that all the satisfaction it has sought after in its seeking unto God, is utterly lost, if this be not admitted. There is neither any foundation left of the communication of love to him, nor means of returning obedience unto God. Besides, all the things that he has been inquiring after, appear on this account in their glory, beauty and reality unto him: so that, that which most staggered him at first in the receiving of the truth, because of its deep mysterious glory, does now most confirm him in the embracing of it, because of its necessity, power, and heavenly excellency.

---

8   See *Of Communion with God the Father, Son, and Holy Ghost, Each Person Distinctly, in Love Grace, and Consolation; or, The Saints' Fellowship with the Father, Son, and Holy Ghost Unfolded* (1657), in *Complete Works of John Owen*, vol. 1.

21. And this is one argument of the many belonging to the things of the Scripture, that upon the grounds before mentioned, has in it, as to my sense and apprehension, an evidence of conviction not to be withstood.

The Design of Scripture

22. Another consideration of the like efficacy, may be taken from a brief view of the whole Scripture with the design of it. The consent of parts or harmony of the Scripture in itself, and every part of it with each other, and with the whole, is commonly pleaded as an evidence of its divine original. Thus much certainly it does evince beyond all possible contradiction, that the whole proceeds from one and the same principle; has the same author; and he wise, discerning, able to comprehend the whole compass of what he intended to deliver and reveal. Otherwise, or by any other, that oneness of spirit, design, and aim, in unspeakable variety and diversity of means of its delivery, that absolute correspondency of it to itself, and distance from anything else, could not have been attained. Now it is certain, that this principle must be *summum*⁹ in its kind; either *bonum*¹⁰ or *malum*.¹¹ If the Scripture be what it reveals and declares itself to be, it is then unquestionably the word of the living God, truth itself; for that it professes of itself, from the beginning to the ending; to which profession all that it reveals answers absolutely, and unquestionably in a tendency to his glory alone. If it be not so, it must be acknowledged that the author of it had a blasphemous design to hold forth himself to be God, who is not so; a malicious design to deceive the sons of men, and to make them believe that they worship and honor God; and obey him when they do not; and so to draw them into everlasting destruction, and that to compass these ends of blasphemy, atheism and malice, he has laid out in a long course of time, all the industry and wisdom that a creature could be made partaker of: now he that should do thus, must be the devil, and none else; no other creature can possibly arrive at that height of obstinacy in evil. Now certainly while God is pleased to continue unto us anything, whereby we are distinguished from the beasts that perish; while there is a sense of a distance between good and evil abiding among men, it cannot fall upon the understanding of any man, that that doctrine which is so holy and pure, so absolutely leading to the utmost improvement of whatever is good, just, commendable and praiseworthy, so suitable to all the light of God, of good and evil that remains in us; could proceed from any one everlastingly hardened in

9   Lat. "highest."
10   Lat. "good."
11   Lat. "evil."

evil, and that in the pursuit of the most wicked design, that that wicked one could possibly be engaged in; namely to enthrone himself, and maliciously to cheat, cousen[12] and ruin the souls of men; so that upon necessity the Scripture can own no author but him, whose it is, even the living God.

As these considerations are far from being the bottom and foundation of our faith, in our assenting to the authority of God in the word; so on the supposition of what is so, they have a usefulness, as to support in trials and temptations, and the like seasons of difficulty: but of these things so far.

12 I.e., deceive.

OF THE INTEGRITY AND PURITY OF THE HEBREW AND GREEK TEXT OF THE SCRIPTURE, WITH CONSIDERATIONS ON THE *PROLEGOMENA* AND *APPENDIX* TO THE LATE *BIBLIA POLYGLOTTA*

Of the Integrity
Contents

Chapter titles have been added by the volume editor.

1

General Principles for Evaluating the Recently Published *Biblia polyglotta*

1. The occasion of this discourse. 2. The danger of supposing corruptions in the originals of the Scripture. 3. The great usefulness of the *Biblia polyglotta*. 4. The grounds of the ensuing animadversions. 5. The assertions proposed to be vindicated laid down. 6. Their weight and importance. 7. Sundry principles in the *Prolegomena* prejudicial to the truth contended for laid down. 8[–9]. Those principles formerly asserted by others. Reasons of the opposition made to them.

THE OCCASION OF THIS DISCOURSE:
THE PUBLICATION OF THE *BIBLIA POLYGLOTTA*

1. When this whole little precedent treatise was finished, and ready to be given out unto the stationer, there came to my hands the *Prolegomena* and *Appendix* to the *Biblia polyglotta* lately published.[1] Upon the first sight of that volume, I was somewhat startled with that bulky collection of various readings, which the *Appendix* tenders to the view of everyone that does but cast an

---

1   The so-called London Polyglot Bible (1657), edited by Brian Walton: Brian Walton, *Biblia sacra polyglotta*, 6 vols. (London: Thomas Roycroft, 1653–1657). The London Polyglot Bible is the last and greatest of the early modern polyglot Bibles that remained a landmark in biblical criticism for several centuries. The *Prolegomena* and *Appendix* are published in vols. 1 and 6 of the collection respectively. The *Prolegomena* has been published separately in numerous editions. The edition cited here will be Brian Walton, *In Biblia polyglotta prolegomena*, 2 vols (Cambridge: J. Smith, 1827–1828). All references in this treatise to *Prolegomena* and *Appendix* refer to the same of the London Polyglot Bible.

eye upon it. Within a while after I found that others also men of learning and judgment, had apprehensions of that work, not unlike those which my own thoughts had suggested unto me. Afterward, considering what I had written, about the providence of God in the preservation of the original copies of the Scripture in the foregoing discourse, fearing least from that great appearance of variations in the original copies, and those of all the translations published with so great care and diligence, there might some unconquerable objections against the truth of what I had asserted, be educed; I judged it necessary to stop the progress of those thoughts, until I could get time to look through the *Appendix*, and the various lections in that great volume exhibited unto us, with the grounds and reasons of them in the *Prolegomena*. Having now discharged that task, and (as things were stated) duty, I shall crave leave to deliver my thoughts to some things contained in them, which possibly men of perverse minds may wrest to the prejudice of my former assertions, to the prejudice of the certainty of divine truth, as continued unto us through the providence of God in the originals of the Scripture.

The Danger of Supposing Corruptions in the Originals of the Scripture

2. What use has been made, and is as yet made in the world, of this supposition, that corruptions have befallen the originals of the Scripture, which those various lections at first view seem to intimate; I need not declare. It is in brief, the foundation of Mohammedanism,[2] the chiefest and principal prop of popery, the only pretense of fanatical antiscripturists, and the root of much hidden atheism in the world.[3] At present there is sent unto me by a

2   In the text: *Alcor. Azoar. 5.*—Owen. Owen is likely to be using Theodor Bibliander's widely used reprint of Robert of Ketton's medieval Latin translation of the Qur'an. For the Azoar that Owen mentions, see Theodor Bibliander, ed., *Machumetis saracenorum principis, eius'que successorum vitae, doctrina, ac ipse Alcoran* (Basel: n.p., 1550), 21–25.

3   In the footnote: Whitak. Cham. Rivet. *de S. S.* Molin. *nov. Pap.* Mestrezat. *Cont. Jesuit. Regourd vid. Card. Perron. respon. ad Reg. mag. Bullen.* l. 5. c. 6.—Owen. "Whitak.": William Whitaker (1548–1595) was an Elizabethan Protestant scholar and Master of St. John's College, Cambridge, who was well known for his Reformed convictions and as an active opponent of Catholic doctrine. "Cham.": Daniel Chamier (1564–1621) was a French Huguenot theologian who established the Academy of Montpellier and was known for his polemical engagement with Roman Catholicism. "Rivet. *de S. S.*": See André Rivet, *Isagoge, seu introductio generalis, ad Scripturam sacram Veteris et Novi Testamenti* (Leiden: I. Commelinus, 1627). André Rivet (1572–1651) was a French Huguenot theologian known for his opposition to Roman Catholicism and for his contribution to the *Synopsis purioris theologiae*. "Molin. *nov. Pap.*": See Pierre du Moulin, *novveauté du papisme* (Geneva: Pierre Chouët, 1627). Pierre Du Moulin (1568–1658) was a Huguenot and anti-Catholic polemicist who spent much of his life in England. "Mestrezat. *Cont. Jesuit. Regourd vid. Card. Perron. respon. ad Reg. mag. Bullen.* l. 5. c. 6.": It is possible that Owen is referring to Jean Mestrezat, *Traicté de l 'Escripture saincte* (Geneva: Jacques Chouët,

very learned person, upon our discourse on this subject, a treatise in English, with the Latin title of *Fides divina*, wherein its nameless author, on this very foundation labors to evert and utterly render useless the whole Scripture.[4] How far such as he may be strengthened in their infidelity by the consideration of these things, time will manifest.

Had there not been then a necessity incumbent on me, either utterly to desist from pursuing any thoughts of publishing the foregoing treatise, or else of giving an account of some things contained in the *Prolegomena* and *Appendix*, I should for many reasons have abstained from this employment. But the truth is, not only what I had written in the first chapter about the providence of God in the preservation of the Scripture, but also the main of the arguments afterward insisted on by me, concerning the self-evidencing power and light of the Scripture, receiving in my apprehension a great weakening by the things I shall now speak unto, if owned and received as they are proposed unto us, I could not excuse myself from running the hazard of giving my thoughts upon them.

The Great Usefulness of the *Biblia polyglotta*

3. The wise man tells us that he considered "all travail and every right work, and that for this a man is envied of his neighbor," which, says he, is "vanity and vexation of spirit" (Eccl. 4:4). It cannot be denied, but that this often falls out through the corruption of the hearts of men, that when works, right works, are with most sore travail brought forth in the world, their authors are repaid with envy for their labor, which mixes all the issues of the best endeavors of men, with vanity, and vexation of spirit. Heirome[5] of old and Erasmus[6] of late, are the usual instances in this kind. That I have any of that

---

1633), 566–76. Jean Mestrezat (1592–1657) was a Huguenot who studied at the Academy of Saumur and is known best for his polemical engagement with the Jesuits François Véron and Alexandre Regourd.

4   In his "Dedicatory Epistle," Owen mentions that he received a copy of this treatise from his friend Seth Ward: *Fides divina: The Ground of True Faith Asserted* (London: n.p., 1657). Seth Ward (1617–1689) was the Savilian Professor of Astronomy at Oxford and later Bishop of Exeter, then Salisbury.

5   I.e., Jerome (347–420), who was a Latin priest, biblical scholar, and historian. Aside from his biblical commentaries, he is best known for his translation of the Bible into Latin (the Vulgate) from the original Greek and Hebrew, which was used as the main translation in the West for the next millennium. In the sixteenth century, the Vulgate became the official authoritative translation for the Catholic Church.

6   Desiderius Erasmus (ca. 1466–1536) was a Dutch Catholic priest and humanist who is most famous for his Latin and Greek editions of the New Testament and for his disputations with Martin Luther on the liberty of the human will.

guilt in a peculiar manner, upon me in reference to this work of publishing the *Biblia polyglotta*, which I much esteem, or the authors and contrivers of it,[7] whom I know not, I can with due consideration, and do utterly deny. The Searcher of all hearts, knows I lie not. And what should possibly infect me with that leaven? I neither profess any deep skill in the learning used in that work, nor am ever like to be engaged in anything that should be set up in competition with it; nor did I ever know that there was such a person in the world, as the chief author of this edition of the Bibles, but by it. I shall then never fail on all just occasions, to commend the usefulness of this work, and the learning, diligence, and pains of the worthy persons that have brought it forth; nor would be wanting to their full praise in this place, but that an entrance into this discourse with their due commendations might be liable to misrepresentations. But whereas we have not only the Bible published, but also private opinions of men, (and collections of various readings really or pretendedly so we shall see afterward), tending some of them as I apprehend to the disadvantage of the great and important truth that I have been pleading for, tendered unto us, I hope it will not be grievous to any nor matter of offense, if using the same liberty, that they, or any of them whose hands have been most eminent in this work have done, I do with (I hope) Christian candor and moderation of spirit, briefly discover my thoughts upon some things proposed by them.

The Grounds of the Ensuing Animadversions

4. The renownedly learned prefacer to the Arabic translation in this edition of it, tells us, that the work of translating the Pentateuch into that language, was performed by a Jew, who took care to give countenance to his own private opinions, and so render them authentic by bringing them into the text of his translation.[8]

It is not of any such attempt, that I have any cause to complain, or shall so do in reference to these *Prolegomena* and *Appendix*; only I could have wished, (with submission to better judgments be it spoken), that in the publishing of the Bible, the sacred text, with the translations, and such naked historical accounts

---

7   In the margin: (Since my writing of this some of the chief overseers of the work, Persons of singular worth, are known to me.)—Owen.

8   Owen is referring to Edward Pococke, who provided the preface to the various lections gathered from the Arabic translation of the Pentateuch in the *Appendix* to the London Polyglot Bible. See Walton, *Biblia sacra polyglotta*, vol. 6, chap. 8, p. 1a. Edward Pococke (1604–1691) was an English biblical scholar and orientalist who specialized in Arabic texts. He was a friend of Owen's.

of their originals and preservation, as were necessary to have laid them fair and open to the judgment of the reader, had not been clogged with disputes and pleas for particular private opinions, imposed thereby with too much advantage on the minds of men, by their constant neighborhood unto canonical truth.

THE ASSERTIONS PROPOSED TO BE VINDICATED LAID DOWN

5. But my present considerations being not to be extended beyond the concernment of the truth which in the foregoing discourse I have pleaded for, I shall first propose a brief abstract thereof, as to that part of it, which seems to be especially concerned, and then lay down what to me appears in its prejudice in the volumes now under debate; not doubting but a fuller account of the whole, will by some or other be speedily tendered unto the learned and impartial readers of them. The sum of what I am pleading for, as to the particular head to be vindicated is; that as the *Scriptures of the Old and New Testament, were immediately, and entirely given out by God himself, his mind being in them represented unto us, without the least inteveniency[9] of such mediums, and ways, as were capable of giving change or alteration to the least iota or syllable; so, by his good and merciful providential dispensation, in his love to his word and church, his whole word as first given out by him, is preserved unto us entire in the original languages; where shining in its own beauty and luster, (as also in all translations so far, as they faithfully represent the originals) it manifests and evidences unto the consciences of men, without other foreign help or assistance, its divine original and authority.*[10]

THEIR WEIGHT AND IMPORTANCE

6. Now the several assertions or propositions contained in this position, are to me such important truths, that I shall not be blamed in the least by my own spirit, nor I hope by any others, in contending for them, judging them fundamental parts of the faith once delivered to the saints; and though some of them may seem to be less weighty than others, yet they are so concatenated[11] in themselves, that by the removal or destruction of any one of them, our interest in the others is utterly taken away. It will assuredly be granted, that the persuasion of the coming forth of the word immediately from God, in

9   I.e., intervention.
10   Italics original.
11   I.e., joined together.

the way pleaded for, is the foundation of all faith, hope, and obedience. But what I pray will it advantage us, that God did so once deliver his word, if we are not assured also, that, that word so delivered, has been by his special care and providence preserved entire and uncorrupt unto us; or that it does not evidence and manifest itself to be his word, being so preserved. Blessed may we say were the ages past, who received the word of God in its unquestionable power and purity, when it shone brightly in its own glorious native light, and was free from those defects and corruptions, which through the default of men, in a long tract of time it has contracted; but for us, as we know not well where to lay a sure foundation of believing, that this book rather than any other does contain what is left unto us of that word of his, so it is impossible we should ever come to any certainty almost of any individual word, or expression whether it be from God or no; far be it from the thoughts of any good man, that God whose covenant with his church, is, that his word and Spirit shall never depart from it (Isa. 59:21; Matt. 5:18; 1 Pet. 1:25; 1 Cor. 11;[12] Matt. 28:20), has left it in uncertainties, about the things that are the foundation of all that faith and obedience which he requires at our hands.

As then I have in the foregoing treatise, evinced as I hope the self-evidencing light and power of the Scripture, so let us now candidly for the sake and in the pursuit of truth, deal with a mind freed from prejudices and disquieting affections, save only the trouble that arises from the necessity of dissenting from the authors of so useful a work, address ourselves to the consideration of what seems in these *Prolegomena* and *Appendix* to impair the truth of the other assertions, about the entire preservation of the word as given out from God, in the copies which yet remain with us. And this I shall do, not doubting, but that the persons themselves concerned, will fairly accept and weigh, what is conscientiously tendered.

SUNDRY PRINCIPLES IN THE *PROLEGOMENA* PREJUDICIAL TO THE TRUTH CONTENDED FOR LAID DOWN

7. As then I do with all thankfulness acknowledge that many things are spoken very honorably of the originals in these *Prolegomena*, and that they are in them absolutely preferred above any translation whatever,[13] and asserted in general as the authentic rule of all versions, contrary to the thoughts of

12   Owen is referring to 1 Cor 11:23.

13   In the margin: *Prolegom.* 7. sect. 17.—Owen. See Brian Walton, *In Biblia polyglotta prolegomena*, 2 vols. (Cambridge: J. Smith, 1827–1828), 1:397–98.

the publisher of the great Parisian Bibles,[14] and his infamous *hyperaspistes*,[15] Morinus;[16] so as they stand in their aspect unto the *Appendix* of various lections, there are both opinions, and principles confirmed by suitable practices, that are of the nature and importance before mentioned.

1. After a long dispute to that purpose,[17] it is determined, that the Hebrew points or vowels and accents, are a novel invention of some Judaical Rabbins, about five or six hundred years after the giving out of the gospel. Hence,

(1) An antiquity is ascribed to some translations, two or three at the least, above and before the invention of these points, whose agreement with the original cannot therefore by just consequence be tried by the present text, as now pointed and accented.

(2) The whole credit of our reading and interpretation of the Scripture, as far as regulated by the present punctuation, depends solely on the faithfulness and skill of those Jews, whose invention this work is asserted to be.

2. The קרי וכתיב [*Qere* and *Ketiv*][18] of which sort are above eight hundred in the Hebrew Bibles,[19] are various lections, partly gathered by some Juduicial Rabbins out of ancient copies, partly their critical amendments.

And therefore after these various lections, as they are esteemed, are presented unto us, in their own proper order wherein they stand in the great Bibles (not surely to increase the bulk of diverse readings, or to present a face of new variety to a less attentive observer but) to evidence, that they are such various lections as above described, they are given us over a second time,[20]

---

14 I.e., the so-called Paris Polyglot Bible (1645). This is the second to last of the major early modern polyglot Bibles, produced under the supervision of Guy-Michel Lejay. See *Biblia: 1. Hebraica, 2. Samaritana, 3. Chaldaica, 4. Graeca, 5. Syriaca, 6. Latina, 7. Arabica: Quibus textus originales totius Scripturae sacrae, quorum pars in editione complutensi*, (Paris: Antonius Vitré, 1645). Guy-Michel Lejay (1588–1674) was an advocate at the French Parliament and is most famous for his patronage of the Paris Polyglot Bible.

15 Gk. "a champion, defender."

16 While the introduction to the Paris Polyglot Bible is written under Lejay's name, Owen suspects it was actually written by Jean Morin. Jean Morin (1591–1659) was a French Catholic priest and scholar most famous for his work on the Samaritan Pentateuch in the Paris Polyglot Bible and for advocating the theory that the Masoretic Text had been corrupted.

17 In the margin: *Prolegom.* 3. sec. 8 & seq.—Owen. Owen here appears to be referring to Walton's extended argument in prolegom. 3, secs. 38–56. See Walton, *Prolegomena*, 1:184–249.

18 Heb., the system of scribal marginalia in the Hebrew Bible to noting the difference between how the Hebrew consonants are written (the *Ketiv*) and how they are to be pronounced (the *Qere*).

19 In the margin: *Prolegom.* 8. sect. 23. etc.—Owen. See Walton, *Prolegomena*, 1:476–79.

20 In the margin: *Append.* P. 5.—Owen. The *Appendix* of the London Polyglot Bible presents the various lections on the Hebrew editions, first according to each book of the Old Testament and, second, according to the classification or arrangement of Louis Cappel, derived from bk. 3 of his

in the method whereinto they are cast by Capellus[21] the great patriarch of these mysteries.

3. That there are such alterations befallen the original,[22] as in many places may be rectified by the translations that have been made of old.

And therefore various lections may be observed and gathered out of those translations,[23] by considering how they read in their copies, and wherein they differed from those which we now enjoy.

4. It is also declared, that where any gross faults or corruptions are befallen the originals,[24] men may by their faculty of critical conjecturing amend them, and restore the native lections that were lost; though in general without the authority of copies, this may not be allowed.

And therefore a collection of various readings out of Grotius,[25] consisting for the most part in such conjectures, is in the *Appendix* presented unto us.[26]

5. The voluminous bulk of various lections, as nakedly exhibited, seems sufficient to beget scruples and doubts in the minds of men, about the truth of what has been hitherto by many pretended concerning the preservation of the Scripture through the care and providence of God.

*Those Principles Formerly Asserted by Others and
the Reasons of the Opposition Made to Them*

8. It is known to all men acquainted with things of this nature, that in all these, there is no new opinion coined or maintained by the learned prefacer to these Bibles. The severals mentioned, have been asserted and maintained by

---

Critica sacra (chaps. 2–13). Owen is referring to the latter. See Walton, *Biblia sacra polyglotta*, vol. 6, chap. 1, pp. 5a–8b. Cf. Louis Cappel, *Critica sacra, sive De variis quae in sacris Veteris Testamenti libris occurrunt lectionibus* (Paris: S&G Cramoisy, 1650), 72–159).

21 Louis Cappel (1585–1658) was a Huguenot and Hebraist at the Academy of Saumur, most controversial for his late dating of Hebrew vowel points and his *Critica sacra*, which promoted the practice of critical emendation of the Hebrew text.

22 In the margin: *Prolegom.* 7. Sec. 12.—Owen. See Walton, *Prolegomena*, 1:381–86.

23 In the margin: *Prolegom.* 6. sect. 8, 9, 10.—Owen. See Walton, *Prolegomena*, 1:338–51.

24 In the margin: *Prolegom.* 6. sect. 12.—Owen. See Walton, *Prolegomena*, 1:352.

25 Hugo Grotius (1583–1645) was a Dutch statesman, lawyer, and humanist who wrote most influentially on natural law. His other works include his *Annotationes in Vetus Testamentum* (included in the *Appendix* of the London Polyglot Bible) and his defense of the satisfaction of Christ against Faustus Socinus.

26 Grotius's annotations are contained within the *Appendix* volume of the "London Polyglot," which contains a number of discrete collections of variant readings and annotations. Grotius's were compiled by Thomas Pierce and are titled *Variantes lectiones ex annotatis viri summi et incomparabilis D. Hugonis Grotii in universa Biblia, cum eisdem de iis judicio, collectae opera ac studio doctissimi viri Thomae Piercii presbyteri, rectoris ecclesiae de Brington in comitatu Northamptoniensi*. See Walton, *Biblia sacra polyglotta*, vol. 6, chap. 15, pp. 37a–58b.

sundry learned men. Had the opinion about them been kept in the ordinary sphere of men's private conceptions in their own private writings running the hazard of men's judgments on their own strength and reputation, I should not from my former discourse have esteemed myself concerned in them. Every one of us must give an account of himself unto God. It will be well for us, if we are found holding the foundation. If we build hay and stubble upon it, though our work perish, we shall be "saved."[27] Let every man in these things be fully persuaded in his own mind, it shall be to me no offense. It is their being laid as the foundation of the usefulness of these *Biblia polyglotta*, with an endeavor to render them catholic, not in their own strength, but in their appendage to the authority, that on good grounds is expected to this work, that calls for a due consideration of them. All men who will find them stated in these *Prolegomena*, may not perhaps have had leisure, may not perhaps have the ability to know what issue the most of these things have been already driven unto, in the writings of private men.

9. As I willingly grant then, that some of these things may, without any great prejudice to the truth, be candidly debated among learned men; so taking them altogether, placed in the advantages they now enjoy, I cannot but look upon them, as an engine suited to the destruction of the important truth before pleaded for; and as a fit weapon put into the hands of men of atheistical minds and principles, such as this age abounds withal, to oppose the whole evidence of truth revealed in the Scripture. I fear with some, either the pretended infallible judge, or the depth of atheism will be found to lie at the door of these considerations. *Hoc Ithacus vellet*.[28] But the debate of the advantage of either Romanists or Atheists from hence, belongs to another place and season. Nor is the guilt of any consequences of this nature charged on the workmen, which yet may be feared from the work itself.

---

27 Owen is alluding to 1 Cor. 3:12, 15.

28 Lat. "This the Ithacan would want." Owen is here using a figurative saying that is slightly adapted from Virgil's *Aeneid*, bk. 2, line 104. For the Latin text and English translation, see Virgil, *Eclogues. Georgics. Aeneid: Books 1–6*, trans. H. Rushton Fairclough, rev. G. P. Goold, Loeb Classical Library 63 (Cambridge, MA: Harvard University Press, 1999), 322–33.

2

Foundational Assumptions about the Integrity of Scripture Outlined and Defended

1. Of the purity of the originals. 2. The αὐτόγραφα of the Scripture lost. 3. That of Moses, how and how long preserved. Of the book found by Hilkiah. 4. Of the αὐτόγραφα of the New Testament. 5. Of the first copies of the originals. The scribes of those copies not θεόπνευστοι. What is ascribed to them. 6. The great and incomparable care of the scribes of it. 7. The whole word of God, in every tittle of it, preserved entire in the copies of the original extant. 8. Heads of arguments to that purpose. 9. What various lections are granted in the original of the Old and New Testaments. [10–12.] Sundry considerations concerning them, manifesting them to be of no importance. [13.] That the Jews have not corrupted the text. The most probable instances considered.

OF THE PURITY OF THE ORIGINALS

1. Having given an account of the occasion of this discourse, and mentioned the particulars that are, all, or some of them, to be taken into further consideration, before I proceed to their discussion, I shall by way of addition and explanation to what has been delivered in the former treatise, give a brief account of my apprehensions concerning the purity of the present original copies of the Scripture, or rather copies in the original languages, which the church of God does now, and has for many ages enjoyed, as her chiefest

treasure; whereby it may more fully appear, what it is, we plead for and defend against the insinuations and pretenses above mentioned.

The Αὐτόγραφα of the Scripture Lost

2. First then, it is granted that the individual αὐτόγραφα[1] of Moses, the prophets, and the apostles, are in all probability, and as to all that we know, utterly perished and lost out of the world. As also the copies of Ezra. The[2] reports mentioned by some to the contrary, are open fictions. The individual ink and parchment, the rolls or books that they wrote, could not without a miracle have been preserved from moldering into dust before this time. Nor does it seem improbable, that God was willing by their loss to reduce us to a nearer consideration of his care and providence in the preservation of every tittle contained in them. Had those individual writings been preserved, men would have been ready to adore them, as the Jews do their own ἀπόγραφα[3] in their synagogues.

The Original of Moses, How Long It Was Preserved, and the Book Found by Hilkiah

3. Moses indeed delivered his original copy of the Pentateuch, in a public assembly unto the Levites, (that is, the sons of Korah) to be put into the sides of the ark, and there kept for a perpetual monument (Deut. 31:25, 26). That individual book was, I doubt not, preserved until the destruction of the temple. There is indeed no mention made of the book of the Law in particular, when the ark was solemnly carried into the holy place after the building of Solomon's temple (2 Chron. 5:4, 5). But the tabernacle of the congregation continued until then. That, and all that was in it, is said to be brought up (verse 5). Now the placing of the book by the sides of the ark,

---

1   Gk. "autographs." Owen has in mind the very first written versions of the Scriptures.
2   In the margin: Adrianus Ferrariensis *Flagellum Judaeor.* lib. 9. c. 2. Rab. Azarias *Meor Henaim.* pa. 13. cap. 9.—Owen. "Adrianus Ferrariensis *Flagellum Judaeor.* lib. 9. c. 2": see Finus Adrianus Ferrariensis, *In Iudaeos flagellum ex sacris Scripturis excerptum* (Venice: Petrum de Nicolinis de Sabio, 1538), 553v–59v. Finus Adrianus Ferrariensis, or Fino Fini (1431–1519), was an Italian orientalist who is best known for his anti-Jewish Christian apology, *In Iudaeos flagellum ex sacris Scripturis excerptum.* "Rab. Azarias *Meor Henaim.* pa. 13. cap. 9": Azariah de' Rossi (ca. 1511–1578) was an Italian Jewish physician and Hebraist who is best known for his *Me'or enayim* ("The Light of the Eyes"), where he deployed critical methods to examine the truthfulness of the Jewish *Haggadah,* or the nonlegal texts contained in the Talmud and Midrash. Here Azariah quotes a report that suggests the discovery of a scroll of the Torah penned by Ezra. For an English translation, see Azariah de' Rossi, *The Light of the Eyes,* trans. Joanna Weinberg (New Haven, CT: Yale University Press, 2001), 194–96.
3   Gk. "original written copies."

being so solemn an ordinance, it was no doubt preserved. Nor is there any pretense to the contrary. Some think the book found by Hilkiah,[4] in the days of Josiah, was this καλὴ παραθήκη,[5] or αὐτόγραφον[6] of Moses, which was placed by the sides of the ark. It rather seems to have been some ancient sacred copy, used in the service of the temple, and laid up there; as there was in the second temple,[7] which was carried in triumph to Rome. For besides that he speaks of his finding it in general in the house of the Lord, upon the occasion of the work which was then done (2 Chron. 34:14–15), which was not, in, or about the holy place, where he, who was high priest, knew full well this book was kept, it does not appear that it was lawful for him to take that sacred *depositum*[8] from its peculiar archives to send it abroad, as he dealt with that book which he found. Nay doubtless it was altogether unlawful for him so to have done, it being placed there by a peculiar ordinance, for a peculiar or special end. After the destruction of the temple, all inquiry after that book is in vain. The author of the Second Book of Maccabees[9] mentions not its hiding in Nebo by Jeremiah, with the ark and altar;[10] or by Josiah, as say some of the Talmudists. Nor were it of any importance if they had. Of the Scripture preserved in the temple at its last destruction, Josephus gives us a full account.[11]

---

4   I.e., the high priest during King Josiah's reign (641–609 BC) who is known for finding a lost copy of the Torah in the Jerusalem Temple (2 Kings 22:8).
5   Gk. "good deposit." Owen is alluding to Paul's injunction in 2 Tim. 1:14.
6   Gk. "an autograph."
7   In the margin: *Joseph: de Bello Judaic. Lib. 7. Cap. 24.*—Owen. For the Greek text in the nineteenth-century critical edition, see *De bello Iudaico*, bk. 7, lines 150–51, in Josephus, *Opera edidit et apparatu critico instruxit*, 7 vols., ed. Benedikt Niese (Berlin: Weidmannos, 1885–1895), 6:590. For the Greek text and an English translation, see Josephus, *The Jewish War*, vol. 3, *Books 5–7*, trans. H. St. J. Thackeray, Loeb Classical Library 210 (Cambridge, MA: Harvard University Press, 1997), 350–51. Owen's citation (which includes a chapter number) reflects extant published editions of the sixteenth and seventeenth centuries, such as the following Latin edition of Josephus's works, published by Frobenius: Josephus, *Antiquitatum iudicarum* [. . .]; *De bello Iudiaco* [. . .]; *contra Apionem* [. . .]; *de imperio rationis* (Basel: Frobenius, 1540), 767–68. Flavius Josephus (37–100) was a first-century Roman Jewish historian who is best known for his The Jewish War and his Jewish history of the world, the Antiquities of the Jews.
8   Lat. "deposit"
9   I.e., the second in a series of deuterocanonical books that portrays the Maccabean history up to 161 BC, with a particular focus on Judas Maccabeus, who led the revolt against the Seleucid Antiochus IV Epiphanes.
10 2 Macc. 2:4–7 indicates that the prophet Jeremiah hid the ark of the covenant and the tabernacle in a cave at Mount Nebo.
11 In the text: *de bello Juda: lib. 7. Cap. 24.*—Owen. For the Greek text in the nineteenth-century critical edition, see *De bello Iudaico*, bk. 7, lines 150–51, 162, in Josephus, *Opera*, 6:590, 92.

The Αὐτόγραφα of the New Testament

4. For[12] the Scriptures of the New Testament, it does not appear, that the αὐτόγραφα of the several writers of it were ever gathered into one volume; there being now no one church to keep them for the rest. The epistles though immediately transcribed for the use of other churches (Col. 4:16), were doubtless kept in the several churches, whereunto they were directed. From those πρωτότυπα,[13] there were quickly ἐκτυπούμενα,[14] transcribed copies given out to "faithful men",[15] while the infallible Spirit yet continued his guidance in an extraordinary manner.

OF THE FIRST COPIES OF THE ORIGINALS

The Scribes of Those Copies Not θεόπνευστοι and What Is Ascribed to Them

5. [Secondly,] for the first transcribers of the original copies, and those who in succeeding ages have done the like work from them, whereby they have been propagated and continued down to us, in a subserviency to the providence and promise of God, we say not, as is vainly charged by Morinus, and Capellus, that they were all or any of them ἀναμάρτητοι and θεόπνευστοι, "infallible" and "divinely inspired," so that it was impossible for them in anything to mistake. It is known, it is granted, that failings have been among them, and that various lections are from thence risen, of which afterward. Religious care and diligence in their work, with a due reverence of him, with whom they had to do, is all we ascribe unto them. Not to acknowledge these freely in them, without clear and unquestionable evidence to the contrary, is high uncharitableness, impiety, and ingratitude. This care and diligence we say, in a subserviency to the promise, and providence of God, has produced the effect contended for. Nor is anything further necessary thereunto. On this account to argue (as some do) from the miscarriages and mistakes of men, their oscitancy[16] and negligence in transcribing the old heathen authors, Homer,[17]

For the Greek text and an English translation, see Josephus, *Jewish War*, 350–51, 354–55. Cf. Josephus, *Antiquitatum et al.* (1540), 767–68.

12 Goold begins this section with "Secondly" (which is absent in the original), when in this editor's judgment it should begin sec. 5.

13 Gk. "originals."

14 Gk. "copied."

15 In the margin: 1 Tim 2:1—Owen. The correct reference is 2 Tim. 2:2.

16 I.e., dullness or carelessness.

17 Homer was a Greek poet who lived sometime between the twelfth and eighth centuries BC, most famously associated with the epic poems *The Iliad* and *The Odyssey*.

Aristotle,[18] Tully,[19] we think it not tolerable in a Christian, or any one that has the least sense of the nature and importance of the word, or the care of God toward his church. Shall we think that men who wrote out books, wherein themselves and others were no more concerned, than it is possible for men to be in the writings of the persons mentioned, and others like them, had as much reason to be careful and diligent in that they did, as those who knew and considered that every letter and tittle that they were transcribing, was part of the word of the great God, wherein the eternal concernment of their own souls and the souls of others did lie. Certainly whatever may be looked for from the religious care and diligence of men, lying under a loving and careful aspect from the promise and providence of God, may be justly expected from them who undertook that work. However we are ready to own all their failings, that can be proved. To assert in this case without proof is injurious.

The Great and Incomparable Care of the Scribes of It

6. The Jews have a common saying among them, that to alter one letter of the Law is no less sin, than to set the whole world on fire; and shall we think that in writing it, they took no more care than a man would do in writing out Aristotle or Plato, who for a very little portion of the world, would willingly have done his endeavor to get both their works out of it? Considering that the word to be transcribed was every tittle and ἰῶτα[20] of it the word of the great God, that, that which was written, and as written was proposed as his, as from him, that if any failings were made, innumerable eyes of men, owning their eternal concernment to lie in that word, were open upon it to discover it, and thousands of copies were extant to try it by, and all this known unto, and confessed by everyone that undertook this work; it is no hard matter to prove their care and diligence to have outgone that of other common scribes of heathen authors. The truth is, they are prodigious things that are related of the exact diligence and reverential care of the ancient Jews in this work, especially when they entrusted a copy to be a rule for the trial and standard of other private copies. Maimonides in הלכות ספר תורה;[21] tells

---

18 Aristotle (384–322 BC) was a Greek philosopher and the most famous student of Plato. Aristotle's physics, logic, ethics, and metaphysics would significantly influence Islamic thought in the Middle Ages and was appropriated into the Latin West most notably by Thomas Aquinas.

19 I.e., Marcus Tullius Cicero (106–43 BC) a Roman lawyer and philosopher who exercised a considerable influence on the Latin language and rhetorical theory and practice.

20 Gk. "jot."

21 In the text: *Chap.* 8.3, 4. —Owen. Maimonides, "Hilchot Sefer Torah," in *Sefer Ahavah* ("Book of the Love of God") of *Mishneh Torah*, chap. 8, secs. 3–4. For a modern Hebrew edition with an English translation, see Maimonides, *Mishneh Torah*, 18 vols., ed. Rabbi Eliyahu Touger (New

us that Ben Asher[22] spent many years in the careful, exact writing out of the Bible. Let any man consider the twenty things, which they affirm to profane a book or copy, and this will further appear. They are repeated by Rabbi Moses [Maimonides].[23] One of them is, שחסר אפילו אות אחת, "if but one letter be wanting"; and another, "If but one letter be redundant." Of which more shall be spoken if occasion be offered.

Even among the heathen, we will scarce think that the Roman pontifices, going solemnly to transcribe the *Sibyls'* verses,[24] would do it either negligently or treacherously, or alter one tittle from what they found written; and shall we entertain such thoughts of them, who knew they had to do with the living God, and that in and about that, which is dearer to him, than all the world besides. Let men then clamor as they please, and cry out of all men as ignorant and stupid which will not grant the corruptions of the Old Testament which they plead for, which is the way of Morinus; or let them propose their own conjectures of the ways of the entrance of the mistakes that they pretend are crept into the original copies, with their remedies, which is the way of Capellus, we shall acknowledge nothing of this nature but what they can prove by undeniable, and irrefragable[25] instances, which as to anything as yet done by them, or those that follow in their footsteps, appears upon the matter to be nothing at all. To this purpose take our sense in the word of a very learned man:

In those books that were written without vowels we have found a certain, constant and altogether similar reading in all copies, [both manuscripts] and printed versions. In just the same way, in all those in which points have been added, we have not observed anything different to any other or in conflict with others. Nor is there anyone who claims that he has seen

---

York: Moznai, 2010), 2:503–6. Moses ben Maimon, or Maimonides (1138–1204) was a highly influential medieval Jewish philosopher, best known for his *Mishneh Torah*, or his attempt to provide a comprehensive codification of the Jewish oral law tradition. Maimonides is also well known for his *The Guide for the Perplexed*, or a theological synthesis of Rabbinic Judaism with the peripatetic tradition.

22 Aaron ben Moses ben Asher (d. 960) was a Tiberian Masorete who is credited with having preserved the most accurate version of the Masoretic Text of the Hebrew Bible, with its vocalization. He has exercised considerable influence on subsequent study of Hebrew grammar.

23 In the text: *Tractat. de libro Legis. cap.* 10.—Owen. Here and following, Owen is citing the twelfth and thirteenth of twenty conditions that will disqualify a copy of the Torah from being deemed an official Torah scroll fit for public Torah reading. See "Hilchot Sefer Torah," chap. 10, sec. 1. For a modern Hebrew edition with an English translation, see Maimonides, *Mishneh Torah*, 2:527–28.

24 I.e., ancient Greek oracles or prophecies that were said to be divinely inspired.

25 I.e., indisputable.

in any place examples of a Hebrew reading different from those that are widely available, provided that we are speaking of those who have followed proper grammatical method. And certainly we judge that it has happened by the counsel and will of God, that when one takes into account the great variety of almost all of the Greek and Latin copies of the same origin and especially of manuscripts in many places, yet a great equivalence, similarity, and constancy of text is preserved in all Hebrew Bibles that are found in our age, in whatever way they were written, whether with consonants alone or furnished with points.[26]

It can, then, with no color of probability be asserted,[27] (which yet I find some learned men too free in granting) namely that there has the same fate attended the Scripture in its transcription, as has done other books. Let me say without offense; this imagination asserted on deliberation, seems to me to border on atheism. Surely the promise of God for the preservation of his word, with his love and care of his church, of whose faith and obedience that word of his is the only rule, requires other thoughts at our hands.

THE WHOLE WORD OF GOD PRESERVED ENTIRE IN THE COPIES OF THE ORIGINAL EXTANT

7. Thirdly, we add that the whole Scripture entire, as given out from God, without any loss, is preserved in the copies of the originals yet remaining;

26 In the text: *Ut in iis libris qui sine vocalibus conscripti sunt, certum constantemque exemplarium omnium, [tum manuscriptorum,] tum excusarum scriptionem similemque omnino comperimus, sic in omnibus etiam iis quibus puncta sunt addita, non aliam cuipiam nec discrepantem aliis punctationem observavimus; nec quisquam est qui ullo in loco diversa lectionis Hebraiae exemplaria [sic: exempla in original] ab iis quae circumferuntur, vidisse se asserat, modo grammaticam rationem observatam dicat. Et quidem Dei consilio ac voluntate factum putamus, ut cum magna Graecorum Latinorumque fere omnium ejusdem auctoris exemplarium, ac praesertim manuscriptorum pluribus in locis varietas deprehendatur, magna tamen in omnibus Hebraicis, quaecunq; nostro saeculo inveniuntur, Bibliis, scriptionis aequalitas, similitudo atq; constantia servetur quocunque modo scripta illa sint, sive solis consonantibus constent, sive punctis etiam instructa visantur; Arias Montan. Praefat. Ad Bibia [sic] Interlin. De varia Hebraicorum librorum scriptione & lectione.*—Owen. Editor's translation. For the Latin text, see Arias Montanus, "De varia Hebraicorum librorum Scriptione et lectione commentatio," in *Biblia Hebraica eorundem Latina interpretatio Xantis Pagnini Lucensis* (Antwerp: Christophori Plantini, 1584), *2b (page numbers with an asterisk refer to unnumbered pages in the original). Benedictus Arias Montanus (1527–1598), a Spanish Catholic priest and scholar, is particularly known for his work on the so-called Antwerp Polyglot Bible.

27 In the margin: *Prolegom. 7. sect. 12.*—Owen. See Brian Walton, *In Biblia polyglotta prolegomena*, 2 vols. (Cambridge: J. Smith, 1827–1828), 1:381–86.

what varieties there are among the copies themselves shall be afterward declared; in them all, we say, is every letter and tittle of the word. These copies we say, are the rule, standard, and touchstone of all translations ancient or modern, by which they are in all things to be examined, tried, corrected, amended, and themselves only by themselves. Translations contain the word of God, and are the word of God, perfectly or imperfectly according as they express the words, sense and meaning of those originals. To advance any, all translations concurring, into an equality with the originals, so to set them by it, as to set them up with it, on even terms, much more to propose and use them as means of castigating, amending, altering anything in them, gathering various lections by them, is to set up an altar of our own by the altar of God, and to make equal the wisdom, care, skill, and diligence of men, with the wisdom, care, and providence of God himself. It is a foolish conjecture of Morinus from some words of Epiphanius,[28] that Origen in his *Octapla* placed the translation of the LXX[29] in the midst,[30] to be the rule of all the rest; even of the Hebrew itself, that was to be regulated and amended by it ("in the midst of all, then, a universal edition had been established so that the Hebrew and other editions might be regulated and amended according to it").[31] The truth is, he placed the Hebrew, in Hebrew characters in the first place as the rule and standard of all the rest; the same in Greek characters in

28 Epiphanius of Salamis (ca. 310–403) was Bishop of Salamis and is best known for his antiheretical polemics, especially his *Panerion*.

29 I.e., the Septuagint, the Greek translation of the Old Testament produced in the second and third centuries BC, and which is attributed in legend to seventy representatives of the twelve tribes of Israel, who independently were said to have produced an identical translation of the Hebrew Bible.

30 While only fragments remain, Owen is referring to what is commonly known as Origen's famous *Hexapla*, which was an early interlinear or polyglot version of the Old Testament, containing (from left to right) the Hebrew text, followed by a Greek transliteration, the translations of Aquila and Symmachus respectively, a recension of the Septuagint (including Theodotion's version, where the Septuagint is missing text), followed by Theodotion's translation. A later edition was said to contain two further Greek translations and was called the *Octapla*, hence Owen's reference here. Origen (ca. 184–253) was a prolific early theologian and biblical exegete who is best known for his allegorical interpretations of Scripture and his influence on Athanasius and the Cappadocian Fathers. The orthodoxy of his views has been hotly debated, through the First and Second Origenist Crises, and especially since his anathema at the Second Council of Constantinople in 553, which resulted in the destruction of most of his works.

31 In the text: *media igitur omnium catholica editio collocata erat, ut ad eam Hebraea caeteraeque editiones exigerentur & emendarentur;* Excercit. lib. 1. cap. 3. pag. 15.—Owen. Editor's translation. Here Owen is citing the 1633 edition of the first part (*pars prior*) of Morin's *Exercitationes*, although the page number is incorrectly recorded as 15 rather than 35. See Jean Morin, *Exercitationes biblicae de Hebraei Graecique textus sinceritate: Pars prior* (Paris: Antonius Vitray, 1633), 35. The second part is sketched only in outline form at the end of this edition. The two parts

the next place, then that of Aquila,[32] then that of Symmachus,[33] after which, in the fifth place followed that of the LXX, mixed with that of Theodotion.[34]

Heads of Arguments to That Purpose

8. The various arguments giving evidence to this truth that might be produced, are too many for me now to insist upon; and would take up more room than is allotted to the whole discourse, should I handle them at large and according to the merit of this cause. [Firstly,][35] the providence of God in taking care of his word, which he has magnified above all his name, as the most glorious product of his wisdom and goodness, his great concernment in this world, answering his promise to this purpose; secondly, the religious care of the church (I speak not of the Romish synagogue) to whom these oracles of God were committed. Thirdly, the care of the first writers in giving out authentic copies of what they had received from God, unto many which might be rules to the first transcribers. Fourthly, the multiplying copies to such a number, that it was impossible any should corrupt them all, willfully or by negligence. Fifthly, the preservation of the authentic copies: first in the Jewish synagogues, then in the Christian assemblies, with reverence and diligence. Sixthly, the daily reading and studying of the word by all sorts of persons ever since its first writing, rendering every alteration liable to immediate observation and discovery, and that all over the world: with, seventhly, the consideration of the many millions that looked on every tittle and letter in this book as their inheritance, which for the whole world they would not be deprived of; and in particular, for the Old Testament (now most questioned). Eighthly, the care of Ezra and his companions, the men of the great synagogue, in restoring the Scripture to its purity, when it had met with the greatest trial that it ever underwent in this world considering the paucity of the copies then extant.[36]

---

were eventually published posthumously in 1660. See Jean Morin, *Exercitationum biblicarum de Hebraei Graecique textus sinceritate, libri duo* (Paris: Gasparus Meturas, 1660).

32 Aquila (2nd c.) produced a Greek translation of the Old Testament of which fragments survived as recorded in Origen's *Hexapla*, and of which fragments from 1–2 Kings and Psalms were discovered in the late nineteenth century.

33 Symmachus (late 2nd c.) is known for his Greek translation of the Old Testament, which was incorporated in Origen's *Hexapla* and *Tetrapla*, and used by Jerome in his preparation of the Vulgate.

34 Theodotion (d. 200) was a Greek Jewish scholar who produced a Greek translation of the Old Testament, which was incorporated by Origen into his *Hexapla*, and which was widely influential in the early church.

35 "1" in the original but altered to be consistent with verbally numbered list.

36 In the margin: *Hierosolymis Babylonica expugnatione deletis, omne instrumentum Judaicae literaturae per Esdram constat restauratum. Tertull. Lib. De Hab. Mal. C. 3.*—Owen. "When

Ninthly, the care of the Masoretes[37] from his days and downward, to keep perfect, and give an account of every syllable in the Scripture, of which see Buxtorfius [Sr.]:[38] with ten; the constant consent of all copies in the world, so that as sundry learned men have observed, there is not in the whole Mishnah,[39] Gemara,[40] or either Talmud,[41] any one place of Scripture found otherwise read, than as it is now in our copies. Eleven, the security we have that no mistakes were voluntarily or negligently brought into the text before the coming of our Savior who was to declare all things, in that he not once reproves the Jews on that account, when yet for their false glosses on the word he spares them not.[42] Twelve, afterward the watchfulness which the two nations of Jews

---

Jerusalem was destroyed at the hands of the Babylonians, every document of Jewish literature is known to have been restored by Esdras." The original locates this citation next to "seventhly," but, as per Goold, it appears to be connected to Owen's eighth observation. Owen is quoting from the first book of Tertullian's *De cultu feminarum*, which in some manuscripts bears the title *De habitu muliebri*. For the Latin text, see Tertullian, *Opera catholica. Adversus Marcionem*, ed. E Dekkers et al., Corpus Christianorum: Series Latina 1 (Turnhout: Typographi Brepolis, 1954), 346. For the English translation, see Tertullian, *Disciplinary, Moral and Ascetical Works*, trans. Rudolph Arbesmann OSA., Sister Emily Joseph Daly, and Edwin A. Quain, Fathers of the Church 40 (Washington, DC: The Catholic University of America Press, 1959), 122. Owen is referring to the great synagogue called by Ezra (or the so-called Men of the Great Assembly) in the period from around 516 to 332 BC. The Great Assembly is known for closing the canon of the Hebrew Bible and included the postexilic prophets Haggai, Zechariah, and Malachi, who are held to be responsible for transmitting the Torah after the Babylonian exile.

37   The Masoretes (ca. 500–ca. 1000) were a community of Jewish scholars dedicated to meticulously preserving and transmitting both the consonantal text of the Hebrew Old Testament and the Jewish oral tradition of vocalization. The Tiberian Masoretes (ca. 600 onward) were a prominent branch of this movement based in the city of Tiberias, next to the sea of Galilee.

38   In the text: *Com: Mas.*—Owen. See Johann Buxtorf Sr., *Tiberias, sive Commentarius Masorethicus triplex* (Basel: J. J. Deckeri, 1665). Johann Buxtorf Sr. (1564–1629) was a notable German Protestant Hebraist who was famous for his posthumously published *Lexicon Chaldaicum, Talmadicum et Rabbinicum*, and his *Tiberius, sive Commentarius Masoreticus triplex*, which disputes Levita's late dating on the origin of the Hebrew vowel points in the Old Testament. Buxtorf Sr.'s legacy was continued by his son Johann Buxtorf Jr.

39   "Mishna" in original, updated to modern spelling convention. The Mishnah is the first collection of Jewish oral tradition called the oral Torah. It was redacted by Judah ha-Nasi in the third century.

40   The Gemara is the Jewish rabbinical commentary on the Mishnah.

41   The Talmud is the combined collection of the Mishnah and Gemara. There are two compilations, an earlier Jerusalem Talmud and the later Babylonian Talmud.

42   In the margin: *Quod si aliquis dixerit Hebraeos libros à Judaeis esse falsatos, audiat Origenem, quid in octavo volumine explanationum Esaiae respondeat quaestiunculae; quod nunquam dominus & apostoli qui caetera crimina arguunt in Scribis & Pharisaeis, de hoc crimine quod erat maximum reticuissent. Sin autem dixerint post adventum Domini & praedicationem apostolorum libros Hebraeos fuisse falsatos cachinnum tenere non potero. Hierom. in c. 6. Esaiae.*—Owen. Editor's translation: "If anyone says that the Hebrew Scriptures were falsified by the Jews, he should hear what Origen says in response to such speculation in volume eight of his explanation of Isaiah, that the Lord and the apostles who charge the Scribes and Pharisees with other crimes,

and Christians, had always one upon another, with sundry things of the like importance, might to this purpose be insisted on. But of these things I shall speak again if occasion be offered.

Various Lections Granted in the Original of No Importance

9. Notwithstanding what has been spoken, we grant that there are, and have been various lections in the Old Testament and the New; for the Old Testament, the *Keri* and *Ketib*;[43] the various readings of Ben Asher and Ben Naphtali;[44] of the Eastern and Western Jews evince it. Of the קרי וכתיב [*Qere and Ketiv*] I shall speak particularly afterward: they present themselves to the view of everyone that but looks into the Hebrew Bible. At the end of the great Rabbinical Bibles (as they are called) printed by Bombergias at Venice, as also in the edition of Buxtorfius [Sr.] at Basel, there is a collection of the various readings of Ben Asher, and Ben Naphtali; of the Eastern and Western Jews; we have them also in this *Appendix*.[45] For the two first mentioned, they are called among the Jews, one of them, R. Aaron the son of R. Moses of the tribe of Asher; the other R. Moses the son of David, of the tribe of Naphtali. They flourished, as is probable among the Jews, about the year of Christ 1030, or thereabouts;[46] and were teachers of great renown, the former in the West or Palestina, the latter in the East, or Babylon. In their exact consideration of every letter, point, and accent of the Bible wherein they spent their lives, it seems they found out some varieties; let any one run them through as they are presented in this *Appendix*, he will find them to be so small, consisting for the most part in unnecessary accents, of no importance to the sense of any word, that they deserve not to be taken notice of. For the various readings of

---

would never have remained silent about this crime that would be the greatest. If, however, after the coming of the Lord and the preaching of the apostles, they [still] said that the Hebrew Scriptures had been falsified, I will not be able to hold back contempt." Owen is quoting from Jerome's commentary on Isa. 6:9–10. For the Latin text, see *Commentariorum in Esaiam*, bk. 3, chap. 6, vv. 9–10, in Jerome, *Commentariorum in Esaiam libri I–XI*, ed. M. Adriaen, Corpus Christianorum: Series Latina 73 (Turnhout: Typographi Brepolis, 1963), 92. For a modern English translation, see *St. Jerome: Commentary on Isaiah; Origen Homilies 1–9 on Isaiah*, trans. Thomas P. Scheck, Ancient Christian Writers 68 (Mahwah, NJ: Newman, 2015), 158.

43 Where Owen uses the English transliteration, spelling has been standardized in this form throughout. Owen's spelling varies.

44 Ben Naphtali or Moses ben David (fl. 890–940) was a Tiberian Masorete who produced an alternative Hebrew text of the Old Testament to ben Asher's received Masoretic Text. Although it has not been preserved, his variations from the Masoretic Text have been, and largely pertain to, the placement of accents in the text.

45 See Brian Walton, *Biblia sacra polyglotta*, 6 vols. (London: Thomas Roycroft, 1653–1657), vol. 6, chap. 1, pp. 8–15.

46 The dates given above are slightly earlier than Owen's.

the oriental, or Babylonian, and occidental or Palestine Jews, all that I know of them (and I wish that those that know more of them would inform me better), is that they first appeared in the edition of the Bible by Bombergius[47] under the care of Felix Pratensis,[48] gathered by R. Jacob Ben Cajim[49] who corrected that impression. But they give us no account of their original. Nor (to profess my ignorance) do I know any that do, it may be some do; but in my present haste, I cannot inquire after them. But the thing itself proclaims their no importance, and Capellus the most skillful and diligent improver of all advantages for impairing the authority of the Hebrew text, so to give countenance to his *Critica sacra*,[50] confesses that they are all trivial, and not in matters of any moment. Besides these, there are no other various lections of the Old Testament. The conjectures of men, conceited of their own abilities to correct the word of God, are not to be admitted to that title. If any other can be gathered, or shall be hereafter out of ancient copies of credit and esteem, where no mistake can be discovered as their cause, they deserve to be considered. Men must here deal by instances not conjectures. All that yet appears, impairs not in the least the truth of our assertion, that every tittle and letter of the word of God, remains in the copies preserved by his merciful providence for the use of his church.

10. As to Jews, besides the mad and senseless clamor in general for corrupting the Scriptures, three things are with most pretense of reason objected against them.[51] The סופרים תקון, *Tikkun Sopherim*; or *correctio scribarum*,[52] by which means it is confessed by Elias, that eighteen places are corrected. But all things are here uncertain, uncertain that ever any such things were done; uncertain who are intended by their *Sopherim*;[53] Ezra and his companions

---

47 Daniel Bomberg (1483–1549) was a famous Venetian printer of Hebrew books, including the Rabbinic Bible, the *Mikraot Gedolot*, and the Babylonian Talmud.

48 Felix Pratensis (d. 1539) was an Italian Jewish convert to Christianity who became an Augustinian friar and was involved in producing Bomberg's first edition of the Rabbinic Bible, the *Mikraot Gedolot* (1516–1517).

49 Jacob ben Chayyim (1470–ca. 1538) was a student of the Masoretic textual notes on the Hebrew Bible and was responsible for making corrections for the printer, Daniel Bomberg in Venice. He was involved in the second edition of Bomberg's Rabbinic Bible, the *Mikraot Gedolot* (1525), which, as Owen alludes here, corrected various errors in the first edition that was edited by Felix Pratensis.

50 See Louis Cappel, *Critica sacra, sive De variis quae in sacris Veteris Testamenti libris occurrunt lectionibus* (Paris: S&G Cramoisy, 1650).

51 Original has "1.," which is omitted by Goold, probably because Owen does not appear to continue the numeration past this point.

52 Heb., Lat. "emendation of the scribes."

53 Heb. "scribes."

most probably; nor do the particular places enumerated discover any such correction; they are all in particular considered by Glassius;[54] but the whole matter is satisfactorily determined by Buxtorfius [Sr.] in his letters to Glassius, printed by him, and repeated again by Amama.[55] Because this thing is much insisted on by Galatinus,[56] to prove the Jews corrupting of the text, it may not be amiss to set down the words of that great master of all Jewish learning:

11. "To your third question concerning the *Tikkun Sopherim*, the Masora notes throughout that eighteen words have been the subject of this criticism. An enumeration of those places [is found] at the beginning of the book of Numbers, and at Psalm 106. In both places, only sixteen are discussed, but in Numbers 12:12, two examples occur, as R. Solomon notes. Now one place eludes me, which I have not been able to discover from any Jewish source so far, nor has that great Mercer come upon it. Galatino has not understood this subject, and adds examples that do not belong. Yes, there also are others who suspect them to be corruptions. Thus far I have not found any one of us, whether from among evangelicals or Catholics, who has explained who those scribes were, and the nature of their תיקונים [*Tikkunim*]. How old those notes regarding the *Tikkun* are, is not clear to me. An older record of them is in the book ספרי [*Sopheri*], which is said to be written before the Babylonian Talmud. However, the Hebrews differ concerning its author and date. In neither Talmud is there any clear mention of those *Tikkun*, when different עיטור סופרים [*Ittur Sopherim*][57] of far less importance are recalled. If those places were ever written differently, Onkelos and Jonathan[58] would also have mentioned it at some point. Nor would Josephus have kept silent, who ascribes

---

54   In the text: *lib. 1 Tract. 1.*—Owen. See Salomon Glass, *Philologiae sacrae, qua totius sacro-sanctae, Veteris et Novi Testamenti Scripturae, tum stylus et literatura tum sensus et genuinae interpretationis ratio expenditur* (Frankfurt : Zacharius Hertelius, 1653), 1–124. Salomon Glass (1593–1656) was a German Hebraist and theologian. Occupying various chairs at universities throughout his career, his most famous work is his *Philologiae sacrae*, through which he made a significant contribution to contemporary biblical criticism.

55   In the text: *Anti: Barb: Bib: lib: 1. pag. 30. 31.*—Owen. See Sixtinus Amama, *Anti-barbarus biblicus* (Franeker: Ludovic and Daniel Elzevir, 1656), 30–31. Sixtinus Amama (1593–1629) was a Dutch Reformed scholar who promoted knowledge of the biblical languages as an essential skill for theology.

56   Pietro Colonna Galatino (1460–1540) was an Italian theologian and anti-Semitic polemicist who had a thorough knowledge of biblical languages. Like Porchetus de Salvaticis's *Victoria Porcheti adversus impios Hebraeos* (Paris: G. Desplains, 1520), his main polemical work, *De arcanis Catholicae veritatis*, also borrowed significantly from Raimund Martini's *Pugio fidei*, though with more adjustments of his own.

57   Heb. "omissions of the scribes."

58   These are the two main Targums, Targum Onkelos on the Penteteuch and the Targum Jonathan on the Prophets.

to the Hebrews the opposite view; namely, that no letter was ever changed in their law by the Hebrew people (lib. i. *contra Apionem*). The Talmudists in Leviticus 27, on the last verse note in different places that none of the prophets were allowed either to make the smallest change or innovation to the Law. In what way, then, would certain common scribes have assumed this audacity to themselves, to amend the letters and meaning of the sacred text?¶[59]

"Accordingly, in view of the silence of all, I whisper in your ear that these *Sopherim* were those sacred authors, Moses and the Prophets, who never wrote anything other than what today may be read as written. But the censorious wise men of the Hebrews, noticing some difficulty in those places, pronounced that those authors ought to speak differently, and to write one of two things in agreement with the proposed text, but that they preferred one over the other and so gave the reading as it is in the text today. So Genesis 18:22, the text reads, 'and Abraham was yet standing before the Lord.' Really? Where it reads (say the wise men), that Abraham came to the Lord, and stood before him; the contrary is stated in what precedes; namely, God came to Abraham, and spoke to him, 'For now I hide from Abraham,' etc. 'The cry of Sodom and Gomorrah is great,' etc. For that reason, Moses ought to write, 'And the Lord was yet standing before Abraham.' But yet it was not proper of Moses to speak of God as being like a slave, whence the תיקון [*Tikkun*] corrected and changed the shape of the discourse in deference to a greater cause, and said, 'And Abraham was standing,' etc. This is why R. Salomon adds that היה לו לכתוב, 'ought to have been written by him' (Moses), (or) 'he ought to write,' 'and the Lord was standing' (not that it was written in a different way before, and that afterward it was corrected by another scribe, or corrupted). Hence R. Aben Ezra at certain places ridicules the censorious, saying there was no need for any *Tikkun*; that is, there is nothing that those censorious wise men may propose that an author ought to speak or write differently from what is there. See also his words on Job 32:3. You have a complicated mystery explained, in a way that many Hebrew writers have also agreed with." Thus far Buxtorfius [Sr.].[60]

59 The ¶ symbol indicates that a paragraph break has been added to Owen's original text.
60 In the text: *Ad tertium quaesitum tuum, de tikkun sopherim, 18 voces hanc censuram subiisse Massora passim notat. Recensio locorum in vestibulo libri Numerorum, & Ps. 106. Utrobique non nisi 16 recensentur, sed in Num. 12:12 duo exempla occurrunt, ut notat R. Solomon. Deest ergo unus locus mihi, quem ex nullo Judaeo hactenus expiscari potui, nec magnus ille Mercerus eum invenit. Galatinus hoc thema non intellexit, & aliena exempla admiscet. Sic & alii qui corruptiones ista esse putant. Nec ullum hactenus ex nostris sive evangelicis sive catholicis vidi, qui explicarit, quae fuerint scribae isti, & quales* תיקונים *ipsorum. Quam antiquae hae notae de*

12. The עיטור סופרים are insisted on by the same Galatinus; but these are only about the use of the letter ו four or five times; which seem to be of the same rise with them foregoing.

That the Jews Have Not Corrupted the Text: The Most Probable Instances Considered

13. But that which makes the greatest cry at present is the corruption of Ps. 22:17;[61] where instead of כארו which the LXX translated ὤρυξαν "they digged" or "pierced," that is, "my hands and feet," the present Judaical copies, as the Antwerp Bibles[62] also, read כארי "as a lion," so depraving the prophecy of our Savior's suffering, "they digged" or "pierced my hands and my feet"; leaving it no sense at all; "as a lion my hands and my feet."

---

tikkun sint, liquido mihi nondum constat. Antiquior ipsarum memoria est in libri ספרי *qui ante Talmud Babylonicum fertur conscriptus. Dissentiunt tamen Hebraei; de ejus autore & tempore. In Talmud neutro ulla plane istius tikkun mentio fit, cum alias* עיטור סופרים *longe minoris negotii in Talmud commemoretur. Si aliter ista loca fuissent aliquando scripta, Onkelos et Jonathan id vel semel expressissent. Nec Josephus reticuisset, qui contrarium Hebraeis adscribit, nullam scilicet unquam literam mutatam fuisse in lege ab Hebraeis popularibus suis, lib. i. contra Apionem. Talmudistae in Lev. 27. vers. ult. diversis locis notant, nec prophetae ulli licitum fuisse vel minimum in lege mutare vel innovare. Quomodo ergo scribae quidam vulgares hanc audaciam sibi arrogassent, textum sacrum in literis & sensu corrigere? In silentio itaque omnium, in aurem tibi dico, Sopherim hosce fuisse ipsos autores sacros, Mosen & Prophetas, qui nunquam aliter scripserunt quam hodie scriptum legitur. At sapientes Hebraeorum nasutiores, animadvertentes inconvenientiam quandam in istis locis, scripserunt, aliter istos autores loqui debuisse, & secundum cohaerentiam propositi textus, sic vel sic scribere, sed pro eo maluisse sic scribere, & id sic efferre, ut illud hodie in textu est. Veluti Gen. 18:22, lectum scriptum, & Abraham adhuc stabat coram Domino. Itane? ubi legitur, inquiunt sapientes, quod Abraham venerit ad Dominum, & steterit coram eo; contrarium dicitur in praecedentibus, Deus scilicet venit ad Abraham, & dixit ad eum: Num ego celo ab Abrahamo, &tc. Clamor Sodomae & Gomorrhae magnus est &tc. Ideoque Moses scribere debuit, Et Dominus adhuc stabat coram Abrahamo. At ita serviliter de Deo loquí non decuit Mosen, unde* תיקון *correxit & mutavit stylum sermonis, honoris majoris causa, & dixit: Et Abraham adhuc stabat &tc. Hinc R. Salamo adjicit* היה לו לכתוב *scribendum ipsi (Mosi) erat, (seu) scribere debebat, Et Dominus stabat; non quod aliter sic scripsit antea, & postea id ab aliis scribis correctum sit, aut corruptum. Hinc R. Aben Ezra, ad aliquot loca irridet nasutos, inquiens, nullo tikkun opus fuisse, id est, nihil esse, quod nasuti isti sapientes putarint, autorem debuisse aliter ibi loqui vel scribere. Vide & eum Job. 32:3. Habes mysterium prolixe explicatum, in quo & multi Hebraeorum impegerunt. [Hucusque Buxtorffius.]*—Owen. Editor's translation. From a letter from Johann Buxtorf Sr. to Salomon Glass. Glass reproduces it in bk. 1 of his *Philologiae sacrae*, dating it to September 1623. See Glass, *Philologiae sacrae*, 40.

61 The issue being discussed here seems to be that there is no *Qere* or oral reading indicated in the margins of the Hebrew text of Ps. 22:17 in the Antwerp Polyglot, while the Septuagint clearly indicates that the oral reading was other than what was printed (the *Ketiv*).

62 One of the major early modern polyglot Bibles, the Antwerp Polyglot or Plantin Polyglot Bible was printed by Christopher Plantin between 1568 and 1573, involving substantial input from the Spanish Hebraist Arias Montanus.

Simyon de Mues[63] upon the place, pleads the substitution of י for ו to be a late corruption of the Jews; at least that כארו was the *Keri*, and was left out by them. Johannes Isaak[64] professes that when he was a Jew, he saw כארו in a book of his grandfather's: Buxtorfe [Sr.] affirms one to have been the *Ketib*, the other the *Keri*, and proves it from the Masora; and blames the Antwerpe Bibles for printing כארי in the line. With him agree, Genebrard,[65] Pagnin,[66] Vatablus,[67] Mercer,[68] Rivet, etc. Others contend that *Cari*,[69] "as a lion," ought to be retained; repeating ὑπὸ κοινοῦ,[70] הקיפוני the verb "They compassed me about"; affirming also that word to signify, "to tear, rend, and strike," so that the sense should be they "tear my hands and feet as a lion." So Voetius;[71] but that כארי cannot be here rendered *sicut leo*,[72] most evince, partly from the anomalous position of the prefix כ with *Camets*,[73] but chiefly from the Masora, affirming that that word is taken in another sense than it is used, (Isa. 38:13); where it expressly signifies "as a lion": the shorter determination is, that from the radix כרה by the epenthesis τοῦ א,[74] and the change which is used often of ו into י (as in the same manner it

63 Siméon Marotte de Muis (1587–1644) was a French Hebraist who objected to Morin's prefer- ence for the Samaritan Pentateuch over the Masoretic Text and is best known for defences of the Hebrew text.

64 In the text: *lib. 2. ad Lindan:*—Owen. See Johannes Isaac, *Defensio veritatis Hebraicae sacrarum Scripturarum* (Cologne: Jacob Soter, 1559), 61–122. Johannes Isaac (1515–1577) was a German Jewish convert to Christianity who was professor of Hebrew at Cologne.

65 Gilbert Génébrard (1535–1597) was a French Benedictine biblical commentator and Hebraist.

66 Santes Pagnino (1470–1541) was an Italian Dominican friar who was a leading philologist, notable for his translation of the Scriptures and his lexical work on the Hebrew text of the Old Testament.

67 Francis Vatablus, or François Vatable (late 1400s–1547) was a French humanist scholar of languages with notable skill in Hebrew and Greek.

68 Jean Mercier (ca. 1510–1570) was a French Hebraist, and a student of François Vatable. Among his students was the notable Huguenot theologian Philippe de Mornay.

69 A transliteration of כארו.

70 Gk. "by common [observation]," referring to something that is repeated by multiple authors.

71 In the text: *de insolubil: Scripturae.*—Owen. See "De Insolubilibus (ut vocant) Scripturae," in Gis- bertus Voetius, *Selectarum disputationum theologicarum* (Utrecht: J. a Waesberge, 1648–1669), pt. 1, disp. 4, pp. 47–63. Gisbertus Voetius (1589–1676) was an influential Dutch Reformed theologian who is famous for his polemical interaction with René Descartes and the impact of Cartesian philosophy on Reformed orthodoxy.

72 Lat. "as a lion."

73 Or kamatz, the Hebrew vowel ˌ that is transliterated "a."

74 The vowel under the first letter of the Hebrew word being discussed here has a different point- ing than would be usual if it were a noun prefixed by a preposition, as in the phrase, "*as* a lion." As such, in Ps. 22:17, this lends support for the word being a verb, "they pierced," and not a preposition attached to a noun. Owen goes on to describe the structural changes that have likely occurred to result in the verb being printed as it is, which is slightly different from what

is, Ezra 10[:44], and the last) in the third person plural, the preterperfect[75] tense of *kal*, is כארי *perfoderunt*, "they digged," or "pierced through my hands and my feet"; but to what purpose is this gleaning after the vintage of Mr. Pococke to this purpose, in his excellent *Miscellanies*?[76]

14. The place of old instanced in by Justine Martyr (Ps. 96:10).[77] Where he charges the Jews to have taken out these words ἀπὸ ξύλου "from the wood"; making the sense, "the Lord reigned from the wood," or the "tree," so pointing out the death of Christ on the cross, is exploded by all: for besides that he speaks of the LXX, not of the Hebrew text, it is evident that those words were foisted into some few copies of that translation, never being generally received, as is manifested by Fuller.[78] And it is a pretty story, that Arias Montanus tells us, of a learned man (I suppose he means Lindanus[79]) pretending that those words were found in a Hebrew copy of the Psalms of venerable antiquity beyond all exception here in England; which copy coming afterward to his hand, he found to be a spurious, corrupt novel transcript, wherein yet the pretended words are not to be found:[80] and I no way doubt, but that we want opportunity to search and sift some of the copies that men set up against the common reading in sundry places of the New Testament, we should find them, not one whit better, or of more worth than he found that copy of the Psalms.

---

one would normally expect for a kal (qal) third person plural verb. But since Hebrew writings have many instances of spelling variations, such changes are quite possible.

75 I.e., an archaic form of perfect tense.

76 See "Appendix Notarum Miscellanea," in Maimonides, *Porta Mosis, sive, Dissertationes aliquot a R. Mose Maimonide, suis in varias Mishnaioth*, ed. Edward Pococke (Oxford: H. Hall, 1655).

77 Justin Martyr (100–165) was a second-century Christian apologist famous for his *First* and *Second Apologies* as well as his *Dialogue with Trypho*. He sought to defend the historical and intellectual credibility of Christianity and was martyred during the reign of Emperor Marcus Aurelius.

78 In the text: *Miscellan: l. 3. Cap. 13.*—Owen. See Nicholas Fuller, *Miscellaneorum theologicorum, quibus non modo Scripturae divinae, set et aliorum classicorum auctorum plurima monumenta explicantur atq; illustrantur* (Strasbourg: sumptibus haeredum Lazari Zetneri, 1650), 352–57. Nicholas Fuller (ca. 1557–1626) was an English Hebraist and philologist most noted for his *Miscellaneorum theologicorum*.

79 Willem van der Lindt (1525–1588) was a Dutch bishop and Catholic apologist.

80 In the text: *Arias Mont. Apparat. De variis lec: Heb. & Mass.*—Owen. From Montanus's Apparatus to the Antwerp Polyglot Bible. See Arius Montanus, *Biblia sacra Hebraice, Chaldaice, Graece, et Latine* (Antwerp: Christoph. Plantinus, 1569–1572).

3

Of Various Lections in the Greek Copies of the New Testament

1. FOR VARIOUS LECTIONS in the Greek copies of the New Testament, we know with what diligence and industry, they have been collected by some, and what improvement has been made of those collections by others. Protestants for the most part have been the chiefest collectors of them; Stephanus,[1] Camerarius,[2] Beza,[3] Camero,[4] Grotius, Drusius,[5] Hensius,[6] D'Dieu,[7] Capellus, all following Erasmus, have had the prime hand in that work. Papists have ploughed with their heifer to disparage the original, and to cry up the Vulgar

1 Robert Estienne (1503–1559), also known as Robertus Stephanus, was a French Protestant classicist and printer who produced editions of the Greek New Testament, including the Textus Receptus (1550), the Vulgate and Erasmus's Latin translation of the New Testament, Pagninus's translation of the Old Testament, and Beza's Latin translation of the New Testament.

2 Joachim Camerarius (1500–1574) was a German Lutheran and classicist who was involved in seeking reconciliation between Protestant and Catholics.

3 Theodore Beza (1519–1605) was a French Reformed theologian who famously succeeded John Calvin in Geneva.

4 John Cameron (1579–1625) was a Scottish theologian most famous for his association with the Academy of Saumur and is known for his biblical annotations published as *Myrothecium evangelicum, hoc est, Novi Testamenti loca quamplurima ab eo.*

5 Johannes van den Driesche (1550–1616) was a Flemish Protestant Hebraist, who taught in Oxford, Leiden, and Franeker. Many of his exegetical contributions were included in the famous compilation of Latin biblical commentaries, *Critici sacri, sive, Doctissimorum sivorum in ss. Biblia annotationes et tractatus.*

6 Daniël Heinsius (1580–1655) was a Dutch classicist and Leiden professor who is best known for his *De tragica constitutione* and his Latin orations. He was a student of the French classicist Joseph Scaliger.

7 Lodewijk de Dieu (1590–1642) was a Dutch Hebraist, biblical exegete, and chronologist who was governor of Walloon College, Leiden.

Latin;[8] a specimen of their endeavors we have in the late virulent *Exercitations* of Morinus. At first very few were observed. What a heap or bulk they are now swelled unto, we see in this *Appendix*.[9] The collection of them makes up a book bigger than the New Testament itself. Of those that went before, most gave us only what they found in some particular copies that themselves were possessors of; some those only which they judged of importance, or that might make some pretense to be considered whether they were proper or no; here we have all, that by any means could be brought to hand, and that whether they are tolerably attested for various lections or no; for as to any contribution unto the better understanding of the Scripture from them; it cannot be pretended. And whither this work may yet grow, I know not.

DISTINGUISHING DIVERSE LECTIONS FROM MERE COPYING ERRORS AND THE DANGER OF REGARDING ERRORS AS GENUINE LECTIONS

2. That there are in some copies of the New Testament, and those some of them of some good antiquity, diverse readings, in things or words of less importance is acknowledged; the proof of it lies within the reach of most, in the copies that we have; and I shall not solicit the reputation of those who have afforded us others, out of their own private furniture. That they have been all needlessly heaped up together, if not to an eminent scandal is no less evident. Let us then take a little view of their rise and importance.

3. That the Grecian, was once as it were the vulgar language of the whole world of Christians is known. The writing of the New Testament in that language in part found it so, and in part made it so. What thousands? Yea, what millions of copies of the New Testament were then in the world, all men promiscuously reading and studying of the Scripture, cannot be reckoned. That so many transcriptions, most of them by private persons, for private use,

---

8 I.e., the Vulgate, Jerome's fourth-century Latin translation of the Bible, which was recognized as the authoritative Latin text by the Catholic Church at the Council of Trent.

9 Owen is referring to the collection of variants by various Protestant scholars on the Greek editions of the New Testament in chap. 16 of the *Appendix* volume of the London Polyglot. See Brian Walton, *Biblia sacra polyglotta*, 6 vols. (London: Thomas Roycroft, 1653–1657), vol. 6, chap. 16, pp. 1–36b. Grotius's collection is contained in chap. 15. See Walton, *Biblia sacra polyglotta*, vol 6, chap. 15, pp. 47a–56b. François Luc de Bruges's collection is also contained in chap. 17, including annotations on both Greek and Latin editions of the New Testament. See Walton, *Biblia sacra polyglotta*, vol. 6, chap. 17, pp. 1a–36b. From Hapsburg Netherlands, François Luc de Bruges (c. 1548–1619) was a Catholic biblical scholar who is noted for his contribution of critical marginalia to the 1574 Leuven edition of the Vulgate.

having a standard of correction in their public assemblies ready to relieve their mistakes, should be made without some variation, is, ἐκ τῶν ἀδυνάτων.[10] From the copies of the first ages, others in the succeeding have been transcribed, according as men had opportunity. From those which are come down to the hands of learned men in this latter age, whereof very few or none at all, are of any considerable antiquity, have men made it their business to collect the various readings we speak of; with what usefulness and serviceableness to the churches of God, others that look on must be allowed their liberty to judge. We know the vanity, curiosity, pride, and naughtiness of the heart of man: how ready we are to please ourselves, with things that seem singular and remote from the observation of the many; and how ready to publish them as evidences of our learning and diligence, let the fruit and issue be what it will. Hence it is come to pass, not to question the credit of any man speaking of his manuscripts, (which is wholly swallowed in this *Appendix*) that whatever varying word, syllable, or tittle, could be by any observed, wherein any book, though of yesterday, varies from the common received copy, though manifestly a mistake, superfluous, or deficient, inconsistent with the sense of the place, yea barbarous, is presently imposed on us as a various lection.

4. As then I shall not speak anything to derogate from the worth of their labor who have gathered all these various readings into one body or volume, so I presume I may take liberty without offense to say, I should more esteem of theirs, who would endeavor to search and trace out these pretenders, to their several originals, and rejecting the spurious brood that has now spawned itself over the face of so much paper, that ought by no means to be brought into competition with the common reading, would reduce them to such a necessary number, whose consideration might be of some other use, than merely to create a temptation to the reader, that nothing is left sound and entire in the word of God.

However now Satan seems to have exerted the utmost of his malice, men of former ages the utmost of their negligence, of these latter ages of their diligence, the result of all which, we have in the present collection in this *Appendix*, with them that rightly ponder things there arises nothing at all to the prejudice of our assertion, as may possibly, God assisting, be further manifested hereafter in the particular consideration of some, or all of these diverse readings therein exhibited unto us. Those which are of importance, have been already considered by others; especially Glassius.[11]

---

10 Gk. "one of those things that is impossible."

11 In the text: *Tract.* 1. *lib.* 1.—Owen. See Salomon Glass, *Philologiae sacrae, qua totius sacrosanctae, Veteris et Novi Testamenti Scripturae, tum stylus et literatura tum sensus et genuinae interpretationis ratio expenditur* (Frankfurt : Zacharius Hertelius, 1653), 1–124.

GENERAL OBSERVATIONS ON THE NEW TESTAMENT LECTIONS CONTAINED IN THE *APPENDIX*

5. It is evident that the design of this *Appendix* was to gather together everything of this sort, that might by any means be afforded; at the present, that the reader may not be too much startled at the fruit of their diligence, whose work and labor it was, I shall only remark concerning it some few things that on a general view of it occur unto me.

6. Firstly, then, here is professedly no choice made, nor judgment used in discerning, which may indeed be called various lections; but all differences whatever that could be found in any copies, printed or written, are equally given out. Hence many differences that had been formerly rejected by learned men for open corruptions, are here tendered us again. The very first observation in the treatise next printed unto this collection in the *Appendix* itself, rejects one of the varieties, as a corruption.[12] So have some others of them been by Arias Montanus, Camero, and many more. It is not every variety or difference in a copy that should presently be cried up for a various reading. A man might with as good color and pretense take all the printed copies he could get, of various editions, and gathering out the *errata typographica*,[13] print them for various lections, as give us many, I shall say the most of those in this *Appendix*, under that name. It may be said indeed, that the composers of this *Appendix* found it not incumbent on them, to make any judgment of the readings, which de facto they found in the copies they perused, but merely to represent what they so found, leaving the judgment of them unto others; I say also it may be so; and therefore as I do not reflect on them, nor their diligence, so I hope they nor others, will not be offended, that I give this notice of what judgment remains yet to be made concerning them.

7. Secondly, whereas Beza, who is commonly blamed by men of all sides and parties, for making too bold upon various lections, has professedly stigmatized his own manuscript, that he sent unto Cambridge, as so corrupt in the Gospel of Luke, that he durst[14] not publish the various lections of it, for fear of offense and scandal, however he thought it had not fallen into the hands of heretics, that had designedly depraved it; we have here, if I mistake not, all the corruptions of that copy given us as various readings; for though I have not seen the copy itself, yet the swelling of the various lections in that Gospel, into a bulk as big or bigger, than the collection of all the New Testament besides the

---

12 Owen appears to be referring to the de Bruge's collection of Greek New Testament lections that is contained in the subsequent chapter of the *Appendix* volume. See Walton, *Biblia sacra polyglotta*, vol. 6, chap. 17, pp. 1a–36b.

13 Lat. "typographical errors."

14 I.e., dare.

[other] Gospels and Acts, wherein that copy is cited 1,440 times, puts it out of all question that so we are dealt withal: now if this course be taken, and every stigmatized copy may be searched for differences, and these presently printed as various readings, there is no doubt but we may have enough of them to frighten poor unstable souls into the arms of the pretended infallible guide;[15] I mean as to the use that will be made of this work, by such persons as Morinus.

8. Thirdly, I am not without apprehensions that *opere in longo obrepsit somnus*,[16] and that while the learned collectors had their hands and minds busied about other things, some mistakes did fall into this work of gathering these various lections. Some things I meet withal in it, that I profess, I cannot bring to any good consistency among themselves; to let pass particular instances, and insist on one only of a more general and eminent importance. In the entrance unto this collection an account is given us of the ancient copies, out of which these observations are made; among the rest one of them is said to be an ancient copy in the library of Emmanuel College in Cambridge: this is noted by the letters "Em": throughout the whole collection. Now whereas it is told us in these preliminary cautions and observations, that it contains only Paul's Epistles, I wonder how it is come to pass, that so many various lections in the Gospels and Acts, as in the farrago[17] itself are fixed on the credit of that book, could come to be gathered out of a copy of Paul's Epistles; certainly here must be some mistake, either in the learned authors of the previous directions, or by those employed to gather the varieties following; and it may be supposed that that mistake goes not alone; so that upon a further consideration of particulars, it may be, we shall not find them so clearly attested, as at first view they seem to be. It would indeed be a miracle, if in a work of that variety many things should not escape the eye of the most diligent observer.

SOME SUGGESTIONS FOR REDUCING
THE NUMBER OF LECTIONS

9. I am not then upon the whole matter, out of hopes but that upon a diligent review of all these various lections, they may be reduced to a less offensive,

---

15 Owen is alluding here to the Papacy.
16 Lat. "sleep has crept on a long labor." This is an allusion to a remark in Horace's *Ars poetica*, line 360: *verum operi longo fas est obrepere somnum*. "When a work is long, a drowsy mood may well creep over it." For the Latin text and English translation, see Horace, *Satires. Epistles. The Art of Poetry*, trans. H. Rushton Fairclough, Loeb Classical Library 194 (Cambridge, MA: Harvard University Press, 1926), 480–81.
17 I.e., hotchpotch.

and less formidable number; let it be remembered that the vulgar copy we use was the public possession of many generations; that upon the invention of printing, it was in actual authority throughout the world, with them that used and understood that language, as far as anything appears to the contrary. Let that then pass for the standard which is confessedly its right and due, and we shall God assisting quickly see, how little reason there is to pretend such varieties of readings, as we are now surprised withal.¶

For (1) let those places be separated, which are not sufficiently attested unto, so as to pretend to be various lections: it being against all pretense of reason, that every mistake of every obscure private copy, perhaps not above two or three hundred years old, (or if older) should be admitted as a various lection, against the concurrent consent of it may be all others that are extant in the world, and that without any congruity of reason, as to the sense of the text where it is fallen out. Men may if they please take pains to inform the world, wherein such and such copies are corrupted, or mistaken, but to impose their known failings on us as various lections, is a course not to be approved.

(2) Let the same judgment, and that deservedly, pass on all those different places, which are altogether inconsiderable, consisting in accents or the change of a letter, not in the least entrenching on the sense of the place, or giving the least intimation of any other sense to be possibly gathered out of them, but what is in the approved reading; to what end should the minds of men be troubled with them or about them, being evident mistakes of the scribes, and of no importance at all.

(3) Let them also be removed from the pretenses which carry their own convictions along with them, that they are spurious, either (1) by their superfluity or redundancy of unnecessary words, or (2) [by] their deficiency in words, evidently necessary to the sense of their places, or (3) [by] their incoherence with the text in their several stations, or (4) [by] evidence of being intended as expository of difficulties, having been moved and assoiled[18] by some of the ancients upon the places, and their resolutions being intimated; or (5) are foisted out of the LXX, as many places out of the New [Testament] have been asserted into that copy of the Old; or (6) are taken out of one place in the same penman, and are used in another, or (7) are apparently taken out of one Gospel, and supplied in another, to make out the sense of the place; or (8) have been corrected by the Vulgar Latin, which has often fallen out in some copies, as Lucas Brugensis shows us on Matthew 17:2, Mark 1:38, 7:4,

18 I.e., cleared.

and sundry other places;[19] or (9) arise out of copies apparently corrupted, like that of Beza in Luke, and that in the Vatican, boasted of by Huntley the Jesuit, which Lucas Brugensis affirms to have been changed by the Vulgar Latin, and which was written and corrected, as Erasmus says, about the [time of the] Council of Florence,[20] when an agreement was patched up between the Greeks and Latins; or (10) are notoriously corrupted by old heretics, as 1 John 5:7. Unto which heads, many, yea the most of the various lections collected in this *Appendix* may be referred; I say if this work might be done with care and diligence (whereunto I earnestly exhort some in this university, who have both ability and leisure for it) it would quickly appear, how small the number is of those varieties in the Greek copies of the New Testament, which may pretend unto any consideration under the state and title of various lections; and of how very little importance they are, to weaken in any measure my former assertion concerning the care and providence of God in the preservation of his word. But this is a work of more time and leisure, than at present I am possessor of; what is to come, $\theta\varepsilon o\tilde{u}$ $\dot{\varepsilon}v$ $\gamma o\acute{u}v\alpha\sigma\iota$ $\kappa\varepsilon\tilde{\iota}\tau\alpha\iota$.[21] In the meantime I doubt not, but to hear tidings from Rome concerning this variety; no such collection having as yet been made in the world.

---

19 For de Bruges's comments on the Greek lections of Matt. 17:2; Mark 1:38 and 7:4, respectively, see Walton, *Biblia sacra polyglotta*, vol. 6, chap. 17, pp. 3b, 5a, 6b.

20 The Council of Florence was an ecumenical council of the Catholic Church, held from 1431–1445. It ended in a short-lived agreement to reunify the Eastern and Western churches.

21 Gk. "lies on the knees of God," an allusion to a line from Homer's *Iliad*, XVII, 514, with very slight variation to the original, where Owen has altered the plural $\theta\varepsilon\tilde{\omega}v$ ("gods") to the singular $\theta\varepsilon o\tilde{u}$ ("God"). For the Greek text and an English translation, see Homer, *Iliad*, vol. 2, *Books 13–14*, trans. A. T. Murray and William F. Wyatt, Loeb Classical Library 171 (Cambridge, MA: Harvard University Press, 1999), 267.

The General Premises of the London Polyglot Bible concerning the Origin and Antiquity of the Hebrew Vowel Points

1. General premises. 2[–3]. Opinions prejudicial to the authority of the originals in the *Prolegomena*, enumerated. 4. The just consequences of these premises. 5. Others engaged in these opinions: of Capellus. 6. Of Origen, Cimenius, Arias Montanus's editions of the Bible.

HAVING NOW DECLARED in what sense, and with what allowance as to various lections, I maintain the assertion laid down in the foregoing treatise, concerning the providential preservation of the whole book of God, so that we may have full assurance, that we enjoy the whole revelation of his will, in the copies abiding among us, I shall now proceed to weigh what may be objected further, (beyond what has already been insisted on) against the truth of it, from the *Prolegomena* and *Appendix* to the *Biblia polyglotta*, at the entrance of our discourse proposed to consideration.

OPINIONS PREJUDICIAL TO THE AUTHORITY OF THE ORIGINALS IN THE *PROLEGOMENA* ENUMERATED

2. To[1] speak somewhat of them in general, I must crave leave to say, and it being but the representation of men's avowed judgments, I hope I may

---

1 Original begins this section with "1.," but the list does not appear to continue beyond this.

188 OF THE INTEGRITY

say without offense, that together with many high and honorable expressions concerning the originals, setting aside the incredible figment, of the Jews corrupting the Bible out of hatred to the Christians, which being first supposed by Justin Martyr (though he speaks of the Septuagint only) has scarce found one or two since to own it, but is rejected by the universality of learned men, ancient and modern, unless some few Papists mad upon their idols, and the thesis preferring in general this or that translation above the original, there is no opinion that I know of, that was ever ventilated among Christians, tending to the depression of the worth, or impairing the esteem of the Hebrew copies, which is not directly, or by just consequence owned in these *Prolegomena*. Thence it is contended that the present Hebrew character is not that used by God himself, and in the old church before the captivity of Babylon, but it is the Chaldean, the other being left to the Samaritans; that the points, or vowels and accents are a late invention of the Tiberian Masoretes, long after sundry translations were extant in the world; that the *Keri* and *Ketib* are critical notes, consisting partly of various lections gathered by the late Masoretes and Rabbins; that considering how ofttimes in likelihood translators read the text before the invention of the points and accents, the present reading may be corrected and amended by them, and that because the old translators had other copies, or different copies from them which we now enjoy. That where gross faults are crept into the Hebrew text, men may by their own conjectures find out various lections, whereby they may be amended; and to this purpose an instance of such various lections, or rather corrections of the original is in the *Appendix* exhibited unto us out of Grotius.[2] That the books of the Scriptures having had the fate of other books; by passing through the hands of many transcribers, they have upon them the marks of their negligence, ignorance and sloth.

3. Now truly I cannot but wish that some other way had been found out to give esteem and reputation to this noble collection of translations, than by espousing these opinions, so prejudicial to the truth and authority of the originals. And it may be justly feared, that where one will relieve himself against the uncertainty of the originals, by the consideration of the various translations here exhibited unto us, being such, as upon trial they will be found to be, many will be ready to question the foundation of all.

---

2 Hugo Grotius's annotations are contained in chap. 15 of the *Appendix*. See Brian Walton, *Biblia sacra polyglotta*, 6 vols. (London: Thomas Roycroft, 1653–1657), vol. 6, chap. 15, pp. 37a–58b.

THE JUST CONSEQUENCES OF THESE PREMISES

4. It is true, the learned prefacer owns not those wretched consequences, that some have labored to draw from these premises; yet it must be acknowledged also, that sufficient security against the lawful deriving those consequences from these premises, is not tendered unto us; he says not, that, because this is the state of the Hebrew language and Bible, therefore all things in it are dubious and uncertain, easy to be turned unto various senses, not fit to be a rule for the trial of other translations, though he knows full well who thinks this a just consequence from the opinion of the novelty of the vowels; and himself grants that all our knowledge of the Hebrew is taken from the translation of the LXX, as he is quoted to that purpose by Morinus.[3] He concludes not, that on these accounts we must rely upon as infallible living judge, and the translation that he shall commend unto us; though he knows full well who do so; and himself gives it for a rule,[4] that at the correction of the original, we have the consent of the guides of the church: I could desire then I say, that sufficient security may be tendered us against these inferences, before the premises be embraced; seeing great and wise men, as we shall further see anon, do suppose them naturally and necessarily to flow from them.

OTHERS ENGAGED IN THESE OPINIONS: CAPELLUS

5. It is confessed that some learned men, even among the Protestants, have heretofore vented these or some of these paradoxes: especially Capellus in his *Arcanum punctationis revelatum*,[5] *Critica sacra*,[6] and other treatises: in the defense whereof, as I hear, he still labors, being unwilling to suffer loss in the fruit of so great pains. What will become of his reply unto Buxtorfius [Sr.] in the defense of his *Critica*, I know not: reports are that it is finished; and it is thought he must once more fly to the Papists by the help of his son, a great zealot among them, as he did with his *Critica* to get it published. The generality of learned men among Protestants are not yet infected with this leaven. Nor indeed do I find his boldness in conjecturing approved in these *Prolegomena*. But let it be free for men to make known their judgments in

3   In the text: *Praefat. ad opusc: Hebrae: Samarit.*—Owen. See "Praefatio" in Jean Morin, *Opuscula Hebraeo-Samaritica* (Paris: Gaspardus Metras, 1657).
4   Original has "it a for rule."
5   See Louis Cappel, *Sôd han-nîqqûd han-nigle, hoc est arcanum punctationis revelatum* [...] *edita a Thoma Erpenio* (Leiden: Johannes Maire, 1624).
6   See Louis Cappel, *Critica sacra, sive De variis quae in sacris Veteris Testamenti libris occurrunt lectionibus* (Paris: S&G Cramoisy, 1650).

the severals mentioned. It has been so, and may it abide so still. Had not this great and useful work been prefaced with the stating of them, it had not been of public concernment (as now it seems to be) to have taken notice of them.

OF ORIGEN, XIMENIUS, AND MONTANUS'S EDITIONS OF THE BIBLE

6. Besides, it is not known whither this inconvenience will grow. Origen in his *Octapla*,[7] as was declared, fixed the Hebrew original as the rule and measure of all translations. In the reviving of that kind of work by Ximenius in the Complutensian Bibles,[8] its station is left unto it. Arias Montanus who followed in their steps (concerning whose performances under his master the king of Spain I may say for sundry excellencies, *Nil oriturum alias, nil ortum tale*[9]) was religiously careful to maintain the purity of the originals, publishing the "Hebrew verity" (as it is called by Hierome, Austin,[10] and others of the ancients) as the rule of examining by it all translations whatever; for which he is since accused of ignorance by a petulant Jesuit, that never deserved to carry his books after him.[11] Michael Le Jay has given a turn to this progress, and in plain terms exalts a corrupt translation above the originals; and that upon the principle under consideration, as is abundantly manifest from Morinus.[12] And if this change of judgment which has been long insinuating itself, by the curiosity and boldness of critics, should break in also upon

7   Original has "octupla."
8   I.e., the so-called Complutensian Polyglot Bible (1514–1517). This was the first of the major polyglot Bibles of the early modern period, patronized by Francisco Jiménez de Cisneros and published by the Complutense University in the Spanish city Alcalá de Henares. See *Vetus Testamentum multiplici lingua nunc primo impressum* (Alcalá de Henares: Arnao Guillén de Brocar, 1514–1517). Francisco Jiménez de Cisneros (1436–1517) was a Spanish Cardinal and statesman, regent of Spain on two occasions, and most famous for his involvement in the Grand Inquisition, his promotion of the Crusades, and for his patronage of the Complutensian Polyglot.
9   Lat. "No one else like him will arise or has arisen." This is an allusion to a line from Horace's *Epistles*, bk. 2, ep. 1, line 17. See Horace, *Satires. Epistles, The Art of Poerty*, H. Rushton Fairclough, Loeb Classical Library 194 (Cambridge, MA: Harvard University Press, 1926), 396–97.
10 Augustine of Hippo (354–430) was the most famous and influential theologian of the Latin patristic era. Aside from his enormous corpus of writings, he is well known for his preference for the Septuagint translation of the Old Testament in his interactions with Jerome over the translation of the Vulgate.
11 In the margin: Morin. *Exercit. De Heb. Text. Sinc.* Lib. 1. Ex. 1. Cap. 4.—Owen. See Morin, *Exercitationes biblicae de Hebraei Graecique textus sinceritate: Pars prior* (Paris: Antonius Vitray, 1633), 19b–23b, esp. 20b–21a.
12 Owen is referring to the so-called Paris Polyglot Bible. As noted above, while the introduction to this Bible is written under Lejay's name, Owen suspects it was actually written by Morin.

the Protestant world, and be avowed in public works, it is easy to conjecture what the end will be. We went from Rome under the conduct of the purity of the originals, I wish none have a mind to return thither again under the pretense of their corruption.

5

Evaluating the Matter concerning the Origin and Antiquity of the Hebrew Vowel Points

1. The original of the points proposed to consideration in particular.
2. The importance of the points to the right understanding of
the Scripture; the testimony of Morinus, Junius, Johannes Isaac,
Cevallerius, and others. 3. The use made by the Papists of the opinion
of the novelty of the points. 4. The importance of the points further
manifested. The extreme danger of making the Hebrew punctuation
arbitrary. 5. That danger evinced by instance. 6. No relief against that
danger on the grounds of the opinion considered. 7. The authors of
the Hebrew punctuation according to the *Prolegomena*: who and what.
Morinus his folly. The improbability of this pretense. 8. The state of the
Jews, the supposed inventors of the points after the destruction of the
temple. 9. Two attempts made by them to restore their religion. The
former under Barchochab with its issue. 10. The second under R. Juda,
with its issue. 11. The rise and foundation of the Talmuds. 12. The
state of the Jews upon and after the writing of the Talmuds. 13. Their
rancor against Christ. 14. Who the Tiberian Massoretes were, that are
the supposed authors of the Hebrew punctuation: their description.
15. That figment rejected. 16. The late testimony of Dr Lightfoot to this
purpose. 17. The rise of the opinion of the novelty of the points. Of
Elias Levita. The value of his testimony in this case. 18. Of the validity
of the testimony of the Jewish Rabbins. 19. Some considerations about
the antiquity of the points; the first from the nature of the punctuation
itself, in reference unto grammatical rules. 20. [The second] from the
Chaldee Paraphrase, and integrity of the Scripture as now pointed.[1]

---

1   The original duplicates this chapter as "IV," affecting the numbering of subsequent chapters.

THE ORIGINAL OF THE POINTS PROPOSED
TO CONSIDERATION IN PARTICULAR

1. This being in my apprehension the state of things among us, I hope I may without offense proceed to the consideration of the particulars before mentioned, from whence it is feared that objections may arise against the purity and self-evidencing power of the Scriptures pleaded for in the foregoing treatise. That which in the first place was mentioned, is the assertion of the points, or vowels and accents to be a novel invention of some Rabbins of Tiberias in Palestina. This the learned author of the *Prolegomena* defends with Capellus his arguments, and such other additions as he was pleased to make use of. To clear up the concernments of our truth in this particular, it will be necessary to consider: (1) What influence in the right understanding of the text these points have, and necessarily must have. (2) What is their original, or who [*sic*] their invention is ascribed unto in these *Prolegomena*. As to the assertive part of this controversy, or the vindication of their true sacred original, some other occasion may call for additions to what is now (by the way) insisted on. And as I shall not oppose them who maintain that they are coevous[2] with the letters, which are not a few of the most learned Jews and Christians; so I nowise doubt, but that as we now enjoy them, we shall yet manifest that they were completed by אנשי כנסת הגדולה, "the men of the great synagogue," Ezra and his companions, guided therein by the infallible direction of the Spirit of God.[3]

THE IMPORTANCE OF THE POINTS TO THE
RIGHT UNDERSTANDING OF SCRIPTURE:
THE TESTIMONY OF MORINUS, JUNIUS,
JOHANNES ISAAC, CAVALLERUS, AND OTHERS

2. That we may not seem ἀεροβατεῖν,[4] or to contend *de lana caprina*,[5] the importance of these points as to the right understanding of the word of God, is first to be considered, and that from testimony and the nature of the thing itself. Marinus, in his preface to his Hebrew Lexicon, tells us that without the

---

2   I.e., of the same age.
3   Like the Buxtorfs, Owen believes the vowel points were added through the Spirit's infallible guidance when the Old Testament canon was formally closed during the Men of the Great Assembly. Cf., e.g., Johann Buxtorf Sr., *Tiberias, sive Commentarius Masorethicus triplex* (Basel: J. J. Deckeri, 1665), 109–10. Here he respectfully acknowledges that with the older Jewish tradition, other Protestants take the view that they were "coevous" with the original consonants.
4   Gk. "to walk on air."
5   Lat. "concerning goat's wool," a Latin expression referring to a futile discussion.

points, "no certain truth can be learned from the Scriptures in that language, seeing all things may be read divers ways, so that there will be more confusion in that one tongue, than was amongst all those at Babylon."[6] Morinus plainly affirms that it is so indeed; instancing in the word דבר,[7] which as it may be variously pointed, has at least eight several significations, and some of them as distant from one another, as heaven and earth. And to make evident the uncertainty of the language on this account, he gives the like instance in *c*, *r*, *s*, in Latin. Junius,[8] in the close of his animadversions on Bellar[mine][9] commends that saying of Johannes Isaac against Lindan:[10] "He that reads the Scriptures without points, is like a man that rides a horse ἀχάλινος,[11] without a bridle; he may be carried he knows not whither."[12] Radulphus Cevallerius[13] goes farther,[14] "As for the antiquity of the vowels and accents (says he) I am of their opinion, who maintain the Hebrew language as the exact pattern of all others, to have been plainly written (with them) from the beginning: seeing that they who are otherwise minded, do not only make doubtful the authority

---

6   In the text (enclosed within parentheses): *Nulla igitur certa doctrina poterit tradi de hac lingua, cum omnia possint diversimodo legi, ut futura sit major confusio unicae hujus linguae, quam illa Babylonis.*—Owen. Owen's translation is immediately preceding in the text. Quotation marks have been inserted. For the Latin text, see "Praefatio," in Marcus Marinus, *Arca noe, thesaurus linguae sanctae novus* (Venice: Iohannis Degara, 1593), 1:*3. Marco Marini (1542–1594) was an Italian Augustinian Hebraist, who was also the Vatican censor of Hebrew books.

7   Heb. "word."

8   Franciscus Junius, the elder (1545–1602), a student of John Calvin, was a widely influential theologian, pastor and biblical scholar throughout Europe. His contributions to Reformed theology include work on the Belgic Confession, the Tremellius-Junius Bible translation, and his *De vera theologia*.

9   In the text: *de verbo Dei. lib. 2. cap. 2.*—Owen. See footnote below following the quotation. Robert Bellarmine (1542–1621) was an Italian Jesuit Cardinal and polemicist, prominent for his contribution to the Counter-Reformation.

10 I.e., Willem van der Lindt.

11 Gk. "unbridled."

12 Owen is referring to this statement of Junius, which he partially quotes as indicated: *Optime Ioannes Isaac dicebat eum qui sine punctis et accidentibus Scripturam legit, similem esse homini equitanti equum* ἀχάλινος. See Franciscus Junius, *Animadversiones ad controversiam primam Christianae fidei, de verbo Dei* (Leiden: C. Raphelengius, 1600), 99.

13 Antoine Rodolphe Chevallier (1523–1572) was a Huguenot Hebraist who came to England under the reign of Edward VI and was eventually appointed Regius Professor of Hebrew at Cambridge.

14 In the text: *Rudiment. ling. Heb. cap. 4. Quod superest de vocalium & accentuum antiquitate, eorum sententiae subscribo, qui linguam Hebraeam, tanquam omnium aliarum* ἀρχέτυπον *absolutissimum plane ab initio scriptam confirmant: quandoquidem qui contra sentiunt, non modo authoritatem sacrae Scripturae dubiam efficiunt, sed radicitus (meo quidem judicio) convellunt, quod absque vocalibus & distinctionum notis, nihil certi firmique habeat.*—Owen. Owen's translation follows in the text. He appears to be citing the edition that was revised by Pierre Chevallier. See Antoine Rudolphe Chevallier and Pierre Chevallier, *Rudimenta Hebraicae linguae* (Geneva: Franciscus Le Preux, 1590), 21.

of the Scriptures, but in my judgment wholly pluck it up by the roots. For without the vowels and notes of distinction, it has nothing firm and certain." In this man's judgment, (which also is my own) it is evident to all, how obnoxious to the opinion now opposed the truth is that I am contending for. To these also may be added the great Buxtorfs, father [Sr.][15] and son [Jr.],[16] Gerard,[17] Glassius,[18] Voetius,[19] Flac. Illyric.,[20] Polan.,[21] Whitaker,[22] Hassret,[23] Wolthius.[24]

---

15 In the margin: *Buxtorf. Tiberius.*—Owen. See Buxtorf Sr., *Tiberias.*
16 In the margin: *De Antiquitate punct.*—Owen. See Johann Buxtorf Jr., *Tractatus de punctorum vocalium* (Basel: L. König, 1648). Johann Buxtorf Jr. (1599–1664) was a Protestant Hebraist and son of Johann Buxtorf Sr. He was involved in the eventual publication of his father's *Concordantiae bibliorum Hebraicae* and *lexicon Chaldaicum, Talmudicum et rabbinicum.* He is well known for his polemical engagement with Louis Cappel over the origin of the Hebrew vowel points, arguing with his father for an early dating that traces their origin to the great synagogue called by Ezra (the so-called Men of the Great Assembly) in the period from around 516 to 332 BC.
17 In the margin: *Exeg. loc. com. Tom. i. de Sa: Sc.*—Owen. See "De Scriptura sacra" in, Johann Gerhard, *Loci theologici,* 9 vols. (Berlin: Gust. Schlawitz, 1863–1885), 1:13–240. Johann Gerhard Sr. (1582–1637) was a German Lutheran theologian, famous for his opposition to Roman Catholicism and his *Loci theologici.*
18 In the margin: *de Text. Heb. Puri:*—Owen. See "De integritate et puritate Hebraei V. Test. codicis" (bk. 1, tract. 1), in Salomon Glass, *Philologiae sacrae, qua totius sacrosanctae, Veteris et Novi Testamenti Scripturae, tum stylus et literatura tum sensus et genuinae interpretationis ratio expenditur* (Frankfurt: Zacharius Hertelius, 1653), 1–124.
19 In the margin: *loc. com. quousque se extendat. Author S. Sa.*—Owen. See "De quaestione hac: quousque se extendat auctoritas Scripturae," in Voetius, *Selectarum disputationum,* pt. 1, disp. 3, pp. 29–47.
20 In the margin: *Clav. Sa: p. 2. Trac. 6.*—Owen. See Matthias Illyricus Flacius, *Clavis Scripturae, seu de sermone sacrarum literarum,* 2 vols. (Basil: per Paulum Quecum, 1567), 2:396–525. Matthias Flacius Illyricus (1520–1575) was a Lutheran theologian who was professor of New Testament at Jena. He is best known for his outlying views about the impact of the fall on the image of God but also made substantial theological contributions such as his *Clavis Scripturae.*
21 Amandus Polanus von Polansdorf (1561–1610), a German Reformed theologian, who was professor of Old Testament and later rector of Basel University. He is best known for his *Syntagma theologiae Christianae:* Amandus Polanus von Polansdorf, *Syntagma theologiae Christianae* (Hanover: Wechel, 1609).
22 William Whitaker (1548–1595) was an Elizabethan Protestant scholar and master of St. John's College, Cambridge, who was well known for his Reformed convictions and as an active opponent of Catholic doctrine.
23 In the margin: *de Templ. Ezec.*—Owen. See Matthias Hafenreffer, *Templum Ezechielis, sive In ix. postrema prophetae capita commentarius* (Tübingen: T. Werlin, 1613). Matthias Hafenreffer (1561–1619) was a German Lutheran theologian and professor at Tübingen best known for his *Loci theologici.*
24 In the margin: *disputant: Jenae.*—Owen. See Johann Jakob Wolf, *Dissertatio de editionis Hebraicae Veteris Testamenti authentica veritate* (Zurich: apud J. Jacobum Bodmerum, 1635). Johann Jakob Wolf (1521–1572) was a Swiss Reformed theologian who was professor of theology at the Zürich Academy and an associate of Heinrich Bullinger.

THE USE MADE BY THE PAPISTS OF THE
OPINION OF THE NOVELTY OF THE POINTS

3. It is well known what use the Papists make of this conceit. Bellarmine maintains that there are errors crept into the original by this addition of the points.[25] "These two opinions being confuted, the third remains which I suppose to be most true, which is that the Hebrew Scriptures are not universally corrupted by the malicious work of the Jews, nor yet are wholly pure and entire, but that they have errors, which have crept in partly by the negligence and ignorance of the transcribers, partly by the ignorance of the Rabbins who added the points: whence we may if we please reject the points and read otherwise."

In the voluminous opposition to the truth made by that learned man, I know nothing more perniciously spoken: nor do yet know how his inference can be avoided, on the hypothesis in question. To what purpose this insinuation is made by him is well known, and his companions in design exactly declare it. That their Hebrew text be corrected by the Vulgar Latin, is the express desire of Gregory de Valentia:[26] and that because the church has approved that translation, it being corrected (says Huntly[27]) by Hierome before the invention of points. But this is put out of doubt by Morinus, who from hence argues the Hebrew tongue to be a very nose of wax, to be turned by men which way they please: and to be so given of God on purpose, that men might subject their consciences to their infallible church.[28] Great has been the endeavor of this sort of men, wherein they have left no stone unturned, to decry the originals. Some of them cry out that the Old Testament is corrupted by the Jews, as (1) Leo Castrius,[29] (2) Gordonius

---

25 In the text: *de Verb. Dei: lib. 2. cap. 2. Hisce duabus sententiis refutatis restat tertia quam ego verissimam puto, quae est, Scripturas Hebraicas non esse in universum depravatas opera & malitia Judaeorum, nec tamen omnino esse integras & puras, sed habere suos errores quosdam, qui partim irrepserint negligentia & ignorantia librariorum, &c: partim ignorantia Rabbinorum qui puncta addiderunt: itaque possumus si volumus puncta detrahere, & aliter legere.*—Owen. Owen's translation follows. This quotation is his abridged version of the original. See Robert Bellarmine, *Opera omnia*, 6 vols. (Naples: Josephum Giuliano, 1856–1862), 1:65a–b.

26 In the text: *Tom. 1. disput. 5. qu. 3.*—Owen. See Gregorio de Valentia, *Commentariorum theologicorum*, 4 vols. (Lyon: Horatio Cardon, 1609), 1:1047–74. Gregorio de Valentia (1550–1603) was a Spanish Jesuit most famous for his *Commentariorum theologicorum* on Thomas Aquinas's *Summa theologiae.*

27 James Gordon (1543–1620), referred to by Owen as Huntley the Jesuit, was a Scottish-born Jesuit scholar of Hebrew and theology and also known as a zealous apologist for the Catholic cause.

28 In the text: *Exercit. l. 1. Exer. 1. c. 2.*—Owen. See Jean Morin, *Exercitationes biblicae de Hebraei Graecique textus sinceritate: Pars prior* (Paris: Antonius Vitray, 1633), 13–30.

29 In the margin: *De Translat. Scripturae.*—Owen. See León de Castro, *Commentaria in Esaiam prophetam, ex sacris Scriptoribus Graecis, et Latinis confecta* (Salamanca: Mathias Gastius,

Huntlaeus,[30] (3) Melchior Canus;[31] (4) Petrus Galatinus,[32] (5) Morinus,[33] (6) Salmeron,[34] (7) Pintus;[35] (8) Mersennus:[36] that many corruptions have crept into it, by negligence, and the carelessness of scribes, so (9) Bellarmine,[37] (10) Genebrard,[38] (11) Sixtus Senensis[39] with most of the rest of them; in these things indeed they have been opposed by the most learned of their own side; as (12) Arias Montanus;[40] (13) Johannes Isaack:[41] (14) Pineda,[42]

1570). León de Castro (1509–1585) was a Spanish professor of theology at Salamanca, famous for his polemical interaction with Arias Montanus's use of the Hebrew and Chaldean text in the Antwerp Polyglot Bible.

30 In the margin: *Controversarium Epitome.*—Owen. See James Gordon, *Controversiarum epitomes* [*tomus primus*] (Poitiers: Ex praelo Antonii Mesnerii, 1612).

31 In the margin: *Loc. Theol.* lib. 2. cap. 13.—Owen. See Melchior Cano, *Opera: In duo volumina distributa* (Madrid: Raymundus Ruiz, 1791–1792), 1:116–30. Melchior Cano (1509–1560) was a Spanish Dominican most famous for his posthumously published *De locis theologicis.*

32 In the margin: *Arcan. Cathol.* lib. 1.—Owen. See Pietro Colonna Galatino, *De arcanis Catholicae veritatis* (Basel: Ioannes Hervagius, 1561), 1–27.

33 In the margin: *Exercit. de Heb. Text. sincer.*—Owen. See Morin, *Exercitationes pars prior.* The numbering in Owen's text stops here and begins again with "7." at Bellarmine. I have amended the list to make it continuous.

34 In the margin: *Prolegom:*—Owen. See Alfonso Salmerón, *Commentarii in evangelicam historiam* [. . .]: *Tomus primus, de prolegomenis in sacrosancta evangelia* (Brescia: sumptibus Matthiae Colosini and Baretii Baretii, 1601). Alfonso Salmerón (1515–1585) was a Spanish Jesuit who was a notable biblical commentator.

35 Hector or Heitor Pinto (1528–1584) was a Portuguese Hieronymite known for his biblical commentaries and devotional writings.

36 In the text: *Animad. in Problem. Georgii Venet, &c. pag. 233.*—Owen. See Marin Mersenne, *Observationes, et emendationes ad Francisci Georgii Veneti problemata* (Paris: Sébastien Cramoisy, 1623), col. 233. Marin Mersenne (1588–1648) was a French Catholic scholar whose writings spanned across a diverse range of fields, including theology, cabalism, antioccult polemics, mathematics, and music.

37 In the margin: *De verbo Dei.* lib. 2.—Owen. See Bellarmine, *Opera*, 1:61–65.

38 In the margin: *In Psal. 21. vers. 19.*—Owen. See Gilbert Génébrard, *Psalmi Davidis: Calendario Hebraeo, Syro, Graeco, Latino, argumentis et commentariis genuinum eorum sensum* [. . .] (Lyon: Horatio Cardon, 1606), 82–83.

39 In the margin: *Bibliothe.* lib. 8. Haeres. 13.—Owen. See Sisto da Siena, *Bibliotheca sancta* (Paris: ex typographia Rolini Theodorici, 1610), 649–53. Sisto da Siena or Sixtus of Siena (1520–1569) was a Jewish convert to Catholicism, who became a Dominican priest and influential biblical scholar.

40 In the margin: *Praefat. ad Bib. interlin.*—Owen. See Arius Montanus, "De varia Hebraicorum librorum Scriptione et lectione commentatio," in *Biblia Hebraica eorundem Latina interpretatio Xantis Pagnini Lucensis* (Antwerp: Christophori Plantini, 1584).

41 In the margin: *respons. ad Lindan.*—Owen. See Johannes Isaac, *Defensio veritatis Hebraicae sacrarum Scripturarum* (Cologne: Jacob Soter, 1559).

42 In the margin: *De rebus Solom. cap. 4. sect. 1.*—Owen. It is likely that Owen has in mind the section to which he referred in the "Dedicatory Epistle", where Pineda objects to Castrius's cavalier treatment of the Hebrew edition. See John de Pineda, *De rebus Salomonis Regis* (Mainz: Antonius

(15) Masius,[43] (16) Ferarius,[44] (17) Andradius[45] and sundry others, who speak honorably of the originals; but in nothing do they so pride themselves, as in this conceit of the novelty of the Hebrew punctuation; whereby they hope, with Abimelech's servants utterly to stop the wells and fountains, from whence we should draw our souls' refreshment.

THE IMPORTANCE OF THE POINTS FURTHER MANIFESTED AND THE EXTREME DANGER OF MAKING THE HEBREW PUNCTUATION ARBITRARY

4. This may serve for a short view of the opinions of the parties at variance, and their several interests in these opinions. The importance of the points is on all hands acknowledged, whether aiming at the honor, or dishonor of the originals. Vowels are the life of words; consonants without them are dead and immovable, by them are they carried to any sense, and may be [carried] to diverse [senses]. It is true that men who have come to acquaintance with the Scriptures by the help of the vowels and accents, being in possession of a habitual notion and apprehension of that sense and meaning which arises from them, may possibly think that it were a facile thing to find out and fix upon the same sense by the help of the *matres lectionis*[46] אהוי,[47] and the consideration of antecedents and consequents with such like assistances. But let them be all taken out of the way (as I shall manifest it is fit they should be, if they have the original assigned to them by the *Prolegomena*) and let men lay aside that advantage they have received from them, and it will quickly appear into what devious ways all sorts of such persons will run. Scarce a chapter, it may be a verse, or a word, in a short time would be left free from perplexing

Hieratus, 1613), 352. John de Pineda (1558–1637) was a Spanish Jesuit scholar, distinguished for his engagement with biblical textual criticism.

43 In the margin: *Praefat. ad Josu.*—Owen. See Andreas Masius, *Iosuae Imperatoris historia* (Antwerp: Christophorus Plantinus, 1574). Andreas Masius (1514–1573) was a Flemish Syriacist who was involved in the production of the Antwerp Polyglot Bible.

44 In the margin: *Prolegom. Biblica.*—Owen. See Nikolaus Serarius, *Prolegomena biblica, et commentaria in omnes epistolas canonicas* (Mainz: Balthasar Lippius, 1612). The work Owen cites was written by Nikolaus Serarius (1555–1609), a French Jesuit biblical commentator who taught ethics, philosophy, and theology in Germany. It is possible Owen or the printer inadvertently confused his name with the Franciscan biblical commentator Johann Ferus (1495–1554).

45 Diogo de Paiva de Andrade (1528–1575) was a Portuguese theologian most famous for his *Defensio Tridentinae fidei Catholicae* and his contributions to the Council of Trent.

46 Lat. "mothers of reading," referring to four particular consonants used in Hebrew to indicate long vowels.

47 I.e., the four Hebrew consonants which make up the *matres lectionis*.

contradicting conjectures. The words are altogether innumerable whose significations may be varied, by an arbitrary supplying of the points. And when the
regulation of the punctuation shall be left to every single person's conjectures
upon antecedents and consequents (for who shall give a rule to the rest) what
end shall we have of fruitless contests? What various, what pernicious senses
shall we have to contend about? Suppose that men sober, modest, humble,
pious, might be preserved from such miscarriages, and be brought to some
agreement about these things, (which yet in these days upon many accounts is
not to be looked for; yea, from the nature of the thing itself seems impossible)
yet this gives us but a human fallible persuasion that the readings fixed on by
them, is[48] according to the mind of God; but to expect such: an agreement is
fond and foolish. Besides who shall secure us against the luxuriant atheistical
wits and spirits of these days who are bold upon all advantages ἀκίνητα κινεῖν,[49]
and to break in upon everything that is holy and sacred; that they will not by
their huckstering, utterly corrupt the word of God? How easy is it to foresee the
dangerous consequents of contending for various readings, though not false
nor pernicious, by men pertinaciously adhering to their own conjectures? The
word of God, as to its literal sense, or reading of the words of it, has hitherto
been ἐξαγώνιον,[50] and the acknowledged touchstone of all expositions; render
this now a μῆλον ἔριδος,[51] and what have we remaining firm and unshaken?

THAT DANGER EVINCED BY INSTANCE

5. Let men, with all their confidence as to the knowledge of the sense and
meaning of the Scriptures which they have already received by such helps
and means as are all of them resolved into the present punctuation of the
Bible, (for all grammars, all lexicons, the whole Masora, all helps to this
language, new and old in the world, are built on this foundation) reduce

---

48 As per original. Goold has "are."
49 Gk. "to move the unmoveable," an Ancient Greek allusion to interfering with a sacred site.
    See, for example, Herodotus, *The Persian Wars*, bk. 6, sec. 134. For the Greek text and English
    translation, see Herodotus, *The Persian Wars*, vol. 3, *Books 5–7*, trans. A. D. Godley, Loeb Clas-
    sical Library 119 (Cambridge, MA: Harvard University Press, 1922), 288–89.
50 Gk. "beyond dispute".
51 Gk. "an object of disputation," literally "an apple of disputation," a reference to the episode
    in Greek mythology when at the wedding of Peleus and Thetis, the uninvited goddess, Eris,
    threw down a golden apple on which was inscribed "For the Fairest" in order to cause a dispute
    among the gods. See, for example, Apollodorus, *Epitome* 3, sec. 2. For the Greek text and En-
    glish translation, see Apollodorus, *The Library*, vol. 2, *Book 3.10–End. Epitome*, trans. James G.
    Frazer, Loeb Classical Library 122 (Cambridge, MA: Harvard University Press, 1921), 172–73.

themselves to such an indifferency, as some of late have fancied as a meet rise for knowledge; and fall seriously to the reading of some of the prophets whose matter is sublime and mystical, and their style elliptical and abstruse, without the help of points and accents: let them fix them, or any figures to answer their sounds arbitrarily, merely on their judgment in the language, and conjectures at the sense of the place, without any advantage from what they have been instructed in, and let us see whether they will agree, as they fabulously report of the LXX translators? Whatever may be the issue of their industry, we need not fear quickly to find as learned as they, that would lay their work level with the ground. I confess considering the days we live in, wherein the bold and curious wits of men, under pretense of critical observations, alluring and enticing with a show of learning have ventured to question almost every word in the Scripture, I cannot but tremble to think, what would be the issue of this supposition, that the points, vowels, and accents are no better guides unto us, than may be expected from those who are pretended to be their authors. The Lord I hope will safeguard his own, from the poison of such attempts; the least of its evil, is not yet thoroughly considered. So that whereas saving to myself the liberty of my judgment, as to sundry particulars both in the impression itself and in sundry translations, I acknowledge the great usefulness of this work, and am thankful for it, which I here publicly testify; yet I must needs say, I had rather that it, and all works of the like kind, were out of the world, than that this one opinion should be received, with the consequences that unavoidably attend it.

NO RELIEF AGAINST THAT DANGER ON THE GROUNDS OF THE OPINION CONSIDERED

6. But this trial needs not be feared. Grant the points to have the original pretended, yet they deserve all regard, and are of singular use for the right understanding of the Scripture: so that it is not lawful to depart from them, without urgent necessity, and evidences of a better lection to be substituted in the room of that refused.[52] But as this relieves us not, but still leaves us within the sphere of rational conjectures. So whether it can honestly be pretended and pleaded in this case, comes nextly to be discovered by the consideration of the supposed authors of this invention.

---

52 Here Owen is voicing the perspective of an imagined interlocutor, hence Goold's insertion of quotation marks.

THE AUTHORS OF THE HEBREW PUNCTUATION
ACCORDING TO THE *PROLEGOMENA*:
WHO AND WHAT, MORINUS'S FOLLY, AND
THE IMPROBABILITY OF THIS PRETENSE

7. The founders of this story of the invention of the Hebrew points, tell us, that it was the work of some Rabbins, living at Tiberias a city in Galilee, about the year of Christ 500, or in the next century, after the death of Hierome, and the finishing of the Babylonian Talmud; the improbability of this story or legend, I am not now to insist upon. Morinus makes the lie lower. He tells us that the Babylonian Talmud was finished but a little before the year 700:[53] that the Masoretes (to whom he ascribes the invention of the points) wrote a long time after the finishing of the Talmud, and the year 700;[54] this long time cannot denote less than some hundreds of years. And yet the same man in his preface to his *Samaritica opuscula*;[55] boasting of his finding Rab. Juda Chiug[56] manifests that he was acquainted with the present punctuation, and wrote about it. Now this rabbi was a grammarian; which kind of learning among the Jews succeeded that of the Masoretes and he lived about the year 1030; so that no room at all seems to be left for this work. That there was formerly a famous school of the Jews, and learned men at Tiberias is granted. Hierome tells us that he hired a learned Jew from thence for his assistance.[57] Among others, Dr. Lightfoot has well traced the shadow of their sanedrym [sic] with their presidents in it, in some kind of succession to that place.[58] That they continued there in any esteem, number or reputation, unto the time assigned by our authors for this work, is not made to

---

53 In the text: *Ex. 2. Cap. 3. par Poster.*—Owen. Owen is referring here to the annotated outline of the *pars posterior* of Morin's *Exercitationes*, published in the 1633 edition. See Morin, *Exercitationes pars prior*, 444. This outline differs from the divisions in the full text of the *pars posterior* that would end up being published in the posthumous edition of 1660.

54 In the text: *p: p: 5. cap. 3.*—Owen. See Morin, *Exercitationes pars prior*, 446.

55 See "Praefatio," in Jean Morin, *Opuscula Hebraeo-Samaritica* (Paris: Gaspardus Metras, 1657).

56 Jehuda Ben-David Chajug (fl. 1020–1040), commonly known as Chiug, is regarded as perhaps the foremost of Hebrew grammarians.

57 In the text: *Epist: ad Chromat:*—Owen. Owen appears to be referring to a remark Jerome made about consulting a Tiberian Jew before translating Chronicles: *ut vobis librum Paralipomenon Latino sermone transferrem, de Tiberiade legis quondam doctorem, qui apud Hebraeos admirationi habebatur, assumpsi.* Editor's translation: "So that I could translate the book of Chronicles into the Latin language for you all, I took up a certain teacher of the law from Tiberias, who was held in admiration among the Hebrews." See "Praefatio Hieronymi in librum Paralipomenon iuxta lxx interpretes," in Jerome, *Opera omnia x*, ed. J. P. Migne, Patrologia Latina 29 (Paris: Vrayet, 1846), 401.

58 In the margin: *Lightfoot Fall of Hierus. Sect. 3. 4. 5. &c.*—Owen. See John Lightfoot, *The Whole Works*, 13 vols. (London: J. F. Dove, 1822), 3:387–93.

appear from any history or record of Jews or Christians; yea it is certain, that about the time mentioned, the chiefest flourishing of the Jewish doctors was at Babylon, with some other cities in the east, where they had newly completed their Talmud, the great pandect[59] of Jewish laws and constitutions as themselves everywhere witness and declare. That any persons considerably learned were then in Tiberias is a mere conjecture. And it is most improbable, considering what destruction had been made of them at Diocaesarea and Tiberias, about the year of Christ 352, by Gallus[60] at the command of Constantius.[61] That there should be such a collection of them, so learned, so authorized; as to invent this work, and impose it on the world, no man once taking notice that any such persons ever were, is beyond all belief. Notwithstanding any entanglements that men by their conjectures may put upon the persuasion of the antiquity of the points, I can as soon believe the most incredible figment in the whole Talmud, as this fable. But this is not my business; let it be granted, that such persons there were; on the supposition under consideration, I am only inquiring what is the state and condition of the present Hebrew pointing, and what weight is to be laid thereon. That the reader then may a little consider what sort of men they were, who are assigned in these *Prolegomena* as the inventors of this artifice of punctuation, I shall take a brief view of the state of the Jews after the destruction of the temple down to the days inquired after.

THE STATE OF THE JEWS, THE SUPPOSED INVENTORS OF THE POINTS, AFTER THE DESTRUCTION OF THE TEMPLE

8. That the Judaical church state continued, not only de facto, but in the merciful forbearance of God so far, that the many thousands of believers that constantly adhered to the Mosaical worship, were accepted with God, until the destruction of the temple; that, that destruction was the ending of the world that then was by fire, and the beginning of setting up solemnly the new heaven and new earth wherein dwells righteousness, I have at large elsewhere declared, and may God assisting yet further manifest in my thoughts on the epistle of Paul to the Hebrews. The time between the beginning of Christ's preaching, to the utter desolation of the city and temple, an open visible rejection of that church, as such was made.

59 I.e., a collection of laws.
60 Constantius Gallus (326–354) ruled the eastern provinces of the Roman Empire and suppressed the Jewish revolt in Palestine in the fourth century (as Owen alludes here).
61 Constantius II (317–361) was Roman emperor, son of Constantine the Great, and cousin of Constantius Gallus.

Thereon an utter separation of the true Israel from it ensued; and the hardened residue became לֹא עַמִּי[62] and לֹא רֻחָמָה[63] a people not in covenant or delight, but of curse and indignation. What their state was for a season, onward both civil and religious many have declared. I shall only insist on the heads of things. In general then, they were most remote from accepting of the punishment of their sin, or considering that God was revenging upon them the quarrel of his covenant to the utmost, having broken both his staves, "Beauty" and "Bands."[64] So far were they from owning their sin in selling of their Messiah, that seeing an end put to all their former worship thereupon, there is nothing recorded of them but these two things, which they wholly in direct opposition unto God gave themselves up unto. (1) They increased in rage and madness against all the followers of Christ, stirring up persecution against them all the world over. Hereunto they were provoked by a great number of apostates, who when they could no longer retain their Mosaical rites with the profession of Christ; being rejected by the churches, fell back again to Judaism or semi-Judaism. (2) A filthy lusting and desire after their former worship now become abominable, and a badge of infidelity, that so their table might become a snare unto them. And what had been for their safety, might now become the means of their utter ruin and hardening. Of the former, or their stirring up of persecution, all stories are full of examples and instances. The latter, or their desires and attempts for the restoration of their worship, as conducing to our present business must be further considered.

TWO ATTEMPTS MADE BY THEM TO RESTORE THEIR RELIGION

The Former under Barchochab, with Its Issue

9. For the accomplishment of a design to restore their old religion, or to furnish themselves with a new, they made two desperate attempts. The first of these was by arms, under their pseudo-Messiah Barchochab,[65] in the days of Adrian.[66] Under the conduct and influencings of this man, to whom one of the chief Rabbins (Akiba[67]) was armor bearer; in the pursuit of a design to restore

---

62 Heb. "not my people." Owen is alluding to Hos. 1:9; 2:1.

63 Heb. "not spared." Owen is alluding to Hos. 1:6, 8.

64 Owen is alluding to Zech. 11:7.

65 Simon Bar Kokhba (d. 135) was a Jewish leader who led the second major Jewish revolt against the Romans in 132–135.

66 Hadrian (76–138) was Roman emperor and cousin of his predecessor, Trajan.

67 Akiva ben Yosef (ca. 50–135) was an early Jewish rabbi who regarded Simon Bar Kokhba as the Messiah and allegedly took part in the revolt against Rome.

their temple and worship, they fell into rebellion against the Romans all the world over. In this work, after they had committed unheard-of outrages, massacres, unparalleled murders, spoils, and cruelties, and had shaken the whole empire, they were themselves in all parts of the world, especially in the city Bether,[68] where was the head of their rebellion, ruined with a destruction, seeming equal to that which befell them at Jerusalem, in the days of Vespasian[69] and Titus.[70]

That the rise of this war was upon the twofold cause mentioned, namely their desire to retain their former worship, and to destroy the Christian is evident. For the first it is expressed by Dio Cassius:

At Jerusalem he founded a city in place of the one which had been razed to the ground, naming it Aelia Capitolina, and on the site of the temple of the god he raised a new temple to Jupiter. This brought on a war of no slight importance nor of brief duration, for the Jews deemed it intolerable that foreign races should be settled in their city and foreign religious rites planted there [etc.].[71]

It was the defiling of the soil whereon the temple stood, which God suffered on set purpose, to manifest their utter rejection, and that the time was come wherein he would be no more worshiped in that place in the old manner, that put them in arms, as that author declares at large. And for the latter, Justin Martyr, who lived at that time informs us of it: "For in the Jewish war which lately happened Bar-Cochba, the leader of the revolt of the Jews, gave orders that Christians alone should be led to terrible punishments, unless they would deny Jesus the Christ and blaspheme."[72] His fury was in an especial manner

68 Original has "Bitter."
69 Vespasian (9–79) was Roman emperor who had previously led the suppression of the Jews in Judea (66–69), which led to the destruction of the Jerusalem Temple and the capture of the city in 70.
70 Titus (39–81) succeeded his father Vespasian as Roman emperor in 79 and was responsible for ending the Jewish rebellion that resulted in the capture of Jerusalem in 70.
71 In the text: *Hist. Rom. lib.* 69. *in vita Had.* ἐς δὲ τὰ Ἱεροσόλυμα πόλιν αὐτοῦ ἀντὶ τῆς κατα-σκαφείσης οἰκίσαντος, ἣν καὶ Αἰλίαν Καπιτωλίναν ὠνόμασε καὶ ἐς τὸν τοῦ θεοῦ τόπον, ναὸν τῷ Διὶ ἕτερον ἀναντεγείροντος, πόλεμος οὔτε μικρὸς οὔτ᾽ ὀλιγοχρόνιος ἐκινήθη. Ἰουδαῖοι γὰρ, δεινόν τι ποιούμενοι τοὺς ἀλλοφύλους τινὰς ἐς τὴν πόλιν σφῶν οἰκισθῆναι, καὶ τὰ ἱερὰ ἀλλότρια ἐν αὐτῇ ἱδρυθῆναι; κλ.—Owen. For the Greek text and the English Translation, see *Epitome of Book* 49, sec. 12, lines 1–2, in Dio Cassius, *Roman History*, vol. 8, *Books 61–70*, trans. Earnest Cary and Herbert B. Foster Loeb Classical Library 176 (Cambridge, MA: Harvard University Press, 1968), 446–47. Dio Cassius or Lucius Cassius Dio (ca. 155–ca. 235) was a Roman historian whose famous history of ancient Rome spanned the arrival of Aeneas and the founding of Rome in 735 BC to AD 229.
72 In the text: *Apol.* 2nd. *ad Anton. Pium:* καὶ γὰρ ἐν τῷ νῦν γεγενημένῳ Ἰουδαϊκῷ πολέμῳ Βαρχοχέβας ὁ τῆς Ἰουδαίων ἀποστάσεως ἀρχηγέτης Χριστιανοὺς μόνους εἰς τιμωρίας δει-

against the Christians, whom he commanded to be tortured and slain, unless they would deny and blaspheme Jesus Christ.[73] And this war they managed with such fury, and for a while success, that after Hadrian had called together against them the most experienced soldiers in the world, particularly Julius Severus[74] out of England, and had slain of them 5,080,000 in battle, with an infinite number besides as the historian speaks by famine, sickness and fire were consumed, he found himself to have sustained so much loss by them, that he began not his letter to the senate in the wonted[75] manner; "If you and your children are in health, it is well; I and the legions are in health"[76] he could not assure them, that it was well with him and his army.

By this second desolation they were very low, made weak and contemptible, and driven into obscurity all the world over. In this state they wandered up and down for some season in all manner of uncertainty. They had not only lost the place of their solemn worship, seeing it wholly defiled, the name of Jerusalem changed into Aelia,[77] and themselves forbid to look toward it upon pain of death,[78] but also being now unspeakably diminished in their number,

---

νὰς, εἰ μὴ ἀρνοῖντο Ἰησοῦν Χριστὸν καὶ βλασφημοῖεν, ἐκέλευεν ἀπάγεσθαι.—Owen. Owen is quoting from what has come to be known as the "First Apology" of Justin Martyr (*Apologia Maior*, chap. 31, sec. 6). For the English translation, see Justin Martyr, *The First and Second Apologies*, trans. Leslie William Barnard, Ancient Christian Writers 56 (New York: Paulist, 1997), 44. For the Greek text, see Justin Martyr, *Iustini Martyris apologiae pro Christianis*, ed. Miroslav Marcovich (Berlin: de Gruyter, 1994), 77.

73 In the text as a discrete sentence: See *Euseb. chron. ad an. Christi* 136.—Owen. Eusebius's *Chronicle* was made famous by Jerome's Latin edition (Eusebius's Greek text has largely been lost). Owen is undoubtedly citing Joseph Scaliger's early seventeenth-century edition, which records that Bar Kokhba's persecution of the Christians actually occurred in 134, while modern editions of the *Chronicle* record it as occurring in 133. As cited in Scaliger, *Chochebas dux Iudaicae factionis nolentes sibi Christianos adversum Romanum militem ferre subsidium omnimodis cruciatibus necat*. Editor's translation: "Barcocheba, leader of a faction of Jews, murders the Christians with every form of torture, since they are not willing to give him reinforcement against the Roman army." See *Chronicorum canonum*, in Joseph Scaliger, *Thesaurus temporum* (Leiden: Thomas Basson, 1606), 167; cf., Eusebius of Caesarea, *Eusebius Werke V: Chronik des Hieronymus*, ed. Rudolf Helm (Berlin: Verlag, 1956), 201. Eusebius of Caesarea (ca. 260–ca. 340) was bishop of Caesarea, a historian of Christianity, a chronologist, a biblical commentator, and a polemicist.

74 Sextus Julius Severus was the early second-century Roman governor of Britain, and the commander who was directly responsible for suppressing the second Jewish revolt led by Simon Bar Kokhba.

75 I.e., usual or habitual.

76 In the text: εἰ αὐτοὶ [τε] καὶ οἱ παῖδες ὑμῶν ὑγιαίνετε, εὖ ἂν ἔχοι· ἐγὼ καὶ τὰ στρατεύματα ὑγιαίνομεν. For the Greek text and the English translation, see *Epitome of Book* LXIX, 14.3, in Cassius, *History*, 450–51.

77 Aelia Capitolina was the official name of the Roman colony that was built under Hadrian on the site of the besieged Jerusalem, post AD 70.

78 In the margin: *Euseb. Hist. lib.* 4. *cap.* 6. *Orosius. lib.* 7. *c.* 13. *Heiron. Com. in. Zech. c.* 11. *vid. Tzemach. David. & Hotting. Hist. ecclesi. nov. Testam.*—Owen. "*Euseb. Hist. lib.* 4. *cap.* 6": for

all hopes of contriving themselves into any condition of observing their old rites and worship was utterly lost.[79]

The Second under R. Judah, with Its Issue

10. Here they sat down amazed for a season; being at their wits' end, as was threatened to them in the curse. But they will not rest so. Considering therefore that their old religion could not be continued without a Jerusalem and a temple, they began a nefarious[80] attempt against God, equal to that of the old world in building Babel, even to set up a new religion, that might abide with them wherever they were, and give them countenance in their infidelity, and opposition to the gospel unto the utmost. The head of this new apostasy was one Rabbi Jehuda,[81] whom we may not unfitly call the Mohammed[82] of the Jews. They term him Hannasi, "the prince," and Hakkadosh, "the holy." The whole story of him and his companions, as reported by the Jews, is well collected by Joseph de Voisin.[83] The sum of the whole concerning this work is

---

an English translation, see Eusebius of Caesarea, *The Church History: A New Translation with Commentary* (Grand Rapids, MI: Kregel, 1999), bk. 4, sec. 6 (p. 138). "*Orosius. lib. 7. c.* 13": see Paul Orosius, *Historiarum adversum paganos libri vii*, ed. Charles Zangemeister, Corpus Scriptorum Ecclesiasticorum Latinorum 5 (Vienna: Apud G. Geroldi filium Bibliopolam Academiae, 1882), 467–69. "*Heiron. Com. in. Zech. c.* 11": see *Commentarium in Zachariam*, bk. 3, chap. 11, in Jerome, *Commentarii in prophetas minores*, ed. M. Adriaen, Corpus Christianorum: Series Latina 76a (Turnhout: Typographi Brepolis, 1970), 848–60. "*vid. Tzemach. David*": see, David Gans, *Chronologia sacra-profana* [Tzemach David], trans. William Henry Vorstius (Leiden: Ioannes Maire, 1644). "*& Hotting. Hist. ecclesi. nov. Testam.*": see Johann Heinrich Hottinger I, *Historiae ecclesiasticae Novi Testamenti* (Zürich: J. H. Hamberger et al., 1651–1667).

79 In the margin: *Dispersi, palabundi et coeli & soli sui extorres, vagantur per orbem sine homine, sine Deo, rege, quibus nec advenarum jure terram patriam saltem vestigio salutare conceditur. Tertull: Apol:*—Owen. *Apologeticum* 21.5. English translation: "Scattered, wanderers, exiles from their own soil and sky, they stray the world over, without man or God for their king; they are not permitted even as foreigners to greet their native land, with so much as a footfall." For the Latin text and the English translation, see Tertullian, *Apology. De Spectaculis. Minucius Felix: Octavius*, trans. T. R. Glover and Gerald H. Rendall, Loeb Classical Library 250 (Cambridge, MA: Harvard University Press, 1966), 104–5. For the critical edition of the Latin text, see Tertullian, *Opera catholica. Adversus Marcionem*, ed. E. Dekkers et al. Corpus Christianorum: Series Latina 1 (Turnhout: Typographi Brepolis, 1954), 123.

80 I.e., wicked.

81 Here Owen is referring to Judah ha-Nasi, or Judah the Prince, or Judah I (ca. 135–217), the first Jewish leader to be given the title "ha-Nasi" or "Prince," who succeeded his father as the leader of the Palestinian Jewish community and, as Owen alludes, was responsible for compiling the Jewish Mishnah.

82 Owen tends to use the spelling "Mahomet." Throughout this edition, his spelling has been adjusted according to the more familiar modern convention.

83 In the text: *observat. In proem: ad pugi: fidei: p.* 26, 27.—Owen. Owen is referring to Joseph de Voisin's annotations or "Observationes," in his edition of Raimund Martini's *Pugio fidei*,

laid down by Maimonides, in his *praefatio* in *Seder Zeraiim*,[84] wherein also a sufficient account is given of the whole Mishnah, with the names of the Rabbins, either implied in it, or occasionally mentioned. This man, about the year of Christ 190, or 200, when the temple had now lain waste almost three times as long as it did in the Babylonish captivity, being countenanced as some of themselves report,[85] by Antoninus Pius,[86] compiled the Jewish Alcoran,[87] or the Mishnah, as a rule of their worship and ways for the future. Only whereas Mohammed afterward pretended to have received his figments by revelation, (though indeed he had many of his abominations from the Talmud) this man pleaded the receiving of his by tradition; the two main engines that have been set up against the word of God. Out of such pharisaical traditions as were indeed preserved among them, and such observances as they had learned and taken up from apostate Christians, as Aquila and others, with such figments as were invented by himself, and his predecessors, since the time of their being publicly rejected and cursed by God, this man compiled the ספר משניות

---

published in 1651. See Raimund Martini, *Pugio Fidei* (Paris: Mathurinus Henault, Ioannes Henault, 1651), 26–27. Joseph de Voisin (1610–1685) was a French Hebraist most famous for his *Theologia Iudaeorum*. De Voisin contributed annotations to an edition of the *Pugio fidei*, which also attributes the work to Raimund Martini.

84 In the text: pag: 36, 37 of the edition of Mr Pococke.—Owen. The text misspells "Zeraim" as "Zeraiim." See Maimonides, *Porta Mosis, sive, Dissertationes aliquot a R. Mose Maimonide, suis in varias Mishnaioth*, ed. Edward Pococke (Oxford: H. Hall, 1655), 35–37.

85 In the margin: *Post haec processu temporis ventum est ad Rabbinu Hakkadosh, cui pax, qui fuit seculi sui phoenix, &c. Ille legem in Israele confirmavit sententiis, dictis, & differentiis ore tradita a Mose, usque ad tempora sua collectis, cum & ipse esset ex iis qui ore tradita referebant. Collectis igitur sententiis & dictis istis, manum admovit componendae Mishnae, quae omnium quae in lege scripta sunt praeceptorum explicationem contineret, partim traditionibus a Mose (cui pax) ore acceptis, partim consequentiis argumentatione elicitis &tc. vid. R. Maimon. praefat. in Zeder.* [sic] *Zeraiim, edit. Pocock.* p. 36, 37, 38.—Owen. Editor's translation: "After these things, in the course of time, it came to Rabbi Hakkadosh (peace be upon the one who was a phoenix in his day!). That man established the law in Israel by the judgments, utterances, and distinctions passed down by mouth from Moses, gathered up to his day, because he himself was from among those who delivered what was passed down by mouth. Therefore, from those gathered judgments and utterances, he put his hand to compiling the Mishnah, which contained an exposition of all the precepts that were written in the law, partly from what had been passed down orally from Moses (to whom be peace), and partly from conclusions drawn by reasoning, etc." This is an expurgated quotation that Owen has actually derived from text spanning pp. 35–37 of Pococke's edition. See Maimonides, *Porta Mosis*, 35–37.

86 Antoninus Pius (86–161) was Roman emperor succeeding Hadrian. The Talmud makes reference to Judah ha-Nasi's friendship with "Antoninus," which, like Owen, some have thought is a reference to Antoninus Pius. However, it is likely to be a reference to his friendship with Pius's successor, Marcus Aurelius Antoninus.

87 I.e., The Qur'an. Owen here is clearly using this label figuratively in a derogative fashion referring to the Mishnah.

Mishnaioth,[88] which is the text of their Talmud, and the foundation of their present religion, under the name of the old oral law. That sundry Christian ceremonies and institutions vilely corrupted were taken up by the Jews of those days, many of them being apostates, as were also some of Mohammed's assistants in compiling of the Alcoran, I shall (God assisting) elsewhere endeavor to evince and manifest. That any gospel observances were taken from the Jews, as being in practice among them, before their institution by Christ, will appear in the issue to be a bold and groundless fancy.

THE RISE AND FOUNDATION OF THE TALMUDS

11. The foundation mentioned being laid in a collection of traditions, and new invention of abominations under the name of old traditions by this rabbi, the following Talmuds are an improvement of the same attempt, of setting up a religion under the curse, and against the mind and will of God; that being rejected by him, and left without king, without prince, without sacrifice, without image, without an ephod, and without a teraphim,[89] and kind of worship, true or false, they might have something to give them countenance in their unbelief. The Talmud of Jerusalem, so called, (for it is the product of many comments on the Mishnae in the city of Tiberias, where Rabbi Juda[90] lived) because it was compiled in the land of Canaan, whose metropolis was Jerusalem, was published about the year of Christ 230, so it is commonly received; though I find Dr. Lightfoot of late,[91] on supposition of finding in it the name of Diocletianus the emperor,[92] to give it a later date. But I confess I see no just ground for the alteration of his judgment, from what he delivered in another treatise before. The Doclet[93] mentioned by the Rabbins was beaten by the children of Rabbi Jehuda Princeps[94] (as himself observes), who lived in the days of one of the Antoninuses,[95] a hundred years before Diocletian. Neither was ever

88 Heb. "Book of the Mishnayoth," i.e., the Mishnah. As per Goold. Original has סכר.
89 I.e., images of some form that functioned as household gods. Cf. Hos. 3:4.
90 Rabbi Judah, or Judah II, was a Jewish sage who is mentioned in the Mishnah and Talmud, and who lived in Tiberius around the mid-third century.
91 John Lightfoot (1602–1675) was a noted Hebraist and biblical scholar, and he held appointments as vice-chancellor of Cambridge and master of St Catharine's College.
92 Diocletian (244–311) was a Roman emperor who brought stability to the empire, while being responsible for the last great empire-wide persecution of Christians.
93 Presumably, this is a shorthand reference to Diocletian.
94 Judah ha-Nasi had two children who succeeded him, Gamaliel III, and Simeon ben Judah ha-Nasi.
95 I.e., Emperors Antonius Pius and his son, Marcus Aurelius.

Diocletian in a low condition in the east, being a Sarmatian born, and living in the western parts; only he went with Numerianus[96] [in] that expedition into Persia, wherein he was made emperor at his return: but this is nothing to my purpose.[97] The Babylonian Talmud so called, because compiled in the land of Babylon, in the cities of Nahardea, Sora, and Pumbeditha, where the Jews had their synagogues and schools, was finished about the year 506 or 510. In this greater work was the mystery of their iniquity finished, and the engine of their own invention for their further obduration[98] perfectly completed. These are now the rule of their faith, the measure of their exposition of Scripture, the directory of their worship, the ground of their hope and expectation.

The State of the Jews upon and after the Writing of the Talmuds

12. All this while the Jews enjoyed the letter of the Scriptures, as they do to this day, yea they receive it sometimes with the honor and veneration due to God alone. God preserved it among them for our present use, their farther condemnation, and means of their future conversion. But after the destruction of the temple, and rejection of their whole church state, the word was no longer committed to them of God, nor were they entrusted with it, nor are to this day. They have it not by promise, or covenant, as they had of old (Isa. 59:21). Their possession of it is not accompanied with the administration of the Spirit, without which, as we see in the instance of themselves, the word is a dead letter, of no efficacy for the good of souls. They have the letter among them, as at one time they had the ark in the battle against the Philistines, for their greater ruin.

Their Rancor against Christ

13. In this state and condition they everywhere discover their rancor and malice against Christ, calling him in contempt and reproach תלוי,[99] who is קדוש קדוש קדוש יהוה צבאות[100] relating monstrous figments concerning him, and their dealing with him, under the name of Jesus the son of Pandira.[101] Some deny that by Jesus the son of Pandira and Stada in the Talmud the blessed Messiah

---

96 Numerian (d. 284) was Roman Emperor in the eastern part of the empire, preceding Diocletian. He was killed on campaign in Persia, at which point Diocletian succeeded him.

97 In the text: See *Lightfoot Chronograph. cap.* 81. *p.* 144.—Owen. Owen is citing from *In chorographicam aliquam terrae Israeliticae.* See John Lightfoot, *Horae Hebraicae et Talmudicae* (Cambridge: John Field, 1658), pt. 1, p. 144.

98 I.e., stubbornness.

99 Heb. "a hanged man."

100 Heb. "Holy, holy, holy is the Lᴏʀᴅ of hosts" (Isa. 6:3 ESV).

101 "Jesus the son of Pandira" (and son of Stada) is an oblique reference that appears in a number of Talmudic-era texts, and in certain editions of the Jerusalem Talmud. Some, like Owen, have

is intended. So did Galatinus[102] and Reuchlins.[103] The contrary is asserted by Reynoldus[;][104] Buxtorfius [Sr.];[105] Vorstius.[106] And in truth the reason pleaded by Galatinus and others, to prove that they did not intend our Savior does upon due consideration evince the contrary. The Jesus (say they) who is mentioned in the Talmud, lived in the days of the Maccabees, being slain in the time of Hyrcanus[107] or of Aristobulus,[108] a hundred years before the death of the true Messiah: so that it cannot be he who is by them intended. But this is invented by the cursed wretches, that it should not appear that their temple was so soon destroyed after their wicked defection from God, in killing of his Son. This is most manifest from what is cited by Genebrard from Abraham Levita in his *Cabala historiae*, where he says, that Christians invented this story that Jesus was crucified in the life of Herod, (that is the tetrarch) that it might appear that their temple was destroyed immediately thereupon: when (says he) it is evident from the Mishnah, and Talmud, that he lived in the time of Alexander, and was crucified in the days of Aristobulus.[109] So discovering the true ground

thought it to be a reference to Jesus of Nazareth, although others (evidently here, Galatino, Reuchlin, and Schickhard) have questioned this association.

102 In the text: *Arcan: Relig. Cathol: lib. 1. cap. 7.*—Owen. See Pietro Colonna Galatino, *De arcanis Catholicae veritatis* (Basel: Ioannes Hervagius, 1561), 25.

103 In the text: *Cabal. lib. 1. p. 636. Guliel: Schickhard: in Prooem. Tarich. p. 83.*—Owen. See Joseph Reuchlin's *De arte Cabalistica*. Owen appears to be citing the edition contained in Paulus Ricci, *Artis Cabalisticae: Hoc est reconditae theologicae et philosophiae, scriptorum: Tomus I* (Basel: Sebastianus Henricpetrus, 1587), 636. For the second citation, see Wilhelm Schickhard Sr., *Tarich, h.e. series regum Persiae* (Tübingen: Theodorus Werlinus, 1628), 83–100. The discussion continues over subsequent pages. Johann Reuchlin (1455–1522) was a German humanist and Hebraist who was a notable Catholic advocate for the authenticity of the Hebrew text of the Old Testament.

104 In the text: *praelec. in lib. Apoc. praelec. 103. p. 405, 406.*—Owen. Owen actually appears to be citing *Praelictio, 153*. See John Rainolds, *Censura librorum apocryphorum Veteris Testamenti*, 2 vols. (Oppenheim: Hieronymus Gallerus, 1611), 2:405–6.

105 In the text: *lexic. Rab. voce* סטד and also in פנדירא.—Owen. See Johann Buxtorf Sr., *Lexicon Chaldaicum, Talmudicum et rabbinicum* (Basel: Ludovicus König, 1639), 1460 (סטד: Stada), 1755 (פנדירא: Pandira).

106 In the text: *not: ad Tzem: Dav:* pag. 264.—Owen. See Gans, *Chronologia sacra-profana*, 264. Owen is referring to the translator of this edition, William Henry Vorstius.

107 John Hyrcanus II (d. 30 BC), son of Alexander Jannaeus, was a Hasmonean high priest and king of Judea.

108 Aristobulus II (d. 49 BC) defeated his older brother Hyrcanus II to become high priest and king of Judea.

109 Abraham Levita or Abraham ibn David (ca. 1110–1180) was a Spanish Jewish historian who authored the chronicle mentioned here, the *Cabala historiae*, or *Sefer ha-Qabbalah*. Génébrard depended on ibn David in his own *Chronologia*, and the last edition of this work contains his Latin abridgement of the *Sefer ha-Qabbalah*. Owen appears to be alluding to a section where ibn David notes that Jewish adversaries claim Jesus was born in the thirty-

why they perverted the whole story of his time: namely lest all the world should see their sin and punishment standing so near together. But it is well that the time of our Savior's suffering and death was affirmed even by the heathens, before either their Mishnah or Talmud were born or thought of, "to scotch the rumor" (he speaks of Nero, and of his firing Rome) "substituted as culprits, and punished with the utmost refinements of cruelty, a class of men, loathed for their vices, whom the crowd styled Christians. Christus, the founder of the name, had undergone the death penalty in the reign of Tiberius, by the sentence of the procurator Pontius Pilatus."[110] To return to our Jews: universally in all their old writings, they have carried on a design of impugning him in his Gospel. For as we need not their testimony, nor anything but the Scripture for their conviction and αὐτοκατακρισία,[111] so to acknowledge the truth, the places cited out of their Talmuds and Gemara, from the Cabalists and other Rabbins, by Martinus Raymundus,[112] Porchetus,[113] Galatinus, Reuchlinus, and

---

eighth year of Caesar Augustus, in the days of Herod, and was crucified in the days of Herod's son Archelaus. He then adds, "However, they probably argue this point so vehemently so they can say that the Temple and kingdom of Israel endured for but a short while after his crucifixion" (*fortassis autem usque eo pugnaciter contendunt, quo dicant templum & regnum Israel post crucifixionem ipsius non nisi paulisper stetisse*): For the Latin text, see "Historica Cabbala sapientis illius, rectorum ornamenti, Rabbi Abraham Levitae Davidis filii" in Gilbert Génébrard, *Chronographiae libri quatuor* (Paris: Ioannes Phillehotte, 1609), 43b. The English translation is adapted from the modern English translation of ibn David's Hebrew text according to the Latin version cited: Abraham ibn Daud, *The Book of Tradition: Sefer ha-Qabbalah*, trans. Gerson D. Cohen (Philadelphia: Jewish Publication Society, 2010), 21. As Owen alludes, ibn David goes on to refer to a "most genuine" (*verissima*) tradition taken from the Mishnah and Talmud indicating Jesus was in fact born during the fourth year of the reign of the Hasmonean King Alexander Jannaeus, and was apprehended at age thirty-six during the third year of the reign of Aristobulus II. See Génébrard, *Chronographiae*, 43b; ibn Daud, *Book of Tradition*, 21–22.

110 In the text: *Abolendo rumori* [. . .] *subdidit reos; et quaesitissimis poenis affecit, quos per flagitia invisos, vulgus Christianos appellabat. Auctor nominis ejus Christus, Tiberio imperitante per Procuratorem Pontium Pilatum supplicio affectus erat. Tacit. Annal. Lib.* 15.—Owen. For the Latin text and the English translation, see Tacitus, *Annals: Books 13–16*, trans. John Jackson, Loeb Classical Library 322 (Cambridge, MA: Harvard University Press, 1937), 282–83. For a critical edition with the Latin text, see Tacitus, *Annals: Book XV*, ed. Rhiannon Ash, Cambridge Greek and Latin Classics, (Cambridge: Cambridge University Press, 2018), 44.

111 Gk. "self-condemnation."

112 Raimund Martini (1220–1284) was Spanish Dominican polemicist who engaged in missionary activity to Jews and Muslims. He was highly competent in Eastern languages and Rabbinic writings and is best known for his anti-Jewish polemic *Pugio fidei*.

113 Porchetus de Salvaticis (d. 1315) was an Italian Carthusian polemicist whose chief anti-Semitic publication, *Victoria Porcheti adversus impios Hebraeos* (Paris: G. Desplains, 1520), closely followed Martini's arguments in *Pugio fidei*.

others, (setting aside Galatinus his *Gale Rezeia*[114] which must be set aside) seem
to be wrested the most of them beside their intentions, as things obscurely,
metaphorically, and mystically written, are easily dealt withal. Their disputes
about the Messiah, when they speak of him of set purpose, as in *Lib. Sanhedrim*,
are foolish contradictious triflings, wherein they leave all things as uncertain,
as if they were wrangling in their wonted manner, *de lana caprina*. So that for
my part, I am not much removed from the opinion of Hulsius[115] that *Aesop's
Fables*[116] are of as much use in Christian religion, as the Judaical Talmud. While
they keep the Scripture, we shall never want weapons out of their own armory
for their destruction. Like the Philistine, they carry the weapon that will serve
to cut off their own heads. Now the Tiberian Masoretes, the supposed inventors of the points, vowels and accents, which we now use, were men living
after the finishing of the last Talmud, whose whole religion was built thereon.

Who the Tiberian Masoretes Were That Are the Supposed
Authors of the Hebrew Punctuation—Their Description

14. Let us then a little, without prejudice or passion, consider who, or what
these men were, who are the supposed authors of this work. (1) Men they
were (if any such were) who had not the word of God committed to them in
a peculiar manner, as their forefathers had of old, being no part of his church
or people, but were only outwardly possessors of the letter, without just right
or title to it; utterly uninterested in the promise of the communication of the
Spirit, which is the great charter of the church's preservation of truth (Isa.
59:21). (2) Men so remote from a right understanding of the word, or the
mind and will of God therein, that they were desperately engaged to oppose
his truth in the books which themselves enjoyed in all matters of importance
unto the glory of God, or the good of their own souls, from the beginning
to the ending. The foundation of whose religion, was infidelity, and one of

114 In his *De arcanis Catholicae veritatis*, Galatino refers to a Christian Kabbalistic apologetic text,
גלי רזייא ("*Gale Razeya*," as per Galatino's Latin translation), which he alleges to be the work of
Rabbi Hakkadosh or Judah ha-Nasi (ca. 135–217), who is famous for compiling the Mishnah.
The text does not actually exist and is likely to be a forgery, a charge that Galatino would emphatically deny. Owen, like others, is clearly doubtful of its existence.
115 In the text: (*lib. 1. pa. 2. dic: sup. de temp. Messiae*).—Owen. See *Dicta sapientum de tempore
adventus Messiae* (bk. 1, pt. 2), in Antonius Hulsius, *Theologiae Iudaicae pars prima de Messia*
(Breda: Abrahamus Subbengius, 1653), 235–528. Antonius Hulsius (1615–1685) was a German
Reformed theologian and philologist. He later became professor of theology and Hebrew at
Leiden.
116 A famous collection of Ancient Greek stories credited to Aesop that from the Renaissance
onward were used for the ethical instruction of children.

their chief fundamentals an opposition to the gospel.[117] (3) Men under the special curse of God, and his vengeance, upon the account of the blood of his dear Son. (4) Men all their days feeding themselves with vain fables, and mischievous devices against the gospel, laboring to set up a new religion under the name of the old, in despite of God, so striving to wrestle it out with his curse to the utmost. (5) Men of a profound ignorance in all manner of learning and knowledge, but only what concerned their own dunghill traditions;[118] as appears in their stories, wherein they make Pyrrhus king of Epirus,[119] help Nebuchadnezzar against Jerusalem; with innumerable the like fopperies.[120] (6) Men so addicted to such monstrous figments, as appears in their Talmuds, as their successors of after ages are ashamed of, and seek to palliate, what they are able; yea for the most part idolaters and magicians, as I shall evince. Now I dare leave it to the judgment of any godly prudent person, not addicted to parties and names of men, who is at all acquainted with the importance of the Hebrew vowels and accents unto the right understanding of the Scripture, with what influence their present fixation has into the literal sense we embrace, whether we need not very clear evidence and testimony, yea undeniable and unquestionable, to cast the rise and spring of them upon the invention of this sort of men.

That Figment Rejected

15. Of all the fables that are in the Talmud, I know none more incredible than this story: that men, who cannot by any story or other record, be made to appear, that they ever were in *rerum natura:*[121] such men, as we have described, obscure, unobserved, not taken notice of by any learned man, Jew or Christian, should in a time of deep ignorance in the place where they lived, among a people wholly addicted to monstrous fables, themselves blinded under the curse of God, find out so great, so excellent a work, of such unspeakable usefulness, not once advising with the men of their own profession and religion,

117 In the margin: *fundament: nonum. apud Maimon. praefat. ad Perek. Chelek. p. 175. Edit. Poc.*— Owen. Owen is referring to a paragraph from Pococke's edition of Maimonides's *Ad Perek Chelek, seu caput decimum tractatus Sanhedrin praefatio,* beginning thus: *Fundamentum nonum est, [de abgrogatione Legis] scil:* . . . Editor's translation: "Fundamental nine is concerning the abrogation of the Law, namely. . . ." For the Latin text, see Maimonides, *Porta Mosis,* 175.
118 In the margin: *Shobet Jehuda,* p. 40.—Owen. See Solomon ibn Verga, *Historia Judaica [Shebeṭ Yehudah],* trans. George van Gent (Amsterdam: Petrus Niellius, 1651), 40.
119 Pyrrhus of Epirus (ca. 318–272 BC) was a Greek king who engaged in heavy warfare with Rome and after whom the term "Pyrrhic victory" was coined.
120 I.e., follies.
121 Lat. "the nature of things."

who then flourished in great abundance at Babylon, and the places adjacent, and impose it on all the world (that receive the Scriptures) and have every tittle of their work received, without any opposition or question, from any person or persons, of any principle whatever; yea so, as to have their invention made the constant rule of all following expositions, comments, and interpretations: *Credat Apella.*[122]

To draw then to the close of this discourse; I must crave liberty to profess, that if I could be thoroughly convinced, that the present Hebrew punctuation were the figment and invention of these men, I should labor to the utmost to have it utterly taken away out of the Bible, nor should [I] (in its present station) make use of it any more. What use such an invention might be of under catholic rules in a way of grammar, I shall not dispute; but to have it placed in the Bible, as so great a part of the word of God, is not tolerable. But blessed be God, things are not as yet come to that pass. I shall only add, that whereas some of the most eminently learned and exercised persons in all the learning and antiquity of the Jews, that these latter ages have produced, have appeared in the confutation of this fancy of the invention of the points by some post-Talmudical Masoretes, I am sorry their respect to the Rabbins has kept them from the management of this consideration, which is to me of so great importance.

The Late Testimony of Dr. Lightfoot to This Purpose

16. To what I have spoken I shall add the words of learned Dr. Lightfoot in his late *Centuria chorograph*, which came to my hands since the finishing of this discourse.[123] In the words of this learned person there is the sum of what I am pleading for. Says he, "I do not admire the Jews' impudence, who found

---

122 Lat. "let Apella believe it." This is a figurative saying drawn from Horace indicating incredulity. Horace remarks, *Credit Iudaeus Apella, non ego* (*Satires*, bk. 1, satire 5, line 100). English translation: "Apella, the Jew, may believe it, not I." For English translation, see Horace, *Satires. Epistles, The Art of Poerty*, H. Rushton Fairclough, Loeb Classical Library 194 (Cambridge, MA: Harvard University Press, 1926), 73.

123 In the text: cap. 81. p. 146. *sunt qui punctata Biblia credunt a sapientibus Tiberiensibus;* (he means Elias only, for other Jews of this opinion there are none). *Ego impudentiam Judaeorum, qui fabulam invenerunt non mirror: Christianorum credulitatem miror, qui applaudunt. Recognosce (quaeso) nomina Tiberiensium, a sita illic primum academia ad eam expirantem: & quidnam tandem invenies, nisi genus hominum, prae Pharisaismo insaniens, traditionibus fascinans & fascinatum, caecum, vafrum, delirum; ignoscant, si dicam magicum & monstrosum? Ad opus tam divinum homines quam ineptos, quam stolidos! Perlege Talmud Hierosolymitanum, et nota qualiter illic se habeant R. Juda, R. Chamnath, Z. Judan, R. Hoshaia, R. Chaija Rubba, R. Chaija Bar Ba, R. Jochanan, reliquique inter Tiberienses grandissimi doctors, quam serio nihil agunt, quam pueriliter seria, quanta in ipsorum disputationibus vafrities, spuma, venenum, fumus, nihil: & si punctata fuisse Biblia in istiusmodi schola potes credere, crede & omnia Talmudica. Opus Spiritus Sancti sapit punctatio Bibliorum, non opus hominum perditorum, exaecatorum,*

out that fable; I admire Christians' credulity who applaud it. Recount I pray the names of the Tiberians from the first foundation of a university there to the expiring thereof, and what do you find, but a sort of men being mad with (or above) the Pharisees, bewitching and bewitched with traditions, blind, crafty, raging; pardon me if I say magical, and monstrous? What fools, what sots as to such a divine work? Read over the Talmud of Jerusalem, consider how R. Juda, R. Chanina,[124] R. Chaija Bar Ba,[125] R. Jochanan,[126] R. Jonathan,[127] and the rest of the great doctors among the Tiberians do behave themselves? How seriously they do nothing? How childish they are in serious things, how much deceitfulness, froth, venom, smoke, nothing, in their disputations: and if you can believe the points of the Bible to proceed from such a school, believe also their Talmuds; the pointing of the Bible savors of the work of the Holy Spirit, not of wicked, blind, and mad men."

The Rise of the Opinion of the Novelty of the Points: Elias Levita and the Value of His Testimony in This Case

17. The Jews generally believe these points to have been from mount Sinai, and so downward by Moses and the prophets; at least from Ezra and his companions, the men of the great synagogue, not denying that the knowledge and use of them received a great reviving by the Gemarists and Masoretes, when they had been much disused; so R. Azarias at large.[128]

Had it been otherwise, surely men stupendously superstitious in inquiring after the traditions of their fathers would have found some footsteps of their rise and progress. It is true, there is not only the opinion, but there are the arguments of one of them to the contrary, namely Elias Levita; this Elias

---

amentium.—Owen. Owen's English translation follows in the text. Owen is quoting from *In chorographicam aliquam terrae Israeliticae.* See Lightfoot, *Horae,* pt. 1, pp. 146–47.

124 Hanina bar Hama (d. ca. 250) was a Jewish Talmudist who was a student of Judah ha-Nasi and is frequently mentioned in the Mishnah and Talmuds.

125 Hiyya bar Abba (fl. late 200s) was a Jewish Palestinian Amora who was a student of Hanina and Joshua ben Levi and is frequently mentioned in the Talmuds.

126 Johanan bar Nappaha (180–279) was a Jewish Amora who is frequently quoted in the Talmuds and is thought to have been responsible for compiling the Jerusalem Talmud.

127 Owen has condensed the list of names in Lightfoot's original, but adds "R. Jonathan." Owen could be referring to Rabbi Jonathan (ben Joseph) who was a Tanna of the second century and is occasionally mentioned in various compilations of the Mishnah. Lightfoot mentions R. Hoshaia or Rabbi Josiah in his list, another second-century Tanna, who was a fellow student alongside Rabbi Jonathan, with whom he is frequently associated.

128 In the text: *Imre Binah. cap.* 59.—Owen. This is a treatise (lit., "Sayings of the Wise") contained within his famous *Me'or enayim.* For an English translation, see Azariah de' Rossi, *The Light of the Eyes,* trans. Joanna Weinberg (New Haven, CT: Yale University Press, 2001).

lived in Germany about the beginning of the Reformation, and was the most learned grammarian of the Jews in that age. Sundry of the first Reformers had acquaintance with him; the task not only of reforming religion, but also of restoring good literature being incumbent on them, they made use of such assistances as were to be obtained then to that purpose. This man (which[129] Thuanus takes notice of) lived with Paulus Fagius, and assisted him in his noble promotion of the Hebrew tongue.[130] Hence haply it is that some of those worthies, unwarily embraced his novel opinion, being either overborne with his authority, or not having leisure to search further after the truth. That the testimony of this one Elias should be able to outweigh the constant attestation of all other learned Jews to the contrary, as Capellus affirms and pleads, and as is insinuated in our *Prolegomena*,[131] is fond to imagine; and the premises of that learned man fight against his own conclusion. It is known says he, that the Jews are prone to insist on everything that makes for the honor of their people and language, and therefore their testimony, to the divine original of the present punctuation being in their own case, is not to be admitted. Only Elias who in this speaks against the common interest of his people is presumed to speak upon conviction of truth. But the whole evidence in this cause is on the other side. Let us grant that all the Jews are zealous of the honor and reputation of their nation and language; as they are: let us grant that they greedily close with everything, that may seem to have a tendency

---

129 In the margin: *Eodem fere tempore Palatinus abolita pontificia authoritate doctrinam Lutheri recepit, eaque de causa Paulum Fagium tabernis Rhenanis in Palatinatu natum Hiedelbergam evocavit. Is sub Volfgango Capitone perfectissimam linguae, sanctae cognitionem adeptus, cum egestate premeretur, Petri Busteri veri locupletis Isnae in qua ille docebat senatoris liberalitate sublevatus Heliam illum Judaeorum doctissimum accersendum curavit, & instituta typographica officina, maximum ad solidam rerum Hebraicarum cognitionem momentum attulit. Thuanus Hist. lib. 2. ad An. 1564. 546.*—Owen. Editor's translation: "At about the same time, the Count Palatine received the teaching of Luther, with papal authority having been abolished, for that reason he summoned to Heidelberg Paul Fagius who had been born in Rheinzabern in the Palatinate. Having obtained a most perfect knowledge of the sacred tongue under Wolfgang Capito, when he was struggling in poverty, he was supported by the generosity of Petrus Busterus, a senator of considerable wealth in Isny, where he was teaching. So he managed to call Elias, that most educated Jew, and having set up a printing press he added great momentum to the sound knowledge of Hebrew matters." Owen's quotation is an abridgment of the original. For the Latin text, in the later Buckley edition, see Jacques Auguste de Thou, *Historiarum sui temporis* (London: Samuel Buckley, 1733), t. 1, bk. 2, p. 59. Jacques Auguste de Thou (1553–1617) was a French historian and Parliamentarian.

130 Paul Fagius (1504–1549) was a German Protestant Hebraist who taught Old Testament at Strasbourg and later at Cambridge. As alluded to in de Thou's comment above, Levita spent 1540–1542 with Fagius overseeing the printing press at Isny.

131 In the margin: *Proleg. 3. sec. 42.*—Owen. See Brian Walton, *In Biblia polyglotta prolegomena*, 2 vols. (Cambridge: J. Smith, 1827–1828), 1:198–200.

thereunto:[132] what will be the issue or natural inference from these premises? Why as nothing could be spoken more honorably of the Jews, while they were the church and people of God, than that of Paul, that to them were committed the oracles of God,[133] so nothing can be imagined or fixed on, more to their honor, since their divorce from God, than that their doctors and masters should make such an addition to the Scripture, so generally acknowledged to be unspeakably useful. And to this purpose Elias who was the father of this opinion, was far from making such deductions thence as some do nowadays; namely, that it is lawful for us to change the vowels and accents at our pleasure; but ties all men as strictly to them as if they had been the work of Ezra; it is Elias then that speaks in his own case; whose testimony is therefore not to be admitted. What was done of old, and in the days of Ezra is ours, who succeed unto the privileges of that church; what has been done since the destruction of the temple, is properly and peculiarly theirs.

OF THE VALIDITY OF THE TESTIMONY OF THE JEWISH RABBINS

18. It may perhaps be thought that by the account given of the Rabbins, their state and condition of old and of late, I might have weakened one great argument which learned men make use of, to confirm the sacred antiquity of the present Hebrew punctuation, taken from the universal consent and testimony of the Jewish doctors, ancient and modern, this one Elias, excepted. Who can think such persons are in anything to be believed. But indeed the case is quite otherwise. Though we account them wholly unmeet for the work that is ascribed unto them, and on supposition that it is theirs, affirm that it had need undergo another manner of trial than as yet out of reverence to its generally received antiquity, it has met withal; yet they were men still, who were full well able to declare what de facto they found to be so, and what they found otherwise. It cannot, I think, be reasonably supposed, that so many men living in so many several ages, at such vast distances from one another, who some of them it may be, never heard of the names of other some of them, should conspire to cozen[134] themselves and all the world besides, in a matter of fact not at all to their advantage. However for my part, whatever can be proved against them, I shall willingly admit. But to be driven out of such a rich possession, as is the present Hebrew punctuation, upon mere surmises and conjectures, I cannot willingly give way or consent.

132 The text has a question mark at this point.
133 Owen is alluding to Rom. 3:2.
134 I.e., deceive.

SOME CONSIDERATIONS ABOUT
THE ANTIQUITY OF THE POINTS

19. It is not my design to give in arguments for the divine original of the present Hebrew punctuation; neither do I judge it necessary for any one so to do, while the learned Buxtorfius [Jr.'s] discourse, *De origine et antiquitate punctorum,*[135] lies unanswered. I shall therefore only add one or two considerations, which to me are of weight, and not as I remember mentioned by him or his father in his *Tiberias,* or any other that I know of in their disputes to this purpose.

The First from the Nature of the Punctuation Itself, in Reference unto Grammatical Rules

First, if the points; or vowels and accents, be coevous with the rest of the letters, or have an original before all grammar of that language (as indeed languages are not made by grammar, but grammars are made by languages) then the grammar of it and them, must be collected from the observation of their use, as they were found in all their variety before any such art, was invented or used; and rules must be suited thereunto; the drawing into rules all the instances that being uniform would fall under such rules, and the distinct observation of anomalous words, either singly, or in exceptions comprehending many under one head, that would not be so reduced, was the work of grammar. But on the other side, if the vowels and accents were invented by themselves, and added to the letters, then the rule and art of disposing, transposing, and changing of them, must be constituted and fixed before the disposition of them; for they were placed after the rules made, and according to them. A middle way that I know of, cannot be fixed on. Either they are of the original writing of the language, and have had rules made by their station therein, or they have been supplied unto it according to rules of art. Things are not thus come to pass by chance; nor was this world created by a casual concurrence of these atoms. Now if the grammar or art was the ground and foundation, not the product of their use, as I am confident I shall never see a tolerable answer given to that inquiry of Buxtorfius the elder in his *Tiberias,*[136] why the inventors of them left so many words anomalous and pointed otherwise than according to rule, or the constant course of the language, precisely reckoning them up when they had so done, and how often

---

135 See Buxtorf Jr., *Tractatus.*
136 See Buxtorf Sr., *Tiberias.*

they are so used, as ‿ and ‿ for ‿ and ‿ for ‿ and the like,[137] when they might, if they had so pleased, have made them all regular, to their own great ease, advantage of their language, and facilitating the learning of it to all posterity, the thing they seem to have aimed at; so I cannot be satisfied why in that long operose[138] and curious work of the Masoretes, wherein they have reckoned up every word in the Scripture, and have observed the irregularity of every letter and tittle, they never once attempt to give us out those catholic rules whereby they, or their masters proceeded in affixing the points; or whence it came to pass, that no learned Jew for hundreds of years after, should be able to acquaint us with that way, but in all their grammatical instructions, should merely collect observations, and inculcate them a hundred times over, according as they present themselves to them by particular instances. Assuredly had this wonderful art of pointing, which for the most part may be reduced to catholic rules, and might have wholly been so, if it were an arbitrary invention limited to no preexisting writing, been found out first, and established as the *norma*[139] and canon of affixing the vowels, some footsteps of it would have remained in the Masora, or among some of the Jews, who spent all their time and days in the consideration of it.

The Second from the Chaldee Paraphrase and the Integrity of the Scripture as Now Pointed

20. Secondly, in the days of the Chaldee Paraphrast,[140] when the prophecies of the humiliation and death of their Messiah were only not understood by them, yet we see into how many several ways and senses they are wrested by that *Paraphrast* to affix some tolerable meaning to them. Take an instance on Isaiah the 53:[141] Jonathan[142] there acknowledges the whole prophecy to be intended of Christ, as knowing it to be the common faith of the church; but

---

137 The vowel points (such as those referred to here) on most Hebrew words are often subject to variation depending on a word's tense, number, gender, affixes, relationship to other words (e.g., nouns in the construct state), or even placement in a verse (such as an accented final vowel). One may also find spelling variations at certain points, particularly in association with vowels.
138 I.e., tedious.
139 Lat. "rule."
140 This is a reference to the Aramaic Targums, which are paraphrases of the Old Testament. The main Targums are the Targum Onkelos on the Penteteuch and the Targum Jonathan on the Prophets. A translation into Aramaic had become necessary by the end of the first-century BC as Hebrew was used only in formal education and in worship.
141 Owen is referring to Isa. 53.
142 I.e., the Targum Jonathan, whose authorship is attributed to Jonathan ben Uzziel, a Tanna who studied under Hillel the Elder during the Roman occupation of Judea.

not understanding the state of humiliation which the Messiah was to undergo, he wrests the words into all forms, to make that which is spoken passively of Christ, as to his suffering from others, to signify actively, as to his doing and exercising judgment upon others. But now more than five hundred years after, when these points are supposed to be invented, when the Rabbins were awake, and knew full well what use was made of those places against them, as also that the prophets (especially Isaiah) are the most obscure part of the whole Scripture, as to the grammatical sense of their words in their coherence without points and accents, and how facile it were, to invert the whole sense of many periods by small alterations, in these rules of reading; yet as they are pointed, they make out incomparably more clearly the Christian faith, than any ancient translations of those places whatever. Johannes Isaac, a converted Jew[143] tells us that above two hundred testimonies about Christ may be brought out of the original Hebrew, that appear not in the Vulgar Latin, or any other translation. And Raymundus Martinus; "They knew that there are things of this kind" (that is who blamed him for translating things immediately out of the Hebrew, not following the Vulgar Latin) "in a great many passages of sacred Scripture that much more evidently and perfectly contain truth supporting the Christian faith in the Hebrew script than in our translation."[144] Let any man consider those two racks of the Rabbins, and swords of Judaical unbelief, Isaiah 53 and Daniel 9; as they are now pointed and accented, in our Bibles, and compare them with the translation of the LXX: and this will quickly appear unto him. Especially has this been evidenced, since the Socinians[145] as well as the Jews, have driven the dispute about the satisfaction of Christ to the utmost scrutiny, and examination of every word in that fifty-third of Isaiah. But yet as the text stands now pointed, and accented, neither Jews nor Socinians (notwithstanding the relief contributed to them by Grotius, wresting that whole blessed prophecy to make application of it unto Jeremiah, thinking therein to outdo the late or modern Jews,

143 In the text: *lib. 1. ad Lindan.*—Owen. See Isaac, *Defensio*, 3–60.

144 In the text: *Noverint quae ejusmodi sunt* [. . .] *in plurimis valde sacrae Scripturae locis veritatem multo planius atque perfectius pro fide Christiana haberi in litera Hebraica quam in translatione nostra: Proem. ad pug. fid. sec. 14.*—Owen. Editor's translation. For the Latin text, see "Proemium," in Martini, *Pugio fidei*, 8.

145 In the margin: *Faustus Socin. de Jesu Christo Servatore. Crellius Cont: Grot. pag. 62.*—Owen. For "*Faustus Socin. de Jesu Christo Servatore*," see Faustus Socinus, *De Iesu Christo servatore* (Kraków: A. Rodecius, 1594). For "*Crellius Cont: Grot. pag. 62*," see Jan Crell, *Ad librum Hugonis Grotii, quem de satisfactione Christi adversus Faustum Socinum senensem scripsit, responsio* (Raków: typis Sternacianis, 1623), 62.

Abarbinel,[146] and others applying it to Josiah, the whole people of the Jews, Messiah Ben Joseph[147] and I know not whom) have been able or ever shall be able, to relieve themselves from the sword of the truth therein. Were such exercitations on the word of God allowable, I could easily manifest, how by changing the distinctive accents, and vowels, much darkness and perplexity might be cast on the contexture of that glorious prophecy. It is known also, that the Jews commonly plead, that one reason why they keep the copy of the law in their synagogues without points is, that the text may not be restrained to one certain sense; but that they may have liberty to draw out various, and as they speak, more eminent senses.

---

146 Isaac ben Judah Abarbanel (1437–1508) was a wealthy Portuguese Jewish financier, philosopher, and biblical exegete. As Owen alludes here, Abarbanel wrote extensively defending the Jewish expectations of the Messiah.

147 Said to be of the tribe of Ephraim, Messiah ben Joseph is an eschatological messianic figure in Jewish writings that is traditionally identified as one of the "craftsmen" in Zech. 1:20.

6

Evaluating the Arguments in Favor of the Late Origin of the Hebrew Vowel Points

1.[1] Arguments for the novelty of the Hebrew points, proposed to consideration. [2–4.] The argument from the Samaritan letters considered and answered. [5.] Of the copy of the Law preserved in the synagogues without points: [6.] The testimony of Elias Levita, and Aben Ezra considered. [7.] Of the silence of the Mishnah, Talmud, and Gemara about the points. [9.] Of the *Keri* and *Ketib*. [10.] Of the number of the points. [11.] Of the ancient translations, Greek, Chaldee, Syriac. [12.] Of Heirome. [13–15.] The new argument of Morinus, in this cause: [16.] The conclusion about the necessity of the points.

ARGUMENTS FOR THE NOVELTY OF THE HEBREW POINTS PROPOSED TO CONSIDERATION

1. But because this seems to be a matter of great importance, wherein the truth formerly pleaded for appears to be nearly concerned, I shall ὡς ἐν παρόδῳ[2] very briefly consider the arguments that are usually insisted on (as in these *Prolegomena*) to prove the points to be a novel invention; I mean of the men, and

---

1   The numbering sequence of these headings in the original corresponds to the numbered observations in this chapter rather than the numbered sections, as per the usual pattern. For consistency, the headings have been renumbered as per the sections.

2   Gk. "as in passing."

at the time before mentioned. Particular instances I shall not insist upon: nor is it necessary I should so do; it has been done already. The heads of arguments which yet contain their strength, are capable of a brief dispatch; which shall be given them in the order wherein they are represented by the *Prolegomena*.[3]

1. THE ARGUMENT FROM THE SAMARITAN LETTERS CONSIDERED AND ANSWERED

2. It is said, then that whereas the old Hebrew letters, were the present Samaritan, the Samaritan letters having been always without points as they yet continue, it is manifest that the invention of the points must be of a later date than the change of the letters, which was in the days of Ezra, and so consequently be the work of the post-Talmudical Masoretes. *Pergula pictoris!*[4] This whole objection is made up of most uncertain conjectures. This is not a place to speak at large of the Samaritans, their Pentateuch and its translation. The original of that nation is known from the Scripture, as also their worship of God, 2 Kings 17. Their solemn excommunication and casting out from any interest among the people of God, is also recorded (Ezra 9; Neh. 6 and 13). Their continuance in their abominations after the closing of the canon of the Scripture is reported by Josephus.[5] In the days of the Machabees[6] they were conquered by Hyrcanus,[7] and brought into subjection by the Jews.[8] Yet their

---

3   In the text: Proleg. 3.38, 39, 40.—Owen. See Brian Walton, *In Biblia polyglotta prolegomena*, 2 vols. (Cambridge: J. Smith, 1827–1828), 1:184–94.

4   Lat. "the workshop of a painter."

5   In the text: *Antiq. lib.*11.*c.*8.—Owen. For the Greek text in the nineteenth-century critical edition, see *Antiquitatum Iudaicarum*, bk. 9, lines 313–47, in Josephus, *Opera edidit et apparatu critico instruxit*, 7 vols., ed. Benedikt Niese (Berlin: Weidmannos, 1885–1895), 3:64–70. For the Greek text and an English translation, see Josephus, *Jewish Antiquities*, vol. 4, *Books I–IV*, trans. Ralph Marcus, Loeb Classical Library 326 (Cambridge, MA: Harvard University Press, 1937), 464–83. Owen's citation (which includes a chapter number) reflects extant published editions of the sixteenth and seventeenth centuries, such as the following Latin edition published by Frobenius in 1540: Josephus, *Antiquitatum et al.* (1540), 301–3. The reference given in this footnote for the nineteenth-century Greek critical edition corresponds to the full chapter division in the 1540 Frobenius edition.

6   I.e., Maccabees. Here Owen is using the label in reference to the Hasmonean dynasty that was founded by a group of Jewish rebels (the Maccabees) who took control of Judea and defeated the Seleucids in the second-century BC.

7   John Hyrcanus I (164–104 BC) was Hasmonean High Priest and leader of the Jews from 134–104 BC. He was responsible for defeating the Samaritans and destroying the Samaritan temple on Mount Gerizim.

8   In the text: *Joseph. Antiq. Lib.* 13: *cap.* 17.—Owen. For the Greek text in the nineteenth-century critical edition, see *Antiquitatum Iudaicarum*, bk. 13, lines 269–300, in Josephus, *Opera*, 3:201–7. For the Greek text and an English translation, see Josephus, *Jewish Antiquities*, vol. 5,

will-worship[9] upon the credit of the tradition of their fathers continued to the days of our Savior, and their hatred to the people of God (John 4). When, by whom, in what character they first received the Pentateuch, is most uncertain; not likely by the priest sent to them; for notwithstanding his instructions they continued in open idolatry; which evidences that they had not so much as seen the book of the Law. Probably this was done when they were conquered by Hyrcanus, and their temple razed after it had stood two hundred years. So also did the Edomites. What diligence they used in the preservation of it, being never committed to them by God, we shall see afterward. That there are any of them remaining at this day, or have been these thousand years past, is unknown. That the letters of their Pentateuch were the ancient Hebrew letters, as Eusebius, Heirome and some of the Rabbins report, seems to me (on the best inquiry I have been able to make) a groundless tradition and mere fable. The evidences tendered for to prove it, are much too weak to bear the weight of such an assertion. Eusebius speaks only on report; *affirmatur;*[10] it was so affirmed, on what ground he tells us not. Hierome indeed is more positive; but give me leave to say, that supposing this to be false, sufficient instances of the like mistakes may be given in him. For the testimony of the Talmud, I have often declared, that with me it is of no weight, unless seconded by very good evidence. And indeed the foundation of the whole story is very vain. The Jews are thought and said to have forgot their own characters in the captivity, and to have learned the Chaldean, upon the account whereof they adhered unto it after their return; when the same men were alive at the burning of the one, and the building of the other temple; that the men of one and the same generation should forget the use of their own letters, which they had been exercised in, is incredible. Besides they had their Bibles with them always, and that in their own character only; whither they had any one other book or no we know not: and whence then this forgetting of one character, and learning of another should arise, does not appear. Nor shall I in such an improbable fiction lay much weight on testimonies, the most ancient whereof is six hundred years later than the pretended matter of fact.

Books V–VIII, trans. Ralph Marcus, Loeb Classical Library 365 (Cambridge, MA: Harvard University Press, 1943), 362–79. Based on the chapter he cites, Owen is seemingly referring to the chapter divisions reflected in the earlier 1540 Frobenius edition rather than that which is included in the later Frobenius edition of Josephus's works. See Josephus, *Antiquitatum et al.* (1540), 350–52. In the later edition, Hyrcanus's defeat of Samaria is narrated in chap. 18 rather than 17; see Josephus, *Opera omnia* (Basel: Frobenius, 1582), 246–48. Goold has altered the chapter reference to "cap. x," reflecting further changes to the chapter divisions in later editions.

9   I.e., self-invented worship.
10   Lat. "it is affirmed."

3. The most weighty proof in this case is taken from the ancient Judaical coins, taken up with Samaritan characters upon them. We are now in
the high road of forgeries and fables: in nothing has the world been more
cheated. But be it granted that the pretended coins are truly ancient; must
it needs follow, that because the letters were then known, and in use, that
they only were so: that the Bible was written with them, and those now in
use unknown. To salve the credit of the coins, I shall crave leave to answer
this conjecture with another. The Samaritan letters are plainly preternatural[11]
(if I may so say) a studied invention; in their frame and figure fit to adorn,
when extended or greatened by way of engraving or embossing anything
they shall be put upon, or cut in. Why may we not think they were invented
for that purpose: namely to engrave on vessels, and to stamp on coin, and
so came to be of some use in writing also. Their shape and frame promise
some such thing. And this is rendered the more probable from the practice
of the Egyptians, who as Clemens Alexan:[12] tells us, had three sorts of letters, one which he calls ἐπιστολογραφική,[13] with which they wrote things
of common use; another termed by him ἱερογραφική,[14] used by the priests
in the sacred writings: and the other ἱερογλυφική:[15] which also was of two

---

11 I.e., beyond the natural.
12 In the text: Αὐτίκα δὲ οἱ παρ᾿ Αἰγυπτίοις παιδευόμενοι, πρῶτον μὲν πάντων τὴν Αἰγυπτίων γραμ-
μάτων μέθοδον ἐκμανθάνουσι, τὴν ἐπιστολογραφικὴν καλουμένην· δευτέραν δε, ἱερατικὴν ᾗ
χρῶνται οἱ ἱερογραμματεῖς· ὑστάτην δὲ καὶ τελευταίαν, τὴν ἱερολυφικὴν ἧς ἡ μέν ἐστι διὰ τῶν
πρωτῶν στοιχείων κυριολογικὴ· ἡ δὲ συμβολική, τῆς δὲ συμβολικῆς ἡ μὲν κυριολογεῖται κατὰ
μίμησιν· ἡ δὲ ὥσπερ τροπικῶς γράφεται, ἡ δὲ ἄντικρυς ἀλληγορεῖται κατά τινας αἰνιγμούς·
ἥλιον γὰρ οὖν γράψαι βουλόμενοι, κύκλον ποιοῦσι· σελήνην δὲ, σχῆμα μηνοειδὲς, κατὰ τὸ
κυριολογούμενον εἶδος. Clem. Alex. stromat. lib. 5.—Owen. "Now those instructed among the
Egyptians learned first of all that style of the Egyptian letters that is called Epistolographic; and
second, the Hieratic, which the sacred scribes practice; and finally, and last of all, the Hieroglyphic,
of which one kind that is by the first elements is literal (Kyriologic), and the other symbolic. Of
the symbolic, one kind speaks literally by imitation, and another writes as it were figuratively; and
another is quite allegorical, using certain enigmas. Wishing to express Sun in writing, they make
a circle; and Moon, a figure like the Moon, like its proper shape." For a modern critical Greek edition, with some minor variations from Owen's quotation, see Stromata bk. 5, chap 4, sec. 20.3–4,
in Clement of Alexandria, Les stromates. Stromata V/1, trans. Pierre Voulet, ed. Alain Le Boulluec,
Sources Chrétiennes 278 (Paris: Les Éditions du Cerf, 2006), 58. For the English translation, see
Clement of Alexandria, The Stromata, or Miscellanies, bk. 5, chap. 4, in Arthur Cleveland Coxe,
Alexander Roberts, and James Donaldson, eds., Ante-Nicene Fathers, vol. 2, Fathers of the Second
Century: Hermas, Tatian, Athenagoras, Theophilus, and Clement of Alexandria (Entire) (Buffalo:
Christian Literature, 1885), 449. Clement of Alexandria (ca. 150–ca. 215) was an early Christian
theologian whose writings reflect his deep familiarity with Hellenistic philosophy and literature.
13 Gk. "letter writing," or certain symbols used in writing letters.
14 Gk. "holy writings," or a form of symbols that are sacred.
15 Gk. "hieroglyphics," or the remaining set of Egyptian symbols out of the three mentioned here.

sorts, simple and symbolical. Seeing then it was no unusual thing to have sundry sorts of letters for sundry purposes, it is not improbable that it was so also among the Jews: not that they wrote the sacred writings in a peculiar character as it were to hide them, which is declaimed against, but only that the other character might be in use for some purposes which is not unusual: I cannot think the Greeks of old used only the uncial letters,[16] which yet we know some did; though he did not, who wrote Homer's *Iliad* in no greater a volume, than would go into a nutshell.

4. But if that should be granted, that cannot be proved, namely that such a change was made; yet this prejudices not them in the least, who affirm Ezra and the men of the great congregation to have been the authors of the points, seeing the authors of this rumor affixed, that as the time wherein the old Hebrew letters were excommunicated out of the church; together with the Samaritans. Nay it cast a probability on the other hand, namely that Ezra laying aside the old letters because of their difficulty, together with the new, introduced the points to facilitate their use. Nor can it be made to appear that the Samaritan letters had never any vowels affixed to them. Postellus affirms that the Samaritans had points in the days of Heirome, and that their loss of them is the cause of their present corrupt reading. "Today they are bereft of those points which they had in the days of Jerome: and [thus] they read [the text] without points in a quite unsound manner":[17] There were always some copies written without vowels, which might be preserved, and the others lost. That people (if we have anything from them,) being wicked, ignorant, sottish, superstitious, idolatrous, rejecters of the greatest part of the Scripture, corrupters of what they had received, might neglect the task of transcribing copies with points, because a matter of so great care and diligence to be performed aright. Nor is it improbable, whatever is pretended to the contrary, that continuing in their separation from the people of God, they might get the Law written in a character of their own choosing, out of hatred to the Jews. Now let any man judge, whither from this heap of uncertainties anything can arise with the face of a witness, to be admitted to give testimony

---

16 I.e., a majuscule script, exclusively in capitals, that was used by Greek and Latin scribes in the fourth to eighth centuries AD.

17 In the text: *Punctis hodie quae habebant Hieronymi temporibus carent: leguntque sine punctis admodum depravatè. Postell. Alphab. 12. lingua.*—Owen. Editor's translation. For the Latin text (which Owen has slightly altered), see "De lingua Samaritana," in Guillaume Postel, *Linguarum duodecim characteribus differentium alphabetum* (Paris: Dionysius Lescuier, 1538), *4. Guillaume Postel (1510–1581) was a French linguist and astronomer with idiosyncratic and controversial religious views, which ultimately led to his arrest and he spent his final years in confinement.

in the cause in hand. He that will part with his possession on such easy terms never found much benefit in it.

2. OF THE COPY OF THE LAW PRESERVED IN THE SYNAGOGUES WITHOUT POINTS

5. The constant practice of the Jews in preserving in their synagogues one book, which they almost adore, written without points, is alleged to the same purpose; for what do they else hereby but tacitly acknowledge the points to have a human original. *Answer:* But it is certain they do not so acknowledge them, neither by that practice, nor by any other way; it being the constant opinion and persuasion of them all, (Elias only excepted) that they are of a divine extract; and if their authority be to be urged, it is to be submitted unto in one thing, as well as in another.[18] The Jews give a threefold account of this practice. First, the difficulty of transcribing copies without any failing, the least rendering the whole book as to its use in their synagogues, profane. [Second,] the liberty they have thereby, to draw out various senses, more eminent as they say, indeed more vain and curious, than they have any advantage to do, when the reading is restrained to one certain sense by the vowels and accents. [Third,][19] to keep all learners in dependence on their teachers, seeing they cannot learn the mind of God, but by their exposition.[20] If these reasons satisfy, not any as to the ground of that practice, they may be pleased to inquire of them for others, who intend to be bound by their authority; that the points were invented by some late Masoretes, they will not inform them. For Jesuitical stories out of China, they are with me for the most part of the like credit with those of the Jews in their Talmud; he that can believe all the miracles, that they work, where men are not warned of their juggling, may credit them in other things. However, as I said, I do not understand this argument; the Jews keep a book in their synagogues without points, therefore the points and accents were invented by the Tiberian Masoretes; when they never read it, or rather sing it, but according to every point and accent in ordinary use. Indeed the whole profound mystery of this business seems to be this; that none be admitted to read or sing the law in their synagogues, until he be so perfect in it, as to be able to observe exactly all points and accents, in a book wherein there are none of them.

18 Original has "2" at this point, but following Goold it has been omitted here as it appears to have been a copying error.
19 "3" in the original, altered to be consistent with verbally numbered list.
20 In the text: Rab: *Azarias: lib. Imre Bina: cap.* 59.—Owen. See Azariah de' Rossi, *The Light of the Eyes*, trans. Joanna Weinberg (New Haven, CT: Yale University Press, 2001), 699–709.

3. THE TESTIMONY OF ELIAS LEVITA
AND ABEN EZRA CONSIDERED

6. The testimony of Elias Levita, not only as to his own judgment, but also as to what he mentions from Aben Ezra[21] and others, is insisted on. They affirm, says he, that we have received the whole punctuation from the Tiberian Masoretes. *Answer:* It is very true, that Elias was of that judgment; and it may well be supposed, that if that opinion had not fallen into his mind, the world had been little acquainted with it at this day. That by receiving of the punctuation from the Tiberians, the continuation of it in their school, not the invention of it is intended by Aben Ezra, is beyond all exception evinced by Buxtorfius [Jr.].[22] Nor can anything be spoken more directly to the contrary of what is intended, than that which is urged in the *Prolegomena* from Aben Ezra,[23] where he affirms that he saw some books examined in all the letters, and the whole punctuation by the wise men of Tiberias; namely to try, whether it were done exactly, according to the patterns they had. Besides all Elias's arguments are notably answered by R. Azarias; whose answers are repeated by Joseph de Voysin in his most learned observations, on the *Proemium* of the *Pugio fidei*.[24] And the same Azarias shows the consistency of the various opinions that were among the Jews about the vowels, ascribing them as to their virtue and force, to Moses, or God on Mount Sinai; as to their figure and character to Ezra; as to the restoration of their use, unto the Masoretes.

4. OF THE SILENCE OF THE MISHNAH, TALMUD,
AND GEMARA, ABOUT THE POINTS

7. The silence of the Mishnah, Gemara, or whole Talmud, concerning the points is further urged. This argument is also at large discussed by Buxtorfius [Jr.], and the instances in it answered to the full: nor is it needful for any man to add anything further, until what he has discoursed to this purpose be removed.[25] See

21 Abraham ibn Ezra (ca. 1089–1167) was an influential Spanish Jewish Hebraist and biblical commentator.
22 In the text: *De Punct. Antiq. p.* 1. *cap.* 3.—Owen. See Johann Buxtorf Jr., *Tractatus de punctorum vocalium* (Basel: L. König, 1648), 11–38.
23 In the text: *comment. in Exod.* 25:31.—Owen. See Abraham ibn Ezra, *Commentary on the Pentateuch: Exodus (Shemot)*, trans. H. Norman Strickman and Arthur M. Silver (New York: Menorah, 1996), 556–57.
24 In the text: pag. 91. 92.—Owen. Owen is referring to Joseph de Voisin's annotations or "Observationes," in his edition of Raimund Martini's *Pugio fidei*, published in 1651: Raimund Martini, *Pugio fidei* (Paris: Mathurinus Henault, Ioannes Henault, 1651), 91a–93b.
25 In the text: See *part.* 1. *cap.* 6.—Owen. See Buxtorf Jr., *Tractatus*, 76–110.

also Glassius[26] who gives instances to the contrary; yea and the Talmud itself in Nedarim, or "of vows" chapter 4 on Nehemiah 8:8 do plainly mention them: and treatises ancienter than the Talmud cited by Rabbi Azarias in *Imre Binah*[27] expressly speak of them. It is to me a sufficient evidence, able to overbear the conjectures to the contrary, that the Talmudists both knew, and in their readings were regulated by the points now in use, in that, as many learned men have observed, there is not one text of Scripture to be found cited in the Talmud, in any other sense, as to the literal reading and meaning of the word, than only that which it is restrained unto by the present punctuation: when it is known that the patrons of the opinion under consideration, yield this constantly as one reason of the LXX translators reading words and sentences otherwise than we read them now in our Bibles; namely, because the books they used were not pointed, whereby they were at liberty to conjecture at this or that sense of the word before them. This is one of the main pillars of Capellus his whole fabric in his *Critica sacra*.[28] And how it can be fancied there should be no variety between our present reading and the Talmudists', upon supposition they knew not the use of points, I know not. Is it possible, on this supposition, there should be such a coincidence between their and our present punctuation; whereon on the same principle, it seems, there are so many variations by the LXX and the Chaldee Paraphrast?

5. OF THE *KERI* AND *KETIB*

9.[29] Of the קרי וכתיב [*Qere* and *Ketiv*] which are pleaded in the next place to this purpose, I shall speak afterward. The difference in them is in the consonants, not in the vowels, which yet argues not that there were no vowels, when they were collected, or disposed as now we find them. Yea that there were no vowels in the copies from whence they were collected (if they were so collected) may be true; but that that collection was made any later for the main of it, than the days of Ezra, does not appear. Now whatever was done about the Scripture in the Judaical church, before the times of our Savior, is manifest to have been done by divine authority, in that it is nowhere by him

---

26 In the text: *lib. 1. Tract. 12 de Text. Hebraei puritat:*—Owen. See "De Integritate et Puritate Hebraei V. Test. Codicis" (lib. i, tract. 1), in Salomon Glass, *Philologiae sacrae qua totius sacrosanctae, Veteris et Novi Testamenti Scripturae, tum stylus et literatura tum sensus et genuinae interpretationis ratio expenditur* (Frankfurt : Zacharius Hertelius, 1653), 1–124.

27 Owen is likely referring to de' Rossi, *The Light of the Eyes*, 702–3.

28 See Louis Cappel, *Critica sacra, sive De variis quae in sacris Veteris Testamenti libris occurrunt lectionibus* (Paris: S&G Cramoisy, 1650).

29 There is no sec. 8.

reproved: but rather the integrity of every word is by him confirmed. But of these things distinctly by themselves afterward we are to speak.

6. OF THE NUMBER OF THE POINTS

10. A sixth argument for the novelty of the points is taken from their number;[30] for whereas it is said all kinds of sounds may be expressed by five vowels, we are in the present Hebrew punctuation supplied with fourteen or fifteen, which as it is affirmed, manifests abundantly that they are not coevous or connatural to the language itself, but the arbitrary, artificial invention of men, who have not assigned a sufficient difference in their force and sound to distinguish them in pronunciation. But this objection seems of small importance. The ground of it is an apprehension, that we still retain exactly the true pronunciation of the Hebrew tongue, which is evidently false. (1) It is now near two thousand years, since that tongue was vulgarly[31] spoken in its purity by any people or nation. To imagine that the true, exact, distinct pronunciation of every tittle and syllable in it, as it was used by them, to whom it was vulgar and natural, is communicated unto us, or is attainable by us, is to dream pleasantly while we are awake. Aben Ezra makes it no small matter that men of old knew aright how to pronounce *Camets Gadol*.[32] Says he[33] "The men of Tiberias, also the wise men of Egypt and Africa knew how to read Kamets Gadol." (2) Even the distinct force of one consonant, and that always radical ע is utterly lost, so that the present Jews know nothing of its pronunciation. (3) Nor can we distinguish now between תב and טק, between ב and ו. Though the Jews tell us that the wise men of Tiberias could do so twelve hundred years ago; as also be-tween ָ and ָ , ָ and ָ , ו and ָ . Nor is the distinct sound of עחהא so obvious unto us. (4) The variety of consonants among many nations, and their ability to distinguish them in pronunciation, makes this of little consideration. The

---

30 The following point contains a technical discussion of the number of distinct sounds made by the various Hebrew vowel points. In summary, Owen is arguing against the premise that due to their large number ("fourteen or fifteen"), the Hebrew vowel points are evidently an arbitrary and late invention of scribes. Rather, he points out that the number of Hebrew vowel symbols is actually smaller than claimed and also that we do not know the exact pronunciation of them or of the Hebrew consonants. This latter point means that contemporary critics cannot claim that the vowel points are an artificial invention due to them being insufficiently distinct from each other, as some of that knowledge of pronunciation has been lost over time. Owen goes on to illustrate the absurdity of the claim by referring to a discourse on English vowel sounds by his friend John Wilkins.

31 I.e., commonly.

32 I.e., the longer form of kamatz, representing the vowel sound "a."

33 In the text: אנשי טבריא גם חכמי מצרים ואפריקא יודעים לקרוא הקמץ גדול.

whole nation of the Germans distinguish not between the force and sound of *t* and *d*, whereas the Arabic *dal* and *dhsal*, *dad*, *ta* and *da* manifest how they can distinguish those sounds. (5) Nor are the Jewish ש שׂ ס ז צ answered distinctly in any other language; to distinguish some of which, good old Hierome had his teeth filed by the direction of his[34] Nicodemus. (6) The truth is, the Hebrews have but ten vowels, five long, and five short, or five great and five less; *sheva* is but a servant to all the rest; and its addition to *segol* and *patha*[*kh*] makes no new vowels. To distinguish between *Camets Hateph*, and *Hateph Camets* there is no color. Seven only of them, as Morinus has manifested out of R. Jehuda Chiug, one of the first grammarians among the Jews, namely ְ ֱ ֳ ֲ ֶ ֵ ֻ they called (of old) kings, or the chief rulers of all the motions of the letters. So that indeed they have not so many figures to distinguish sounds by, with all their vowels, as have the Greeks. Besides the seven vowels they have twelve diphthongs, and three of them as to any peculiar sound as mute as *sheva*. It is true, Pliny tells us that Simonides Melicus[35] found out two of the vowels, η and ω, as he did also two consonants, ζ and ψ: but surely he did so, because he found them needful to answer the distinct sounds used in that language, or he had deserved little thanks for his invention.[36] Speaking lately with a worthy

---

34 In the margin: *Veni rursum Hierosolymam, & Bethlehem ubi labore pretii Bartemium Judaeum nocturnum habui praeceptorem, timebat enim Judaeos, & exhibebat se mihi alium Nicodemum. Hieron. Epist. ad Oceanum.*—Owen. Editor's translation: "In turn, I went to Jerusalem and Bethlehem where I had Bartemaeus, a Jew, as a hired teacher, and he proved himself to me to be another Nicodemus." For the critical edition of the Latin text, with minor variations from Owen's quotation, see *Ad Pammachium et Oceanum (Epist. 84)*, sec. 3, in Jerome, *Epistulae II*, 71–120, ed. Isodore Hilberg, Corpus Scriptorum Ecclesiasticorum Latinorum 55 (Vienna: Verlag der Österreichischen Akademie der Wissenschaften, 1996), 123.

35 Simonides of Ceos (ca. 556–468 BC) was a Greek poet who is credited by Pliny for inventing the four letters of the Greek alphabet Owen mentions here.

36 In the margin: *Literas semper arbitror Assyrias fuisse, sed alii apud Egyptios a Mercurio, ut Gellius; alii apud Tyros* [*sic: Syros*] *repertas volunt: utique in Graeciam intulisse e Phoenice Cadmum sexdecim numero, quibus Trojano bello adjecisse quatuor hac figurâ* θ ξ φ χ. *Palimedem totidem, post eum Simonidem Melicum* ζ η ψ ω, *quarum omnium vis in nostris cognoscitur; Plinius Nat. Hist.* lib. 7. Cap. 56. *Quae quis in vita invenerit.*—Owen. English translation: "I am of the opinion that the Assyrians have always had writing, but others, e.g., Gellius, hold that it was invented in Egypt by Mercury, while others think it was discovered in Syria; both schools of thought believe that Cadmus imported an alphabet of 16 letters into Greece from Phoenecia and that to these Palamedes at the time of the Trojan war added the four characters θ ξ φ χ, and after him Simonides the lyric poet added another four, ζ η ψ ω, all representing sounds recognized also in the Roman alphabet." For the Latin text and this English translation, with minor variations from Owen's quotation, see *Naturalis historia*, bk. 7, chap. 56, line 192, in Pliny the Elder, *Natural History*, vol. 2, *Books 3–7*, trans. H. Rackham, Loeb Classical Library 352 (Cambridge, MA: Harvard University Press,

learned friend,[37] about a universal character, which has been mentioned by many, attempted by divers, and by him brought to that perfection, as will doubtless yield much, if not universal satisfaction unto learned and prudent men, when he shall be pleased to communicate his thoughts upon it to the world; we fell occasionally on the difference of apert sounds[38] or vowels, which when I heard him with good reason affirm to be eight or nine, remembering this argument about the Hebrew points, I desired him to give his thoughts in a few words the next day, which he did accordingly; now because his discourse seems evidently to discover the vanity of this pretense, that the Hebrew vowels are an arbitrary invention from their number, I have here inserted it:[39]

Apert sounds are either	Simple: vowels
	Double: diphthongs

(1) Apert simple sounds	Formally
are distinguishable	Accidentally

[1] The formal difference is that which does constitute several letters, and must depend upon the various apertion,[40] required to the making of them, together with the gravity or acuteness of the tone which is made by them. According to which there are at least eight simple vowels, that are by us easily distinguishable, namely,

{1}	E	*magis acutum*:[41] as in "he," "me," "she," "ye," etc.
{2}		*minus acutum*:[42] as the English, "the"; the Latin "*me*," "*te*," "*se*," etc.

1942), 634–637. The Loeb translation is altered slightly to reflect the variations in Owen's quotation.

37 In the margin: Dr. Wilkins *Ward: of Wad. Col.*—Owen. Owen is referring to John Wilkins (1614–1672), a scientist and philosopher who was also an Establishment clergyman, Warden of Wadham College, Oxford, and later Bishop of Chester. He was a notable advocate of a more lenient approach to religious nonconformity. Wilkins is the author of the celebrated *Essay towards a Real Character and Philosophical Language*, which advocates for a new universal scholarly language, and on the grounds of his phronological expertise, Owen here appeals to his authority.

38 Here Owen is referring to the "open" or "free" sound that is made when vowels are pronounced in English.

39 Owen speaks of having taken this table of distinct vowel sounds in English from John Wilkins, following some personal correspondence. The table has been reproduced here much as it appears in the Goold edition.

40 I.e., the degree to which the mouth is opened upon pronunciation of particular vowels.

41 Lat. "more sharp" vowel sounds.

42 Lat. "less sharp" vowel sounds.

{3}	I or Y	which are both to be accounted of one power and sound: "shi," "di," "thy," "my"
{4}	A	*magis apertum:*[43] "all," "tall," "gall," "wall"
{5}		*minus apertum:*[44] "ale," "tale," "gale," "wale"
{6}	O	*rotundum, minus grave:*[45] as the English, "go," "so," "no"; the Latin, "*do.*"
{7}		*magis grave et pingue:*[46] as the English, "do," "to," "who"
{8}	U	as in "tu," "use," "us," etc.

So many apert simple sounds there are evidently distinguishable, I would be loath to say that there neither are, nor can be any more; for who knows, how many other minute differences of apertion, and gravity, may be now used, or here after found out by others, which practice and custom, may make as easy to them as these are to us.

[2] But besides this formal difference, they are some of them accidentally distinguishable from one another, with reference to the quantity of time required to their prolation,[47] whereby the same vowel becomes sometimes long [and sometimes] short:

So, E *min. acut.*	Long: "mete," "steme"
	Short: "met," "stem"
I	Long: "alive," "give," "drive," "title," "thine"
	Short: "live," "give," "driven"—i.e., "tittle," "thin"
A, *min. apert.* A.	Long: "bate," "hate," "cate," "same," "dame"—"ae"
	Short: "bat," "hat," "cat," "sam," "dam"
O *rotund.*	Long: "one," "none," "note," etc.—"oe" vel "oa"
	Short: "one" (non Lat.), "not"
U	Long: "use," "tune," "pule," "acute"—"ue"
	Short: "su," "tun," "pull," "cut"

The other remaining vowels, namely, E *magis acut.*, A *magis apert.*, and O *magis grave*,[48] do not change their quantities, but are always long.

(2) Diphthongs are made of the complexion of two vowels in one syllable, where the sounds of both are heard. These are:

---

43 Lat. "more open" vowel sounds.
44 Lat. "less open" vowel sounds.
45 Lat. "round, less heavy" vowel sounds.
46 Lat. "more heavy and fat" vowel sounds.
47 I.e., actual pronunciation.
48 Lat. "more heavy"—a reference to vowel sounds.

{1} Ei, ey:	"hei," Lat. "They"
{2} Ea:	"eat," "meat," "seat," "teat," "yea," "plea"
{3} Eu, ew:	"heu," Lat. "Few," "dew"
{4} Ai, ay:	"aid," "said," "pay," "day"
{5} Au, aw:	"audience," "author," "law," "draw"
{6} Oi, oy:	"point," "soil," "boy," "toy"
{7} Ou, ow:	"rout," "stout," "how," "now"
{8} Ui, uy:	"bui," "juice"
{9} Eo:	"yeoman," "people"

How other diphthongs (which have been used) may be significant for the expression of long vowels, see noted above.

There is then very little weight to be ventured upon the strength of this objection.

7. OF THE ANCIENT TRANSLATIONS, GREEK, CHALDEE, SYRIAC

11.[49] It is further pleaded that the ancient translations the Greek, the Chaldee and Syriac, do manifest that at the time of their composing the points were not invented; and that because in sundry places it is evident that they read otherwise, or the words with other points (I mean as to the force and sound, not figure of them) than those now affixed. For this purpose very many instances are given us out of the LXX especially by Capellus: Grotius also takes the same course. But neither is this objection of any force to turn the scale in the matter under consideration. Somewhat will in the close of this discourse be spoken of those translations. The differences that may be observed in them especially in the former, would as well prove, that they had other consonants, that is that the copies they used had other letters and words than ours, as other vowels. Yea if we must suppose that where they differ from our present reading, they had other and better copies, it is most certain that we must grant ours to be very corrupt. *Hoc Ithacus vellet*; nor can this inference be avoided, as shall God willing be further manifested if occasion be administered. The truth is, the present copies that we have of the LXX do in many places so vary from the original, that it is beyond all conjecture what should occasion it. I wish some would try their skill upon some part of Job, the Psalms and

---

49 In the text: *Proleg.* 8.46. *Sect.* 11.—Owen. Owen is actually citing Walton's *Prolegomena,* prolegom. 3, sec. 46. See Walton, *Prolegomena,* 1:212–14.

the Prophets, to see if by all their inquiries of extracting various lections, they can find out how they read in their books, if they rendered as they read; and we enjoy what they rendered. Symeon de Muys tells us a very pretty story of himself to this purpose:[50] as also how ridiculous he was in his attempt. But I shall recall that desire; the Scripture indeed is not so to be dealt withal; we have had too much of that work already. The rabbinical אל תקרא[51] is not to be compared, with some of our critics Temura[52] and Notaricon.[53] Of the Chaldee Paraphrase I shall speak afterward. It seems not to be of the antiquity pretended. It is not mentioned by Josephus, nor Origen, nor Hierome; but this will not impeach its antiquity. But whereas it is most certain that it was in high esteem and reverence among all the Jews before the time assigned for the punctuation of the points, it seems strange that they should in disposing of them, differ from it voluntarily in so many places. Secondly, besides, though these translators or any of them, might use copies without vowels, as it is confessed that always some such there were, as still there are, yet it does not follow at all that therefore the points were not found out nor in use. But more of this when we come to speak distinctly of these translations.

8. OF JEROME

12. Of the same importance is that which is in the last place insisted on, from the silence of Hierome and others of the ancients, as to the use of the points among the Hebrews. But Hierome saw not all things, not the Chaldee Paraphrase, which our authors suppose to have been extant at least four hundred years before him; so it cannot be made evident that he mentioned all that he saw. To speak expressly of the vowels he had no occasion, there was then no controversy about them. Nor were they then distinctly known by the names whereby they are now called. The whole current of his translation argues

---

50 In the text: *Assert. Heb. Vind. Sect.* 1.—Owen. It is hard to be certain exactly what Owen is referring to here by "sect. 1." He likely has in mind a reference from the first of the three polemical treatises de Muis composed against Jean Morin (cf. Owen's similar remark in the "Dedicatory Epistle"). While originally published separately, the three treatises are published under the title, *Triplex assertio veritatis Hebraicae adversus exercitationes Ioannis Morini*, in Siméon Marotte de Muis, *Opera omnia in duos tomos* (Paris: Mathurinus et Ioannes Henault, 1650), 2:129–258.

51 Heb. "do not read so, but so," a Talmudical rule indicating a word should be understood differently from how it is written, without changing the way it is written.

52 I.e., Temurah, a Kabbalistic method of swapping letters of the Hebrew alphabet in the words of the Bible to create new spiritual or mystical meanings.

53 I.e., Notarikon, another Kabbalistic method of creating spiritual meaning from the biblical text by using the first or last letter of words to create a new acronym, word, or idea.

that he had the Bible as now pointed. Yea, learned men have manifested by instances that seem of irrefragable evidence, that he had the use of them. Or it may be he could not obtain a pointed copy, but was instructed by his Jew in the right pronunciation of words. Copies were then scarce, and the Jews full of envy: all these things are uncertain. See Munster.[54] The truth is, either I cannot understand his words, or he does positively affirm, that the Hebrew had the use of vowels; in his *Epistle to Evagrius*: "Neither does it indicate whether it may be called 'Salim' or 'Salem,' since the Hebrews use vowels in the midst of letters on rare occasions";[55] if they did it *perraro*,[56] they did it; and then they had them; though in those days to keep up their credit in teaching, they did not much use them; nor can this be spoken of the sound of the vowels, but of their figures. For surely they did not seldom use the sounds of vowels, if they spoke often: and many other testimonies from him may be produced to the same purpose.

9. THE NEW ARGUMENT OF MORINUS IN THIS CAUSE

13. Morinus in his late *Opuscula Hebraea Samaritica*, in his digression against the Hebrew points and accents, the first part:[57] brings in a new argument to prove that the *puncta vocalia*[58] were invented by the Jewish grammarians, however the distinction of sections might be before.[59] This he attempts out of a discourse of Aben Ezra concerning the successive means of the preservation of the Scripture: first by the men of the great synagogue, then by the Masoretes,

---

54 In the text: *Praefat. Ad Bib.*—Owen. See "Praefatio" in Sebastian Münster, *Hebraica Biblia*, t. 1 (Basel: n.p., 1534).

55 In the text: *Epist.* 126: *Nec refert utrum Salem an Salim nominetur, cum vocalibus in medio litteris perraro utantur Hebraei.*—Owen. Editor's translation. For a modern critical edition, see *Ad euangelium presbyterum de Melchisedech (Epist. 73)*, sec. 8, in Jerome, *Epistulae II, 71–120*, 21.

56 Lat. "on very rare occasion."

57 In the text: *pag:* 209.—Owen. The digression begins on page 207, but the first quotation from ibn Ezra is on page 209. See Jean Morin, *Opuscula Hebraeo-Samaritica* (Paris: Gaspardus Metras, 1657), 207–25 (for the entire digression).

58 Lat. "the vowel points."

59 In the following paragraphs, Owen refers to Morin's suggestion that ibn Ezra testifies that the vowel points were invented by the Masoretes and the Jewish grammarians who followed them. Owen maintains that ibn Ezra's discourse does not necessarily support this assertion. To his mind, ibn Ezra does not explicitly ascribe the creation of the vowel points to the Masoretes, and in any event Morin's inference regarding the grammarians does not line up. If the grammarians are said to have known about matters of grammar and the vowel points, they could not have invented them, he argues. On the distinction between the *reges* (kings) and *ministri* (servants), or the *matres* (mothers) and *filias* (daughters), or the long and short vowels, see Owen's discussion above (sec. 10).

then by the grammarians. As he assigns all these their several works, so to the grammarians the skill of knowing the progresses of the holy tongue, the generation of the kingly points and of *sheva*, as he is by him there cited at large. After he labors to prove by sundry, instances that the *puncta vocalia* are by him called *reges*, and not the accents as is now the use. And in the *Addenda* to his book prefixed to it, he triumphs upon a discovery that the vowels are so called by Rabbi Jehuda Chiug the most ancient of the Jewish grammarians. The business is now it seems quite finished; and he cries out; "We do not need more [evidence] from the eyes of others. Now we are eyewitnesses."[60] A sacrifice is doubtless due to this drag of Morinus. But *quid dignum tanto?*[61]

14. The[62] place insisted on by him out of Aben Ezra, was some years before produced, weighed and explained by Buxtorfe [Jr.] out of his מאזְנֵי לְשׁוֹן הַקֹּדֶשׁ[63] or "the standard of the holy tongue:"[64] and it is not unlikely, from Morinus his preface to his consideration of that place, that he fixed on it some years ago, that he learned it from Buxtorfius [Jr.], by the provision that he lays in against such thoughts; for what is it to the reader when Morinus made his observations; the manner of the men of that society in other things gives sufficient grounds for this suspicion. And Simeon de Muys intimates that he had dealt before with the father as he now deals with the son:[65] himself with great and rare ingenuity acknowledging what he received of him. "You will tell me I have taken all these things from Buxtorf, will you not? I will certainly borrow something if it is necessary."[66] But what is the great discovery here made? [First,][67] that the

---

60 In the text: *Oculis aliorum non egemus amplius*, αὐτόπται *nunc sumus.*—Owen. Editor's translation. For the Latin text, see *"Addenda p. 218. L. 7."* in Morin, *Opuscula.*

61 Lat. "What [does he offer] worthy of so much [admiration]?" This is an abbreviated quotation from Horace, *Ars poetica*, line 138. For the Latin text and an English translation, see Horace, *Satires. Epistles, The Art of Poerty*, trans. H. Rushton Fairclough, Loeb Classical Library 194 (Cambridge, MA: Harvard University Press, 1926), 462–63.

62 Original begins this section with "1," but the list does not seem to continue; hence Goold has left it out.

63 The pointing in the text is difficult to make out. Goold has altered the pointing as follows: מאזְנֵי לְשׁוֹן הַקֹּדֶשׁ. This alteration reflects its appearance in Buxtorf's text.

64 In the text: *De Punct. Orig. Part.* 1. *Pag.* 13. 14. *Cap.* 3. See Buxtorf Jr., *Tractatus*, 13–14.

65 In the text: *Censur. In Excercitat.* 4. *Cap.* 7. *Pag:* 17.—Owen. Owen is referring to "Censura in exercitat. Quartae caput septimum," in *Censura in aliquot capita exercitationum ecclesiasticarum in utrumque Samaritanorum Pentateuchum* [*Assertio Hebraicae veritatis I*]. See de Muis, *Opera omnia*, 2:171a–73a.

66 In the text: *Ass. Text. Heb. Ver. Cap.* 5. *Dicesve me haec omnia mutuatum a Buxtorfio? Quidni vero mutuor, si necesse erit.*—Owen. Editor's translation. For the Latin text (with minor difference), see *Assertio* [*Hebraicae veritatis*] *III. Castigationis animadversionum M. Ioanni Morini, Blesensis, in censura exercitationum ecclesiasticarum ad Pentateuchum Samaritanum,"* pt. 1, chap. 5, in de Muis, *Opera omnia*, 2:223a.

67 Absent in original but added as per numbered list which follows.

puncta vocalia are some of them called *reges*; the accents have now got that appellation, some of them are *reges*, and some *ministri*: so that the present state of things, in reference to vowels and accents is but novel. Secondly, that the grammarians invented these *regia puncta* as Aben Ezra says.[68]

15. But I pray what cause of triumph or boasting is in all this goodly discovery? Was it ever denied by any, that the casting of the names of the vowels and accents, with the titles was the work of the grammarians; Was it not long since observed by many that the five long vowels with ˑ and ˒ were called of old *reges*? And that the distinction of the vowels into long and short was an invention of the Christians rather than Jewish grammarians; the Jews calling them some absolutely *reges*, some great and small, some *matres et filias*? But then says he, the grammarians were the inventors of these points, why so? Aben Ezra refers this unto the work of the grammarians, to know the progresses of the holy tongue, the generation of those kings, etc.: but can anything be more evident against his design than his own testimony? It was the work of the grammarians to know these things, therefore not to invent them; did they invent the radical and servile letters? Surely they also then invented the tongue; for it consists of letters radical and servile, of points and accents; and yet this is also ascribed to them by Aben Ezra. But it is well that Morinus has at length lighted upon R. Jehuda Chiug: His opinion before was collected out of Kimchi,[69] Ephodius,[70] Muscatus,[71] and others. But

68 Morin cites ibn Ezra's remark that the grammarians were responsible for "having made additions and advancements for the understanding of the sacred tongue, of its emergence, of its beginning, and of the generations of the kingly points [*punctorum regum*], of the silent *sheva*, of pronunciation, of the servile letters, of the servants, of the radicals." Editor's translation of Morin's Latin translation of ibn Ezra's Hebrew text, *Sefer Tsaḥot*, likely quoting the Venetian edition published by Daniel Bomberg in 1546: Morin, *Opuscula*, 212–13. The inference is that since ibn Ezra explicitly goes on to define the "kings" (*reges*) as the vowel points, the points themselves must have been invented by the grammarians. This is in distinction from a reference ibn Ezra makes earlier to the preservation of the "kings and servants" (*reges . . . et ministros*) by the Men of the Great Assembly, which Morin takes to be referring to the Hebrew accents rather than the points, later explicitly divided into "kings and servants" by the grammarians. Cf. Morin, *Opuscula*, 215. By contrast, commenting on the same passage, Buxtorf Jr. takes this earlier mention of the "kings" (*reges*) to be referring to the vowel points rather than the accents (and as evidence of their early dating), on the very grounds that ibn Ezra goes on to speak of the *reges* in reference to the points: Buxtorf Jr., *Tractatus*, 15.
69 Owen is likely referring to either Moses (Moses: ca. 1127–ca. 1190) or his better-known brother David Kimhi or Kimchi (1160–1235), both of whom were sons of Joseph Kimchi. Theirs was a family of medieval Hebrew grammarians and biblical commentators.
70 Profiat Duran or Isaac ben Moses ha-Levi (ca. 1360–1412), was otherwise known as Ephodius or Ephodeus, from his Hebrew Grammar, מעשה אפד (*The Making of the Ephod*). He was a physician, philosopher, and grammarian who was forcibly converted to Christianity.
71 Judah Moscato (1530–1593) was an Italian Jewish poet and rhetorician.

what says he now himself? For aught appears, by what we have quoted by Morinus, he is like to prove a notable witness of the antiquity of the points. It may be well supposed that Morinus, writing on set purpose against their antiquity would produce that testimony which in his whole author was most to his purpose; and yet he fixes on one, wherein this ancient grammarian who lived about the years of Christ [AD] 1150, or 1200; gives us an account of the points, with their names without the least intimation of anything to the impeachment of their divine original; so also the same Aben Ezra (on Ps. 9:7):[72] tells us, of one Adonis Ben Iafrad[73] who long before this R. Jehuda found for in an ancient copy. And therefore when Morinus comes to make the conclusion of his argument, discovering it seems himself the folly of the pretense, that the points were invented by the grammarians, the last sort of men mentioned by Aben Ezra, he says, "It is beyond every doubt, and clearer than the midday light to conclude that Aben Ezra believed the origin of all the vowel points came from the Tiberian Masoretes, and the grammarians who followed them."[74] But of these Masoretes there is not one word in the premises, nor is any such thing assigned unto them by Aben Ezra; but quite another employment, of making a hedge about the Law by their observations on all the words of it; and had he dreamed of their inventing the points, he would sure enough have assigned that work to them; and as for the grammarians, his own testimony lies full to the contrary.

THE CONCLUSION ABOUT THE NECESSITY OF THE POINTS

16. And these are the heads of the arguments insisted on by Capellus and others, and by these *Prolegomena*, to prove the Hebrew punctuation to be an invention of the Jews of Tiberias five hundred years or more after the incarnation of Christ. *Brevis cantilena, sed longum epiphonema.*[75] As I have not here designed to answer them at large, with the various instances produced to give countenance unto them, (nor is it needful for any so to do, until the answer already given to them be removed) so by the specimen given of their

---

72 For a modern English translation, see Abraham ibn Ezra, *Commentary on the First Book of Psalms: Chapters 1–41*, trans. H. Norman Strickman (Boston: Academic Studies Press, 2009), 80.

73 Dunash ben Labrat (ca. 920–ca. 990) was a medieval Jewish poet and early Hebrew grammarian.

74 In the text: *procul omni dubio est, et luce meridiana clarius Aben Ezram sensisse omnium vocalium punctationem a Masorethis Tiberiensibus, et grammaticis, qui hos sequuti sunt, originem ducere.*—Owen. Editor's translation. For the Latin text, see Morin, *Opuscula*, 221.

75 Lat. "A short song, but one that needs a long explanation."

nature and kind, the sober and pious reader may easily judge whether there be any force in them, to evert the persuasion opposed by them; grounded on the catholic tradition and consent of the Jews, the uncontradicted reception of them absolutely, without the least opposition all the world over by Jews and Christians, the very nature of the punctuation itself following the genius of the language not arising or flowing from any artificial rules, the impossibility of assigning any author to it since the days of Ezra, but only by such loose conjectures and imaginations as ought not to be admitted to any plea and place in this weighty cause; all attended with that great uncertainty, which without their owning of these points to be of divine original we shall be left unto, in all translations and expositions of the Scripture. It is true; while the Hebrew language was the vulgar tongue of the nation, and was spoken by everyone uniformly everywhere, it had been possible, that upon a supposition that there were no points, men without infallible guidance and direction might possibly affix notes and figures, which might with some exactness answer the common pronunciation of the language, and so consequently exhibit the true and proper sense and meaning of the words themselves. But when there had been an interruption of a thousand years in the vulgar use of the language, it being preserved pure only in one book; to suppose that the true and exact pronunciation of every letter, tittle and syllable was preserved alive by oral tradition, not written anywhere, not commonly spoken by any, is to build towns and castles of imaginations, which may be as easily cast down as they are erected, yet unless this be supposed, (which with no color of reason can be supposed, which is yet so, by Capellus and the learned author of the *Prolegomena*) it must be granted, that the great rule of all present translations, expositions, and comments, that have been made in the church of God for some hundreds of years, is the arbitrary invention of some few Jews, living in an obscure corner of the world under the curse of God, in their unbelief and blindness.¶

The only relief in the *Prolegomena*, against this amazing inference, is, as was said, that the Masoretes affixed not the present punctuation arbitrarily, (so also Capellus) but according to the tradition they had received. What weight is to be laid upon such a tradition for near a thousand years (above according to Morinus) is easily to be imagined. Nor let men please themselves with the pretended facility of learning the Hebrew language without points and accents, and not only the language, but the true and proper reading and distinction of it in the Bible. Let the points and accents be wholly removed, and all apprehensions of the sense arising, by the restraint and distinction of the words as now pointed; and then turn in the drove of the learned critics of this age upon the naked consonants, and we shall quickly see what woeful work, yea havoc of sacred truth will be made among them. Were they shut up in several cells, I should scarcely expect the harmony and agreement among them, which is fabulously reported to have been in the like case among the LXX. The Jews say, and that truly,[76] "No man can lift up his tongue to read without punctuation." And, "If we concede authority to their opinion [*rationi*] in this and similar matters, every book will be changed, in letters, words, and sentences, and thus the meaning itself will also be changed."[77]

And thus have I with all possible brevity vindicated the position formerly insisted on, from this grand exception, which might be justly feared from the principles laid down in the *Prolegomena*.

---

76 In the text: איש את לשונו על הקהאה בלצריו לא ירים. Goold has corrected what appear to be a number of typographical errors in the original in accordance with Owen's translation that follows: איש את לשונו על הקראה בלנקוד לא ירים.

77 In the text: *Si rationi in his & similibus dominium concedamus, toti mutabuntur libri, in literis, vocibus, & sententiis, & sic res ipsa quoque mutabitur. Lib. Cosri. 1. Par. 3. Pag. 28.*—Owen. Editor's translation. Owen appears to be quoting this from the younger Buxtorf's paraphrase of this pericope in his *Tractatus de punctorum vocalium* (see Buxtorf Jr., *Tractatus*, 84), as opposed to Buxtorf's separately published translation of the *Liber Cosri* itself, which is somewhat different: see Johann Buxtorf Jr., *Liber Cosri* (Basel: Georgius Deckerus, 1660), 198. Moreover, the original mistakenly notes "*pag.* 28," when in fact this should be sec. 28.

7

The Nature of the *Keri* and *Ketib* Considered

1. Of the קרי וכתיב [*Qere* and *Ketiv*]. Their nature and original.
2. The difference is in the consonants. 3. Morinus' vain charge
on Arias Montanus. 4. The senses of both consistent. 5. Of "The
Great Congregation": the spring and rise of these various readings.
6. The judgment of the *Prolegomena* [and *Appendix*] about them,
their order given twice over in the *Appendix*. 7. The rise assigned to
them. 8. Considered. 9. Of Capellus his opinion and the danger of it.

THE NATURE AND ORIGINAL OF THE *KERI* AND *KETIB*

1. We are not as yet come to a close. There is another thing agitated in these *Pro-legomena*, and represented in the *Appendix*, that may seem to derogate from the universality of my assertion, concerning the entire preservation of the original copies of the Scripture. The קרי וכתיב [*Qere* and *Ketiv*] or the *scriptio*[1] and *lectio*,[2] or *scriptum*[3] and *lectum*,[4] is that which I intend. The general nature of these things is known to all them that have looked into the Bible. One word is placed in the line, and another in the margin; the word in the line having not the points or vowels affixed to it that are its own, but those that belong to the word in the margin; of this sort there are in the Bible 840, or thereabouts; for some of the late

1 Lat. "writing."
2 Lat. "reading."
3 Lat. "what is written."
4 Lat. "what is read."

editions by mistake or oversight, do differ in the precise number. All men that have wrote any considerations on the Hebrew text have spoken of their nature in general; so has the author of these *Prolegomena*. As to our present concernment, namely to manifest that from them no argument can arise as to the corruption of the original, the ensuing observations concerning them may suffice.

THE DIFFERENCE IS IN THE CONSONANTS

2. [First],[5] all the difference in these words is in the consonants, not at all in the vowels. The word in the margin owns the vowels in the line, as proper to it; and the vowels in the line seem to be placed to the word whereunto they do not belong, because there is no other meet place for them in the line where they are to be continued as belonging to the integrity of the Scripture.

MORINUS'S VAIN CHARGE ON ARIAS MONTANUS

3. Morinus to manifest his rage against the Hebrew text, takes from hence occasion to quarrel with Arias Montanus, and to accuse him of ignorance and false dealing.[6]

The pretense of his quarrel he makes to be, that Arias affirms the greatest part of these various lections to consist in some differences of the points; for which purpose he cites his words out of his preface to his collection of various lections. "The largest proportion of the variety in these readings consists of a discrepancy in such points, as is demonstrated in the whole of this Masora, or in the volume of various readings."[7] Whereunto he subjoins, "It is an astonishing assertion that not even a single thing was fixed in the points. He himself added a list of a great number [of discrepancies] at the end of his preface. But all the variations are in the letters, not the points. I quite confidently write that of all the various readings which the Jews call קרי וכתיב, *Qere* and *Ketiv*, with which Arias concerns himself, absolutely none relates to the points. Again, quite confidently, etc."[8] Would not any man think

5   Original has "1." Goold begins a list here, adding "2." To the beginning of sec. 4, and numbering Owen's "thirdly" at the beginning of sec. 7 as "3." In this editor's judgment, Owen is not here beginning a list that is continued at sec. 4 and sec. 7.

6   In the text: *De Heb. Text. Sincer. Excer.* 1. *Cap.* 4. *Pag.* 40.—Owen. See Jean Morin, *Exercitationes biblicae de Hebraei Graecique textus sinceritate: Pars prior* (Paris: Antonius Vitray, 1633)

7   Here Morin is quoting Montanus.

8   In the text: *Maxima in his lectionibus Varietatis pars in hujusmodi punctorum discrepantia Consistit, ut toto hujus Mazzoreth sive variarum lectionum volumine demonstratur.* [...] *Mira assertio ne una quidem in punctis sita est. Catalogum plurimorum ipse ad finem praefationis*

but that the man had made here some great discovery, both as to the nature of the קרי וכתיב [*Qere* and *Ketiv*] as also to the ignorance of Arias, whom he goes on to reproach as a person unacquainted with the Masora, and with the various lections of Ben Asher, and Ben Naphtali, of the Eastern and Western Jews, at the end of the Venetian Bibles;[9] which Bibles he chiefly used in the printing of his own. And yet on the other hand, men acquainted with the ability and great discerning of Arias, will be hardly persuaded, that he was so blind and ignorant as to affirm the greatest part of the variety he spoke of consisted in the changing of vowels, and immediately to give instances, wherein all he mentions consists in the change of consonants only. But what if all this should prove the ignorance and prejudice of Morinus? First to his redoubled assertion about the difference of the *Keri* and *Ketib* in the consonants only, wherein he speaks as though he were blessing the world with a new and strange discovery, it is a thing known *lippis et tonsoribus*,[10] and has been so since the days of Elias Levita; what then intended Arias Montanus to affirm the contrary? "Here is the very ink of the cuttlefish; here is venom unadulterate";[11] he speaks not at all of the קרי וכתיב [*Qere* and *Ketiv*], but merely of the anomalous pointing of words, in a various way from the genius of the tongue, as they are observed and reckoned up in the Masora, of other varieties he speaks afterward; giving a particular account of the *Keri* and *Ketib*, which whether he esteemed various lections or no, I know not. *Non si te ruperis aeques*.[12] But all are ignorant, who are not of the mind of an aspiring Jesuit.

---

adtexuit. Et [sic: At in Morin's text] *Varietates omnes sunt in literis, nulla in punctis. Confidentius scribo omnium variorum lectionum quas Judaei appellant* קרי וכתיב *Keri & Ketib: de quibus agit Arias nulla prorsus ad puncta pertinet. Iterum confidentius, &c.*—Owen. Editor's translation. For the Latin text, see Morin, *Exercitationes pars prior*, 40.

9 Owen is referring here to the two editions of Bomberg's Rabbinical Bible or *Mikraot Gedolot* (1516–1517; 1525).

10 Lat. "to the blind and barbers," a figurative expression that is an allusion to a remark in Horace's *Satires*, bk. 1, satire 7, line 3. The original refers to a tale that is *omnibus et lippis notum et tonsoribus esse*; "known [. . .] to every blear-eyed man and barber." For the English translation, see Horace, *Satires. Epistles, The Art of Poerty*, trans. H. Rushton Fairclough, Loeb Classical Library 194 (Cambridge, MA: Harvard University Press, 1926), 91.

11 In the text: *Hic nigri [sic] succus loliginis: haec est Aerugo mera*—Owen. This is an allusion to a line from Horace's *Satires*, bk. 1, satire 4, lines 100–101, with slight variation to the original. For the English translation, see Horace, *Satires*, 57.

12 Lat. "not if you burst yourself will you be equal to the task." The 1658 text appears at this point to be corrupt and the text given is an emendation. The 1658 text reads "*superis*" with the Errata suggesting that this should be replaced with the word "*capuis*." The latter reading has no meaning. If we accept the reading "*superis*," then Owen's meaning would be "not even if you make yourself equal to the gods." However, the present edition proposes that the 1658 printed text

THE SENSES OF BOTH CONSISTENT

4. That the difference in the sense taking in the whole context, is upon the matter very little or none at all; at least each word, both that in the line and that in the margin, yields a sense agreeable to the analogy of faith.

Of all the varieties that are found of this kind, that of two words, the same in sound but of most distinct significations, seems of the greatest importance; namely לֹו and לֹא, fourteen or fifteen times where לֹא, "not," is in the text; the margin notes לֹו, "to him," or "his," to be read. But yet though these seem contrary one to the other, yet wherever this falls out, a sense agreeable to the analogy of faith arises fairly from either word. As to give one or two instances: Psalm 100:3, הוּא עָשָׂנוּ וְלֹא אֲנַחְנוּ,[13] "He hath made us, and not we ourselves," the *Keri* in the margin is וְלֹו,[14] "his," giving this sense; "He hath made us, and his we are"; the verb substantive being included in the pronoun. So Isaiah 63:9, בְּכָל־צָרָתָם לֹא צָר,[15] "In all their afflictions (or straits), no straitness"; so the כתיב [*Ketiv*]. The קרי [*Qere*], לֹו, "Straitness or affliction was to him," or "he was straitened" or "afflicted": in the first way, God signifies that when they were in their outward straits, yet he was not straitened from their relief; in the other, that he had compassion for them, was afflicted with them, which upon the matter is the same; and the like may be showed of the rest.

OF "THE GREAT CONGREGATION": THE SPRING AND RISE OF THESE VARIOUS READINGS

5. I confess I am not able fully to satisfy myself in the original and spring of all this variety, being not willing merely to depend on the testimony of the Jews, much less on the conjectures of late innovators. To the uttermost

---

includes a misreading of the word "*ruperis*" (by substitution of the long *s* (ſ) of early modern typesetting). This would mean that Owen is slightly misquoting and abbreviating a citation from Horace, *Satires*, bk. 2, satire 3, lines 319–20, "'*non, si te ruperis,*' inquit / '*par eris.*'" ("'Though you burst yourself,' said he, 'you'll never be as large'"). Horace tells the story of a mother frog who tries to swell up to the size of a large beast that has trodden on her young but is told that she can never make herself large enough. The story intends to illustrate someone trying to take on a task for which they can never be adequate. For the Latin text and translation, see Horace, *Satires*, 180–81. We are grateful to Professor Paul Botley for suggesting this corruption in the text.

13 The pointing in *Biblia Hebraica Stuttgartensia* is שׂ instead of שׁ. See *Biblia Hebraica Stuttgartensia*, ed. Karl Elliger and Wilhelm Rudolph (Stuttgart: Deutsche Bibelgesellschaft, 1983). Hereafter cited as *BHS*.

14 Pointed in the original text. Unpointed in Goold: ולו.

15 For ב in the first word, modern editions such as *BHS* read, בְּ.

length of my view, to give a full account of this thing, is a matter of no small difficulty. Their venerable antiquity, and unquestionable reception by all translators gives them sanctuary from being cast down from the place they hold by any man's bare conjecture. That which to me is of the greatest importance, is, that they appear most of them to have been in the Bibles, then, when the oracles of God were committed to the Jews, during which time we find them not blamed for adding or altering one word or tittle. Hence the Chaldee Paraphrast often follows the τὸ [the] קרי [Qere] which never was in the line whatever some boastingly conjecture to the contrary: and sometimes the τὸ [the] כתיב [Ketiv]. That which seems to me most probable is, that they were collected for the most part of them, by the אנשי כנסת הגדולה, "the men of the great congregation." Some indeed I find of late (I hope not out of a design to bring all things to a further confusion about the original) to question whether ever there were any such thing as the great congregation. Morinus calls it a Judaical figment. Our *Prolegomena* question it.[16] But this is only to question, whether Ezra, Nehemiah, Joshuah, Zechariah, Haggai and the rest of the leaders of the people in their return from the captivity, did set a sanhedrin according to the institution of God, and labor to reform the church and all the corruptions that were crept either into the word or worship of God. I see not how this can reasonably be called into question, if we had not to confirm it the catholic tradition of Jews and Christians. Neither is it called the great congregation from its number, but eminency of persons. Now on this supposition it may be granted that the קרי [Qere] on the books of these men themselves Ezra and the rest, were collected by the succeeding churches. Unless we shall suppose with Ainsworth,[17] that the word was so received from God, as to make both necessary. And if we know not the true cause of its being so given, we have nothing to blame but our own ignorance, this not being the only case wherein we have reason so to do. Our last translation generally renders the word in the margent[18] noting also the word in the line where there is any considerable difference. Those who have leisure for such a work, may observe what choice is used in this case by old and modern translators. And if they had not believed them to have had an authoritative original beyond the impeachment of any man in these days, they could not fairly and honestly have used both line and margin as they have done.

16 In the text: *Prol.* 8. *Sect.* 22.—Owen. See Brian Walton, *In Biblia polyglotta prolegomena*, 2 vols. (Cambridge: J. Smith, 1827–1828), 1:474–76.
17 Henry Ainsworth (1571–1622) was an English Brownist and renowned commentator on the Hebrew Bible.
18 I.e., margin.

THE JUDGMENT OF THE *PROLEGOMENA*
AND *APPENDIX* ABOUT THEM

6. What says now our *Prolegomena*, with the *Appendix* unto these things.

[First,][19] we have them in the *Appendix* represented unto us in their own order according as they are found in the books of the Scriptures; and then over again, in the order and under the heads that they are drawn and driven unto by Capellus; a task, that learned man took upon himself, that he might in the performance of it, give some countenance to his opinion, that they are for the most part critical emendations of the text, made by some late Masoretes, that came no man knows whence; that lived no man knows where, nor when. Thus whereas these *Keri* and *Ketib*, have the only face and appearance upon the matter, of various lections upon the Old Testament, (for the Jews, collections of the various readings of Ben Asher and Ben Naphtali, of the oriental and occidental Jews, are of no value, nor ever had place in their Bible and may be rejected) the unwary viewer of the *Appendix* is presented with a great bulk of them, their whole army being mustered twice over in this service.[20]

The Rise Assigned to Them by the *Prolegomena*

7. But this inconvenience may be easily amended, nor am I concerned in it. Wherefore [secondly,][21] for the rise of them it is said that some of them are the amendments of the Masoretes or Rabbins, others, various lections out of divers copies. That they are all, or the most part of them critical amendments of the Rabbins is not allowed; for which latter part of his determination, we thank the learned author; and take leave to say that in the former we are not satisfied:[22] the arguments that are produced to prove them not to have been from Ezra, but the most part from post-Talmudical Rabbins are capable of a very easy solution which also another occasion may discover; at present I am gone already too far beyond my intention, so that I cannot allow myself any farther digression.

That Judgment Considered

8. To answer briefly. Ezra and his companions might be the collectors of all those in the Bible, but their own books; and those in their own books might

19 "1." In the original but altered to be consistent with verbally numbered list that follows.
20 Cf. Brian Walton, *Biblia sacra polyglotta*, 6 vols. (London: Thomas Roycroft, 1653–1657), vol. 6, chap. 1, pp. 8–15.
21 Original has "thirdly," but Owen appears to be drawing out a second observation from the *Prolegomena*, continuing from the first that is raised in sec. 6.
22 In the text: *Prol.* 8. 23, 24, 25.—Owen. See Walton, *Prolegomena*, 1:476–83.

be added by the succeeding church. The oriental and occidental Jews, differ about other things as well as the *Keri* and *Ketib*. The rule of the Jews, that the *Keri* is always to be followed, is novel; and therefore the old translators might read either, or both, as they saw cause. There was no occasion at all why these things should be mentioned by Josephus, Philo, Origen: Heirome says indeed on Isaiah 49:5 that Aquila rendered that word, "to him," which is written with ל and א not ל and ו. But he makes it not appear that Aquila read not as he translated, that is by the קרי [*Qere*].[23] And for what is urged of the Chaldee and LXX, making use of the *Keri* and *Ketib*, it is not intended that they knew the difference under these names, but that these differences were in their days. That the word now in the margin was in the line until the days of the pretended Masoretes, is not to be said nakedly but proved, if such a novel fancy expect any credit in the world. That the Judaical Rabbins have made some alterations in the text of their own accord, at least placed words in the margin, as to their consonants, supplying their vowels in the line, where they ought not to have place; that there were various lections in the copies after the Talmud, which have been gathered by some obscure Jews, no mention being made of those collections in the Masora, or any of their grammarians, is the sum of the discourse under consideration. When all this, or any part of it, is proved by testimony, or evident reason, we shall further attend unto it.

OF CAPELLUS, HIS OPINION, AND THE DANGER OF IT

9. In the meantime I cannot but rejoice, that Capellus his fancy about these things, than which I know nothing more pernicious to the truth of God, is rejected. If these hundreds of words were the critical conjectures and amendments of the Jews, what security have we of the mind of God as truly represented unto us, seeing that it is supposed also, that some of the words in the margin were sometimes in the line; and if it be supposed, as it is, that there are innumerable other places of the like nature, standing in need of such amendments, what a door would be opened unto curious pragmatical wits, to overturn all the certainty of the truth of the Scripture, everyone may see. Give once this liberty to the audacious curiosity of men, priding themselves in their critical abilities, and we shall quickly find out what woeful state and condition the truth of the Scripture will be brought unto. If the Jews have made

23 See *Commentariorum in Esaiam*, bk. 13, chap. 49, vv. 5–6, in Jerome, *Commentariorum in Esaiam libri XII–XVIII. In Esaia parvula adbreviatio*, ed. M. Adriacn, Corpus Christianorum: Series Latina 73a (Turnholti: Typographi Brepolis, 1963), 537. Jerome, *Isaiah* [Jerome; Origen], 617.

such amendments and corrections of the text, and that to so good purpose, and if so much work of the like kind yet remain, can any man possibly better employ himself, than with his utmost diligence to put his hand to this plough. But he that pulls down a hedge, a serpent shall bite him.

8

The Proper Use of Translations

1. Of gathering various lections by the help of translations.
2. The proper use and benefit of translations. Their new pretended
use. 3. The state of the originals on this new pretense. 4. Of the
remedy tendered to the relief of that state. 5. No copies of old
differing in the least from those we now enjoy, from the testimony
of our Savior. 6. No testimony new or old to that purpose.
7. Requisites unto good translations. 8. Of the translations in
the *Biblia polyglotta*: of the Arabic. 9. Of the Syriac. 10. Of the
Samaritan Pentateuch. 11. Of the Chaldee Paraphrase. 12. Of the
Vulgar Latin. 13. Of the LXX [Septuagint]. 14. Of the translations
of the New Testament: of the Persian. 15. Of the Ethiopian.
16. The value of these translations as to the work in hand.
17. Of the supposition of gross corruption in the originals. 18. Of
various lections out of Grotius. 19. Of the *Appendix* in general.

OF GATHERING VARIOUS LECTIONS BY
THE HELP OF TRANSLATIONS

1.[1] Because it is the judgment of some, that yet other objections may be raised
against the thesis pleaded for, from what is affirmed in the *Prolegomena* about
gathering various lections by the help of translations, and the instances of
that good work given us in the *Appendix*, I shall close this discourse with the
consideration of that pretense.

1 Original has "Sect. 5."

THE PROPER USE AND BENEFIT OF TRANSLATIONS
AND THEIR NEW PRETENDED USE

2. The great and signal use of various translations, which hitherto we have esteemed them for, was the help afforded by them in expositions of the Scripture. To have represented unto us in one view the several apprehensions and judgments of so many worthy and learned men, as were the authors of these translations, upon the original words of the Scripture, is a signal help and advantage unto men inquiring into the mind and will of God in his word. That translations were of any other use formerly, was not apprehended. They are of late presented unto us under another notion: namely, as means and helps of correcting the original, and finding out the corruptions that are in our present copies, showing that the copies which their authors used, did really differ from those which we now enjoy, and use. For this rare invention we are, as for the former, chiefly beholden to the learned and most diligent Capellus, who is followed, as in sundry instances himself declares, by the no less learned Grotius. To this purpose the scene is thus laid. It is supposed of old there were sundry copies of the Old Testament differing in many things, words, sentences, from those we now enjoy. Out of these copies some of the ancient translations have been made. In their translations they express the sense and meaning of the copies they made use of. Hence by considering what they deliver, where they differ from our present copies, we may find out, (that is, learned men who are expert at conjectures may do so) how they read in theirs. Thus may we come to a further discovery of the various corruptions that are crept into the Hebrew text, and by the help of those translations amend them. Thus Capellus. The learned author of our *Prolegomena* handles this business.[2] I do not remember that he anywhere expressly affirms, that they had other copies than those we now enjoy; but whereas (besides the *Keri* and *Ketib*, the various readings of Ben Asher, and Ben Naphtali, of the eastern and western Jews) there are through the neglect, oscitancy, and frailty of the transcribers, many things befallen the text, not such failings as happening in one copy, may be easily rectified by others, which are not to be regarded as various lections, nor such as may be collected out of any ancient copies, but faults, or mistakes in all the copies we enjoy, or have ever been known, by the help and use of translations, conjecturing how they read in their books, either with other words, or letters, consonants or points, we may collect various lections, as out of the original; what this opinion upon the matter differs

2   In the text: *Prol.* 6.—Owen. See Brian Walton, *In Biblia polyglotta prolegomena*, 2 vols. (Cambridge: J Smith, 1827–1828), 1:318–53.

from that of Capellus I see not; for the difference between our copies, and those of old, are by him assigned to no other original; nor does Capellus say that the Jews have voluntarily corrupted the text; but only that alterations are befallen it, by the means and ways recounted in the *Prolegomena*. To make this evident by instances, we have a great number of such various lections gathered by Grotius in the *Appendix*.[3] The truth is, how that volume should come under that name, at first view I much wondered. The greatest part of it, gives us no various lections of the Hebrew text as is pretended; but various interpretations of others from the Hebrew. But the *Prolegomena* solve that seeming difficulty. The particulars assigned as various lections, are not different readings collected out of any copies extant, or ever known to have been extant, but critical conjectures of his own for the amendment of the text, or at most conjectures upon the reading of the words by translators, especially the LXX and Vulgar Latin.

THE STATE OF THE ORIGINALS ON THIS NEW PRETENSE AND THE REMEDY TENDERED TO THE RELIEF OF THAT STATE

3. Let us now consider our disease intimated, and the remedy prescribed; together with the improbability of the one, and the unsuitableness of the other as to the removal of it; being once supposed. The distemper pretended is dreadful, and such, as it may well prove mortal to the sacred truth of the Scripture. The sum of it as was declared before, is that of old there were sundry copies extant, differing in many things from those we now enjoy, according to which, the ancient translations were made; whence it is come to pass, that in so many places they differ from our present Bibles even all that are extant in the world; so Capellus; or that there are corruptions befallen the text (varieties from the αὐτόγραφα) that may be found by the help of translations, as our *Prolegomena*.

4. Now whereas the first translation that ever was, as is pretended, is that of the LXX, and that of all others, excepting only those which have been translated out of it, does most vary and differ from our Bible, as may be made good by some thousands of instances, we cannot but be exceedingly uncertain in finding out wherein those copies, which as it is said, were used by them, did differ from ours, or wherein ours are corrupted; but are left unto endless uncertain conjectures. What sense others may have of this distemper I know not; for my own part I am

---

3   Hugo Grotius's annotations are contained in chap. 15 of the *Appendix*. See Brian Walton, *Biblia sacra polyglotta*, 6 vols. (London: Thomas Roycroft, 1653–1657), vol. 6, chap. 15, pp. 37a–58b.

solicitous for the Ark; or the sacred truth of the original; and that because I am fully persuaded that the remedy and relief of this evil, provided in the translations, is unfitted to the cure, yea fitted to increase the disease. Some other course then must be taken. And seeing the remedy is notoriously insufficient to effect the cure, let us try whether the whole distemper be not a mere fancy, and so do what in us lie[s] to prevent that horrible and outrageous violence, which will undoubtedly be offered to the sacred Hebrew verity, if every learned mountebank[4] may be allowed to practice upon it, with his conjectures from translations.

No Copies of Old Differing in the Least from Those We Now Enjoy, Inferred from the Testimony of Our Savior

5. Firstly, it is well known that the translation of the LXX, if it have the original pretended, and which alone makes it considerable, was made and finished three hundred years or near thereabout, before the incarnation of our Savior, it was, in that time and season wherein the oracles of God were committed to the Jews while that church and people were the only people of God, accepted with him, designed by him keepers of his word for the use of the whole church of Christ to come, as the great and blessed foundation of truth. A time when there was an authentic copy of the whole Scripture, as the rule of all others kept in the temple; now can it be once imagined that there should be at that time such notorious varieties in the copies of the Scripture through the negligence of that church, and yet afterward neither our Savior nor his apostles take the least notice of it; yea does not our Savior himself affirm of the word that then was among the Jews, that not ἰῶτα ἕν or μία κεράια of it,[5] should pass away or perish, where let not the points but the consonants themselves with their apices[6] be intended or alluded unto in that expression; yet of that word which was translated by the LXX, according to this hypothesis, and which assuredly they then had if ever, not only letters and tittles, but words, and that many, are concluded to be lost. But that no Jew believes the figment we are in the consideration of, I could say, *credat Apella*.

---

4 I.e., a quack or deceiver.

5 Owen is alluding to Matt. 5:18, where Christ alludes to the smallest particles of the Greek script in saying that "not an iota" (ἰῶτα ἕν) and "not a dot" (μία κεράια) "will pass from the Law until it is accomplished" (ESV). Owen infers that it would be inconceivable for Christ to speak this way of the Old Testament Law if the Hebrew text may be emended by translations drawn from the Septuagint, on the grounds that the Hebrew text was already corrupted by the time the Septuagint was produced.

6 I.e., plural of *apex*. This is technically a reference to the acute accent placed over a consonant, but here Owen is using it figuratively as a reference to the Hebrew accent marks (in distinction from the vowel points), implying that Christ had even these in mind when making his remark in Matt. 5:18.

No Testimony New or Old to That Purpose

6. Secondly, waiving the consideration of our refuge in these cases, namely the good providence and care of God in the preservation of his word, let the authors of this insinuation prove the assertion; namely that there was ever in the world any other copy of the Bible, differing in any one word from those that we now enjoy; let them produce one testimony, one author of credit, Jew or Christian, that can, or does, or ever did, speak one word to this purpose. Let them direct us to any relic, any monument, any kind of remembrance of them, and not put us off with weak conjectures, upon the signification of one or two words, and it shall be of weight with us? Is it meet that a matter of so huge importance, called into question by none but themselves, should be cast and determined by their conjectures? Do they think that men will part with the possession of truth upon so easy terms? That they will be cast from their inheritance by divination? But they will say is it not evident that the old translators did make use of other copies, in that we see how they have translated many words, and places, so as it was not possible they should have done, had they rendered our copy according to what we now read; but will indeed this be pleaded? May it not be extended to all places, as well as to any? And may not men plead so for every variation made by the LXX from the original; [that] they had other copies than any that now are extant; better all old translations should be consumed out of the earth, than that such a figment should be admitted. That there are innumerable other reasons to be assigned of the variations from the original; as the translators' own inadvertency, negligence, ignorance, (for the wisest see not all,) desire to expound and clear the sense, and, as it was likely, of altering and varying many things from the original, with the innumerable corruptions and interpolations that have befallen that translation, indifferently well witnessed unto by the various lections exhibited in the *Appendix*, it were easy to manifest; seeing then, that neither the care of God over his truth, nor the fidelity of the Judaical church while the oracles of God were committed thereunto, will permit us to entertain the least suspicion, that there was ever in the world any copy of the Bible differing in the least from that which we enjoy, or that those we have are corrupted as is pretended; and seeing that the authors of that insinuation cannot produce the least testimony to make it good μένωμεν ὥσπερ ἐσμὲν[7] through the mercy and goodness of God in the entire unquestionable possession of his oracles once committed to the Jews, and the faith therein once committed to the saints.

7 Gk. "we may remain as we are."

But now to suppose, that such indeed has been the condition of the holy Bible in its originals as is pretended let us consider whether any relief in this case be to be expected from the translations exhibited unto us with much pains, care, and diligence in these *Biblia polyglotta*, and so at once determine that question, whether this be any part of the use of translations, be they ever so ancient, namely to correct the originals by, leaving further discussion of sundry things in and about them to other exercitations.

REQUISITES UNTO GOOD TRANSLATIONS

7. That all, or any translation, may be esteemed useful for this purpose, I suppose without any contention it will be granted: [Firstly,][8] that we be certain concerning them, that they are translated out of the originals themselves, and not out of the interpretations of them that went before them; for if that appear, all their authority as to the business inquired after, falls to the ground, or is at best resolved into that former, whence they are taken, if they are at agreement therewith; otherwise they are a thing of naught; and this one consideration, will be found to lay hold of one moiety[9] of these translations:

Secondly, that they be of venerable antiquity, so as to be made when there were other copies of the original in the world besides that which we now enjoy.

Thirdly, that they be known to be made by men of ability and integrity, sound in the faith, and conscientiously careful not to add or detract from the originals they made the translation out of; if all these things at least, concur not in a translation, it is most undeniably evident that it can be of no use, as to assist in the finding out what corruptions have befallen our copies; and what is the true lection of any place about which any differences do arise. Let us then, as without any prejudice in ourselves, so without (I hope) any offense to others, very briefly consider the state and condition of the translations given us in the *Biblia polyglotta* as to the qualifications here laid down.

OF THE TRANSLATIONS IN THE *BIBLIA POLYGLOTTA*

Of the Arabic

8. Let us then take a view of some of the chiefest of them without observing any order; seeing there is no more reason for that which is laid down in this *Appendix* than for any other that may be fixed on; I shall begin with the

---

8 "(1.)" in the original but altered to be consistent with the verbally numbered list that follows.
9 I.e., a part.

Arabic, for the honor I bear to the renownedly learned publisher of it and the various lections of the several copies thereof;[10] and the rather because he has dealt herein with his wonted candor, giving in a clear and learned account of the original and nature of that translation, which I had for the substance of it, received from him in a discourse before, wherein also he gave me a satisfactory account concerning some other translations, which I shall not need now to mention; though I shall only say his judgment in such things is to be esteemed at least equal, with [that of] any now alive.[11]

[First,][12] then he tells us upon the matter that this translation is *a cento*[13] made up of many ill-suited pieces, there being no translation in that language extant; I speak of the Old Testament; Secondly, for the antiquity of the most ancient part of it was made about the year 4,700 of the Jews' account, that is, of Christ [AD] 950. Thirdly, it was as to the Pentateuch, translated by R. Saadias Haggaon.[14] Fourthly, that it is interpreted and changed in sundry things by some other person. Fifthly. That he who made these changes seemed to have so done that he might the better thereby δουλεύειν ὑποθέσει[15] as to some particular opinion of his own, whereof sundry instances are given. Sixthly, that he seems to have been a Mohammedan, or at least much to have favored them, as appears from other evidences, so from the inscription of his work with that solemn motto taken out of the Alcoran, *In nomine Dei miseratoris, misericordia.*[16] Seventhly,[17] it may be thought also that some other, a Jew or a Samaritan had his hand in corrupting the last translation. Eighthly, who thought to stamp a divine authority upon his particular opinions. Ninthly, that the foundation of this translation now printed being that of Saadias, it is

10 Owen is referring to Edward Pococke. Walton corrects a number of minor infelicities he perceives in Owen's account here, not least pointing out that Pococke was not the "publisher" of the Arabic version contained in the London Polyglot: rather, at the request of the publisher, he insists, Pococke collated copies of the Pentateuch and produced a preface to the lections in the *Appendix*. See Brian Walton, *The Considerator Considered: or, A Brief View of Certain Considerations upon "the Biblia polyglotta," the "Prolegomena" and "Appendix" Thereof* (London: Thomas Roycroft, 1659), 171–76.
11 For the following, Owen is drawing upon Pococke's preface: see Walton, *Biblia sacra polyglotta*, vol. 6, chap. 8, p. 1a.
12 Numbering absent in original. Goold adds "First" to align with numbering that follows.
13 Lat. "a patchwork of different sources."
14 Saadia Gaon (ca. 882–942) was a Jewish philosopher and biblical exegete from Babylonia who produced an Arabic translation of the Pentateuch. Owen here implies that he flourished slightly later than the year he is now believed to have died in Baghdad.
15 Gk. "to serve a pretext."
16 Lat. "In the name of God the mercifcul, mercy." This is a Latin translation of the Basmala, which is recited before each chapter of the Qur'an.
17 Original duplicates this point as "Sixthly," affecting the numbering of subsequent points.

observable that he professes, that he did both add and detract according as he thought meet, that so he might set out, the hidden (cabalistical[18]) understanding of the Scripture. Tenthly, that the other Arabic translations that are extant, are out of the LXX: either immediately, or by the Syriac which was translated out of it: on these and the like heads does that oracle of the Eastern learning, who has not only (as some) learned the words of some of those languages, but searched with great diligence and judgment into the nature of the learning extant in them, and the importance of the books we have, discourse in that preface. It is the way of sciolists[19] when they have obtained a little skill in any language or science to persuade the world that all worth and wisdom lie therein; men thoroughly learned, and whose learning is regulated by a sound judgment, know that the true use of their abilities consists in the true suiting of men to a clear acquaintance with truth. In that kind, not only in this particular are we beholding[20] to this worthy learned person.¶

I suppose there will not need much arguing, to prove that this translation though exceeding useful in its own place, and kind, yet is not in the least a fit remedy to relieve us, against any pretended corruption in the original, or to gather various lections different from our present copy by; well may it exercise the ability of learned men, to consider wherein and how often it goes, off from the rule of faith; but rule in itself, and upon its own account, coming short of all the necessary qualifications laid down before, it is none.

Should I now go to gather instances of the failings of this translation, open and gross, and so proceed with the rest, I think I might make a volume near as big as that of the various lections, now afforded us: but I have another manner of account to give of my hours than so to spend them.

Of the Syriac

9. Whether the Syriac translation be any fitter for this use, anyone who shall be pleased to consider and weigh it, will easily discover.[21] It seems indeed to have been made out of the original, at least for some part of it; or that the translation of the LXX has been in many things changed since this was made, which I rather suppose. But when, where, or by whom, it does not appear; nor does it in many things seem to have any respect at all unto the Hebrew;

---

18 I.e., Kabbalistic, pertaining to an ancient tradition of esoteric Jewish mystical interpretation of Scripture.

19 I.e., persons who feign learning.

20 I.e., beholden.

21 While Owen is more measured in his assessment of the Syriac translation, Walton vehemently dismisses any of his lingering equivocation. See Walton, *The Considerator Considered*, 176–80.

the note at the close of the Prophets I suppose to proceed rather from the scribe of that individual copy, than the translator; but that the reader may see what hands it has passed through, he may take it as it is rendered by the learned author of the annotations on that translation; "Here ends Malachi, or the twelve books of the prophets, whose words are continually present to us, Amen. And from their prayers, and the prayers of all the saints, of their companions, and especially of the Virgin, who bore God, the mother of all the saints who intercedes on behalf of the race of Adam, may God be gracious to the sinful reader and writer, and to everyone participating with them, whether by word or deed";[22] but this good conclusion is as I suppose from the scribe, the usual negligence of whom in his work is frequently taxed in the collection of various readings.[23]

Now though I confess this translation to be very useful in many things, and to follow the original for the most part, yet being made as yet I know neither when nor by whom, in sundry places evidently following another corrupt translation, having passed through the hands of men ignorant and suspicious, against whose frauds and folly, by reason of the paucity of copies we have no relief, I question whether it may be esteemed of any great use or importance, as to the end inquired after.

Of the Samaritan Pentateuch

10. Of the Samaritan Pentateuch both original and translation we shall not need to add much;[24] what the people from whom it has its denomination were, is known; nor have the inquiries of Scaliger, or Morinus, added anything to what is vulgarly known of them from the Scripture, and Josephus; in a word, an idolatrous, superstitious, wicked people they were, before they were subdued by Hyrcanus;[25] afterward they continued in the separation from the true church of God; and upon the testimony of our Savior had not salvation among them. When they received their Pentateuch is uncertain;

22 In the text: *Explicit Malachias sive libri 12 prophetarum, quorum oratio perpetuo nobis adsit, Amen; precibusque ipsorum, precibusque omnium sanctorum, sodalium ipsorum praesertim virginis, quae Deum peperit, omnium sanctorum matris quae pro genere Adami intercedit, propitius sit Deus lectori & scriptori peccatori, & omnibus sive verbo sive opere, ipsis participantibus.*—Owen. Editor's translation. For the Latin text, see Walton, *Biblia sacra polyglotta*, vol. 6, chap. 3, p. 39b.
23 In the text: as *pag. 8 & alibi.*—Owen. Presumably, Owen is referring to repeated references to scribal errors in the Syrian version: e.g., at Lev. 10:4; 17:8; 18:7. See Walton, *Biblia sacra polyglotta*, vol. 6, chap. 3, p. 8a–b.
24 For Walton's response to Owen's assessment of the Samaritan Pentateuch, see Walton, *The Considerator Considered*, 180–87.
25 I.e., Hyrcanus I.

uncertain also how long they kept it; that they corrupted it while they had it, is not uncertain; they are charged to have done so by the Jews in the Talmud, and the instance they give abides to this day (Deut. 11:30). They have added *Sichem*[26] to the text, to give countenance to their abominations. And openly in Deut. 27:4: where God gives a command that an altar should be set up on mount Ebal, they have wickedly and nefariously corrupted the text and put in Gerizim. Now one such voluntary corruption made on set purpose to countenance a sin, and false worship, is enough to lay low the authority of any copy whatever. The copy here printed was brought out of the east from Damascus not long since. It appears to have been 230 years old says Morinus in the account of it.[27] As I said before, that any Samaritans do as yet remain is uncertain; some few Jews there are that walk in that way, here and there a few families.¶

Now that this Pentateuch which was never as such committed to the church of God, that had its rise no man knows by whom, and that has been preserved no man knows how, known by few, used by none of the ancient Christians, that has been voluntarily corrupted by men of corrupt minds to countenance them in their folly, should be of any authority upon its own single account to any end or purpose, especially to vie with the Hebrew text, men that have not some design that they publicly own not, will scarce contend. The places instanced in by Morinus[28] to prove its integrity above the Hebrew copy, as to the solution of difficulties by it, in Genesis 11:29, 31, Exodus 12:40; do evidently prove it corrupt; any man that will consider them will find the alterations purposely made to avoid the difficulties in those places, which is one common evidence of corruption. In Genesis 11:31 sixty years are cut off from the life of Terah to make the chronology agree; and that of Exodus 12:40, "The dwelling of the children of Israel and their fathers, when they dwelt in the land of Canaan, and in the land of Egypt, was 430 years," is a plain comment or exposition on the text, nor would Hierome, who had this copy, make any use of it, in these difficulties. Might I go over the rest of Morinus his instances whereby he seeks to credit his Samaritan copy, which we have in these *Biblia polyglotta*, I could manifest that there is scarce one of them, but yields a clear argument of corruption in it, upon some of the best grounds that we have to judge of the sincerity or corruption of any copy;

26 I.e., Shechem.
27 In the text: *Opusc. Samar. praefat: ad Translat. Samarat:*—Owen. See Jean Morin, *Opuscula Hebraeo-Samaritica* (Paris: Gaspardus Metras, 1657).
28 In the footnote: *Morin: cap. i. Exercit:* 4.—Owen. See Jean Morin, *Exercitationes biblicae de Hebraei Graecique textus sinceritate: Pars prior* (Paris: Antonius Vitray, 1633), 37–45.

and if this Pentateuch had been of any credit of old, it would not have been omitted, yea as it seems utterly rejected as a thing of naught, by Origen, in his diligent collection of the original and versions.

But we are in a way and business, wherein all things are carried to and fro by conjectures; and it were no hard task to manifest the utter uncertainty of what is fixed on as the original of this Pentateuch, by the author of the *Prolegomena*, or to reinforce those conjectures which he opposes; but that is not my present work; nor do I know that ever it will be so. But I must for the present say; that I could have been glad, that he had refrained the close of his discourse:[29] wherein from the occasional mention of the Samaritan Liturgy, and the pretended antiquity of it, he falls not without some bitterness of spirit on those who have laid aside the English service book; it were not (in the judgment of some) imprudently done, to reserve a triumph over the sectaries; to some more considerable victory, than any is to be hoped from the example of the Samaritans: were they all barbers, and porters, and alehouse keepers, yet they might easily discern, that the example and precedent of a wicked people, forsaken of God, and forsaking of him, to whom the promise of the Spirit of supplications, was never made, nor he bestowed upon them, is not cogent unto the people of Christ under the new testament; who have the promise made good unto them. And much more unto the same purpose will some of them be found to say, when men of wisdom and learning who are able to instruct them, shall condescend personally so to do. But I shall forbear, what might further be spoken.

Of the Chaldee Paraphrase

11.[30] The Chaldee Paraphrase is *a cento* also. The Targum of Jonathan is ancient, so also is that of Onkelos; they are supposed to have been made before,

---

29 In the text: *Sect. 2.*—Owen. Owen actually appears to be referring to prolegom. 11, sec. 23 of Walton's *Prolegomena*. Here Owen takes exception to a remark Walton makes about the Nonconformists' refusal to adopt the liturgy of the English prayer book, citing the example of the Samaritan liturgy. Somewhat implausibly, Walton dismisses Owen's objection on the grounds that he was chiefly intending to uphold the example of the Jews (whom the Samaritans followed) in his remark. See Walton, *The Considerator Considered*, 185–87. In the *Prolegomena*, Walton refers to the extemporaneous public "prattling" and "babbling" of "barbers, porters, and shopkeepers" in churches and concludes that "even from the Jews themselves and their imitators the Samaritans, their practice is proven to be of one error and novelty" (*quorum praxis vel ab ipsis Judaeis, eorumque aemulis Samaritanis, erroris et novitatis arguitur*). See Walton, *Prolegomena*, 2:357.

30 Section number missing in original.

or about the time of our Savior. Some of the Jews would have Jonathan to have lived not long after Ezra. Others that he was the chief disciple of Hillel about a hundred years before Christ's incarnation; some are otherwise minded, and will not own it to be much older than the Talmud: but as yet I see no grounds sufficient to overthrow the received opinion. The other parts, of the Scripture were paraphrased at several times, some above five hundred years after our Savior, and are full of Talmudical fancies, if not fables; as that on the Canticles. That all these Targums are of excellent use is confessed, and we are beholding to the *Biblia polyglotta* for representing them in so handsome an order and place, that with great facility they may be compared with the original. But as to the end under consideration, how little advantage is from hence to be obtained these few ensuing observations will evince. [Firstly,][31] It was never the aim of those paraphrasts to render the original text exactly *verbum de verbo*;[32] but to represent the sense of the text, according as it appeared to their judgment; hence it is impossible to give any true account how they read in any place, wherein they dissent from our present copies, since their endeavor was to give us the sense as they thought rather than the bare and naked importance of the words themselves; hence Elias says of them,[33] "Behold the Targumists observed not sometimes the way of grammar." Secondly, it is evident, that all the Targums agreed to give us often mystical senses, especially the latter, and so were necessitated to go off from the letter of the text. Thirdly, it is evident that they have often made additions of whole sentences to the Scripture, even the best of them, from their own apprehensions or corrupt traditions, whereof there is not one tittle or syllable in the Scripture nor ever was. Fourthly, what careful hands it has passed through, the bulky collection of various lections given in this *Appendix* does abundantly manifest; and seeing it has not lain under any peculiar care and merciful providence of God, whether innumerable other faults and errors, not to be discovered by any variety of copies, as it is happened with the Septuagint, may not be got into it who can tell. Of these and the like things we shall have a fuller account when the *Babylonia* of Buxtorfe the father [Sr.], (promised some while since by the son to be published;[34] and, as we are informed by the

---

31 "1." in the original, but altered to be consistent with subsequent verbally numbered list.

32 Lat. "word for word."

33 In the text: והנה המתרגמים לא שמרו לפעמום דרך הדקדוק.—Owen. As per Goold. The pointing in the original is difficult to make out. Owen's translation follows in the text.

34 In the text: *Vindic. veritat. Heb. p.* 2. *chap.* 10. *pag.* 337.—Owen. The pagination appears to be incorrect. Buxtorf Jr. makes reference to his father's *Babylonia* on p. 713 (pt. 2, chap. 10) of the work Owen cites: "The reader will discover examples of all these things at some point in my father's *Babylonia*" (*Horum omnium exempla Lector aliquando inveniet in Patris mei Babylonia*).

learned annotator on this *Paraphrase* in his preface in the *Appendix*, lately
sent to the publishers of this Bible) shall be put out; so that we have not as
yet arrived at the remedy provided for the supposed distemper.

Of the Vulgar Latin

12. Of the Vulgar Latin, its uncertain original, its corruptions and barbarisms,
its abuse, so much has been spoken, and by so many already, that it were to
no purpose to repeat it over again: for my part I esteem it much the best in
the whole collection exhibited unto us, excepting the interlineary of Arias;[35]
but not to be compared to sundry modern translations, and very unfit to
yield the relief sought after.

Of the Septuagint

13. The LXX is that which must bear the weight of the whole.[36] And good
reason it is indeed, that it should answer for the most of the rest; they being
evidently taken out of it, and so they are oftentimes worse, yet they are now
better than that is. But here again all things are exceedingly uncertain, nothing almost is manifest concerning it, but that it is woefully corrupt; its rise
is uncertain; some call the whole story of that translation into question as
though there had never been any such persons in *rerum natura*, the circumstances that are reported about them and their works, are certainly fabulous;
that they should be sent for upon the advice of Demetrius Phalereus,[37] who
was dead before, that they should be put into seventy-two cells or private
chambers; that there should be twelve of each tribe, fit for that work, are all
of them incredible.[38]

See Johann Buxtorf Jr., *Anticritica: Seu vindiciae veritatis Hebraicae* (Basel: Ludovicus Rex, 1653),
713. At any rate, the forthcoming work to which Owen is referring is Buxtorf Sr.'s *Babylonia,
sive Commentarius criticus in universum Targum, sive paraphrasin bibliorum Chaldaicum* (Universitätsbibliothek Basel, MS F IX 41), which was never published but was used by Walton in his
comments on the Targums in the London Polyglot Bible. Walton intended to publish it in the
Polyglot, but evidently received it too late. See Walton, *The Considerator Considered*, 187–88.

35 See Arias Montanus, "De varia Hebraicorum librorum Scriptione et lectione commentatio," in
Biblia Hebraica eorundem Latina interpretatio Xantis Pagnini Lucensis (Antwerp: Christophori
Plantini, 1584)

36 Walton believes he has already sufficiently resolved all of Owen's doubts about the Septuagint
in prolegom. 9 of his *Prolegomena* to the London Polyglot Bible. See Walton, *The Considerator
Considered*, 189–91. Cf. Walton, *Prolegomena*, 2:1–190.

37 Demetrius of Phalerum (ca. 350–ca. 280 BC) was an Athenian statesman, rhetorician, and
Peripatetic philosopher.

38 In the text: See *Scal. ad Euseb. fol. 123. Wouwer Syntag. cap. 11.*—Owen. See, respectively,
Animadversiones in chronologica Eusebii, in Scaliger, *Thesaurus temporum* (Leiden: Thomas

Some of the Jews say that they made the translation out of a corrupt Chaldee Paraphrase, and to me this seems not unlikely. Josephus, Austin, Philo,[39] Hierome, Zonaras[40] affirm that they translated the Law or Pentateuch only; Josephus affirms this expressly, "For not even he," says he, "came to obtain all our records: it was only the portion containing the Law which was delivered to him from those who were sent to interpret it":[41] and this is a received opinion: whence we have the rest is unknown. Take to this purpose the ensuing chapter out of Drusius.

The common Greek translation is not of the seventy translators, contrary to the way it was once regarded.

I believe no one today doubts that that translation, which is rendered in the common tongue among the Greeks, is in reality not of the seventy translators. For if nothing else, there are innumerable places in it which betray a great ignorance of the Hebrew tongue. He who does not see in this edition a singular negligence in reading and the laziness unworthy of such men, sees nothing, even if Eusebius Jerome always seems to attribute it to the seventy translators in his histories. We too when we produce a reference from it use the common name rather than the true. We follow the example of Jerome, who, we suspect, believed that the translation was not at all fashioned by those men, but so wanted nevertheless always to call it by the received name that he would not offend the Greeks. We certainly have no doubt that he had some hesitation over those authors. And the following confirms us in that opinion: he writes that Josephus and nearly every school of the Jews claimed that only the five books of Moses were translated by the seventy translators. Moreover, he writes this not once, but often (as on Ezek. 5. pag. 343, & pag. 371, & 373, & Mic. 2. pag. 150. In the edition of his books published at Antwerp).[42]

Basson, 1606), 123a–b; *De Graeca et Latina bibliorum interpretatione syntagma*, in Johann von Wowern, *Epistolarum centuriae ii* (Hamburg: Heringius, 1609), 77–86.

39 Philo of Alexandria (ca. 20 BC–ca. AD 50) was a Jewish philosopher who lived in Alexandria, and was known for his attempts to harmonize Scripture with Stoic philosophy.

40 Joannes Zonarus (fl. 12th c.) was a Byzantine theologian and historian.

41 In the text: οὐδὲ γὰρ [. . .] πᾶσαν ἐκεῖνος ἔφθη λαβεῖν τὴν ἀναγραφὴν, ἀλλ' αὐτὰ μόνα τὰ τοῦ νόμου παρέδοσαν οἱ πεμφθέντες ἐπὶ τὴν ἐξήγησιν. *Proem. ad Antiquit.*—Owen. For the Greek text in the nineteenth-century critical edition, see *Antiquitatum Iudaicarum*, bk. 1, lines 12–13, in Josephus, *Opera: Edidit et apparatu critico instruxit*, 7 vols., ed. Benedikt Niese (Berlin: Weidmannos, 1885–1895), 1:6. For the Greek the text and the English translation, see Josephus, *Jewish Antiquities*, vol. 1, *Books 1–3*, trans. H. St. J. Thackeray, Loeb Classical Library 242 (Cambridge, MA: Harvard University Press, 1930), 6–7. The Loeb translation is slightly modified.

42 In the text: *Observat, lib. 6. chap. 9. Vulgatam translationem Graecam non esse LXX interpretum, contra quam olim existimatum fuit.*

Let it be granted that such a translation was made, and that of the whole Bible, by some Alexandrian Jews, as is most probable; yet it is certain, that the αὐτόγραφον⁴³ of it, if left in the library of Alexandria, was consumed to ashes in Caesar's wars;⁴⁴ though Chrysostom⁴⁵ tells us that the Prophets were placed in the temple of Serapis, "even to this day, the translated books of the prophets remain there":⁴⁶ "and they abide there," says he, "unto this day"; how unlikely this is, any man may guess, by what Hierome, who made another manner of inquiry after those things than Chrysostom, affirms concerning the incurable various copies of that translation wanting an umpire of their differences. We know also what little exactness men in those days, before the use of grammar attained in the knowledge of languages, in their relation to one another; and some learned men do much question even the skill of those interpreters,

Jerome, a holy and learned man, perceived that that Latin speakers lacked a true and genuine reading of the law and the prophets, because the edition of the seventy translators, which at that time was most highly regarded among the Greeks and Latins everywhere (needless to say improperly), was altered in many places, the truth having been indeed greatly corrupted through scribes and copyists. This is very clear to anyone who compares that edition with the true Hebrew version. Consequently, I sometimes grant

---

Translatio ea quae vulgo apud Graecos habetur, quin LXX interpretum non sit, nemini hodie dubium esse arbitror nam si nihil aliud, innumeri in ea loci sunt, qui arguunt magnam imperitiam sermonis Ebraici; sed & negligentiam singularem in legendo, & oscitantiam tantis viris indignam qui in ea editione non videt, nihil videt; etsi Eusebius, Hieronymus passim in monumentis suis eam Septuaginta interpretibus attribuere videtur. Nos quoq; cum aliquid inde proferimus usitato magis quam vero nomine utimur, exemplo videlicet Hieronymi, quem suspicamur, licet crederet interpretationem eam a viris illis elaboratam minime fuisse, ne offenderet Graecos voluisse tamen recepto nomine semper appellare. Certe quin dubitaverit super iisdem authoribus, nihil dubitamus, nam vel hoc nos in ea opinione confirmat, quod scribit Josephum, omnemque adeo scholam Judaeorum quinque tantum libros Mosis a Septuaginta interpretibus translatos esse asserere, scribit autem hoc non semel, sed saepius, ut Ezech. v. pag. 343, et pag. 301, et 372 et Mich. ii. pag. 150. Libris Antwerpiae vulgatis.—Owen. Editor's translation. For the Latin text, see Johannes van den Driesche, *Observationum libri xii* (Antwerp: Aegidius Radaeus, 1584), 132–33

43 Gk. "the original."
44 The famous Library of Alexandria was thought to have been set ablaze during the Alexandrian war of Julius Caesar in 48 BC.
45 John Chrysostom (ca. 347–407) was Archbishop of Constantinople, a prolific writer, and one of the most famous preachers in Christian history.
46 In the text: μέχρι νῦν ἐκεῖ τῶν προφητῶν αἱ ἑρμηνευθεῖσαι βίβλοι μένουσιν: *ad Judaeos*. Editor's translation. For the. Greek text, see *Adversus Iudaeos* I.6, in John Chrysostom, *Opera omnia*, t. 1, ed. J. P. Migne, Patrologia Graeca 48 (Paris: Migne, 1862), 851.

that they were not sufficiently skilled in the Hebrew language, a point we are compelled to admit, albeit unwillingly, otherwise they would not have fallen into mistakes so shamefully in many passages.[47]

If moreover the ability be granted, what security have we of their principles and honesty. Cardinal Ximenius, in his preface to the edition of the Complutensian Bibles, tells us, (that which is most true, if the translation we have be theirs) that on sundry accounts they took liberty in translating according to their own mind; and thence conclude[s], "Whence the translation of the seventy-two is sometimes superfluous, sometimes wanting";[48] it is sometimes superfluous, sometimes wanting; but suppose all these uncertainties might be overlooked, yet the intolerable corruptions, that (as is on all hands confessed) have crept into the translation, make it altogether useless as to the end we are inquiring after; this Hierome in his *Epistle to Chromat.* at large declares, and shows from thence the necessity of a new translation.[49] Yea Bellarmine himself says, that though he believes the translation of the LXX to be still extant, yet it is so corrupt and vitiated, that it plainly appears to be another.[50]

He that shall read and consider what Hierome has written of this translation even then when he was excusing himself, and condescended to the utmost to waive the envy that was coming on him, upon his new translation, in the

47 In the text: so *Munster. Praefat: ad Biblia; Videbat Hieronymus vir pius & doctus, Latinos vera & genuina legis atque prophetarum destitutos lectione, nam LXX interpretum editio, quae tunc ubiq; locorum receptissima erat apud Graecos & Latinos nedum perperam plerisque in locis versa fuit, verum per scriptores atque scribas plurimum corrupta, id quod & hodie facile patet conferenti editionem illam juxta Hebraicam, veritatem, ut interim fatear illos non admodum peritos fuisse linguae Hebraicae id vel quod inviti cogimur fateri, alioquin in plurimis locis non tam foede lapsi fuissent.*—Owen. Editor's translation. For the Latin text, see "Praefatio," in Sebastian Münster, *Hebraica Biblia*, t. 1 (Basel: n.p., 1534), *2.

48 In the text: *Unde translatio Septuaginta duum, quandoque est superflua quandoque diminuta.*—Owen. Editor's translation. For the Latin text, see "Prologus in Hebraicum Chaldaicumque dictionarium," in *Vetus Testamentum multiplici lingua nunc primo impressum* (Alcalá de Henares: Arnao Guillén de Brocar, 1514–1517), 1:*2b.

49 It is probable that Owen is here referring to Jerome's preface to the Vulgate translation of Chronicles (specifically addressed to Chromatius), where he outlines various reasons for the corruption of the Septuagint, not least through Origen's emendations from Theodotion's translation. See "Incipit prologus Sancti Hieronymi in libro paralipomenon," in *Biblia sacra iuxta Vulgatam versionem*, 5th ed.], ed. Roger Gryson (Stuttgart: Deutsche Bibelgesellschaft, 2007), 546–47. A number of Jerome's prefaces to his translation of various Old Testament books in the Vulgate take up this point, and are repeated in his *Apology against Rufinus*. See *Apologia adversus libros Rufini*, bk. 2, secs. 25–33, in Jerome, *Opera Omnia II–III*, ed. J. P. Migne, Patrologia Latina 23 (Paris: Vrayet, 1845), 448–55.

50 In the text: lib. 2, *de Verbo Dei, cap.* 6.—Owen. See Robert Bellarmine, *Opera omnia*, 6 vols. (Naples: Josephum Giuliano, 1856–1862), 1:68a–71a.

second book of his *Apology against Rufinus*;[51] repeating and mollifying[52] what he had spoken of it in another place, will be enabled in some measure to guess of what account it ought to be with us. In brief he tells us, it is corrupt, interpolated; mingled by Origen with that of Theodotion marked with asterisks and obelisks; that there were so many copies of it, and they so varying, that no man knew what to follow; tells us of a learned man who on that account interpreted all the errors he could light on for Scripture; that in the book of Job take away what was added to it by Origen, or is marked by him, and little will be left; his discourse is too long to transcribe; see also his *Epistle to Chromatius* at large to this purpose.[53] Let the reader also consult the learned Masius, in his preface to his most learned comment on Joshua.[54]

TRANSLATIONS OF THE NEW TESTAMENT

The Persian

14. For the translations of the New Testament that are here afforded us, little need be spoken;[55] of the antiquity, usefulness, and means of bringing the Syriac into Europe, an account has been given by many, and we willingly acquiesce in it: the Ethiopian and Persian are novel things, of little use or value, yea I suppose it may safely be said they are the worst and most corrupt that are extant in the world; the Persian was not translated out of the Greek, as is confessed by the learned annotator upon it: "The present place truly has adequately demonstrated that the Persian had not consulted the Greek codex."[56] Yea in how many things he goes off from the Greek, Syriac, Arabic, yea goes directly contrary to the truth; is both acknowledged by its publisher, and is manifest from the thing itself; I know no use of it, but only to show that such a useless thing is in the world.

The Ethiopian

15. Nor is the Ethiopian one whit better; a novel endeavor of an illiterate person: he tells us that John when he wrote the Revelation was Archbishop,

51 In the text: *Cap. 8. 9.*—Owen. See *Apologia adversus libros Rufini*, bk. 2, secs. 25–35, in Jerome, *Opera II–III*, 448–56.
52 I.e., appearing.
53 See "Incipit Prologus Sancti Hieronymi in Libro Paralipomenon," in *Vulgatam*, 546–47.
54 See Andreas Masius, *Iosuae imperatoris historia* (Antwerp: Christophorus Plantinus, 1574), 1–7.
55 For Walton's response to Owen's complaints about the *Persian* and *Ethiopian* translations of the New Testament, see Walton, *The Considerator Considered*, 191–93.
56 In the text: *Praesens [vero] locus satis arguit, Persam Graecum codicem haud consuluisse; in Luc. 10. & 41.*—Owen. Editor's translation. See the annotations on the Persian edition of the Gospels on Luke 10:41, Walton, *Biblia sacra polyglotta*, vol. 6, chap. 7, p. 63b.

of Constantia, or Constantinople, etc.: It is to no purpose to go over the like observations that might be made on these translations; if any man has a mind to be led out of the way, he may do well to attend unto them. Whether some of them be in use now in the world I know not, I am sure it is well if they be not; had I not seen them, I could not have imagined any had been so bad: would I make it my business to give instances of the mistakes, ignorance, falsifications, errors and corruptions of these translators, whoever they were (Jews or Christians, for I am not without some ground of thinking that Jews have had their hands in them for money)[57] my discourse, as I said before, would swell into a volume, and unless necessitated, I shall avoid it.

THE VALUE OF THESE TRANSLATIONS AS TO THE WORK IN HAND

16. From what has been spoken it may abundantly appear, that if there are indeed such corruptions, mistakes, and errors crept into the original; as some have pretended, there is no relief in the least provided for the security of truth, by any of the translations exhibited unto us in these late editions of the Bible; themselves being of an uncertain original, corrupt, and indeed of no authority from themselves, but merely from their relation to that whose credit is called in question; for my own part as I said before, I allow them their proper use, and place; and am thankful to them by whose care and pains we are made partakers of them; but to endeavor by them to correct the Scripture, to gather various lections out of the original as say others, for my part I abhor the thought of it, let others do as seem good unto them. And if ever I be necessitated to speak in particular of these translations, there are yet in readiness further discoveries to be made of them.

OF THE SUPPOSITION OF GROSS CORRUPTION IN THE ORIGINALS

17. There remains only as to my purpose in hand that some brief account be taken of what is yet further insinuated, of the liberty to observe various lections in the Bible upon supposition of gross corruptions that may be crept into it, as also of the specimen of various lections gathered out of Grotius

---

57 Cf. Walton, *The Considerator Considered*, 193: "How the Jews should have a hand in any of the translations is a fancie which I think never lodged in any mans breast but his own, nor can he shew any ground for it."

his *Annotations*, and somewhat of the whole bulk of them as presented unto us in the *Appendix*.[58]

For the corruptions supposed, I could heartily wish that learned men would abstain from such insinuations unless they are able to give them some pretense by instances; it is not spoken of this or that copy, which by the error of the scribes or printers may have important mistakes found in it. There is no need of men's critical abilities to rectify such mistakes, other copies are at hand for their relief. It is of the text without such suppositions, that this insinuation is made; now to cast scruples into the minds of men, about the integrity and sincerity of that, without sufficient ground or warrant, is surely not allowable. It is not good to deal so with men or their writings, much less with the word of God. Should any man write that in case of such a man's theft, or murder, who is a man of unspotted reputation, it were good to take such or such a course with him, and publish it to the world, would their stirring of such rumors be looked on as a honest, Christian, and candid course of proceeding? And is it safe to deal so with the Scripture? I speak of Protestants; for Papists, who are grown bold in the opposition to the originals of the Scripture, I must needs say, that I look upon them as effectually managing a design of Satan to draw men into atheism. Nor in particular do I account of Morinus his *Exercitations* one whit better.[59] It is readily acknowledged, that there are many difficult places in the Scripture, especially in the historical books of the Old Testament. Some of them have by some been looked at as ἄλυτα.[60] The industry of learned men of old, and of late Jews and Christians, has[61] been well exercised in the interpretation and reconciliation of them: by one, or other, a fair and probable account is given of them all. Where we cannot reach the utmost depth of truth, it has been thought meet, that poor worms should captivate their understandings to the truth and authority of God in his word. If there be this liberty once given that they may be looked on as corruptions, and amended at the pleasure of men, how we shall be able to stay before we come to the bottom of questioning the whole Scripture, I know not. That then which yet we insist upon, is, that according to all rules of equal procedure, men are to prove such corruptions before they entertain us with their provision of means for remedy.

58 Hugo Grotius's annotations are contained in chap. 15 of the *Appendix*. See Walton, *Biblia sacra polyglotta*, vol. 6, chap. 15, pp. 37a–58b.
59 See Morin, *Exercitationes pars prior*.
60 Gk. "incomprehensible" or "unresolved."
61 Original has "have."

OF VARIOUS LECTIONS OUT OF GROTIUS

18. For the specimen of various lections gathered out of Grotius his *Annotations*, I shall not much concern myself therein; they are nothing less than various lections of that learned man's own observations; set aside; [first,][62] the various lections of the LXX, and Vulgar Latin of Symmachus, Aquila, and Theodotion, wherein we are not concerned. Secondly, the *Keri* and *Ketib* which we have oftentimes over and over in this volume. Thirdly, the various readings of the oriental and occidental Jews which we have also elsewhere. Fourthly, conjectures how the LXX, and Vulgar Latin read, by altering letters only. Fifthly, conjectures of his own how the text may be mended, and a very little room will take up what remains; by that cursory view I have taken of them, I see not one word that can pretend to be a various lection; unless it belong to the *Keri* and *Ketib*, or the difference between the oriental and the occidental Jews: so that as I said before, as to my present design I am not at all concerned in that collection; those that are may further consider it.

OF THE *APPENDIX* IN GENERAL

19. As short an account will seem for the general consideration of the whole bulky collection of various lections that we have here presented unto us; for those of the several translations we are not at all concerned in them: where any or all of them fail, or are corrupted, we have a rule blessed be God, preserved to rectify them by. For those of the originals I have spoken to them in particular; I shall only add, that we have some of them both from the Old and New Testament given us thrice over at least, many of the *Keri* and *Ketib*, after a double service done by them, are given us again, the third time by Grotius, so also are those of the New Testament by the same Grotius, and Lucas Brugensis.[63]

---

62 "1." in the original, but altered to be consistent with verbally numbered list that follows.

63 François Luc de Bruges's collection of New Testament annotations is also contained in the *Appendix* volume of the London Polyglot and includes annotations on both Greek and Latin editions of the New Testament. See Walton, *Biblia sacra polyglotta*, vol. 6, chap. 17, pp. 1a–36b. He also compiled a collection of annotations on the Vulgate Old Testament.

PART 2

WORKS ON THE LORD'S SUPPER

TWENTY-FIVE DISCOURSES SUITABLE TO THE LORD'S SUPPER

*Delivered Just before the Administration
of That Sacred Ordinance*

———

By the Reverend and Learned

John Owen, D.D.

Of the Last Age.

———

Never before Printed.

———

*Hebrews 11:4.
He being dead yet speaketh.*

———

London:
Printed for J. Buckland, in the
Pater-noster-Row; T. Field,
in Cheapside; E. Dilly, in the
Poultry; and G. Keith,
in the Gracechurch-street. 1760.
[Price Bound Two Shillings]

Twenty-Five Discourses Suitable to the Lord's Supper

Contents

The chapter titles have been supplied by the editor. The dates of the discourses, when given, are
original.

To Mrs. Cooke of Stoke Newington

MADAM,

Four years ago the world was favored through your means with a volume of Doctor Owen's sermons which never before appeared in print; and it is at your instance that the following *Sacramental Discourses* of that same venerable divine are now made public. Hereby, madam, you at once express your high value and just esteem for the memory and works of that incomparable author, with your generous concern, and prevailing desire of being serviceable to the cause of Christ, a cause much more dear to you than all the worldly possessions with which the providence of God has blessed you.

With the greatest sincerity it may be said, your constant affection to the habitation of God's house, your steady adherence to the peculiar doctrines of Christianity, your kind regards to the faithful ministers of the gospel, your extensive benevolence to the indigent and the distressed, your affability to all you converse with, and, in a word, your readiness to every good work, are so spread abroad, that, as the apostle says to the Thessalonians, "There is no need to speak any thing."

That the Lord would prolong your valuable life, daily refresh your soul with the dew of his grace, and enable you, when the hour of death approaches, to rejoice in the full prospect of eternal life through our Lord Jesus Christ, is the prayer,

Madam,
Of your affectionate and obedient servant,
Richard Winter.

Tooke's Court,
Cursitor Street,
March 4, 1760.

Preface to the 1760 Edition

THE PRECEDING DEDICATION is sufficient to acquaint the public, that these *Sacramental Discourses* are the genuine productions of that great man of God, Doctor John Owen, who was for some time in the last age vice-chancellor of Oxford. They enter the world through the same channel as his *Thirteen Sermons* on various occasions published four years since,[1] namely, they were at first taken in shorthand from the Doctor's mouth, and by the late Sir John Hartopp,[2] Baronet, Mrs. Cooke's pious grandfather, were transcribed into longhand.

Mr. Matthew Henry has this note in his annotations on 2 Kings 2, "There are remains of great and good men, which, like Elijah's[3] mantle, ought to be gathered up, and preserved by the survivors; their sayings, their writings, their examples; that as their works follow them in the reward of them, they may stay behind in the benefit of them."[4] Not that our faith is to stand in the wisdom of men; the Bible alone is the standard of truth; and there we are bid to go by the footsteps of the flock; and to keep the paths of the righteous. There is a strange itch in the minds of men after novelties; and it is too common a case, that they who are for striking out something new in divinity are ready to pour contempt on the valuable writings of those who are gone before them; and even the most learned, peaceable and pious men shall not

---

1 Cf. John Owen, *Thirteen Sermons Preached on Various Occasions. By the Reverend and Learned John Owen, D.D. Of the Last Age. Never before Printed* (London: For J. Buckland, fold by E. Dilly, 1756).

2 Sir John Hartopp (ca. 1637–1722) was a Nonconformist Parliamentarian who was son-in-law to Charles Fleetwood, Owen's friend and patron in the years following the Restoration. Hartopp was responsible for taking shorthand notes of Owen's sermons, which were expanded in longhand form in the posthumous collections of sermons published in 1721, 1756, and 1760.

3 "this" in Henry's original.

4 See Henry's commentary on 2 Kings 2:13–18. Matthew Henry, *An Exposition of the Old and New Testament*, 6 vols. (Philadelphia: Ed. Barrington and Geo. D. Haswell, 1828), 2:570.

escape their unrighteous censures. This is notorious in the conduct of those who embrace the new scheme.

If we inquire of the former age, we shall find there flourished in it some of the greatest and best of men, for whose printed works many acknowledge they have abundant cause to bless God to eternity. Among these the writings of Doctor Owen shine with a peculiar luster in the judgment of judicious Christians; and I am persuaded they who peruse them with the spirit of love and of a sound mind, will be as far from asserting, that in his manner of maintaining the doctrine of faith, his "right arm appeared to be weakened," as from saying, that his right eye was darkened, and unable to discern the object of it.

As to the following discourses, which the Doctor calls *Familiar Exercises*, they are now printed in hopes they will be made useful, through the divine blessing, to assist the meditations of Christians of all denominations in their approaches to the Lord's Table, seeing they are so well adapted to answer that sacred purpose.

Several Things Suitable for the Acting of Faith

October 10, 1669

For he hath made him to be sin for us, who knew no sin; that
we might be made the righteousness of God in him.

2 CORINTHIANS 5:21

I SHALL NOT ENTER into the opening of this Scripture, but only propose some few things that may be a suitable subject for your present meditation.

There are three things concerning God the Father; three things concerning the Son; and three things concerning ourselves, all in these words that I have mentioned, and all suitable for us to be acting faith upon.

1. I would remember, if the Lord help me, the sovereignty of God the Father, his justice, and his grace. His sovereignty,—"He made him"; God the Father made him. His justice,—"He made him to be sin"; a sacrifice and an offering for sin. And his grace, "that we might be made the righteousness of God in Christ."

(1) The sovereignty of God. I could mention, that this sovereignty of God extends itself to all persons chosen, and show for whom Christ should be made sin; for he was not made sin for all, but for them who became the righteousness of God in him. Also the sovereignty of God over things, dispensing with the law so far, that He suffered for sin, "who knew no sin"; and we, who had sinned, were let go free. The sovereignty of God in appointing the Son to this work; He "made him"; for none else could. He was the servant of the Father: so that the whole foundation of this great transaction lies in the

sovereignty of God over persons and things, in reference unto Christ. Let us then remember to bow down to the sovereignty of God in this ordinance of the Lord's Supper.

(2) There is the justice of God. He "made him to be sin," imputed sin unto him, reckoned unto him all the sins of the elect, caused all our sins to meet upon him, made him a sin offering, a sacrifice for sin, laid all the punishment of our sins upon him. To this end he sent him forth to be a propitiation for sin, to declare his righteousness. The Lord help us to remember that his righteousness is in a special manner exalted by the death of Christ. He would not save us any other way but by making him sin.

(3) There is the grace of God [which] manifests itself in the aim and design of God in all this matter. What did God aim at? It was that we might become "the righteousness of God in him"; that we might be made righteous, and freed from sin.

2. There are three things that lie clear in the words, that we may call to remembrance, concerning the Son. There is his innocency, his purity, he "knew no sin." There is his sufferings, he was made "to be sin": and there is his merit. It was that we might become "the righteousness of God in him." Here is another object for faith to meditate upon.

(1) There are many things in Scripture that direct us to thoughts of the spotless purity, righteousness and holiness of Christ, when we think of his sufferings. A Lamb of God, "without spot."[1] He "did no sin, nor had any guile in his mouth."[2] He was "holy, harmless, undefiled, separate from sinners."[3] Faith should call this to mind in the sufferings of Christ, that he "knew no sin." That expression sets sin at the greatest distance from Jesus Christ.

(2) The sufferings of Christ; he was made sin, a comprehensive word, that sets out his whole sufferings. Look, whatever the justice of God, the law of God, whatever the threatenings of God did require to be inflicted as a punishment for sin, Christ underwent it all. They are dreadful apprehensions that we ourselves have, or can take in concerning the issue and effect of sin, from the wrath of God, when under convictions, and not relieved by the promises of the gospel. But we see not the thousandth part of the evil of sin, that follows inseparably from the righteousness and holiness of God. The effects of God's justice for sin will no more enter into our hearts fully to apprehend, than the effects of his grace and glory will; yet whatever it was, Christ underwent it all.

---

1   1 Pet. 1:19.
2   1 Pet. 2:22.
3   Heb. 7:26.

(3) Then there is the merit of Christ, which is another object of faith that we should call over in the celebration of this ordinance. Why was he made sin? It was that we might become "the righteousness of God in him." It is answerable to that other expression in Galatians 3:13–14. He has borne the curse, "was made a curse for us." To what end? That "the blessing of faithful Abraham might come upon us"; or, that we might be completely made righteous. The design of our assembling together, is to remember, how we come to be made righteous; it is, by Christ's being made sin.

3. We may see three things concerning ourselves.

(1) Our own sin and guilt: he was made sin "for us." If Christ was made sin for us, then we were sinners.

(2) We may remember our deliverance; how we were delivered from sin, and all the evils of it. It was not by a word of command, or power, or by the interposition of saints or angels, or by our own endeavors; but by the sufferings of the Son of God. And,

(3) God would have us remember and call to mind the state whereinto we are brought, which is a state of righteousness; that we may bless him for that which in this world will issue in our righteousness, and in the world to come, eternal glory.

These things we may call over for our faith to meditate upon. Our minds are apt to be distracted; the ordinance is to fix them: and if we act faith in an especial manner in this ordinance, God will be glorified.

The Special Object of Faith in This Ordinance, the Peculiar Communion with Christ in This Ordinance, and the Use of This Ordinance

November 26, 1669

The cup of blessing which we bless, is it not the communion
of the blood of Christ? The bread which we break, is
it not the communion of the body of Christ?

1 CORINTHIANS 10:16

THERE IS, IN THE ORDINANCE of the Lord's Supper an especial and peculiar communion with Christ in his body and blood to be obtained. One reason why we so little value the ordinance, and profit so little by it, may be, because we understand so little of the nature of that special communion with Christ, which we have therein.

THE SPECIAL OBJECT OF FAITH IN THIS ORDINANCE

We have this special communion upon the account of the special object that faith is exercised upon in this ordinance, and the special acts that it puts forth in reference to that, or those objects. For the acts follow the special nature of their objects. Now,

1. The special object of faith, as acted in this ordinance, is not the object of faith, as faith; that is, the most general object of it, which is the divine

veracity: "He that hath received his testimony, hath set to his seal, that God is true" (John 3:33). The divine veracity, or the truth of God, that is the formal object of faith, as faith; and makes our faith to be divine faith. But now this is not the special object of faith in this ordinance, but something that does suppose that.

2. The special object of faith, as justifying, is not the special object of faith in this ordinance. The special object of faith, as justifying, is the promise, and Christ in the promise, in general, as the Savior of sinners: so when the apostle called men to "Repent and believe," he tells them, "The promise is unto you" (Acts 2:38–39). And, I suppose, I need not insist upon the proof of this, that the promise, and Christ in the promise, as Savior and Redeemer, is the object of faith, as it is justifying. But this also is supposed in the actings of faith in this ordinance; which is peculiar, and gives us peculiar communion with Christ. Therefore,

3. The special and peculiar object of faith, the immediate object of it, in this ordinance, in its largest extent is,

(1) The human nature of Christ, as the subject wherein mediation and redemption was wrought. Christ is considered to come as a sacrifice; that is laid down as the foundation of it (Ps. 40:6); "A body hast thou prepared me" (Heb. 10:5); which is synecdochically[1] taken for the whole human nature. Faith, when it would lead itself unto the sacrifice of Christ, which is here represented, does in an especial manner consider the human nature of Christ; that God prepared him a body for that end. This we are to have peculiar regard unto when we come to the administration, or participation of this ordinance; for that end we now celebrate it. Nay,

(2) Faith goes further, and does not consider merely the human nature of Christ, but considers it as distinguished into its integral parts, into body and blood; both which have a price, value, and virtue given unto them by their union with his human soul; for both the body of Christ and the blood of Christ, upon which the work of our redemption is put in Scripture, have their value and worth from their relation unto his soul; as soul and body, making the human nature, had its value and worth from its relation unto the Son of God: otherwise, he says of his body, "Handle" it, it is but "flesh and bones."[2] But where the body of Christ is mentioned, and the blood of Christ is mentioned, there is a distribution of the human nature into its integral parts, each part retaining its relation to his soul, and from thence

---

1 I.e., where a part of something is indicated figuratively in reference to the whole (so, here, the body of Christ is a reference to his whole human nature).

2 Luke 24:39.

is its value and excellency. That is the second peculiar in the object of faith in this ordinance.

(3) There is more than this: they are not only considered as distinguished, but as separate also; the blood separate from the body, the body left without the blood. This truth our apostle, in this chapter and the next, does most signally insist upon; namely the distinct parts of this ordinance, one to represent the body, and the other to represent the blood; that faith may consider them as separate.

The Papists, we know, do sacrilegiously take away the cup from the people: they will give them the bread, but they will not give them the cup: and as it always falls out, that one error must be covered with another, or else it will keep no man dry under it; they have invented the doctrine of concomitance;[3] that there is a concomitance, that is, whole Christ is in every kind, in the bread, and in the wine; the one does accompany the other; which is directly to overthrow the ordinance upon another account, as it is to represent Christ's body and blood as separated one from the other: Our Lord Jesus blessed the bread and the cup, and said, "This is my body"; ["This is my blood";][4] which cannot be spoken distinctly, unless supposed to be separate.

Here then is a threefold limitation of the act of faith, even in this ordinance, in a peculiar manner restraining it to a special communion with God in Christ; that it has a special regard to the human nature of Christ: to his human nature, as consisting of body and blood; and as it respects them as separated body and blood.

Yea, (4) it respects them as separate in that manner. You all along know that I do not intend these objects of faith as the ultimate object; for it is the person of Christ that faith rests in; but those immediate objects that faith is exercised about, to bring it to rest in God: it is exercised about the manner of this separation; that is, the blood of Christ comes to be distinct, by being shed; and the body of Christ comes to be separate, by being bruised and broken. All the instituted sacrifices of old did signify this, a violent separation of body and blood; the blood was let out with the hand of violence, and so separated, and then sprinkled upon the altar, and then toward the holy place; and then the body was burned distinct by itself: so the apostle tells us, it is the cup "which we bless," and the bread "which we break": the cup is poured out, as well as

3   The doctrine of concomitance, as Owen goes on to explain, maintains that receipt of the Lord's Supper in one kind entails a receipt of both kinds. The restriction of the Lord's Supper to one kind (the bread) for the laity was first formally upheld by the Catholic Church at the Council of Constance in 1415.
4   Matt. 26:26, 28.

the bread broken, to remind faith of the violent separation of the body and blood of Christ. From this last consideration of faith acting itself upon the separation of the body and blood of Christ, by way of violence, it is led to a peculiar acting of itself upon all the causes of it; whence it was, that this body and this blood of Christ were represented thus separate; and by inquiring into the causes of it, it finds a moving cause,—a procuring cause,—an efficient cause,—and a final cause; which it ought to exercise itself peculiarly upon always in this ordinance.

First, a moving cause; and that is, the eternal love of God in giving Christ in this manner, to have his body bruised, and his blood shed. The apostle, going to express the love of God toward us, tells you it was in this, that he "spared not his own Son" (Rom. 8:32). One would have thought, that the love of God might have wrought in sending his Son into the world; but it also wrought in not sparing of him. Thus faith is called in this ordinance, to exercise itself upon that love which gives out Christ not to be spared.

Secondly, it reflects upon the procuring cause; whence it is, or what it is, that has procured it, that there should be this representation of the separated body and blood of Christ; and this is even our own sin: he "was delivered for our iniquities,"[5] given for our transgressions, died to make reconciliation and atonement for our sins: they were the procuring cause of it, upon such considerations of union and covenant, which I shall not now insist upon. It leads faith, I say, upon a special respect to sin, as the procuring cause of the death of Christ. A natural conscience on the breach of the law leads the soul to the consideration of sin, as that which exposes itself alone to the wrath of God and eternal damnation; but in this ordinance we consider sin as that which exposed Christ to death; which is a peculiar consideration of the nature of sin.

Thirdly, there is the efficient cause. Whence it was that the body and blood of Christ was thus separated; and that is threefold, principal, instrumental, and adjuvant.[6]

What is the principal efficient cause of the sufferings of Christ? Why, the justice and righteousness of God. God hath set him forth "to be a propitiation," "to declare his righteousness" (Rom. 3:25). Whence it is said, he spared him not;[7] he caused all our sins to meet upon him, "the chastisement of our peace was upon him."[8]

5 Rom. 4:25.
6 I.e., something that gives aid or assistance.
7 Owen is alluding to Rom. 8:32.
8 Isa. 53:5.

Again; there is the instrumental cause; and that is the law of God. Whence did that separation, which is here represented unto us, ensue and flow? It came from the sentence of the law, whereby he was hanged upon the tree.

Moreover, the adjuvant cause, was those outward instruments, the wrath and malice of men: "For of a truth against thy holy child Jesus, whom thou hast anointed, both Herod, and Pontius Pilate, with the Gentiles, and the people of Israel, were gathered together" (Acts 4:27).

Faith considers the cause whence it was that Christ was thus given up, the eternal love of God; the procuring cause was our own sins; and if once faith takes a view of sin, as that which has nailed Christ to the cross, it will have a blessed effect on the soul; and it considers the efficient cause, which is the justice and righteousness of God. The law of God was the instrument in the hand of righteousness, which was holpen[9] on by those outward instruments, who had a hand in his suffering; but none in his sacrifice.

Fourthly, faith considers in this matter the end of this separation of the body and blood of Christ, which is thus represented; and that is ultimately and absolutely the glory of God. He set him forth for the declaration of his righteousness (Rom. 3:25; Eph. 1:6); God aimed at the glorifying of himself. I could easily manifest unto you, how all the glorious properties of his nature are advanced, exalted, and will be so to eternity, in this suffering of Christ. The subordinate ends are two; I mean, the subordinate ends of this very peculiar act of separation of the body and blood; [1] it was to confirm the covenant. Every covenant of old was to be ratified and confirmed by sacrifice; and in confirming the covenant by sacrifice, they divided the sacrifice into two parts, and passed between them before they were offered; and then took it upon themselves, that they would stand to the covenant, which was so confirmed. Jesus Christ, being to confirm the covenant (Heb. 9:16), the body and blood of Christ, this sacrifice, was to be parted, that this covenant might be confirmed. And, [2] a special end of it was for the confirming and strengthening of our faith. God gives out unto us the object of our faith in parcels: we are not able to take this great mysterious fruit of God's love in gross, in the lump; and therefore he gives it out, I say, in parcels. We shall have the body broken to be considered; and the blood shed is likewise to be considered. This is the peculiar communion which we have with Christ in this ordinance; because there are peculiar objects for faith to act itself upon in this ordinance above others.

9 I.e., helped.

THE NATURE OF THE ORDINANCE WITH
ITS PECULIAR COMMUNION

The very nature of the ordinance itself gives us a peculiar communion; and there are four things that attend the nature of this ordinance that are peculiar. It is commemorative, professional, eucharistical, and federal.

1. The ordinance is commemorative: "Do this in remembrance of me."[10] And there is no greater joy to the heart of sinners, and a man knows not how to give greater glory to God, than to call the atonement of sin unto remembrance. It is observed in the offering for jealousy (Num. 5:15). If a man was jealous, and caused an offering to be brought to God, God allowed neither oil, nor frankincense; and the reason is, because it was to bring "sin to remembrance." But how sweet is that offering that brings to our remembrance the atonement made for all our sins? That is pleasing and acceptable unto God, and sweet unto the souls of sinners.

2. It has a peculiar profession attending it. Says the apostle, doing this, "ye show forth the Lord's death till he come"; you make a profession and manifestation of it (1 Cor. 11:26). And give me leave to say it, they that look toward Christ, and do not put themselves in a way of partaking of this ordinance, they refuse the principal part of that profession which God calls them unto in this world. The truth is, we have been apt to content ourselves with a profession of moral obedience; but it is a profession of Christ's institution by which alone we glorify him in this world. I will have my death shown forth, says Christ, and not only remembered. The use of this ordinance is to show forth the death of Christ. As Christ requires of us to show forth his death, so surely he has deserved it by his death.

3. It is peculiarly eucharistical: there is a peculiar thanksgiving that ought to attend this ordinance. It is called the "The cup of blessing," or the "The cup of thanksgiving":[11] the word εὐλογία[12] is used promiscuously for "blessing" and "thanksgiving." It is called "The cup of blessing," because of the institution, and prayer for the blessing of God upon it; and it is called "The cup of thanksgiving," because we do in a peculiar manner give thanks to God for Christ, and for his love in him.

4. It is a federal ordinance, wherein God confirms the covenant unto us, and wherein he calls us to make a recognition of the covenant unto God. The covenant is once made; but we know that we stand in need that it should

---

10   Luke 22:19; 1 Cor. 11:24.

11   1 Cor. 10:16.

12   Gk. "blessing" or "thanksgiving."

be often transacted in our souls, that God should often testify his covenant unto us, and that we should often actually renew our covenant engagements unto him. God never fails, nor breaks his promises; so that he has no need to renew them, but testify them anew: we break and fail in ours, so that we have need actually to renew them. And that is it which we are called unto in this ordinance, which is the ordinance of the great seal of the covenant in the blood of Christ.

Upon all these accounts have we special communion with Christ in this ordinance. There is none of them but I might easily enlarge upon; but I name these heads; and my design is to help my own faith and yours from roving, in the administration of this ordinance, or from a general acting of itself, to fix it to that which is its particular duty; that we may find no weariness nor heaviness in the administration: here in these things is there enough to entertain us forever, and to make them new and fresh to us. But while we come with uncertain thoughts, and know not what to direct our faith to act particularly upon, we lose the benefit of the ordinance.

THE USE OF THE ORDINANCE

For the use, it is,

1. To bless God for his institution of his church, which is the seat of the administration of this ordinance, wherein we have such peculiar and intimate communion with Christ. There is not one instance of those which I have named, but if God would help us to act faith upon Christ in a peculiar manner through it, would give new strength and life to our souls. Now in the church we have all this treasure. We lose it, I confess, by our unbelief and disesteem of it, but it will be found to be an inestimable treasure to those that use it, and improve it in a due manner.

2. Does God give us this favor and privilege, that we should be invited to this special communion with Christ in this ordinance? Let us prepare our hearts for it in the authority of its institution. Let us lay our souls and consciences in subjection to the authority of Christ, who has commanded these things, and who did it in a signal manner the same night wherein he was betrayed. So that there is a special command of Christ lies upon us; and if we will yield obedience to any of the commands of Christ, then let us yield obedience to this. Prepare your souls for special communion with him then, by subjugating[13] them thoroughly to the authority of Christ in this ordinance.

---

13 I.e., bringing something under control.

3. It will be good for us all to be in a gradual exercising of our faith unto these special things, wherein we have communion with Christ. You have heard sundry particulars: here is an object of your faith that is given to be represented unto you in this ordinance, that God has prepared Christ a body, that he might be a sacrifice for you, and that this body was afterward distinguished into his body strictly so taken, and his blood separated from it; and this in a design of love from God, as procuring the pardon of our sins, as tending to the glory of God, and the establishing of the covenant. Train up a young faith in the way it should go, and it will not depart from it when old.[14] And new things will be found herein every day to strengthen your faith, and you will find much sweetness in the ordinance itself.

---

14 Owen is alluding to Prov. 22:6.

Discourse 3

The Two Immediate Ends
of This Ordinance

December 10, 1669

The cup of blessing which we bless, is it not the communion
of the blood of Christ? The bread which we break, is
it not the communion of the body of Christ?

1 CORINTHIANS 10:16

I HAVE BEEN TREATING somewhat about the special communion which believers have with Christ in the ordinance of the Lord's Supper. There remains yet something farther to be spoken unto for our direction in this great work and duty; and this is taken from the immediate ends of this ordinance. I spoke, as I remember, the last day to the specialty of our communion, from the consideration of the immediate ends of the death of Christ: now I shall speak to it in reference unto the immediate ends of this ordinance; and they are two, one whereof respects our faith and our love, and the other respects our profession; which two make up the whole of what is required of us. For as the apostle speaks, "With the heart man believeth unto righteousness, and with the mouth confession is made unto salvation" (Rom. 10:10). Both these ends, that which respects our faith and love, and that which respects our profession, are mentioned by our apostle in the next chapter [of 1 Corinthians]; verse 24 there is mention of that end of this ordinance which respects our faith, now that is recognition. Recognition is a calling over, or a commemoration of the death of Christ; "Do this," says he, "in remembrance of me." That which respects our profession is a representation and declaration of the Lord's death. When you eat this bread, and drink this cup, you show forth (1 Cor. 11:26), ye declare, ye manifest "the Lord's death till he come." These are the two immediate great ends of this ordinance, a recognition of the death of Christ, which respects our faith and love; and a representation of it, which respects our profession; both are required of us.

THE FIRST END: THAT WHICH RESPECTS FAITH AND LOVE

There is that which respects our faith. The great work of faith is to make things that are absent, present to a soul, in regard to their sweetness, power, and efficacy; whence it is said to be "the evidence of things not seen";[1] and it looks backward unto the causes of things; and it looks forward unto the effects of things; to what has wrought out grace, and to what grace is wrought out; and makes them in their efficacy, comfort and power, to meet and center in the believing soul.

Now there are three things in reference unto the death of Christ that faith in this ordinance does recognize, call over, and commemorate. The first is, the faith of Christ in and for his work. The second is, the obedience of Christ. And the third is the work itself.

Faith Recalls Christ's Faith

1. Faith calls over the faith of Christ. Christ had a double faith in reference to his death; one with respect unto himself, and his own interest in God; and the other in respect to the cause whose management he had undertaken, and the success of it. He had faith for both these.

(1) The Lord Christ had faith in reference to his own person, and to his own interest in God. The apostle, declaring that because the children were "partakers of flesh and blood," Christ also did "partake of the same" (Heb. 2:14); that so he might die to deliver us from death, brings that text of Scripture, verse 13 in confirmation of it, which is taken out of Psalm 18:2. "And again," says he, "I will put my trust in him." How does this confirm what the apostle produces it for? Why from hence, that in that great and difficult work that Christ did undertake, to deliver and redeem the children, he was all along carried through it by faith and trust in God. He trusted in God, says he, and that made him undertake it: and he gives a great instance of his faith,

1 Heb. 11:1.

when he was departing out of the world. There are three things that stick very close to a departing soul: the giving up of itself, the state wherein it shall be when it is given up, and the final issue of that estate. Our Lord Jesus Christ expressed his faith as to all three of them. As to his departure, he "cried with a loud voice, Father, into thy hands I commend my spirit: and having said thus, he gave up the ghost" (Luke 23:46). What was his faith as to what would become of him afterward? That also he expresses, "For thou wilt not leave my soul in hell, neither wilt thou suffer thine Holy One to see corruption" (Ps. 16:10). My soul shall not be left under the state of the dead, whereunto it is going; nor my body see corruption. What was his faith as to the future issue of things? That he expresses, verse 11, "Thou wilt show me the path of life"; (which is his faith for his rising again): "in thy presence is fulness of joy, at thy right hand are pleasures for evermore"; where he was to be exalted: And these words, "Father, into thy hands I commend my spirit," were the first breaking forth of the faith of Christ toward a conquest. He looked through all the clouds of darkness round about him toward the rising sun; through all storms, to the harbor, when he cried those words with a loud voice, and gave up the ghost. And by the way, it is the highest act of faith upon a stable bottom and foundation, such as will not fail, to give up a departing soul into the hands of God, which Jesus Christ here did for our example. Some die upon presumptions, some in the dark; but faith can go no higher than, upon a sure and stable ground, to give up a departing soul into the hands of God; and that for these reasons, to show the faith of Christ in this matter.

[1] Because the soul is then entering into a new state, whereof there are these two properties that will try it to the utmost; that it is invisible, and that it is unchangeable. I say, there are two properties that make this a great act of faith; {1} the state is invisible. The soul is going into a condition of things that "eye hath not seen, nor ear heard";[2] that nothing can take any prospect into but faith alone. However men may talk of the invisible state of things, which our souls are departing into, it is all but talk and conjecture, besides what we have by faith. So that to give up a soul cheerfully and comfortably into that state, is a pure act of faith.

{2} It is unchangeable. It is a state wherein there is no alteration. And though all alterations should prove for the worse, yet it is in the nature of man to hope good from them. But here is no more alteration left: the soul enters into an unchangeable state. And,

2   1 Cor. 2:9.

[2] The second reason is, because the total sum of a man's life is now cast up, and he sees what it will come to. While men are trading in the world, though they meet with some straits and difficulties, yet they have that going on which will bring in something this way, or that way. But, when it comes to this, that they can go no farther, then see how things stand with a departing soul; the whole sum is cast up, there is no more venture to be made, no more advantage to be gained, he must stand as he is. And when a man takes a view of what he is to come to, he needs faith to obtain a comfortable passage out of it. And,

[3] Even death itself brings a terror with it, that nothing can conquer but faith; I mean, conquer duly. He is not crowned that does not overcome by faith. It is only to be done through the death of Christ. He delivered "them who through fear of death were all their lifetime subject to bondage."[3] There is no deliverance that is true and real, from a bondage frame of spirit to death, but by faith in Christ.

I touch on this by the way, to manifest the glorious success the faith of Christ had, who, in his dying moments, cried out, "Father, into thy hands I commend my spirit": and this is that we are to call over in the remembering of his death. It is a very great argument the apostle uses to confirm our faith, when speaking of the patriarchs of old, he says, all these "died in faith."[4] But that "all" is nothing to this argument, that Jesus Christ, our head and representative, who went before us, he "died in faith." And this is the principal inlet into life, immortality, and glory, the consideration of the death of Christ, dying in that faith that he gave up his soul into the hands of God, and was persuaded God would not leave his soul in hell, nor suffer his Holy One to see corruption; but that he would show him the path of life, and bring him to his right hand, where there are pleasures for evermore.

(2) Christ had a faith for the cause wherein he was engaged. He was engaged in a glorious cause, a great undertaking, to deliver all the elect of God from death, hell, Satan and sin; to answer the law, to undergo the curse, and to bring his many children unto glory. And dreadful oppositions lay against him in this his undertaking. See what faith he had for his cause; "The Lord God will help me, therefore shall I not be confounded: therefore have I set my face like a flint, and I know that I shall not be ashamed: He is near that justifieth me; who will contend with me? [. . .] Who is mine adversary? Let him come near to me. Behold the Lord God will help me; who is he that

---

3   Heb. 2:15.
4   Heb. 11:13.

shall condemn me?" (Isa. 50:7–9). "Who is mine adversary?" Or (as in the Hebrew), Who is the master of my cause? I have a cause to plead; who is the master of it? I am engaged in a great cause, says he, and I am greatly opposed; they seek to make me ashamed, to confound me, to condemn me: but here is faith for his cause; the Lord God will justify me, says he. It was with Christ as it would have been with us under the covenant of works; man ought to have believed he should be justified of God, though not by Jesus Christ; so here, he had faith that he should be justified. God will justify me; I shall not be condemned in this cause that I have undertaken.

It is matter of great comfort and support, to consider, that when the Lord Jesus Christ had in his eye all the sins of all the elect upon the one hand, and the whole curse of the law and the wrath of God on the other, yet he cried, I shall not be confounded, "I shall go through it, I shall see an end of this business, and make an end of sin, and bring in everlasting righteousness; and God will justify me in it."[5] We are in an especial manner to call to remembrance the faith that Christ had for his cause; and we ought to have the same faith for it now, for this great conquest of overcoming the devil, sin, death, hell, and the saving of our souls: he has given us an example for it.

There is one objection lies against all this, and that is this: but did not Christ despond in his great agony in the garden, when he cried three times, "Father, if it be possible, let this cup pass from me?"[6] And in that dreadful outcry upon the cross, which he took from the twenty-second Psalm, a prophecy of him, "My God, my God, why hast thou forsaken me?"[7] Does not Christ seem to repent here, and to despond?

I answer; in this difficult inquiry two things are to be stated; first, in reference to his person, that it was impossible, Christ should have the indissolubility of his personal union utterly hid from him. He knew the union of his human nature unto the Son of God could not be utterly dissolved, that could not be utterly hid from him; so that there could not be despair properly so called in Christ. And, secondly, this is certain also, that the contract he had with the Father, and the promises he had given him of being successful, could never utterly be hid from him. So that his faith, either as to his person or cause, could not possibly be utterly ruined: but there was a severe and terrible conflict in the human nature, arising from these four things.

First, from the view which he was exalted to take of the nature of the curse that was then upon him. For the curse was upon him, he was "made a curse

5 Quotation marks original.
6 Matt. 26:39.
7 Matt. 27:46.

for us, as it is written; cursed is every one that hangeth on a tree" (Gal. 3:13). Give me leave to say, Jesus Christ saw more into the nature of the curse of God for sin, than all the damned in hell are able to see; which caused a dreadful conflict in his human soul upon that prospect.

Secondly, it arose from hence; that the comforting influences of the union with the divine nature were restrained. Jesus Christ was in himself "a man of sorrows," and "acquainted with grief":[8] but yet all the while there were the influences of light and glory from the divine nature to the human by virtue of their union; and now they are restrained, and instead of that, was horrible darkness, and trembling, and the curse, and sin and Satan round about him; all presenting themselves unto him: which gave occasion to that part of his prayer, "Deliver my soul from the sword, my darling from the power of the dog. Save me from the lion's mouth," etc. (Ps. 22:20–21). There was the sword in the curse of the law, and the dog and the lion, or Satan, as it were, gaping upon him, as if ready to devour him; for it was the hour and power of darkness, dread and terror: besides, there were cruel men, which he compares to the "bulls of Bashan,"[9] which rent him. This caused that terrible conflict.

Thirdly, it was from the penal desertion of God. That he was under a penal desertion from God, is plain; "My God, my God, why hast thou forsaken me?" And when I say so, I know little of what I say, I mean, what it is to be under such penal desertion. For the great punishment of hell, is an everlasting penal desertion from God.

Fourthly, it was from the unspeakable extremity of the things that he suffered. Not merely as to the things themselves which outwardly fell upon his body; but as unto that sword of God, which was awakened against him, and which had pierced him to the very soul. The advantage which he had in his sufferings by his divine union, was that which supported and bore him up under that weight which would have sunk any mere creature to nothing. His heart was enlarged to receive in those pains, that dread and terror, that otherwise he could not have received: and notwithstanding all this, as I showed before, Christ kept up his faith in reference to his person, and kept up his faith in reference to his cause; and a great example he has given unto us, that though the dog and the lion should encompass us, though we should have desertion from God and pressures more than nature is able to bear, yet there is a way of keeping up faith, trust and confidence through all, and not to let go our hold of God.

8   Isa. 53:3.
9   Ps. 22:12.

Now this is the first thing we are to call over in remembrance of Christ, in reference to his death: that faith he had, both for his person and his cause, in his death. For if you remember any of the martyrs that died, you will stick upon these two things, more than upon the flames that consumed them; they expressed great faith of their interest in Christ; and in reference to the cause they died for. They are things you will remember. And this you are to remember of him, who was the head of the martyrs, our Lord Jesus Christ's faith.

Faith Recalls Christ's Obedience

2. We are to call over his obedience in his death. The apostle does propose it unto us; "Let this mind be in you which was in Christ Jesus; who, when he was in the form of God, and thought it not robbery to be equal with God, made himself of no reputation, and took upon him the form of a servant, and became obedient unto death, even the death of the cross" (Phil. 2:5–6, etc.). We are to call over the mind of Christ in suffering. And the following things the Scripture does peculiarly direct us to consider in the obedience of Christ unto death: the principle of it, which was love, readiness to and for it, submission under it, his patience during it. They are things the Scripture minds us of concerning the obedience of Christ in his death.

(1) Consider his love, which is one of the principal things to be regarded in this obedience of Christ. The love wherewith it was principled: he "loved me," says the apostle, "and gave himself for me" (Gal. 2:20). "Hereby perceive we the love of God, because he laid down his life for us" (1 John 3:16). It was his love did it; who "loved us, and washed us from our sins in his own blood" (Rev. 1:5). This gives life to the whole sufferings of Christ, and to our faith too. It was a high act of obedience to God, that he laid down his life; but that obedience was principled with love to us.

And now, I pray God to enable me to consider this with my own soul, what that love would stick at that did not stick at this kind of death we have been speaking of. If Jesus Christ had reserved the greatest thing he was to do for us unto the last, we had not known but his love might have stuck when it come to that; I mean, when it came to the curse of the law, though he had done other things. But having done this, he that would not withdraw, nor take off from that, because he loved us, what will he stick at for the future? Our hearts are apt to be full of unkind and unthankful thoughts toward him, as though, upon every dark and black temptation and trial he would desert us, whose love was such as he would not do it when himself was to be deserted and made a curse. Call over then the love of Christ in this obedience. Yea; but love prevails sometimes, you will say, with many to do things that they have no great mind to: we come very difficultly to do some things, when yet out of love we will not deny them. But it was not so with Christ; his love was such that he had,

(2) An eternal readiness unto his work. There are two texts of Scripture inform us of it; Proverbs 8:30–31, where the Holy Ghost describes the prospect that the Wisdom of God, that is, the Son of God took of the world, and the children of men, in reference to the time he was to come among them; "I was," says he, "daily his delight, rejoicing always before him; rejoicing in the habitable part of his earth, and my delights were with the sons of men." He considered what work he had to do for the sons of men, and delighted in it. The fortieth Psalm expounds this, verses 6–8, "Sacrifice and offering thou didst not desire; mine ears hast thou opened: burnt-offering and sin-offering hast thou not required. Then said I, lo, I come: in the volume of the book it is written of me," etc. Sacrifice and burnt offering will not take away sin, says he; then, "lo, I come." But does he come willingly? Yea; "I delight," says he, "to do thy will, O my God; yea, thy law is within my heart." What part of the will of God was it? The apostle tells you, offering "the body of Jesus Christ once for all"; "By the which will we are sanctified" (Heb. 10:10). He came not only willingly, but with delight. The baptism he was to be baptized with, he was straitened till it was accomplished. The love he had unto the souls of men, that great design and project he had for the glory of God, gave him delight in his undertaking, notwithstanding all the difficulties he was to meet with.

(3) We are to remember his submission to the great work he was called unto. This he expresses, "The Lord God," says he, "hath opened mine ear, and I was not rebellious, neither turned away back: I gave my back to the smiters, and my cheeks to them that plucked off the hair; I hid not my face from shame and spitting" (Isa. 50:5–6). The Lord God called him to it, and he was not rebellious, but submitted unto it.

There is one objection arises against this submission, and that is the prayer of Christ in the garden; "Father, if it be possible, let this cup pass from me."

I answer: that was an expression of the horror which was upon the human nature, which we mentioned before. But there were two things that Christ immediately closed upon, which gave evidence to this submission, that he did not draw back, nor rebel, nor hide himself, nor turn away his face from shame and spitting, one was this, Father, "thy will be done"[10] says he; and the other was this, that he refused that aid to deliver him which he might have had: "Know ye not that I could pray the Father, and he would give me more

10 Matt. 26:42.

than twelve legions of angels?"[11] He then suffered under the Roman power, and their power was reduced to twelve legions. Says he, I could have more than these; which argues his full submission unto the will of God.

(4) We are to call over his patience under his sufferings, in his obedience, "He was oppressed, and he was afflicted, yet he opened not his mouth: he is brought as a lamb to the slaughter, and as a sheep before her shearers is dumb, so he openeth not his mouth" (Isa. 53:7). The highest expressions of an absolute, complete and perfect patience: though he was afflicted, and though he had all manner of provocations, "though he was reviled, he reviled not again."[12] The apostle tells us, "He endured the cross" (that is, he patiently endured it, as the word signifies), and "despised the shame, that he might sit down at the right hand" of God (Heb. 12:2).

You see then the end of this ordinance of the Lord's Supper, is to stir us up to call over the obedience of Christ, both as to his love in it, as to his readiness for it, submission to the will of God in it, and patience under it.

Faith Recalls the Death of Christ Itself

3. Faith is to call over the work itself, and that was the death of Christ. I shall not now be able to manifest under what consideration in this ordinance faith calls over the death of Christ; but these are the heads I shall speak unto. It calls it over as a sacrifice, in that it was bloody; it calls it over as shameful, in that it was under the curse; it calls it over as bitter and dreadful, in that it was penal. It was a bloody, shameful, and penal death; as bloody, a sacrifice; as cursed, shameful; and as it was penal, it was bitter. In the work of faith's calling over these things there is a peculiar work of love also. Says our Savior, "Do this in remembrance of me." These are the words we would use unto a friend, when we give him a token or pledge, remember me. What is the meaning of it? Remember my love to you; my kindness for you; remember my person. There is a remembrance of love toward Christ to be acted in this ordinance, as well as a remembrance of faith; and as the next object of faith is, the benefits of Christ, and thereby to his person; so the next object of love, is the person of Christ, and thereby to his benefits; I mean, as represented in this ordinance. Remember me, says he, that is, with a heart full of love toward me. And there are three things wherein this remembrance of Christ by love in the celebration of this ordinance does consist: delight in him, thankfulness unto him, and the keeping of his word. He that remembers Christ with love, has these three affections in his heart.

11   Matt. 26:53.
12   1 Pet. 2:23.

(1) He delights in him. The thoughts of Christ are sweet unto him, as of an absent friend; but only in spiritual things we have this great advantage, we can make an absent Christ present to us. This we cannot in natural things. We can converse with friends only by imagination. But by faith we make Christ present with us, and delight in him.

(2) There is thanksgiving toward him. That love which is fixed upon the person of Christ will break forth in great thankfulness, which is one peculiar act of this ordinance: the cup "which we bless," or give thanks for.[13]

(3) It will greatly incline the heart to keep his word. If ye are my disciples, "if ye love me, keep my commandments."[14] Every act of love fixed upon the person of Christ gives a new spring of obedience to all the ordinances of Christ: and the truth is, there is no keeping up our hearts unto obedience to ordinances, but by renewed acts of obedience upon the person of Christ: this will make the soul cry, when shall I be in an actual observation of Christ's ordinance, who has thus loved me, and washed me with his own blood, that has done such great things for me?

This is the end of the death of Christ, which concerns our faith and love; the end of commemoration, or calling to remembrance.

THE SECOND END SIGNALED: THE PROFESSION OF CHRIST'S DEATH

There is an end of profession also; which is, to "show the Lord's death till he come."[15] But this must be spoken to at some other time. If we come to the practice of these things, we shall find them great things to call over; namely the whole frame of the heart of Christ in his death, and his death itself, and our own concern therein, and the great example he has set unto us. Some of them, I hope, may abide upon our hearts and spirits for our use.

---

13   1 Cor. 10:16.
14   John 14:15.
15   1 Cor. 11:26.

The Ways and Uses of "Showing" the Lord's Death in This Ordinance

December 24, 1669

*As often as ye eat this bread, and drink this cup, ye
do show the Lord's death till he come.*

1 CORINTHIANS 11:26

TWO WAYS WE SHOW THE LORD'S DEATH

One end, you see, of this great ordinance, is to show the Lord's death, to declare it, to represent it, to show it forth, hold it forth; the word is thus variously rendered. And in the especial ends of this ordinance it is, that we have special communion with our Lord Jesus Christ.

Now there are two ways whereby we show forth the Lord's death; the one is, the way of representation to ourselves; and the other is, a way of profession unto others.

The Way of Representation to Ourselves

1. The way of representation to ourselves. The work of representing Christ aright to the soul, is a great work. God and men are agreed in it; and therefore God when he represents Christ, his design is to represent him to the faith of men. Men that have not faith have a great desire to have Christ represented to their fancy and imagination; and therefore when the way of representing Christ to the faith of men was lost among them, the greatest part of their religion was taken up in representing Christ to their fancy. They would make pictures and images of his cross, resurrection, ascension, and everything he did.

There are three ways whereby God represents Christ to the faith of believers; the one is, by the word of the gospel itself as written; the second is, by the ministry of the gospel, and preaching of the word; and the third in particular is, by this sacrament, wherein we represent the Lord's death to the faith of our own souls.

By the Word

(1) God does it by the word itself. Hence are those descriptions that are given of Christ in Scripture, to represent him desirable to the souls of men. The great design of the book of Canticles[1] consists for the most part in this, in a mystical, allegorical description of the graces and excellencies of the person of Christ, to render him desirable to the souls of believers; as in the fifth chapter, from the ninth verse to the end, there is nothing but that one subject. And it was a great promise made to them of old, "Thine eyes shall see the King in his beauty" (Isa. 33:17). The promises of the Old Testament are much spent in representing the person of Christ beautiful, desirous, and lovely, to the faith of believers. And you will see in 2 Corinthians 3:18 what is the end of the gospel: "We all with open face beholding as in a glass the glory of the Lord, are changed into the same image from glory to glory, even as by the Spirit of the Lord." The gospel is the glass here intended; and looking into the glass, there is an image appears in it, not our own, but the representation the gospel makes of Jesus Christ is the image that appears in the glass. The work and design of the gospel is to make a representation of Christ unto us, As Christ makes a representation of the Father, and therefore he is called his image, "the image of the invisible God,"[2] why so? Because all the glorious properties of the invisible God are represented to us in Christ, and we looking upon the image of Christ in this glass, that is the representation made of him in the gospel; it is the effectual means whereby the Spirit of God transforms us into his image.

This is the first way whereby God does this great work of representing Christ unto the faith of men, which men having lost, have made it their whole religion to represent Christ unto their fancy.

By the Ministry of the Word

(2) The second way is, by the ministry of the word. The great work of the ministry of the word is to represent Jesus Christ. The apostle Paul tells us, "O foolish Galatians, who has bewitched you, that you should not obey the truth, before whose eyes Jesus Christ hath been evidently set forth cruci-

---

1 I.e., Song of Songs.
2 Col. 1:15.

fied among you?" (Gal. 3:1). He is *depictus crucifixus*,[3] crucified before their eyes. How was this? Not before their bodily eyes; but the apostle had in his preaching made such a lively representation unto their faith of the death of Christ, that he was as one painted before them. One said well on this text, of old the apostles did not preach Christ by painting, but they painted him by preaching; they did in so lively a manner represent him.

Abraham's servant, in the 24th chapter of Genesis, that was sent to take a wife for his son Isaac, is by all granted to be, if not a type, yet a resemblance of the ministers of the gospel, that go forth to prepare a bride for Christ. And what does he do? Truly he is a great example; when he came to the opportunity, though he had many things to divert him, yet he would not be diverted. There was set meat before him to eat, but he said, "I will not eat, till I have told my errand."[4] Nothing should divert the ministers of the gospel, no not their necessary meat, when they have an opportunity of dealing with souls on behalf of Christ. What course does Abraham's servant take? He says, "I am Abraham's servant; and the LORD has blessed my master greatly, and he is become great, and he hath given him flocks and herds, and silver and gold, and men-servants and maid-servants, and camels and asses."[5] What is all this to Isaac? He was to take a wife for Isaac, not for Abraham. He goes on; "And Sarah, my master's wife, bare a son to my master when she was old, and unto him hath he given all that he hath."[6] The way to procure this wife for Isaac was to let them know, that this great man, Abraham, had given all he had to Isaac. And it is the work of ministers of the gospel to let the people know, that God the Father has given all things into the hands of his Son; they are to represent Christ as Abraham's servant does here his master Isaac, as one who inherited all the goods of Abraham; so Christ is the appointed heir of all things, of the kingdom of heaven, the whole household of God. They are to represent him thus to the souls of men, to make him desirable to them. This is the great work of ministers, who are ambassadors of God; they are sent from God to take a wife for Christ, or to make ready a bride for him from among the children of men.

Through the Ordinance of the Lord's Supper

(3) The special way whereby we represent Christ unto our souls through faith, is in the administration of this ordinance, which I will speak to upon the great end of showing forth the death of the Lord.

---

3   Lat. "set forth as crucified" (cf., Gal. 3:1).
4   Gen. 24:33.
5   Gen. 24:34–35.
6   Gen. 24:36.

Now the former representations were general, this is particular; and I cannot at this time go over particulars. I bless the Lord my soul has many times admired the wisdom and goodness of God in the institution of this one ordinance, that he took bread and wine for that end and purpose, merely arbitrary, of his own choice, and might have taken anything else, what he had pleased; that he should fix on the cream of the creation, which is an endless storehouse, if pursued, of representing the mysteries of Christ. When the folly of men goes about to invent ceremonies that they would have significant; when they have found them out, they cannot well tell what they signify. But though I do acknowledge, that all the significancy of this ordinance depends upon the institution, yet there is great wisdom in the fitting of it; the thing was fitted and suited to be made use of to that end and purpose.

One end of the ordinance itself is to represent the death of Christ unto us; and it represents Christ with reference to these five things. [1] It represents him with reference to God's setting him forth. [2] In reference to his own passion. [3] In reference to his exhibition in the promise. [4] To our participation of him by believing: and, [5] To his incorporation with us in union.

[1] The great end of God in reference to Christ as to his death was, his setting of him forth, "Whom God has set forth to be a propitiation" (Rom. 3:25). And in the very setting forth of the elements in this ordinance there is a representation of God's setting forth his Son, of giving him out for this work, of giving him up unto it, to be a propitiation.

[2] There is a plain representation of his passion, of his suffering and death, and the manner of it. This, with all the concerns of it, I treated of the last Lord's day, under the head of Recognition, or calling over the death of Christ, do this "in remembrance of me";[7] and so I shall not again insist upon it.

[3] There is a representation of Christ in it, as to the exhibition and tender[8] of him in the promise. Many promises are expressed in invitations, "Ho! Every one that thirsts, come,"[9] take, eat: there is a promise in it. And in the tender that is made even of the sacramental elements, there is the exhibition of Christ in the promise represented to the soul. I told you before, God has carefully provided to represent Christ unto our faith, and not to our fancy; and therefore there is no outward similitude and figure. We can say concerning this ordinance, with all its representations, as God said concerning his appearing to Moses upon mount Horeb, you saw no similitude.[10] God has

7   1 Cor. 11:24.
8   I.e., offer.
9   Isa. 55:1.
10 Owen is alluding to Deut. 4:12.

taken care there shall be no natural figure, that all representations made may stand upon institution. Now there is this tender with an invitation. The very elements of the ordinance are a great representation of the proposal of Christ to a believing soul. God holds out Christ as willing to be received, with an invitation. So, we show forth the Lord's death.

To Our Reception of Him

(4) There is in this ordinance a representation of Christ as to our reception of him; for hereon depends the whole of the matter. God might make a feast of fat things, and propose it to men; but if they do not come to eat, they will not be nourished by it. If you make a tender of payment to a man, if he does not receive it, the thing remains at a distance, as before. Christ being tendered to a soul, if that soul does not receive him, he has no benefit by it. All these steps you may go. There may be God's exhibition of Christ, and setting of him forth; there may be his own oblation and suffering, laying the foundation of all that is to come; there may be an exhibition of him in the promise, tender, and invitation, and yet if not received, we have no profit by all these things. What a great representation of this receiving is there in the administration of this ordinance, when everyone takes the representation of it to himself, or does receive it?

Of Our Incorporation in Christ

(5) Fifthly and lastly. It gives us a representation of our incorporation in Christ; the allusion whereto, from the nature of the elements' incorporation with us, and being the strength of our lives, might easily be pursued. This is the first way of showing forth the Lord's death.

The Second Way: In Its Profession to Others

2. I shall now speak a few words to the profession of it among ourselves, and to others.

Let me take one or two observations, to make way for it.

The Importance of Visible Profession

(1) That visible profession is a matter of more importance than most men make of it. As the apostle says, "With the heart man believes unto righteousness, and with the mouth confession is made unto salvation" (Rom. 10:10). Look, how indispensably necessary believing is unto righteousness, to justification; no less indispensably necessary is confession or profession unto salvation. There is no man that does believe with his heart unto righteousness,

but he will with his mouth (which is there taken by a synecdoche for the whole of our profession) make confession unto salvation. This is that which brings glory to God. The apostle tells us, that men, "by the experiment of this ministration, glorify God for your professed subjection unto the gospel of Christ" (2 Cor. 9:13). Glory does not arise out of obedience so much as by your profession of it; by the giving them experiment[11] both of your faith and the reality of it, and that by this fruit of your profession.

Now profession consists in these two things; [1] In an abstinence from all things with reference to God and his worship, which Christ has not appointed. [2] In the observation and performance of all things that Christ has appointed.

Men are apt to think, that abstinence from the pollutions that are in the world through lust, the keeping themselves from the sins and defilements of the world, and inclining to that party that is not of the world, is profession. These things are good: but our profession consists in the observation of Christ's commands, what he requires of us. "Go teach them." What to do? "Whatsoever I have commanded" them; "and, lo, I am with you always" to "the end of the world."[12] There is an expression, wherein our Savior puts a trial of our love to him upon the keeping of his sayings; "He that loveth me not, keepeth not my sayings" (John 14:24). To keep the sayings of Christ, is to observe the commands of Christ which is the perfect trial of our love to him.

The Special Profession of Christ in This Ordinance

(2) There is in this ordinance a special profession of Christ. There is a profession of him against the shame of the world; a profession of him against the curse of the law; and a profession of him against the power of the devil. All our profession does much center, or is mightily acted in this ordinance.

[1] The death of our Lord Jesus Christ was in the world a shameful death, and that with which Christians were constantly reproached, and which hardly went down with the world. It is a known story, that when the Jesuits preached the gospel, as they call it, in China, they never let them know of the death of Christ, till the Congregation *De propaganda fide*[13] commanded it; for the world is mightily scandalized at the shameful death of the cross.

Now in this ordinance we profess the death of Christ, wherein he was crucified, as a malefactor, against all the contempt of the world. It was a great

---

11 I.e., proof.

12 Matt. 28:20.

13 *De propaganda fide* is an abbreviated title of the Catholic Congregation, *Sacra congregatio de propaganda fide* ("The Sacred Congregation for the Propagation of the Faith"), founded by Pope Gregory XV in 1622 to coordinate the missionary expansion of the Catholic Church.

part of the confession of the Christians of old, and there is something in it still: here we come solemnly before God, and all the world, and profess that we expect all our life and salvation from the death of this crucified savior.

[2] In our profession we show forth the death of the Lord in the celebration of this ordinance, in opposition to the curse of the law; that whereas the curse of the law does lay claim to us because we are sinners, here we profess that God has transferred the curse of the law to another who underwent it. So they did with the sacrifices of old, when they had confessed all the sins and iniquities of the people over the head of the goat, then they sent him away into destruction. So it is in this ordinance: here we confess all our sins and iniquities over the head of this great sacrifice, and profess to the law and all its accusations, that there our sins are charged. Who shall lay anything to our charge? And who shall condemn? It is Christ that died.[14] We confront the claim of the law, shake off its authority as to its curse, and profess to it that its charge is satisfied.

[3] We make a profession against the power of Satan. For the great trial of the power and interest of the devil in, unto, and over the souls of men, was in the cross of Jesus Christ. He put his kingdom to a trial, staked his all upon it, mustered up all the strength he had got, all the aids that the guilt of sin and the rage of the world could furnish him with. Now, says Christ, "is your hour, and the power of darkness."[15] He comes to try what he can do; and what was the issue of the death of Christ? Why, says the apostle, he "spoiled principalities and powers" and triumphed over them in his cross.[16] So that in our celebration of the death of Christ, we do profess against Satan, that his power is broken, that he is conquered, tied to the chariot wheels of Christ, who has disarmed him.

This is the profession we make when we show forth the Lord's death, against the shame of the world, against the curse of the law, and the power of hell. This is the second general end of this ordinance, and another means it is whereby we have especial communion with Christ in it; which was the thing I aimed at from the words I had chosen. And now I have gone through all I intend upon this subject.

THE USE OF THE ORDINANCE IN SHOWING FORTH THE LORD'S DEATH

A word or two of use, and I have done.

---

14 Owen is alluding to Rom. 8:33–34.
15 Luke 22:53.
16 Col. 2:15.

1. It is a very great honor and privilege to be called of God unto this great work of showing forth the death of Christ. I think it is as great and glorious a work as any of the children of men can be engaged in, in this world. I have showed you formerly, how all the acts of the glorious properties of God's nature center themselves in this infinite, wise, holy product of them, the death of Christ: and that God should call us to represent and show forth this death. The Lord forgive us where we have not longed to perform this work as we ought; for we have suffered carnal fears and affections, and anything else, to keep us off from employing ourselves in this great and glorious work.

The grace and mercy of God in this matter is ever to be acknowledged, in that he has called us to this great and glorious work.

2. Then surely it is our duty to answer the mind of God in this work; and not to attend to it in a cold, careless and transient manner. But methinks we might rejoice in our hearts when we have thoughts of it, and say within ourselves, come, we will go and show forth the Lord's death. The world, the law, and Satan, are conquered by it: blessed be God that has given us an opportunity to profess this. O that our hearts may long after the season for it, and say, when shall the time come?

3. We may do well to remember what was spoken before concerning the great duty of representing God to our souls, that we may know how to attend to it. I would speak unto the meanest of the flock, to guide our hearts and thoughts which are too ready to wander, and are so unprofitable for want of spiritual fixation. We would fain trust to our affections rather than to our faith, and would rather have them moved, than faith graciously to act itself. And when we fail therein, we are apt to think we fail in our end of the ordinance, because our affections were not moved. Set faith genuinely at work, and we have the end of the ordinance. Let it represent Christ to our souls, as exhibited of God, and given out unto us, as suffering, as tendered to us, and as received and incorporated with us.

Discourse 5

Preparation Necessary
for This Ordinance

January 7, 1670

But let a man examine himself, and so let him eat
of that bread, and drink of that cup.

1 CORINTHIANS 11:28

I HAVE BEEN TREATING of that special communion which believers have
with Christ in the administration of the ordinance of the Supper of the
Lord; and thought I should have treated no more of that subject; having
gone through all the particulars of it, which were practical, such as might be
reduced to present practice. But I remember I said nothing concerning preparation for it, which yet is a needful duty: and therefore I shall a little speak
to that also; not what may doctrinally be delivered upon it, but those things,
or some of them at least, in which every soul will find a practical concern
that intends to be a partaker of that ordinance to benefit and advantage: and
I have taken these words of the apostle for my groundwork: "But let a man
examine himself, and so let him eat of that bread, and drink of that cup."[1]

There were many disorders fallen in this church at Corinth; and that various ways, in schisms and divisions, in neglect of discipline, in false opinions,
and particularly in a great abuse of the administration of this great ordinance
of the Supper of the Lord. And though I do not, I dare not, I ought not to
bless God for their sin; yet I bless God for his providence. Had it not been

1 1 Cor. 11:28.

313

for their disorders, we had all of us been much in darkness as to all church way. The correction of their disorders contains the principal rule for church communion and the administration of this sacrament that we have in the whole Scripture; which might have been hid from us, but that God suffered them to fall into them on purpose, that through their fall in them, and by them, he might instruct his church in all ages to the end of the world.

The apostle is here rectifying abuses about the administration of the Lord's Supper, which were many; and he applies particular directions to all their particular miscarriages, not now to be insisted on; and he gathers up all directions into this one general rule that I have here read, "Let a man examine himself, and so let him eat," etc.[2] Now, this self-examination extends itself unto the whole due preparation of the souls of men for the actual participation of this ordinance. And I shall endeavor by plain instances out of the Scripture (which is my way in these familiar exercises) to manifest that there is a preparation necessary for the celebration, or observance of all solemn ordinances—and I shall show you what that preparation is, and wherein it does consist. And then I shall deduce from thence what is that particular preparation which is incumbent upon us, in reference unto this special ordinance, that is superadded unto the general preparation that is required unto all ordinances.

NECESSARY PREPARATION FOR THE CELEBRATION OF SOLEMN WORSHIP

First, I shall manifest, that there is a preparation necessary for the celebration of solemn worship. We have an early instance of it in Genesis 35:1–5. In the first verse, "God said unto Jacob, 'Arise, go up to Bethel, and make there an altar unto God.'" It was a solemn ordinance Jacob was called unto, to build an altar unto God, and to offer sacrifice. What course did he take? You may see, and "Jacob said unto his household, and to all that were with him, 'Put away the strange gods that are among you, and be clean, and change your garments; and let us arise, and go up to Bethel, and I will make there an altar unto God'" (Gen. 35:2–3). I will not engage, says he, in this great duty without a preparation for it; and, says he, the preparation shall be suitable. Peculiar, special preparation (to observe that by the way) for any ordinance, consists in the removal of that from us which stands in peculiar opposition to that ordinance, whatever it be. I am to build an altar unto God: put away the strange gods; and accordingly he did so.

2 1 Cor. 11:28.

When God came to treat with the people in that great ordinance of giving the law, which was the foundation of all following ordinances, "The LORD said unto Moses, 'Go unto the people, and sanctify them to day, and to morrow; and let them wash their clothes, and be ready against the third day. For the third day the LORD will come down [...] upon mount Sinai'" (Ex. 19:10–11). I will not insist on these typical preparations, but only say, it sufficiently proves the general thesis, that there ought to be such a preparation for any meeting with God in any of his ordinances. Says he, sanctify yourselves, etc., and on the third day I will come. God is a great God, with whom we have to do. It is not good to have carnal boldness in our accesses and approaches to him; and therefore, he teaches us, that there is a preparation due. And what weight God lays upon this, you may see (2 Chron. 30:18–20). A multitude of people came to the sacrifice of the Passover; but, says he, they "had not cleansed themselves," there was not due preparation; but "Hezekiah prayed for them, saying, 'the good LORD pardon every one, that prepareth his heart to seek God, the LORD God of his fathers, though he be not cleansed according to the purification of the sanctuary.' And the LORD hearkened to Hezekiah, and healed the people." Perhaps the people might have thought it enough, that they had their personal qualification, that they were believers, that they had prepared their hearts to seek the Lord God of their fathers; a thing most persons trust unto in this matter. No, says the king, in praying for them, they did prepare their hearts for the Lord God of their fathers; but they were not prepared "according to the purification of the sanctuary." There is an instituted preparation, as well as a personal disposition, which if not observed, God will smite them: God had smote the people; given them some token of his displeasure: they come with great willingness and desire to be partakers of this holy ordinance; yet because they were not prepared according to the purification of the sanctuary God smites them.

It was an ordinance of God that Paul had to perform, and we would have thought it a thing that he might easily have done, without any great forethought, but it had that weight upon his spirit that with all earnestness he begs the prayers of others, that he might be carried through the performance of it; "Now I beseech you, brethren, for the Lord Jesus Christ's sake, and for the love of the Spirit, that ye strive together with me in your prayers to God for me; [...] that my service which I have for Jerusalem may be accepted of the saints" (Rom. 15:30–31). He had a service to do at Jerusalem. He was gathering the contributions of the saints (an ordinance of God) to carry them up to the poor of Jerusalem; and it was upon his heart, that this his service might find acceptance with them; therefore he begs with all his soul, "I beseech you, brethren," etc. So great weight did he lay upon the performance of an ordinance, that one would think might be easily passed over, without any great regard.

The caution we have is to the same purpose: "Keep thy foot when thou goest into the house of God; and be more ready to hear, than to give the sacrifice of fools, for they consider not that they do evil" (Eccl. 5:1). I shall not stand upon the particular exposition of any of these expressions, but it is a plain caution of diligent consideration of ourselves in all things we have to do in the house of God. A bold venturing upon an ordinance is but "the sacrifice of fools." "Keep thy foot," look to thy affections; "be more ready to hear," says he; that is, to attend unto the command, what God requires from you, and the way and manner of it, than merely to run upon a sacrifice, or the performance of the duty itself.

I will name one place more, "I will wash mine hands in innocency, so will I compass thine altar, O LORD" (Ps. 26:6).

I have a little confirmed this general proposition, that all take for granted; and I fear we content ourselves for the most part with the state and condition of those mentioned, who prepared their hearts to meet the Lord God of their fathers, not considering how they may be prepared according to the purification of the sanctuary.[3] You will ask, what is that preparation?

PREPARATION HAS REFERENCE UNTO GOD, TO OURSELVES, AND TO THE ORDINANCE ITSELF

This question brings me to the second general head I propounded to speak unto: I answer, that the general preparation that respects all ordinances has reference unto God, to ourselves, to the ordinance itself.

Preparation with Respect to God

1. It has respect unto God. This is the first thing to be considered; for this he lays down as the great law of his ordinances. "I will be sanctified in them that draw nigh unto me" (Lev. 10:3). God is, in the first place, to be considered in all our drawings nigh unto him; as that is the general name of all ordinances, a drawing nigh, an access unto God. "I will be sanctified," etc. Now God is to be considered three ways, that he may be sanctified in any ordinance: as the author, as the object, as the end of it. I shall speak only to those things that lie practically before us, and are indispensably required of us in waiting upon God in any and every ordinance.

---

3 Owen is alluding here to 2 Chron. 30:19.

Considering God as the Author of Ordinances

(1) Our preparation in reference unto God consists in due consideration of God as the author of any ordinance wherein we draw nigh unto him. For this is the foundation of all ordinances. "As I live, saith the Lord, every knee shall bow to me, and every tongue shall confess" to me (Rom. 14:11). A practical sense of the authority of God in every ordinance, is that which is required in the very first place for our preparation. I know full well how that the mind of man is [apt] to be influenced by general convictions and particular customs. Particular usages built upon general convictions carry most people through their duties: but that is no preparation of heart. There is to be an immediate sense of the authority and command of God.

Considering God as the Object of Ordinances

(2) We are to consider God in Christ, as the immediate object of that worship which in every ordinance we do perform. You will ask, What special apprehensions concerning God are particularly necessary to this duty of preparation for communion with God in an ordinance? I answer; two are particularly necessary, that should be practically upon our thoughts in every ordinance, the presence of God, and the holiness of God. As God is the object of our worship, these two properties of God are principally to be considered in all our preparations.

First, the presence of God. When Elijah derided the worshipers of Baal, the chief part of his derision was, "he is in a journey" (1 Kings 18:27); you have a god that is absent, says Elijah: and the end of all idolatry in the world, is to feign the presence of an absent deity. All images and idols are set up for no other end, but to feign the presence of what really is absent. Our God is present, and in all his ordinances. I beg of God, I may have a double sense of his presence, [1] a special sense of his omnipresence. God requires, that we should put in all ordinances a specialty of faith upon his general attributes. Jacob, when God appeared unto him, though but in a dream, awaked out of sleep, and said, "Surely the LORD is in this place, and I knew it not" (Gen. 28:16). I would say so concerning every ordinance whereunto I go; the Lord is in that place. I speak now only concerning his real presence: for if idolaters adorn all their places of worship with pictures, images and idols, that they might feign the presence of a god; I ought to act faith particularly upon the real presence of the immense and omnipresent God. He bids us consider it in the business of his worship, "Am I a God at hand, saith the LORD, and not a God afar off?" (Jer. 23:23) Consider my glorious presence is everywhere. As we ought always wherever we are, and whatever we do, to carry a sense with us of the presence of God, to say, God is here, that we may not be surprised in our journeys, or in anything that may befall us, suppose a broken leg or a broken arm; then we may say, God is in this place, and I knew it not: so, particularly where we have to do in his ordinances, let there be an antecedent remembrance that God is in that place.

[2] We are to remember the gracious presence of God. There was a twofold presence of God of old, the one temporary, by an extraordinary appearance; the other standing, by a continued institution. Wherever God made an extraordinary appearance, there he required of his people to look upon him to have a special presence: it was but temporary, when God appeared to Moses in the bush: "Draw not nigh," says God: "put off the shoes from off thy feet: for the ground whereon thou standest is holy";[4] because of God's special appearance: but the next day, as far as I know, sheep fed upon that holy ground. It was no longer holy than God's appearance made it so. So he said to Joshua, when he was by Jericho, "Loose thy shoe from off thy foot, for the place whereon thou standest is holy" (Josh. 5:15). It was a temporary appearance of God; there was his special presence. It was so on the institution of the tabernacle and temple; God instituted them, and gave his special presence to them by virtue of his institution. Our Savior tells us, all this is departed under the gospel, you shall no longer worship God, says he, "neither in this mountain, nor yet at Jerusalem"; but he that worships God "must worship him in spirit and in truth" (John 4:21).[5] Is there no special presence of God remains then? Yea; there is a special presence of God in all his ordinances and institutions. Whenever "I record my name" (as the name of God is upon all his institutions), "I will come unto you, and I will bless you," says God in Exodus 20:24. Let us exercise our thoughts then to this especial promised presence of God in every ordinance and institution: it belongs greatly to our preparation for an ordinance. It was no hard thing for them, you may think, of old, where God had put his presence in a place, to go thither, and expect the presence of God; things that are absent are hard; things that are present are not so. But it is no harder matter for us to go and expect God's presence in his instituted ordinances now, than for them to go to the temple; considering God, as the object of our worship, is no less present with us.

Secondly, the second property which is principally to be considered in God in his ordinances, as he is the object of them, is his holiness. This is

4   Ex. 3:5.
5   With 4:24.

the general rule that God gives in all ordinances: "Be ye holy, for I the LORD your God am holy."[6] And Joshua tells the people what they were principally to consider in serving the Lord. "We will serve the LORD," say the people: says Joshua, "you cannot serve" him, for he is "an holy God" (Josh. 24:19); intimating, that they were to have due apprehensions of his holiness; and without it there is no approaching unto him in his service. The apostle gives a great and plain rule to this purpose; "let us have grace," says he, "whereby we may serve God acceptably, with reverence and godly fear." What does he propose now as the principal reason why he requires this preparation? "For," says he, "our God is a consuming fire" (Heb. 12:28–29). What property of God is expressed by this word "consuming fire?" It is the holiness of God, the purity of God's nature, that can bear no corrupt, nor defiled thing. It is set forth by that metaphorical expression, "a consuming fire." As fire is the most pure and unmixed element, and so powerful of itself as that it will consume and destroy everything that is not perfectly of its own nature; so is God, says he, "a consuming fire"; and in all your serving of him, and approaches unto him, labor to obtain a frame of spirit that becomes them who have to do with that God who is so pure and holy.

I do but choose out these things, which in the way of ordinances, I would say, are, I may say, desire, should be most upon my heart and spirit: I might easily enlarge it to other considerations. But let these two considerations dwell upon our minds, as our preparation for our access unto God; thoughts of his glorious and gracious presence, and of his holiness. "Holiness becometh thine house, O LORD, for ever" (Ps. 93:5). That is the second thing with respect to God, as the object of all the ordinances of our worship.

Considering God as the End of Ordinances

(3) Our preparation respects God as he is the end of ordinances; and that to these three purposes, if I could insist upon them. He is the end of them, as we aim in them to give glory unto him: he is the end of them, as we aim in them to be accepted with him; he is the end of them, as we aim in them to be blessed by him. These are the three things that are our end in all ordinances that we celebrate.

The first is,[7] the general end of all that we do in this world; we are to do all to the glory of God: it is the immediate end of all our worship. If I am a father, says he, "where is mine honour?" (Mal. 1:6) Where is my glory? Do you come

---

6   Lev. 19:2.
7   Original reads, "1st, The first is."

to worship me? You are to give me honor as to a father, glory as to a master, as to a lord. We come to own him as our Father, acknowledge our dependence upon him as a Father, our submission to him as our Lord and master, and thus give glory to him. He has never taken one step to the preparing of his heart according to the preparation of the sanctuary, in the celebration of ordinances, who has not designed in them to give glory unto God.

Secondly, another end is, to be accepted with him; according to that great promise, which you have. You "shall make your burnt-offerings upon the altar, [. . .] and I will accept you, saith the Lord God" (Ezek. 43:27). It is a promise of gospel times; for it is in the description of the new, glorious temple. We come to God to have our persons and offerings accepted by Jesus Christ. And,

Thirdly, to be blessed according to his promise. That God will bless us out of Zion.[8] What the particular blessings are we look for in particular ordinances, in due time, God assisting, I shall acquaint you with, when we come to the special and particular preparation for that ordinance we aim at. But this is necessary to all, and so to that.

Preparation with Respect to Ourselves

2. This preparation respects ourselves. There are three things which I desire my heart may be prepared by in reference to the ordinances of God.

(1) The first is indispensably necessary, laid down in that great rule, "If I regard iniquity in my heart, the Lord will not hear me" (Ps. 66:18); that I bring a heart to ordinances without regard to any particular iniquity. We have the dreadful instance of Judas, who came to that great ordinance of the Passover with regard to iniquity in his heart, which particular iniquity was covetousness, and went away with the Devil in his whole mind and soul.

Ezekiel 14:4 is another place to this purpose:

Therefore speak unto them, and say unto them, Thus saith the Lord God, Every man of the house of Israel that setteth up his idols in his heart, and putteth the stumbling-block of his iniquity before his face, and cometh to the prophet, I the Lord will answer him that cometh, according to the multitude of his idols.

There is no more effectual course in the world to make poor souls incorrigible, than to come to ordinances, and to be able to digest under them a regard to iniquity in our hearts. If we have idols, God will answer us according to our

---

8   Owen is alluding to Ps. 128:5.

idols. What is the answering of men according to their idols? Why plainly, it is this, allotting them peace while they have their idols; you shall have peace with regard to iniquity; you come for peace, take peace; which is the saddest condition any soul can be left under: you shall have peace and your idols together. Whenever we prepare ourselves, if this part of our preparation be wanting, if we do not all of us cast out the idols of our hearts, and cease regarding of iniquity, all is lost.

(2) The second head of preparation on our own part, is self-abasement, out of a deep sense of the infinite distance that is between God and us, whom we go to meet. I have taken upon myself to speak to the great possessor of heaven and earth, who am but dust and ashes. Nothing brings God and man so near together, as a due sense of our infinite distance. "Thus saith the high and lofty One who inhabiteth eternity, whose name is Holy; I dwell in the high and holy place, with him also that is of a contrite and humble spirit" (Isa. 57:15).

(3) A heart filled with love to ordinances, is a great preparation for an ordinance. How does David, in the 84th Psalm, pant and long and breathe after the ordinances of God! To love prayer, to love the word, is a great preparation for both. To love the presence of Christ in the Supper, is a great preparation for it. To keep a habitual frame of love in the heart for ordinances.

I would not load your memories with particulars. I mention plain practical things unto those, for whose spiritual welfare I am more particularly concerned; that we may retain them for our use, and know them for ourselves; and they are such as I know more or less (though perhaps not so distinctly) all our hearts work after, and in these things our souls do live.

Preparation with Respect to Any Ordinance Itself

3. Our preparation in reference unto any ordinance itself; which consists in two things;

(1) A satisfactory persuasion of the institution of the ordinance itself; that it is that which God has appointed. If God should meet us, and say, who has required these things at your hands? And Christ should come and tell us, every plant that my heavenly Father has not planted shall be plucked up: or, in vain do you worship me, teaching for doctrines the commandments of men: How would such words fill the hearts of poor creatures with confusion, if engaged in such ways that God has not required? We must be careful then that for the substance of the duty, it be appointed of God.

(2) That it be performed in a due manner. One failure herein, what a disturbance did it bring upon poor David? It is observed by many, that search the whole course of David's life, that which he was most eminent in, which

God did so bless him for, and own him in, was his love to the ordinances of God. And I cannot but think with what a full heart David went to bring home the ark; with what longings after God; with what rejoicings in him; with what promises to himself what glorious things there would be after he had the ark of God to be with him: and yet, when he went to do this, you know what a breach God made upon him, dashed all his hopes, and all the good frame in him: God made a breach upon Uzzah; and it is said, the thing God did displeased David, it quite unframed him, and threw a damp on his joy and delight for the present. But he afterward gathers it up, he spoke to the Levites, "Sanctify yourselves, both ye and your brethren, that ye may bring up the ark of the LORD God of Israel unto the place that I have prepared for it; for because ye did it not at the first, the LORD our God made a breach upon us; for that we sought him not after the due order" (1 Chron. 15:12–13). He sought him, says he, but "not after the due order." And what that due order was, he shows in the next verses, where he declares, that the Levites carried the ark upon their own shoulders, with the staves thereon, as Moses commanded, according to the word of the Lord; whereas before, they carried it in a cart, which was not for that service. It is a great thing to have the administration of an ordinance in the due order. God lays great weight upon it, and we ought to take care that the order be observed.

This is what we have to offer to you concerning the two general propositions, that there is a preparation required of us for the observance of all solemn ordinances; and that this preparation consists in a due regard to God, to ourselves, and to the ordinance, whatever it be. To God, as the author, as the object, and as the end of ordinances; to ourselves, to remove that which would hinder, not to regard iniquity, to be self-abased in our hearts with respect to the infinite distance that there is between God and us, and with a love unto ordinances: with respect unto the ordinance itself, that it be of God's appointment for the matter and manner. These things may help us to a due consideration, whether we have failed in any of them, or not.

I have mentioned nothing but what is plain and evident from the Scripture, and what is practicable; nothing but what is really required of us; such things as we ought not to esteem a burden, but an advantage: and whereinsoever we have been wanting we should do well to labor to have our hearts affected with it; for it has been one cause why so many of us have labored in the fire under ordinances, and have had no profit nor benefit by them. As I said before, conviction is the foundation, custom is the building of most in their observation of ordinances. Some grow weary of them; some wear them on their necks as a burden; some seek relief from them, and do not find it; and is it any wonder, if this great duty be wanting? Having neither considered God, nor ourselves, in what we go about? And above all things take heed of that deceit I mentioned, which is certainly very apt to impose itself upon us, that where there is a disposition in the person there needs no preparation for the duty. There was a preparation in those whom God broke out upon, because they were not prepared according to the preparation of the sanctuary; that is, in that way and manner of preparation; they had not gone through those cleansings which were instituted under the law.

Discourse 6

Preparation for This Ordinance Continued

January 21, 1670

But let a man examine himself, and so let him eat
of that bread, and drink of that cup.

1 CORINTHIANS 11:28

I HAVE BEEN TREATING in sundry of these familiar exercises about communion with Jesus Christ in that great ordinance of the Lord's Supper, intending principally, if not solely, the instruction of those who have, it may be, been least exercised in such duties. I have spoken something of preparation for it, and on the last opportunity of this kind I did insist upon these two things, that there is a preparation required unto the due observance of every solemn ordinance: and I did manifest, what in general was required to that preparation. I have nothing to do at present, but to consider the application of those general rules to the special ordinance of the Supper of the Lord. For the special preparation for an ordinance consists in the special respect which we have to that ordinance in our general preparation: and I shall speak to it plainly, so as that the weakest, who are concerned, may see their interest in it, and have some guidance to their practice.

And there are two things which may be considered to this purpose, the time wherein this duty is to be performed; and, the duty of preparation itself.

THE TIME WHEREIN THE DUTY IS TO BE PERFORMED

First, the time of the performance of the duty; for that indeed regards as well what has been said concerning preparation in general, as what shall now be farther added concerning preparation in particular, with respect to this ordinance.

Time has a double respect unto the worship of God, as a part of it; so it is when it is separated by the appointment of God himself; and as a necessary adjunct of those actions whereby the worship of God is performed; for there is nothing can be done, but it must be done in time, the inseparable adjunct of all actions.

And therefore having proved that a preparation is necessary, I shall prove that there is a time necessary, for there can be no duty performed, but it must be performed, as I said, in some time.

For the right stating of that therefore, I shall give you these rules.

1. That there is a time antecedent to the celebration of this ordinance to be set apart for preparation unto it. The very nature of the duty, which we call preparation, does inevitably include this, that the time for it must be antecedent to the great duty of observing the ordinance itself. So the evening before the Passover is called the "preparation" of the Passover (Matt. 27:62), time set apart for the preparation of it.

2. The second rule is this, that there is no particular set time, neither as to the day, or season of the day, as to the beginning or ending of it, that is determined for this duty, in the Scripture: but the duty itself being commanded, the time is left unto our own prudence, to be regulated according to what duty does require; so that you are not to expect that I should precisely determine this or that time, this or that day, this or that hour, so long or so short; for God has left these things to our liberty, to be regulated by our own duty and necessity.

3. There are three things that will greatly guide a man in the determination of the time, which is thus left unto his own judgment, according to the apprehension of his duty.

(1) That he chooses a time wherein the preparation of it may probably influence his mind and spirit in and unto the ordinance itself. Persons may choose a time for preparation when there may be such an interposition of worldly thoughts and business, between the preparation and the ordinance, that their minds may be no way influenced by it in the performance and observation of the duty. The time ought to be so fixed, that the duty may leave a savor upon the soul unto the time of the celebration of the ordinance itself, whether it be the preceding day, or whether it be the same day. The work is lost unless a man endeavors to keep up a sense of those impressions which he received in that work.

(2) Providential occurrences and intimations are great rules for the choosing of time and season for duties. Paul comes to Athens (Acts 17), and in all probability he intended not to preach immediately upon his journey. He intended to take some time for his refreshment. But observing the wickedness of the place, that they were "wholly given to idolatry" (Acts 17:16), and observing their altar to "the unknown God" (Acts 17:23). He laid hold of that hint of providence, that intimation given him by God's providence from these things, and immediately fell upon his work, which God blessed with great success. There be a thousand ways, if I may so say, wherein an observing Christian may find God hinting and intimating duties unto him. The sins of other men, their graces, mercies, dangers, may be all unto us intimations of a season for duty. Were none of us ever sent to God by the outrageous wickedness of others? By the very observation of it? And it is a sign of a good spirit to turn providential intimations into duties. The psalmist speaks to that purpose, "I will guide thee by mine eye" (Ps. 32:8–9), says he. The next words are, "Be not as the horse or as the mule which hath no understanding, whose mouth must be held in with bit and bridle" (Ps. 32:9). God loves a pliable spirit, that upon every look of his eye will be guided to a duty. But those who are like horses and mules, that must be held with a strong rein, that will not be turned, till God puts great strength to it, are possessed with such a frame of spirit as God approves not. You are left at liberty to choose a time, but observe any intimation of providence that may direct to that time.

(3) Be sure to improve surprisals with gracious dispositions, I mean, in the approach of solemn ordinances. Sometimes the soul is surprised with a gracious disposition, as in Canticles, "Or ever I was aware, my soul made me like the chariots of Amminadib" (Song 6:12). I knew it not, says the church, I was not aware of it, but I found my soul in a special willing manner drawn forth to communion with Christ. Is God pleased at any time to give us such gracious surprisals with a holy disposition to be dealing with him, it will be the best season; let it not be omitted.

These things will a little direct us in the determination of the time for preparation, which is left unto our own liberty.

4. Take care, that the time designed and allotted, does neither too much entrench upon the occasions of the outward man, nor upon the weakness of the inward man. If it does, they will be too hard for us. I confess, in this general observation which professors are fallen into, and that custom which is in the observation of duties, there is little need to give this rule. But we are not to accommodate our rule unto our corruptions, but unto our duties; and so there is a double rule in Scripture fortifies this rule; the one is that great

rule of our Savior, that God will have mercy and not sacrifice.[1] Where these duties of observing sacrifices do sensibly entrench upon duties of mercy, God does not require it; which has a great regard even unto our outward occasions. And the other rule is this, that bodily exercise profits little. When we assign so long a time as wearies out our spirits, and observe the time because of the time, it is bodily exercise; when the vigor of our spirits is gone, which is a sacrifice God delights not in. As Jacob told Esau, if the cattle were driven beyond their pace they would die;[2] so we find by experience, that though with strong resolutions we may engage unto duties in such a manner as may entrench upon these outward occasions, or those weaknesses, they will return, and be too hard for us, and instead of getting ground, they will drive us off from ours; so that there is prudence to be required therein.

5. Let not the time allotted be so short as to be unmeet for the going through with the duty effectually. Men may be ready to turn their private prayers into a few ejaculations, and going in or out of a room may serve them for preparation for the most solemn ordinance. This has lost us the power, the glory, the beauty of our profession. Never was profession held up to more glory and beauty, than when persons were most exact in their preparation for the duties of their profession; nothing will serve their turn, but their souls having real and suitable converse with God, as unto the duty that lies before them.

6. The time of preparation is to be extended and made more solemn upon extraordinary occasions. The intervention of extraordinary occasions must add a solemnity to the time of preparation, if we intend to walk with God in a due manner. These extraordinary occasions may be referred to three heads; particular sins, particular mercies, particular duties.

First, is there an interveniency[3] upon the conscience of any special sin, that either the soul has been really overtaken with, or that God is pleased to set home afresh upon the spirit, there is then an addition to be made unto the time of our preparation, to bring things to that issue between God and our souls, that we may attend upon the ordinance, to hearken what God the Lord will now speak, and then he will speak peace. This is the first principal extraordinary interveniency that must make an addition to the time of preparation for this ordinance.

Secondly, the interveniences of mercies. The ordinance has the nature of a thank offering, and is the great medium, or means of our returning praise unto God, that we can make use of in this world. And then are we truly thankful

---

1   Owen is alluding to Hos. 6:6.
2   Owen is alluding to Gen. 33:13.
3   I.e., intervention.

for a temporal mercy, when it engages our hearts to thank God for Christ, by whom all mercies are blessed to us. Has God cast in any special mercy, add unto the special preparation, that the heart may be fit to bless God for him, who is the fountain and cause of all mercies.

Thirdly, special duties require the like. For it being the solemn time of our renewing covenant with God, we stand in need of a renewal of strength from God if we intend to perform special duties; and in our renewing covenant with God, we receive that especial strength for these special duties.

These rules I have offered you concerning the time of this great duty of preparation, which I am speaking unto; and I shall add one more, without which you will easily grant that all the rest will fall to the ground, and with which God will teach you all the rest; and that is, be sure you set apart some time. I am greatly afraid of customariness in this matter. Persons complain that in waiting upon God in that ordinance, they do not receive that entertainment at the hand of God, that refreshment which they looked for. They have more reason to wonder, that they were not cast out, as those who came without a wedding garment.[4] That is not only required of us, that we come with our wedding garment, which every believer has, but that we come decked with this garment. A man may have a garment that may fit very ill, very unhandsomely, about him. The bride decks herself with her garments for the bridegroom. We are to do so for the meeting with Christ in this ordinance, to stir up all the graces God has bestowed upon us, that we may be decked for Christ. There lies the unprofitableness under that ordinance, that though God has given us the wedding garment that we are not cast out, yet we take not care to deck ourselves, that God and Christ may give us refreshing entertainment when we come into his presence. Our failing herein evidently and apparently witnesses to the faces of most professors, that this is the ground of their unprofitableness under that ordinance. So much for the time.

THE DUTY OF PREPARING FOR THE
ORDINANCE OF THE LORD'S SUPPER

Secondly, I shall now speak a little to the duty itself of preparation for that ordinance; remembering what I spoke before of preparation in general unto all solemn ordinances, which must still be supposed.

Now the duty may be reduced to these four heads, meditation, examination, supplication, expectation. And if I mistake not, they are all given us in one

---

4   Owen here alludes to the parable of the wedding banquet in Matt. 22:1–14.

verse; and though not directly applied to this ordinance, yet to this among other ways of our intimate communion with Christ: "I will pour upon the house of David, and upon the inhabitants of Jerusalem, the spirit of grace and of supplications; and they shall look upon me whom they have pierced; and they shall mourn for him, as one mourneth for his only son, and shall be in bitterness for him, as one that is in bitterness for his first-born" (Zech. 12:10). There is (1) Meditation: "They shall look upon him"; this is no otherwise to be performed but by the meditation of faith. Our looking upon Christ is by believing meditation. Looking argues the fixing of the sight; and meditation is the fixing of faith in its actings. Looking is a fixing of the eye; faith is the eye of the soul: and to look is to fix faith in meditation. And there is, (2) Examination which produces the mourning here mentioned. For though it is said, "They shall mourn for him"; it was not to mourn for his sufferings; for so he said, "weep not for me";[5] but to mourn upon the account of those things wherein they were concerned in his sufferings. It brings to repentance; which is the principal design of this examination. (3) There is supplication; for there shall be poured out a spirit of grace and supplication. And, (4) There is expectation; which is included also in that of looking unto Christ.

Meditation

1. The first part of this duty of preparation consists in meditation: and meditation is a duty, that by reason of the vanity of our own minds, and the variety of objects which they are apt to fix upon, even believers themselves do find as great a difficulty therein as any.

I shall only mention those special objects which our thoughts are to be fixed upon in this preparatory duty: and you may reduce them to the following heads.

(1) The principal object of meditation in our preparation for this ordinance, is the horrible guilt and provocation that is in sin. There is a representation of the guilt of sin made in the cross of Christ. There was a great representation of it in the punishment of angels: a great representation of it is made in the destruction of Sodom and Gomorrah; and both these are proposed unto us in a special manner (2 Pet. 2:4–6), to set forth the heinous nature of the guilt of sin: but they come very short, nay, give me leave to say, that hell itself comes short of representing the guilt of sin in comparison of the cross of Christ. And the Holy Ghost would have us mind it, where he says, he was made "sin for us" (2 Cor. 5:21). See what comes of sin, says he, what demerit, what

5 Luke 23:28.

provocation there is in it; to see the Son of God praying, crying, trembling, bleeding, dying, God hiding his face from him; the earth trembling under him; darkness round about him; how can the soul but cry out, O Lord, is this the effect of sin! Is all this in sin! Here then take a view of sin. Others look on it in its pleasures and the advantages of it; and cry, is it not a little one? as Lot of Zoar. But look on it in the cross of Christ, and there it appears in another hue. All this is from my sin, says the contrite soul.

(2) The purity, the holiness, and the severity of God, that would not pass by sin, when it was charged upon his Son. He set him forth "to declare his righteousness" (Rom. 3:25). As there was a representation of the guilt of sin, so there was an everlasting representation of the holiness and righteousness of God in the cross of Jesus Christ. He spared him not. And may the soul say, is God thus holy in his nature, thus severe in the execution of his wrath, so to punish, and so to revenge sin, when his Son undertook to answer for it? How dreadful is this God! How glorious! What a consuming fire! It is that which will make sinners in Zion cry, "Who among us shall dwell with the devouring fire? Who among us shall dwell with everlasting burnings?" (Isa. 33:14). Consider the holiness and the severity of God in the cross of Christ, and it will make the soul look about him, how to appear in the presence of that God.

(3) Would you have another object of your meditation in this matter; let it be the infinite wisdom and the infinite love of God that found out this way of glorifying his holiness and justice, and dealing with sin according to its demerit. "God so loved the world as to send his only begotten Son" (John 3:16). And "Herein is love," love indeed! That God sent his Son to die for us (1 John 4:10). And the apostle lays it upon "the manifold wisdom of God" (Eph. 3:10). Bring forth your faith; be your faith never so weak, never so little a reality, do but realize it, and do not let common thoughts and notions take up and possess your spirits: here is a glorious object for it to work upon, to consider the infinite wisdom and love that found out this way. It was out of love unsearchable. And now what may not my poor sinful soul expect from this love? What difficulties can I be entangled in, but this wisdom can disentangle me? And what distempers can I be under, but this love may heal and recover? There is hope, then, says the soul, in preparation for these things.

(4) Let the infinite love of Jesus Christ himself be also at such a season had in remembrance. "Who loved me, and gave himself for me" (Gal. 2:20). "Who loved us, and washed us" from our sins "in his own blood" (Rev. 1:5). "Who when he was in the form of God, and thought it no robbery to be equal with God, [...] humbled himself, and became obedient unto death, even the death of the cross" (Phil. 2:6–8). This was "the grace of our Lord Jesus Christ,

that though he was rich, yet for your sakes he became poor, that ye through his poverty might be rich" (2 Cor. 8:9). The all-conquering and all-endearing love of Christ, is a blessed preparative meditation for this great ordinance.

(5) There is the end, what all this came to; this guilt of sin, this holiness of God, this wisdom of grace, this love of Christ; what did all this come to? Why, the apostle tells us, he has "made peace through the blood of his cross" (Col. 1:20). The end of it all was to make peace between God and us; and this undertaking issued in his blood, that was able to do it, and nothing else; yea, that has done it. It is a very hard thing for a soul to believe that there is peace made with God for him and for his sin; but really trace it through these steps, and it will give a great deal of strength to faith. Derive it from the lowest, the deepest pit of the guilt of sin; carry it into the presence of the severity of God, and so bring it to the love of Christ, and the issue which the Scriptures testify of all these things was, to make peace and reconciliation.

Some may say, that they would willingly meditate upon these things, but they cannot remember them, they cannot retain them, and it would be long work to go through and think of them all; and such as they have not strength and season for.

I answer, first, my intention is not to burden your memory, or your practice, but to help your faith. I do not prescribe these things, as all of them necessary to be gone through in every duty of preparation; but you all know, they are such as may be used, every one of them singly in the duty: though, they that would go through them all again and again, would be no losers by it, but will find something that will be food and refreshment for their souls. But,

Secondly, let your peculiar meditation be regulated by your peculiar present condition. Suppose, for instance, the soul is pressed with a sense of the guilt of any sin, or of many sins; let the preparative meditation be fixed upon the grace of God, and upon the love of Jesus Christ, that are suited to give relief unto the soul in such a condition. Is the soul burdened with senselessness of sin? Does it not find itself so sensible of sin as it would be? But rather, that it can entertain slight thoughts of sin; let meditation be principally directed unto the great guilt of sin as represented in the death and cross of Christ, and to the severity of God as there represented. Other things may lay hold upon our carnal affections, but if this lay not hold upon faith, nothing will.

I have one rule more in these meditations; does anything fall in that does peculiarly affect your spirits, as to that regard which you have to God? Set it down. Most Christians are poor in experience; they have no stock; they have not laid up anything for a dear year, or a hard time: though they may have had many tokens for good, yet they have forgotten them. When your hearts are raised by intercourse between God and yourselves in the performance of this duty, be at pains to set them down for your own use; if anything does immediately affect your spirits, you will be no loser by it; it is as easy a way to grow rich in spiritual experiences as any I know. This is the first part of this duty of preparation; which with the rules given may be constantly so observed, as to be no way burdensome nor wearisome to you; but very much to your advantage. The other duties I shall but name, and so have done.

Examination

2. There is examination. Examination is the word in my text, and that duty which most have commonly spoke unto, that have treated anything about preparation for this ordinance. It respects principally two things, namely repentance and faith.

(1) Our examination as to repentance, as far as it concerns preparation unto this duty, may be referred to three heads,

First, to call ourselves to account, whether indeed we have habitually that mourning frame of spirit upon us which is required in them who converse with God in the cross of Jesus Christ. They shall look upon him whom they have pierced, and mourn.[6] There is an habitual mourning frame of spirit required in us, and we may do well to search ourselves about it, whether it is maintained and kept up or no? Whether worldly security and carnal joys do not devour it? For spiritual joys will not do it. Spiritual joys will take off nothing from spiritual mourning; but worldly security and carnal joy and pleasures will devour that frame of spirit.

Secondly, our examination as to repentance respects actual sins, especially as for those who have the privilege and advantage of frequent and ordinary participation of this ordinance. It respects the surprisals that have befallen us (as there is no man that does good and sins not) since we received the last pledge of the love of God in the administration of that ordinance. Friends, let us not be afraid of calling ourselves to a strict account. We have to do with Him that is greater than we, and knows all things. Let us not be afraid to look into the book of conscience and conversation, to look over our surprisals, our neglects, our sinful failings and miscarriages. These things belong to this preparation, to look over them and mourn over them also. I would not be thought to myself or you to prescribe a hard burden in this duty of preparation. It is nothing but what God expects from us, and what we must do if we intend any communion with him in this ordinance. I may add;

---

6   Owen is loosely quoting Zech. 12:10.

Thirdly, whether we have kept alive our last received pledges of the love of God? It may be at an ordinance we have received some special intimations of the goodwill of God. It is our duty to keep them alive in our spirits; and let us never be afraid we shall have no room for more. The keeping of them makes way for what further is to come. Have we lost such sensible impressions, there is then matter for repentance and humiliation.

(2) Examination also concerns faith; and that in general and in particular. In general: is not my heart hypocritical? Or do I really do what in this ordinance I profess? Which is placing all my faith and hope in Jesus Christ for life, mercy, salvation, and for peace with God. And in particular, do I stir up and act faith to meet Christ in this ordinance? I shall not enlarge upon these things that are commonly spoken unto.

Supplication

3. The third part of our preparation, is supplication; that is, adding prayer to this meditation and examination. Add prayer, which may inlay and digest all the rest in the soul. Pray over what we have thought on, what we have conceived, what we have apprehended, what we desire, and what we fear; gather all up into supplications to God.

Expectation

4. There belongs unto this duty, expectation also; that is, to expect that God will answer his promise, and meet us according to the desire of our hearts. We should look to meet God, because he has promised to meet us there; and we go upon his promise of grace, expecting he will answer his word and meet us. Not going at all adventures, as not knowing whether we shall find him or not; God may indeed then surprise us as he did Jacob when he appeared unto him, and made him say, God "is in this place, and I knew it not."[7] But we go where we know God is. He has placed his name upon his ordinances, and there he is; go to them with expectation, and rise from the rest of the duties with this expectation.

This is the substance of what might be of use to some in reference unto this duty of preparation for this great and solemn ordinance, which God has graciously given unto any of you the privilege to be made partakers of.

Have we failed in these things or in things of a like nature? Let us admire the infinite patience of God, that has borne with us all this while, that he has not cast us out of his house, that he has not deprived us of these enjoyments,

---

7 Gen. 28:16.

which he might justly have done, when we have so undervalued them, as far as lay in us, and despised them; when we have had so little care to make entertainment for the receiving of the great God and our Lord Jesus Christ, who comes to visit us in this ordinance. We may be ready to complain of what outward concerns, in and about the worship of God, some have been deprived of. We have infinite more reason to admire, that there is anything left unto us, any name, any place, any nail, any remembrance in the house of God; considering the regardlessness which has been upon our spirits in our communion with him. Go away, and "sin no more, lest a worse thing" befall us (John 5:14). If there be in any, that have not risen up in a due manner in this duty, any conviction of the necessity and usefulness of it, God forbid we should be found sinning against this conviction.

The Sacramental Representation of Christ in This Ordinance

July 7, 1673

I SHALL SHOW BRIEFLY what it is to obtain a sacramental part of Jesus Christ in this ordinance of the Lord's Supper.

It is a great mystery, and great wisdom and exercise of faith lie in it, how to obtain a participation of Christ. When the world had lost an understanding of this mystery for want of spiritual sight, they contrived a means to make it up, that should be easy on the part of them that did partake, and very prodigious on the part of them that administered. The priest, with a few words, turned the bread into the body of Christ; and the people have no more to do but to put it into their mouths, and so Christ is partaken of. It was the loss of the mystery of faith in the real participation of Christ, that put them on that invention.

Neither is there in this ordinance, a naked figure, a naked representation: there is something in the figure, something in the representation, but there is not all in it. When the bread is broken, it is a figure, a representation that the body of Christ was broken for us; and the pouring out of the wine is a figure and representation of the pouring of the blood of Christ, or the pouring forth of his soul unto death. And there are useful meditations that may arise from thence. But in this ordinance there is a real exhibition of Christ unto every believing soul.

I shall a little inquire into it, to lead your faith into a due exercise in it, under the administration of this ordinance.

First, the exhibition and tender of Christ in this ordinance is distinct from the tender of Christ in the promise of the gospel; as in many other things, so it is in this: in the promise of the gospel the person of the Father is principally looked upon, as proposing and tendering Christ unto us: in this ordinance, Christ tenders himself, "This is my body," says he; "this do in remembrance of me."[1] He makes an immediate tender of himself unto a believing soul; and calls our faith unto a respect to his grace, to his love, to his readiness to unite, and spiritually to incorporate with us. Again,

Secondly, it is a tender of Christ, and an exhibition of Christ under an especial consideration; not in general, but under this consideration, as he is, as it were, newly (so the word is) sacrificed; as he is a new and fresh sacrifice in the great work of reconciling, making peace with God, making an end of sin, doing all that was to be done between God and sinners, that they might be at peace.

Christ makes a double representation of himself, as the great Mediator upon his death, and the oblation and sacrifice which he accomplished thereby.

He presents himself unto God in heaven, there to do whatever remains to be done with God on our behalf, by his intercession. The intercession of Christ is nothing but the presentation of himself unto God, upon his oblation and sacrifice.

He presents himself unto God to do with him what remains to be done on our part, to procure mercy and grace for us.

He presents himself unto us in this ordinance, to do with us what remains to be done on the part of God; and this answers to his intercession above, which is the counterpart of his present mediation, to do with us what remains on the part of God, to give out peace and mercy in the seal of the covenant unto our souls.

There is this special exhibition of Jesus Christ, and it is given directly for this special exercise of faith, that we may know how to receive him in this ordinance.

1. We receive him as one that has actually accomplished the great work (so he tenders himself) of making peace with God for us; for the blotting out of sins, and for the bringing in everlasting righteousness. He does not tender himself as one that can do these things. It is a relief when we have an apprehension that Christ can do all this for us: nor does he tender himself as one that will do these things upon any such or such conditions, as shall be prescribed unto us. But he tenders himself unto our faith, as one that has done these things; and as such are we to receive him, if we intend to glorify him in this ordinance; as one that has actually done this, actually made peace for us, actually blotted out our sins, and purchased eternal redemption for us.

1   Luke 22:19; 1 Cor. 11:24.

Brethren, can we receive Christ thus? Are we willing to receive him thus? If so, we may go away and be no more sorrowful. If we come short herein, we come short of that faith, which is required of us in this ordinance. Pray let us endeavor to consider, how Jesus Christ does hereby make a tender of himself unto us, as one that has actually taken away all our sins, and all our iniquities, that none of them shall ever be laid unto our charge: and to receive him as such, is to give glory unto him.

2. He tenders himself as one that has done this work by his death; for it is the remembrance of his death in a peculiar manner that we celebrate. What there is of love, what there is of efficacy, of power and comfort in that, what there is of security, I may have occasion another time to speak unto you. At present this is all I would offer; that for the doing of these great things, for the doing the greatest, the hardest things that our faith is exercised about, which are the pardon of our sins, and the acceptation of our persons with God, for the accomplishment hereof, he died an accursed death; and that death had no power over him, but the bands of it were loosed; he rose from under it, and was acquitted. Let us act faith on Jesus Christ, as one that brings with him mercy and pardon, as that which was procured by his death, against which lies no exception. I could show you that nothing was too hard for it, that nothing was left to be done by it, which we are to receive.

3. To be made partakers of him in this sacramental tender by submitting unto his authority in his institutions, by assenting unto the truth of his word in the promise that he will be present with us, and give himself unto us, and by approving of that glorious way of making peace for us which he has trodden and gone in, in his sufferings, and in our stead: to get a view of Christ, as tendering himself unto every one of our souls in this ordinance of his own institution, as him who has perfectly made an end of all differences between God and us, and who brings along with him all the mercy and grace that is in the heart of God, and in his covenant: to have such a view of him, and so to receive him by faith, that it shall be life unto our souls, is the way to give glory unto God, and to have peace and rest in our own bosoms.

4. And lastly, in one word, faith is so to receive him, as to enable us to sit down at God's Table, as those that are the Lord's friends; as those that are invited to feast upon the sacrifice. The sacrifice is offered, Christ is the sacrifice, God's Passover; God makes a feast upon it, and invites his friends to sit down at his Table, there being now no difference between him and us. Let us pray that he would help us to exercise faith to this purpose.

Discourse 8

The Duty of Remembering Christ's Sufferings in This Ordinance

November 2, 1673

YOU KNOW I USUALLY SPEAK a few words to prepare us for this ordinance: you know it is an ordinance of calling to remembrance, "Do in remembrance of me." There was under the Old Testament but one sacrifice to call anything to remembrance; and God puts a mark upon that sacrifice, as that which was not, as it were, well pleasing unto him, but only what necessity did require, and that was the sacrifice of jealousy. Says God, there shall be no oil in it (a token of peace); there shall be no frankincense (that should yield a sweet savor), for it is an offering to bring "iniquity to remembrance" (Num. 5:15): this great ordinance of the Lord's Supper, is not to call iniquity to remembrance, but it is to call to remembrance the putting an end to iniquity: God will make an end of sin; and this ordinance is our solemn remembrance of it.

REMEMBERING THE SUFFERINGS OF CHRIST IN THIS ORDINANCE

Now there are sundry things that we are to call to remembrance. I have done my endeavor to help you to call the love of Christ to remembrance. The Lord I trust has guided my thoughts now to direct you to call the sufferings of Christ unto remembrance. I know it may be a suitable meditation to take up your minds and mine, in and under this ordinance. It is our duty in this holy ordinance solemnly to call to remembrance the sufferings of Christ.

It is said of the preaching of the gospel, that Jesus Christ is therein "evidently set forth" crucified before our eyes (Gal. 3:1). And if Christ is evidently crucified before our eyes in the preaching of the gospel, Christ is much more evidently crucified before our eyes in the administration of this ordinance, which is instituted for that very end.

And certainly, when Christ is crucified before our eyes, we ought deeply to consider his sufferings. It would be a great sign of a hard and senseless heart in us, if we were not willing in some measure to consider his sufferings upon such an occasion. We are, therefore, solemnly to remember them.

Well, shall I a little mind myself and you, how we may, and how we ought to call to remembrance the sufferings of Christ.

Let us remember that we ourselves were obnoxious unto these sufferings. The curse lay doubly upon us. The original curse, ("In the day that thou eatest thereof, thou shalt surely die"[1]) lay upon us all. The consequent curse, "Cursed be every one who continueth not in all things that are written in the book of the law to do them";[2] that also lay upon us all; we were under both, the original and the consequent curse. We know what is in the curse, even all the anger and wrath that a displeased holy God can and will inflict upon sinful creatures to all eternity. In this state and condition then, all lay upon us, and all must lie upon us; unless we come to have an interest in the sufferings of Christ, there is no relief for us. I will not insist upon calling to your mind, that heaven and earth, and all God's creation combining together, could not have procured relief for one of our souls. Christ, the Son of God, offered himself, and said, "Lo, I come."[3] Indeed, it was a good saying of David, it was nobly said, when he saw the angel of the Lord destroying the people with a pestilence, Lord, says he, it is I and my father's house that have sinned; but as for these sheep, these poor people, what have they done? It was otherwise with Christ; he came in the place of sinners, and said, let not these poor sheep die. If God would by faith give your souls and mine a view of the voluntary substitution of Jesus Christ in his person in our room and on our behalf, it would comfort and refresh us. When the curse of God was ready to break forth upon us, God accepted of this tender, of this offer of Christ: "Lo, I come [. . .] to do thy will,"[4] to be a sacrifice: and what did he do? Why, says he, this God did; then if he will come, if he will do it, let him plainly know how the case stands; the curse is upon them, wrath is upon them, punishment must be undergone; my holiness, faithfulness,

---

1 Gen. 2:17.
2 Gal. 3:10.
3 Owen is alluding to Ps. 40:7 and Heb. 10:7.
4 Heb. 10:7.

righteousness, and truth, are all engaged. Yet says Christ, "Lo, I come." Well, what does God do? He tells you, "All we like sheep have gone astray, we have turned every one to his own way, and the LORD hath caused all our iniquities to meet on him" (Isa. 53:6). God so far relaxed his own law, that the sentence shall not fall upon their persons, but upon their substitute, one that has put himself in their place and stead. Be it so; all their iniquities be upon thee; all the iniquities of this congregation, says God, be upon my Son Jesus Christ.

Well, what then did he suffer? He suffered that which answered the justice of God. He suffered that which answered the law of God. He suffered that which fully repaired the glory of God. Brethren, let us encourage ourselves in the Lord. If there be any demands to be made of you or me, it must be upon the account of the righteousness and justice of God; or, upon the account of the law of God; or, upon the account of the loss that God suffered in his glory by us. If the Lord Jesus has come in, and answered all these, we have a good plea to make in the presence of the holy God.

1. He suffered all that the justice of God did require. Hence it is said, that God set him forth "to be a propitiation through faith in his blood, to declare his righteousness for the forgiveness of sins" (Rom. 3:25). And you may observe, that the apostle uses the very same words in respect of Christ's sufferings, that he uses in respect of the sufferings of the damned angels. God spared him not (Rom. 8:32). And when he would speak of the righteousness of God in inflicting punishment upon the sinning angels, he does it by that very word, God spared them not.[5] So that whatever the righteousness of God did require against sinners, Christ therein was not spared at all. What God required against your sins and mine, and all his elect, God spared him nothing, but he paid the utmost farthing.[6]

2. The sufferings of Christ did answer the law of God. That makes the next demand of us. The law is that which requires our poor, guilty souls to punishment in the name of the justice of God. Why, says the apostle, he "hath redeemed us from the curse of the law, by being made a curse for us" (Gal. 3:13). By undergoing and suffering the curse of the law, he redeemed us from it.

3. He suffered everything that was required to repair and make up the glory of God. Better you and I and all the world, should perish, than God should be endamaged[7] in his glory. It is a truth, and I hope God will bring all our hearts to say, Christ has suffered to make up that. The obedience that was in the sufferings of Christ, brought more glory to God, than the disobedience

---

5 Owen is alluding to 2 Pet. 2:4.
6 I.e., a unit of currency worth a quarter of a penny.
7 I.e., damaged.

of Adam, who was the original of the apostasy of the whole creation from God, brought dishonor unto him. That which seemed to reflect great dishonor upon God was, that all his creatures should as one man fall off by apostasy from him. God will have his honor repaired, and it is done by the obedience of Christ much more. There comes, I say, more glory to God by the obedience of Christ and his sufferings, than there did dishonor by the disobedience of Adam; and so there comes more glory by Christ's sufferings and obedience upon the cross, than by the sufferings of the damned forever. God loses no glory by setting believers free from suffering, because of the sufferings of the Son of God. This was a fruit of eternal wisdom.

THE DUTIES THAT FOLLOW A REMEMBRANCE OF CHRIST'S SUFFERINGS

Now, having thus touched a little upon the sufferings of Christ, what shall we do in a way of duty?

1. Let us by faith consider truly and really this great substitution of Jesus Christ; the just suffering for the unjust; in our stead, in our room, undergoing what we should have undergone. The Lord help us to admire the infinite holiness, righteousness, and truth, that is in it: we are not able to comprehend these things in it; but if God enables us to exercise faith upon it, we shall admire it. Whence is it that the Son of God should be substituted in our place? Pray remember, that we are now representing this infinite effect of divine wisdom in substituting Jesus Christ in our room, to undergo the wrath and curse of God for us.

2. Let us learn from the cross of Christ, what indeed is in our sins; that when Christ, the Son of God, in whom he was always well pleased, that did the whole will of God, was in his bosom from all eternity, came and substituted himself in our room, God spared him not. Let not any sinner under heaven that is estranged from Christ, ever think to be spared. If God would have spared any, he would have spared his only Son. But if he will be a mediator of the covenant, God will not spare him, though his own Son. We may acquaint you hereafter, what it cost Christ to stand in the room of sinners. The Lord from thence give our hearts some sense of that great provocation that is in sin, that we may mourn before him, when we look upon him whom our sins have pierced.

3. Will God help us to take a view of the issue of all this, of the substitution of Jesus Christ, placing him in our stead, putting his soul in the place of our souls; his person in the place of our persons; of the commutation of punish-

ment, in which the righteousness, holiness and wisdom of God laid that on him which was due unto us. What is the issue of all this? It is to bring us unto God; to peace with God, and acquitment from all our sins; and to make us acceptable with the righteous, holy and faithful God; to give us boldness before him; this is the issue. Let us consider this issue of the sufferings of Christ, and be thankful.

Discourse 9

Instructions for Different Sorts of Sinners in Approaching the Lord's Table

February 22, 1674

IT IS THE TABLE OF THE LORD that we are invited to draw nigh unto. Our Lord has a large heart and bountiful hand; has made plentiful provision for our souls at this Table; and he says unto us by his Spirit in his word, eat, O my friends, yea, drink abundantly. It is that feast that God has provided for sinners. And there are three sorts of sinners that I would speak a word unto, to stir them up unto a due exercise of faith in this ordinance, according as their condition does require. There are such as are not sensible of their sins, so as they ought to be; they know they are not; they are not able to get their hearts affected with their sins, as they desire. There are some that are so burdened, and overpressed with the sense of their sins, that they are scarce able to hold up under the weight of them; under the doubts and fears wherewith they are distressed. And there are sinners, who are in enjoyment of a sense of the pardon of sin; and do desire to have hearts to improve it in thankfulness and fruitfulness.

Something of these several frames may be in us all; yet it may be, one is predominant, one is chief; one in one, another in another; and therefore I will speak a few words distinctly to them all.

THOSE UNABLE TO AFFECT THEMSELVES OF THEIR SIN

1. There are sinners who are believers, who cannot get their hearts and spirits affected with sin so as they ought, and so as they desire. There is not a sadder

complaint of the church, as I know, in the whole book of God, than that, why hast thou "hardened our heart from thy fear?" (Isa. 63:17). Poor creatures may come unto that perplexity through an apprehension of the want of a due sense of the guilt of sin, as to be ready thus to cry out, why is it thus with me? Why am I so senseless under the guilt of all the sins that I have contracted? I have a word of direction unto such persons. Are there such among us? It is a direction unto faith to be acting in this ordinance. It is that which we have, they shall look unto him "whom they have pierced," and mourn (Zech. 12:10). Why, brethren, Christ is represented unto us in this ordinance, as he was pierced, as his precious blood was poured out for us. Let us act faith, if God help us, in two things.

(1) Upon the dolorous[1] sufferings of Christ, which are represented here unto us. Let us take a view of the Son of God under the curse of God.

(2) Remember that all these sufferings were for us; they shall look upon him "whom they have pierced," and then "mourn." The acting of faith upon the sufferings of Christ, as one that suffered for us, is the great means in this ordinance to bring our hearts to mourn for sin indeed. Therefore pray, let us beg of God, whoever of us are in any measure under this frame, that our insensibleness of the guilt and burden of sin may be our great burden. Let us try the power of faith in this ordinance, by getting our hearts affected with the sufferings of Christ in our behalf. Let us bind it to our hearts and consciences; and may the Lord give a blessing.

THOSE OVERBURDENED BY THEIR SIN

2. There are others who, it may be, are pressed under the weight of their sins; walk mournfully, walk disconsolately. I know there are some so, in the condition expressed by the psalmist, "Innumerable evils have compassed me about, mine iniquities have taken hold upon me, so that I am not able to look up; they are more than the hairs of mine head; therefore my heart faileth me" (Ps. 40:12). Some may be in that condition that their hearts are ready to fail them, through the multitude of their iniquities taking hold upon them. What would you direct such unto in this ordinance? Truly, that which is given, "As Moses lifted up the serpent in the wilderness, even so must the Son of man be lifted up; that whosoever believeth in him should not perish, but have eternal life" (John 3:14–15). The Lord Jesus Christ was lifted up, as Moses lifted up the serpent in the wilderness; and here he is lifted up, as bearing all

---

1   I.e., sorrowful.

our sins in his own body upon the tree. Here is a representation made unto poor sinners whose hearts are most burdened; here is Jesus Christ lifted up with all our sins upon the tree. Let such a soul labor to have a view of Christ as bearing all our iniquities, that believing on him we should not perish, but have life everlasting. God has appointed him to be crucified evidently before our eyes, that every poor soul that is stung with sin, ready to die by sin, should look up unto him, and be healed; and virtue will go forth, if we look upon him, for by "his stripes we are healed."[2]

THOSE SENSIBLE OF PARDON SEEKING TO BE THANKFUL AND FRUITFUL

3. There may be some that live in full satisfaction of the pardon of their sins, and are solicitous how their hearts may be drawn forth unto thankfulness and fruitfulness. Remember that place, "To him that loved us, and washed us from our sins in his own blood, [. . .] to him be glory and dominion for ever and ever" (Rev. 1:5–6). Remember this, that whatever your state and condition be, you have here a proper object for faith to exercise itself upon; only be not wanting unto your own comfort and advantage.

2   Isa. 53:5.

Discourse 10

The Presence of Christ in This Ordinance

May 17, 1674

Teaching them to observe all things whatsoever I have commanded
you: and, lo, I am with you alway, even unto the end of the world.

MATTHEW 28:20

BY "THE END OF THE WORLD" we are to understand the consummation of all things; when all church work is done, and all church duties are over; when the time comes that we shall pray no more, hear no more, no more administer ordinances; but till then, says Christ, take this for your life and for your comfort, do what I command you, and you shall have my presence with you.

There are three things whereby Christ makes good this promise, and is with his church to the end of the world.

First, by his Spirit. Wherever, says he, "two or three are gathered together in my name, there I am in the midst of them" (Matt. 18:20), by his quickening, guiding, directing Spirit, as a Spirit of grace and supplication, as a Spirit of light and holiness, and as a Spirit of comfort.

Secondly, Christ is present with us by his word. Says the apostle, "Let the word of Christ dwell in you richly" (Col. 3:16), or plentifully. And how then? Then, says he, Christ dwells in us "by faith" (Eph. 3:17). The word dwells in us plentifully, if mixed with faith; and Christ dwells in us; he is present with us by his word.

Thirdly, Christ is present with us in an especial manner in this ordinance. One of the greatest engines that ever the devil made use of to overthrow the faith of the church, was by forging such a presence of Christ as is not truly in this ordinance, to drive us off from looking after that great presence which is true. I look upon it as one of the greatest engines that ever hell set on work. It is not a corporeal presence; there are innumerable arguments against that; everything that is in sense, reason, and the faith of a man, overthrows that corporeal presence. But I will remind you of one or two texts wherewith it is inconsistent. The first is that in John 16:7. "Nevertheless," says our Savior, "it is expedient for you that I go away; for if I go not away, the Comforter will not come unto you." The corporeal presence of Christ, and the evangelical presence of the Holy Ghost, as the comforter, in the New Testament, are inconsistent. I must go away, or the comforter will not come. But, he so went away as to his presence, as to come again with his bodily presence, as often as the priests call. No, says Peter. "The heavens must receive" him (Acts 3:21). For how long? Till "the time of the restitution of all things." I go away as to my bodily presence, or the comforter will not come; and when he is gone away, the heaven must receive him until the time of the restitution of all things. We must not therefore look after such a presence.

I will give you a word or two, what is the presence of Christ with us in this ordinance; what is our duty; and how we may meet with Christ when he is thus present with us; which is the work I have in hand. Christ is present in this ordinance in an especial manner three ways, by representation, by exhibition, by obsignation,[1] or sealing.

PRESENCE BY REPRESENTATION

1. He is present here by representation. So in a low, shadowy way God was present in the tabernacle, in the temple, in the ark and mercy seat; they had a representation of his glory. But Christ here has given us a more eminent and clear representation of himself. I will name but two things:

(1) A representation of himself, as he is the food of our souls.

(2) A representation of himself, as he suffered for our sins.

These are two great ways whereby Christ is represented as the food of our souls, in the matter of the ordinance; and Christ as suffering for our sins is represented in the manner of the ordinance; both by his own appointment. The apostle says, Jesus Christ was evidently crucified before their eyes (Gal. 3:1). Evidently crucified, does not intend particularly this ordinance, but

---

1   I.e., the ratification of something formally by seal.

the preaching of the gospel, which gave a delineation, a picture and image of the crucifixion of Christ unto the faith of believers. But of all things that belong unto the gospel, he is most evidently crucified before our eyes in this ordinance; and it is agreed on all hands, that Christ is represented unto the soul in this ordinance. How shall we do this? Shall we do it by crucifixes, pictures and images? No; they are all cursed of that God who said, "Thou shalt not make unto thyself any graven image."[2] But that way by which God himself, and Christ himself has appointed to represent these things unto us, that he blesses, and makes effectual. This way, as I have often showed, is the way that was chosen by the wisdom and goodness of Jesus Christ; the name of God is upon it; it is blessed unto us, and will be effectual, if we are not wanting to ourselves.

PRESENCE BY EXHIBITION

2. Christ is present with us, by way of exhibition; that is, he does really tender and exhibit himself unto the souls of believers in this ordinance, which the world has lost, and knows not what to make of it. They exhibit that which they do not contain. This bread does not contain the body of Christ, or the flesh of Christ; the cup does not contain the blood of Christ, but they exhibit them; both do as really exhibit them to believers, as they partake of the outward signs. Certainly we believe that our Lord Jesus Christ does not invite us unto this Table for the bread that perishes, for outward food; it is to feed our souls. What do we think then? Does he invite us unto an empty, painted feast? Do we deal so with our friends? Here is something really exhibited by Jesus Christ unto us, to receive, besides the outward pledges of bread and wine. We must not think the Lord Jesus Christ deludes our souls with empty shows and appearances. That which is exhibited is himself, it is his flesh as meat indeed, and his blood as drink indeed; it is himself as broken and crucified that he exhibits unto us. And it is the fault and sin of every one of us if we do not receive him this day, when an exhibition and tender is made unto us, as here by way of food. To what end do we receive it? Truly we receive it for these two ends, for incorporation, for nourishment.

(1) We receive our food, that it may incorporate and turn into blood and spirits, that it may become one with us; and when we have so done,

(2) Our end and design is, that we may be nourished, nature strengthened, comforted and supported, and we enabled for the duties of life.

2   Ex. 20:4.

Christ does exhibit himself unto our souls, if we are not wanting unto ourselves, for these two things, incorporation and nourishment; to be received into union, and to give strength unto our souls.

PRESENCE BY SEALING

3. Christ is present in this ordinance by way of obsignation: he comes here to seal the covenant; and therefore the cup is called, the "new testament in the blood" of Christ;[3] how in the blood of Christ? It is the new covenant that was sealed, ratified, confirmed and made so stable as you have heard, by the blood of Jesus Christ. For from the foundation of the world, no covenant was ever intended to be established, but it was confirmed by blood; and this covenant is confirmed by the blood of Christ; and he comes and seals the covenant with his own blood in the administration of this ordinance.

WHAT IS REQUIRED OF US TO ENJOY CHRIST'S PRESENCE IN THE ORDINANCE

Well, if Jesus Christ be thus present by way of representation, exhibition and obsignation, what is required of us, that we may meet him, and be present with him? For it is not our mere coming hither that is a meeting with Christ; it is a work of faith: and there are three acts of faith whereby we may be present with Christ, who is thus present with us.

1. The first is by recognition, answering his representation. As Christ in this ordinance does represent his death unto us, so we are to remember it, and call it over. Pray consider how things were done formerly in reference unto it. The Paschal Lamb[4] was an ordinance for remembrance; it is a night to be had in remembrance; and this they should do for a remembrance; and it was to be eaten with bitter herbs: there was once a year a feast wherein all the sins, iniquities and transgressions of the children of Israel were called to remembrance; and it was to be done by greatly afflicting of their souls. If we intend to call to remembrance the death of Christ, we may do well to do it with some bitter herbs; there should be some remembrance of sin with it, some brokenness of heart for sin, with respect to him who was pierced and broken for us. Our work is to call over and show forth the death of Christ. Pray, brethren, let us a little consider whether our hearts be suitably affected

---

3   Owen is alluding to 1 Cor. 11:25.
4   I.e., the lamb sacrificed in the Jewish Passover feast.

with respect to our sins which were upon Jesus Christ when he died for us, or no; lest we draw nigh unto him with the outward bodily presence, when our hearts are far from him.

2. If Christ is present with us by way of exhibition, we ought to be present by way of admission. It will not advantage you or me that Christ tenders himself unto us, unless we receive him. This is the great work; herein lies the main work upon all the members of the church. When we are to dispense the word, the first work lies upon ministers; and when the work is sufficiently discharged, they will be a good savor unto God in them that believe, and in them that perish: but in this ordinance, the main work lies upon yourselves. If in the name of Christ we make a tender of him unto you, and he be not actually received, there is but half the work done; so that you are in a peculiar manner to stir up yourselves, as having a more especial interest in this duty, than in any other duty of the church whatsoever, and you may take a better measure of yourselves by your acting in this duty, than of us by our acting in the ministry. Let Christ be received into your hearts by faith and love upon this particular tender that he assuredly makes in this ordinance of himself unto you; for, as I said, he has not invited you unto an empty painted feast or Table.

3. Know what you come to meet him for, which is, to seal the covenant; solemnly to take upon yourselves again the performance of your part of the covenant. I hope I speak in a deep sense of the thing itself, and that which I have much thought of. This is that which ruins the world, the hearing that God has made a covenant of grace and mercy, it is preached to them, and declared unto them, and they think to be saved by this covenant, though they themselves do not perform what the covenant requires on their part. What great and glorious words do we speak in the covenant, that God gives himself over unto us to be our God! Brethren, there is our giving ourselves unto God (to answer this) universally and absolutely. If we give ourselves unto the world, and to our lusts, and to self, we are not to expect any benefit by God's covenant of grace. If it is not made up by our sealing of the covenant of grace, or by a universal resignation of ourselves, in all that we are and do unto him, we do not meet Jesus Christ; we disappoint him when he comes to seal the covenant. Where is this people, says Christ, that would enter into covenant with me? Let it be in our hearts to see him seal the covenant of grace as represented in this ordinance; and to take upon ourselves the performance of what is required of us, by a universal giving up ourselves unto God.

Discourse 11

Scripture to Consider When Meditating Upon Christ's Sufferings in This Ordinance

August 9, 1674

I SHALL NOW PRODUCE some few places of Scripture, one especially, that may administer occasion unto you for the exercise of faith, the great duty required of us at this time. You may do well to think of these words of the prophet concerning Jesus Christ, concerning his sufferings and death, which we are here gathered together in his name to remember. They are, "He shall see of the travail of his soul, and shall be satisfied" (Isa. 53:11).

There are two things that the Holy Ghost minds us of in these words: first, that Jesus Christ was in a great travail of soul to bring forth the redemption and salvation of the church. Secondly, he minds us that Jesus Christ was satisfied, and much rejoiced in the consideration of the effects and fruits of the travail of his soul.

I shall speak a word to both, and a word to show you how both these things are called over in this ordinance, both the travail of the soul of Christ, and his satisfaction in the fruit of that travail.

THE TRAVAIL OF CHRIST'S SOUL

First, Christ was in a great travail of soul to bring forth the redemption and salvation of the church. It was a great work that Christ had to do. It is usually said, we are not saved as the world was made, by a word; but there was travail in it; it is the word whereby the bringing forth of children into the world is expressed; the travail of a woman; and there are three things in that travail, an agony of mind, outcrying for help, and sense of pain; all these things were in the travail of the soul of Christ. I will name the Scriptures to call them to your remembrance.

1. He was "in an agony" (Luke 22:44). An agony is an inexpressible conflict of mind about things dreadful and terrible. So it was with Christ. No heart can conceive, much less can tongue express the conflict that was in the soul of Jesus Christ with the wrath of God, the curse of the law, the pains of hell and death, that stood before him in this work of our redemption. There was an agony.

2. There was an outcrying for help, "Who in the days of his flesh [. . .] offered up prayers and supplications with strong crying and tears unto him that was able to save him" (Heb. 5:7). Such is the outcry of a person in travail, crying out unto them that are able to save them. So it was with Jesus Christ when he was in the travail of his soul about our salvation. He made these strong cries unto God, to him that was able to save him.

3. There was pain in it, which is the last thing in travail; so that he complained that the pains of hell had taken hold upon him. Whatever pain there was in the curse of the law, in the wrath of God; whatever the justice of God did ever design to inflict upon sinners was then upon the soul of Jesus Christ; so that he was in travail. That is the first thing I would mind you of; that in the bringing forth the work of our redemption and salvation, the Lord Jesus was in travail.

CHRIST'S SATISFACTION IN THE
FRUITS OF HIS TRAVAIL

Secondly, it was a satisfaction, a rejoicing unto the Lord Jesus Christ, to consider the fruits and effects of this travail of his soul, which God had promised he should see. He was satisfied in the prospect he had of the fruit of the travail of his soul. So the apostle tells us, that, "for the joy that was set before him," which was the joy of bringing us unto God, of being the captain of salvation unto them that should obey him, he "endured the cross" and despised "the shame" (Heb. 12:2); he went through all with a prospect he had of the fruit of his travail; there would joy come out of it; the joy that was set before him, as he speaks, where God presents unto him what he shall have by this travail, what he shall get by it; says he, "The lines are fallen unto me in a pleasant place, yea I have a goodly heritage" (Ps. 16:6). It is the satisfaction that Jesus Christ (who is there spoken of only in that psalm) takes in the fruit of the travail of his soul; he is contented with it. He does not do as Hiram, who when Solomon gave him the twenty cities in the land of Galilee, calls them, "Cabul";¹ they were dirty, and they displeased him (1 Kings 9:11–13), etc. No; but, "The lines are fallen unto me in a pleasant place"; he rejoiced in his travail. It is expressed, in my apprehension, to the height in Jeremiah 31:25–26. "I have satiated the weary soul, and I have replenished every sorrowful soul." What follows? "Upon this I awaked, and beheld, and my sleep was sweet unto me." They are the words of Jesus Christ; and he speaks concerning his death, wherein he was as asleep in the grave. Now consider what was the effect and fruit of it? It was sweet unto Jesus Christ after all the travail of his soul, that he had "satiated the weary soul," and "replenished every sorrowful soul."

In one word, both these things, the travail of the soul of Christ, and the satisfaction he took in the fruit of his travail, are represented unto us in this ordinance.

There is the travail of the soul of Christ to us in the manner of the participation of this ordinance, in the breaking of the bread, and in the pouring out of the wine, representing unto us the breaking of the body of Christ, the shedding of his blood, and the separation of the one from the other, which was the cause of his death. Now though these were outward things in Christ (because the travail of his soul cannot be represented by any outward things, wherein the great work of our redemption lay) we are in this ordinance to be led through these outward things to the travail of the soul of Christ: we are not to rest in the mere outward act or acts of the breaking of the body of Christ, and pouring out of his blood, the separation of the one from the other, and of his death thereby, but through all them we are to inquire, what is under them? There was Christ's making his soul an offering for sin; there was Christ's being made a curse under them, Christ's travail of soul in an agony to bring forth the redemption and salvation of the church.

Brethren, let us be able by faith not only to look through these outward signs to that which makes the representation itself unto us, the body and blood of Christ; but even with them and through them to the travail of the soul of Christ; the work that he was doing between God and himself for the redemption of the church.

And here is also a representation made unto us of that satisfaction the soul of Christ received in the fruit of his travail, having appointed it in a particular manner to be done in remembrance of him. No man will appoint a remembrance of that which he does not delight in. When Job had no more delight in his life, he desired that the time of his birth might never be remembered.

1   I.e., signifying "good for nothing" or something displeasing in Hebrew.

When God brought the children of Israel out of Egypt, whereby he exalted his glory, he appointed a Passover, and said, it is a day greatly to be remembered;[2] because the people had a great deliverance, and God received great glory and great satisfaction, therefore it was greatly to be remembered. We are to celebrate this ordinance in remembrance of Christ, and therefore there is a representation of that satisfaction which Jesus Christ did receive in the travail of his soul, so that he never repented him of one groan, of one sigh, of one tear, of one prayer, of one wrestling with the wrath of God. It is matter of rejoicing and to be remembered; and do you rejoice in the remembrance of it.

Again; it is apparent from hence, because this ordinance is in an especial manner an ordinance of thanksgiving; the bread that is blessed, or which we give thanks for; the cup which is blessed: Christ gave thanks. Now if hereby we give thanks, it is to call to remembrance, not merely the travail of Christ's soul, but the success of that travail; hereby all differences were made up between God and us; hereby grace and glory were purchased for us, and he became the captain of salvation unto us.

To shut up all, here is by Christ's institution bread and wine provided for us; but it is bread broken and wine poured out. There are two things in it, there is the weak part that is Christ's, there is the nourishing part that is given unto us: the Lord Christ has chosen by this ordinance to represent himself by these things that are the staff of our lives; they comprise the whole nourishment and sustenance of our bodies. He has so chosen to represent them by breaking and pouring out, that they shall signify his sufferings; here are both, as the bread is broken, and as the wine is poured out, there is the representation of the travail of the soul of Christ to us: as bread is received, and the cup, which is the means of the nourishment of man's life, here is the fruit of Christ's death exhibited unto us, and his sufferings. The Lord help us to look into the satisfaction that Christ received from this, that we may be partakers of the one and the other.

---

2   Owen is alluding to Ex. 12:14.

Discourse 12

Attaining Conformity to Christ's Death in This Ordinance

February 21, 1675

WE ARE MET HERE TO REMEMBER, to celebrate and set forth the death of Christ, to profess and plead our interest therein. And there are two things that we should principally consider in reference to ourselves, and our duty, and the death of Christ. The first is, the benefits of it, and our participation of them. And the second is, our conformity unto it; both are mentioned together by the apostle in Phil. 3:10. "That I may know him, and the power of his resurrection, and the fellowship of his sufferings, being made conformable unto his death."

CONFORMITY TO CHRIST'S DEATH

I shall speak a word or two (upon this occasion of remembering the death of Christ) unto the latter clause, of our "being made conformable unto his death," wherein a very great part of our due preparation unto this ordinance does consist; and for the furtherance whereof we do in an especial manner wait upon God in this part of his worship. Therefore I shall in a few words mind you wherein we ought to be conformable unto the death of Christ, and how we are advantaged therein by this ordinance.

We are to be conformable unto the death of Christ, in the internal, moral cause of it, and in the external means of it.

The cause of the death of Christ, was sin. The means of the death of Christ, was suffering. Our being conformable unto the death of Christ, must respect sin and suffering.

The procuring cause of the death of Christ was sin. He died for sin; he died for our sin; our iniquities were upon him, and were the cause of all the punishment that befell him.

Wherein can we be conformable unto the death of Christ with respect unto sin? We cannot die for sin. Our hope and faith is, in and through him, that we shall never die for sin. No mortal man can be made like unto Christ in suffering for sin. Those that undergo what he underwent, because they were unlike him, must go to hell and be made more unlike him to eternity. Therefore the apostle tells us, that our conformity unto the death of Christ with respect unto sin lies in this, that as he died for sin, so we should die unto sin; that, that sin which he died for, should die in us. He tells us so, we are "planted together in the likeness of his death" (Rom. 6:5); we are made conformable unto the death of Christ, planted into him, so as to have a likeness to him in his death. Wherein? Knowing "that our old man is crucified with him," says he (Rom. 6:6). It is the crucifixion of the old man, the crucifying of the body of sin, the mortifying of sin, that makes us conformable unto the death of Christ; as to the internal moral cause of it, that procures it. See another apostle tells us, "Forasmuch then as Christ hath suffered for us in the flesh, arm yourselves likewise with the same mind; for he that hath suffered in the flesh, hath ceased from sin; that he no longer should live the rest of his time in the flesh to the lusts of men, but to the will of God" (1 Pet. 4:1–2). Here is our conformity to Christ, as he suffered in the flesh, that we should no longer live to our lusts, nor unto the will of man, but unto the will of God. And, brethren, let me tell you, he who approaches unto this remembrance of the death of Christ, that has not labored, that does not labor for conformity to his death in the universal mortification of all sin, runs a hazard to his soul, and puts an affront upon Jesus Christ. O let none of us come in a way of thankfulness to remember the death of Jesus Christ, and bring along with us the murderer whereby he was slain. To harbor with us, and bring along with us to the death of Christ, unmodified lusts and corruptions, such as we do not continually and sincerely endeavor to kill and mortify, is to come and upbraid Christ with his murderer, instead of obtaining any spiritual advantage; what can such poor souls expect?

To be conformable unto the death of Christ as to the outward means, is to be conformable unto him in suffering. We here remember Christ's sufferings. And I am persuaded, and hope I have considered it, that he who is unready to be conformable unto Christ in suffering, was never upright and sincere in endeavoring to be conformable unto Christ in the killing of sin; for we are called as much to the one as to the other. Christ has suffered for us, "leaving us an example,"[1] that we should also suffer when we are called thereunto. And our unwillingness to suffer like unto Christ arises from some unmortified corruption in our hearts, which we have not endeavored to subdue, that we may be like unto Christ in the mortification and death of sin.

FOUR THINGS REQUIRED FOR CONFORMITY TO CHRIST'S DEATH

There are four things required, that we may be conformable unto the death of Christ in suffering; for we may suffer, and yet not be like unto Christ in it nor by it.

1. The first is, that we suffer for Christ. Let none "suffer as a murderer, or as a thief, or as an evil-doer," etc.; "but if any man suffer as a Christian, let him not be ashamed." (1 Pet. 4:15–16). To suffer as a Christian is to suffer for Christ; for the name of Christ; for the truths of Christ; for the ways of Christ; for the worship of Christ.

2. It is required, that we suffer in the strength of Christ; that we do not suffer in the strength of our own will, our own reason, our own resolutions; but that we suffer, I say, in the strength of Christ. When we suffer aright, it is given unto us "in the behalf of Christ, not only to believe on him," but to suffer for him (Phil. 1:29). As all other graces are to be derived from Christ, as our head and root, stock and foundation; so in particular that grace which enables us to suffer for Christ, must be from him. And we do well to consider whether it be so or no; for if it be not, all our sufferings are lost, and not acceptable to him. It is a sacrifice without salt, yea without a heart, that will not be accepted.

3. It is required, that we suffer in imitation of Christ, as making him our example. We are not to take up the cross but with design to follow Christ. Take up the cross, is but half the command; take up the cross, "and follow me,"[2] is the whole command; and we are to suffer willingly and cheerfully, or we are the most unlike Jesus Christ in our sufferings of any persons in the world. Christ was willing and cheerful: "Lo, I come [. . .] to do thy will";[3] "I have a baptism to be baptized with, and how am I straitened till it be accomplished!"[4] says he. And,

4. We are to suffer to the glory of Christ.

1   1 Pet. 2:21.
2   Matt. 16:24.
3   Heb. 10:7.
4   Luke 12:50.

These are things wherein we ought to endeavor conformity to the death of Christ, that we now remember. I pray, let none of us trust to the outward ordinance, the performance of the outward duty. If these things be not in us, we do not remember the Lord's death in a right manner.

HOW THE STRENGTH REQUIRED FOR SUCH CONFORMITY IS ATTAINED

How may we attain the strength and ability from this ordinance to be made conformable to his death? That we may not come and remember the death of Christ, and go away and be more unlike him than formerly?

There is power to this end communicated to us, doctrinally, morally, and spiritually.

There is no such sermon to teach mortification of sin, as the commemoration of the death of Christ. It is the greatest outward instruction unto this duty that God has left unto his church; and I am persuaded which he does most bless to them who are sincere. Do we see Christ evidently crucified before our eyes; his body broken, his blood shed for sin, and is it not of powerful instruction to us, to go on to mortify sin? He that has not learned this, never learned anything aright from this ordinance, nor did he ever receive any benefit from it. There is a constraining power in this instruction to put us upon the mortification of sin; God grant we may see the fruit of it. It has a teaching efficacy; it teaches, as it is peculiarly blessed of God to this end and purpose. And I hope many a soul can say, that they have received that encouragement and that strength by it, as that they have been enabled to more steadiness and constancy in fighting against sin, and have received more success afterward.

There is a moral way whereby it communicates strength to us; because it is our duty now to engage ourselves unto this very work, meeting at the death of Christ, it is our duty to engage ourselves unto God, and that gives strength. And I would beg of you all, brethren, that not one of us would pass through or go over this ordinance, this representation of the death of Christ, without a fresh obligation to God to abide more constant and vigorous in the mortification of sin; we all need it.

And lastly, a spiritual beholding of Christ by faith, is the means to change us into the image and likeness of Christ. Beholding the death of Christ by faith as represented to us in this ordinance, is the means to change us into his image and likeness, and make us conformable unto his death, in the death of sin in us.

1. Take this instruction from the ordinance, as you believe in Christ, as you love him, as you desire to remember him, sin ought to be mortified, that we may be conformed unto him in his death.

2. That we do every one of us bring our souls under an engagement so to do, which is required of us in the very nature of the duty.

3. That we labor by faith so to behold a dying Christ, that strength may thence issue forth for the death of sin in our souls.

Discourse 13

The Nature, Use, and Administration of the Ordinance Itself

April 18, 1675

I HAVE GENERALLY on this occasion fixed on something particular that may draw forth and guide present meditation; but I shall at present enter on what may be further carried on, and speak a little to you about the nature and use of the ordinance itself, in which, it may be, some of us (for there are of all degrees and sizes of knowledge in the church) may not be so well instructed. God has taught us, that the using of an ordinance will not be of advantage to us, unless we understand the institution, and the nature and the ends of it. It was so under the Old Testament, when their worship was more carnal, yet God would have them to know the nature and the reason of that great ordinance of the Passover, as you may see in Exodus 12:24–27. "And ye shall observe this thing for an ordinance to thee and to thy sons for ever. And it shall come to pass, when ye be come to the land which the LORD will give you according as he hath promised, that ye shall keep this service. And it shall come to pass, when your children shall say unto you, What mean ye by this service? That ye shall say, It is the sacrifice of the LORD's Passover," etc. Carry along with you the institution; it is the ordinance of God, you shall keep this service: then you must have the meaning of it, which is this, it is the Lord's Passover; and the occasion of the institution was this, the Lord passed over our houses when he smote the Egyptians, and delivered us out of Egypt.[1] There is a great mystery in that word, "It is the sacrifice of the LORD's Passover": their deliverance was by the blood of a sacrifice; it was a sacrifice which made

---

1 Owen is loosely quoting the remainder of Ex. 12:27.

them look to the great sacrifice, "Christ our Passover," who was "sacrificed for us."[2] And there is a mystical instruction: it is the Lord's Passover, says he; it was a pledge and sign of the Lord's passing over, and sparing the Israelites, for it was not itself the Lord's Passover. Christ says, "This is my body,"[3] that is, a pledge and token of it. Under the Old Testament, God would not have his people to observe this great service and ordinance, but they should know the reason of it, and the end and rise of it, that it might be a service of faith.

All these things are clearly comprised in reference unto this ordinance of the Lord's Supper in those words of the apostle,

> For I have received of the Lord that which also I delivered unto you, that the Lord Jesus, the same night in which he was betrayed, took bread. And when he had given thanks he brake it; and said, Take, eat, this is my body which is broken for you: this do in remembrance of me. After the same manner also he took the cup when he had supped, saying, This cup is the new testament in my blood; this do ye as oft as ye drink it in remembrance of me. For as often as ye eat this bread, and drink this cup, ye do show the Lord's death till he come. (1 Cor. 11:23–26)

You have both the institution and the nature, the use and ends of this ordinance in these words; and I shall speak so briefly to them and under such short heads, as those who are young and less experienced may do well to retain.

THE INSTITUTION OF THE ORDINANCE

First, there is the institution of it; I received it, said he, from the Lord; and he received it on this account, that the Lord appointed it; and if you would come in faith unto this ordinance, you are to consider two things in this institution:

1. The authority of Christ. It was the Lord: the Lord, the head and king of the church; our Lord, our lawgiver, our ruler, he has appointed this service; and if you would have your performance of it an act of obedience, acceptable to God, you must get your conscience influenced with the authority of Christ, that we can give this reason in the presence of God, why we come together to perform this service, it is because Jesus Christ our Lord has appointed it; he has required it of us: and what is done in obedience to his command, that is a part of our reasonable service, and therein we are accepted with God.

2 1 Cor. 5:7.
3 Luke 22:19.

2. In the institution of it there is also his love, which is manifested in the time of its appointment; the Lord Jesus, in that "same night in which he was betrayed." One would think that our Lord Jesus Christ, who knew all the troubles, the distresses, the anguish, the sufferings, the derelictions of God, which were coming upon him, and into which he was just now entering, would have had something else to think of besides this provision for his church. But his heart was filled with love to his people; and that love which carried him to all that darkness and difficulty that he was to go through, that love at the same time did move him to institute this ordinance for the benefit and advantage of his church. And this I shall only say, that that heart which is made spiritually sensible of the love of Jesus Christ in the institution of this ordinance, and in what this ordinance does represent, is truly prepared for communion with Christ in this ordinance. O let us all labor for this in particular, if possible, that through the power of the Spirit of God we may have some impressions of the love of Christ on our hearts! Brethren, if we have not brought it with us, if we do not yet find it in us, I pray let us be careful to endeavor that we do not go away without it. Thus you have what is to be observed in the institution itself, the authority and the love of Christ.

THE USE AND ENDS OF THE ORDINANCE

Secondly, I shall speak to the use and ends of this ordinance, and they are three: (1) recognition, (2) exhibition, (3) profession.[4]

RECOGNITION

1. Recognition, that is, the solemn calling over and remembrance of what is intended in this ordinance.

There is a habitual remembrance of Christ, what all believers ought continually to carry about them: and here lies the difference between those that are spiritual and those that are carnal; they all agree that Christians ought to have a continual remembrance of Christ; But what way shall we obtain it? Why, set up images and pictures of him in every corner of the house and chapel, that is to bring Christ to remembrance; that way carnal men take for this purpose. But the way believers have to bring Christ to remembrance is by the Spirit of

---

4   In this discourse, Owen will only discuss "recognition," leaving "exhibition" to discourse 14. Owen does not return to discuss "profession," at least in the order of the discourses as they are presented in their posthumous publication. However, the way in which the Lord's Supper entails a "profession" of faith is a subject he discusses in discourse 4 above.

Christ working through the word. We have no image of Christ but the word; and the Spirit represents Christ to us thereby, wherein he is evidently crucified before our eyes. But this recognition I speak of, is a solemn remembrance in the way of an ordinance, wherein unto the internal actings of our minds there is added the external representation of the signs that God has appointed, do this "in remembrance of me." It is twice mentioned, in verses 24, 25.

Concerning this remembrance we may consider two things, (1) what is the object of this remembrance, or recognition; and, (2) what is the act of it. What we are to remember, and what is that act of remembrance that is acceptable to God in this ordinance.

(1) What is the object of this remembrance. The object of this remembrance principally is Christ: but it is not Christ absolutely considered; it is Christ in those circumstances wherein he then was: do it in remembrance of me says he, as I am sent of God, designed to be a sacrifice for the sins of the elect, and as I am now going to die for that end and purpose; so do it in remembrance of me. Wherefore there are these four things that we are to remember of Christ as proposed in those circumstances wherein he will be remembered. And I will be careful not to mention anything but what the meanest of us may bring into present exercise at the ordinance.

[1] Remember the grace and love of God, even the Father, in sending Christ, in setting him forth and proposing him to us. This is everywhere mentioned in Scripture. We are minded of this in Scripture whenever we are called to thoughts of the death of Christ. "God so loved the world" as to give "his only begotten Son" (John 3:16). God set him forth "to be a propitiation through faith in his blood" (Rom. 3:25). "God commendeth his love to us in that while we were yet sinners, Christ died for us" (Rom. 5:8). Remember, I pray you, the unspeakable grace and love of God in sending, giving, and setting forth Jesus Christ to be the propitiation.

Now how does this ordinance guide us in calling this love and grace of God to remembrance? Why in this, in that it is in the way of a furnished Table provided for us. So God has expressed his love in this matter. "In this mountain shall the LORD of hosts make unto all people a feast of fat things, a feast of wines on the lees, of fat things full of marrow, of wines on the lees well refined" (Isa. 25:6). The preparation of the Table here is to mind us to call to remembrance the love and grace of God, in sending and exhibiting his Son Jesus Christ to be a ransom and propitiation for us. That is the first thing.

[2] Remember in particular the love of Jesus Christ, as God-man, in giving himself for us. This love is frequently proposed to us with what he did for us; and it is represented peculiarly in this ordinance. "Who loved me, and gave

himself for me,"[5] says the apostle. Faith will never be able to live upon the last expression, "gave himself for me," unless it can rise up to the first, "who loved me." "Who loved us, and washed us from our sins in his own blood," etc. (Rev. 1:5–6).

I think we are all satisfied in this, that in calling Christ to remembrance we should in an especial manner call the love of Christ to remembrance. And that soul in whom God shall work a sense of the love of Christ in any measure (for it is past comprehension, and our minds and souls are apt to lose themselves in it, when we attempt to fix our thoughts upon it), that he who is God-man should do thus for us, it is too great for anything but faith, which can rest in that which it can no way comprehend, if it go to try the depth, and breadth, and length of it, to fathom its dimensions, and consider it with reason; for it is past all understanding; but faith can rest in what it cannot comprehend. So should we remember the love of Christ, of him who is God-man, who gave himself for us, and will be remembered in this ordinance.

[3] We shall not manage our spirits aright as to this first part of the duty, the end of the ordinance in recognition, unless we call over and remember what was the ground upon which the profit and benefit of the sufferings of Christ does redound[6] to us.

Let us remember that this is no other but that eternal covenant and compact that was between the Father and the Son, that Christ should undertake for sinners, and that what he did in that undertaking should be done on their behalf, should be reckoned to them and accounted as theirs. So our Savior speaks, "Sacrifice and offering thou didst not desire: mine ears hast thou opened: burnt-offering and sin-offering hast thou not required. Then said I, Lo, I come; in the volume of the book it is written of me," etc. (Ps. 40:6–7).

Christ does that in our behalf which sacrifice and burnt offerings could not perform. We have this covenant declared at large, "Yet it pleased the Lord to bruise him, he hath put him to grief: when thou shalt make his soul an offering for sin, he shall see his seed," etc. (Isa. 53:10–11). Pray, brethren, be wise and understanding in this matter, and not children in calling over and remembering Christ in this ordinance. Remember the counsel of peace that was between them both, when it was agreed on the part of Christ to undertake and answer for what we had done; and upon the part of God the Father, that upon his so doing, righteousness, life and salvation should be given to sinners.

5 Gal. 2:20.
6 I.e., rebound or return.

[4] Remember the sufferings of Christ. This is a main thing. Now the sufferings of Christ may be considered three ways, {1} The sufferings in his soul. {2} The sufferings in his body. {3} The sufferings of his person in the dissolution of his human nature, soul and body, by death itself.

{1} Remember the sufferings in his soul: and they were of two sorts, 1st, privative; his sufferings in the desertion and dereliction of God his Father; and, 2ndly, positive; in the emission of the sense of God's wrath, and the curse of the law on his soul.

1st, the head of Christ's sufferings was in the divine desertion, whence he cried out, "My God, my God, why hast thou forsaken me?"[7] It is certain, Christ was forsaken of God; he had not else so complained; forsaken of God in his soul; how? The divine nature in the second person did not forsake the human; nor did the divine nature in the third person forsake the human, as to the whole work of sanctification and holiness, but kept alive in Christ all grace whatsoever, all grace in that fullness whereof he had ever been partaker. But the desertion was as to all influence of comfort and all evidence of love from God the Father, who is the fountain of love and comfort, administered by the Holy Ghost. Hence some of our divines have not spared to say, that Christ did despair in that great cry, "My God, my God," etc. Now despair signifies two things, a total want of the evidence of faith, as to acceptance with God; and a resolution in the soul to seek no farther after it, and not to wait for it from that fountain. In the first way Christ did despair; that is, penal only; in the latter he did not, that is, sinful also. There was a total interception of all evidence of love from God, but not a ceasing in him to wait upon God for the manifestation of that love in his appointed time. Remember Christ was thus forsaken that his people might never be forsaken.

2ndly, there were sufferings positive in his soul when he was made sin and a curse for us, and had a sense of the wrath and anger of God on his soul. This brought those expressions concerning him, and from him; he "began to be sore amazed," and said, "My soul is exceeding sorrowful, even unto death."[8] He was "in an agony."[9] I desire no more for my soul everlastingly to confute that blasphemy, that Christ died only as a martyr to confirm the truth he had preached, but the consideration of this one thing. For courage, resolution and cheerfulness are the principal virtues and graces in him who dies only as a martyr; but for him who had the weight of the wrath of God and the curse of the law upon his soul, it became him to be "in an agony," to

7 Ps. 22:1.
8 Mark 14:33–34.
9 Luke 22:44.

sweat "great drops of blood,"¹⁰ to cry out, "My God, my God, why hast thou forsaken me?" Which, had he been called to for nothing else but barely to confirm the truth he had preached, he would have done without much trouble or shaking of mind.

{2} I shall not now speak of the sufferings in his body, which I am afraid we do not consider enough. Some poor souls are apt to consider nothing but the sufferings of his body, and some do not enough consider them. We may call this over some other time, as also the sufferings of his person in the dissolution of his human nature, by a separation of the soul from the body, which was also comprised in the curse.

Do this "in remembrance of me." What are we to remember? These are things of no great research; they are not hard and difficult, but such as we all may come up to the practice of in the administration of this very ordinance. Remember the unspeakable grace and love of God in setting forth Christ to be a propitiation. Remember the love of Christ who gave himself for us, notwithstanding he knew all that would befall him on our account. Remember the compact and agreement between the Father and the Son, that what was due to us he should undergo, and the benefit of what he did should redound to us: remember the greatness of the work he undertook for these ends; in the sufferings of his whole person, when he would redeem his church with his own blood.

(2) One word for the act of remembrance, and I have done. How shall we remember? Remembrance in itself is a solemn calling over of what is true and past; and there are two things required in our remembrance; the first is, faith; and the second is, thankfulness.

First, faith; so to call it over as to believe it. But who does not believe it? Why, truly, brethren, many believe the story of it, or the fact, who do not believe it to that advantage for themselves, as they ought to do. In a word, we are so to believe it, as to put our trust for life and salvation in those things that we call to remembrance. Trust and confidence belong to the essence of saving faith. So remember these things as to place your trust in them. Shall I gather up your workings of faith into one expression? The apostle calls it, the receiving the atonement (Rom. 5:11). If God help us afresh to receive the atonement at this time, we have discharged our duty in this ordinance; for here is the atonement proposed from the love of God, and from the love of Christ by virtue of the compact between the Father and the Son, through the sufferings and sacrifice of Christ, in his whole person, soul and body.

10 Luke 22:44.

Here is an atonement with God proposed unto us; the working of our faith is to receive it, or to believe it so as to approve of it as an excellent way, full of wisdom, goodness, holiness; to embrace it and trust in it.

Secondly, remember that among the offerings of old which were appointed to shadow out the death of Christ, there was a thank offering, for there was a burning of the fat upon the altar of thank offering,[11] to signify there was thankfulness to God always as part of the remembrance of the sacrifice that Christ made for us. Receive the atonement, and be thankful.

The Lord lead us into the practice of these things.

---

11   Owen is alluding to the offering of thanksgiving described in Lev. 7:12–15.

Discourse 14

The Nature, Use, and Administration of the Ordinance Itself Continued

THE LAST TIME I SPOKE TO YOU on this occasion, I told you that the grace of God, and our duty in this ordinance, might be drawn under the three heads of recognition, or calling over, of exhibition, and of profession.[1] The first of these I then spoke unto, and showed you what we are to recognize or call over therein.

EXHIBITION AND RECEPTION[2]

2. The second thing is, exhibition and reception; exhibition on the part of Christ, reception on our part, wherein the essence of this ordinance does consist. I shall briefly explain it to you, rather now to stir up faith unto exercise, than to instruct in the doctrine. And that we may exercise our faith aright, we may consider, (1) who it is that makes an exhibition, that offers, proposes, and gives something to us at this time in this ordinance. (2) What it is that is exhibited, proposed, and communicated in this ordinance. And, (3) how or in what manner we receive it.

(1) Who is it that makes an exhibition? It is Christ himself. When Christ was given for us, God the Father gave him, and set him forth to be a propitiation; but in this exhibition it is Christ himself, I say, that is the immediate exhibiter. The tender that is made of, whatever it be, it is made by Christ. And, as our faith stands in need of directions and boundaries to be given to it in this holy duty, it will direct our faith to consider Jesus Christ present

---

1 See note above. Owen does not return to discuss "profession" in the published order of the discourses presented here. He discusses the subject in that which is published as discourse 4.

2 Continuing from discourse 13.

among us by his Spirit, and by his word, making this tender, or this exhibition unto us. It is Christ that does it, which calls out our faith unto an immediate exercise on his person.

(2) What is it Christ does exhibit and propose to us? [1] Not empty and outward signs. God never instituted such things in his church. From the foundation of the world he never designed to feed his people with such outward symbols. Those under the Old Testament were not empty, though they had not a fullness like those under the New: they had not a fullness, because they had respect to what was yet to come, and could not be filled with that light, that grace, that evidence of the things themselves, as the present signs are, which are accomplished. Christ does not give us empty signs.

Nor, [2] does Christ give us his flesh and blood, taken in a carnal sense. If men would believe him, he has told us a long time ago, when that doubt arose upon that declaration of his eating his flesh and drinking his blood, (though he did not then speak of the sacrament, but of that which was the essence and life of it), "How can this man give us his flesh to eat?" (John 6:52). He told us, that eating his flesh profited nothing, in that way they thought of eating it; for they apprehended, as the Papists do now, that they were to eat flesh, body, bones, and all. Why, says he, "The flesh profits nothing"; "it is the Spirit that quickens";[3] that power that is to be communicated to you is by the Spirit. So that Christ does not give us his flesh and blood in a carnal manner, as the men at Capernaum thought, and others look for. This would not feed our souls.

But then, what is it that Christ does exhibit, that we may exercise our faith upon? I say, it is himself as immediately discharging his great office of a priest, being sacrificed for us. It is himself as accompanied with all the benefits of that great part of his mediation in dying for us. May the Lord stir up our hearts to believe that the tender Christ makes unto us is originally and principally of himself, because all the benefits of his mediation arise from that fountain and spring, when God purchased the church with his own blood. A way this is which the Lord Jesus Christ, who is the wisdom of God, has found out and appointed to make a special tender of his person to our souls, to be received by us. And he tenders himself in the discharge of his mediation in the most amiable and most glorious representation of himself to the soul of a sinner. Christ is glorious in himself, in all his offices, and in all the representations that are made of him in the Scripture unto our faith; but Christ is most amiable, most beautiful, most glorious to the soul of a believing sinner, when he

---

3 John 6:63.

is represented as dying, making atonement for sin, making peace for sinners, as bearing our iniquities; satisfying the wrath of God, and curse of the law, to draw out our hearts unto faith and love. Christ in this ordinance makes such a representation of himself as bleeding for us, making atonement for our sins, and sealing the everlasting covenant: and he proposes himself unto us with all the benefits of his death, of that redemption he wrought out for us, peace with God, making an end of sin, bringing in everlasting righteousness, and the like. I intend only to remind you of these things, for we are at a loss sometimes as to the exercise of faith in and under this duty.

(3) There remains to be considered, reception; for unless it be received, there is nothing done to any saving purpose. Notwithstanding all this tender that is made, the issue of all the benefit and consolation lies upon receiving.

There are two ways whereby we do receive Christ: [1] we receive him sacramentally, by obedience in church order. And [2] we receive him spiritually and really by faith, or believing in him.

[1] We receive him sacramentally. This consists in the due and orderly performance of what he has appointed in his word for this end and purpose, that therein and thereby he may exhibit himself to our souls. It does not consist (as some have thought) in partaking of the elements; that is but one part of it, and but one small part. Our sacramental reception consists in the due observation of the whole order of the institution according to the mind of Christ.

[2] Spiritually, we receive him by faith: and if we could rightly understand that special act of faith which we are to exercise in the reception of Christ when he does thus exhibit himself to us, then should we glorify God, then should we bring in advantage to our own souls.

I have but a word to say, and that is this, it is that acting of faith which is now required of us which draws nearest unto spiritual, sensible experience. Faith has many degrees and many acts, some at a kind of distance from the object in mere reliance and recumbency; and many other acts of faith make very near approaches to the object, and rise up to sensible experience. It should be (if God would help us) such an act of faith as rises up nearest to a sensible experience. It is that which the Holy Ghost would teach us by this ordinance, when we receive it by eating and drinking, which are things of sense; and things of sense are chosen to express faith wrought up to an experience. And they who had some apprehension hereof, that it must be a peculiar acting of faith and rising up to a spiritual experience, but finding nothing of the light and power of it in their own souls, gave birth to transubstantiation, that they might do that with their mouths and teeth which they could not do with their souls.

Faith should rise up to an experience in two things, {1} in representation. {2} In incorporation.

{1} The thing we are to aim at, to be carried unto by faith in this ordinance is, that there may be a near and evident representation of Christ in his tender unto our souls; faith being satisfied in it; faith being in this matter the evidence of things not seen, making it exist in the soul, making Christ more present to the soul than he would be to our bodily eyes, if he were among us; more assuredly so. Faith should rise up to evidence in that near and close representation it makes of Christ in this exhibition of himself.

And, {2} faith is to answer the end of eating and drinking, which is incorporation. We are so to receive Christ, as to receive him into a spiritual incorporation, that the flesh and blood of Christ as communicated in this ordinance through faith may be turned and changed in our hearts into spiritual vital principles, and unto growth and satisfaction. These are the three things we receive by nourishment, and wherein incorporation does consist, there is an increase and quickening of vital principles, there is growth, and there is satisfaction in receiving suitable food and nourishment. Faith, I say, should rise up to these three things in its acts. I mention these things to direct the actings of our faith in this holy administration.

Discourse 15

The Present Exercise of Faith in This Ordinance

September 5, 1675

I SHALL OFFER A FEW WORDS to direct you in the present exercise of faith in this ordinance. I design no more but to give occasion to that particular exercise of faith which is now required of us, whereby we may sanctify the name of God in a due manner, give glory to him by believing, and receive establishment unto our own souls: and I would do it by minding you of that word of our Lord Jesus Christ in John 12:32. "And I, if I be lifted up from the earth, will draw all men unto me."

What he means by his lifting up, the evangelist expounds in the next words, which are these, "This he spake signifying what death he should die."[1] So that the lifting up of Christ on the cross, is that which he lays as the foundation of his drawing sinners unto him. No sinner will come near to Christ unless he be drawn; and to be drawn is to be made willing to come unto him, and to follow him in chains of love. Christ draws none to him, whether they will or no, but he casts on their minds, hearts and wills the cords of his grace and love, working in them powerfully, working on them kindly, to cause them to choose him, to come to him and to follow him. "Draw me; we will run after thee."[2] The great principle and fountain from whence the drawing efficacy and power of grace does proceed is, from the lifting up of Christ. Drawing grace is manifested in, and drawing love proceeds from the sufferings of Jesus Christ on the cross.

1 John 12:33.
2 Song 1:4.

But that which I would just mind you of at present is this, that the look of faith unto Christ as lifted up, is the only means of bringing our souls near to him. Our faith is often expressed by looking unto Christ: "Look unto me," says he, "and be ye saved, all the ends of the earth" (Isa. 45:22). The conclusion is, that those who so look unto him shall be justified and saved. "Behold me, behold me" (Isa. 65:1). And it is the great promise of the efficacy of the Spirit poured out upon us, that we shall look upon him whom we have pierced (Zech. 12:10). God calls us to look off from all other things, look off from the law, look off from self, look off from sin, look only unto Christ. Is Christ said to be lifted up in his death? And to die that manner of death wherein he was lifted up on the cross? So it was expressed in the type; the brazen serpent was lifted up on a pole, that those who were smote with the fiery serpents might look to it.[3] If the soul can but turn an eye of faith unto Jesus Christ as thus lifted up, it will receive healing; though the sight of one be not so clear as the sight of another. All had not a like sharpness of sight that looked to the brazen serpent; nor have all the like vigor of faith to look to Christ; but one sincere look to Christ is pleasing to him, so as he says. "Thou hast ravished my heart, my sister, my spouse, thou hast ravished my heart with one of thine eyes" (Song 4:9). A soul sensible of guilt and sin, that casts but one look of faith to Christ as lifted up, it even raises the heart of Christ himself, and such a soul shall not go away unrefreshed, unrelieved.

Now, brethren, the end of this ordinance is to lift up Christ in representation: as he was lifted up really on the cross, and as in the whole preaching of the gospel Christ is evidently crucified before our eyes, so more especially in the administration of this ordinance. Do we see, then wherein the special acting of faith in this ordinance does consist? God forbid we should neglect the stirring up our hearts unto the particular acting of faith in Jesus Christ, who herein is lifted up before us. That which we are to endeavor in this ordinance is to get a view by faith, faith working by thoughts, by meditation, acting by love, a view of Christ as lifted up, that is, as bearing our iniquities in his own body on the tree. What did Christ do on the tree? What was he lifted up for, if it was not to bear our sins? Out of his love and zeal to the glory of God, and out of compassion to the souls of men, Christ bore the guilt and punishment of sin, and made expiation for it. O that God in this ordinance would give our souls a view of him! I shall give it to myself and to you in charge at

---

3 Owen is alluding to that occasion when Moses made a brass ("brazen") snake and lifted it up so that the Israelites would look to it for healing from their envenomation by the snakes God sent in judgment for their sin (Num. 21:6–9). Christ interprets the event as a typological representation of his redemptive mission in John 3:14.

this time: if we have a view of Christ by faith as lifted up, our hearts will be drawn nearer to him. If we find not our hearts in any manner drawn nearer to him, it is much to be feared we have not had a view of him as bearing our iniquities. Take therefore this one remembrance as to the acting of faith in the administration of this ordinance, labor to have it fixed upon Christ as bearing sin, making atonement for it, with his heart full of love to accomplish a cause in righteousness and truth.

The Present Exercise of Faith in This Ordinance Continued

October 31, 1675

TO WHET OUR MINDS, and lead us to a particular exercise of faith and love in this duty, I shall add a few words from that Scripture which I have already spoken something to, upon this occasion, namely, John 12:32. "And I, if I be lifted up from the earth, will draw all men unto me."

THE ENDS OF CHRIST BEING "LIFTED UP"

This lifting up, as I said before, was the lifting up of Christ on the cross, when as the apostle Peter tells us, he "bore," or, as the word is, he carried up, "our sins in his own body on the tree."[1] Christ died for three ends, (1) to answer an institution. (2) To fulfil a type; and, (3) To be a moral representation of the work of God in his death.

1. It was to answer the institution, that he who was hanged on a tree was accursed of God (Deut. 21:23). There were many other ways appointed of God to put malefactors to death among the Jews; some were stoned, in some cases they were burned with fire; but it is only by God appointed, that he that was hanged on a tree was accursed of God: and Christ died that death, to show, that it was he who underwent the curse of God, as the apostle shows. He was "made a curse for us, as it is written, cursed is every one that hangs on a tree" (Gal. 3:13).

2. Christ died that death to fulfil a type. For it was a bloody and most painful death, yet it was a death wherein a bone of him was not broken, typified

1   1 Pet. 2:24.

of him in the paschal lamb, of which not a bone was to be broken. Christ was lifted up on the cross to fulfill that type, that though his death was bitter, lingering, painful, shameful, yet not a bone was broke; that everyone might have a whole Christ, an entire Savior, notwithstanding all his suffering and rending on our behalf.

3. He was so lifted up that it might be a moral representation unto all, to answer that other type also of the serpent lifted up in the wilderness; so that he was the person that might say, "Behold me, behold me."[2] He was lifted up between heaven and earth, that all creatures might see God had set him forth to be a propitiation.

And I, when I am lifted up, what will he then do? When I have answered the curse, when I have fulfilled the types, when I have complied with the will of God in being a propitiation, I will draw all men unto me. It is placed upon Christ's lifting up; now that is actually past; nor was it done merely while Christ was hanging on the cross. There are two ways whereby there is a representation made of Christ being lifted up, to draw men unto him.

(1) By the preaching of the word. So the apostle tells us, that Jesus Christ was "evidently set forth crucified" among them, before their eyes (Gal. 3:1). The great end of preaching the word is to represent evidently Christ crucified; it is to lift up Christ that he may draw sinners unto him. And, (2) it is represented in this ordinance of the Lord's Supper, wherein we show forth his death. Christ is peculiarly and eminently lifted up in this ordinance, because it is a peculiar and eminent representation of his death.

THE WAYS CHRIST DRAWS SINNERS TO HIMSELF IN THIS ORDINANCE

Now there are two ways of Christ's drawing persons to himself, (1) his way of drawing sinners to him, by faith and repentance. (2) His way of drawing believers to him, as to actual communion with him.

Christ draws sinners to him by faith and repentance, as he is lifted up in the preaching of the word; and he draws believers to him, as unto actual communion, as by the word, so in an especial manner by this ordinance. I shall only speak a word on the latter, how Christ is lifted up in this ordinance that represents his death unto us, or, how he draws us into actual communion with him.

1. He does it by his love. The principal thing that is always to be considered in the lifting up of Christ, is his love. "Who loved me," says the apostle,

2   Isa. 65:1.

"and gave himself for me":[3] and, who "loved us, and washed us from our sins in his own blood."[4] I could show you, that love is attractive, that it is encouraging and constraining. I will only leave this with you, whatever apprehensions God in this ordinance shall give you of the love of Christ, you have therein an experience of Christ's drawing you, as he is lifted up, unto actual communion with him. It is of great concernment to you. Christ is never so lovely unto the soul of a sinner as when he is considered as lifted up, that is, as undergoing the curse of God, that a blessing might come upon us. O that he who has loved us, and because he has loved us, would draw us with the cords of his loving-kindness, as God says he does, "Yea, I have loved thee with an everlasting love, therefore with loving-kindness have I drawn thee" (Jer. 31:3).

2. The sufferings of Christ in soul and body are attractive of, and do draw the souls of believers to him. "They shall look on me whom they have pierced," and "mourn."[5] It is a look to Christ as pierced for sin under his sufferings that is attractive to the souls of believers in this ordinance, because these sufferings were for us. Call to mind, brethren, some of these texts of Scripture; see what God will give you out of them. He was made "sin for us, who knew no sin, that we might be made the righteousness of God in him."[6] He was "made a curse for us";[7] and he "bore our sins in his own body on the tree";[8] and died, "the just for the unjust, that he might bring us unto God."[9] If Jesus Christ be pleased to let in a sense of his sufferings for us by these Scriptures upon our souls, then we have another experience of his drawing us, as he is lifted up.

3. Christ draws us as he is lifted up, by the effects of it. What was he lifted up for? It was to make peace with God through his blood. "God was in Christ reconciling the world unto himself,"[10] When? When he "made him to be sin for us, who knew no sin."[11] It is the sacrifice of atonement; it is the sacrifice wherewith the covenant between God and us was sealed. This is one notion of the Supper of our Lord. Covenants were confirmed with sacrifice. Isaac made a covenant with Abimelech, and confirmed it with sacrifice.[12] So it was

---

3   Gal. 2:20.
4   Rev. 1:5.
5   Zech. 12:10.
6   2 Cor. 5:21.
7   Gal 3.13.
8   1 Pet. 2:24.
9   1 Pet. 3:18.
10 2 Cor. 5:19.
11 2 Cor. 5:21.
12 Owen is alluding to Gen. 26:26–33.

with Jacob and Laban;[13] and in both places, when they had confirmed the covenant with a sacrifice, they had a feast upon the sacrifice. Christ by his sacrifice has ratified the covenant between God and us, and invites us in this ordinance to a participation of it. He draws us by it to faith in him as he has made an atonement by his sacrifice.

These are some of the ways whereby Christ draws the souls of believers unto communion with him in this ordinance, that represents him as lifted up, by expressing his love, by representing his sufferings, and tendering the sealing of the covenant as confirmed with a sacrifice, inviting us to feed on the remainder of the sacrifice that is left to us for the nourishment of our souls. O that he would cast some of these cords of love upon our souls! For if he should be lifted up, and we should not come, if we should find no cords of love cast upon us to draw us into actual communion, we should have no advantage by this ordinance.

WHAT IS REQUIRED OF US TO COME INTO COMMUNION WITH CHRIST IN THIS ORDINANCE

How shall we come in actual communion unto Christ in this ordinance upon his drawing? What is required of us? Why,

1. We are to come by faith, to receive the atonement (Rom. 5:11). We come to a due communion with Christ in this ordinance, if we come to receive the atonement made by his death, as full of divine wisdom, grace and love, and as the truth and faithfulness of God is confirmed in it, to receive and lay hold on this atonement, that we may have peace with God. "Let him take hold of my strength," and he shall be at "peace with me" (Isa. 27:5). Brethren, here is the arm of God, Christ the power of God, Christ lifted up. We ourselves have sinned and provoked God, what shall we do? Shall we set briers and thorns in battle array against God? No, says he, I will pass through and devour such persons: What then? "Let him take hold of my strength," of my arm, and be at peace. God speaks this to every soul of us in this lifting up of Christ. Now receive the atonement as full of infinite wisdom, holiness and truth.

2. Faith comes and brings the soul to Christ as he is thus lifted up, but it is always accompanied with love, whereby the soul adheres to Christ when it is come.

Does faith bring us to Christ on his drawing, to receive the atonement? Set love at work to cleave unto him, to take him into our hearts and souls, and to abide with him.

---

13 Owen is alluding to Gen. 31:43–55.

3. It is to come with mourning and godly sorrow, because of our own sins. Look unto him whom we have pierced, and mourn. These things are very consistent. Do not think we speak things at random: they are consistent in experience, that we should receive Christ as making an atonement, and have peace with God in the pardon of our sins, and nevertheless mourn for our own iniquities. The Lord give experience of them in your hearts.

Let us now pray that some of these cords wherewith he draws the souls of believers, may be on our souls in this ordinance.

The Exchange between Christ and the Sinner Represented in the Ordinance

WHEN WE HAVE OPPORTUNITY of speaking to you on these occasions, it is for the direction of the exercise of your faith in this ordinance in a due manner. Here is a representation of the death of Christ; and there is in the word a representation of that which we should principally consider, and act faith with respect unto in the representation that is made in this ordinance, and that is of a blessed change and commutation that is made between Christ and believers, in the imputation of their sins unto him, and in the imputation of his righteousness unto them: and the principal part of the life and exercise of faith, consists in a due consideration and improvement thereof. God taught this to the church of the Old Testament in the type of the offering of the scapegoat. "And Aaron shall lay both his hands on the head of the live goat, and confess over him all the iniquities of the children of Israel, and all their transgressions in all their sins, putting them upon the head of the goat," etc. (Lev. 16:21).

THE IMPUTATION OF THE SINNER'S INIQUITIES AND GUILT TO CHRIST, AND THE ACT OF FAITH THEREIN

Aaron was not only to confess all the sins and iniquities of the people over the head of the goat, but he was to put all their sins upon him. Here is a double act, the confession of sin, which is, as it were, the gathering of all their sins together; and the putting of them on the goat, to give a lively representation of it unto faith. So God did instruct Aaron to the putting of the guilt of our iniquities typically upon the sacrifice, really upon Jesus Christ.

He does not say, he shall bear the punishment, but he shall take the sin itself, that is, as to the guilt of it, and carry it quite away: and therefore in the sacrifice appointed in Deuteronomy 21 for expiation of an uncertain murder, when a man was killed, and none knew who killed him, so none was liable to punishment, but there was guilt upon the land; then the elders of the city that was nearest the place where the murder was committed, to take away the guilt, were to cut off the neck of an heifer by God's appointment, and that took away the guilt. Thus did God instruct the church under the Old Testament in this great sovereign act of his wisdom and righteousness, in transferring the guilt of sin from the church unto Christ. Therefore the prophet says, "the LORD has laid on him the iniquities of us all" (Isa. 53:6). What then? "By his stripes we are healed" (Isa. 53:5). The stripes were all due to us; but they were due to us for our iniquities, and for no other cause. Now our iniquities being transferred to Christ, all the stripes came to be his, and the healing came to be ours. To the same purpose the apostle says, he was made "sin for us, who knew no sin, that we might be made the righteousness of God in him."[1] As we are made the righteousness of God in him, so he is made sin for us. We are made the righteousness of God in him by the imputation of his righteousness unto us; for our apostle is to be believed, that righteousness is by imputation; God imputes righteousness, says he. We have no righteousness before God but by imputation, and when we are made righteous, the righteousness of God, which God ordains, approves and accepts, it is the righteousness of Christ imputed to us. And how is he made sin for us? Because our sin is imputed to him. Some will say, he was made sin for us, that is, a sacrifice for sin; be it so; but nothing could be made an expiatory sacrifice, but it had first the sin imputed to it. Aaron shall put his hands on the goat, confessing all their sins over his head; be their sins on the head of the goat, or the expiatory sacrifice was nothing.

The same exchange you have again in Galatians 3:13–14, he was "made a curse for us." The curse was due to us, and this Christ was made for us: and to confirm our faith, God did institute a visible pledge long beforehand, to let us know he was made a curse for us; he had made it a sign of the curse for one to be hanged on a tree, as it is written, "Cursed is every one that hangs on a tree." What then comes to us? Why, "the blessing" of faithful Abraham.[2] What is that? "Abraham believed God, and it was accounted to him for righteousness."[3] Justification and acceptance with God is the blessing of

---

1   2 Cor. 5:21.
2   Gal. 3:14.
3   Gal. 3:6.

faithful Abraham. Here is the great exchange represented to us in Scripture in these things, that all our sins are transferred upon Christ by imputation, and the righteousness of Christ transferred to us by imputation. Both these are acts of God, and not our acts. It is God who imputes our sin to Christ; he has made him to be sin for us; and it is God who imputes the righteousness of Christ to us; it is God that justifies.[4] He who made Christ to be sin, he also makes us to be righteousness. These acts of God we ought to go over in our minds by faith, which is that I now call you to.

The way to apply the benefits and advantage of this great commutation to our souls, is in our minds by faith to seal to these acts of God. Christ in the gospel, and especially in this ordinance, is evidently crucified before our eyes (Gal. 3:1). God has set him forth to be a propitiation; so he is declared in this ordinance, and Christ at the same time calls us to him, come unto me: "look unto me, [. . .] all the ends of the earth."[5] Come with your burdens; come you that are heavy laden with the guilt of sin. What God has done in a way of righteous imputation, that we are to do in this ordinance in a way of believing. We are, by the divine help, to lay our sins by faith on Jesus Christ by closing with that act of God which is represented to us in the word, that God has imputed all our sins to Jesus Christ. Let you and I and all of us say amen by faith, so be it, O Lord. Let the guilt of all our sins be on the head of Jesus Christ; and therein admire the goodness, the grace, the love, the holiness, the infinite wisdom of God in this matter. If we were able to say amen to this great truth, we should have the comfort of it in our souls, to acquiesce in it, to find power and reality in it.

THE IMPUTATION OF CHRIST'S RIGHTEOUSNESS TO THE SINNER, AND THE ACT OF FAITH THEREIN

Then the other act of God is the imputation of the righteousness of Christ to us. It is not enough to us, that our sins are all carried away into a land not inhabited; we stand in need of a righteousness whereby we may be accepted before God. He makes us to be the righteousness of God; we do not make ourselves so, but are made so by the imputation of the righteousness of Christ.

Our second act of faith that God may stir us up unto in this ordinance, is to receive the atonement. So the apostle expresses it (Rom. 5:11), we receive together with it all the fruits of the atonement.

---

4   Owen is alluding to Rom. 8:33.
5   Isa. 45:22.

Now if the Lord will be pleased to stir up our hearts from under their deadness, to gather them in from their wanderings, to make us sensible of our concern, to give us the acting of faith in this matter, that truly and really the holy God has laid all our iniquities upon Christ, and tenders to us life, righteousness, justification, and mercy by him, we shall then have the fruit of this administration.

Discourse 18

Preparing Our Minds for the Exercise of Faith and Communion with God in This Ordinance

April 16, 1676

I SHALL OFFER A FEW WORDS with a view to prepare our minds to the exercise of faith and communion with God in this ordinance: and because we ought to be in the highest exercise of faith in this ordinance, I shall take occasion from those words which express as high an acting of faith, I think, as any is in the Scripture, I mean those words of the apostle in Galatians 2:20. "I am crucified with Christ; nevertheless I live; yet not I, but Christ liveth in me; and the life which I now live in the flesh, I live by the faith of the Son of God, who loved me, and gave himself for me."

THE ACT OF FAITH IN THIS ORDINANCE

Our inquiry now is, how we may act faith? It acts two ways,

1. By way of adherence, cleaving to, trusting and acquiescing in God in Christ, as declaring his love, grace and goodwill in his promises. This is the faith whereby we live, whereby we are justified; the faith without which this ordinance will not profit, but disadvantage us; for without this faith we cannot discern the Lord's body, we cannot discern him as crucified for us: this is that we are in an especial manner to examine ourselves about in reference to a participation of this ordinance, for self-examination is a gospel institution proper for this ordinance. And this is the faith whereby we are in Christ, without which a participation of the outward signs and pledges of Christ will

not avail us. So then with faith thus acting we are to be qualified and prepared unto a participation of this ordinance.

2. Another way by which faith ought to act in this ordinance, is that of special application. "Who loved me, and gave himself for me," this is faith acting by particular application. I hope the Lord has given us that faith whereby we may be prepared for this ordinance: and now I am to inquire and direct you a little in that faith which you may act in this ordinance; I say, it is this faith of special application to our own souls that God now requires we should act; and I prove it thus, it is because in this ordinance there is a proposition, tender and communication of Christ to everyone in particular: in the promise of the gospel Christ is proposed indefinitely to all that believe; and so the faith I mentioned before, of acquiescence in him, answers what is required of us by virtue of the promise in the gospel; but in this ordinance, by God's institution Christ is tendered and given to me and to thee, to everyone in particular; for it is by his institution that the elements in this ordinance are distributed to every particular person, to show, that there is a tender and communication of Christ to particular persons. Now such a particular communication is to be received by this particular faith, the faith of application, to receive him to our own souls.

And then moreover, one great end of the ordinance is manifestly, that it requires the acting of faith in a particular way of application to every one of us; it is for a farther incorporation of Christ in our souls; it is for receiving Christ as nourishment, as the bread that came down from heaven, as giving his body and blood for spiritual food. Now everyone knows, that whatever feasts be prepared in the world, unless everyone in particular takes his own portion, and eats and digests it, it will not turn to nourishment unto him. This particular act of application answers that eating, drinking and digesting, which the nature of the ordinance does require. So, brethren, this is that I aim at, that it is our duty in this ordinance to act a particular faith as to the application of Christ and all his benefits, each one to his own soul.

THE SPECIAL OBJECT OF FAITH

You will say then, what is the special object of this special faith? Truly that which the apostle tells us here, it is special love, in the first place; and it is the special design of the death of Christ, in the next place: "who loved me, and gave himself for me." The object you ought to fix upon in the exercise of this faith of application to your own souls is the special love of Christ, that Christ had a special love, not only to the church in general; but the truth is,

Christ had a special love for me in particular. It will be a very hard thing for you or me to rise up to an act of faith, that Christ has a love for us in particular, unless we can answer this question, Why should Christ love you or me in particular? What answer can I give hereto, when I know he does not love all the world? I can give but this answer to it, even because he would. I know nothing in me, or in any of you, that can deserve his love. Was there ever such a thing heard of, that Christ should have a particular love for such as we are? Would ever any person go and fix his love on a creature who was all over leprous? Is this the manner of man? Truly Christ would never have fixed his love upon any of our poor, defiled, leprous souls, but upon this one consideration, I know I can cleanse them, and I will. He loved us.

But what will he do with such deformed, polluted creatures as we are? Why, he "loved the church, and gave himself for it," that he might wash and purify it, and "present it to himself a glorious church, not having spot or wrinkle, or any such thing."[1] Though we are altogether deformed and defiled, though no example, no instance can be given in things below, or among the creatures, of any fixing love on such as we are; yet Christ has done it out of sovereign grace, with this resolution, that he would cleanse us with his own blood to make us fit for himself.

O that God would help you and me to some firm unshaken acts of faith, that Jesus Christ did out of sovereign grace love us in particular, and that in pursuit of this love he has washed us in his blood, to make us lovely and meet for himself! This is love to be adored and celebrated in time and to eternity.

This special love of Christ is not only to be considered by us in this special acting of faith, as free and undeserved, but it is to be considered as invincible, that would break through all oppositions, or whatever stood in the way, that nothing should hinder or turn him aside in his design of doing good to our souls. It is a glorious pitch that the spouse rises to in Canticle 8:7. "Many waters cannot quench love, neither can the floods drown it; if a man would give all the substance of his house for love, it would utterly be contemned"; speaking of her own love to Christ; nothing could quench, nothing could drown it, nothing could make a purchase of it from her, but her love was invincible and would carry her through all difficulties. O how much more was the love of Christ? For our love being once fixed on Christ, meets with no difficulties of that nature that the love of Christ met withal when it was fixed on us. What did the love of Christ meet with when it was fixed on us? That we must take along with us, namely the curse of the law was the first thing

1   Eph. 5:25–27.

that presented itself to him: "The soul that sinneth, it shall die."[2] "Cursed is every one that continues not in all things written in the book of the law to do them."[3] That he was to make his soul an offering for sin, was presented to him. We are to look on this love of Christ as sovereign and free, and with a design of making our souls lovely; so invincible also, that it broke up the eternal obstacles, that nothing could stand before it until it had accomplished his whole work and design: "who loved me, and gave himself for me."

I speak on this manner, and of these things, to encourage and direct the weakest and most unskillful in the mysteries of the gospel, to instruct them in the exercise of faith in this ordinance; and therefore, I say, that as this special faith (which I proved to you to be our duty in this ordinance) is to respect the love of Christ, so it is to respect more especially the peculiar acting of the love of Christ, whereby he gave himself for us; gave himself! How is that? Truly thus, brethren; the Lord help me to believe it, that I stood before the judgment-seat of God, charged with my original apostasy from him, and with all the sins of my life multiplied above the hairs of my head, and being ready to perish, to have the sentence pronounced against me; then Christ came and stood in my place, putting the sinner aside, and undertaking to answer this matter; "Let the poor sinner stand aside a while; come enter into rest, abide here in the cleft of the rock, I will undertake thy cause, and plead it out at God's judgment-seat."[4] In this undertaking, God spared him not: as if God should say, if you will stand in the place of the sinner, and undertake his cause, then it must go with you as with him; I will not spare. "Lo, I come," says Christ, notwithstanding this, "to do thy will, O God";[5] whatever thou dost require to make good this cause I have espoused, lo, I come to do it.

So Christ loved me and gave himself for me. Everlasting rest and peace will dwell upon our souls, if the Lord will be pleased to help us to exercise faith on Christ's love in this ordinance, wherein all these things are represented to us.

---

2 Ezek. 18:20.
3 Gal. 3:10.
4 Quotation marks original.
5 Heb. 10:7.

Discourse 19

Exercising Faith in the Death of Christ in This Ordinance

June 11, 1676

I am crucified with Christ, nevertheless I live; yet not I, but Christ liveth in me; and the life which I now live in the flesh, I live by the faith of the Son of God, who loved me, and gave himself for me.

GALATIANS 2:20

THE EXERCISE OF FAITH IN THE DEATH OF CHRIST

The apostle in this place is expressing the vigor, and indeed the triumph of the life of faith, "nevertheless I live." To show the excellency of that life, says he, "yet not I, but Christ liveth in me," etc. That which I would to our purpose observe from these words is this, that the exercise of faith on the death of Christ ("who loved me, and gave himself for me") is the very life of faith. This is that we are now called to, to the exercise of faith on the death of Christ; and I cannot more recommend it to you than by this observation, to show that the life of faith does greatly consist in this peculiar exercise of it upon the death of Christ. And that,

1. Because Christ in his death as the ordinance of God for the salvation of believing sinners, is the proper and peculiar object of faith, as it justifies and saves. Now when faith is in its exercise upon its direct immediate proper object, it is like a person that is feeding on his proper food, which gives refreshment, spirits and strength; for faith and its object are in Scripture set out as an appetite and food; and especially it is so represented to us in this

ordinance, where the spiritual food of our souls is conveyed to our faith under the symbol and representation of food to our bodies, which we eat and drink. Therefore, brethren, our faith is in its proper place, it is about its proper work, it is directing the soul to its special food when it is exercised about the death of Christ, as the ordinance of God for the salvation of sinners.

2. As the death of Christ is thus the immediate and direct object of our faith, for God has set him forth as "a propitiation" for sin, "through faith in his blood,"[1] which is the proper object of faith as it justifies, so the ultimate and supreme object of our faith is, the properties of God as manifested and glorified in the death of Christ; that you shall see how faith has its plain and full work in coming to this, "who loved me, and gave himself for me." The properties of God are God himself; the properties of God as manifested and glorified are God's name; and God himself and his name are the supreme and ultimate object of our faith and trust. All the inquiry then is, what special properties of the nature of God, God did design to manifest and glorify in the death of Christ, so as we should make them the special ultimate object of our faith, that which faith will find rest and satisfaction in, and wherein it will give glory to God? For the reason why God has made faith the alone instrument, and no other grace, of justification, and so of salvation, it is not because it is so fitted and suited to receive in us, as that it is the only grace whereby we give glory to God, and can do so.

HOW TO EXERCISE FAITH IN CHRIST'S DEATH IN THIS ORDINANCE

Now let us see, that we may know how to exercise faith therein, what are those properties of the divine nature which God designs to manifest and glorify in the death of Christ, that our faith may stand in, and be fixed upon them. I find several things that God distinctly proposes of his divine excellency for our faith to fix upon in the death of Christ.

1. His righteousness: "Whom God hath set forth to be a propitiation through faith in his blood to declare his righteousness" (Rom. 3:25). I shall not now show how, or wherein; but to me, this it is that manifests his righteousness in granting forgiveness of sin in the death of Christ, in that he caused all our iniquities to meet upon him. Remember, brethren, we are here to give God the glory he designed to himself in sending Christ to die for us; and he tells us plainly what it was, and therefore it is expected of us, that we should

1 Rom. 3:25.

give glory to him. Let us labor to be in the actual exercise of faith, whereby we may declare the righteousness of God in this thing.

2. God designed to glorify his love. This is more particularly insisted on than any property of God in this matter. "God so loved the world" as to send "his only begotten Son" (John 3:16). "God commended his love unto us, that when we were sinners Christ died for us" (Rom. 5:8). "Herein is love, not that we loved God, but that he loved us, and sent his Son to be the propitiation for our sins" (1 John 4:10). There is no property of the nature of God which he does so eminently design to glorify in the death of Christ as his love. That we may know that God is love; that the Father himself loves us, he has sent Jesus Christ out of his eternal love to save sinners; and if we have not due apprehensions of these things, it is not our appearing in this place that will give glory to God.

3. God does design to glorify his grace or pardoning mercy. "He has made us accepted in the Beloved," "to the praise of the glory of his grace" (Eph. 1:6). This God purposed, to make his grace in pardoning sinners very glorious by giving Christ to die for us.

4. God designed to glorify his wisdom. "He has abounded towards us in all wisdom and prudence" (Eph. 1:8). There appeared "the manifold wisdom of God" (Eph. 3:10). "Christ the power of God, and the wisdom of God" (1 Cor. 1:24).

Now let us gather up these things. The special ultimate act[2] of faith whereby we are justified, are those divine properties of God's nature which he designed to manifest in the death of Christ, his righteousness, his love, his grace, his wisdom.

The reason therefore why the life of faith does consist in its exercise on the death of Christ is, because the death of Christ is the immediate proper object of faith, as the ordinance of God for the salvation of sinners; and because the glorious properties of the nature of God, which are manifested in the death of Christ, are the ultimate object of our faith, wherein we give glory to him, and find rest to our own souls.

Let us then be called on and be stirred up to this exercise of faith upon this present occasion. And to that end,

1. We might consider the deplorable condition of all our souls without this blessed provision and ordinance of God for our deliverance by the death of Christ. We had been in a deplorable condition, the wrath of God abiding on us, had not God made this a blessed way for our deliverance.

---

2   The context indicates this is likely to be an error and that Owen intends "object," as per Goold.

2. If you would be found acting faith in this matter, labor to come up to a firm, vigorous assent of your minds, not only that these things are true, but that this is the way wherein God will be glorified to eternity. The truth of it is, that person who is firmly satisfied and heartily pleased, that this way of the death of Christ for the salvation of sinners by the forgiveness of sin, is the way whereby God is, and will be glorified, I say, that person is a true believer. Now let not your assent be only to this thing, that it is true, that Christ came into the world to save sinners; but to this, that this is the way whereby God is, and will be glorified. He will be glorified in pardoning such guilty creatures as we are, in imputing righteousness to such sinners as we are. He is glorified in laying all our iniquities on Christ. By this way, his righteousness, his love, grace and wisdom are all manifested; this is God's being glorified. If our souls come up to a free close with these things, that all these properties are manifested in this way, that is an act of faith, and may the Lord help us unto it.

3. Let us gather up our minds to this institution, whereby these things are represented to us. Here is represented the death of Christ, the immediate object of our faith, as God's ordinance. If the Lord help us to see it so represented to us, as that divine righteousness and wisdom, love and grace do all center therein, and appear eminently to our souls, we shall have communion with God in this ordinance.

Discourse 20

The Love of Christ in His Death for Sinners

September 3, 1676

YOU HAVE BEEN MINDED OF, and instructed in the nature and benefit of our love to God; and I shall take occasion thence a little to mind you of the love of Christ unto us, the love in an especial manner which he showed in dying for us, which is that we are here gathered together to remember and celebrate, not barely the death of Christ, but that which is the life of that death, the love of Christ in his death. And I would ground it on that which the apostle speaks in Romans 5:5. "The love of God is shed abroad in our hearts by the Holy Ghost, which is given unto us."

This is that which I know you all long for, and prize above life; the "loving-kindness" of God "is better than life."[1] Why so? "For," says he, "when we were yet without strength, in due time Christ died for the ungodly."[2]

An apprehension of the love of Christ as dying for us ungodly creatures, is that which is shed abroad in our hearts by the Holy Ghost. Do not let your minds go upon uncertainties: when the Holy Ghost gives you a due apprehension of Christ's love in dying for ungodly sinners, as we are, then is this love shed abroad in our hearts. The apostle there proceeds to show how great this love was in that Christ died; he died, not for good men, and righteous men, and for friends, but he died for the ungodly, for sinners, and for enemies.[3] This was great love indeed. We are here to remember that love of Christ

---

1 Ps. 63:3.
2 Rom. 5:6.
3 Owen is alluding to Rom. 5:7–8, 10.

wherewith he gave himself to death for us, when we were enemies, and would have continued so to eternity, had he not loved us and given himself for us.

Brethren, if we barely remember the love of Christ in the way of an ordinance and our hearts be not powerfully affected with it, we are in danger of being disadvantaged by our attendance. Pray remember it; you know how plainly I use to speak on these occasions; I say, we have frequent opportunities of remembering the love of Christ in dying for us, in this ordinance representing of it; but if our hearts be not powerfully influenced and affected by it, we shall be losers by the frequency of ordinances.

I will add one word more; according as our hearts are affected with the love of Christ, so will be our love to Christ, and no otherwise. And truly, even that faith which discovers too much selfishness is very dangerous. If we come here to act faith, to look for no other effect of it, but what evidence and sense we have of the pardon of our own sins, how our consciences may be quieted and cleared, faith ends in self; it is dangerous, lest it should be only a branch from, and commensurate with convictions. True faith acting itself on Christ in this ordinance will work by love unto Christ: I would not say, principally, or in the first place; I know poor creatures are apt to look after themselves, and their own relief; but it will so work also: and truly, brethren, this it will not do, we shall not have faith working by love toward him, unless we have some sense of the love of Christ on our hearts.

WAYS TO KNOW WHETHER OUR HEARTS ARE UNDER THE INFLUENCE OF CHRIST'S LOVE

How shall we know, whether our hearts are under the powerful influence of the love of Christ in dying for us? Why, the love of Christ in dying for us has three properties with it, which will have an influence on our souls, if we are affected with it.

1. It has a transforming power, property, and efficacy with it. They are plain truths I am speaking, but of great concern to our souls, to know whether we are affected with the love of Christ or not. If we are rightly affected with it, I say, it will transform and change our whole souls in some measure into the likeness of Christ. How so? I will tell you in the most familiar manner I am able; if you are affected with the love of Christ, it lays hold upon and possesses your affections; the affections being possessed, stir up many thoughts; thoughts are the very image of the soul, represent it, to show you what the soul is: and those things concerning which your thoughts do most abound, that carries the frame of the soul. Let a man profess what he will, if his thoughts

are generally conversant about earthly and worldly things, he has an earthly and worldly mind; and if [his] thoughts are conversant about sensual things, he has a sensual and carnal mind; for whatever he may outwardly say, as he thinks so is he; there is the image and likeness of the soul.

Now if we are affected with the love of Christ, it will beget in our souls many thoughts of Christ, in our lying down and in our rising up, in our beds, in our ways, on our occasions, as well as in ordinances. If indeed our hearts are affected with the love of Christ, our thoughts of Christ will abound, and those thoughts will work again on our affections, and conform our souls more and more unto the image of Jesus Christ. That man who thinks much of the earth, because affected with it, his soul is like the earth; and that man who thinks much on the love of Christ, because he is affected with it, his soul is like Christ.

If it has been thus with us, brethren, in our preparation for this ordinance, or at any time, that thoughts of Christ have not abounded, verily there has been a failing in us. Let us strive for the future to amend it, that we may find the love of Christ begetting in us many thoughts of him, working upon our affections, and with a transforming power change the frame of our souls into his own likeness.

Again, 2. The love of Christ, if we are affected with it, has an attractive power: "And I, if I be lifted up [. . .], will draw all men unto me" (John 12:32). I cannot stay to show you the drawing power and efficacy there is in the love of Christ when dying on the cross; but this I will say, it is that which converted the world of all that did believe. It was the love of Christ, set forth in his death as one crucified for them, that drew all men unto him. "When I am lifted up, when I have accomplished, manifested and evidenced the un-speakable love which I have for the sinful sons of men, in being lifted up for them, I will draw them unto me."[4] If you have a true sense, brethren, of the love of Christ in dying for you, it will draw your souls unto him. "Draw me, we will run after thee" (Song 1:4). I do not now speak to you about the first drawing of Christ, which is as unto believing; I hope Christ has so drawn all our souls, but the following efficacy of the love of Christ to draw souls that do believe nearer unto him. Whoever is sensible of this attractive power of the death of Christ, it will have this efficacy upon him, it will have adherence and delight; it will cause him more to cleave to Christ. The soul will cleave to Christ with delight that is affected with the attractive drawing power of his loving-kindness in his death. There is a great deal in that word, cleave unto

4   Quotation marks original.

Christ with love and delight, with the best of our affections and dearest of our valuations, to cleave to him with trust, and to him alone. I do but remind you of what you know, that you may reduce it into practice. Pray in this ordinance, labor to have such a sense of the drawing power of the love of Christ in his death, that you may resolve to cleave unto him with full purpose of heart, to cleave unto this Christ who has thus loved us.

3. Whenever we are affected with the love of Christ, it is accompanied with a constraining power. "The love of Christ constraineth us" (2 Cor. 5:14), and that constraint is unto obedience; it constrains us to judge that we ought to live to him who died for us. It is a blessed thing, brethren, to walk in our obedience under a sense of the constraining efficacy of the love of Christ. Take but this one word to discover to you, whether you walk in your obedience under a sense of the constraining power of Christ, it comprehends all others. "His commandments are not grievous" (1 John 5:3). When a soul works out of love, what it does is "not grievous." And the inward and outward commands of Christ will be grievous to all that are not under the constraining power and efficacy of his love.

I have no more to say but only to tell you, that we should labor to have our hearts affected with the love of Christ in this ordinance. I have showed you the danger, if it be otherwise; and given you some ways to examine your hearts, whether they are so affected or not. The Lord grant that where they are, it may be increased; and where they are not, that God would renew it by his Spirit in us.

Being Affected by the Love That "Passeth Knowledge"

October 29, 1676

WE HAVE HAD, through the providence of God, so good and so seasonable a word unto the present occasion, that there is no need, as well as but little time to offer any thing farther unto you. Yet a few words in compliance with what we have heard, may not be altogether unseasonable, or unuseful.

Our business and duty is to set forth the sufferings and death of our Lord Jesus Christ, and therein principally to call to mind his love. What you have heard may very well occasion us to think of that passage of the apostle wherein he earnestly prays for them: "and to know the love of Christ which passeth knowledge" (Eph. 3:19).

This is a peculiar kind of expression; the meaning is, that we may know that experimentally which we cannot know comprehensively; that we may know that in its power and effects, which we cannot comprehend in its nature and depths. A weary person may receive refreshment from a spring who cannot fathom the depths of the ocean from whence it does proceed. And if we would have our hearts in this ordinance, and at other times, affected with the love of Christ, which is the thing we are to aim at (to know his love, and to experience the power of it) it is of great advantage to us to consider, that it is such a love as passes knowledge, that our faith concerning it must issue in admiration, not comprehension.

I shall name two or three things that may give a little sense of this love as it passes knowledge.

1. The love of Christ is the fountain and spring of all the glory that is in heaven, or shall be there unto all eternity. God's eternal glory is eternally the same; "from everlasting to everlasting thou art God";[1] but all the created glory that is in heaven, or that ever shall be there, springs out of the love of Christ. It is true, the angels were not redeemed by him, but they were confirmed by him. They were not recovered out of a lost estate by him, but they were continued in their first estate by him. Hence it is that God gathered all things in heaven and earth unto a head in him (Eph. 1:10). And there is a great deal to the same purpose in that expression of the apostle, when he had mentioned principalities and powers, "in him all things consist" (Col. 1:17), they have their consistence in him. All would dissolve and fall to nothing, if they had not their consistence in Jesus Christ. Certainly this is a love that passes knowledge, that is the fountain and spring of all the glory that is in heaven. If God help us by faith to look within the veil, and to take a view of all those glories wherewith the holy God is encompassed, we shall see that this love is the fountain and spring of them, the interposition of Christ saved the creation, and brought in that everlasting glory that shall dwell in heaven. God knows this love, God understands the way of it; but as to us it passes knowledge.

Again, 2. This love of Christ passes the comprehension and knowledge of angels; and therefore Peter tells us, speaking of the sufferings of Christ and the glory that followed, "which things," says he, "the angels desire to" bow down and "look into" (1 Pet. 1:12). The angels in heaven live in an admiration of the love of Christ unto sinners, that is, that love he expressed in suffering, and in the glory that did ensue. And, oh! What thoughts ought we to have of this love, who have all the benefits of it? The angels had no benefit by the sufferings of Christ, but their benefit and advantage ensued on the assumption of the human nature to bring the creation into a consistence, and in his interposition between God and all his creatures. They admire and adore it. What ought such poor creatures as we are to do? It may well be said to pass our knowledge, for it passes the knowledge of all the angels in heaven.

3. It passes knowledge, in that the effects of it in Christ himself pass all our knowledge and comprehension.

To give but two instances, (1) his condescension to assume our human nature passes all our comprehension. No man can fully understand the mystery of the assumption of our nature into the personal subsistence of the Son of God. Some dispute whether we shall understand the mystery of the

---

1 Ps. 90:2.

incarnation in heaven; here we believe it. It is love which passes knowledge that the eternal Son of God should take our nature into personal union with himself; it is that we may admire, and ought to admire; and God help us, we are such poor earthly creatures that we cannot admire it as we ought; though it be much in our nature to admire what we cannot comprehend.

(2) We cannot fully understand his passion and sufferings. God alone knows what is in the curse of the law; we do not know it. God alone knows what is the true desert of sin; it cannot be fully understood by any but himself. They who undergo it must suffer to eternity; there is no end; they never see, never knew what sin deserved. How do we know then what Christ suffered, when the punishment due to our sin, when all our iniquities met upon him, with the curse of the law? God only knows what is in these things; the fruits and effects of this love in himself, in his incarnation and passion, are past our knowledge, therefore the love itself surpasses our knowledge.

4. Give me leave to say, the very fruits of it in ourselves do pass knowledge. No man that lives knows what there is in these three general heads of the fruits of Christ's love, in justification and pardon of sin, in the renovation and sanctification of our natures, and in the inhabitation and consolations of the Holy Spirit. No man living can find out these things to perfection. None of us fully understands and comprehends what it is to be justified in the sight of God, to have sin pardoned, to have our natures renewed, and transformed into the likeness of God, and to have the Holy Ghost dwell in us. The love of Christ therefore passes all knowledge, for the very fruits of it in ourselves are beyond what we can comprehend; there is a greatness in them we cannot reach unto. Why then, my brethren, let us labor to have our hearts affected with this love. If God would be pleased to give unto every one of us some sense and impression of the greatness of this love of Christ, glance it into our hearts, beam it upon us in this ordinance, we should have cause to bless him all the days of our lives. The faith and light of it issue in admiration; the light of glory will bring us to comprehension. Let us have such a sense as may cause us to admire what we cannot now comprehend.

EXHORTATIONS TO KINDLE ADMIRATION FOR CHRIST'S LOVE

1. I could speak something, but I will not now, to the actings of faith in admiration; it being the proper nature of faith to issue itself in the admiration of that which is infinite. If we can get our souls up to a holy admiration of this love, we have some gracious sense of it upon our hearts, if we can go no farther.

2. Let us learn to run up all the mercies we are partakers of, whatsoever it be we value, to the proper spring: "who loved me, and gave himself for me."[2] If we have any relief, or supply, or refreshment of soul, in a sense of pardon of sin, in spiritual light or consolation, pray let us exercise ourselves to run up all these things to the fountain: it is all from the love of Christ, that unspeakable love which passes knowledge.

3. In this let us be ashamed, seeing the love of Christ to us is such as passes our knowledge, our love to him is so weak, that sometimes we know not whether we have any or not. For this let us be greatly humbled. This is not the way to answer that love which passes knowledge, to know not whether we love Christ again or not. Let us be ashamed for our want of love.

4. And lastly, let us abound in praise and thanksgiving for his love, and all the fruits of it.

For my part I do not know, whether that vision in Revelation 5:9 does express the rejoicing of the church above, or the duty of the church below; but both I am sure are of so near affinity, that apply it to which you will, you do not miss it. And what do they there? Why, it is said, "They sang a new song, saying, Thou art worthy to take the book and to open the seals of it; for thou wast slain and hast redeemed us to God by thy blood out of every kindred, and tongue, and people, and nation, and hast made us unto our God kings and priests," etc.[3] And it is said again, "Worthy is the Lamb that was slain to receive power, and riches, and wisdom, and strength, and honor, and glory, and blessing";[4] and again he repeats it in verse 13. I say, I know not whether this be a representation of the rejoicing of the church above, or a representation of the duty of the church below; but I can conclude from it, that the enjoyment of the one and the duty of the other, consist greatly in continual giving praise and thanks to Christ for his unspeakable love in our redemption.

---

2   Gal. 2:20.
3   Rev. 5:9–10.
4   Rev. 5:12

Discourse 22

The Eternal Love of the Father for the Son the Foundation of All Love in Creation

February 18, 1676

WE ARE MET HERE to remember the death of Christ in the way and by the means that he himself has appointed, and in remembering the death of Christ we are principally to remember the love of Christ; who "loved us, and washed us from our sins in his own blood";[1] and that which on our part is required herein is faith in Christ who died for us, and love to Christ who loved us so as to give himself an offering and a sacrifice to God for us.

1. That which I would now observe is this (to make way for the stirring up of our love), that the person of Christ is the adequate complete object of the love of God, and of the whole creation that bears the image of God, I mean, the church of God above, the angels and saints; and the church of God below in believers, which are the creation that has the image of God upon it.

The person of Christ is the first complete object of the love of God the Father. A great part (if I may so speak, and I must so speak) of the essential blessedness of the holy Trinity consists in the mutual love of the Father and the Son, by the Holy Ghost, which is the love of them both.

That which I would now take notice of, I say, as the foundation of all is this, that the divine nature in the person of the Son is the only full, resting, complete object of the love of God the Father. I will give you a place or two of Scripture for it, and so go on to another instance, "Then," says he, that is,

---

1 Rev. 1:5.

from everlasting, was I "by him, as one brought up with him, and I was daily his delight, rejoicing always before him" (Prov. 8:30), that is, as the special object of his love; as among you men, one that is brought up with you, as your child is. The delight of the Father from all eternity was in the Son. The ineffable love and mutual delight of the Father and the Son by the Spirit, is that which is the least notion we have of the blessedness of the eternal God. "The only begotten Son who is in the bosom of the Father" (John 1:18). Pray observe it, that I speak yet only of the divine person of Christ antecedent unto his incarnation, and the ineffable mutual love of the blessed persons in the holy Trinity, which Jesus Christ wonderfully sets out in John 17. There is his relation unto God, he is "the only be-gotten Son," by eternal generation; what follows? He is "in the bosom of the Father," is in the Father's eternal infinite love. Herein is God's love; and everything else of love is but a free act of the will of God, a free emanation from this eternal love between the Father and the Son. God never did anything without himself, but the end of it was to manifest what is in himself. The old and new creation that God has wrought was to manifest what was in himself. God made this world to manifest his power and wisdom; God made the new world by Jesus Christ to manifest his grace, his love, goodness, etc.

The sole reason why there is such a thing as love in the world, among the creatures, angels or men, that God ever implanted it in the nature of rational creatures, it was, that it might shadow and represent the ineffable eternal love that the Father had unto the Son, and the Son unto the Father by the Spirit.

Contemplative men of old did always admire love, wherein they would have the life, luster and glory of all things to consist, but they could never see the rise of it: and they traced some things to this, that God necessarily loved himself; and it is true, it cannot otherwise be; but God's loving of himself, absolutely as God, is nothing but his eternal blessed acquiescence in the holy, self-sufficing properties of his nature. This they had some reach after; but of this eternal ineffable love of the Father to the Son, and of the Son to the Father, by the Spirit, that they had no conjecture of. Yet this is the fountain and springhead; and all such things as love in the old and new creation, as I said, is but to resemble and shadow out this great prototype of divine love. I acknowledge there is little discerned of these things, by reason of the weakness of our understandings; but the Scripture has so directly declared to us the mutual love of the Father and the Son (which truly is of such singular use, that I would fix persons upon it in conceiving of the doctrine of the Trinity), that it is matter of admiration and thankfulness to us. Here lies the foundation of all love, whereunto we hope to reduce our love unto Christ, namely in the unchangeable love of the Father to the Son.

2. The person of Christ as vested with our nature, and undertaking the work of mediation, is the first object of the Father's love, wherein there is any mixture of anything without himself.

The first love of God the Father to the Son is that which we call *ad intra*,[2] where the divine persons are objects of one another's actings; the Father knows the Son, and the Son knows the Father; the Father loves the Son, and the Son loves the Father; and so consequently of the Holy Ghost, the medium of all these actings.

But now, I say, the first act of the love of God the Father, wherein there is anything *ad extra*,[3] or without the divine essence, is the person of Christ, considered as invested with our nature. And had not the love of God been fixed in the first place in all things upon the person of Christ, there would have been no redundancy to us, nor communication of love unto us. From the first eternal love of God proceeds all love that was in the first creation; and from this second love of God to the person of Christ, as incarnate, proceeds all the love in the second creation. See how God expresses it in a prospect of what he should be, "Behold my servant whom I uphold, me elect in whom my soul delighteth" (Isa. 42:1). And this is singular in the whole Scripture, that God spoke the same words twice from heaven immediately, and they were these, "This is my beloved Son, in whom I am well pleased"; at his baptism (Matt. 3:17), and at his entrance on his sufferings, which was the voice which came "from the excellent glory" (Matt. 17:5).[4] I would observe this unto you, because I think it is what God would have us take notice of, the emphasis in the words, behold my servant, mine elect, my Son, my beloved Son! What of him? In whom I rest, in whom I am well pleased and delighted. All of them emphatical words. Says God, let the sons of men (I speak it from heaven again and again) take notice of this, that the infinite love of my whole soul is fixed on the person of Jesus Christ, as incarnated. And you will find the Lord Jesus Christ pleading this as the ground of that trust committed unto him, and all that he received, "The Father loveth the Son, and has given all things into his hand" (John 3:35). "The Father loveth the Son, and showeth him all things that himself doth, and he will show him greater works than these" (John 5:20).

---

2 Lat. "toward that which is within," used in reference to discussing God's attributes, relations, and decrees from the perspective of God himself, rather than in relation to his works.
3 Lat. "toward that which is outside," used in reference to discussing God's activity and revelation of himself in relation to his external works.
4 Owen is also quoting Peter's allusion to this event in 2 Pet. 1:17.

He lays the foundation of all the trust that God the Father committed unto him, in the peculiar love of the Father to him, as the Son incarnate.

Truly I shall not go beyond this foundation to manifest to you, that the person of Christ is the complete, adequate object of the love of the Father. The great satisfaction of the soul of God wherein he rests and delights, consists in love to Christ as incarnate.

I will make but this one inference from it; proportionable to the renovation of the image and likeness of God upon any of our souls, is our love to Jesus Christ. He that knows Jesus Christ most is most like unto God, for there the soul of God rests, there is the complacency[5] of God; and if we would be like to God, have pledges in ourselves of the renovation of this image upon us, it must be in the gracious exercise of our love to the person of Jesus Christ. And pray let me observe it to you, the world, that is full of enmity to God, does not exercise its enmity against God immediately under the first notion of God, but exercises its enmity against God in Christ: and if we return to God by the renovation of his image, we do not exercise our love to God immediately as God, but our love to God by and in Christ; that ye through him might believe in God. Here is a trial, brethren, of our return to God, and of the renovation of his image in us, namely in our love to Jesus Christ. There God and man do meet, there God and his church above and below center. The Lord grant that this ordinance may be the means to stir up our hearts more to the exercise of this grace!

---

5 I.e., delight.

Brief Instructions for Believers Unacquainted With the Nature of the Ordinance

July 8, 1677

I SHALL SPEAK TO THEM who have a mind to be found performing their duty; but it may be, it does not occur to them what is particularly required of them. They are such as are least acquainted with this mystery that I would have most respect unto, that nothing of God's provision in his house may be lost to his children for want of understanding aright to come to his Table, where he makes this provision.

I pray you brethren, exercise your thoughts unto the institution of this ordinance, wherein you exercise your obedience; unto the proposition of Christ in this ordinance, wherein consists the peculiar acting of your faith; and unto the exhibition of Christ in this ordinance, which is the ground of your thankfulness.

What shall I do that I may please God now, please Jesus Christ, and benefit my own soul, in the administration of this ordinance?

Why, 1. Consider the institution of it, wherein we have the authority of Jesus Christ put forth, and acting toward our souls. "Do this in remembrance of me."[1] Labor therefore to bring your hearts into an actual obedience to the authority of Jesus Christ in what we are about. This the Lord Jesus does require at our hands. We do not come here in a customary manner to satisfy our convictions, because we ought to come; we do not come here merely to make use of our privilege, but our hearts are to bow to the authority of Jesus

---

1 Luke 22:19; 1 Cor. 11:24.

413

Christ. Consider, I pray you, the institution of this ordinance, and labor to bring your souls into actual obedience to Jesus Christ. We do it because Christ has required it of us. If our hearts are in that frame, that we are here upon the command of Christ, to do what he has appointed, and we can recommend our consciences unto him, that it is in obedience to his command that we are here, then our obedience is in exercise.

2. Consider the proposition that is made of Jesus Christ in this ordinance to us, that our faith may be in its proper exercise.

The Lord take off our hearts from the consideration of the outward signs merely. Christ in his love, Christ in his bloodshed, agony and prayer, Christ in his death is here proposed before us. You show forth the Lord's death.[2] Who proposes it? He that has appointed these things proposes it. And there is the engagement of the faithfulness of God and Christ in this proposition and tender that is made of Jesus Christ; and it is a peculiar way, and as I could prove, full of love, that God has found out a way to propound Christ as dying, and crucified, to all our souls. Therefore stir up your hearts to this. To every one of you there is by the grace and faithfulness of God a proposal of Jesus Christ in his death, and all the benefits of it, unto your souls. The whole question is, whether you will stir up your hearts to a new and fresh receiving of Jesus Christ who is thus proposed and tendered unto you, evidently crucified before your eyes, offered to you by the love and faithfulness of God? But if we do not endeavor every one of us in the participation of this ordinance a fresh acceptance of Jesus Christ, we do what we can to make God a liar, as though he was not tendered unto us. The especial exercise of your faith in this ordinance is upon the love, grace and faithfulness of God, proposing and tendering of Christ unto you, the death of Christ, and the benefits of Christ in this way which he has chosen; submit unto it, and embrace it.

3. As your obedience is required with respect to the institution (we give this account before God, angels and men, that we are here in obedience to the command of our Lord Jesus Christ); and as faith is required with respect to the proposition of Christ, whereby he is evidently proposed and tendered by God unto us, so in this ordinance to them that believe there is an exhibition of Christ: Christ is really exhibited and communicated to the souls of men who exercise faith upon him in this ordinance; really exhibited with all the benefits of his death. And want of receiving by faith in particular Christ as exhibited and communicated in this ordinance is the great ground of our want of profiting by it, and thriving under it; of our want of receiving strength, joy

---

2   Owen is alluding to 1 Cor. 11:26.

and life by it; because we do not exercise ourselves to the receiving of Christ as he is exhibited, as God does really give him out, and communicate him to them that do believe.

That there is such an exhibition of Christ appears (1) by the sacramental relation there is between the outward elements and the thing signified. This is my body, says Christ; this bread is so; and this is my blood.[3] It is the body of Christ and the blood of Christ, that we are invited to the participation of. If there was no more in this ordinance exhibited, but only the outward elements, and not by virtue of sacramental relation upon God's institution, the body and blood of Christ, his life and death and merits exhibited unto us, we should come to the Lord's Table like men in a dream, eating and drinking, and be quite empty when we have done, for this bread and wine will not satisfy our souls.

(2) As it is plain from the sign and the thing signified, that there is a grant, or a real communication of Jesus Christ unto the souls of them that do believe, so it is evident from the nature of the exercise of faith in this ordinance; it is by eating and drinking. Can you eat and drink unless something is really communicated? You are called to eat the flesh and drink the blood of the Son of man; unless really communicated we cannot eat it nor drink it. We may have other apprehensions of these things, but our faith cannot be exercised in eating and drinking, which is a receiving of what is really exhibited and communicated. As truly, my brethren, as we do eat of this bread and drink of this cup, which is really communicated to us, so every true believer does receive Christ, his body and blood, in all the benefits of it, that are really exhibited by God unto the soul in this ordinance: and it is a means of communicating to faith.

We come to receive a crucified Christ, come to be made partakers of the body and blood of the Lord, to have the Lord Jesus really united to our hearts more and more. The Lord open our hearts to embrace the tender, receive the exhibition, take in Jesus Christ as food, that he may be incorporated in our hearts by faith, that he may dwell in us plentifully, more and more; that we may go away refreshed by this heavenly food, this glorious feast of fat things which the Lord has made in his mount for his people. The whole of our comfort depends on our particular receiving of Christ by faith, and carrying him away by believing.

3   Alluding to Luke 22:19–20.

Discourse 24

The Importance of Seeking an Experience of the Power of Christ's Death

September 30, 1677

WE ARE MET TOGETHER AGAIN by the patience and kindness of God for the celebration of this great ordinance, and therein to show forth the death of the Lord.

I have often spoken to you on this occasion concerning the nature of this ordinance, the expression of the love of God, and Christ that is in it and the especial acts of faith and love that are required of us in this ordinance.

I have one word now somewhat of another nature, but yet such as I judge not unseasonable; and it is to this purpose, that we, who so frequently enjoy the privilege of the representation of the death of Christ unto us, ought to be very diligent in inquiring after an experience of the power of the death of Christ in us. Without this our privilege will not be to our advantage.

THE POWER AND EFFICACY OF CHRIST'S DEATH

The power and efficacy of the death of Christ, which we now remember in a peculiar manner, is twofold,

1. Toward God, as the consummation of the sacrifice of atonement. This we have often spoke to.

2. Toward our own souls; toward the church, and that is to be an example, a precedent, a pattern of what is to be wrought in us. In this sense the power of the death of Christ is its efficacy to conformity with Christ in his death. It

is to be "crucified with Christ," as the apostle speaks (Gal. 2:20). Power comes forth from the death of Christ, if received by faith in a due manner, to render us conformable to him in the death of sin in us. The apostle has a great and glorious word concerning himself. "Always bearing about in the body the dying of the Lord Jesus" (2 Cor. 4:10). I acknowledge the words are usually applied to the representation of the sufferings of Christ in the sufferings of the ministers of the gospel, concerning which the apostle there discourses; but the antithesis in the following words, "That the life of Jesus" might be "manifest in our body," does certainly lead to a larger sense. Then, brethren, we may have an experience of the power of Christ in us, when we can say, we always carry about with us the dying of the Lord Jesus, to carry it in our meditation, to carry it in our conversation, to carry it in our constant universal endeavors for conformity to it; and without this we have not experience of the power of his death in us, and it will not avail us to have the nature of his death represented to us.

WHAT IT MEANS TO CARRY THE DEATH OF CHRIST ABOUT US

1. We are always to carry about the dying of Jesus Christ, in our thoughts and meditations. O that our thoughts were much fixed upon it! I verily believe that the life of faith does answer in proportion to our thoughts about the dying of Jesus. The dying of Jesus comprises the love from whence he died, the death itself he died, and the end for which he died. Let us carry about us always thoughts hereof, for his sake who loved us and who died for us. Meditate more on these things.

2. In our conversation. It is not a time to reflect upon any, unless I did it upon myself. But truly, brethren, I am afraid we do not carry about and manifest to all the dying of the Lord Jesus in our conversation; to perform all things, so as it may appear and be made manifest to ourselves and others, that our hearts are set upon his dying love, that we have not such quick, such active, and vigorous affections to the world, and the things of the world, nor that fury of diligence after them and in them, as other men have, and we have had; we cannot do it; the dying of the Lord Jesus crucifies our hearts. These are hard words I know; how far from our practice! But if we live not in an endeavor after it, in all things to manifest that our hearts are full of the dying of the Lord Jesus, we have not experience of the power of it in our souls. These things depend on one another. If we dwelt more upon this subject in our meditations, we should manifest it, and carry it about and represent it more in our conversation.

3. Carry it about in a constant endeavor for conformity to Jesus Christ in all things in his death. Did Christ die, and shall sin live? Was he crucified in the world, and shall we have quick and lively affections to the world? O where is the temper and spirit of that apostle who by the cross of Christ, was crucified to the world, and the world crucified to him?[1] If there be any among us that should be indulgent to the life of any one lust or corruption, that soul can have no experience of the power of the death of Christ in himself, cannot carry about him the dying of Christ. Endeavor to destroy sin that we may be like unto Christ.

I will not make particular application of these things to all the concerns of our walk, but leave it with you, with this word, begging of you, and my own heart, and of God for us all, that having these blessed representations of the death of Christ to us, we may have no rest in our spirits but when we have experience of the power of the death of Christ in us.

---

1   Owen is alluding to Gal. 6:14.

The Peculiar Spiritual Communion with Christ, and His Substantial Incorporation within a Believer through This Ordinance

September 20, 1682

IT IS A COMMON RECEIVED NOTION among Christians, and it is true, that there is a peculiar communion with Christ in this ordinance, which we have in no other ordinance; that there is a peculiar acting of faith in this ordinance which is in no other ordinance. This is the faith of the whole church of Christ, and has been so in all ages. This is the greatest mystery of all the practicals[1] of our Christian religion, a way of receiving Christ by eating and drinking, something peculiar that is not in prayer, that is not in the hearing of the word, nor in any other part of divine worship whatsoever; a peculiar participation of Christ, a peculiar acting of faith toward Christ. This participation of Christ is not carnal, but spiritual. In the beginning of the ministry of our Lord Jesus Christ, when he began to instruct them in the communication of himself, and the benefit of his mediation to believers, because it was a new thing, he expresses it by eating his flesh and drinking his blood, "Unless ye eat the flesh and drink the blood of the Son of Man, ye have no life in you" (John 6:53). This offended and amazed them. They thought he taught them to eat his natural flesh and blood. "How can this man give us his flesh to eat?"[2] They thought he instructed them to be cannibals. Whereupon he gives that everlasting

1   I.e., practices.
2   John 6:52.

rule for the guidance of the church, which the church forsook, and thereby ruined itself, says he, "It is the Spirit that quickens; the flesh profits nothing. The words that I speak [. . .], they are spirit and they are life."[3] It is a spiritual communication, says he, of myself unto you; but it is as intimate, and gives as real an incorporation, as if you did eat my flesh and drink my blood. The church, forsaking this rule of a spiritual interpretation, ruined itself, and set up a monster instead of this blessed mysterious ordinance.

We may inquire therefore how faith does peculiarly act itself toward Christ in this ordinance, whereby we have a distinct participation of Christ otherwise than we have by and in any other ordinance whatsoever. And I would mention four things unto you, which you may make use of.

1. That faith has a peculiar respect to the sole authority of Christ in the institution of this ordinance.

All other ordinances draw upon the light of nature, and upon the moral law, as prayer, preaching the word, and singing of psalms to the praise of God; but this, that we should receive Jesus by eating of bread, and drinking of wine, it has no respect to the light of nature, or the moral law at all; and we should as soon choose to honor God by sacrifices, and eating the flesh of them, if it were not for the authority of Jesus Christ. Herein does faith give honor to Christ in his kingly office. This is the most direct profession of the subjection of our souls and consciences to the authority of Christ, in all our religion. We can give no other reason, we can take no allusion from things, but merely this, Christ would have it so.

2. Faith has a peculiar respect to the love of Christ in dying for us, making the atonement for us by his blood, and therein the glorifying of the wisdom, love, and grace of God the Father. Faith is led into special communion with Christ as dying for us to make the atonement, and therein we give glory to Christ in his priestly office in a peculiar manner in this ordinance, it respecting the sacrifice of Christ, whereby he made atonement for us.

3. Faith has respect to this special manner of the exhibition of Christ to the souls of believers, under the outward signs and symbols of bread and wine by his institution, making such a sacramental union between the thing signified and the sign, that the signs remaining to be what they are in themselves, they are unto us the thing that is signified by virtue of the sacramental union that Christ has appointed between his body and blood, and the benefits of it; and this bread and wine, though not changed at all in themselves, yet they become to us by faith, not what they are in themselves, but what is signified by them,

---

3   John 6:63.

the body and blood of Christ. Herein we give glory to Christ in his prophetical office. It is he who has revealed, taught and instructed his church in this truth which depends on the sacramental union which follows by his institution. That is the third thing wherein faith peculiarly acts itself in this ordinance.

4. The fourth thing is, the mysteriousness, which I leave to your experience, for it is beyond expression, the mysterious reception of Christ in this peculiar way of exhibition. There is a reception of Christ as tendered in the promise of the gospel, but here is a peculiar way of his exhibition under outward signs, and a mysterious reception of him in them really, so as to come to a real substantial incorporation in our souls. This is that which believers ought to labor after an experience of in themselves; to find that indeed under these four considerations, they submit to the authority of Jesus Christ in a peculiar manner, giving him the glory of his kingly office; mixing faith with him as dying and making atonement by his blood, so giving him the glory and honor of his priestly office; much considering the sacramental union that is by his institution between the outward signs and the thing signified, thus glorifying him in his prophetical office; and raising up their souls to a mysterious reception and incorporation of him, receiving him to dwell in them, warming, cherishing, comforting and strengthening their hearts.

I have mentioned these things as those which lie in your practice, and to obviate that (if I may mention it) which you may be tried with. There is but one plausible pretense that our adversaries, who design to oppress us, have in this business: If, say they, there be not a real presence and a real substantial transmutation of the elements into the substance of the body and blood of Christ, show you a way whereby you may have a peculiar communion with Christ any more than in the word preached. We say, we have in these things experience of a peculiar communion with Christ in a way made proper to this ordinance, which is not to be found in any other ordinance.

THE LORD'S SUPPER FULLY CONSIDERED, IN A REVIEW OF THE HISTORY OF ITS INSTITUTION. WITH MEDITATIONS AND EJACULATIONS SUITED TO THE SEVERAL PARTS OF THE ORDINANCE.

*To Which Are prefixed Three Discourses
Delivered at the Lord's Table,*

By the reverend and learned
John Owen, D.D.

*Never before Published:
And Some Remarks on the Plain
Account of the Sacrament.*

London:
Printed by J. Buckland, at the
Buck in Pater-noster-
Row; and R. Lobb, Bookseller in Chelmsford.
1750.

Three Discourses Delivered at the Lord's Table

Contents

The chapter titles have been supplied by the editor. The dates of the discourses are original.

Advertisement to the 1750 Edition

THE THREE FOLLOWING DISCOURSES were given me by a worthy gentleman, who assured me that they were taken from Dr. Owen's mouth by one who was a member of the church of which he was pastor: and they are published, not merely to gratify the curiosity of those who have a veneration for the works and memory of that learned divine, but because they give us, as far as they go, a just notion of the Lord's Supper.

J. Greene
CHIPPING ONGER,
MARCH 26, 1750.

Discourse 1

The Act and Object of Faith in This Ordinance

June 8, 1673

FAITH IS BOUNDED in every ordinance by its objects and acts.

The general object of saving faith respecting God is the truth of his word and promises (Rom. 15:8). The special object of our faith in this ordinance is the sufferings and death of Christ. Herein he is "evidently set forth" crucified before our eyes.[1] And we must act faith upon three things with respect to his death.

First, the personal love of Christ to our persons; from whence it was that he died for us, so says the apostle "who loved me and gave himself for me" (Gal. 2:20). Were we helped to raise up our hearts by faith to apprehend Christ's love to our persons, it would greatly help us in this ordinance. The Lord lift us up above our fears, and give us a view by faith, not only of the love of Christ in general, but that he personally loved us, even this whole church.

Secondly, the sufferings of Christ. In this ordinance we are to act faith upon his death, as therein undergoing the punishment due to our sins. It is to mind us that he made "his soul an offering for sin,"[2] that he "suffered [. . .] the just for the unjust,"[3] bearing "our sins in his own body on the tree,"[4] that they should not come into judgment.

Thirdly, the effects of Christ's death, which was the making an atonement for all our sins, the making peace between God and our souls, bringing in

1 Gal. 3:1.
2 Isa. 53:10.
3 1 Pet. 3:18.
4 1 Pet. 2:24.

everlasting righteousness. Under the law we find, that "the blood of bulls and of goats, and the ashes of a heifer sprinkling the unclean, sanctified to the purifying of the flesh," and the people were thereby legally cleansed; "How much more shall the blood of Christ, who through the eternal Spirit offered himself [. . .] to God," purge our consciences "from dead works to serve the living God?" (Heb. 9:13–14).

The acts of faith in this ordinance are, first, recognition. That faith which is exercised on the death of Christ that is past, is to call it over, and make it present to the soul. It is to realize it, and bring it before us. It is not a bare remembrance of it, but such a one as makes it present. And where there is faith there is the same advantage to a believing soul in the participation of this ordinance, as there would have been if we had stood by the cross.

Secondly, faith works by reflecting to humiliation. They shall look on him whom they have pierced, and mourn for all their unkindness and unthankfulness to their Savior.[5] And when we come to this work in this ordinance, self-abasement, self-abhorrence, and brokenness of heart will be acted, and flow forth in abundance of love to Jesus Christ.

Thirdly, another act of faith in this ordinance is, thankfulness to God for his wisdom and grace, in contriving this way of our salvation, and thankfulness to Christ, in whom was this mind, that "being in the form of God," and thinking it no "robbery to be equal with God," he "took upon him the form of a servant [. . .], and became obedient unto death, even the death of the cross,"[6] that he might save us from our sins. If the Lord be pleased to lead us to act faith in any of these things, in some signal and eminent manner, we shall find an advantage in this ordinance.

5   Owen is alluding to Zech. 12:10.
6   Phil. 2:6–8.

Discourse 2

The Sacramental Participation of Christ in This Ordinance

July 6, 1673

TO HELP YOU in the exercise of faith in the administration of this ordinance, I would briefly show what it is to have a sacramental participation of Jesus Christ.

When the world had lost the understanding of this mystery, for want of spiritual light, they contrived a means to make it up, very easy on the part of them that partake of it, and very prodigious on the part of the priest. For he, by a few words, turns the bread into the body of Christ, and the people have no more to do but to receive it, as such, into their mouths. It was the loss of the understanding of this mystery that put them upon that invention.

There is indeed a figure or representation in this ordinance, but that is not all; when the bread is broken it is a figure, a representation that the body of Christ was broken for us. But there is also a real exhibition of Christ unto every believing soul. This is distinct from the tender of Christ in the promises of the gospel. In the promises, the person of the Father is particularly looked upon as proposing and tendering Christ to us. In this ordinance, as God exhibits him, so Christ makes an immediate tender of himself, and calls our faith to have respect to his grace, to his love and to his readiness, to unite and spiritually incorporate with us. He tenders himself to us not in general but under a special consideration, namely as having made an end of sin, and done all that was to be done between God and sinners that they might be at peace.

Christ made a double presentation of himself. First, as the great mediator, when he offered himself a sacrifice on the cross for the accomplishing [of] the work of man's redemption. Secondly, he presented himself to God in heaven, there to do whatever remained to be done with God on our behalf by his intercession. The intercession of Christ is the presentation of himself to God upon his oblation and sacrifice. He presents himself to God to do with him what remains to be done on our part to procure mercy and peace for us; and he presents himself to us in this ordinance (which answers to that intercession of Christ above, and is a counterpart of it) to do what remains to be done on the part of God; to give in peace, and mercy, and the sealed covenant to us.

There is this special exhibition or tender of Jesus Christ; and this directs to a special exercise of faith, that we may know how to receive him in this ordinance. And first, let us receive him as one that hath actually accomplished the great work of making peace with God for us; blotting out our sins, and bringing in everlasting righteousness. Secondly, as one that has done this work by his death. It is a relief when we have an apprehension that Christ can do all this for us: but he does not tender himself to us as one that can or will do it upon such and such conditions as shall be prescribed but as one that has done it, and so we must receive him, if we intend to glorify God in this ordinance, namely as having blotted out all our sins, and purchased for us eternal redemption.

Let us act faith on Jesus Christ, as one who brings along with him mercy and pardon, procured by his death; all the mercy and grace that are in the heart of God and in the covenant. To have such a view of him, and so to receive him by faith is the way to give glory to God, and to have peace, and rest in our own bosoms.

Discourse 3

The Exhibition and Receipt of Christ in This Ordinance

August 10, 1673

TO A DUE ATTENDANCE on this ordinance it is requisite, not only that we be in a spiritual frame, but that we endeavor to bring and fix our hearts to some special thoughts with respect to this special ordinance; wherein the principal act on the part of God, and the principal act on our part, with respect to Christ, are gloriously represented.

The great act of God, with reference to Christ, is the exhibiting of him. God did two ways exhibit Christ.

First, there was, as I may call it, on the part of God, a legal exhibition of Christ, mentioned by the apostle, "Whom God hath set forth to be a propitiation through faith in his blood, to declare his righteousness for the remission of sins [. . .]; that he might be just, and the justifier of him which believeth in Jesus" (Rom. 3:25–26). This I call God's legal exhibition of Christ, when he set him forth to undergo the curse of the law, that we might be blessed. This setting forth of Christ is here represented in this ordinance when the bread is broken. And this is that which you may exercise your faith on in this ordinance, that as the bread is here set forth to be broken, so God, to declare his own righteousness, has set forth Christ to be bruised and broken, to undergo the sentence of the law. Thus we have a gracious sight of God's holiness in this ordinance.

Secondly, he does exhibit Jesus Christ in the promises of the gospel. And it might be with some respect to this ordinance, that the gospel invitations, which have the nature of promises, were in the Old Testament set forth by eating and drinking. "Ho, every one that thirsteth, come ye to the waters, and he that hath no money; come ye, buy and eat, yea come, buy wine and milk without money and without price" (Isa. 55:1). God having provided Jesus Christ to be the food of our souls, he does propose and exhibit him in the gospel as such. And what a blessed representation is there hereof in this ordinance? Here God makes a visible tender of Christ, as exhibited in the promises of the gospel for the life, food and strength of our souls. To answer the promises, he here makes this tender unto us.

Thus you see the principal act of God in this ordinance, is the exhibiting of Jesus Christ unto us. The great act on our part, with respect to Christ, which is also represented in this ordinance, is the reception of him by faith. It is not enough that God has set forth Christ to declare his righteousness, and in the promises of the gospel. Unless we receive Christ, we shall come short of all the design of grace and mercy therein. "As many as received him, to them gave he power to become the sons of God; even to them that believe on his name" (John 1:12).

If there be anything that is brought and tendered to you, unless you receive it, there is nothing done. Things are but in the same state wherein they were. Notwithstanding all the tenders that God makes of Jesus Christ in both the ways mentioned, if there be not an act of faith in receiving him, we shall have no benefit by it. Now can anything be more lively represented to us with respect to Christ, who is tendered to us, than our receiving of the bread in this sacrament. But if we act not faith therein, it will be but a bare representation. Therefore, if we believe that God is in good earnest with us in the tender that he makes of Christ, let us not be backward on our part, that the sacrament rites may not be empty signs to us.

PART 3

COLLECTED WORKS
ON ECCLESIOLOGY

THE WORKS INCLUDED in the remainder of this volume appeared in two collections published after Owen's death in 1683. *Several Practical Cases of Conscience Resolved*; *Reflections on a Slanderous Libel*; *A Letter concerning the Matter of the Present Excommunications*; *A Discourse concerning the Administration of Church Censures*; *Of Infant Baptism, and Dipping*; and *Of Marrying after Divorce in Case of Adultery* all appeared in *A Complete Collection of the Sermons of the Reverend and Learned John Owen* (1721). The other two, *An Answer unto Two Questions* and *Twelve Arguments, against Any Conformity of Members of Separate Churches to the National Church*, were published in *Seventeen Sermons Preach'd by the Reverend Dr. John Owen* (1720). Since these works appeared in collections, not all of them include title pages (with detailed publishing information) like those included in the preceding works in this volume.

SEVERAL PRACTICAL
CASES OF CONSCIENCE
RESOLVED

Delivered in Some Short Discourses
at Church Meetings

Several Practical Cases of Conscience Resolved

Contents

The chapter titles have been supplied by the editor. The dates of the discourses, when given, are original.

Discourse 1

Conviction of Sin and Looking to Christ

January 28, 1672

Question. What conviction of a state of sin, and of the guilt of sin, is necessary to cause a soul sincerely to look after Christ?

Answer

There is one thing only that I shall at present speak to, and that is this: What is the lowest condition that has the nature of conviction in sincerity, so as that souls may not be discouraged from closing with Christ, because they have had no greater convictions of sin? And I shall speak to it on this account; because, although the things that have already been spoken by others are true, and such, as those who have spoken them have found to be true by the word, and their own experience; yet, it may be, others have not come up in their experience unto such a distinct observation of the work of conviction, as has been laid down; [so] that they may be discouraged. For seeing conviction is so indispensably necessary, some may say, it has not been thus and thus with me, according as has been declared. Therefore I would only show what I judge to be so necessary, as that without it a soul cannot be supposed sincerely to have closed with Christ. And we having all made our profession of choosing and closing with Christ, as I would be loath to say anything that might discourage any, lest they should have failed in the very necessary work of conviction; so I would not betray the truth of God, nor the souls of any.

Therefore I shall place it upon this: What Jesus Christ does indispensably call men unto, in order to believing in him, that is indispensably required of them. And this I shall manifest out of two or three places of Scripture: "I came not to call the righteous, but sinners to repentance" (Mark 2:17). Now this calling them unto repentance, is a calling them unto it by the faith which is in him. The apostle says, it "is a faithful saying, and worthy of all acceptation, that Jesus Christ came into the world to save sinners" (1 Tim. 1:15). What kind of sinners does Christ call? Whom he calls to repentance, he calls to faith; and whom he calls to faith, that they may truly believe; they are sinners, opposed unto them that are righteous: "I came not to call the righteous, but sinners to repentance." ¶[1]

The "righteous": who are those righteous? The Scriptures tell us of these very men, that there were two sorts of them: First, such as trusted in themselves that they were righteous, and despised other men. As long as a man trusts in himself that he is righteous, Christ does not call that man to believe. So long as a man is persuaded that his condition is good enough, he shall do well enough, that man has no warrant to believe. Another description of these very persons, though upon another occasion, is given by the apostle Paul, where he says, they were "ignorant of the righteousness of God, and went about to establish their own righteousness" (Rom. 10:3). Though they did not come to trust in themselves for righteousness; yet sought righteousness as it were by the works of the law, and went about to establish their own righteousness. Jesus Christ does not call these men to believe: these righteous persons have no ground for believing. What is the conclusion? Lost sinners, says Christ, this is that I require of you. So that this is what I assert to be indispensably necessary; namely, that they are so far convinced that they are sinners as to state and course, that they are not righteous in themselves, and can have no righteousness in themselves. I say therefore, when a person is not really convinced that he is not righteous, he is not under the call of Jesus Christ: and if he does believe this, he is under a sovereign dispensation, and let not such despond.

Another direction of Christ is, "The whole need not the physician, but they that are sick" (Matt. 9:12). There are in my apprehension two things in a sick person that have need of a physician: first, he has an uneasiness. A man who is sick, though he would shift it, yet his uneasiness will cause him to send for a physician. Says Christ, I come to such persons who say they can find

---

1 Luke 5:32. The ¶ symbol indicates that a paragraph break has been added to Owen's original text.

no rest nor ease in their present condition. It may be, they have often tried this and that, and see all will not do, they are sick still; conscience reflects, and their hearts are burdened, and they must have relief, or they shall not be free. Secondly, there is a fear that it will end in death. This puts the sick person upon sending for a physician. When the soul is made uneasy in its state and condition, can find no rest nor ease, it thinks, if I abide here, I shall be lost forever. This soul does Christ call; this man will be at the charge of a physician, cost what it will.

There is another word of Christ, [which] very remarkably speaks just to the same purpose, "Come unto me all ye that labour, and are heavy laden, and I will give you rest" (Matt. 11:28). A soul finding itself under want, laboring after something, whereby it may be accepted with God. I will not confine this to extraordinary instances, for sometimes he is found of them that sought him not; but the ordinary case of a laboring soul, before closing with Christ, is to abstain from sin, pray more or less, be found in duties, and under strong desires to be accepted with God. And what is the end of these labors and endeavors? They labor and are weary; that is, they see their labor comes to no effect; they do not find rest, and peace, and acceptance with God. And here is the turning point, "Thou art wearied in the largeness of thy way; yet saidst thou not there is no hope" (Isa. 57:10). When the soul has labored for acceptance with God, and comes to be weary, says Christ: "Come unto me." No, says the light of nature, come unto me, trust unto your own endeavors. Says the soul, I will try what it will do; I will not say, there is no hope. Says another, I will not say so, I will go unto Christ: this is he whom Christ calls.

Now these things I do account indispensably necessary, antecedently to believing, as to the substance of them. And this, I hope, has been found in all our souls. And if we have obtained so far, we need not then question whether our close with Christ be sincere or not. This is all that I dare assert to be absolutely and indispensably necessary: many pretend to believe though they never were convinced thoroughly that they were not righteous; never were sick in their lives, never had fears that they should die. These are contrary to the express rule Christ has given, "I came not to call the righteous but sinners"; not those that say, there is hope; but those that say, there is no hope.

Discourse 2

Evidences of True Conversion

February 7, 1672

*Question. Seeing the act of closing with Christ is secret and hidden, and
the special times and seasons of our conversion unto God are unknown
unto most: What are most certain evidences and pledges, that we
have cordially and sincerely received Christ, and returned unto God?*

Answer

I do acknowledge the inquiry is very large and such as we may be straitened
in, through the abundance of it. I shall only speak plainly some few things
that to me are an evidence of a sincere closing with Christ, and receiving of
Christ, such as I know have been of use unto some.

First, when there is a permanency and abiding in the choice we have
made of Christ, notwithstanding opposition against it, that we shall be sure
to meet withal, I do not speak to the nature of the choice, or the means of it,
how the mind is prepared for it; but I speak unto the poorest, the weakest of
the flock, that may be inquiring, whether they have made a sincere choice of
Christ or not; I say, they may try it by the permanency and abiding in their
choice against opposition.

And there are two sorts of oppositions that will try us and shake us; as to
our choice, as I have found it, if I have had any experience of these things.
(1) Opposition from charges of the guilt of sin, and the law. (2) Opposition
from temptations unto sin.

1. There will, even after sincere believing and closing with Christ, be many
a heavy charge brought against a soul from the law, and the guilt of sin in the

conscience. Now in such a case the inquiry is: What the soul abides by, when it is shaken? Why truly, if a man go only upon mere convictions, on such shaking impressions of the guilt of sin, he will be very ready, and inclined in his own mind, to tack about to some other relief. He puts out fair for his voyage, the storm arises, the ship will not carry him, he must tack about for another harbor. I have known it so with some, and experienced when the wind has set very strong that way with myself: when the guilt of sin has been charged with all its circumstances, the soul has been very hardly able to keep its hold, yet notwithstanding resolved, I will trust to Christ; but it has been tacking about to self again, I must remedy this, have relief for this from myself, I cannot abide by it, and live wholly upon Christ, and when the storm is over, then I will out to sea again. I say this is no good sign to me, when things are so: but when a soul in all those charges, that sometimes come upon it, abides the issue, here I will trust upon Christ, let the worst come upon me; this I call a permanency in our choice against opposition. I hope you have experience of it.

2. There must be a permanency in our choice of Christ against temptations unto sin, as well as against the charges from sin. Truly the former of abiding with Christ against the charges from sin, is our daily work. It is sometimes more high and pressing, but it is our daily work. But there are also temptations unto sin, it may be to the neglect of our duty, or to a compliance in any evil way (which we are subject unto while in the body) and perhaps great sins. Here Joseph's reply applied to Christ, is that which does argue our choice of Christ to be sincere. How shall I do this great wickedness, and sin against God? When the soul can draw a prevailing argument from that: how shall I do this, and relinquish my Lord Christ? I will not do this against him, whom I have chosen. This is a good argument, if frequently reiterated, that our choice of Christ is sincere.

Secondly, growing up in a love unto the person of Christ is a great evidence to me of a sincere choice of Christ. It is a blessed field that is before me, but I shall but hint things unto you. When the soul has received Christ, it cannot but study Christ: and though it is no argument against the sincerity of a man's faith and grace, that he does principally regard the offices, and graces of Christ, and the benefits we have by him, yet it is an argument against the thrift[1] and growth of it. For a thriving faith and grace will come to respect principally the person of Christ. I mean this: when the soul studies the person of Christ, the glory of God in him, of his natures, the union of them in one person, of

1 I.e., thriving.

his love, condescension, and grace; and the heart is drawn out to love him, and cry, doubtless I count all things but loss and dung for the excellency of Christ Jesus my Lord:[2] "What is thy beloved more than another beloved? [...] My beloved is white and ruddy, the chiefest among ten thousand";[3] "he is altogether lovely";[4] to see an excellency, a desirableness in the person of Christ, so as to grow in admiration and love of him, is to me an evidence, that when all fails besides, will greatly support the soul and persuade it, that its choice is true. Nay, it is one of the most spiritual evidences; for I much question, whether an unregenerate man can love Christ for his own sake at all. But it is a good sign of growth, when our love to the person of Christ grows, when we meditate much upon it, and think much about it. I could show you wherein the beauty of Christ's person does much consist, but I have not time now to do it.

Thirdly, another evidence to me of the soul's having made a sincere choice of Christ is, when it continues to approve, judge well of, and every day more and more to see the glory, the excellency, the holiness, the grace which is in the way of salvation by Jesus Christ, approves of it as not only a necessary way, a way it has betaken itself to, because it must unavoidably perish in any other way; but when it approves of it to be a most excellent way, in pardoning sin freely through the atonement he has made, and the imputation of his righteousness unto us; while the righteousness, the holiness, and the grace of God in all this is glorified. Says the soul, what a blind, wretched creature was I, that I did not see an excellency in this way before? It is better than the way of the law, and the old covenant; I approve of this way with all my heart; if all other ways were set before me, and made possible, I would choose this way of going to God by Jesus Christ, as the best way, that brings most glory to God, and most satisfaction unto the creature, and is most suited to the desires of my heart; I would have no other way. "I am the way, the truth, and the life,"[5] says Christ; and this I will abide by, whatsoever becomes of me, replies the soul; though I should perish, I will abide by it, since God has given me such a discovery of the glory of saving sinners by Christ, that is inferior to nothing but the glory of heaven. I see that glory to God in it, that exaltation to Christ, whom I would love, that honor to the Holy Spirit, and safety to my own soul, that I will abide by it. A growing in the approbation of this way gives some assurance that we have made a true and sincere choice of Christ.

2   Owen is paraphrasing Phil. 3:8.
3   Song 5:9–10.
4   Song 5:16.
5   John 14:6.

Give me leave to add this one thing more,

Fourthly, that a delight in obedience unto God by Christ, in the ways of his own appointment, is a great evidence that we have chosen Christ, and he us; chosen him as our king, prophet, and priest. The ways of the worship of God in his church and ordinance are the ways and worship of God in Christ, which he has appointed: take these things abstractedly and in themselves, and we should be apt to say of them, as was said of Christ, there is no beauty in them, nor glory, that they should be desired.[6] There is much more outward beauty and glory in other ways that Christ has not appointed. But if we love the ways Christ has appointed, because he has appointed them, then we choose those ways because we have chosen him to be our king; and that is it which gives them beauty and life. And when the ways of Christ's appointment grow heavy and burdensome to us, we are weary of them, and are willing to have our neck from under the yoke; it is a sign we grow weary of him, who is the author of them, and this is a great sign that we never made a right and sincere choice of him.

Many other things might be offered as evidences of sincere closing with Christ; but these are some which have been of use to me, and I hope they may be so unto some of you.

---

6   Owen is paraphrasing Isa. 53:2.

Discourse 3

Our Participation in the Particular Sins of the Day

Question. What concern have we in the sins of the day wherein we live?

Answer

All sins may be referred to two heads, First, irreligion. Secondly, immorality.

First, irreligion. And that may be reduced to two heads: atheism, and false worship: you may add also particularly, the contempt of all instituted worship. It takes up much of the sins against the first table; however at present I shall only speak of the first of them.

As to atheism then, it may be no age can parallel that wherein we live, consider all the ways whereby the atheism of man's heart may discover itself. For take it absolutely and in the seat of it, it is found only in the heart of man; unless some one or other prodigious instance breaks out sometime, as we have had in our days; but otherwise, "The fool hath said in his heart there is no God."[1] The heart is the seat of atheism.

But we consider the ways whereby this atheism may and does manifest itself.

1. By horrid, cursed, blasphemous swearing, which is a contempt of the name of God. And when did it ever more abound in this nation?

2. By reproaching of the Spirit of God. Perhaps this is the peculiar sin of the nation at this day, and that the like has not been known, or heard of, in any nation under the sun.

---

1 Ps. 14:1.

3. By scoffing, at all holy things, at the Scriptures, at everything that carries a reverence and fear of God; so that a man who dares profess a fear of God in what he does, makes himself a scorn.

4. Contempt of all God's providential warnings, is another proof of atheism. Never had a nation more warnings from God's providence, nor ever were they more despised. These things, brethren, are not done in a corner, they are perpetrated in the face of the sun. The steam of them darkens the whole heaven, and they abound more and more every day.

Secondly, shall we go to the other head, viz. immorality, and see how it is there? It would be an endless thing to go over the sins that reign among us; oppression, blood, uncleanness, sensuality, drunkenness, all to the height raging and reigning in the nation. I mention these things as a matter to be bewailed before the Lord by us this day, and we ought to be affected with the consideration of them.

Unto this great prevalency and predominancy of sin in the whole nation, there is added a strange and unspeakable security. The truth is, men were a little awakened one while in the nation, when the judgments of God, the pestilence, the fire, the sword, and the year after another warning from heaven were upon us; then there was a little awakening, like a man out of a dead sleep that lifts up his head and rubs his eyes for a time. But I can say this, that it is now towards forty years since God enabled me to observe something in the world, and to my knowledge, I never observed this nation in that state of security, wherein it is at this day. For even in former times there were warnings continually that God had a controversy with the nation, and those that had any fear of God spoke one to another about it, and we saw and found their warnings were not in vain. But here is now a general security. Men complain of straits, want, poverty, and the like; but as to anything wherein God has to do with the world, either my observation does greatly deceive me, or I never saw I think so general a security as at this day in this nation. And this security has reached us all, even the churches of God themselves.

These things are matter of fact. The whole question is: whether we are greatly to be concerned in these things or not. They are the sins of wicked men, and they are the sins of the persecutors of God's people and the like; and what have we to do with them?

The psalmist of old said, that rivers of waters ran down his eyes, because men did not keep the law of God.[2] And you know that God does set a special mark upon those, not that are free from the abominations of the age; but upon

2 Owen is paraphrasing Ps. 119:136.

those that mourn for the abominations, that are in the midst of us. It will not be enough for us, that we are free from those abominations, unless we are found to mourn for them. Brethren, our own hearts know we are guilty in this matter, and that we had need seek the face of God this day to give us a deeper sense of these things, than we have obtained. The name of God is blasphemed, the Spirit of God reproached, a flood of iniquity spreads itself over the nation, the land of our nativity, over the inheritance of Christ, over a nation professing the Reformed religion; all things go backward; everything declines. Indeed, brethren, if you will not, I do acknowledge here before you, and to my own shame, I have great guilt upon me in this matter, that I have not been sensible of the abominations of the nation, so as to mourn for them and be humbled for them, as I ought to have been. And you will do well to search your hearts, and consider how it is with you; whether indeed you have been affected with these things, or whether you have not thought all is well, while all has been well with yourselves and families, and it may be with the church that may have no trouble upon that account. The security that is upon the nation is dismal, and, I may say, I see no way or means whereby the nation should be freed from this security. The conduct of the ministry which they are under generally, is not able to free them from this security, nor the dispensation of the word; that it seems to be a security from God to lead on the nation to judgment, the means for the removal of it, and the awakening of us being laid aside. And if it comes this way, or that way, any way, though we see not the morning of it, you will find yourselves concerned in it. "Who may abide the day of his coming!"[3]

We may do well, brethren, to consider the state of the church of God in the world, among ourselves, and our own condition. I need not tell you how it is in the world; but this I can say, that to my apprehensions, the interest of Christ and the gospel was never so fast going down in the world since it came into it, as at this day. I will give you my reason of what I say. When the gospel was first planted, and brought into the world, the devil was not able to bring the church into its apostasy under six, or seven, or eight hundred years, and that by degrees. Since the time of the Reformation, the church was progressive for about seventy years; it stood at a stay about the same proportion of time, and ever since it has been going backward, straitened in all places, the power of it decays, and the peace of it is taken away, and destruction everywhere seems to lie at the door. Many indeed are in great misery and distress: some I have heard of lately, sold for slaves for the testimony of their conscience. How is

3   Mal. 3:2.

it with the church of Christ in this nation? Truly some [are] in great poverty, in great affliction, in great distress; and I am afraid, we and others have not hearts to relieve them as we ought to do in a due manner: however, let us help them with our prayers. And that which is worst of all, there seems to me, I must acknowledge it, to be a very great decay in all churches of Christ in the nation, especially among those of us who have had most peace, most prosperity. That which we call zeal for God is almost quite lost among us. Some of us have almost forgot whether there be such a thing as the cause and interest of Christ in the world. We who have cried and prayed about it, and had it upon our hearts, have sat down in our narrow compass, and almost forgot there is such a thing as the interest of Christ in the world, so as to have an active zeal for the ordinances of God according to rule, as God requires of us. Our primitive love, how is it decayed?[4] Value of the ordinances of Christ, and the society of his people for edification, how cold are we grown in these things? How little is the church society upon our hearts, which some of us remember, when it was the very joy of our souls? Truly we have reason to lift up our cry to God, that he would return and visit the churches, and pour out a new, fresh, reviving spirit upon them, that we fall not under the power of these decays, till we come to formality, and God withdraws himself from us, and leaves us, which he seems to be at the very point of doing.

Then, brethren, let us remember our own church, that God would in an especial manner revive the spirit of life, power, and holiness among us: that he would be pleased to help the officers of the church to discharge their duty, and not suffer them to fall under any decay of grace or gifts, unfitting of them to the discharge of their office to the edification of the church: that he would give them also to beware and take heed of formality, as to the exercise of gifts in their administration; and that he would take care of us, since we are apt to fall under these things. Let us pray, that we may be acted by the Spirit of God, and enlivened by the grace of God in all things we do.

Have any of us any particular occasions in reference to temptations, trials, and troubles, we may bear it upon our hearts to the Lord this day. This is much better than by multiplying a company of formal bills. The Lord help us to know the plague of our own hearts, and to be enabled to plead with the Lord upon this opportunity, for grace and mercy to help us in every time of need.

---

4 Owen here is alluding to Christ's letter to the church in Ephesus, where he charges them of having forsaken their first love (Rev. 2:4).

Recovering from Spiritual Decay

March 24, 1675/1676

Question. How may we recover from a decay of the principle of grace?

Answer

We have been speaking concerning the decay of the principle of grace; and I will now offer you some few thoughts that may be applied unto our recovery from the decay of this principle; in doing which, I shall tell you no more than I think I have found myself.

If we would recover spiritual life, we must come as near as we can unto, and abide as much as we are able at the wellhead of life. Christ is the spring of our spiritual life; he is every way our life. It is in a derivation of life from Christ, and in conformity to him, that we must look for our spiritual life.

Before I mention how we should approach unto, and lie at this wellhead of life, let me observe to you this one thing: that when there is a general contagious disease, the plague, or the like, every man will look to his health and safety with reference to other occasions, but will be most careful in regard to the general contagion. Now if forsaking this spring of life be the plague of the age, and the plague of the place where we live, and the plague of Christians, we ought to be very careful, lest this general contagion should reach us more or less, one way or other. It is evident to me, who have some advantage to consider things, as much as ordinary men, that the apostasy, the cursed apostasy that spreads itself over this nation, and whose fruits are in all ungodliness and uncleanness, consists in an apostasy from, and forsaking the person of Christ. Some write of how little use the person of Christ is in religion, none, but to declare the doctrine of the gospel to us. Consider the preaching and talk of men. You have much preaching and discourse about virtue and vice; so it was among the philosophers of old; but Jesus Christ is laid aside, quite as a thing forgotten, as if he was of no use, no consideration in religion; as if men knew not at all how to make any use of him, as to living to God.

This being the general plague, as is evident, of the apostasy of the day wherein we live, if we are wise we shall consider very carefully, whether we ourselves are not influenced, more or less, with it; as where there is a general temptation, it does, more or less, try all men, the best of believers, and prevail, more or less, upon their spirits. I am afraid we have not, some of us, that love for Christ, that delight in him, nor do make that constant abode with him, as we have done. We have very much lost out of our faith, and our affections, him, who is the life and center, the glory and the power of all spiritual life, and of all we have to do with God, Jesus Christ himself. I brought it in only to let us know, that if we would revive our spiritual life (and believe it, if any of us are not concerned in our spiritual decays, these are sapless things, and will be heard with as much weariness, as spoken), we are to abide more at the wellhead of life: it is the direction of our Lord Jesus Christ, abide in me, unless ye abide in me, ye can bring forth no fruit. And every such branch shall be so and so purged.[1]

But you will say: How shall we do so? How shall we abide, more than we have done, at this wellhead of life?

1. We are to abide at the wellhead of life by a frequency of the acts of faith upon the person of Christ. Faith is that grace, not only whereby we are implanted into Christ, but whereby we also abide in him: if so, methinks the frequent actings of faith upon the person of Christ, are a drawing near to the wellhead of life. And though we are to put forth the vigor, the earnestness, the watchfulness of our hearts unto obedience; yet a ceasing to continue in the acting of faith upon the person of Christ, even under the vigor of our own endeavors by those general, outward desires of walking with God, and living to him, will weaken us, and we shall find ourselves losers by it. Do you all understand me? I am not teaching the wise, and more knowing of the flock; I would speak unto the meanest. I say, suppose we should resolve with great earnestness, diligence, watchfulness to abide in duties, in inward duties, to watch over our hearts, which is required of us; yet, if in our so doing we are taken off thereby from frequent actings of faith upon Christ, as the spring of our life; we shall decay under all our endeavors, watchfulness, and multiplication of duties. Wherefore, my brethren, let me give you this advice, that you

---

1   Owen is alluding here to John 15:4–6.

would night and day, upon your beds, in your ways, upon all occasions, have the exercise of faith upon the person of Christ; faith working by a view of him as represented in the gospel, by trust in him, and by invocation of him, that he may be continually nigh unto you. And you cannot have him nigh unto you, unless you make yourselves by these actings of faith, through his grace, continually nigh unto him: so you will abide at the wellhead.

I could show you those excellent advantages that we should have by continually being near to Christ, who is the overflowing spring of grace, and from whence it will issue out to us, if we abide with him, be nigh to him, and keep up to this wellhead.

2. Abide with him in love. Oh, the warm affections for Christ, which some of you can witness concerning yourselves, that your hearts have been filled withal toward Christ, when you have been under his call to believe on him! And it is a marvelous way of abiding with Christ, to abide with him by love, which is called cleaving to God and Christ; it is the affection of adhesion, and gives a sense of union.

How, then, shall we get our hearts to abide with Christ by love?

This is a subject that if I were to preach upon, how many things would presently offer themselves to us, from the excellency of his person, from the excellency of his love, from our necessity of him, the advantages and benefits we have by him, and his kindness toward us? All these things, and many more, would quickly present themselves unto us.

But I will name but one thing, and I name it the rather, because I heard it mentioned in prayer since I came in: labor to have your hearts filled with a love to Jesus Christ, as there is in him made a representation of all divine excellencies. This was God's glorious design. It is not to be separated from his design of glorifying himself in the work of redemption; for a great part of God's glorious design in the incarnation of Christ, was in him to represent himself unto us who is "the image of the invisible God," "the express image of his person."[2] Now if you do but consider Christ, as God is gloriously represented unto you in him, you will find him the most proper object for divine love, for that love which is wrought in your hearts by the Holy Ghost, for that love that has sweetness, complacency, satisfaction in it. Then let us remember that we exercise our minds to consider Christ, as all the lovely properties of the divine nature and counsels of his will, as to love and grace, are manifested by Christ.

If we would abide at the wellhead of life, we must abide in these things: and let love be excited to Christ under this especial consideration, as he who

2 Col. 1:15; Heb. 1:3, respectively.

represents the supreme object of your love, God himself, in all the glorious properties of his nature.

3. Add meditation hereunto; study Christ more, and all the things of Christ; delight more in the hearing and preaching of Christ: he is our best friend: let not the difficulties of the mystery of his person and grace deter you. There are wonderful things of the counsels of heaven, and of the glory of the holy God in the person of Christ, as the head of the church; if you would be found inquiring into them; an unsearchable treasure of divine wisdom, grace and love, are laid up in Christ; therefore meditate upon them more. Let me assure you, this will prove the best expedient for the recovery of our spiritual life. And I will abide by this doctrine to eternity, that without it we shall never recover spiritual life to the glory of God in Christ.

4. And then, brethren, seeing we have in the next place felt decays in the midst of the performance of multiplied duties, labor to bring spirituality into your duties.

What is that, you will say, and wherein does it consist?

It is the due exercise of every grace that is required to the discharge of that duty. Let every such grace be in its due exercise, and that is to be spiritual in duty: as, for instance; would a man be spiritual in all his prayers? Let him then consider what grace, and what exercise of grace is required to this duty: a due fear and reverence of the name of God, faith, love, and delight in him; an humble sense of his own wants, earnest desires of supply, dependence upon God for guidance, and the like. We all know that these are the graces required to the discharge of this duty of praying by the Holy Ghost. And let these graces be in a due exercise, and then you are spiritual in this duty. Is the duty charity, giving a supply to the poor? There is to be a ready mind, a compassionateness of heart, and obedience unto the command of Christ in that particular; these are the graces required to the discharge of that duty, and to watch against the contrary vices. So that if we would bring spirituality into duty, it is to exercise the graces that are required by the rule to the performance of that duty.

I shall only farther give you this one caution: have a care that your head in notion, and your tongue in talk, do not too fast empty your hearts of truth: we are apt to lay it up in our heads by notions, and bring it forth in talk, and not let it be in our hearts; and this weakens spiritual life greatly. We hear the word preached, and it is of great concernment what account we shall give of the word that has been preached unto you; for we that preach must give an account of our preaching; and so must you of what you hear: and many a good word is spoken truly, and yet we see but little fruit of it. And the reason of this is, that some when they hear it, take no farther regard of it, but "let it slip," as the apostle speaks (Heb. 2:1). And if we complain of the treacherousness of our memories, it is the most harmless way of the slipping out of the word. It is not the treachery of our memories, but of our hearts and affections, that makes the heart like a broken vessel, that makes all the rents in it where the water runs out, as the comparison is. The word slips out by putting your affections into carnal exercise; and it quickly finds its way to depart from the heart that gives it no better entertainment. We talk away a sermon, and the sense of it; which robs us both of the sermon, and the fruit of it. A man hears a good word of truth, and instead of taking the power of it into his heart, he takes the notion of it into his mind, and is satisfied therewith: but this is not the way to thrive. God grant that we may never preach to you anything, but what we may labor to have an experience of the power of it in our own hearts, and to profit ourselves by the word, wherewith we design to profit others. And I pray God grant that you also may have some profit by the word dispensed to you, that it slip not out through carnal affections, and be not drawn out through notions and talk, with a regardlessness to treasure it up in your hearts.

These things we are diligently to attend unto, if we would recover our spiritual losses that we are complaining of, and that not without just cause.

Approaching the Whole Person of Christ in Devotion and Worship

April 7, 1676

*Question. It was queried by some, How we may make our
application unto Christ, not in general; but under what
notion and apprehension of the person of Christ?*

Answer

Because some seem to apprehend there might be danger in terminating our
worship upon the nature of Christ as a creature, I shall give you my thoughts
and directions in it. And,

First, you must observe, we are to have no conceptions in our acting of any
duty toward Christ or about him, but with respect unto his person; as he is
God and man in one person. It is not lawful for us to have any apprehensions
of Christ, to make any application to him as man only. Nor is it lawful for us to
have any apprehensions of him as God only. But all our apprehensions of Christ,
and all our addresses unto him, must be as God and man in one person. So he
is, and so he will be to all eternity. The union is inseparable and indissoluble.
And for any man to make his application unto Christ either as God, or as man,
is to set up a false Christ, Christ is God and man in one person, and no other.
So in all our actings of faith upon him, and applications unto him, we ought
to consider him, as he was the "seed of David,"[1] and as "God over all, blessed

---

1   Rom. 1:3.

for ever,"[2] in one person. This makes the great idolatry among the Papists, in the image of Christ they represent the human nature of Christ separated from his Deity, for they can make no representation of one, that is God and man in one person: hereby they become guilty of double idolatry, referring the mind unto one that is a man, and no more; and doing it by means of an image.

Secondly, the person of Christ is the immediate and proper object of all divine worship. The worship of Christ is commanded in the first commandment. By worship, I intend faith, love, trust, subjection of soul, invocation on the name of Christ, every act of the soul and mind, whereby we ascribe infinite divine excellencies unto God, which is the worship of the mind. It is the will of God "that all men should honour the Son, even as they honour the Father" (John 5:23). How do we honor the Father? By divine faith, trust, love, and worship, making him our end and our reward. So the Son is to be honored. And as to the divine person of the Son of God, being of the same nature, essence, and substance with the Father, there is no dispute of that among them by whom his Deity is acknowledged.

Thirdly, the divine person of the Son of God lost nothing of his glory and honor, that was due unto him, by the assumption of our human nature. Though thereby he became the Son of man, as well as the Son of God, a Lamb for sacrifice; yet he is still in his whole and entire person, the object of all that worship I spoke of before; and the whole church of God agrees together in giving that worship unto him,

> And when he had taken the book, the four beasts, and four and twenty elders fell down before the Lamb, having every one of them harps, and golden vials full of odours, which are the prayers of saints. And they sung a new song, saying, thou art worthy to take the book, and to open the seal thereof, for thou wast slain, and hast redeemed us unto God by thy blood, out of every kindred, and tongue, and people, and nation; [...] and I beheld, and I heard the voice of many angels round about the throne, and the beasts, and the elders, and the number of them was ten thousand times ten thousand, saying with a loud voice, worthy is the Lamb that was slain, to receive riches, and wisdom, and strength, and honour, and glory, and blessing. And every creature which is in heaven, and on the earth, and under the earth, and such as are in the sea, and all that are in them, heard I, saying, blessing, and honour, and glory, and power, be unto him that sitteth upon the throne, and unto the Lamb for ever and ever. (Rev. 5:8–9, 11–13)

2 Rom 9:5.

Jesus Christ is here distinguished from the Father; there is "he that sitteth upon the throne"; and "the Lamb"; and he is considered as incarnate, as a Lamb slain: and yet there is all the glory, honor, praise, and worship, that is given to him that sits upon the throne, the Father, given to Jesus Christ, God and man, the Lamb slain, who has redeemed us with his blood.

Fourthly, this person of Christ, God-man must not be so much as severed by any conception of the mind. For distinction, as God and man he may be considered two ways, either absolutely in himself, or in the discharge of his mediatory office. And this double consideration produces a double kind of worship to the person of Christ.

1. Consider Christ absolutely in his own person, as the Son of God incarnate, and so he is the immediate and ultimate object of our faith, prayer, and invocation. So that a man may lawfully, under the guidance and conduct of the Spirit of God, direct his prayer immediately to the person of Christ. You have the example of Stephen in his last prayer. "Lord Jesus," says he, "receive my spirit."[3] These were the words of our Lord Jesus Christ, when he died: "Father, into thy hands I commend my spirit."[4] And Stephen, when he died, committed his spirit into the hands of Jesus Christ: "Lord Jesus" (for that is the name of the Son of God incarnate, he shall be called "Jesus, for he shall save his people from their sins"[5]) into thy hands I commit my spirit. So that a person may make an immediate address in his prayers and supplications unto the person of Christ, as God and man. I look upon it as the highest act of faith that a believer is called unto in this world, to resign a departing soul into his hands, letting go all present things, and future hopes; to resign, I say, a departing soul quietly and peaceably into the hands of Christ. Now this, Stephen did with respect unto Jesus: "Lord Jesus, receive my spirit." There he left himself by faith. So we may apply ourselves unto him upon any other account, in the acting of faith upon any other occasion.

2. Consider Christ in the discharge of his mediatory office. And under that formal consideration, as discharging his mediatory office; he is not the ultimate object of our faith and invocation; but we call upon God, even the Father in the name of Jesus Christ. We through Christ have believed in God, says Peter in one of his epistles.[6] And it implies a contradiction to have it otherwise: for the calling him mediator shows he is a means between God and

---

3 Acts 7:59.
4 Luke 23:46.
5 Matt. 1:21.
6 Owen is alluding to 1 Pet. 1:21.

us; and so it is contradictory to say, our faith is terminated on his mediatory office. This he calls asking the Father in his name. You "shall ask the Father in my name":[7] that is, expressly plead the intervention of the mediation of Christ. And so the apostle tells us in that grand rubric and directory of church worship, by whom "we have access by one Spirit unto the Father" (Eph. 2:18). The Father is proposed as the ultimate object of access in our worship; and the Spirit is the effecting cause, enabling us unto this worship; and the Son is the means whereby we approach unto God.

All that I shall add hereunto is this: seeing there is in Scripture a double worship of Christ that is immediate (for his person is considered absolutely, and as mediator between God and man) which of these ought we principally to apply ourselves unto?

I answer plainly,

(1) Our direction for solemn worship in the church, generally respects Christ as mediator in Scripture. The general worship that is to be performed unto God in the assemblies of the saints, does look upon Christ as executing his mediatory office; and so our address is unto the throne of grace by him. By him we enter into the holy place; through him, and by him unto God. "I bow my knees unto (God) the Father of our Lord Jesus Christ" (Eph. 3:14). God, considered as the Father of our Lord Jesus Christ, is the proper, ultimate object of the solemn worship of the church.

(2) In treating and dealing about our own souls, under the conduct of the Spirit of God, it is lawful and expedient for us in our prayers and supplications to make addresses to the person of Christ, as Stephen did.

7   John 16:23.

Seeking Spiritual Grace from Christ

April 19, 1676

Question. How may we make our addresses to Christ for the exercise
of grace; that is, that we may have grace strengthened, and be
ready, for all exercise? Or, How may we make application to Christ
that we may receive grace from him to recover from decays?

Answer

I think the direction given by our Savior himself is so plain, and does so fall in with our experience, that we need not look much farther. Says he, unless you abide in me, you cannot bear fruit.[1] The business we aim at is fruit-bearing; which consists as much in the internal vigorous actings of grace, as in the performance of outward duties; to be faithful in our minds and souls, as well as in our lives. The way for that, says our Savior, is, abide in me. And unless we do so, he tells us plainly, do we whatever we will else, we cannot bring forth fruit. So that the whole of our fruitfulness depends upon our abiding in Christ: there cannot then be much more said unto this business, but to inquire a little, what it is to abide in Christ.

Certainly it is not a mere not going off from Christ, as we say, a man abides, when he does not go away. For I hope, that under all the decays we have complained of, and want of fruitfulness; yet we have not left Christ, and gone away from him. We have so far abode in him, as the branch abides in the root, from whence it has its communication and supplies. Therefore

---

1 Owen is alluding to John 15:4–6.

there is something in particular included in this abiding in Christ, dwelling in Christ, and Christ dwelling in us.

And there seems to be this in it, that to abide in Christ, is to be always nigh unto Christ, in the spiritual company of Christ, and in communication with Christ. It does not lie in a naked, essential act of believing, whereby we are implanted into Christ, and will not go from him; but there is something of an especial, spiritual activity of soul in this abiding in Christ, it is abiding with him, and in his presence.

And as this abiding with Christ must be by some acts of our souls, let us consider what acts those are, which may give a little farther light into this matter. And, first, it must be certainly by some act of our minds. Secondly, by some act of our wills. Thirdly, by some act of our affections. And thus we abide with Christ, which is the way certainly to bring forth fruit.

First, there is an abiding with Christ in our minds. Now this to me is in contemplation, and thoughts of him night and day: "I sought him on my bed, in the night,"[2] says the spouse: to consider very much the person of Christ, to contemplate upon him as vested with his glorious office, and as entrusted and designed by the Father to this work. "We all," says the apostle, "with open face beholding the glory of the Lord, as in a glass, are changed into the same image from glory to glory by the Spirit of the Lord."[3] My brethren! That which you and I are aiming at, is to be "changed into the same image"; that is, into the image and likeness of the glory of God in Christ. I dare boldly say, that by those of us, who have reason to have daily apprehensions of our going out of the world, and leaving this state of things, that we have no greater desire, nor is there anything more frequent in our minds than this, that we may be more and more changed into that image before we go out of this world; for we are looking after perfection in likeness to Christ. Therefore aged Christians especially will bear witness, that there is nothing now we long for more, than to be more and more changed into the image and likeness of Christ. How shall we get to this? Why, says he, the way is by looking steadily upon Christ, as a man looks with an optic glass to an object at a great distance. We behold him, says he, by looking steadily upon Christ himself, and the glory of God in him. Now there is a wonderful large object for us to behold; for when you look upon the glory of God in Christ, you have what you please of Christ for the object of your eye and view; the person of Christ, the office of Christ, the merit of Christ, the example of Christ, the death of Christ, and

---

2 Song 3:1.
3 2 Cor. 3:18.

what you will, so you be much intent in your thoughts and minds, much in immediate contemplation about Christ. I do not know how you find it, brethren; but it is the advice I would give you, who are aged Christians, and not likely to continue long in this world, to exercise yourselves in immediate contemplations upon Christ. All the teachings you have had from ministers, the principal end of them have been to enable you to this; and really if I know anything, we shall find them accompanied with a sweet, transforming power, beyond what we have had experience of in other ways and duties: "We shall be changed into the same likeness."

Well then, we abide with Christ in the acts of our mind, by immediate thoughtfulness and contemplation upon Christ in the night, and upon our beds, and in our walkings, and by the wayside, and in times we set apart for meditation, we are greatly to labor after an intuitive view of Christ, that is a direct view in the contemplation of Christ.

Secondly, if you will abide with Christ, there must be an acting of your will in it also, and that is in great diligence and carefulness about that obedience which Christ does require in all the instances of it. This is a great way of abiding with Christ, when we labor to have our wills in a readiness unto all the instances of obedience that Christ requires at our hands. Let that be the question, whether it be the will of God that we should do thus, or not. And if it be so, pray let us be ready to show we do abide with Christ, by yielding cheerful and willing obedience to him in this instance and duty which he calls us unto, and so in all other things. I would have every one of us think often of this matter, what it is Christ requires of me personally, in a way of duty and obedience. And I would have us labor to have in great readiness all things which Christ requires of us. And especially, brethren, I would have this in a readiness, that Christ requires of me to walk very circumspectly, and carefully, to keep myself from spots, and pollution, and defilements by converse in the world. This Christ requires at all times, in all instances, and upon all occasions. What have we been preaching? What have former teachers been instructing us in? All that you are taught is, that you should come to the knowledge of all instances of duty, and the way of them, which Christ requires at your hands. And "if you know these things, happy are you if ye do them."[4]

This is your fruit bearing, a direct contemplation upon Christ; wherein I would beg, that both you and my own soul might be found more to abound, while we are in this world, and you will find Christ in the discharge of this duty will make very near approaches, and frequent visits to your hearts,

---

4 John 13:17.

more in the discharge of this duty, than of any other; and to have our hearts in a readiness to comply with every instance of obedience Christ requires at our hands.

Thirdly, there is an abiding with Christ in point of affection. There may be love and delight in all these things; if there be not, very spiritual contemplations will be a bar. There is no duty, that is required of any man in this world so spiritual, so heavenly, so evangelical, but through want of love and delight a man may be slothful in performing of it. I may tie myself to do so this hour, or that hour, and have no benefit to my own soul, nor give any glory unto God, if there be not love and delight in it. They will sweeten the duty, and refresh the heart of God and man, Christ and us. So labor, brethren, and pray greatly for it, that you may abide with Christ with delight, that you may find a sweetness and refreshment in it, and that every season of retiring unto Christ may bring a kind of spiritual joy and gladness to your hearts. Now you have a great opportunity, having shaken off the occasions of life and other concernments, to dwell with Christ, now it is a good time.

Discourse 7

Threats to Our Faith When in Prayer

March 22, 1676

Question. When our own faith is weakened as to the hearing of
our prayers; when we ourselves are hindered within ourselves
from believing the answer of our prayers; have no ground to
expect we should be heard, or ground to believe we are heard:
What are those things, that greatly weaken our faith, as to the
answer of our prayers; that though we continue to pray, yet our
faith is weakened as to the hearing of our prayers? And what
are the grounds that weaken men's faith in such a state?

Answer

If our hearts are not duly prepared to the consideration of the great and
glorious properties, presence, and holiness of God, and duly affected with
them in our preparation for prayer, it is certain we can have no faith for the
hearing of our prayers.

It is also of great importance, that we consider aright in what state the things
we seek for are promised; whether temporal things, that are left to God; or spiritual, that lie under a promise, and so we may press God immediately about them.

There are two things that are certainly great weakeners of our faith as to
God's hearing our prayers.

First, the one is, that intermixture of self, which is apt to creep into our
prayers, in public especially, in the congregation and assemblies, self-repu-
tation in the exercise of gifts, or whatever it be, weakens our faith as to the
expectation of God's hearing our prayers.

Secondly, the other is, that we pray with earnestness and fervency, with noise and clamor of speech; but do not industriously pursue the things we pray for. Unless we watch and follow after these things, we shall not have ground of faith for the hearing of our prayers. As for instance; when the soul is burdened with a corruption, there is nothing we are more fervent in prayer unto God against; yet when we have done this, we take no more care to get it mortified. Where is our faith, that our prayers may be heard in this thing! We must pursue our prayers, or it will weaken our faith as to the hearing of them. We all pray; but do we believe that God will hear and answer our prayers?

I shall not speak unto the nature of that faith we exercise, or what assurance we may have of God's hearing our prayers; but I will tell you plainly what hinders in us the answer of our prayers.

1. We are not clear that our persons are accepted. God had respect unto Abel, and his offering; and not unto Cain, and his offering. We can have no more faith that our prayers are heard, than we have faith that our persons are accepted. How many of us are dubious, and know not whether we believe or no? or are the children of God or no? According as our faith is, as to the acceptance of our persons; so ordinarily our faith will be, as to the hearing of our prayers. I do acknowledge, that sometimes under extraordinary darkness, or temptation, while a person does not at all know, nor has any assurance, what is his own condition, whether approved, or rejected of God; yet the Holy Spirit of God many times gives assurance of the hearing of that prayer, which is poured out in the anguish of the soul. But let us bring things unto a good issue between God and our souls, and not complain that our prayers are not heard, when we are negligent to come unto the assurance of faith about the acceptance of our persons. We have had many days of prayer, and have not seen that return of our prayer, that we designed. This evil lies at the bottom; that we have been dubious as to our state of acceptance with God. Let us labor to amend it.

2. Another thing is this; pray while you will, you will not believe your prayers are answered, if you indulge any private lust, or do not vigorously endeavor the mortification of it, according to what the Scripture and duty require. If any lust arises in the soul, and we do not immediately engage to mortify it, as God requires, it will break out, and weaken our faith in all our prayers. Therefore if you will be helped to believe the answer of your prayers, labor to search your hearts. Do not think that no corruption is indulged, but such as break out into open sin. It may be, you do not know the corruption you indulge; labor therefore to find it out, and you will find how your faith is weakened thereby.

3. Again, want of having treasured up former experiences of the hearing of prayer. We have not provided as we ought in this matter. If we had laid up manifold experiences of God's having heard our prayers, it would strengthen our faith that God does hear them. It may be some have prayed all their days, God has kept their souls alive, that they have not wickedly departed from God, and they have obtained particular mercies; why such ought to keep a constant record of God's hearing their prayers. Every discovery made of Christ that draws our souls more to love him, and engages us to cleave unto him, is our experience of God's hearing our prayers.

4. I might add; when we ourselves are not sensible that we arise unto that fervency of prayer, that is required of them that believe. If we pray in the congregation, in our closets, or families, and when we have done are not sensible that we have risen up unto that fervency that is required, we cannot believe our prayers are answered.

It is the duty of all men to pray unto the Lord; but it is incumbent on none more than those, who have really and sincerely given up themselves unto God, and yet in truth have no comfortable persuasion concerning their condition. That is a state wherein I am so far from discouraging prayer, that it is your season for prayer, in the whole course of your lives. When Paul was first called, before such time as he had evidence of the pardon of his sins, it is said: "behold, he prays."[1] If they truly attend unto their state and condition, they may be sure to be the persons of whom also it will be said, behold, they pray. And even in these prayers they may exercise faith, when they have not faith to believe that their prayers are heard. But while in this condition, it will be hard to believe that their prayers are heard, when they cannot believe that their persons are accepted.

---

1   Acts 9:11.

Discourse 8

Identifying Habitual Sin

Question. When may any one sin, lust, or corruption
be esteemed habitually prevalent?

Answer

I shall premise some few things, before I come to answer the question.

First, all lusts and corruptions whatsoever, have their root and residence in our nature, the worst of them. For, says the apostle, "Every man is tempted [. . .] of his own lust" (James 1:14). Every man has his own lust, and every man has all lust in him; for this lust or corruption is the depravation of our nature, and it is in all men. And in the root and principle of it, it is in all men even after their conversion. So says the apostle concerning believers, "The flesh lusteth against the Spirit, [. . .] so that ye (believers) cannot do the things that ye would" (Gal. 5:17). What does the flesh lust unto? Why it lusts unto the works of it. What are they? Adultery, fornication, uncleanness, licentiousness, idolatry, witchcraft, hatred, strife, sedition, heresy, envy, murder, drunkenness, reveling, and such like.[1] The flesh lusts unto all these things in believers, the worst things that can be mentioned. Whence is that [saying] of our Savior, which yields to me a doctrine that is a sad truth; but so plain that, nothing can be more. He foretells marvelous troubles, great desolations and destructions that shall come upon the world, and befall all sorts of men, and says it is a day that as "a snare shall [. . .] come on all them that dwell on the face of the whole earth."[2] Nothing makes me more believe that day, that

1 Owen is alluding to Gal. 5:19–21.
2 Luke 21:35.

473

terrible day of the Lord, is coming upon the face of the whole earth, than this, that it comes "as a snare." Men do not take notice of it, do you therefore take heed to yourselves, you that are my disciples, believers, "take heed to yourselves, lest at any time your hearts be overcharged with surfeiting and drunkenness, and the cares of this life, and so that day come upon you at unawares."[3] The doctrine I observe from thence is this: that the best of men have need to be warned, to take care of the worst of sins in the approach of the worst of times. Who would think, when such troubles, distresses, desolations were coming upon a nation, in that place the disciples of Christ should be in danger of being overtaken with surfeiting,[4] and drunkenness, and the cares of this life? Yet he, who is the wisdom of God, knew how it would be with us. Nay, what if a man should say from observation, that professors are never more in danger of sensual, provoking sins, than when destruction is lying nearest at the door? "In that day," says he, "take care."

Secondly, another thing I would premise is this, that this root of sin abiding in us, as I have showed, will upon its advantage work unto all sorts of evils; which should give us a godly jealousy over our souls, and over one another. Says the apostle, sin "wrought in me all manner of concupiscence" (Rom. 7:8).

Thirdly, if it be so, that sin does thus always abide in us, and will upon occasions work to all its fruit, to all manner of concupiscence; then the mortification of sin is a continual duty, that we ought to be exercised in all our days. "Ye are dead, and your life is hid with Christ in God" (Col. 3:3). A blessed state and condition! I desire no better attainment in this world, than this holds out. But what duty does the apostle infer from thence? "Therefore," says he, "mortify your members, which are upon the earth." What, I pray? "Fornication, uncleanness, inordinate affections, evil concupiscence, and covetousness which is idolatry."[5] The mortification of sin is a duty incumbent upon the best of saints.

Fourthly, the fourth thing I would premise is this: that a particular sin does not obtain a signal prevalency without it has some signal advantage: for our corrupt nature is universally and equally corrupt, but a particular sin obtains prevalency by particular advantages.

It would be too long to speak of all those advantages; I shall name two, whereunto others may be reduced.

1. The inclination of constitution gives particular advantages unto particular sins. Some may be very much inclined to envy; some to wrath and

3 Luke 21:34.
4 I.e., overconsumption.
5 Col. 3:5.

passion; and others to sensual sins, gluttony, drunkenness, uncleanness, to name the things which our Savior names and warns us of. It is with respect hereunto, that David said, he would keep himself from his iniquity,[6] as some think. I have only this to say, that it has been much from the fallacy of the devil, that men have been apt to plead constitution, and the inclination of their constitution to the extenuation of their sin, when indeed it is an aggravation. I am apt to be passionate in my nature, says one; I am sanguine, says another, and love company. They make their natural inclinations to be a cover and excuse for their sin. But this I must say as my judgment, that if grace does not cure constitution sins, it has cured none; and that we can have no trial of the efficacy of grace, if we have it not in curing constitution sins. The great promise is, that it shall change the nature of the wolf and the lion, of the bear, the asp, the cockatrice, and that they shall become as lambs; which it can never do, if it does not change it by a habitual counterworking of inclinations arising from constitution. If grace being habitual does not change the very inclination of constitution, I know not what it does. That is the first advantage whereby particular sins come to have signal advantage and prevalency.

2. Outward occasions. And I refer them unto two heads.

(1) To education, particular sins get advantage by education. If we do even in education instruct our children to pride by their fineries, and deportment to themselves, if we teach them to be proud, we heap dry fuel upon them, till such time as lust will flame. Let us take heed of this. It is an easy thing to bring forth a proud generation by such means.

(2) Society in the world, according to occasion of life, is that which inflames particular corruptions. According as men delight in their converse, so corruption will be provoked and heightened by it.

I have spoken all these things previously to show you where lies the nature and principle of the danger we are going to inquire into, and how it comes to that condition.

Now I shall inquire a little into the question itself: How we may know whether a particular corruption is habitually predominant or no?

Brethren, I take it for granted, the vilest of those lusts which our Savior and his apostles warn us against to mortify and crucify, may be working in the hearts and minds of the best of us; and that a particular lust may be habitually prevalent, where for particular reasons it never brings forth outward effects; therefore look to yourselves. I say then, when the mind and soul is

6   Owen is alluding to Ps. 18:23.

frequently and greatly, as there are occasions, urged upon and pressed with a particular lust and corruption, this does not prove that particular lust and corruption to be habitually prevalent; for it may be a temptation. This may all proceed from the conjunction of temptation with indwelling sin, which will make it fight, and war, and use force, and lead captive.

But suppose a person be in that condition, how shall he know whether it be a temptation in conjunction with indwelling sin in general? Or, whether it be an habitual prevalency of a particular corruption?

I answer,

1. It is not from the prevalency of corruption these three ways.

(1) If the soul be more grieved with it, than defiled by it, it is a temptation, and not a lust habitually prevalent. In this case, when a heart is so solicited with any sin, sin and grace are both at work, and have their contrary aims. The aim of grace is to humble the soul, and the aim of sin to defile it. And the soul is so far defiled, as by the deceitfulness and solicitations of sin, consent is obtained. Defilement arises not from temptation, as active upon the mind; but from temptation, as admitted with consent: so far as it consents, whether by surprisal, or long solicitations, so far it is defiled. It is otherwise, if the soul is more grieved with it, than defiled by it.

(2) It is so, when the soul can truly, and does look upon that particular corruption, as its greatest and most mortal enemy. It is not soldiers who have ruined my estate, nor a disease that has taken away my health, nor enemies who have ruined my name or opposed me; but this corruption, which is my great and mortal enemy. When the soul is truly under this apprehension, then it is to be hoped, it is the power of temptation; and not the prevalency of lust, or corruption.

(3) It is so also when a man maintains his warfare and his conflict with it constantly, especially in those two great duties of private prayer and meditation; which if once the soul is beat off from, it is driven out of the field, and sin is conqueror. But so long as a man maintains the conflict in the exercise of grace in those duties, I look upon it as a temptation, and not an habitual, prevalent lust.

2. I shall now proceed to show when a corruption is habitually prevalent. And here is a large field before me, but I shall only speak some few things.

(1) When a man does choose, or willingly embrace known occasions of his sin, that sin is habitually prevalent. There is no man that has the common understanding of a Christian, and has any corruption or lust working in him, but he knows what are the occasions that provoke it. No man unless he is profligately wicked can choose sin for sin's sake. But he who knows what are the occasions that stir up, excite, and draw forth any particular corruption, and

does choose them, or willingly embrace them, there is the habitual prevalency of sin to a high degree in the mind of that man, whosoever he be: for sin is to be rejected in the occasion of it, or it will never be refused in the power of it.

(2) Let a man fear it is so, when he finds arguments against it to lose their force. No man is under the power of particular corruption, but will have arguments suggested to his mind from fear, danger, shame, ruin, against continuing under that corruption. When a man begins to find these arguments abate in their force, and have not that prevalency upon his mind, they have had, let him fear there is an habitual prevalency of his corruption.

(3) When a man upon conviction is turned out of his course, but is not turned aside from his design, when he traverses his way like the wild ass: in her occasion who shall turn her aside? If you meet her, or pursue her, you may turn her out of her way; but still she pursues her design. Men meet with strong convictions of sin, strong rebukes and reproofs; this a little puts them out of their way, but not from their design or inclination, the bent of their spirit lies that way still, and the secret language of their heart is, that it was free with me, to be as in former days. Certainly a corruption is habitually prevalent, if it seldom or never fails to act itself under opportunities and temptations. If a man who trades cheats every time he is able to do so, he has covetousness in his heart. Or if a man whenever opportunity and occasion meet together to drink, does it to excess; this is a sign of an habitual corruption, if he be not able to hold out scarce at any time against a concurrence of temptation and opportunity.

3. When the soul, if it will examine itself, will find it is gone from under the conduct of renewing grace, and is at the best but under the evidence of restraining grace. Believers are under the conduct of renewing grace, and I grant that sometimes, when under the power of corruption and temptation, even they have broken the rule of renewing grace, God will keep them in order by restraining grace, by fear of danger, shame, and infamy; by outward considerations set home upon the mind by the Spirit of God, which keeps them off from sin; but this is but sometimes. But if a man finds his heart wholly got from under the rule of renewing grace, and that he has no leading or conduct but restraining grace, his sin has got the perfect victory over him; that is, he would sin on to the end of his life, were it not for fear of shame, danger, death, and hell; he is no longer acted by renewing grace, which is faith and love, faith working by love. A man who has a spiritual understanding may examine himself, and find under what conduct he is.

4. Lastly, when there is a predominant will in sinning, then lust is habitually prevalent. Sin may entangle the mind, and disorder the affections, and yet not be prevalent; but when it has laid hold upon the will, it has the mastery.

Discourse 9

The Conflict between Habitual
Sin and the Spiritual State

April 19, 1677

Question. Whether lust or corruption habitually
prevalent, be consistent with the truth of grace?

Answer

This is a hard question, there are difficulties in it, and it may be it is not precisely to be determined. I am sure we should be wonderfully careful what we
say upon such a question, which determines the present and eternal condition
of the souls of men.

Supposing we retain something of what was spoken in stating a lust or
corruption so habitually prevalent, because this is the foundation of our
present inquiry, I shall bring what I have to say upon this question to a few
heads, that they may be remembered.

I say then,

First, it is the duty of every believer to take care, that this may never be his
own case practically. We shall meet with straits enough, and fears enough,
and doubts enough about our eternal condition, though we have no lust,
nor corruption habitually prevalent. Therefore, I say, it is the duty of every
believer to take care this may never be his case. David did so, "Who can understand his errors?" says he. "Cleanse thou me from secret faults. Keep back
thy servant also from presumptuous sins: [. . .] then shall I be upright, and
free from the great offense" (Ps. 19:12–13). He acknowledges his errors and

sins, and prays for cleansing, purifying, pardon; but for presumptuous sins, sins with a high hand, and every habitual corruption which has something of presumption, Lord, "keep back thy servant from them," says he. The apostle's caution is to the same purpose, "Looking diligently, lest any man fail of the grace of God, lest any root of bitterness spring up" (Heb. 12:15). There is the root of bitterness in everyone, which I look upon as a corruption in some measure habitual, if it springs up unto great defilement. And I beseech you, brethren, beg of God for your own souls and mine, that we may be careful this is never our case.

Secondly, the second thing I would observe is this: whatever may be said concerning its consistency with grace, it is certainly inconsistent with peace. I wish we could remember what description was given before of this prevalent corruption, that we might consider the things now applied unto it. Here though I would be as tender, as of the apple of mine eye in these things, I will not fear to say this: that the peace which any one has concurring with a prevalent corruption, is security, not peace. I know men may be at great peace under prevalent corruptions, and live upon good hopes, that they shall be accepted with God, that it shall be well with them in the latter end; and that they shall have power one time or other against this corruption, and will leave it when it is seasonable, and strive against it more than they have done. But all such peace is but security. Under prevalent corruption there is a drawing back; for I would state the matter thus: a person who is a professor, and has kept up to duties and obedience, till some lust has gotten strength by constitution, temptations, or occasions of life, and has drawn him off from his former renovation in walking with God; there is then a drawing back. Now, says the apostle, "If any man draw back, my soul shall have no pleasure in him" (Heb. 10:38). And when God has no pleasure according to the several degrees of backsliders (it may be that is meant of final apostasy) he does not intimate anything that is a ground of peace to that soul. So, "For the iniquity of his covetousness I was wroth," and hid myself from him (Isa. 57:17). If there be an incurable iniquity of covetousness, or any other iniquity, whether manifest unto us or no, God is angry and does hide himself from us. I pray, brethren, let us examine our peace; and if we find we have a peace that can maintain its ground and station under prevalent corruption, trust no more to that peace, it will not stand us in stead when it comes to a trial.

Thirdly, the third thing I would say is this, that if a prevalent corruption be not inconsistent with the truth of grace, it is certainly inconsistent with the true exercise of grace. It is not indeed inconsistent with the performance of duties, but it is inconsistent with the true exercise of grace in the performance of duties. It is often seen and known, that persons under prevalent corruption will multiply duties, thereby to quiet conscience, and to compensate God for what they have done amiss. Persons may multiply prayers, follow preaching, and attend to other duties, when they use all these things, through the deceitfulness of sin, but as a cloak unto some prevailing corruption. But in all those duties there is no true exercise of grace.

The true determination of this question depends upon a right exposition of 1 John 2:15, if we could understand that verse, it determines this point: "Love not the world, neither the things that are in the world: if any man love the world, the love of the Father is not in him." There is the question, whether prevalent corruption is inconsistent with true grace? I know the words may have this construction, if any man do make the world his chiefest good, if any man put the world in the place of God, then the love of the Father is not in him; he has either received no love from God, or he has no love to God, as a Father in Christ. But indeed, the apostle speaking unto believers, I am apt to think, speaks not of the whole kind, but degrees: if there is a prevalency of love of the world, there is no prevalency of the actings of the love of the Father; that they do not concern the habitual principles of the love of the world, and of the love of the Father, but the prevailing actings of the one and the other. And accordingly it may be said of all other graces whatsoever, that where there is a prevalency of the acting of sin, there is a suspension of the exercise of grace. Brethren, if any of us have been under the power of prevalent corruption (I will be still tender, and speak what ought to be received and believed, whether people do or not) it is much to be feared, we have lost all our prayers and hearing, because we have not had a true exercise of grace in them. Some exercise there may be, but a due and true exercise of grace will be laid asleep by prevalent corruption. And therefore let us take heed of prevalent corruption, as we would take heed of losing all things that we have wrought, our praying, hearing, suffering, charity, for want of a due exercise of grace in them.

Fourthly, I shall grant this, that spiritual life may be in a swoon, when the spiritual man is not dead. There is a kind of deliquium[1] of the spirits, called swooning away, that may befall believers, which suspends all acts of life, when yet the man is not dead. So I say, though I should see a man through the prevalency of corruption have all the evidences of a spiritual life cast into a swoon, yet I will not presently conclude the spiritual man is dead. Take the case of David, from the time of his great fall and transgression in the matter of

---

1   I.e., a loss of vitality.

Uriah until the coming of Nathan the prophet. Persons are generally inclined to believe that the spiritual life was in a swoon, when the spiritual man was not dead. His fall, as an honest man said, beat the breath out of his body, and he lay a long time like a man dead, by reason of that power, which one signal sin left in his soul. And take that as a great instance, that one sin, not immediately taken off by great humiliation, leaves great and even habitual inclinations in the soul to the same sin. So that some ascribed it unto the corruption of our nature. For it is a great and difficult question in divinity, how one particular sin, as the sin of Adam was, should bring in habitual corruption to our nature. To which some answer thus: that any one, single, moral act performed with a high hand, has great obliquity[2] in it, disposing our whole nature to corruption. David by that single act of flagrant wickedness did continue in it for so long a space of time, till Nathan came and administered some good spirits to him that relieved him out of his swoon. Wherefore I say that I will not judge a person to be spiritually dead, whom I have judged formerly to have had spiritual life, though I see him at present in a swoon as to all evidences of the spiritual life. And the reason why I will not judge so, is this, because if you judge a person dead, you neglect him, you leave him; but if you judge him in a swoon, though never so dangerous, you use all means for the retrieving of his life. So ought we to do to one another and our own souls.

Fifthly, there is a prevalency of sin that is inconsistent with true grace, which may befall those who have been professors. So the apostle does plainly declare, "Know ye not that to whom ye yield yourselves servants to obey, his servants ye are to whom ye obey; whether of sin unto death, or of obedience unto righteousness." (Rom. 6:16). There is such a serving of sin, as puts a man into a contrary state.

Sixthly, I shall add but one thing more, and that is this: there may be a corruption, sin, or lust habitually prevalent as to whatsoever evidences the person in whom it is, or others can discern; and yet the root of the matter, the root of spiritual life be notwithstanding in the person.

Suppose then there is such a prevalency, that the soul judges to be habitual, how shall we know, whether the root of the matter be in such a person or no?

If the soul has anything left of spiritual life, there will be something of vital operations in that soul. Now the vital operations that give evidence the soul is not absolutely slain by prevalent corruption, are opposition, and humiliation. So long as the soul, though it be never so much captivated, is conscious to

---

2 I.e., immorality.

itself of a sincerity in the opposition it makes, there is an evidence of a vital operation, as likewise where it is constant in its humiliation on that account.

But if it be farther inquired, how it may be known that this humiliation is sincere?

I answer, it cannot be known from its vigor and efficacy; for that overthrows the question. For if the opposition was vigorous and effectual, it would break the power of lust and corruption, so that it would be no more prevalent. But two ways it may be known.

1. By its constancy. If the root of the matter be still in us, there will be a constant opposition to every act of any prevailing corruption whatsoever. I do not speak about violent temptations, but ordinary cases, in which I know not whence we should conclude the root of the matter is in that man, who does not make a sincere opposition to every instance of the acting of prevalent corruption. If a man can pass over one and another instance of prevalent corruption without any humiliation for it, the holy sovereign God show him grace and mercy; but it is to me "the way of a serpent upon a stone,"[3] I see it not, I know it not.

2. It is sincere if it be from its proper spring, that is, if the opposition be not from conviction, light, or conscience only; but from the will of the poor sinner. I would do otherwise, I would have this sin destroyed, I would have it rooted out, that it should be no more in me, my will lies against it, however it has captivated my affections, and disturbed my course.

This is all I dare say upon this question: that there may be a habitual prevalency of corruption, which may seem so to them in whom it is, as also to those who converse with them, and yet the root of the matter is in them. We may know the root of the matter by the acting of spiritual life, in opposition going before, and humiliation coming after. We may know the sincerity of these vital actings by their constancy, and by their spring, if we are constant in them, and if they arise from our wills.

---

3   Prov. 30:19.

Instructions for Responding to Habitual Sin

May 4, 1677

Question. What shall a person do who finds himself under the power of a prevailing corruption, sin, or temptation?

Answer

I shall premise only this one thing, and then inquire whether it belongs to us or no.

This prevalency has many degrees. It may be a prevalency to outward scandal, or to the utter loss of inward peace, or to the disquieting and divesting of us of that tranquility of mind, usually which Christ calls us unto. Now, pray consider, that I speak to it equally and in every degree. And perhaps there may be none of us, but at one time or other, after inquiry, will have had experience in one degree or other, either to disquietment, loss of peace, or scandal.

What shall such a person then do, who finds it so with him?

I answer,

First, he should labor to affect his mind with the danger of it. It is not conceivable how subtle sin is to shift off an apprehension of the danger of it. Notwithstanding this, says the man, yet I hope I am in a state of grace, and shall be saved, and come to the issue of it at one time or other: and so the mind keeps off a due sense of the danger of it. I beseech you, brethren and sisters, if this is your condition, labor to affect your minds that this state, as far as I know, will end in hell. And let not your minds be relieved from the apprehension, that upon due and good grounds of faith, these ways go down to the chambers of death. Do not please yourselves imagining you are members of the church, and have good hopes of salvation by Jesus Christ; but consider whither this tends; and affect your minds with it.

Secondly, when the person is affected with the danger of it, the next thing to be done is, to burden his conscience with the guilt of it. For the truth is, as our minds are upon many pretenses slow to apprehend the danger of sin; so our consciences are very unwilling to take the weight of the burden of it, as to its guilt. I speak not of men of seared consciences, that lay what weight you will upon them, will feel none; but even of the consciences of renewed men, unless they use all the ways and means whereby conscience may be burdened, as by apprehensions of the holiness of God, of the law, of the love of Christ, and of all those things whereby conscience must be made to feel the weight of its guilt. No sooner does it begin to be made a little sick with a sense of the guilt of sin, but it takes a cordial presently. Here this sin has taken place, it has contracted this and that guilt; I have been thus long negligent in this or that duty, I have thus long engaged in this and that folly, and been so given up unto the world; I must take to Christ by faith, or I am undone: it is afraid of making its load. But let conscience bear the burden, and not easily shift it off, unless it can, by true faith guided by the word, load it upon Christ, which is not a thing of course to be done.

Thirdly, what shall we do in case we have this apprehension of its danger, and can be thus burdened with its guilt? Pray for deliverance. How? You will say, there is in the Scriptures mention of "roaring" (Ps. 32:3). The voice of my roaring. And likewise of shouting (Lam. 3:8), I shouted and cried. This is a time to pray, that God would not hide his face from our roaring, nor shut out our prayers when we shout unto him; that is, to cry out with all the vigor of our souls. Christ is able to succor and help them that make an outcry to him. The word signifies so, and our word succor, signifies a running in to help a man who is ready to be destroyed. These may seem hard things to us, but it is a great thing to save our souls, and to deliver ourselves from the snares of Satan.

Fourthly, treasure up every warning, and every word that you are convinced was pointed against your particular corruption. There is none of you who may have the power of particular corruptions, but God at one time or other in his providence or word gives particular warning, that the soul may say, this is for me, I must comply with it; but it is like a man that sees his face in a glass, and goes away, and immediately forgets what manner of man he was:[1] there

---

1 Owen is alluding to James 1:23–24.

is an end of it. But if God give you such warnings, set them down, treasure them up, lose them not, they must be accounted for. "He that being often reproved, hardens his heart, shall perish suddenly, and that without remedy."[2]

Fifthly, I shall mind you of two rules, and so have done.

1. In your perplexities, as to the power of sin, exercise faith, that notwithstanding all, you see and find that you are almost lost and gone, there is a power in God, through Christ, for the subduing and conquering of it.

2. It is in vain for any to think to mortify a prevailing sin, who does not at the same time endeavor to mortify all sin, and to be found in every duty. Here is a person troubled and perplexed with a temptation or corruption, both are the same in this case: he cries, O, that I were delivered; I had rather have deliverance than life; I will do my endeavor to watch against it. But it may be this person will not come up to a constancy in secret prayer; he will go up and down, and wish himself free, but will not be brought up to such duties wherein those lusts must be mortified. Therefore take this rule along with you; never hope to mortify any corruption whereby your hearts are grieved, unless you labor to mortify every corruption by which the Spirit of God is grieved; and be found in every duty, especially those under which grace thrives and flourishes.

---

2   Prov. 29:1.

Discourse 11

Responding to Difficult Seasons of Divine Providence

Question. What is our duty with respect to dark and difficult
dispensations of God's providence in the world?

Answer

In answer unto this question, three things are to be considered.

First, what are, in a Scripture sense, those things that make a season of providence dark and difficult? Secondly, what are the open signs of the coming and passing of such a season over us? Thirdly, what are our special duties in reference to our entering into, and passing through such a season?

First, what are those things that make a season of providence dark and difficult?

I find four things in Scripture that make a dark season of providence; and if I mistake not, they are all upon us.

1. The long-continued prosperity of wicked men. This you are sensible is the most known case of all the Old Testament (Ps. 73; Jer. 12:1–3; Hab. 1:4, 13, and many other places). The holy men of old did confess themselves in great perplexity at the long-continued prosperity of wicked men, and their long-continued prosperity in ways of wickedness. Give but this one farther circumstance to it, the long-continued prosperity of wicked men, in their wickedness, when the light shines round about them to convince them of that wickedness, and God speaks in and by the light of his word against them, that is a trial. When all things were wrapped up in darkness and idolatry, it is no wonder at the patience of God; but when things come in any place

to that state, that many continue prosperous in wickedness when the day is upon them that judges them, it is a difficulty.

2. It is a difficult season of providence, when the church is continued under persecution and distress in a time of prayer, when they give themselves to prayer. The difficulty seems mentioned, "O Lord, [. . .] how long wilt thou smoke against the prayer of thy people?" (Ps. 80:4). This made it hard, that God should afflict his church, and keep her under distresses, and suffer the furrows to be made long upon her back, and continue her under oppression from one season to another, there may be evident reason for that. But, says God, "Call upon me in the time of trouble,"[1] and I will hear. God has promised to hear the church. Will not God avenge the elect, that call upon him day and night? He will do it speedily.[2] Now when God seems to be angry with the prayers of his people, that is a difficult season: when they cry and shout and God shuts out their prayers, that makes a dark providence.

As the other difficulty is evidently upon us; so I hope we have this difficulty to conflict withal, that the anger of God continues to smoke against the prayers of his people, as having stirred up many a blessed cry to himself, for there is a time when he will hear and answer their prayers.

3. It is a dark and difficult dispensation of providence, when the world, and nations of the world are filled with confusion and blood, and no just reason appearing why it should be so. When our Savior foretells a difficult season, he says, there shall be terrible times, such as never were; nation shall rise against nation, and kingdom against kingdom, and there shall be wars, bloodshed, and earthquakes; and the very elect shall hardly escape (Matt. 24; Luke 21). Therefore God calls such a time, "a day of darkness," yea, "of thick darkness" (Joel 2:2). A dark gloomy day. There is nothing to be seen in all the confusions that are in the world at this day, but that the frogs or unclean spirits are gone forth to stir up the lusts of men to make havoc of one another.

4. It adds greatly to the difficulty of a season, when we have no prospect whither things are tending, and what will be their issue.

There are two ways whereby we may have a prospect of things that are in being: by the eye of God's providence, when we perceive which way that looks: and by Scripture rule. The truth is, we are in a time wherein no man can discern a fixed eye of providence looking this way or that way. What will be the issue of these things; whether it will be the deliverance of the church, or the desolation of the nation and straitening of the church; whether God

---

1 Ps. 50:15.
2 Here Owen is paraphrasing Luke 18:7–8.

will bring good out of them in this generation, or any other time, none knows: this makes it difficult. "We see not our signs" (have no tokens what God intends to do), "neither is there among us any to tell us how long" (Ps. 74:9).

There is none of these things but make a season difficult, and providence dark; but when all of them concur together, they cannot but greatly heighten it: and I think they are all upon us.

Secondly, what are the open signs of the coming and passing of such a season over us?

There are three tokens or outward evidences of a difficult season. It is so,

1. When God's patience is abused. You know that place, "Because judgment is not speedily executed upon an evil work, therefore the heart of the sons of men is fully set in them to do evil" (Eccl. 8:11). Things pass thus; men fall into wickedness, great wickedness; their consciences fly in their faces, and they are afraid; the power of their lusts carries them into the same wickedness again, and their consciences begin to grow a little colder than they were; no evil comes of it; and judgment is not speedily executed; and so their hearts at last come to be wholly set to do evil. Hence others that look on say, here are men given up to all wickedness, surely judgment will speedily come upon these men; judgment does not come, God is patient, and so they themselves turn as wicked as the former. Abusing of God's patience is an evident sign of a dispensation of the displeasure of God in his providence: and if ever it was upon any, it is upon us, and men learn it more and more every day. Everyone talks of other men's sins, and seeing no judgment falls upon them, they give up themselves to the same sins.

2. It is so when God's warnings are despised: "When thine hand is lifted up, they will not see." That is a difficult season, for, says God, "The fire of thine adversaries shall consume them."[3] Never had people more warnings than we have had; warning in heaven above, and warning on the earth beneath; warnings by lesser judgments, and warnings by greater; and warnings by the word. God's hand has been lifted up, but who takes notice of it? Some despise it, and others talk of it as a tale to be told, and there is an end of it. Who sanctifies the name of God in all the warnings that are given us? "The Lord's voice crieth unto the city" (Mic. 6:9), but it is only "the man of wisdom," of substance, that sees the name of God in these his cries unto the city by his warnings from heaven and earth, signs and tokens, and great intimations of his displeasure.

3. An inclination in all sorts of people to security, and to take no notice of these things. I have spoken unto this business of security formerly, and I pray

3 Isa. 26:11

God warn you and myself of it; for I believe none of us are such strangers to our hearts, but we can say, that under all these warnings there is an inclination to security; if God did not prevent it, we should fall fast asleep under all the judgments that are round about us.

Any of these things shows that we are under a difficult dispensation of providence; but where all concur, God be merciful to such a people: it is the opening of the door to let out judgments to the uttermost.

Now if this be such a season, as I do verily believe we are all sensible it is; then,

Thirdly, what shall we do? What are our special duties in reference to our entering into, and passing through such a season?

I might speak unto the peculiar exercise of those graces which are required unto such a season; as faith, resignation to the will of God, readiness for his pleasure, waiting upon God, weanedness from the world, and the like; but I will only give you three or four duties, which are peculiarly hinted in such a season, and so have done.

1. Our first duty is, that we should meet together, and confer about these things (Mal. 3:16–17). A good plan in difficult seasons, such as some of us have seen. The day of the Lord was coming that would burn as an oven:

> Then they that feared the Lord, spake often one to another, and the Lord hearkened and heard it, and a book of remembrance was written before him for them that feared the Lord, and that thought upon his name. And they shall be mine, saith the Lord of hosts, in that day when I make up my jewels, and I will spare them as a man spareth his own son that serveth him.

When was this? In a time of great judgment, and great sin: when they called the proud happy, and they that wrought wickedness were set up, and they that tempted God were even delivered: that is, appeared to be delivered.[4] It is the great duty of us all, as we have opportunity and occasion, to confer about these things; about the causes of them; what arises from the profane, wicked world; what from a persecuting, idolatrous world; and (wherein we are more concerned) what from a professing generation; and see how we can sanctify the name of God in it. We might have as great advantages as any under the face of heaven for the discharge of this duty, if we did but make use of that prize which God has put into our hands; but if we are fools and have no heart to improve it, the blame will be our own. You have

---

4   Owen is paraphrasing Mal. 3:15.

opportunities for meeting and assembling; I fear there are cold affections in your private meetings, I wish there be not. It may be some thrive and grow; I hope so: and others are cold and backward, it is not a season for it. If God would help us to manage this church aright and as we ought to do, there can be no greater advantage under such a season, than we enjoy; but we want voluntary inspection; and the Lord lay it not to our charge we have deferred it so long. Much want of love might have been prevented, many duties furthered, and many evils removed, if we had come up to the light God has given to us. But we are at a loss, and God knows we suffer under it for want of discharging our duty.

That is the first thing, to speak often one to another; to sanctify the name of God by a humble, diligent inquiry into the causes of these dispensations, and preparation for these things.

2. The second duty in such a season is, for every one of us privately to inquire of Jesus Christ in prayer and supplication, what shall be the end of these things?[5] You have a great instance of it,

> Then I heard one saint speaking, and another saint said unto that certain saint which spake, how long shall be the vision concerning the daily sacrifice, and the transgression of desolation, to give both the sanctuary and the host to be trodden under foot? And he said unto me, unto two thousand and three hundred days; then shall the sanctuary be cleansed. (Dan. 8:13–14)

I suppose there is something of the ministry of angels in it; for this saint inquires, but the answer is made to Daniel: one saint said unto another saint, "And he said unto me." But the speaking saint was Jesus Christ. There was the Holy One that spoke, which he calls פַּלְמוֹנִי, "a certain saint"; but the derivation of the word is, one that reveals secrets. There was application made unto Jesus Christ, who is the revealer of secrets, to know how long. And you will find in the Scriptures, in difficult dispensations, that is very many times the request of the saints to God: How long? "How long shall it be to the end of these wonders?" and, "O my Lord, what shall be the end of these things?" (Dan. 12:6, 8). There is a humble application by faith and prayer unto Jesus Christ to know the mind of God in these things, that will bring satisfaction in to our souls. Do not leave yourselves to wander in your own thoughts and imaginations. It is impossible but we shall be debating things, and giving a rational account of them; but all will not bring us satisfaction. But let us go

---

5   Owen is alluding to Dan. 12:8.

to Jesus Christ, and say to him: "O Lord, how long?"[6] And he will give in secret satisfaction to our souls.

This is the second thing: frequently confer about these things; and press Jesus Christ to give your souls satisfaction as to these dispensations. And then,

3. Another peculiar duty, required in such a season, is to mourn for the sins that are in the world. That is recommended to us (Ezek. 9). When God had given commission unto the sword to slay both old and young, he spared only them that mourned for the abominations that were done in the land. We come short in our duty in that matter, in [not] being affected with the sins of the worst of men. God being dishonored, the Spirit of God blasphemed, the name of God reproached in them; we ought to mourn for their abominations. We mourn for the sins among God's people; but we ought also to mourn for those abominations others are guilty of; for their idolatries, murders, bloodshed, uncleanness, for all the abominations that the lands about us, as well as our own, are filled with. It is our duty in such a season to mourn for them, or we do not sanctify the name of God, and shall not be found prepared for those difficult dispensations of God's providence, which are coming upon us.

4. The fourth and last peculiar duty, which I shall mention, is to hide ourselves. And how shall we do that? The storm is coming, get an ark, as Noah did; when the flood was coming upon the world, which is stated for a precedent of all judgments in future times. There are two things required to provide an ark; fear, and faith.

(1) Fear: "By faith Noah being [. . .] moved with fear prepared an ark."[7] If he had not been moved with the fear of God's judgments, he would never have provided an ark. It is a real complaint, we are not moved enough with the fear of God's judgments. We talk of dreadful things, as can befall human nature, and expect them every day; but yet we are not moved with fear. "Yet were they not afraid," says Jeremiah, "nor rent their garments."[8] Nor do we do so. Habakkuk, upon the view of God's judgments, was in another frame, "When I heard," says he, "my belly trembled: my lips quivered at the voice: rottenness entered into my bones, and I trembled in myself that I might rest in the day of trouble" (Hab. 3:16). This is the way to find rest in the day of God's judgments; we are afraid of being esteemed cowards for fearing God's judgments. And then,

(2) We cannot well provide an ark for ourselves, unless we be guided by faith, as well as moved by fear. "By faith" Noah "prepared an ark." How many things there are to encourage faith, you have heard; the name, the properties

6 E.g., Ps. 79:5.
7 Heb. 11:7.
8 Jer. 36:24.

of God, and the accomplishment of the promise of God. By virtue of all those properties encourage faith in providing an ark.

But you will say, we are yet at a loss, what this providing of an ark, and hiding of ourselves is. "A prudent man foresees the evil, and hides himself."[9] God calls us to enter into the chamber of providence, and hide ourselves till the indignation be over past. If we knew what this was, we should apply ourselves unto it, I will tell you what I think in one instance: give no quiet to your minds, until by some renewed act of faith you have a strong and clear impression of the promises of God upon your hearts, and of your interest in them. If it be but one promise, it will prove an ark. If under all these seasons, moved with fear, acted by faith, we can but get a renewed sense and pledge of our interest in any one promise of God, we have an ark over us that will endure, whatever the storm be. Think of it, and if nothing else occur to you, apply your minds to it, that you may not wander up and down at uncertainties; but endeavor to have a renewed pledge of your interest in some special promise of God, that it belongs unto you, and it will be an ark in every time of trouble that shall befall you.

9   Prov. 22:3.

Discourse 12

Spiritual Encouragements for Responding to Difficult Seasons of Divine Providence

March 14, 1678

I DID AT TWO MEETINGS inquire among ourselves, what was required in the time of approaching judgments and calamities that the world has been, and is like to be filled withal. And God was pleased to guide us to the discovery of the necessary exercise of many graces, and the necessary attendance unto many duties for that end and purpose. And we did design to spend our time this day, to beg that God would give us those graces, and stir them up by his Spirit unto a due exercise; and that he would help us unto such a performance of those duties, that when the Lord Christ shall come by any holy dispensation of his providence, we may be found of him in peace. That was the especial occasion of allotting the present time unto this duty; no ways excluding the reasons, occasions, and matter of prayer, which at other times we attend to for ourselves, the church, and the nation.

I would offer a few words that may stir us up unto this duty.

The Scripture does everywhere, upon all such occasions, call expressly unto us for a special preparation by the exercise of grace in reformation and holiness. "Judgment must begin at the house of God": and "what will be the end of them that obey not the gospel?"[1] What then is our duty? Why, says he, "seeing [. . .] that all these things shall be dissolved" (all this outward frame of things), "what manner of persons" ought we "to be in

---

1 1 Pet. 4:17.

all holy conversation and godliness?"[2] Brethren! We ought at all times to attend unto "all holy conversation and godliness": but, says the apostle, the approach of judgment is a peculiar motive thereunto: seeing that all these things are to be dissolved. It is true, seeing Christ has died for us, washed us in his blood, and given his Holy Spirit unto us; what manner of persons ought we to be? But the great motives are not exclusive of occasional exercises, but give an addition unto them. Take heed that ye be not overtaken with surfeiting and drunkenness, with any excess in the use of the creature. What if it be so? Then that day will come upon you at unawares.[3] The day when all shall be dissolved; the day of judgment, the day of approaching calamities. You ought at all times to take care of these things, but if your minds are not influenced in the consideration of the approach of that day, you are not my disciples. I do not at all speak unto what preparations are required.

I could also reflect on those places, where God expresses his great displeasure against such, who did not labor for a peculiar preparation upon approaching calamities. "I called for mourning, and fasting, and girding with sackcloth"; and you betook yourselves unto feasting on all occasions: "Surely," says the Lord, "this iniquity shall not be purged from you till ye die" (Isa. 22:12–14). And it is reckoned among the sins of the most profligate persons, that when God's hand is lifted up, and ready to strike, they will not see, so as to learn righteousness (Isa. 26:11).

Let us therefore beg for grace. Though God multiplies warnings, makes appearances of mercy, and then writes death upon them, and entangles everything in darkness; yet our work goes slowly on in preparation. Cry earnestly unto God for such supplies of his grace and Spirit, that may effectually bring us unto him; that we may no longer abide in the frame wherein we are.

There are three things, and no more, that I know of (others may be named, but they may be reduced unto these three heads), that are required of us in reference unto approaching judgments. And there is not one of them through which we can pass, or which we can perform in a due manner comfortably unto ourselves, and unto the glory of God, without we have some singular and eminent preparation for it. And they are these,

First, that we ourselves stand in the gap, to turn away the threatened judgments.

2   2 Pet. 3:11.
3   Owen is here alluding to and paraphrasing Luke 21:34.

Secondly, that we may be fit for deliverance, if it please the Lord graciously to give it unto us, says Christ, speaking of great calamities; "lift up your heads, for the day of your salvation draws nigh."[4]

Thirdly, that we may cheerfully and comfortably go through the calamities, if they shall overtake us.

These three are comprehensive of all the threats of approaching judgments and darkness that encompass us at this day. Now there is not one of them that we can be any way fit for, unless our hearts and lives are brought into an extraordinary preparation, according as God calls and requires. I do not know whether we believe these things, or no, but they will be shortly found to be true.

First, who dares among us to propose himself to stand in the gap, to divert judgments from the nation, otherwise than in a formal manner, who is not prepared by these things we have spoken of, and has not some good and comfortable persuasion of his own personal interest in Christ, and has not freed himself from those sins that have procured these judgments, and who lives not in a resignation of himself unto the will of God? Who dares to do this? We shall provoke God, if we think to stand in the gap, and turn away judgments from the nation; when we see ourselves are concerned in procuring those judgments.

Secondly, we cannot be meet for deliverance, unless we are thus prepared. I have heard a notion preached, and spoken upon other occasions, which I confess I never liked; and the more I consider it, the more I dislike it; and that is, that God in the deliverance of his people works for his own name's sake, that he may have all the glory, that it shall be seen merely to be of grace; and therefore he will oftentimes deliver his people, when they are in an unreformed and unreforming condition, that he may shame them and humble them by his mercy and grace afterward. I know no rule of Scripture upon which this notion may be grounded, nor one instance or example whereby it may be made out.

Here lies the truth of it: when there are two things concurring in the deliverance of the church, God will deliver them notwithstanding all their sins and unworthiness, without any previous humiliation in themselves. First, when God has fixed and limited a certain season in his word and promise for their deliverance. And secondly, when antecedent unto their deliverance they want means for humiliation. God delivered the children of Israel out of Egypt, when they were in a very bad condition, an ignorant, stubborn, faithless

4 Luke 21:28.

generation. But both these things were concurring. God was engaged in point of his promise, that at the end of four hundred and thirty years he would visit and deliver them. And they were deprived of all ordinances of worship in Egypt: not a sacrifice could they offer, while they were there; not a Sabbath, I believe, though it is not expressed in Scripture, could they observe. The way of worship and knowledge of God was taken from them. So when God delivered the children of Israel out of Babylon, they were in no very good condition; but God was engaged in point of promise as to that time, that at the end of seventy years they should be delivered. And in Babylon they had no means for instruction or reformation, no temple, no sacrifice, these were denied. But whenever God does afford unto persons all the means of grace for humiliation, reformation, and turning unto himself, it may be as good as ever they shall in this world; that God did ever deliver that people out of their distresses, when they refused to be reformed, humbled, or to turn unto him, neither instances of Scripture, nor God's dealing with his church will make this good. Therefore it is vain for us to expect anything of this nature. If indeed for so many years we had been thrown into a wilderness condition, and had no preaching, no assemblies, no administration of ordinances, no warnings or charges from God; we might have expected the Lord would have given us deliverance. But to us who have had all these things, and yet will not make use of what we have now at present, we have no ground to expect any such thing. Therefore, I confess, neither by rule, instance or example, do I expect deliverance, until God come in to work a thorough change and reformation in our hearts and lives, which makes it very necessary to be preparing to meet God in the way of his judgments.

Thirdly, the third thing that may lie before us is, how we may cheerfully go through the calamities which may overtake us. I will say no more unto that, because it is that which we did expressly insist upon in our former discourse. As to the best of us, who have been long in the ways of God, woeful will be our surprisal, when the days of calamity come, if we have lived in negligence of complying with the calls and warnings of God, that we have had, to bring ourselves unto a more even and better frame. We shall find our strength to fail us, and have our comforts to seek; and be left to inward darkness, when outward darkness increases, and not know whither to cause our sorrows to go.

These things, brethren, I thought fit to mention unto you, that, if it be the will of God, they may be of use to take us off from those false hopes, and false expectations, which we are wonderfully ready to feed ourselves withal in such a day as this is wherein we live. It is high time for us to be calling upon God for this end.

Discourse 13

Spiritual Encouragement in Difficult Seasons of Divine Providence

THE PROPHET DANIEL TELLS US, when he understood by books, namely, the writings of the prophet Jeremiah, that the time wherein the great contest between Babylon and the church was to have its issue, was come to a point; then, says he, "I set my face [. . .] to seek the Lord with prayer, and supplications, and fasting."[1] And if you will read his prayer, you will find nothing of confidence, nothing of self-ascription, but a deep acknowledgment of sin: we, our kings, our princes, our fathers, our church, have all sinned; so as that to us belongs shame, and confusion of face.[2] And never had such shame and confusion of face befallen the church, as would have befallen them, if they had been disappointed in that trial. But he adds, unto you "belong mercies and forgiveness."[3] There he issues the whole business, upon mercy and forgiveness, though he knew by books that the time was come.

Truly, brethren, we do not know by any Scripture revelation, as he did, that the time is come wherein the long contest and conflict between Babylon and the church will have its issue; but it looks like it in the book of providence, and so like it, that it is a plain duty we should give ourselves unto prayer and supplication, that it do not issue in shame and confusion of face, which belongs unto us by reason of our sins. It is that contest which is now under consideration, and which seems to be coming to its issue, and all men are in expectation of it. It is the greatest, save one, that ever was. For the greatest contest that ever was in this world, was between the person and the gospel

1 Dan. 9:3.
2 Owen is paraphrasing Dan. 9:8.
3 Dan. 9:9.

501

of Christ on the one hand; and the devil and the pagan world on the other. And the next to that is the contest between Christ in his offices and grace, in his gospel and worship; and antichrist. And it is at this day upon its trial, in as signal an instance as ever it received. The question is, as to us and our posterity; whether Christ, or antichrist; whether the worship of God, or of idols; whether the effusion, and waiting for the effusion of the Spirit of God in his worship, or all manner of superstitious impositions. This is the present contest; and it may be under heaven there never was a more signal instance of the issue of this contest, than will be in these nations in these days; I do not say presently or speedily, but this you all know, is our state.

I mention it only to let you know, that there is more than an ordinary earnestness and fervency of spirit, and wrestling with God required of us at this day, for the case[4] of Zion, the interest of Christ, and defeating of his adversaries. What way God will work we know not. If he be at work, he has said, that when a flood was cast out of the mouth of the dragon, to swallow up the woman everywhere (and we have had a flood cast out of the mouth of the dragon to swallow up the whole interest of Christ in this nation) the earth lifted up herself, and helped the woman, and turned aside the flood.[5] Good old Eli's heart trembled for the ark of God.[6] The interest of God, and the truths of Christ are yet among us; but hardly beset by the Philistines: and whether they may not take them I know not, God only knows. But assuredly, brethren, our hearts ought now to tremble for the ark of God, that God would continue it among us, and not give his glory into the hands of the adversary.

I have mentioned these things, only for this end, that if God will, our hearts may be a little warmed upon all occasions in this great contest and conflict between Christ and antichrist, to come in with our prayers to the help of the Lord, and of the ark of the Lord, that we may see a blessed issue of this trial, and not be covered with that shame and confusion of face which belong unto us.

---

4   As per original. The meaning is "cause."
5   Owen is paraphrasing Rev. 12:15–16 here.
6   Here Owen is referring to 1 Sam. 4:12–18, where the priest Eli dies from the shock of hearing that the Philistines have captured the ark of the covenant.

Discourse 14

Spiritual Reformation in a Difficult Season of Divine Providence

February 15, 1680

THIS MEETING IS FOR CONFERENCE, and I would ask you a few questions.

First, whether do you think there are extraordinary calls and warnings of God toward this nation at this time?

Secondly, if there be, what is the voice of these calls?

Thirdly, whether any sort of men, believers, or churches, are exempted from attending unto, and complying with these calls of God? For there lies a reserve in our hearts. The nation is very wicked (I shall not repeat the sins of the nation); the warning is general to the nation, the body of the people, and God testifies his displeasure against them. Now the inquiry is, whether there be any rule, that we, who profess ourselves believers, and a church, should count ourselves exempted from a particular compliance with these extraordinary calls of God, that they are for others, and not for us? "If the scourge slay suddenly, he will laugh at the trial of the innocent" (Job 9:23). And the good figs went first into captivity.

Fourthly, what have we done hitherto in order to it, that may evidence itself to be an answer to a compliance with these calls of God, which we have owned here before the Lord? We have been speaking of it, and it becomes me to judge that we have had good and sincere desires after it. And neither the church, nor anyone in the church, shall have any reflections from me beyond evidence. It becomes me to judge, that we have had in ourselves good intentions, and sincere endeavors after it; though they have been, it may be, no way suitable or proportionable to the present occasion: and therefore I must say, that in an eminent and extraordinary manner, as yet, we have done nothing; we have not consulted of it yet, what we should do, and what it is in particular that the Lord our God requires of us; nor declared our designs and intentions for a universal compliance with these great calls of God, for repentance and turning unto the Lord. I mourn over myself night and day, I mourn over you continually. I do not see that life and vigor in returning unto God, either in our persons, or in our church relation, as I could desire. And give me leave to say from an experience in my own heart, I am jealous over you. We may proceed to consider something of outward duties afterward; but as yet we are not at all come to it, but only to inquire into our hearts what we have done in compliance with these calls of God in the reformation and change of our hearts, and vigor of spirit in walking with him. I speak it with all tenderness, that none might take offense; but I do acknowledge to you, that I have not myself attained, nor can I, though I am laboring to bring my heart to that frame, which God requires in us all at this time: I find many obstructions: if you have attained, I shall rejoice in it with all my heart and soul; but if not, help them that are laboring after it. I intend no more at present but this, to settle upon our souls a conviction that we have not as yet answered the calls of God in the heart; for if we have all apprehensions we have complied, the work is at an end.

I hope we may in due time go on to consider all the ways and instances whereby we may reform and return unto God; but in the meantime I offer this to you, that unless the foundation of it be laid in a deep and broken sense of our past miscarriages and present frames, and I can see in the church some actings of a renewed spirit with vigor and earnestness to pursue our recovery and return to God, I shall much despond in this thing. But let us be persuaded that we are to lay this foundation, I desire we may agree upon this, that it is our duty to get a deep sense upon our hearts (as the first thing God aims at in his calls) of our past miscarriages, and of our present dead, wretched frame, in comparison of that vigor liveliness, and activity of grace that ought to be found in us. Ought we not to lay the foundation here? If so, then we ought to apply ourselves unto it. It may be, though it be so with some, that they have such a lively, vigorous acting of faith in a deep and humble sense of their past miscarriages, yet it is not so with others; and we are looking for the edification of the whole. And therefore, brethren, do we judge it our present duty to labor to affect our hearts deeply with a sense of our present unanswerable frame unto the mind of God and Christ, and of our past miscarriages?

If it be so, let us every day pray, that God would keep this thing in the imagination of the thoughts of our hearts, not only of ourselves, but of one another. Observe the phrase of the Holy Ghost: when you come to the thoughts of the heart, you think you can go no farther; but says David, I pray, O Lord, preserve this "in the imagination of the thoughts of the heart of thy people":[1] that is, in the first internal framing of our thoughts. There must be a frame acting and coining thoughts (if I may so say) continually in us to this purpose. But I recommend this to you, that if this be a truth, and we are convinced it is our duty to labor to affect our hearts with a sense of the unanswerableness of our souls, and the frame of our minds unto the will of God and the holiness of Christ, who is coming to visit his churches, what manner of persons ought we to be?[2] Not such as we have been. We should labor for a deep sense of this, and I hope it may not be unsuitable unto you; for if any of us have any corruption, temptation, or disorder in our spirits and ways to conflict withal, in vain, believe me, shall we contend against it, unless we lay this foundation.

I know one great means for the beginning, and carrying on of this work, is by earnest crying unto God by prayers and supplications, and humiliations. I am loath to issue it there, I have seen so many days of humiliation without reformation, that I dare not issue it there, we shall make use of them as God shall help us. I desire the church would do so, if they find in themselves a sense of duty and a heart crying to God in sincerity and truth. I have now been very long, though very unprofitable, in the ministration of the word; and I have observed the beginning of churches, and wish I do not see the end of them in this their confidence of mere profession, and the observation of these duties of humiliation. God knows, I have thought often of this thing, and, I say, I dare not issue it there. Let us have as many as we have hearts for, and no more; and as many as shall end with reformation, but no more. But let us all begin among ourselves; and who knows but that God may give wisdom to this church? I am ready to faint, and give over, and to beg of the church, they would think of some other person to conduct them in my room without these disadvantages. The last day will discover I have nothing but a heart to lead you in the ways of God to the enjoyment of God.

---

1   1 Chron. 29:18.

2   Owen is paraphrasing 2 Pet. 3:10–11.

AN EXPOSTULATORY LETTER TO THE AUTHOR OF THE LATE SLANDEROUS LIBEL AGAINST DR. O.

With Some Short Reflections Thereon

Reflections on a Slanderous Libel

SIR,[1]

It is upon your desire, and not in any compliance with my own judgment or inclination, that I have taken a little consideration of a late slanderous libel published against me.[2] I have learned, I bless God, to bear and pass by such reproaches, without much trouble to myself, or giving the least unto others. My mind and conscience are not at all concerned in them, and so far as my reputation seems to be so, I am very willing to let it go. For I cannot entertain a valuation of their good opinion, whose minds are capable of an impression from such virulent calumnies. Besides I know that there is nothing absolutely new in these things under the sun. Others also have met with the like entertainment in the world in all ages, whose names I shall not mention, to avoid the envy in comparing myself with them. I acknowledge that it is a dictate of the law of nature, that where others do us open wrong, we should do ourselves right, so far as we lawfully may. But I know also, that it is in the power of everyone to forgo the prosecution of his own right, and the vindication of himself, if thereby there arise no detriment unto others. That which alone in this case may be feared, is lest offense should be taken against my person to the disadvantage of other endeavors, wherein I desire to be useful in the world.

---

1 The original 1671 edition of the letter is appended without any title to an anonymous letter to George Vernon, rebuking him for his treatment of Owen. See John Owen, "[Reflections]," in *An Expostulatory Letter to the Author of the Slanderous Libel against Dr. O. With Some Short Reflections Thereon* (London: n.p., 1671). Thomas Overbury, who was sympathetic to Owen's views, was a neighbor of Vernon's and, according to Peter Toon, a future member of Owen's London congregation. See Peter Toon, *God's Statesman: The Life and Work of John Owen, Pastor, Educator, Theologian* (Exeter, UK: Paternoster, 1971), 138.

2 George Vernon [s.n.], *A Letter to a Friend concerning Some of Dr. Owens Principles and Practices: With a Postscript to the Author of the Late Ecclesiastical Polity, and an Independent Catechism* (London: J. Redmayne for Spencer Hickman, 1670).

But against this also I have the highest security, from that indignation and contempt wherewith this libel is entertained by all persons of ingenuity and sobriety. Not out of any respect therefore to myself, or my own name (things of little or no consideration in or to the world) nor out of a desire that this paper should ever pass farther, than to your own hand, and thence to the fire; but to give you some account of this pamphlet whose author it seems is known unto you, I have both perused it, and made some short reflections upon it, which I have herewith sent unto you.

The whole design of this discourse is, *per fas et nefas*,[3] to endeavor the defamation of a person, who to his knowledge never saw the author of it, and is fully assured never gave him the least provocation unto any such attempt. For when I am told who he is, I am as wise and knowing unto all his concernments as I was before. And yet it is not only my reputation, but considering my present state and condition, with the nature of his libelous aspersions, my further outward trouble in the world, that he aims at; from which he seems to be much displeased that I am secured by the righteousness of the government, and laws under which I live. Now however he pleased himself in this attempt, yet there is no man but may give as tolerable an account by the law of God, the customs of civilized nations, and in the estimation of wise and honest men, of robbing persons on the highway, and spoiling them of their goods, as he can do of this undertaking. It is true! Some others have of late dealt not much otherwise with me, wherein how far they have satisfied themselves and others, time will discover. But yet according to the present custom and manner of men, they may give some tolerable pretense to what they have done. For they sufficiently declare that they were provoked by me, though no such thing was intended; and it is abundantly manifest, that they had no other way left them to give countenance unto some fond imaginations which they have unadvisedly published, but by petulant reviling of him, by whom they thought they were detected. And such things have not been infrequent in the world. But as for this author, one wholly unknown to me, without the compass of any pretense of the least provocation from me, to accommodate the lusts and revenges of others with that unruly evil, a mercenary tongue full of deadly poison, without the management of any difference, real or pretended, merely to calumniate and load me with false aspersions, as in the issue they will prove, is an instance of such a depraved disposition of mind, such a worthless baseness of soul; such a neglect of all rules of morality, and principles of human conversation, such a contempt of Scripture precepts

3   Lat. "by fair or unfair means."

innumerable, as it may be can scarcely be paralleled in an age, among the vilest of men. Something I confess, of this nature is directed unto in the casuistical divinity, or modern policy of the Jesuits. For they have declared it lawful to reproach and calumniate anyone who has done them an injury, or otherwise reflected on the honor of their society. And notable instances of their management of this principle, are given us by the ingenious discoverer of their mysteries. But they always require a previous injury or provocation to justify themselves in this filthy kind of revenge. And hereby is our author freed from the suspicion of having been influenced by their suggestions. For he has gone in a way whereon they never attempted to set a foot before him; and scorning a villainy that has a precedent, he seems to design himself an example in the art of sycophantry. However the same author has directed men unto the best way of returning an answer unto false and calumnious accusations, whatever be their occasion. For he tells us, that Valerianus Magnus[4] an honest Capuchin friar, being so dealt withal by a Jesuit, made not any defense of his own innocency, any further than by adjoining unto all the instances of his charge *Mentiris impudentissime.*[5] And this you will immediately find to be the substance of that answer which this book deserves. For setting aside things relating to the former public troubles and disorders in these nations, from the venom of all reflections from whence, I am secured, by the government, law and interest of the kingdom, all which in this revival of them, are notoriously abused and trampled on, and there is no one thing charged on me in the whole libel, but that either in the matter or manner of its relation, is notoriously false. The task I acknowledge of making this discovery would be grievous and irksome unto me, but that I must not account anything so, which may fall out among men in the world; and do remember him who, after he had done some public services, whereof others had the advantage, was forced to defend his own house against thieves and robbers.

The whole discourse is a railing accusation, such as the angel dare not bring against the devil, but such as has many characters and lineaments upon it, of him who was a false accuser and murderer from the beginning.[6] Neither is it capable of a distribution into any other parts but those of railing and false accusations. And for the first, seeing he has manifested his propensity unto it, and delight in it, he shall by me be left to the possession of that honor and reputation, which he has acquired thereby. Besides his way of managery has

---

4 Valerianus Magnus or Valérien Magni (1586–1661) was an Italian Capuchin missionary who engaged in a protracted controversy with the Jesuits.
5 Lat., "you lie most shamelessly."
6 Owen is here alluding to Christ's remark about the devil in John 8:44.

rendered it of no consideration. For had it been condited[7] to the present gust of the age, by language, wit, or drollery,[8] it might have found some entertainment in the world. But downright dirty railing, is beneath the genius of the times, and by common consent condemned to the Bear-Garden[9] and Billingsgate.[10] His charges and accusations, wherein doubtless he placed his principal hopes of success (though I much question whether he knew what he aimed at in particular or no), may in so many instances be called over, as to discover unto you with what little regard to Christianity, truth, or honesty, they have been forged and managed by him.¶[11]

I shall begin with what he calls my practices, and then proceed to the principles he mentions, which is the best order his confused rhapsody of slanders can be reduced unto, though inverting that which he projected in his title.¶

One of the first charges I meet withal upon the first head is, that I was one of them who promised Cromwell[12] his life upon his last sickness, and assured him that his days should be prolonged.[13] This I confess he manages somewhat faintly and dubiously, the reason whereof I cannot guess at, it being as true as those other tales, in the report whereof he pretends to more confidence. And I have no answer to return but that of the friar before mentioned, *Mentitur impudentissime*,[14] for I saw him not in his sickness, nor in some long time before. Of the same nature is what he affirms of my being the "instrument" in the "ruin" of his son Richard,[15] with whose setting up, and pulling down, I had no more to do, than himself. And such are the reasons which he gives, for that which never was. For the things he instances in, were my own choice, against all importunities, to the contrary; so that the same answer must be returned again, *Mentitur impudentissime*. He charges me, that in writing against the Papists, I reflected "upon the authority of the king, as to his power in matters of religion,"[16] which he repeats again, and calls it a covert undermining of

---

7 I.e., seasoned with spice.
8 I.e., humor.
9 I.e., a place of coarse entertainment.
10 I.e., a fish market in London.
11 The ¶ symbol indicates that a paragraph break has been added to Owen's original text.
12 Oliver Cromwell (1599–1658) led the Parliamentary army's campaign against Charles I and was Lord Protector of England during the Interregnum from 1653–1658. Owen was, for a time, his chaplain.
13 In the text: (pag. 9).—Owen. See Vernon [s.n.], *Letter*, 9.
14 Lat., "He lies most shamelessly."
15 In the text: (pag. 28).—Owen. See Vernon [s.n.], *Letter*, 28. Richard Cromwell (1626–1712), son of Oliver, was briefly Lord Protector of England following his father's death until his forced resignation, after which he lived abroad in relative obscurity.
16 In the text: (pag. 10).—Owen. See Vernon [s.n.], *Letter*, 10.

"the just authority of the king."[17] Still the same answer is all that can be given. His majesty's supremacy, as declared and established by law, is asserted and proved in the book he intends.[18] Nor is there any word in the places quoted by him in his margin, that will give the least countenance to this false calumny. Besides the book was approved by authority, and that by persons of another manner of judgment and learning, than this pitiful scribbler, who are all here defamed by him. He charges me with countenancing an accusation against the reverend Bishop of Chester, then warden of Wadham College;[19] which is a known lie, and such I believe the bishop if he be asked, will attest it to be. And so he says, I received a "commission" from Oliver to carry "*gladium ferri*";[20] but *Mentitur impudentissime*; for I never received commission from any man, or company of men in this world; nor to my remembrance did I ever wear a sword in my life. His whole thirty-fourth page, had there been anything of wit, or ingenuity in fiction in it, I should have suspected to have been borrowed from Lucian's *Vera historia*,[21] concerning which he affirmed, that he wrote that which he had never seen, nor heard, nor did any one declare unto him.[22] For it is only a confused heap of malicious lies, which all that read and know, laugh at with scorn. Such likewise is the ridiculous story he tells, of my ordering things so, that members of parliament should have a book, which he calls mine, "laid in their lodgings" by "unknown hands"; whereof there is not anything in substance or circumstance that can lay the least pretense to truth; but it is an entire part of his industrious attempt to carry the whetstone.[23] The same must be said concerning what he reports of passages between me, and the then lord chancellor; which as I have good witness to prove the mistake that fell out between us, not to have been occasioned by

17 In the text: (pag. 34).—Owen. See Vernon [s.n.], *Letter*, 34.

18 In the text: (pag. 404–6).—Owen. Owen is referring to his own *A Vindication of the Animadversions on Fiat Lux*. See John Owen, *A Vindication of the Animadversions on Fiat Lux: Wherein the Principles of the Roman Church, as to Moderation, Unity and Truth Are Examined* (London: For Ph. Stephens, 1664), 404–6.

19 In the text: (pag. 12).—Owen. See Vernon [s.n.], *Letter*, 12. Owen is here referring to John Wilkins (1614–1672), a scientist and philosopher who was also an Establishment clergyman, Warden of Wadham College, Oxford, and later Bishop of Chester. He was a notable advocate of a more lenient approach to religious nonconformity.

20 Lat. "a sword of iron." In the text: (pag. 14).—Owen. See Vernon [s.n.], *Letter*, 14.

21 Owen is referring to the satirical work of Lucian of Samosata (ca. 125–180), which ridicules authors who tell fanciful tales.

22 Here Vernon accuses Owen, among other things, of trying to solicit from the king's counsels the progress of his efforts at promoting liberty of conscience in religious matters, so as to tip off his fellow independents of the outcome. See Vernon [s.n.], *Letter*, 34.

23 In the text: (pag. 66).—Owen. See Vernon [s.n.], *Letter*, 66.

me, so I much question, whether this author was informed of the untruths he reports, by Doctor Barlow,[24] or whether ever he gave him his consent to use his name publicly for a countenance unto such a defamatory libel.[25] It was endless and useless to call out, the remaining instances of the same kind, whereof I think there is scarce a page free in his book, unless it be taken up with quotations. And I am sure that whosoever will give the least credit unto any of his stories and assertions, will do it at the utmost peril of being deceived. And where anything he aims at, has the least of truth in it, he does but make it a foundation to build a falsehood upon. Such are his ingenious repetitions of some things I should say, fourteen or fifteen years ago, in private discourses; which yet supposing them true in the terms by him reported, as they are not, contain nothing of immorality, nothing of injury unto, or reflection on others. Surely this man must be thought to study the adorning and freedom of conversation, who thus openly traduces a person, for words occasionally, and it may be hastily spoken, without the least injury to any, or evil in themselves, fourteen or fifteen years after. And these also are such as he has taken upon mere reports, for I believe he will not say, that ever he spoke one word with me himself in his life. How anyone can safely converse with a man of this spirit and humor, I know not.¶

I shall wholly pass by his malicious wresting and false applications of the passages he has quoted out of some things published by me; for as for the greatest part of those small perishing treatises, whence he and others have extracted their pretended advantages, it is many years since I saw them, some of them twenty at the least; nor do I know, how they have dealt in repeating their *excerpta*,[26] which with so much diligence they have collected; that they are several times wrested and perverted by this malicious scribbler unto things never intended by me, that I do know.

One discourse about *Communion with God*,[27] I find there is much wrath stirred up against; and yet upon the severe scrutiny which it has in several hands undergone, nothing can be found to lay to its charge, but one passage

---

24 Thomas Barlow (ca. 1607–91) was a Reformed theologian, and later post-Restoration bishop of Lincoln, who was Owen's tutor while he was a student at Oxford.

25 Vernon refers to an incident where Owen had allegedly broken faith with the Lord Chancellor, Edward Hyde, for preaching to a group in his own home against his instruction. Owen evidently appealed to Barlow to mediate with Hyde, and Vernon recounts that Hyde responded to Barlow, saying that Owen was a "perfideous person, in that he had violated the engagements before specified, and therefore that he would have nothing to do with him, but leave him to the penalty of those laws he had transgressed." Vernon [s.n.], *Letter*, 39–40.

26 Lat. "excerpts."

27 *Complete Works of John Owen*, vol. 1.

concerning some differences about external worship; which they needed not to have put themselves to so much trouble, to have found out and declared. But as for this man, he makes such inferences from it, and applications of it, as are full of malice and poison, being not inferior in these good qualifications unto any of his other prodigious tales. For from what I speak concerning the purity of instituted worship, he concludes, that I judge, that all who in the worship of God make use of the Common Prayer,[28] are not loyal to Christ, nor have communion with God, nor can promote the interest of the gospel; all which are notoriously false, never thought, never spoken, never written by me: and I do believe, that many that have used that book in the public administrations have been as loyal to Christ, had as much communion with God, and been as zealous to promote the interest of the gospel, as any who have lived in the world these thousand years. For men are accepted with God according to what they have, and not according to what they have not.¶

The next charge I can meet withal in this confused heap, which is like the grave, a place of darkness without any order, is no less than of perjury. And this principally he does on such an account, as is not at all peculiar to me; but the reproach he manages is equally cast on the greatest part of the kingdom by this public defamer. And I suppose others do, though I do not know the prudence of encouraging such a slanderous libeler, to cast firebrands among peaceable subjects; and to revive the remembrance of things, which the wisdom, clemency and righteousness of his majesty, with, and by the law of the land, upon the best and most assured principles of piety and policy, have put into oblivion. And it also seems strange to me, how bold, he and some other scribblers make, by their interesting the sacred name of his majesty, and his concerns in their impertinent squabblings, as they do on all occasions. But such things are of another cognizance, and there I leave them. What is peculiar to myself in this charge, is represented under a double instance; (1) of the oath of canonical obedience, which I took and violated: and (2) of the university oath.¶[29]

For the first, although I could easily return an answer unto the thing itself, yet as to what concerns me, I shall give no other, but *Mentitur impudentissime*, I never took any such oath.¶

And for the other I doubt not to speak with some confidence, that the intention and design of the oath, was observed by me with as much conscience and diligence, as by any who have since acted in the same capacity wherein

28 I.e., the Book of Common Prayer.
29 I.e., an oath that pledged allegiance to the statutes of the University of Oxford.

I was at that time reflected on. And upon the provocation of this man, who-ever he be, I do not fear to say, that considering the state and condition of affairs, at that time in the nation and the university, I do not believe there is any person of learning, ingenuity, or common modesty, who had relation in those days unto that place, but will grant at least, that notwithstanding some lesser differences from them, about things of very small importance, I was not altogether useless to the interests of learning, morality, peace, and the preservation of the place itself; and further I am not concerned in the ingratitude and envy of a few illiterate and malicious persons, as knowing that "the disparagement which they are passing around by word of mouth is a treasure-trove for fools."[30]

But if all these attempts prove successless, there is that yet behind, which shall justify the whole charge, or at least the author in filling up his bill, with so many prodigious falsities. And this is my blaspheming the Lord's Prayer, which is exaggerated with many tragical expressions, and hideous exclama-tions, as indeed who can lay too heavy a load on so horrid a crime. But how if this should not prove so: how if by all his outcries he should but adorn and set forth his own forgeries? This I know, that I do, and ever did believe, that that prayer is part of the canonical Scripture, which I would not willingly blaspheme. I do believe that it was composed by the Lord Jesus Christ him-self, and have vindicated it from being thought a collection and composition of such petitions as were then in use among the Jews, as some learned men had, I think unadvisedly, asserted it to be. I do and ever did believe it the most perfect form of prayer that ever was composed; and the words of it so disposed by the divine wisdom of our blessed Savior, that it comprehends the substance of all the matter of prayer to God. I do and did always believe, that it ought to be continually meditated on, that we may learn from thence, both what we ought to pray for, and in what manner; neither did I ever think a thought, or speak a word unsuitable to these assertions. Wherein then does this great blasphemy lie? Unto two heads it must be reduced: (1) that I judge not, that our Lord Jesus Christ in the giving of this prayer unto his disciples, did prescribe unto them the precise use or repetition of those words, but only taught them what to pray for, or how. Now although it may be this man does not, yet all men of any tolerable learning or reading know, that this assertion relating only to the different interpretations of one expression, indeed of one word, in one of the evangelists, has been owned and allowed

---

30 In the text: *Obtrectatio est stultorum thesaurus, quem in linguis gerunt.*—Owen. Editor's translation.

by learned men of all parties and persuasions. He may, if he please, consult Grotius,[31] Musculus,[32] and Cornelius à Lapide,[33] to name one of a side for his information. But (2) I have delivered other things concerning the use of it, in my book against the Socinians.¶[34]

Whereunto I shall only say, that he who differs from others in the manner of the use of anything, may have as reverent an esteem of the thing itself as they; and herein I shall not give place unto any man that lives on the earth with respect unto the Lord's Prayer. It is true, I have said that there were manifold abuses in the rehearsal of it among people ignorant and superstitious; and did deliver my thoughts, it may be too freely and severely against some kind of repetition of it. But as for the ridiculous and impudent charge of blasphemy hence raised by this pitiful calumniator, I am no way concerned in it. No more am I, with that lie which has been now reported to the satiety of its first broachers and promoters: namely, that I should put on my hat upon the repetition of it; it was as I remember about fifteen years ago, that such a rumor was raised, by I know not whom, nor on what occasion. It was somewhat long before I heard any whisper of it, as is the manner in such cases. But so soon as I did attain a knowledge that such a slander had been reported and scattered abroad, I did cause to be published in English and French, a declaration of its notorious falsity; in the year 1655.[35] But so prone are many to give entertainment to false reproaches of them whom on any account they are displeased with, so unwilling to part with a supposed advantage against them, though they know it to have been put into their hand by the mistakes, folly, or malice of others, that the same untruth has been several times since, repeated and republished, without the least taking notice that it was publicly denied, condemned, and the authors of it challenged to give any tolerable account of their report. Only of late, one learned person, meeting it afresh, where its admittance would have been to his advantage (namely, Mr. Durel, in

---

31 Hugo Grotius (1583–1645) was a Dutch statesman, lawyer, and humanist who wrote most influentially on natural law. His other works include his *Annotationes in Vetus Testamentum*, and his defense of the satisfaction of Christ against Faustus Socinus.

32 Wolfgang Musculus (1497–1563) was a German Reformer who taught theology in Bern and is famous for his biblical commentaries and *Loci communes sacrae theologiae*.

33 Cornelius à Lapide (1567–1637) was a Flemish Jesuit and exegete, noted for his biblical commentaries.

34 Owen is referring to his *Vindiciae Evangelicae; or, The Mystery of the Gospel Vindicated and Socinianism Examined*. See *Complete Works of John Owen*, vols. 2–3.

35 Owen's diffidence about the frequent repetition of the Lord's Prayer in public worship is something he later expresses in his *A Discourse of the Work of the Holy Spirit in Prayer*, in *Complete Works of John Owen*, vol. 8. As he indicates here, however, in 1655 he set about responding to exaggerated representations of his view on the matter.

his answer unto the apology of some nonconformists),[36] had the ingenuity to acknowledge the public disclaimure[37] of any such practice so long since made and published, and thereon at least to suspend his assent to the report itself.¶

I am sir, quite weary of repeating the instances of this man's notorious falsehoods and unjust accusations, I shall therefore overlook the remainder of them on this head, that I may give you one of his intolerable weakness and ignorance. And this lies in his attempt to find out contradictions between what I have written in several places about toleration and liberty of conscience.[38] For because I say, that pernicious errors are to be opposed and extirpated[39] by means appointed, proper, and suitable thereunto; as also that it is the duty of the magistrate to defend, protect, countenance and promote the truth, the man thinks that these things are inconsistent with liberty of conscience, and such a toleration or forbearance, as at any time I have pleaded for. But if any man should persuade him to let those things alone, which either he has nothing to do withal, or does not understand, it may be he would accommodate him with a sufficient leisure, and more time than he knows well how to dispose of.¶

His last attempt is upon some sayings which he calls my principles, in the representation whereof, whether he has dealt with any greater regard to truth and honesty, than are the things we have already passed through shall be briefly considered. The first as laid down in the contents prefixed to this sorry chapter, is in these words; that success in business does authoricate[40] its cause, and that if God's providence permit a mischief, his will approves it.[41] There are two parts you see of this principle; whereof the first is, that success will justify a cause in business; that is as I take it any one; and secondly, that

---

36 Owen is likely referring to John Durel, *A View of the Government and Publick Worship of God in the Reformed Churches beyond the Seas. Wherein Is Showed Their Conformity and Agreement with the Church of England, as It Is Established by the Act of Uniformity* (London: J. G. for R. Royston, 1662).

37 I.e., disclaimer.

38 In the text: (page 67).—Owen. See Vernon [s.n.], *Letter*, 67. In particular, Vernon here cites from Owen's "Countrey Essay for the Practice of Church-Government." See John Owen, *A Vision of Unchangeable Free Mercy, in Sending the Means of Grace to Undeserved Sinners [. . .] : In a Sermon Preached before the Honourable House of Commons, April 29. Being the Day of Publike Humiliation. Whereunto Is Annexed, A Short Defensative about Church-Government, (with a Countrey Essay for the Practice of Church-Government There) Toleration and Petitions about These Things* (London: G. M. for Philemon Stephens, 1646). See *Complete Works of John Owen*, vol. 18.

39 I.e., completely destroyed.

40 I.e., authorize.

41 Owen is closely paraphrasing the table of contents for pp. 44–45 of Vernon's tract. See Vernon [s.n.], *Letter*, *2 (page numbers with an asterisk refer to unnumbered pages in the original).

which God permits, he does approve. Now as both parts of this principle are diabolically false, so in their charge on me also; so that I must betake myself again, to the example of the friar, and say *Mentitur impudentissime*. A cause is good or bad before it has success one way or other. And that which has not its warranty in itself, can never obtain any from its success. The rule of the goodness of any public cause, is the eternal law of reason, with the just legal rights and interests of men. If these make not a cause good, success will never mend it. But when a cause on these grounds is so indeed, or is really judged such by them that are engaged in it, not to take notice of the providence of God in prospering men in the pursuit of it, is to exclude all thoughts of him and his providence from having any concern in the government of the world. And if I, or any other, have at any time applied this unto any cause not warranted by the only rule of its justification, it no way reflects on the truth of the principle which I assert, nor gives countenance to the false one, which he ascribes unto me. For the latter clause of this pretended principle, that if God's providence permit a mischief, his will approves it, I suspect there is some other ingredient in it, besides lying and malice; namely stupid ignorance. For it is mischief in a moral sense that he intends, nothing being the object of God's approbation or disapprobation, on any other account. It would therefore seem very strange, how anyone who has but so much understanding as to know that this principle would take away all differences between good and evil, should provide himself with so much impudence as to charge it on me.⁋

Another principle, in pursuit of the same design, he lays down as mine, namely, that saints may retain their holiness in the act of sinning, and that whatever law they violate, God will not impute it to them as a sin.[42] There seem to be two parts of this principle also. The first is, that saints may retain their holiness in the act of sinning; I know not well what he means by this part of his principle, and yet do for some reasons, suppose him to be more remote from the understanding of it, than I am, although the words are his own. If he means that the act of sinning is not against, or an impeachment of holiness, it is a ridiculous contradiction. If he means that every actual sin does not deprive the sinner of all holiness; he is ridiculous himself if he asserts that it does, seeing there is no man that doeth good and sins not.[43] The framing of the last clause of this principle smells of the same cask: and as it is charged on me is false. Whatever law of God any man breaks it is a sin, is so judged of God, and by him imputed so far unto the sinner, as to judge him guilty

---

42 In the text: (pag. 46).—Owen. Owen is closely paraphrasing the table of contents for pp. 46–47 of Vernon's tract. See Vernon [s.n.], *Letter*, *2. Cf. 46.

43 Owen is alluding to Eccl. 7:20.

thereof whoever he be. But God does not impute every sin unto believers unto judgment and condemnation. And if he can understand anything in the books quoted by him, he will find that there is no more in them toward what he reflects upon, but that God will by his grace, preserve true believers from falling into such sins, as whereby they should totally and finally lose their faith, fall from grace, and be cast out of God's covenant. This principle I own, and despise his impotent, ignorant, and ridiculous defamation of it.¶

His third principle is about praying by the Spirit, which he charges at the highest rate, as that which will destroy all government in the world. I know well enough whence he has learned this kind of arguing. But I have no reason to concern myself particularly in this matter. The charge, for ought I know, as here proposed, falls equally on all Christians in the world; for whether men pray by a book, or without a book, if they pray not by the Spirit, that is, by the assistance of the Spirit of God, they pray not at all. Let therefore the Scripture and Christianity answer for themselves, at present in this charge, I am not particularly concerned.¶

Thus sir, I have complied with your desire, unto a perusal of this confused heap of malicious calumnies, which otherwise I had absolutely in silence put off to the judgment of the great day. It may be this author has scarce yet cast up his accompt,[44] nor considered what it is to lend his fingers to others to thrust into the fire, which they would not touch themselves. For while they do, or may if they please, enjoy their satisfaction in his villainy and folly, the guilt and shame of them will return in a cruciating sense upon his own understanding and conscience. When this shall befall him, as it will do assuredly, if he be not utterly profligate, he will find no great relief in wishing that he had been better advised; nor in considering that those who rejoice in the calumny, do yet despise the sycophant.

Finis.

44 I.e., account.

A LETTER CONCERNING THE MATTER OF THE PRESENT EXCOMMUNICATIONS

London:
Printed for Benjamin Alsop,
at the Angel and Bible in
the Poultry, over-against the Church. 1683.

A Letter concerning the Matter of
the Present Excommunications

SIR,

You judge aright, that at my last being in London, I did consider the unusual hurry of excommunications against those called Dissenters; and because of the novelty of the proceedings therein, I did moreover endeavor my own satisfaction, as unto the design, causes, and ends of them: and I found it a thing easily attainable, without difficulty, or curiosity of inquiry. For whereas there is no covering of religion, nor any thing appertaining thereunto, save only a name or title cast upon them, they openly discover themselves of what sort they are, and what they belong unto. And among many other indecencies where with they are accompanied, one seemed to me to be very notable; and this is, the collection of whole droves together by summons and citations; then dealing with them in such a clamorous manner as makes a representation of a public market or fair for chaffering[1] about souls. But that, I found, which did principally affect the minds of men, was the event which these proceedings do tend unto, and will produce; and they generally concluded, that they would be highly prejudicial, if not ruinous unto all trust and trade, among the peaceable subjects of the kingdom. For they said, that if the commissaries would do as in the old Roman proscriptions in the time of Sylla and of the triumvirate afterward,[2] and set up the names of all that were to be proceeded against, in public tables, to be exposed to the view of all; those concerned, might shift for themselves, as well as they could, and the residue

---

1 I.e., haggling.
2 Owen is referring to the ancient Roman proscriptions, in particular that of Lucius Cornelius Sulla (82 BC), which consisted of a published list of enemies of the state, followed by a similar proscription of Octavian, Mark Antony, and Marcus Lepidus (the second Roman "triumvirate").

of mankind might be at liberty to follow their own occasions; but while they retain an unmeasurable reserve in their own breasts, as unto persons to be ruined by them, so as that they know not whose names, their own, or of those with whom they are concerned, they shall see the next day affixed on the church doors in order unto excommunication, it deprives them of all repose in the law of the land, or public justice, and breaks all their measures about the disposal of their affairs. How far this is already come to pass, you that are in the place, know better than I; but sure I am, that the very rumor of it gives a general discomposure unto the minds of men.

Hearing no other discourse of these things, I was somewhat surprised with your letter, wherein you required my thoughts what influence these excommunications may have on the consciences of them who are so excommunicated; for I did not think there would have been any question made about it: but since you are pleased to make the inquiry, I shall for the satisfaction of my respects unto you (though as unto any other end I judge it needless), give you a brief account of my judgment concerning these proceedings, which is the same for the substance of it, with that of all sober persons with whom I ever conversed.

Excommunication is the name of a divine institution of Christ, wherein, and in whose due and just administration, the consciences of Christians are, or ought to be highly concerned; and this, as for other causes, so principally because it is the only sure representation of the future judgment of Christ himself; he did appoint it for this end, that so it might be. Providential dispensations are various, and no certain judgment can be made on them, as unto the final and eternal determination of things and causes; no man knows love or hatred by the things of that nature that are before him;[3] but this is ordained by the law of Christ to be a just representation of his future judgment, with a recognition of the cause which he will proceed upon: therefore it is divinely instructive, in what he himself will do in the great day; it is a *futuri judicii praejudicium*:[4] but he will scarcely be thought well advised, who shall send men to Doctors' Commons,[5] to learn the way and manner of Christ's judgment of his church, with the causes which he will proceed upon. He himself gives another account of it (Matt. 25:32 unto the end of the chapter); of what he there declares, there is neither name, nor thing found among the men of these practices which we treat about. The mentioning of them, would be looked on as a sedition against their authority; or else make them ashamed,

---

3 Owen is alluding to Eccl. 9:1.
4 Lat. "a prejudgment of the future judgment."
5 I.e., the London society of civil lawyers.

as a thief when he is found: but for any sort of person to undertake the administration and execution of the sentence of excommunication against others, not making it their design to represent the judgment of Christ toward impenitent sinners, is to bid defiance to him and his gospel. Wherefore no person whatever, wise or unwise, good or bad, can be concerned in these excommunications, in conscience, or on a religious account; I speak not only of them who are forced to suffer by them, but of them also by whom they are administered and denounced: for it is impossible that men should be so far forsaken of all understanding, as to imagine that the proceedings therein, do belong unto the gospel, or Christian religion, any otherwise but as a debasement and corruption of it; neither is any man ever the less of the communion of the Church of England by those excommunications; though he may by force be debarred from some advantages that belong thereunto. Neither is the communion of any church to be valued, from which a man may be really and effectually expelled by such means: for this excommunication is not only null as to the efficacy of its sentence on the account of its maladministration; but it is not in any sense that which it is called, and which it pretends to be. Idols are called gods, but we know they are nothing in the world: so is this proceeding called excommunication, but is no such thing at all. If a man should paint a rat or an hedgehog, and write over it, that it is a lion, no man would believe it so to be, because of its magnificent title. All that it can pretend unto is a political engine, used to apply the displeasure of some, upon an accidental advantage, unto them whose ruin they design; and therein a satisfaction unto revenge, for discountenancing their supposed interest. That there is any acting in it of the authority of Christ, any representation of his love, care, and tenderness toward his church, anything that is instructive in his mind or will, any *praeludium*[6] of the future judgment, no man I suppose does pretend; nor I am sure can do so, without reflecting the highest dishonor imaginable on Christ himself, and the gospel.

To make these things yet more evident, and to show how remote the present excommunications are, from all possibility of affecting the consciences of any, I shall briefly pass through the consideration of those things, which principally belong unto them, and whereunto all their efficacy is resolved; and that which first offers itself, is the persons by whom they are administered: the truth is, there is such a variety of scenes in this tragedy, and such different actors in it, from apparitor[7] with whom it begins, unto the jailer with

6 Lat. "prelude."
7 I.e., an official who delivers a court summons.

whom it ends, that it seems not easy, whom to ascribe the animating power and authority that is in it, unto: but yet on a little consideration the matter is plain enough. The ministers of the parishes wherein the excommunicated persons are supposed to dwell, by whom the sentence of excommunication is rehearsed out of a paper from the court, have no concernment herein; for they know nothing of the causes, or reasons of it, nor of the process therein, nor do pretend unto any right, for the cognizance of them; nor do for the most part know the persons at all, on whose qualifications alone, the validity or invalidity of the sentence do depend; nor can give an account to God or man of what is done, as to right and equity; and therefore I no way doubt, but that these who are learned and pious among them, do hardly bear the yoke of being made such properties those acts and duties which appertain unto their ministerial function; but it is known who they are, who begin the work, and carry on the process of it until its final execution; and I shall say no more concerning them, but this alone, that how meet soever they may be for the transaction of civil affairs, or for the skillful managing of that work herein, which they suppose committed unto them; yet as unto anything wherein conscience may be affected with the authority of Jesus Christ, they can be of no consideration in it. If any man can but pretend to believe, that our Lord Jesus by an act, grant, law or institution of his, by any signification of his mind or will has committed, or do commit, the keys of the kingdom of heaven, the power of binding and loosing, of expelling out of, and admitting into his church, unto these or such persons, he has assuredly confidence enough to pretend unto a persuasion of whatever he pleases. They do not believe it themselves; nor among themselves, pretend unto any such thing; but only a power to execute their own laws or canons. They do not judge that any personal, moral or spiritual qualifications, are required unto ecclesiastical administrations; which yet to deny, is to undermine all religion, without which they may be fit for all church duties, who are no better than that archdeacon of Oxford, who being charged with immoralities in his conversation, justified himself by the soundness of his faith, affirming that he believed three Gods in one person; and besides he believed all that God himself did believe: let a man out of interest, or fear, or ignorant superstition, strive never so much to affect his conscience with the excommunications of such men, he will never be able to effect it.

But be the personal qualifications of those intended, what they please, the question is, how they came by that power and authority herein, which they pretend unto? They are chancellors, archdeacons, commissaries, officials, with their court attendants, of whom we speak. I confess these horrid names, with the reports concerning them, and their power, are enough to terrify poor harmless men, and make them fear some evil from them. But excommunication is that which no man knows on what grounds to fear, from these names, titles, and offices: for that is the name of a divine ordinance instituted by Christ in the gospel, to be administered according to the rule and law thereof; but these names, and those unto whom they do belong, are utterly foreign unto the Scriptures, and as unto this work, to the practice of the church for a thousand years; what therefore is done by them of this kind, must of necessity be utterly null, seeing that as such, they have no place in the church themselves by the authority of Christ. But however it be undeniably evident, that they have no relation unto the Scripture, nor can have any authority from Christ, by virtue of any law or institution of his, nor countenance given unto them by any practice of the primitive church; yet what they do in this kind, being pretended acts of power and authority, an authority for them must be pleaded by them: but then it may be justly demanded of them, What it is? Of what nature and kind? How it is communicated unto them, or derived to them from others? This is that which those who are excommunicated by them, are principally concerned to inquire into, and, which themselves in the first place are obliged to declare and evince: unless men are satisfied in conscience, that those who act against them have just authority so to do, or in what they do, it is utterly impossible they should be concerned in conscience in what is done against them, or be any ways obliged thereby: here therefore they abide until they are satisfied in this just and necessary demand.

But here all things are in confusion; they can declare neither what authority is required unto what they do, nor how they came to possess that which they pretend unto.

If it be from Christ, how comes it to operate on the outward concerns of men, their liberties and estates? If it be merely of man, whence do they give the name, and pretense of a divine ordinance unto what they do? If any should follow the clue in this labyrinth, it is to be feared that it would lead them into the abyss of papal omnipotency.

As they exercise this power in courts of external jurisdiction, and forms of law, they will not deny, I suppose, but that it is from the king; but why do they not then act that power in the king's name; for what is not done by his name, is not done by his authority.

Ministers do not preach, nor administer sacraments in the name of the king, for they do it not by his authority, or by virtue of authority derived from him; nor do parents govern their children or families in his name, but their own; because authority for it, is their own by the law of God and nature; but that exercise of power which externally affects the civil rights and liberties of men, must be in the king's name, or the foundations of the government of the nation are shaken—but I make it not my concernment what name or style they use in their courts. Let it be granted for their own security, that they have all their power and authority from the king, it must be therewithal granted of what nature it is, namely, civil and not spiritual, but why then do what they do, not go under the name of a civil order, constitution, or penalty, but of an ordinance or institution of Jesus Christ? Are not these things in their own nature everlastingly distinct? and is not conscience hereby fully absolved from any respect unto it, as such an ordinance which in this supposition it neither is, nor can be. It is easily discernible, how these things tend unto the utter confusion of all things in religion.

If it be said, that the power of it, as it is excommunication, is originally seated in the prelates, by virtue of their office, and is communicated unto these sorts of persons, by commission, delegation, or deputation, under their seals; it will yield no relief: for this fiction of the delegation of office power, or the power of office, unto any, without giving them the office itself, whereunto that power belongs, is gross and intolerable. Let it be tried, whether the bishops can delegate the power of ministerial preaching the word, and administration of the sacraments, unto any persons, without giving them the office of the ministry. If excommunication be an act of office power, authority to administer it, cannot be delegated unto any without the office itself, whereunto it do belong; for these things are inseparable. I certainly believe it is the duty and concernment of some men, to state proceedings of this nature on better foundations, that the exercise of such solemn duties of Christian religion be not exposed to utter contempt, nor men led by a discovery of false pretenses of divine institutions, to despise the things themselves that are so abused.

It were easy from many other considerations to demonstrate the nullity of these men's pretended authority, with respect unto excommunication, as it is an ordinance of the gospel, in which respect alone, the consciences of men are concerned; and as unto their power over the civil rights and interests of men, those troubled by them, must shift as well as they can.

But yet further, the manner of the administration of the present excommunications do evidence their invalidity and nullity. That which they pretend unto, as has been said, is a divine ordinance, an institution of Jesus Christ; and this declares in general how it ought to be administered by them who have authority for it, and are called thereunto: for it hence follows, that it ought to be accompanied with an humble reverence of him and his authority, diligent attendance unto his law, and the rule of his word in all things, with solemn reiterated invocation of his holy name, for his presence, guidance, and assistance: where these things are neglected in the administration of any divine ordinances, it is nothing but the taking the name of God in vain, and the profanation of his worship. It may be some will despise these consider-ations; I cannot help it, they do it at their utmost peril; it is conscience alone which I respect in this discourse; they who have any such thing, will think these things reasonable.

Again, the especial nature of this institution do[es] require an especial frame of mind in its administration; for it is the cutting off of a member of the same body with them, which cannot be without sense and sorrow. To cut off any one from a church, who was never a member of it by his own consent, nor do[es] judge himself so to be, is ridiculous; hence St. Paul calls the execution of this censure, "bewailing" (2 Cor. 12:21), denominating the whole action from the frame of mind wherewith it ought to be performed; and he that shall dare to decree or denounce this sentence without sorrow and compassion for the sin, and on the person of him that is excommunicated, plays a game with things sacred for his advantage, and shall answer for his presumption.

Besides, as was before observed, it is an instituted representation of the Lord Christ, and his judgment in, and of the church at the last day. If the consideration hereof, be once out of the minds of them by whom it is ad-ministered, they must unavoidably err in all that they do; much more if it be never once in them; but this they ought to take on their souls and consciences, that what they do, Christ himself if present would do, and will do the same at the last day; for so he will deal with all impenitent sinners, he will denounce them accursed, and deliver them to Satan. There is undoubtedly required from hence a reverential care and circumspection in all that is done herein: to make a false representation of Christ in these things, that is, his wisdom, authority, holiness, love, and care toward the church, is the worst and most deformed image, that can be set up: what higher indignity can be offered to his gracious holiness, than to act and represent him as furious, proud, pas-sionate, unmerciful, and delighting in the ruin of those that openly profess faith in him, and love unto him? God forbid that we should think that he has any concern in such ways and proceedings.

Whereas also, the next end of this censure is not destruction, but edi-fication, or the repentance and recovery of lapsed sinners, it ought to be accompanied with continual fervent prayers for this end. This the nature of the thing itself requires, this the Scripture directs unto, and such was the practice of the primitive church.

If we are Christians, we are concerned in these things as much as we are in the glory of Christ, and the salvation of our own souls. If we only make a pretense of religious duties, if we only erect an image of them for our own advantage, we may despise them, but at our peril.

How well these things are observed in the present excommunications, is notorious. Once to mention them, is to deserve a second thunderbolt: an account of them as to matter of fact, will be shortly given; at present I shall only say, that there is not any transaction of affairs in any kind among men civilized, wherein there is a greater appearance and evidence of turbulent passions, acting themselves in all manner of irregularities, more profaneness of expression, more insolent insultations, more brawling, litigious proceedings, more open mixtures of money demands in pretended administrations of right and equity, than there are in the public proceedings about them: shall any Christian suppose that the Holy Spirit of God, on whom alone depends the efficacy of all divine ordinances unto their proper end, will immix his holy operations in or with this furious exertion of the lusts of men? If this be looked on as the complement of Christian discipline, or the last and utmost actings of the authority of Christ toward men in this world, it must needs be a temptation unto men of atheistical inclinations: certainly greater scandal cannot be given; and it is the interest of some, at least for the preservation of a veneration to their office, to dispose of proceedings in this case, in such a way and manner, as may administer occasion of consideration unto them concerned, and not be carried on as at present, with laughter, indignation and confusion; and if Dissenters are to be destroyed, it is desired, that the work were left unto the penal statutes, which as now prosecuted and interpreted, are sufficient for it; rather than that the name of religion, and a divine ordinance, should merely for that end be exposed to contempt.

The last thing that I shall trouble you with at present is, the consideration of the persons against whom the present excommunications are blustered, with the pretended causes of them. These are they whom they call Dissenters, concerning whom we may inquire what they are, and the cause of this pretended ecclesiastical severity toward them. And as unto the first part of the inquiry, they are such as believe and make open profession of all the articles of the Christian faith; they do so, as they are declared in the Scripture; nor is the contrary charged on them. There is nothing determined by the ancient councils to belong unto Christian faith, which they disbelieve; nor do they own any doctrine condemned by them: they profess an equal interest of consent in the harmony of Protestant confessions, with any other Protestants whatever. They own the doctrine of the Church of England as established by law, in nothing receding from it; nor have they any novel, or uncatholic opinion of their own.

It is therefore utterly impossible to separate them from the communion of the catholic church in faith; or to cast them from that Rock whereon they are built thereby. They do also attend unto divine worship in their own assemblies; and herein they do practice all that is agreed on by all Christians in the world, and nothing else; for they do not only make the Scripture the sole rule of their worship, so as to omit nothing prescribed therein to that purpose, nor to observe anything prohibited thereby; but their worship is the very same with that of the catholic church in all ages; nothing do they omit that was ever used by it, nothing do they observe that was ever condemned by it; and this must be the principle and measure of catholic union in worship, if ever there be any such thing in the earth; to expect it in any other observances, is vain and foolish. Offering prayers and praises to God in the name of Jesus Christ, reading the Holy Scripture, and expounding of it; singing of psalms to God, preaching of the word, with the administration of the sacraments of baptism and the Lord's Supper; in a religious observation of the Lord's Day, unto these ends; all according as God do enable them by his Spirit, is the sum and substance of the worship of the catholic church, wherein all Christians are agreed: these things the Scripture do prescribe, and these things the church in all ages has observed: all differences about this worship, which have filled the world with inhuman contentions, arose from men's arbitrary addition of forms, rites, modes, ceremonies, languages, cringings, adorations, which they would have observed in it, whereof the Scripture is silent, and primitive antiquity utterly ignorant—and it may be it will be one day understood, that the due observance of this catholic worship, according as God enables any thereunto, leaving others at liberty to use such helps unto their devotion, as they shall think meet; is the only communion of worship in the church, which the Scripture requires, or which is possible to be attained: about the imposition of other things, there ever were, since they were, and ever will be, endless contentions. Wherefore these Dissenters practicing nothing in the worship of God, but what is approved by all Christians, particularly by the Church of England, omitting nothing that either the Scripture or catholic tradition directs unto, they are, notwithstanding this pretended excommunication, secure of communion with the catholic church in evangelical worship.

Moreover, they plead, that their conversation is unblameable; that they are peaceable in the civil government, and useful among their neighbors; if they do evil in these things, let them that prosecute them, bear witness of the evil; but if they do well, why are they smitten? If they can be charged with any immoralities, with any disobedience unto the rule and precept of the gospel; those by whom they are thus prosecuted, are highly concerned, if not in conscience, yet in honor and interest, to manage the charge against them, that some countenance may be given unto their proceedings: for "the law is not made" (as penal) "for a righteous man, but for the lawless, and disobedient; for the ungodly, and for sinners; for unholy and profane";[8] and if it be otherwise with the laws about these excommunications, they neither belong to nor are derived from the law of God.

There are indeed great clamors against them, that they are schismatics and separatists, and things of the like nature; that is, that they are Dissenters: but in this case the whole force of any inference from hence, is built on this supposition, that it is the will of Christ, that those who profess faith in him, and obedience unto him, unblameably, should be excluded from an interest in, and participation of these ordinances of divine worship, which are of his own institution, who will not comply with, and observe such rites and practices in that worship, as are not so, but confessedly of human invention. But no color of proof can be given hereunto; for it is directly contrary unto express Scripture rule, to the example of the apostolical churches, and unheard of in the world, before the branded usurpation of Victor Bishop of Rome:[9] an assertion of it, is to prostitute the wisdom, authority, and love of Christ toward his disciples, unto the wills of men, oftentimes prepossessed with darkness, ignorance and superstition, and other lusts, as shall be more fully manifested, if there be occasion. Let any color be given unto this supposition from Scripture or antiquity, and the whole cause shall be given up; yet thus is it, and no otherwise, in the matter of the present excommunications; persons of all sorts, every way sound in the faith, unreprovable in the catholic worship of the gospel, professing love and obedience unto Jesus Christ, without blame, are excluded, what lies in them, who manage these excommunications from those ordinances, of divine worship, which the Lord Christ has appointed and enjoined, without pretense of any other cause or reason, but only their not observance, in that worship, of what he has not appointed. He that can believe this to be the will of Christ, neither knows him, nor his will as it is revealed in his word; and the consciences of men are sufficiently secure from being concerned in that, wherein such an open defiance is bid unto evangelical precepts and rules, with apostolical examples.

---

8   1 Tim. 1:9.

9   Pope Victor I (d. 199) is most famous for his role in the Quartodeciman controversy, where he controversially excommunicated Polycarp and his followers for maintaining that the Easter feast should occur on the fourteenth day of the month of Nissan (following the Jewish Passover custom) rather than on a Sunday.

And further, to manifest the iniquity of these proceedings, while these Dissenters are thus dealt withal, all sorts of persons, ignorant, profane, haters of godliness, and openly wicked in their lives, are allowed in the full communion of the church, without any disciplinary admonition or control: but as this serves to acquit them from any concernment in what is done against them; so nothing can be invented that tends more directly to harden men in their sins and impenitency; for while there is a pretense of church censures, they will be apt to think, that they are sufficiently approved of Christ and the church, seeing their displeasure is no way declared against them; so they are not Dissenters, they have reason to judge that they are safe here, and shall be so to eternity; let them look to themselves who deserve to be excommunicated. Is this the rule of the gospel? Is this the discipline of Christ? Is this the representation of his future judgment? Is this the way and manner of the exercise of his authority in the church, a declaration of what he owns, and what alone he disavows? God forbid that such thoughts should have any countenance given unto them.

Ecclesiastical laws have been always looked on as cobwebs, that catch the smaller flies, while the greater break them at their pleasure, but among those lesser, to spare those that are noxious or poisonous, and to cast the net over the innocent and harmless, is that which the spider gives no pattern of, nor can imitate.

I shall not mention the avowed end and design of these present excommunications; only I shall say, they are such, as many good men tremble to consider the horrible profanation of things sacred, which they manifest to be in them.

There are also many other things which evidence the nullity of these proceedings, which may be pleaded if there be occasion; what has already been spoken, is abundantly sufficient to satisfy my engagement unto you, namely, that the consciences of men are not at all concerned in the present excommunications.

It may be it will be said, that all this while we have been doing just nothing, or that which is to no purpose at all, as not concerning the present case; for these of whom we treat, pretend no power in *foro interiore*,[10] or the court of conscience, or unto nothing that should immediately affect it. Their authority is only in *foro exteriore*,[11] in the court of the church, which it seems is at Doctors'

10 Lat. "in the internal court." As Owen suggests, it is a reference to the domain or judgment of the conscience.
11 Lat. "in the external court." Owen uses the expression here in reference to the ecclesiastical court.

Commons: wherefore by their sentence of excommunication, they oblige men only as unto their outward concernments; as unto what concerns conscience, they leave that unto the preachers of the word: it may be it will be so pleaded; but before they quit their hands well of this business, they will understand, that excommunication itself is nothing but an especial way of the application of the word unto the consciences of sinners, unto their edification; and that which is not so, pretend what it will, is nothing at all; unto the dispensers, therefore, of the word, it do alone belong; and whereas the apostle tells us, that the weapons of our Christian warfare are not carnal, but mighty, through God, to bring into captivity every thought unto the obedience of Christ;[12] they seem herein to say, that the weapons of their warfare are carnal, and mighty through the aid of somebody, to cast men into prison, or to bring their persons into captivity: and indeed this outward court of theirs, is part of that court without the temple, which is trodden down by the Gentiles, and shall not be measured in the restoration of the worship of God; yea the distinction itself is silly, if anything be intended by this outward court, but only the outward declaration of what is, or is supposed to be effected in the inward, or the mind and consciences of men. But let it be what it will; those who have neither name, nor place, nor office in the church by divine institution, who attend not at all in what they do unto any rule of the Scripture; nor can, nor do pretend any authority from Christ, in and for what they do, are no way to be heeded in this matter, but only as the instruments of external compulsion, which for the sake of the public peace, is to be submitted unto with quietness and patience.

I find, I confess, by the books with me, sent us weekly into the country, that in this state of things some of the reverend clergy do manifest great compassion toward the Dissenters, in writing and publishing many discourses containing persuasives unto, and arguments for conformity, whereby they may be freed from their troublesome circumstances: but I must needs commend their prudence in the choice of the season for this work, as much as their charity in the work itself: for the conformity they press, needs no other recommendation at this time; nor need they use any other arguments for it, but only that it is better than being hanged, or kept in perpetual durance, or stifled in prisons, or beggared, they and their families; or be starved in exile. And it has been always observed, that arguments which march with halberts,[13] bills, staves, sergeants, bailiffs, writs, warrants, and capiases,[14] are very forcible and prevalent.

12 Owen is alluding to 2 Cor. 10:4–5.
13 I.e., weapons consisting of a battle axe and pike mounted on a pole.
14 I.e., arrest warrants.

But I have done, and shall leave it unto others to declare what mischiefs do ensue on these proceedings, on civil accounts, and what an inroad is made by them on the government of the kingdom. For a new tenure is erected by them, whereon all men must hold their birthright privileges, especially that which is the root whereon they all do grow, namely, their personal liberty. They hold them no longer by the law of the land, nor can pretend unto security, while they forfeit them not by that law; they are all put into the power of chancellors, archdeacons, commissaries, and officials; they may deprive them of them all at their pleasure, against the protection of that law under which they are born, and which has been looked on as the only rule and measure of the subjects' liberties, privileges, and possessions. These things tend not only to the disturbance, but the ruin of all peace and trust among men, and of all good government in the world.

And if they should excommunicate all that by the law of Christ are to be excommunicated on the one hand, and all that are to be so by their own law on the other, and then procure capiases for them all, it is to be feared, the king might want subjects to defend his realms against his enemies, unless he should do as they did of old at Rome in great distresses, open the jails, and arm the prisoners; or it may be the lesser part would at length find it troublesome to keep the greater in prison. But these things concern not you nor me. I beg your excuse, as not knowing whether you will judge this hasty writing too little for the cause, or too much for a letter. As it is, accept it from [. . .]

Finis.

A DISCOURSE
CONCERNING THE
ADMINISTRATION OF
CHURCH CENSURES

A Discourse concerning the Administration of Church Censures

SEVERAL QUESTIONS TO BE CONSIDERED

Question 1: May a true church of Christ err or mistake in the administration of church censures?

Answer

A true church of Christ may err or mistake in the administration of the censures, or any act of discipline; whereby members of it, who are true members of Christ, may be injured, and sundry other inconveniences may ensue. And this is not unduly supposed:

1. Because no particular church is absolutely infallible, either in doctrine or administrations, especially in such points or things as overthrow not the foundation of faith or worship.

2. Because churches are more obnoxious and liable to error and mistake in their administrations and discipline, than in doctrine. For all doctrines of truth are absolutely determined and revealed in the Scripture, so that there is no principle, means, nor cause of mistake about them, but what is only in the minds of men that inquire into them and after them. But the administration of the censures of the church has respect unto many fallible mediums, requiring testimonies, evidences, and circumstances, which of themselves may lead a church acting in sincerity into many mistakes; especially considering how much in the dark unto us for the most part are the principles, causes, and ends of actions, the frames of men's spirits in and after them; all which in such cases deserve much consideration.

3. Churches have erred in not administering the censures of the gospel, according unto order and their duty (1 Cor. 5:2).

4. The experience of all ages confirms the truth of this supposition. The first church censure, after the death of the apostles, that is remaining on any

record, was that of the church of Corinth against some of their elders; wherein how they miscarried, is evident from the epistle of the church of Rome unto them about that matter.[1]

Corollary

In case any question arise about the administration of any church censure in a church of Christ, it ought to be very jealous, lest it have in matter or manner miscarried therein; seeing absolutely they may do so, and seeing there are so many ways and means whereby they may actually be induced into mistakes.

Question 2: Is it necessary that such maladministrations be rectified?

Answer

It is necessary such maladministrations should be rectified, by some way or means of Christ's appointment. And it is so,

1. First on the part of the censures themselves. And that,

(1) Because of their nullity; for they are null, and bind not.

[1] *In foro coeli*.[2] They bind not in heaven; for the Lord Christ ratifies nothing in heaven, but what is done in his name, by his commission, and according to his word. In some or all of which every maladministration fails.

[2] Nor *in foro conscientiae*:[3] for conscience is not bound, nor will bind on mere external, ecclesiastical authority, where the person is indeed free, and judges himself to be so according unto rule.

Only such censures may be said to bind for a season, in some cases, in the church, but that *quoad ordinem exteriorem et mere ecclesiasticum*,[4] with respect unto outward order, that the peace of the church be not troubled, until mistakes may be rectified; but not *quoad ordinem internum et mere spiritualem*,[5] with reference unto the dependence of the whole church on Christ the head.

(2) Because of the consequents of them. Disadvantage to the gospel, prejudice to the ways of Christ, and the utter impairing the authority of all church censures must needs ensue, if there be no way to rectify such mistakes, or if they are left unrectified; as may easily be manifested.

---

1 Owen is referring to the very early letter attributed to Clement of Rome, "The First Epistle of Clement to the Corinthians." For the English text, see *The Apostolic Fathers, Justin Martyr, Irenaeus*, vol. 1 of *Ante-Nicene Fathers*, ed. Arthur Cleveland Coxe, Alexander Roberts, and James Donaldson, (Buffalo, NY: Christian Literature Publishing, 1885), 5–21.
2 Lat. "in the heavenly court."
3 Lat. "in the court of the conscience."
4 Lat. "with respect to the external and merely ecclesiastical order."
5 Lat. "with respect to the internal and merely spiritual order."

2. This is also necessary on the part of the church, supposed to have erred. For whereas all church power is for edification, that which is unduly put forth and exercised, is rather for destruction; the guilt whereof every church ought to rejoice in being delivered from; especially considering that there is much more evil in condemning the righteous, than in acquitting the wicked, though both of them be an abomination.

3. On the part of the persons unduly, or unjustly separated from the church by such censures. This is so evident that it need no confirmation.

4. On the account of all other churches, holding communion with the church which has (as it is supposed to have) miscarried. The reasons hereof will afterward be made to appear.

Corollary

This relief, by what means soever it is to be obtained, is of great use to the churches of Christ, and of great concernment unto their peace and edification.

Question 3: How may such [mal]administrations be rectified?

Answer

The rectifying such maladministrations, may be (and is ordinarily no otherwise to be expected) by the advice and counsel of other churches, walking in the same fellowship and ordinances of the gospel with that church so failing, as is supposed. And this to be given upon the hearing and understanding of the whole proceedings of that church in the administration supposed irregular.

This being the principal thing aimed at, must be further considered. And,

1. The way, or means, whereby other churches come to the knowledge of such supposed miscarriages in any church of their communion, may be considered. Now, this is either,

(1) By public report. So the Israelites took notice of the fact of the Reubenites and Gadites in building an altar, which thereupon they sent to inquire about: they heard say they had done it (Josh. 22:11). So the apostle took notice of the miscarriage of the church of Corinth in the case of the incestuous person (1 Cor. 5:1). And this is a sufficient ground of inquiry, or of desiring an account of any church, in such cases.

(2) By information of particular persons, whom they judge holy and faithful. So the apostle took notice of the dissensions in the church of Corinth: they were declared unto him by them of the house of Chloe (1 Cor. 1:11).

(3) By an account given unto them by any church, requiring their advice in any case of difficulty, either before or after the administration of censures.

So the church at Antioch gave an account of their troubles and differences to the church at Jerusalem (Acts 15).

(4) By the addresses of the persons injured, or supposing themselves to be so; which to make, while they judge themselves innocent, is their indispensable duty; either directly, by seeking advice or counsel from them; or by desiring admission into the fellowship of the gospel with them, which they cannot grant, without an inquiry into the causes of their separation from any other church, or society.

Corollary

Where there is a concurrence of the most ways, or means of information, there ought to be the more diligence in the inquiry.

Hence it follows, that it is the duty of churches walking in the same order and fellowship of the gospel, upon such information or complaint, as before mentioned, of any undue administration of church censures, especially of excommunication by any church among themselves, to inquire by their messengers into the cause and manner of it, to the end that they may give their joint advice and counsel in the matter. And it is the duty of the church complained of, or informed against, to give them an account of all their proceedings in that case, with their reasons for their procedure, and to hearken unto, and consider the advice, that shall be offered and given unto them.

2. This will appear sufficiently confirmed, if we consider, in order unto a right judgment of the grounds whereon this way and practice is asserted,

(1) That this advice of churches in communion to be given and taken, is no ordinary or standing ordinance of the church as to its practice, though it be as unto its right; but is only to be made use of in extraordinary cases, and such as should not occur, although they will, and for this cause it is more sparingly mentioned in the Scripture.

(2) That it is, and may be fully proved to be the duty of all churches, by previous advice with other churches in cases of difficulty, to prevent this consequent counsel, which being after a sentence given, must needs be attended with many difficulties.

(3) That the practice of the churches, as to discipline, is no longer recorded in the Scripture, than they had the direction and help of the apostles, which supplied all extraordinary emergencies among them; so that many instances of this practice among them are not to be expected, and it is of the care and wisdom of our Lord Jesus that we have any.

(4) That we must here be content with such arguments and testimonies, as we act upon in other ordinances and things belonging to the worship and order of the churches; such as the distribution of elders into teaching and

ruling, the administration of the sacraments by officers only, gesture in the sacrament of the Supper, observation of the first day of the week, and the like.

ARGUMENTS SUPPORTING THESE CONCLUSIONS

These things being premised, the order above expressed, is confirmed,

Argument 1

1. From the light and law of nature, with the unalterable reason of the thing itself. Hence are churches directed unto this order and practice.

There is somewhat that is moral in all ordinances. Some of them are wholly so as to their matter and substance, and founded in the light of nature, being only directed as to their principle, manner, and end, in the gospel; such is excommunication itself, as might easily be made to appear. And from hence a direction unto duty, and an indispensable obligation unto obedience does arise. That which is moral in any ordinance does no less oblige us to an observation of it, than that which is of mere institution. And it obliges us because it is moral. And the Lord Christ being in all things the Lord of our consciences, what we do therein, we do it in obedience unto him.

Now that the order established is thus grounded and warranted, appears by the ensuing rules, taken from the light of nature:

(1) *Quod omnes tangit, ab omnibus tractari debet.*[6] All men are to consider that, wherein the concernment of all does lie, according to their respective interests. What is the ground and reason, why all the members of a church do consider, determine, give their counsel and consent, in the case of any persons being cast out of their society? It is warranted by virtue of this rule. They all have communion with such a person, and must all withdraw communion from him, and therefore must consider the reason of his excision or cutting off. Now a church in its censures does not eject any one from the enjoyment of ordinances numerically only, that is, in that one society; but specifically, that is, from the ordinances of Christ in all churches. Hence it becomes the concernment of other churches, even as many as the person ejected may seek communion from; and therefore it is to be considered by them, with respect unto their own duty of walking toward him.

(2) *Cujus est judicare, ejus est cognoscere.*[7] Whoever is to judge, is to take cognizance of the fact, and the reason of it. This is to be done according to the several

---

6   Lat. "That which touches everyone ought to be discussed by everyone."
7   Lat. "Whoever is to judge is to have an understanding of it."

interests that men may have in the matter under consideration; which in some is of jurisdiction, which in this case we admit not of; in others of counsel and advice. Now other churches are not allowed in this case to be merely passive and indifferent, but must make a determination in it. This is evident on supposition of the injured person's offering himself to their communion: for they must reject him, or receive him. In both they judge, and therein must take cognizance, by hearing the matter from the church; and so on both sides. And unless this be allowed, no church can, or ought to expect, that any other church will reject from communion any whom they reject, merely because they are rejected; unless they suppose their judgment to be absolutely a rule unto any other churches to walk by, in their observation of the commands and institutions of Christ.

(3) On the part of the persons supposed to be injured, every man by the law of nature is obliged to undertake *inculpatam sui tutelam*,[8] the just defense of his own innocency, by all lawful ways and means. And as absolutely the way, means, and measure of this defense are left unto a man's own prudence; so there is a rule given unto it, wherever the glory of God, or of the good of his neighbor is concerned: if either of these suffer by his wrong, he is obliged to vindicate his own innocency, nor is at liberty to suffer false imputations to lie upon him. It is in such cases a man's sin not to do so. And in the case under consideration this can be done only by an address unto other persons, for their assistance according to their interest. An interest of jurisdiction in civil courts, or in churches, in this case there is none. The interest of private persons herein is of compassion, prayer, and private advice; the interest of churches is a cognizance of the cause, with advice and judgment thereon. And for persons or churches not to give assistance in this case, according to truth and equity, is their sin.

That these are principles of the light of nature, and the natural reason of such things, appears from the general allowance of them so to be, and their constant practice among all men, walking according to that light and law.

Corollary

If churches, as they are assemblies and societies of men in communion for the same end, observe not the indispensable rules of societies, they cannot as such be ordinarily preserved in their being and communion.

Argument 2

2. The way and order laid down is directed unto, warranted, and confirmed, by general rules of the Scripture.

---

8   Lat. "a defense of his own innocence."

(1) On the part of the church supposed to err in its administrations. There are sundry general rules, which declare it to be their duty to give an account unto other churches, of their proceedings therein, and to consider their advice. Some of these may be named. As,

[1] That they "give none offence [. . .] to the church of God" (1 Cor. 10:32). Give "no offence in any thing, that the ministry be not blamed" (2 Cor. 6:3). Upon a supposition, or information, or complaint of maladministration of any ordinance, offense may be taken, and that, if accompanied (as it may be) with much appearing evidence, justly. And in this case the church has no way to clear itself from having indeed given offense, but by giving an account of their proceedings and the reason thereof. And without this it cannot be avoided, but that offenses will be multiplied among the churches of Christ, and that to the utter ruin of their mutual communion. Thus when Peter, by the special command and direction of God, went and preached the gospel to the Gentiles, many, not knowing the grounds of his so doing, nor his warrant for it, took offense at it, and charged him with irregular walking (Acts 11:2, 3). In this case, he does not defend himself by his apostolical authority and privilege, nor in a few words tell them he had a warrant for what he did; but to remove all doubts, questions, and causes of offense, he distinctly repeats the whole matter, and all the circumstances of it: an example of so great importance, that the Holy Ghost thought meet at large to express his account and defense, though the matter of it was set down immediately before (Acts 10, 11).

[2] That they "be ready always to give an answer" (that is, an account) "of the hope" that is in them (and consequently of their practice suitable thereunto) "with meekness and fear" (1 Pet. 3:15). This proves it *a minore ad majus:*[9] if they should be ready thus to answer every man, much more many churches of God, and that in and about things of their mutual edification.

[3] That in particular they clear themselves, when suffering under any imputation, or being in danger of so doing. "What carefulness it wrought in you, [. . .] what clearing of yourselves [. . .]: In all things you have approved yourselves to be clear in this matter" (2 Cor. 7:11). And this on many accounts is the duty of a church in the case proposed: the glory of God, the honor of Christ, their own peace and edification, with the peace and credit of all other churches, require it of them. Nor can this duty be any otherwise performed, but by this giving an account of their own proceedings, and receiving the advice of other churches therein. And if this be not done freely, with readiness and submission of mind, there is no way left to preserve the peace and

---

9 Lat. "[an argument derived] from the lesser to the greater."

communion of churches. Those who suppose they may in such cases act in a way of jurisdiction and church power, can attain the end by them aimed at, by virtue of the censures which they do administer. But in this way of counsel and advice, unless those who are concerned to give an account of themselves, will do it with meekness, gentleness, mutual trust and confidence suitable unto the conduct of the Spirit of Christ, in obedience unto his institutions, the whole end of it will be in danger to be frustrated.

(2) On the part of other churches.

[1] All churches, walking in the same order and fellowship of the gospel, are mutually debtors to each other for their good and edification. "Their debtors they are" (Rom. 15:27). And this debt in this case can no otherwise be paid, but by the way prescribed.

[2] What the apostles did, might do, and ought to do toward one another, who were all equal by virtue of their common interest in the same work, that one church may do, and ought to do toward another, or many churches toward one: but one apostle might take cognizance of the ways and walking of another, and withstand, advise, or reprove him, if in anything he failed, and walked not with a right foot (Gal. 2:11, 14).

Corollary

General rules, containing the grounds and reasons of particular institutions, are sure guidance and direction in and unto their observation.

Argument 3

3. The way and order expressed is warranted by necessity; as that without which the peace of communion, and edification of the churches cannot be preserved and carried on. As,

(1) On the part of the church whose administrations are questioned. The persons censured (which is ordinary) may in their own vindication, or by way of undue reflection, not to be discovered without a just examination, impair their reputation with other churches, or many members of them, whereby it may suffer and be exposed to sundry inconveniences. In this case a church can have no relief, but by reporting the matter unto other churches, so seeking their advice and counsel, whereby they may receive great encouragement, comfort, and boldness in the Lord, if found to have proceeded according unto rule.

(2) On the part of other churches. A church may either causelessly, or with just cause, cast out or withdraw communion from such a number of their members, as bearing themselves on their own innocency and right, may

continue in a society, and plead that the power, authority, and privilege of the church do abide with them. How in this case shall other churches know with which of these societies they may and ought to hold communion, unless they may and ought to examine and consider the causes of the dissension between them? And they may justly, and ought to withhold communion from that party of them, which shall refuse to tender their case unto such consideration.

(3) On the part of the persons supposed to be injured; and that either for their restoration, or their conviction and humiliation. For,

[1] If they are innocent, it is meet that they should be heard, as the Israelites heard the Reubenites; and necessary that they should be restored. Now it being supposed that the church which has rejected them, will not rescind their own act without new light and evidence, which for many reasons is not like[ly] to spring from among themselves; this is the only way left for that necessary relief, which the Lord Christ requires to be given. For what is our duty toward a person repenting, in reference to his restoration, is certainly our duty toward a person who has not sinned, when his innocency shall be discovered.

[2] For their conviction and humiliation, if they be found offenders. While they see not the right regularity of the church's proceedings with them; while they are able to justify themselves in their own consciences, and their hearts condemn them not, it is not to be expected that the sentence of excommunication, which works only by the means of men's light and conviction, will have its effect upon them. But when there shall be the concurrence of many churches, in the approbation of the censure inflicted on them, which probably will be accompanied with a contribution of new light and conviction, it is a most useful means to bring them to humiliation and repentance. It was an aggravation of the censure inflicted on the incestuous Corinthian, that it was given out against him by "many" (2 Cor. 2:6), that is, by the common consent of the church: and it will add thereunto when the censure shall be confirmed and approved by the concurrent advice of many churches.

Corollary

The Lord Christ having provided all things necessary for the peace and edification of his church, in all things that are evidently of that importance, his mind and will is diligently to be inquired after.

Argument 4

4. This whole order and practice are grounded on especial warrant and approbation, recorded Acts 15. Concerning which we may observe,

(1) That the occasion there mentioned fell out in the providence of God, and the practice upon it was guided by the Holy Ghost, that it might be an example and rule for the churches of Christ, in cases of a like concernment unto them in all ages, and so has the force and warranty of an institution. As it was in the case, that gave occasion unto deacons (Acts 4),[10] a matter of fact wherein was some disorder, rectified by a practice answering the necessity of the churches, became an institution for order in all future ages.

(2) That in that synod things were not determined by immediate inspiration, but the truth was searched out, and the mind of the Holy Ghost searched into by reasonings, arguings, and the consideration of Scripture testimonies, whereby they were guided in their conclusion and determination.

(3) That the institution and rule given is not in its exercise to be confined to that particular case, and instance there mentioned (which to do would overthrow many other rules and observations which we admit) but it is to be extended in proportion, and parity of reason, unto all cases of a like nature. For the reason of any law is the rule of its interpretation; and so it is of any institution. That that which gives offense and trouble unto any church, that wherein many churches are concerned, that which in any church hinders edification, and disturbs the faith or peace of any of its members, whether it be in doctrine or practice, that is not, or cannot be composed in any one church, should be considered, advised upon, and determined by more churches holding communion together, and meetings for that purpose by their messengers, is the sense, meaning, design and importance of this institution.

Corollary

To deny an institution of so great necessity to the peace and edification of the churches, will give great countenance unto men, who supposing such defects, are ready to supply them with their own inventions.

Argument 5

5. The order asserted is confirmed by the practice of the first churches, after the decease of the apostles. For when the church of Corinth had by an undue exercise of discipline deposed some of their elders, the church of Rome taking cognizance of it, wrote unto them, reproving their rashness, and advised their restoration. And when the church of Antioch was afterward troubled with the pride, and false opinions of Paulus Samosatenus,[11]

10 Owen is referring to Acts 6.
11 Paul of Samosata (200–275), one time Bishop of Antioch, is best known for his advocacy of Monarchianism, an anti-Trinitarian heresy stressing the oneness of God, and adoptionism,

the neighboring bishops or elders came unto the church, and joined their consent in his deposition.

Objections Considered

Some things are, or may be objected unto this course of proceeding among the churches of Christ, which shall therefore be briefly considered and answered.

Objection 1

This way of proceeding will abridge the liberty, and destroy the privileges of particular churches, which ought to be carefully preserved as the ground and foundation of the whole superstruction[12] of church order.

Answer

1. Particular churches have certainly no liberties or privileges, that are inconsistent with, and do contradict either the light of nature, moral equity, general rules of the Scripture, or the reasons and ends of all institutions, and of the edification of the whole body of Christ. And on these, as has been declared, is this way and course of proceeding grounded.

2. Other churches taking care about their own concernments and duty according to the will and appointment of Christ, namely, in considering whom they receive into, and whom they are to deny communion unto, with the cause thereof, do not, nor can truly abridge the liberties or privileges of any church whatever. For the duty of many churches will never interfere with the due liberty of anyone. And this is all upon the matter that they do in this case; which must be granted them, unless we will say, that the actings of one church, and those it may be irregular, shall not only abridge all other churches of their liberty, but hinder them also from performing their duty.

3. I do not see how counsel and advice can abridge the liberty of any church or person. Certainly to guide, direct, and assist any in the acting of their liberty, is not to abridge it, but rather to strengthen it. For liberty acted not according to rule, is licentiousness. A man in the use of his liberty may be going to do himself some notable injury; he that shall stop him by counsel and persuasion, with the prevalency and authority of reason, does not take away his liberty, but guides him aright in the use of it.

4. Wherein is the abridgment pretended? Is a church by this means hindered from the free use and acting of its own judgment, in taking in what

---

or the heresy that Jesus was born as a mere man and was only subsequently infused with the divine Logos.

12   I.e., edifice.

members it seems good, in watching over them according to the rule, in admonishing, reproving, or casting them out, if they find just and sufficient cause so to do? To hinder, or obstruct a church in any of these acts or actings by any authority, sentence, or determination, by any act or acts whatever, is utterly disclaimed: so that this is but a pretense.

5. When a case has difficulty in it, and such mostly, if not universally have all cases, wherein there will be found the least appearance of a grievance in the execution of censures, or pretense for seeking redress; a church has not liberty, has no privilege to secure it from previous[ly] seeking the advice of other churches, which is their duty by many rules of Scripture. We must not pretend unbounded liberty against known duty. And as a church does not seek previous advice from other churches, that they may obtain power to execute their censures, which they have in themselves; no more does this following advice any way cut them short in the use or execution of their power, but only direct them. And if a church have not this liberty by rule before censure in difficult cases, as it has not, no more has it after a censure, whereby the necessity of advice and counsel may be increased.

Objection 2

This way of proceeding will erect a jurisdiction or judicature in some churches over others, which is not to be allowed.

So some have spoken, who have not, it may be, duly weighed either what jurisdiction, properly so called, is; or how great an evil it is to cast a reproach upon the right ways of the Lord. In answer I say,

Answer

1. Excommunication itself, whatever men may suppose, is no proper act of jurisdiction. For jurisdiction in any sense is an adjunct of office, and the acts of it are acts of office and power. But so is not excommunication. For it is not an authoritative act of the officers of the church, but a judicial sentence of the whole church. Now the whole church is not in office. The whole body is not an eye. What is then done by it, is no act of office power, but a declaration of a judgment according to especial institution. And if excommunication itself may be exercised without any jurisdiction; surely that exercise may be consulted and advised about, without any pretense thereunto.

2. To constitute a jurisdiction it is required that there be, first, an office power stated in them that claim it; and a duty in others on the same account

to submit unto them; secondly, an authoritative acting by virtue of that office power, with an obligation from that authority, formally considered, unto obedience; with sundry other things, which in this matter are utterly disclaimed.

3. A right understanding of the true state of the question, of what is granted, and what asserted in this matter, will with them that love peace and truth fully obviate such objections as these. For,

(1) It is granted that all church power and authority, for the administration of all the ordinances and institutions of the gospel, is entrusted with a particular congregation.

(2) That there is no judicature,[13] no church assembly vested with church power and authority, without, above, or beyond a particular church, that should either contribute authority unto such a church for its actings, or authoritatively control it in its actings, to order or change its proceeding in anything, as by virtue of any authority received unto that purpose.

(3) That in case any person be not satisfied with the administration of the church, whereof he is a member, but finds himself aggrieved thereby, he cannot appeal unto any church, or churches, or assemblies of churches, as having power or authority to revoke, or disannul the sentence or act of the church, wherewith he is offended; either in pretense that the church without their concurrence and consent had not power to pass any such act, or that they have authority to control their acts, or can on any account authoritatively interpose in their administrations.

(4) It is then granted, that the power of excommunication in the preceding acts unto it, and full execution of it, is placed in a particular congregation, without respect unto any superior authority, but that of Christ and his word. These things are acknowledged; but that it should hence follow, that in case of supposed maladministration of ordinances, and the complaint of persons pretending to be injured thereby, other churches are not by virtue of Scripture rules, institution of our Lord Jesus, warrant of the light of nature, on their communion and common interest, to inquire into the matter, and take cognizance of it, that no offense be given or taken, that they may know how to discharge aright their duty toward both the church and the persons aggrieved, and give their advice in the common concernment of all the churches, there is no pretense to surmise. And for a church to say, that because they have power to do what they do, they will therefore in such things neither desire advice, nor take advice, nor hearken unto counsel, nor give account of their

13 I.e., judiciary.

proceedings to them that are or may be offended, or that require an account of them, is scarce agreeable to the Spirit of Christ, or the rule of his word.

Objection 3

This is the way to frustrate the sentence of excommunication, and to prevent the due efficacy of it upon the persons censured, yea to harden them in their sin and offense.

Answer

1. Concerning whom are these things feared? Were the advice mentioned, and the counsel to be had and given to be among heathens, enemies of the church, or of the ways of Christ, or of the especial way and order of church fellowship, which in this discourse is supposed, such events might be feared. But to pretend to fear, that other churches of Christ, walking in the same order and communion with ourselves, and whom we ought to look on in all things as like-minded with ourselves, as to their aim at the glory of God, and edification of the church, should by their counsel and advice frustrate the end of any ordinance of Christ, is a surmise that ought not to be indulged unto. Yea, we have herein cause to admire the wisdom, and bless the care of our Lord Jesus Christ, who has provided this help for us, to strengthen and confirm us in the ways of truth and righteousness, or to direct us where we are or may be mistaken.

2. Where excommunication is not administered but in a due manner, and for just causes, there will appear little trouble or difficulty in this matter. Let the cause or matter of it be as it ought to be, such a sin or sins, as the mind or conscience of a believer, of an enlightened person free from open prejudices, will at first view condemn in himself and others, and this, or these sins, persisted in after due admonition; and there will indeed be left no pretense of grievance, or complaint in those that are censured. But if it be administered in dubious cases, we shall find that this way of counsel is so far from being an obstruction of its efficacy, as that it is the only means to render it effectual.

3. No man will complain or address himself unto the relief declared, if he be convinced in his conscience that he is not injured, but that he is indeed guilty of the crimes charged on him, and that by Scripture rule they are such as deserve that censure. In this case no man will be so foolish or obstinate as to seek for relief. And if he should do so, he can possibly expect nothing, but to have his bonds made strong. But now suppose that a person be not so convinced, neither before nor after sentence denounced against him, but looks on himself as innocent and injured, either in part, or in whole, in matter

or manner of proceeding, what effect can be expected of his excommunication? We are deceived, if we look that this ordinance should have any effect upon men, but by the conviction of their minds and consciences. It works doctrinally only, though peculiarly by virtue of especial institution. And in this case it is evident how this way may further, and that it cannot possibly obstruct the effects of this censure, as was in part before declared.

4. The address being but once to be made, this is the only way to bind the guilty person, and that without delay, and to give him a sense of his sin; which it is supposed that before he had not.

5. It is our duty not to cast even persons that are excommunicated under new temptations. Now he that is aggrieved with the sentence denounced against him, and supposes himself injured (which while he does so, he cannot be humbled for his sin) if he supposes he has no way of relief left unto him, that is, that his case can no more come under advice or counsel; he will be exposed unto temptations to irregular ways, and so cast off the yoke, which he supposes grievous and injurious.

Objection 4

The pattern urged for this course of proceeding (Acts 15), concerns only doctrines, and not the administration of censures, which was not then, nor there in question. And therefore in the like case only may the like course be taken.

Answer

1. The way of mutual counsel and advice among churches, pleaded for, is not built only upon that instance and example, as has before been evinced. There are many more grounds of it, reasons for it, and directions about it, than what are, or can be comprised in any one particular instance.

2. There is frequently, if not always, some doctrinal mistake in the bottom of all maladministration. For whereas the nature of the sin proceeded against, and the rule proceeded by, ought in the first place to be doctrinally and dogmatically stated, here usually is the beginning of the mistake and error of any church. This therefore falls confessedly under that example of Acts 15.

3. Though that assembly made a doctrinal determination of the things in difference, yet the formal reason of the consideration of those things was the offense that was given, and that the churches were troubled. So that the pattern is to be extended unto all things whereby the peace of the church is disturbed.

4. Maladministration may tend to the subversion of the church, and the ruin of the souls of men, no less than false doctrines. As suppose a church

should admit known Arians, or Socinians into their society, supposing they have liberty so to do, may not other churches both consider the fact, and unless they alter their proceeding, withhold communion from them? Instances innumerable of the same kind may be given.

Objection 5

Churches have the sole power of admitting members into their society; by virtue of which admission they are not only received into a participation of the privileges of the church in that particular society, whereof they are members; but also into the communion of all other churches of Christ. Now this is daily practiced by churches, without any further inspection into their actions by others. Those admitted are received upon their testimony into their admission. And why shall not churches have the same trust reposed in them, as to the exclusion of any members from them; and expect that their testimony alone in the fact should satisfy, for their exclusion from all other churches, and their communion?

Answer

1. The cases indeed are parallel, and the power of every church is no less for the exclusion of any of their members, than for their admission. Nor ought their testimony to be of less weight in the one, than in the other.

2. Ordinarily, and where there is no ground of further consideration, the actings of a church of Christ in both these cases are, and ought to be granted, and taken to be according unto rule; so that other churches do acquiesce as to their concernments in the judgment of all the several churches of their communion.

3. There may be mistakes in admission, as well as in the exclusion of members. And some there are, who do very much scruple complete communion with many churches, principally upon this account, that they proceed not on right grounds in their admission of members; and such cannot but grant that, on occasion the grounds of their own admission may, and ought to be questioned and examined.

4. No church has such an absolute power in the admission of members, but that in cases of difficulty; and such as may in their determination one way or other give offense, they are bound to seek, and to take the advice of other churches with whom they hold communion.

5. Suppose it be reported or intimated by any of the ways that were before mentioned, that a church in communion with others, had admitted into their society an Arian, or Socinian, a seducer, or a person of a flagitious life, given

to corrupt the manners of others; shall not the other churches of the same communion, to whom the matter is so reported, or declared, and who are offended thereat, require an account of that church's proceeding therein, to know whether it be as it is reported, or no? And is not that church, so represented or reported of, obliged to give a full and punctual account of their proceedings, and to receive advice thereupon? Let any consider the instances before given, the nature of the thing itself, the rule of the Scripture in such cases, and determine. The case is directly the same as to excommunication. "But if any man seem to be contentious, we have no such custom, neither the churches of God" (1 Cor. 11:16).

AN ANSWER UNTO TWO QUESTIONS:

By the late Judicious John Owen, D.D.

———

*With Twelve Arguments against
Any Conformity to Worship,
Not of Divine Institution.*

———

*Zech. 7:7. Should you not hear the words, which
the Lord hath cry'd by the former Prophets?
Rom. 14:22. Happy is he that condemneth not
himself in that thing, which he alloweth.*

———

London:
Printed for Joseph Marshall, at the Bible in
Newgate-Street. 1720.

AN ANSWER UNTO TWO QUESTIONS

An Answer unto Two Questions

Contents

Question 1

Whether persons, who have engaged unto reformation, and
another way of divine worship, according to the word of
God, as they believe; may lawfully go unto, and attend on,
the use of the Common Prayer Book in divine worship?

Answer

1. We suppose herein, all that has been pleaded against that kind of service, as to its matter, form, imposition, use, end and consequents; which are all of them duly to be considered, before the practice inquired after can be allowed. But,

2. The present question, is not about the lawfulness or unlawfulness of forms of prayer in general; nor about the lawfulness of that form, or those forms, which are prescribed in the Common Prayer Book, as unto their matter and manner of composure, absolutely considered; nor yet about the expediency of the whole system of worship limited thereunto: but it respects all these things, and the like, with reference unto the persons described in the inquiry. And as unto the persons intended in the inquiry, we judge this practice unlawful unto them, as contrary unto sundry rules of the Scripture, and wherein it is condemned.

1. It is contrary unto that general, rule in those cases given us by the apostle, "If I build again the things that I destroyed, I make myself a transgressor" (Gal. 2:18). To destroy or dissolve anything in the worship of God, is, to lay it aside, and remove it out of that worship, as that which we have no divine obligation unto. So the apostle destroyed the legal ceremonies whereof he there speaks, and no otherwise. To build again, is to admit into the worship of God as useful unto the edification of the church. And these are contrary,

so as that, if the one be a duty, the other in the same case, or with respect unto the same things, is a sin. If it were a duty to destroy, it is a sin to build; and if it be a duty to build, it was a sin to destroy. He that does both, makes himself unavoidably a transgressor.

But, we have in this sense, as unto ourselves, destroyed this form of worship; that is, we have omitted it, and left it out in the service of the church, as that, which we had no divine obligation unto, and as that, which was not unto edification; if we now build it again, as it is done in the practice inquired after, we make ourselves transgressors, either by destroying or building.

And there is strength added unto this consideration, in case that we have suffered any thing on the account of the forbearance of it; as the same apostle speaks in the same case, "Have ye suffered so many things in vain? if it be yet in vain" (Gal. 3:4). It is a great folly to lose our own sufferings: "Are ye so foolish?" (Gal. 3:3).

2. It is contrary unto that great rule, "Whatsoever is not of faith is sin" (Rom. 14:23). For that anything which a man does in the worship of God, may be of faith, it is necessary that he be convinced or persuaded that it is his duty so to do (Matt. 28:20; Isa. 1:12; Deut. 4:2).

It is no rule in the worship of God, that we should do what we can, or that we have a liberty to do this or that, which we yet suppose, all circumstances considered, that we are not divinely obliged to do. In all things in general, and in particular duties or instances, we must have an obligation on our consciences, from the authority of God, that so we ought to do, and that our not doing of it, is a neglect of a duty, or it is not of faith. The performance of anything in the worship of God, has in it, the formal nature of a duty, given it, by its respect unto divine authority. For a duty to God, that is not an act of obedience with respect unto his authority, is a contradiction.

Wherefore, no man can (that is, lawfully and without sin) go to, and attend on this kind of religious worship, but he, who judges his so doing to be a duty, that God requires of him, and which it would be his sin to omit, every time he goes unto it. God will not accept of any service from us on other terms. Whether this be the judgment of those who make the inquiry as unto what they do they may do well to consider.

3. It is contrary to the rule delivered, "Ye brought that which was torn, and the lame, and the sick; thus ye brought an offering. Should I accept this of your hand saith the LORD. But cursed be the deceiver, that hath in his flock a male, and voweth and sacrificeth unto the LORD a corrupt thing: for I am a great King saith the LORD of hosts" (Mal. 1:13–14). We are obliged by all divine laws, natural, moral and positive, to serve God always with our

best. The obligations hereunto are inseparable, from all just conceptions of the divine nature, and our relation thereunto. No man can think aright of God, and that it is his duty to serve him, but must think it to be so with the best that he has. To offer him anything when we have that which is better, or which we judge to be better, is an act of profaneness and not obedience. In all sacrifices, the blood and the fat were to be offered unto God. Wherefore he that attends unto this service, does avow to God that it is the best that he has, and if it be not so, he is a deceiver.

If it be objected hereon, that by virtue of this rule so understood, as that we are always obliged to the use of that which we judge best in the worship of God, we are bound to leave this or that ministry or church, if we judge that the administrations are better among others; it is answered, that the rule respects not degrees, where the whole administration is according to the mind of God, but different kinds of worship, as worshiping by a limited prescribed form, and worshiping by the assistance of the Spirit of God, are.

4. It is contrary unto that rule, "Let all things be done to edifying" (1 Cor. 14:26). Whatsoever does not promote edification, is excluded out of the worship of the church by virtue of this rule. Nor can it be a duty in us to give countenance thereunto, or to make use of it. It is said, that prayer is the worship of God; these forms of it are only a determination of the manner of it, or an outward means of that worship. Let it be supposed; although it be certain that as prescribed they are parts of the service. They are therefore means that are a help and furtherance unto edification in prayer, or they are an hindrance of it; or they are of no use or signification one way or the other. If it be said, that they are an help unto edification, and are found so by experience, in the exclusion of any other way of worship; then I ask, why they are not constantly used? Why do we at any time, in any place refuse the aid and help of them, unto this great end, of all things that are done in the church? But this can be pleaded only by those, who contend for the constant use of them in the worship of God, with whom at present we are not concerned.

If it be acknowledged, that indeed they are an hindrance unto edification, which is more promoted without them, yet are they not in themselves unlawful; I say as before, that is not the present question. We inquire only, whether the use of them by those who judge them hindrances unto edification, be not contrary to the rule mentioned, let all things be done unto edifying. For the things of the third sort that are of no use, nor signification at all, they can have no place, nor be of any consideration in the worship of God.

5. It is inconsistent with that sincerity in profession that is required of us. Our public conjunction with others, in acts and duties of religious worship, is

a part of that profession which we make; and our whole profession, is nothing but the declaration of the subjection of our souls unto the authority of Christ, according unto the gospel. Wherefore, in this conjunction in worship, we do profess, that it is divinely required of us, and that it is part of that obedience which we owe to Jesus Christ. And if we do not so judge it, we are hypocritical in what we do, or the profession that we make; and to deny, that our practice is our profession in the sight of God and men, is to introduce all manner of licentiousness into religion.

6. Such a practice is in very many instances, contrary unto the great rule of not giving offense.[1] For it is unavoidable, but that many will be given and taken, and some of them of pernicious consequence unto the souls of men. In particular,

First, woe will be unto the world because of these offenses. For hence our adversaries, will take occasion, to justify themselves, in their most false and injurious charges against Dissenters, unto the hardening of them in their ways. As (1) they accuse them as factious and seditious, in that they will not do what they can do, and what by the present practice they own to be the mind of God, that they should do (or else expressly play the hypocrites), for the sake of peace, order and obedience unto magistrates. (2) That they pretend conscience, wherein indeed it is not concerned in their own judgment, seeing on outward considerations, which conscience can have no regard unto, they can do what is required. On these apprehensions, they will justify themselves in their security, and harden themselves in their sins, it may be to their perdition. Woe be unto them by whom such offenses come!

Secondly, by this practice, we cast in our suffrage on the part of persecutors against the present sufferers in the nation. For we justify what is done against them, and condemn them in their sufferings, as having no just cause or warranty for what they do; as we declare by our practice of what they refuse. There is no man who complies in this matter, but it is a part of his profession, that those who refuse so to do, and are exposed to sufferings thereon, do not suffer according to the will of God, nor do their sufferings redound unto his glory. And no offense or scandal can be of a higher nature!

Thirdly, differences and divisions will on this practice, unavoidably arise between churches themselves, and members of the same church, which will be attended with innumerable evil consequences unto the dishonor of the gospel, and it may be to the loss of all church communion.

Fourthly, many will be induced, on the example of others, especially if they be persons of any reputation in the church, who shall so practice, to follow

---

1   Here Owen is alluding to 1 Cor. 10:32.

them against their own light, having the great weight of the preservation of their liberties, and goods lying on the same side. And, experience will quickly show, what will be the event hereof, either in total apostasy, or that terror of conscience which they will find no easy relief under, as it has fallen out with some already. And,

Fifthly, it is a justification of our adversaries in the cause wherein we are engaged, (1) in their church state, (2) in a reading ministry, (3) in their casting us out of communion on the present terms, (4) in their judgment concerning us on the point of schism, as might easily be manifested.

Lastly, there is in this practice, a visible compliance with the design of the prescription of this form of service, unto the sole use of the church in the duties of divine worship. And this, in the nature of the thing itself, is an exclusion of the exercise of the gifts of the Holy Spirit in that worship, which is given and continued by Christ, to this very end, that the church may be edified in divine worship, and the due performance of it. And whether this answers our loyalty unto Christ in his kingly office, ought to be well inquired into.

And we shall hereby, on a mere act of outward force, join with them in church communion, who have cast us out of their communion, by the imposition of principles and practices in divine worship, no way warranted by the Scripture, or authority of Christ: who allow us no church state among ourselves: nor will join in any one act of church communion with us! Who persecute us even unto death, and will not be satisfied with any compliance, without a total renunciation of our principles, and practice in the worship of God, and giving away our whole cause about the state of the church, and other divine institutions! Besides, at present we shall seem to be influenced by a respect unto their excommunications, which as they are managed, and administered at present, are not only a high profanation of a sacred ordinance, but suited to expose Christian religion unto scorn and contempt.

Question 2

A second inquiry is, Whether the persons before mentioned, and
described, may lawfully and in a consistency with, or without
a renunciation of their former principles and practice, go to,
and receive the sacrament of the Lord's Supper in the parish
churches, under their present constitution, and administration?

Answer

It appears that they may not, or cannot so do. For,

1. Their so doing, would be an ecclesiastical incorporation in the church, wherein they do partake: for, a voluntary conjunction, in the highest act of communion, with any church, according to its order and institution, warranted by its own authority, is an express incorporation with it; whereby a man is constituted a formal member of it, unto all ends and purposes of privilege, right and duty. The church state is owned hereby, its authority submitted unto in its right and exercise; nor is it otherwise interpreted of them unto whom they so join themselves. But this is a virtual, yea, an express renunciation of their own present church state in any other society, and necessitates a relinquishment of their former practice.

It will be said, that a member of one particular church, may partake of the sacrament of the Lord's Supper in another, without incorporating or becoming a stated member of that church wherein he does so partake.

It is answered, that he may do so by virtue of that communion, which is between the church whereof he is a member, and that church wherein he does so partake. For he is admitted unto that participation, by virtue of that communion, and not on his own personal account. If it be otherwise, where any one is received unto the participation of this ordinance, there he is admitted unto entire membership, and is engaged unto all the duties thereunto belonging.

And thus is it in this case, for those unto whom they join themselves herein, if but occasionally, do first, own no church state in this nation, but their own, secondly, admit of none unto this sacrament, by virtue of their communion with any other church, or any churches not of their own constitution. Nor, thirdly, will administer it unto any, but those whom they claim to be their own, as living in their parishes, in opposition unto any other church state whatever.

Wherefore it is impossible, that any man should be a member of one church, and communicate in this ordinance in another, which condemns that whereof he is, as schismatical, and receives him as one belonging unto itself only, but he does professedly renounce the communion of that church, wherein he was; and is by them that receive him, esteemed so to do! And no reserves of a contrary judgment, or resolution in his own mind, will relieve any man in conscience or reputation, against the testimony of his practical profession!

2. They do hereby profess a spiritual incorporation with those, or that church wherein they do so communicate; namely, that they are one body and one bread with them; that they all "drink into one Spirit" (1 Cor. 10:17; 12:13). How they can do this in those places where they judge the generality of them to be profane and ignorant, without sinning against their own light, is not to be understood.

It is said, that no persons, in this or any other ordinance of divine worship, are polluted, or made guilty by the sins of others, with whom they do communicate. It is answered, that this is not at present inquired into. That which such persons are charged with, is their own sin only, in making a profession of spiritual incorporation, or becoming of one body, one bread with them, and of drinking into the same Spirit with them, when they do not esteem them so to be, in the exercise of love without dissimulation. The neglect also of other express duties, which we owe unto those, who stand in that union with us, will necessarily follow hereon. Neither do such persons, as so communicate, intend to take on themselves an obligation unto all those duties which are required of them, toward those with whom they profess themselves to be one spiritual body, which is an open prevarication against Scripture rule.

3. They would hereby, not only justify the whole service of the liturgy, but the ceremonies also enjoined to be used in the administration of the sacrament. For the rule of the church wherewith they join, is that whereby they are to be judged. Any abatement that may be made of them in practice, is on both sides an unwarrantable self-deceiving, inconsistent with Christian

ingenuity and sincerity. But hereby they do not only condemn all other present Dissenters, but all those also of former days and ages, ministers and others, who suffered under deprivation, imprisonment and banishment, in their testimony against them.

If they shall say, they do not approve what is practiced by others, though they join in the same worship and duties of it with them; I say, this is contrary to the language of their profession, unto Scripture rule (Rom. 14:22), and is indefensible in the sight of God and good men, and unworthy of that plain, open, bold sincerity, which the gospel requires in the professors of it.

4. The posture of kneeling, in the receiving of this sacrament, is a peculiar act of religious adoration, which has no divine institution or warranty; and is therefore at best, an act of will worship not to be complied withal.

It is said that kneeling is required not as an act of worship or religious adoration, but only as a posture decent and comely, because the sacrament is delivered with a prayer unto everyone. But,

(1) That delivery of it with a prayer unto everyone, is uninstituted, without primitive example, contrary to the practice at the first institution of the ordinance, unsuited unto the nature of the communion required, and a disturbance of it.

(2) He that prays stands, and he that does not pray kneels: which must be on another consideration. For,

(3) Prayer is not the proper exercise of faith, in the instant of receiving of this sacrament, as is evident from the nature and use of it.

(4) The known original of this rite, does render it not only justly to be suspected, but to be avoided.

On these considerations, which might be enlarged, and many others that might be added, it is evident, that the practice inquired into, with respect unto the persons at first intended, is unlawful; and includes in it a renunciation of all the principles of that church communion, wherein they are engaged. And whereas, some few have judged it not to be so, they ought to rectify their mistake in their future walking!

TWELVE ARGUMENTS, AGAINST ANY CONFORMITY OF MEMBERS OF SEPARATE CHURCHES, TO THE NATIONAL CHURCH

Twelve Arguments, against Any Conformity of Members of Separate Churches, to the National Church

POSITION

It is not lawful for us, to go to and join in public worship by the Common Prayer, because that worship itself, according to the rule of the gospel, is not lawful.

Some things must be premised to the confirmation of this position.

As first, the whole system of liturgical worship, with all its inseparable dependencies, are intended. For as such, it is established by law, and not in any part of it only: as such, it is required that we receive it, and attend unto it. It is not in our power, it is not left to our judgment or liberty, to close with, or make use of any part of it, as we shall think fit.

There are in the Mass Book many prayers and praises directed to God only, by Jesus Christ, yet it is not lawful for us thereon to go to Mass, under a pretense of joining only in such lawful prayers as, we must not affect[1] their drink offerings of blood, so, we must not take up their names into our lips. We must have no communion with them.

2. It is to be considered as armed with laws: first, such as declare and enjoin it, as the only true worship of the church: secondly, such as prohibit, condemn, and punish, all other ways of the worship of God in church assemblies; by our communion and conjunction in it, we justify those laws.

3. This conjunction by communion in the worship of the liturgy, is a symbol, pledge, and token of an ecclesiastical incorporation with the church of England in its present constitution, it is so in the law of the land[2] it is so in the

---

1   In the footnote: Ps. 16.4.—Owen.
2   In the footnote: In the Canon of the Church.—Owen.

common understanding of all men; and by these rules, must our profession and practice be judged, and not by any reserves of our own, which neither God nor good men will allow of.

4. Wherefore, he that joins in the worship of the Common Prayer, does by his practice make profession that it is the true worship of God, accepted by him, and approved of him, and wholly agreeable to his mind, and to do it with other reserves, is hypocrisy, and worse than the thing itself without them. "Happy is he who condemneth not himself" in the things "which he alloweth."[3]

5. There may be a false worship of the true God as well as a worship of a false god:[4] such was the worship of Jehovah the Lord by the calf in the wilderness: such was the feast unto the Lord, ordained by Jeroboam "in the eighth month, on the fifteenth day of the month," the which "he devised of his own heart."[5]

On these suppositions the proposition laid down, is proved by these following arguments.

FIRST ARGUMENT

Religious worship not divinely instituted and appointed, is false worship, not accepted with God; but the liturgical worship intended, is a religious worship not divinely instituted, nor appointed, *ergo*, not accepted of God.

The proposition is confirmed by all the divine testimonies, wherein all such worship is expressly condemned;[6] that especially where the Lord Christ restrains all worship to his alone command.

It is answered to the minor proposition, that the liturgical worship is of Christ's appointment, as to the substantials of it, though not as to its accidentals, namely, prayers and praises, not unto its outward rites and forms, which do not vitiate the whole;

But it is replied,

1. There is nothing accidental in the worship of God: everything that belongs to it, is part of it,[7] some things are of more use, weight, and importance, than others; but all things that duly belong unto it, are parts of it, or of its substance: outward circumstances are natural and occasional, not accidental parts of worship.

---

3   In the footnote: Rom. 14.23.—Owen. Owen is citing Rom. 14:22.
4   In the footnote: Exod. 32.56.—Owen. Owen is alluding to Ex. 32:5–6.
5   In the footnote: 1 Kings. 12.32, 33.—Owen.
6   In the footnote: Deut. 4.2 chap. 12.32. Prov. 30.6. Jer. 7.31. Isaiah 29.13. Mat. 28.20.—Owen.
7   In the footnote: Mat. 23.23.—Owen.

2. Prayers and praises absolutely considered, are not an institution of Christ, they are a part of natural worship, common to all mankind. His institution respects only the internal form of them, and the manner of their performance: but this is that which the liturgy takes on itself, namely, to supply and determine the matter, to prescribe the manner and to limit all the concerns of them to modes and forms of its own, which is to take the work of Christ out of his hands!

3. Outward rites and modes of worship, divinely instituted, and determined, do become thereby necessary parts of divine worship,[8] therefore such as are humanly instituted, appointed and determined, are thereby made parts of worship, namely, of that which is false, for want of a divine institution.

4. Prayer and praise are not things prescribed and enjoined in and by the liturgy, it is so far from it, that thereby all prayers and praises in church assemblies, merely as such, are prohibited; but it is its own forms, ways, and modes, with their determination and limitation alone, that are instituted, prescribed, and enjoined by it; but these things have no divine institution, and therefore are so far false worship.

SECOND ARGUMENT

That which was in its first contrivance, and has been in its continuance, an invention, or engine to defeat, or render useless the promise of Christ unto his church, of sending the Holy Spirit in all ages, to enable it unto a due discharge, and performance of all divine worship, in its assemblies; is unlawful to be complied withal, nor can be admitted in religious worship, but such is the liturgical worship. *Ergo*, etc.

That the Lord Jesus Christ did make such a promise, that he does make it good, that the very being and continuance of the church (without which it is but a dead machine) does depend thereon, I suppose will not be denied, it has been sufficiently proved. Hereon the church lived and acted for sundry ages, performing all divine worship in their assemblies, by virtue of the gifts and graces of the Holy Spirit, and no otherwise.

When these things were neglected, when the way of attaining them, and the exercise of them, appeared too difficult to men of carnal minds, this way of worship, by a prescribed liturgy, was insensibly brought in, to render the promise of Christ, and the whole work of the Holy Spirit in the administration of gifts, useless, and thereupon two things did follow;

---

8 In the footnote: Lev. 1.15.—Owen.

First, a total neglect of all the gifts of the Holy Spirit in the administration of church worship and ordinances.

Secondly, when a plea for the work of the Holy Spirit began to be revived, it produced all that enmity, hatred, and contempt of and against the Spirit of God himself, and his whole work in the church which the world is now filled withal. All the reproaches that are daily cast upon the Spirit of prayer; all that contempt and scorn, which all duty, of religious worship, performed by his aid and assistance, are entertained withal, arise from hence alone, namely, from a justification of this devised way of worship, as the only true way and means thereof.

Take away this, and the wrath and anger of men against the Spirit of God, and his work, in the worship of the church, will be abated; yea the necessity of them will be evident. This we cannot comply with, lest we approve of the original design of it, and partake in the sins which proceed from it.

THIRD ARGUMENT

That in religious worship, which derogates from the kingly office of Jesus Christ, so far as it does so, is false worship.

Unto this office of Christ, it inseparably belongs, that he be the sole lawgiver of the church, in all the worship of God. The rule of his government herein is, teach men to observe and do whatsoever I command.[9]

But the worship treated about, consists wholly in the institutions, commands, prescriptions, orders, and rules of men, and on the authority of men alone, do all their impositions on the practice of the church depend; what is this but to renounce the kingly office of Christ in the church?

FOURTH ARGUMENT

That which gives testimony against the faithfulness of Christ in his house, as a Son and Lord of it, above that of any servant, is not to be complied withal, let all his disciples judge.

Unto this faithfulness of Christ, it does belong, to appoint and command all things whatever in the church, that belong to the worship of God; as is evident from his comparison with Moses herein, and his preference above him; but the institution and prescription of all things in religious worship, of things never instituted or prescribed by Christ in the forms and modes of them, arises from a supposition of a defect, in the wisdom, care and faithfulness

---

9 Here Owen is alluding to Matt. 28:20.

of Christ, whence alone a necessity can arise, of prescribing that in religious worship, which he has not prescribed.

FIFTH ARGUMENT

That which is a means humanly invented, for the attaining of an end in divine worship, which Christ has ordained a means for, unto the exclusion of the means so appointed by Christ, is false worship, and not to be complied withal.

The end intended, is the edification of the church, in the administration of all its holy ordinances. This, the service book is ordained and appointed by men for, or it has no end or use at all; but the Lord Christ has appointed other means for the attaining the end, as is expressly declared,[10] he has given gifts to men for the work of the ministry, "for the edifying of the body":[11] that is, in all gospel administrations; but the means ordained by Christ, namely, the exercise of spiritual gifts in gospel administrations, unto the edification of the church is excluded, yea, expressly prohibited in the prescription of this liturgical worship; the pretense of men's liberty to use their gifts in prayer before their sermons, and in preaching is ridiculed, they are excluded in all the solemn worship of the church.

SIXTH ARGUMENT

That which has been, and is obstructive of the edification of the church, if it be in religious worship, it is false worship; for the end of all true worship is edification; but such has been, and is this liturgical worship.

For first, it puts an utter stop to the progress of the reformation in this nation, fixing bounds to it, that it could never pass.

Secondly, it has kept multitudes in ignorance.

Thirdly, it has countenanced and encouraged many in reviling and reproaching the Holy Spirit and his work.

Fourthly, it has set up and warranted an ungifted ministry.

Fifthly, it has made great desolations in the church. First, in the silencing of faithful and painful[12] ministers. Secondly, in the ruin of families innumerable. Thirdly, in the destruction of souls!

It is not lawful to be participant in these things, yea the glory of our profession, lies, in our testimony against them!

10 In the footnote: Eph. 4.7. 8. 11.—Owen.
11 Eph. 4:12.
12 I.e., painstaking.

SEVENTH ARGUMENT

That practice, whereby we condemn the suffering saints of the present age, rendering them false witnesses for God and the only blamable cause of their own sufferings, is not to be approved; but such is this practice, and where this is done on a pretense of liberty, without any plea of necessary duty on our part, it is utterly unlawful.

EIGHTH ARGUMENT

That practice, which is accompanied with unavoidable scandal, engaged in only on pretense of liberty, is contrary to the gospel, but such is our joining in the present public worship. It were endless to reckon, up all the scandals which will ensue hereon.

That which respects our enemies; must not be omitted; will they not think? Will they not say? That we have only falsely and hypocritically pretended conscience for what we do, where we can on outward considerations comply with that which is required of us? Woe to the world, because of such offenses, but, woe to them also, by whom they are given.

NINTH ARGUMENT

That worship, which is unsuited to the spiritual relish of the new creature, which is inconsistent with the conduct of the Spirit of God in prayer, is unlawful: for the nature, use, and benefit of prayer are overthrown hereby, in a great measure.

Now let anyone consider, what are the promised aids of the Holy Spirit, with respect unto the prayers of the church, whether as to the matter of them, or as to the ability for their performance, or as to the manner of it, and he shall find, that they are all rejected and excluded by this form of worship; comprising (as is pretended) the whole matter, limiting the whole manner, and giving all the abilities for prayer, that are needful or required, and this has been proved at large!

TENTH ARGUMENT

That which overthrows, and dissolves our church covenant, as unto the principal end of it, is as unto us unlawful.

This end is, the professed joint subjection of our souls and consciences unto the authority of Christ in the observation of all whatever he commands, and nothing else in the worship of God; but by this practice, this end of the church covenant is destroyed, and thereby the church covenant itself is broken; for we do and observe that which Christ has not commanded, and while some stand unto the terms of the covenant which others relinquish, it will fill the church with confusion and disorder.

ELEVENTH ARGUMENT

That which contains a virtual renunciation of our church state, and of the lawfulness of our ministry, and ordinances therein, is not to be admitted, or allowed.

But this also is done by the practice inquired into, for, it is a professed conjunction with them in church communion and worship, by whom our church state and ordinances are condemned as null. And this judgment they make of what we do, affirming, that we are gross dissemblers, if after such a conjunction with them, we return any more into our own assemblies. In this condemnation we do outwardly and visibly join!

TWELFTH ARGUMENT

That which deprives us of the principal plea for the justification of our separation from the Church of England, in its present state, ought not justly to be received or admitted; but this is certainly done by a supposition of the lawfulness of this worship, and a practice suitable thereunto, as is known to all who are exercised in this case. Many other heads of arguments, might be added to the same purpose, if there were occasion.

OF INFANT BAPTISM,
AND DIPPING

Of Infant Baptism, and Dipping
Contents

Of Infant Baptism

1. THE QUESTION IS NOT, whether professing believers, Jews or Gentiles, not baptized in their infancy, ought to be baptized. For this is by all confessed.

2. Neither is it whether, in such persons the profession of saving faith, and repentance ought not to go before baptism. This we plead for, beyond what is the common practice of those who oppose us.

Wherefore testimonies produced out of authors, ancient or modern, to confirm these things, which consist with the doctrine of infant baptism, are mere tergiversations,[1] that belong not to this cause at all; and so are all arguments produced unto that end out of the Scriptures.

3. The question is not, whether all infants are to be baptized, or not. For according to the will of God some are not to be baptized; even such, whose parents are strangers from the covenant. But hence it will follow, that some are to be baptized: seeing an exception confirms both rule and right.

4. The question is only concerning the children, or infant seed of professing believers, who are themselves baptized. And,

First, they by whom this is denied, can produce no testimony of Scripture, wherein their negation is formally, or in terms included, nor any one asserting what is inconsistent with the affirmative: for it is weak beneath consideration to suppose, that the requiring of the baptism of believers, is inconsistent with that of their seed. But this is to be required of them, who oppose infant baptism, that they produce such a testimony.

Secondly, no instance can be given from the Old or New Testament, since the days of Abraham; none from the approved practice of the primitive church, of any person or persons born of professing, believing parents, who were themselves made partakers of the initial seal of the covenant, being then in infancy, and designed to be brought up in the knowledge of

1   I.e., equivocations.

God, who were not made partakers with them of the same sign and seal of the covenant.

Thirdly, a spiritual privilege once granted by God unto any, cannot be changed, disannulled, or abrogated without an especial, divine revocation of it, or the substitution of a greater privilege and mercy in the room of it. For,

1. Who shall disannul what God has granted? What he has put together, who shall put asunder? To abolish, or take away any grant of privilege made by him to the church, without his own express revocation of it, is to deny his sovereign authority.

2. To say, a privilege so granted may be revoked, even by God himself, without the substitution of a greater privilege and mercy in the room of it, is contrary to the goodness of God, his love and care unto his church; contrary to his constant course of proceeding with it from the foundation of the world, wherein he went on in the enlargement, and increase of its privileges, until the coming of Christ. And to suppose it under the gospel, is contrary to all his promises, the honor of Christ, and a multitude of express testimonies of Scripture.

Thus was it with the privileges of the temple, and the worship of it granted to the Jews; they were not, they could not be taken away without an express revocation, and the substitution of a more glorious, spiritual temple, and worship in their room.

But now the spiritual privilege of a right unto, and a participation of the initial seal of the covenant was granted by God unto the infant seed of Abraham (Gen. 17:10).

This grant therefore must stand firm forever, unless men can prove or produce,

1. An express revocation of it by God himself, which none can do either directly, or indirectly, in terms or any pretense of consequence.

2. An instance of a greater privilege, or mercy granted unto them in the room of it; which they do not once pretend unto, but leave the seed of believers while in their infant state, in the same condition with those of pagans and infidels, expressly contrary to God's covenant.

All this contest therefore is to deprive the children of believers of a privilege once granted to them by God, never revoked as to the substance of it, assigning nothing in its room, which is contrary to the goodness, love, and covenant of God, especially derogatory to the honor of Jesus Christ and the gospel.

Fourthly, they that have the thing signified, have right unto the sign of it: or those who are partakers of the grace of baptism, have a right to the administration of it; so Acts 10:47.

But the children of believers are all of them capable of the grace signified in baptism, and some of them are certainly partakers of it, namely, such as die in their infancy (which is all that can be said of professors) therefore they may and ought to be baptized. For,

1. Infants are made for, and are capable of eternal glory or misery, and must fall dying infants into one of these estates forever.

2. All infants are born in a state of sin, wherein they are spiritually dead, and under the curse.

3. Unless they are regenerated or born again, they must all perish inevitably (John 3:3). Their regeneration is the grace whereof baptism is a sign or token. Wherever this is, there baptism ought to be administered.

Fifthly, God having appointed baptism as the sign and seal of regeneration, unto whom he denies it, he denies the grace signified by it. Why is it the will of God, that unbelievers and impenitent sinners should not be baptized? It is because not granting them the grace, he will not grant them the sign. If therefore God denies the sign unto the infant seed of believers, it must be because he denies them the grace of it; and then all the children of believing parents dying in their infancy must without hope be eternally damned. I do not say, that all must be so, who are not baptized; but all must be so whom God would have not baptized.

But this is contrary to the goodness and law of God, the nature and promises of the covenant, the testimony of Christ reckoning them to the kingdom of God, the faith of godly parents, and the belief of the church in all ages.

It follows hence unavoidably, that infants who die in their infancy, have the grace of regeneration, and consequently as good a right unto baptism as believers themselves.

Sixthly, all children in their infancy are reckoned unto the covenant of their parents, by virtue of the law of their creation.

For they are all made capable of eternal rewards and punishments, as has been declared.

But in their own persons, they are not capable of doing good or evil.

It is therefore contrary to the justice of God, and the law of the creation of humankind, wherein many die before they can discern between their right hand and their left, to deal with infants any otherwise but in and according to the covenant of their parents, and that he does so (see Rom. 5:14).

Hence I argue,

Those who by God's appointment, and by virtue of the law of their creation, are and must of necessity be included in the covenant of their parents, have the same right with them unto the privileges of that covenant, no express exception being put in against them. This right it is in the power of none to deprive them of, unless they can change the law of their creation.

Thus it is with the children of believers with respect unto the covenant of their parents; whence alone they are said to be holy (1 Cor. 7:14).

Seventhly, Christ is "the messenger of the covenant" (Mal. 3:1). That is, of the covenant of God made with Abraham. And he was the "minister of the circumcision, for the truth of God, to confirm the promises made to the fathers" (Rom. 15:8). This covenant was that he would be a God unto Abraham and to his seed.[2]

Now if this be not so under the New Testament, then was not Christ a faithful messenger, nor did confirm the truth of God in his promises.

This argument alone will bear the weight of the whole cause against all objection. For,

1. Children are still in the same covenant with their parents, or the truth of the promises of God to the fathers was not confirmed by Christ.

2. The right unto the covenant, and interest in its promises wherever it be, gives right unto the administration of its initial seal, i.e. to baptism, as Peter expressly declares (Acts 2:38–39). Wherefore,

The right of the infant seed of believers unto baptism, as the initial seal of the covenant, stands on the foundation of the faithfulness of Christ, as the messenger of the covenant, and minister of God, for the confirmation of the truth of his promises.

In brief, a participation of the seal of the covenant is a spiritual blessing. This the seed of believers was once solemnly invested in by God himself; this privilege he has nowhere revoked, though he has changed the outward sign, nor has he granted unto our children any privilege or mercy in lieu of it now under the gospel, when all grace and privileges are enlarged to the utmost; his covenant promises concerning them which are multiplied, were confirmed by Christ as a true messenger and minister; he gives the grace of baptism unto many of them, especially those that die in their infancy; owns children to belong unto his kingdom; esteems them disciples, appoints households to be baptized without exception. And who shall now rise up, and withhold water from them?

This argument may be thus further cleared, and improved.

Christ is "the messenger of the covenant" (Mal. 3:1), that is, the covenant of God with Abraham (Gen. 17:7). For,

1. That covenant was with and unto Christ mystical (Gal. 3:16). And he was the messenger of no covenant, but that which was made with himself and his members.

---

2   Owen is alluding here to Gen. 17:7.

2. He was sent, or was God's messenger, to perform and accomplish the covenant and oath made with Abraham (Luke 1:72–73).

3. The end of his message, and of his coming was, that those to whom he was sent, might be "blessed with faithful Abraham"; or, that "the blessing of Abraham" promised in the covenant, might come upon them (Gal. 3:9, 14).

To deny this, overthrows the whole relation between the Old Testament and the New; the veracity of God in his promises, and all the properties of the covenant of grace, mentioned 2 Samuel 23:5.

It was not the covenant of works, neither originally, or essentially; nor the covenant in its legal administration; for he confirmed and sealed that covenant, whereof he was the messenger; but these he abolished.

Let it be named what covenant he was the messenger of, if not of this. Occasional additions of temporal promises do not in the least alter the nature of the covenant.

Herein he was the "minister of the circumcision for the truth of God, to confirm the promises made to the fathers" (Rom. 15:8). That is undeniably the covenant made with Abraham, enlarged and explained by following promises. This covenant was, that God would be a God unto Abraham and to his seed; which God himself explains to be his infant seed (Gen. 17:12), that is, the infant seed of every one of his posterity, who should lay hold on, and avouch[3] that covenant, as Abraham did, and not else. This the whole church did solemnly for themselves and their posterity, whereon the covenant was confirmed and sealed to them all (Ex. 24:7–8). And everyone was bound to do the same in his own person; which if he did not, he was to be cut off from the congregation, whereby he forfeited all privileges unto himself and his seed.

The covenant therefore was not granted in its administrations unto the carnal seed of Abraham as such; but unto his covenanted seed, those who entered into it, and professedly stood to its terms.

And the promises made unto the fathers were, that their infant seed, their buds, and offspring, should have an equal share in the covenant with them (Isa. 22:24; 44:3; 61:9). "They are the seed of the blessed of the LORD, and their offspring with them" (Isa. 65:23). Not only themselves who are the believing, professing seed of those who were blessed of the Lord by a participation of the covenant (Gal. 3:9), but their offspring also, their buds, their tender little ones, are in the same covenant with them.

To deny therefore that the children of believing, professing parents, who have avouched God's covenant, as the church of Israel did (Ex. 24:7–8), have

---

3 I.e., to affirm.

the same right and interest with their parents in the covenant, is plainly to deny the fidelity of Christ in the discharge of his office.

It may be it will be said, that although children have a right to the covenant, or do belong unto it, yet they have no right to the initial seal of it. This will not suffice; for

1. If they have any interest in it, it is either in its grace or in its administration. If they have the former, they have the latter also, as shall be proved at any time. If they have neither, they have no interest in it; then the truth of the promises of God made unto the fathers was not confirmed by Christ.

2. That unto whom the covenant or promise does belong, to them belongs the administration of the initial seal of it, is expressly declared by the apostle (Acts 2:38–39), be they who they will.

3. The truth of God's promises is not confirmed, if the sign and seal of them be denied: for that whereon they believed, that God was a God unto their seed, as well as unto themselves was this; that he granted the token of the covenant unto their seed, as well as unto themselves. If this be taken away by Christ, their faith is overthrown; and the promise itself is not confirmed, but weakened, as to the virtue it has to beget faith and obedience.

Eighthly, particular testimonies may be pleaded and vindicated, if need be, and the practice of the primitive church.[4]

---

4 The editor of the 1721 collection of sermons in which this tract was published notes that Owen also defends the doctrine of infant baptism in a number of places in his Hebrews commentary. See John Owen, *A Complete Collection of the Sermons of the Reverend and Learned John Owen, D.D. Formerly Published: With an Addition of Many Others Never before Printed. Also Several Valuable Tracts, Now First Published from Manuscripts: And Some Others, Which Were Very Scarce. To Which Are Added His Latin Orations, Whilst Vicechancellor of Oxford, Taken from His Own Copies. And to the Whole Are Prefix'd Memoirs of His Life: Some Letters Written by Him upon Special Occasions: And His Funeral Sermon, Preach'd by Mr. David Clarkson* (London: John Clark, 1721), 578. Likewise, see Gatiss, *Cornerstones of Salvation: Foundations and Debates in the Reformed Tradition* (Welwyn Garden City, UK: Evangelical Press, 2017), 181–82.

A Vindication of Two Passages
in Irenaeus against the
Exceptions of Mr. Tombs

Being a Master, therefore, He also possessed the age of a master, not despising or evading any condition of humanity, nor setting aside in himself that law which He had appointed for the human race, but sanctifying every age, by that period corresponding to it which belonged to himself. For He came to save all through means of Himself—all, I say, who through Him are born again to God—infants, and children, and boys, and youths, and old men. He therefore passed through every age, becoming an infant for infants, thus sanctifying infants; a child for children, thus sanctifying those who are of this age, being at the same time made to them an example of piety, righteousness, and submission; a youth for youths, becoming an example to youths, and thus sanctifying them for the Lord. So likewise He was an old man for old men, that He might be a perfect Master for all, not merely as respects the setting forth of the truth, but also as regards age, sanctifying at the same time the aged also, and becoming an example to them likewise. Then, at last, He came on to death itself, that He might be "the first-born from the dead, that in all things He might have the pre-eminence" [Col. 1:18], the Prince of life, existing before all, and going before all.[1]

---

1 In the text: *Adversus Haereses*, Lib. 2. cap. 39. *Magister ergo existens, magistri quoque habebat aetatem, non reprobans nec supergrediens hominem, neque solvens suam legem in se humani generis, sed omnem aetatem sanctificans per illam quae ad ipsum erat similitudinem. Omnes enim venit per semetipsum salvare, omnes, inquam, qui per eum renascuntur in Deum, infantes, & parvulos, & pueros, & juvenes, & seniores. Ideo per omnem venit aetatem; & infantibus infans factus, sanctificans infantes; in parvulis, parvulus, sanctificans hanc ipsam habentes aetatem,*

593

Thus there are as many schemes of "redemption" as there are teachers of these mystical opinions. And when we come to refute them, we shall show in its fitting-place, that this class of men have been instigated by Satan to a denial of that baptism which is regeneration to God, and thus to a renunciation of the whole [Christian] faith.[2]

Mr. Tombs tells us, this proves not infant baptism, because though it be granted, that in Justin Martyr, and others of the ancients, to be regenerated, is to be baptized; yet it does not appear that Irenaeus meant it so in this place, unless it were proved it is so only meant by him and the ancients. Nor does Irenaeus[3] term *baptism*, regeneration; but says thus, "to the denying of baptism of that regeneration which is unto God."[4] But that indeed the word *renascuntur*, "are born again," is not meant of baptism, is proved from the words and the scope of them. For,

1. The words are, *per eum renascuntur*, "by him," that is, Christ, "are born again." And it is clear from the scope of the speech about the fullness of his age, as a perfect master, that "by him" notes his person according to his human nature. Now, if then, "by him are born again," be as much as by him are baptized, this should be Irenaeus's assertion: that by Christ himself in his human body, infants, and little ones, and boys, and young men, and elder men, are baptized unto God. But this speech is most manifestly false; for neither did Christ baptize any at all in his own person, "Jesus himself did

---

    simul & exemplum illis pietatis effectus, & justitiae & subjectionis; in juvenibus juvenis, exemplum juvenibus fiens, & sanctificans Domino; sic & senior in senioribus, ut sit perfectus magister in omnibus, non solum secundum expositionem veritatis, sed & secundum aetatem sanctificans simul & seniores, exemplum ipsis quoque fiens; deinde & usque ad mortem pervenit, ut sit primogenitus ex mortuis, ipse primatum tenens in omnibus, princeps vitae, prior omnium, & praecedens omnes.—Owen. For the English translation, see Irenaeus, *Against Heresies* 2.22.4, in *The Apostolic Fathers, Justin Martyr, Irenaeus*, vol. 1 of *Ante-Nicene Fathers*, ed. Arthur Cleveland Coxe, Alexander Roberts, and James Donaldson, (Buffalo, NY: Christian Literature Publishing Company, 1885), 391. The Latin term *magister* that has been translated throughout as "master" is, in the context, referring specifically to a "schoolmaster" or "teacher." For the Latin text, see the nineteenth-century critical edition, Irenaeus, *Sancti Irenaei episcopi Lugdunensis: libros quinque adversus haereses*, ed. W. Wigan Harvey, 2 vols. (Cambridge: Typis Academicis, 1857), 1:330.

2   In the text: Lib. 1. cap. 18. Ὅσοι γάρ εἰσι ταύτης τῆς γνώμης μυσταγωγοί, τοσαῦται καὶ ἀπολυτρώσεις. Ὅτι μὲν εἰς ἐξάρνησιν τοῦ βαπτίσματος τῆς εἰς Θεὸν ἀναγεννήσεως, καὶ πάσης τῆς πίστεως ἀπόθεσιν ὑποβέβληται τὸ εἶδος τοῦ ὑπὸ τοῦ σατανᾶ, ἐλέγχοντες αὐτοὺς ἀπαγγελοῦμεν ἐν τῷ προσήκοντι τόπῳ.—Owen. For the English translation, see Irenaeus, *Against Heresies* 1.21.1 (345). For the Greek text, see the nineteenth-century critical edition, Irenaeus, *Sancti Irenaei episcopi Lugdunensis*, 1:181.

3   In the text: Lib. 1. cap. 18.—Owen.

4   Owen's translation.

not baptize, but his disciples" (John 4:1–2); nor did the disciples baptize any infant at all, as may be gathered from the whole New Testament.

2. The word which Irenaeus expresses, whereby persons are born again to God by Christ, is applied to the example of his age, as the words and scope show. But he was not in his age, an example of every age by his baptism, as if he did by it sanctify every age; for then he should have been baptized in every age, but in respect of the holiness of his human nature, which did remain in each age, and so exemplarily sanctify each age to God, so as that there was no age but was capable of holiness by conformity to his example.

3. Irenaeus's words are: "He came to save all through means of Himself—all, I say, who through Him are born again to God—infants, and children" etc.[5] Now if the meaning were, that Christ came to save all that were baptized by him, or by his appointment, then he came to save Simon Magus, or whoever are, or have been baptized rightly. But in that sense the proposition is most palpably false, and therefore that sense is not to be attributed to his words.

4. Christ is by Irenaeus said to sanctify as a perfect master, not only according to the exposition of truth, but also as "an example to them of piety, justice, and subjection."[6] But this is to be understood, not in respect of his baptism only, but his whole life, in which he was an example, even as an infant, for then he did willingly empty himself, "took upon him the form of a servant," etc. (Phil. 2:7–8).

By all which reasons (says Mr. Tombs) I presume the readers who are willing to see truth, will perceive this passage of Irenaeus to be wrested by pedobaptists against its meaning, to prove a use of pedobaptism in his time.

Answer 1. The phrase of "born again to God,"[7] is so constantly used by the ancients for baptism, that it may be referred to the conscience of Mr. Tombs, or any one, who has been conversant in their writings, whether they would not have judged and granted that it was here intended, if mention had not been made of infants and little ones. The ensuing exceptions therefore are an endeavor to stifle light in favor of an opinion, which is not unusual with some.

2. "Through Him,"[8] is the same with "through means of Himself,"[9] in the words immediately foregoing; that is, by himself in his mediation, grace, and

---

5 In the text: *Omnes enim venit per semetipsum salvare, omnes, inquam, qui per eum renascuntur in Deum, infantes, & parvulos.*—Owen. The English translation here and in subsequent locations as per that which is cited above.

6 Owen's translation.

7 In the text: *renascuntur in Deum.*—Owen.

8 In text: *Per eum.*—Owen.

9 In the text: *per semetipsum.*—Owen.

ordinances. And to suppose that if baptism be intended, he must baptize them in his own person, is a mere cavil; for all that are born to God by baptism to this day, are so by him.

3. The words, εἰς ἐξάρνησιν τοῦ βαπτίσματος τῆς εἰς Θεὸν ἀναγεννή-σεως, "unto the denial of the baptism of regeneration unto God,"[10] do plainly declare that by "are born again"[11] he intends the baptism of regeneration, as being the means and pledge of it; in allusion to that of the apostle, λούτρον παλιγγενεσίας[12] (Titus 3:5).

4. It is remarkable in the words of Irenaeus, that in expressing the way and means of the renascency[13] of infants, he mentions nothing of the example of Christ, which he adds unto that of all other ages.

5. The example of Christ is mentioned as one outward means of the regeneration of them, who were capable of its use and improvement; of his being an example of baptism, nothing is spoken: nor was Christ in his own person an example of regeneration unto any; for as he was not baptized in all ages, so he was never regenerated in any, for he needed no regeneration.

6. It is well that it is so positively granted that Christ does sanctify infants; which, seeing he does not do so to all universally, must be those of believing parents; which is enough to end this controversy.

7. The meaning of Irenaeus is no more, but that Christ passing through all ages, evidenced his design to exclude no age, to communicate his grace unto all sorts and ages; and he mentions old men, because his judgment was, that Christ was fifty years old when he died.

8. It was the constant opinion of the ancients, that Christ came to save all that were baptized; not intending his purpose and intention with respect unto individuals, but his approbation of the state of baptism, and his grant of the means of grace.

---

10 Owen's translation.

11 In the text: *renascuntur.*—Owen.

12 Gk. "the washing of regeneration" (Titus. 3:5 ESV).

13 I.e., rebirth or regeneration.

Of Dipping

Βάπτω used in these scriptures (Luke 16:24, John 13:26, Rev. 19:13), we translate "to dip." It is only to touch one part of the body. That of Revelation 19:13 is better rendered, "stained by sprinkling."

In other authors, it is *tingo*,[1] *immergo*,[2] *lavo*,[3] or *abluo*:[4] but in no other author ever signifies, "to dip," but only in order to washing, or as the means of washing. It is nowhere used with respect unto the ordinance of baptism.

The Hebrew word, טָבַל,[5] is rendered by the LXX[6] (Gen. 37:31), by μολύνω, "to stain by sprinkling," or otherwise; mostly by βάπτω. Second Kings 5:14 they render it by βαπτίζω,[7] and nowhere else. In verse 10, Elisha commands him [Naaman] "to wash"; therefore that in verse 14 is, that "he washed." Exodus 12:22 is, to put the top of the hyssop into blood, to sprinkle it. First Samuel 14:27, to take a little honey with the top of a rod: in neither place can dipping or plunging be intended. Leviticus 4:6, 17; 9:9, and in other places, it is only to touch the blood, so as to sprinkle it.

βαπτίζω signifies "to wash," and instances out of all authors may be given, Suidas,[8] Hesychius,[9] Julius Pollux,[10] Phavorinus,[11] and Eustathius.[12]

---

1 Lat. "I wet."
2 Lat. "I immerse or plunge."
3 Lat. "I wash or bathe."
4 Lat. "I wash away or cleanse."
5 Heb. "to dip or dip into" (*Qal*), although Owen here qualifies this rendering based on the way it is translated in the Septuagint.
6 I.e., the Septuagint.
7 Gk. "I wash" (or "I dip or plunge," a rendering to which Owen only consents in a qualified sense below).
8 Owen is likely referring to a late fifteenth-century Greek lexicon edited by Demitrius Chalcondylas.
9 Owen is likely referring to the famous Greek lexicon produced by Hesychius of Alexandria (fl. 5th c.).
10 Owen is likely referring to the *Onomasticon*, or the Greek thesaurus of Julius Pollux (fl. 2nd c.).
11 Owen is likely referring to the Greek lexicon of Phavorinus produced in 1523.
12 Owen is referring to Eustathios of Thessalonica (ca. 1115–ca. 1195), who was an Archbishop of Thessalonica, theologian, and famous commentator on Greek literature.

It is first used in the Scripture (Mark 1:8; John 1:33), and to the same purpose (Acts 1:5). In every place it either signifies "to pour," or the expression is equivocal. I "baptize you with water," but "he shall baptize you with the Holy Ghost";[13] which is the accomplishment of that promise, that the Holy Ghost should be poured on them.

For the other places (Mark 7:3–4), νίπτω and βαπτίζω are plainly the same, both "to wash." Luke 11:38 is the same with Mark 7:3. No one instance can be given in the Scripture wherein βαπτίζω does necessarily signify either "to dip," or "plunge."

Βαπτίζω may be considered either as to its original, natural sense, or as to its mystical use in the ordinance.

This distinction must be observed concerning many other words in the New Testament, as ἐκκλησία,[14] χειροτονία,[15] and others, which have a peculiar sense in their mystical use.

In this sense, as it expresses baptism, it denotes "to wash" only, and not "to dip" at all: for so it is expounded (Titus 3:5; Eph. 5:26; Heb. 10:22; 1 Pet. 3:21). And it signifies that communication of the Spirit, which is expressed by "pouring out" and "sprinkling" (Ezek. 36:25), and expresses our being washed in the blood of Christ (Titus 2:14; Heb. 9:14, 19, 23).

Wherefore in this sense, as the word is applied unto the ordinance, the sense of dipping is utterly excluded. And though as a mere external mode it may be used, provided the person dipped be naked; yet to urge it as necessary, overthrows the nature of the sacrament.

For the original and natural signification of it, it signifies, "to dip, to plunge, to dye, to wash, to cleanse."

But I say, (1) it does not signify properly "to dip" or "plunge," for that in Greek is ἐμβάπτω and ἐμβαπτίζω. (2) It nowhere signifies "to dip," but as a mode of, and in order to washing. 3. It signifies the "dipping" of a finger, or the least touch of the water, and not plunging the whole. 4. It signifies "to wash" also in all good authors.

I have not all those quoted to the contrary. In the quotations of them whom I have, if it be intended, that they say, it signifies "to dip," and not "to wash," or "to dip" only, there is neither truth nor honesty in them by whom they are quoted.

Scapula[16] is one, a common book, and he gives it the sense of *lavo, abluo*, "to wash," and "wash away."

---

13 Matt. 3:11.
14 Gk. "assembly or church."
15 Gk. "laying on of hands or ordination."
16 Owen is referring to the Greek-Latin dictionary of Johann Scapula published in 1628.

Stephanus,[17] is another, and he expressly in sundry places assigns *lavo* and *abluo* to be also the sense of it.

Aquinas is for dipping of children, provided it be done three times in honor of the Trinity; but he maintains pouring or sprinkling to be lawful also; affirming that Laurentius,[18] who lived about the time 250, so practiced. But he meddles not with the sense of the word, as being too wise to speak of that which he understood not; for he knew no Greek.[19]

In Suidas,[20] the great treasury of the Greek tongue, it is rendered by *madefacio*,[21] *lavo, abluo, purgo*,[22] *mundo*.[23]

The places in the other authors being not quoted, I cannot give an account of what they say. I have searched some of them in every place wherein they mention baptism, and find no one word to the purpose. I must say, and will make it good, that no honest man who understands the Greek tongue, can deny the word to signify "to wash," as well as "to dip."

It must not be denied but that in the primitive times they did use to baptize both grown persons and children oftentimes by dipping; but they affirmed it necessary to dip them stark naked, and that three times; but not one ever denied pouring water to be lawful.

The apostle, is dehorting[24] from sin (Rom. 6:3–5), exhorting to holiness and new obedience, and gives this argument from the necessity of it, and our ability for it, both taken from our initiation into the virtue of the death and life of Christ expressed in our baptism; that by virtue of the death and burial of Christ, we should be dead unto sin, sin being slain thereby; and by virtue of the resurrection of Christ, we should be quickened unto newness of life, as Peter declares (1 Pet. 3:21). Our being "buried with him,"[25] and our being "planted together in the likeness of his death," and "in the likeness of his resurrection,"[26] is the same with "our old man being crucified with him"

---

17 Owen may be referring to the Greek lexicon begun by Robert Estienne, or Robertus Stephanus, and completed by his son, published in 1573.

18 St. Laurence (225–258) served as an archdeacon of Rome during the papacy of Sixtus II and was martyred during the Valerian persecution.

19 Owen is referring to Thomas Aquinas's remarks on baptism in his *Summa theologiae*, par. 3, q. 66, art. 7.

20 Owen is referring to a Byzantine encyclopedic lexicon known as the *Suda* or *Souda*, after Suidas, the lexicographer to whom it was once attributed.

21 Lat. "I make wet or moisten."

22 Lat. "I cleanse or purify."

23 Lat. "I make clean or cleanse."

24 I.e., dissuading.

25 Rom. 6:4.

26 Rom. 6:5.

verse 6, and the destroying of the body of sin, and our being raised from the dead with him; which is all that is intended in the place.

There is not one word, nor one expression, that mentions any resemblance between dipping under water, and the death and burial of Christ, nor one word that mentions a resemblance between our rising out of the water, and the resurrection of Christ. Our being "buried with him by baptism into death," verse 4, is our being "planted together in the likeness of his death," verse 5. Our being "planted together in the likeness of his death" is not our being dipped under water, but the crucifying of the old man, verse 6. Our being raised up with Christ from the dead is not our rising from under the water, but our "walking in newness of life," verse 4, by virtue of the resurrection of Christ (1 Pet. 3:21).

That baptism is not a sign of the death, burial, and resurrection of Christ, is clear from hence; because an instituted sign is a sign of gospel grace participated, or to be participated. If dipping be a sign of the burial of Christ, it is not a sign of a gospel grace participated; for it may be where there is none, nor any exhibited.

For the major: if all gospel ordinances are signs and expressions of the communication of the grace of Christ, then baptism is so: but this is the end of all gospel ordinances, or else they have some other end; or are vain and empty shows.

The same individual sign cannot be instituted to signify things of several natures. But the outward burial of Christ, and a participation of the virtue of Christ's death and burial, are things of a diverse nature, and therefore are not signified by one sign.

That interpretation which would enervate the apostle's argument and design, our comfort and duty, is not to be admitted. But this interpretation that baptism is mentioned here as the sign of Christ's burial, would enervate the apostle's argument and design, our comfort and duty. And therefore it is not to be admitted.

The minor is thus proved: the argument and design of the apostle, as was before declared, is to exhort and encourage unto mortification of sin and new obedience, by virtue of power received from the death and life of Christ, whereof a pledge is given us in our baptism. But this is taken away by this interpretation: for we may be so buried with Christ and planted into the death of Christ by dipping, and yet have no power derived from Christ for the crucifying of sin, and for the quickening of us to obedience.

OF MARRYING AFTER
DIVORCE IN CASE
OF ADULTERY

Of Marrying after Divorce
in Case of Adultery

IT IS CONFESSED BY ALL, that adultery is a just and sufficient cause of a divorce betwixt married persons.

This divorce, say some, consists in a dissolution *vinculi matrimonialis*,[1] and so removes the marriage relation, as that the innocent person divorcing, or procuring the divorce, is at liberty to marry again.

Others say that it is only a separation *a mensa et thoro*,[2] and that on this occasion, it does not, nor ought to dissolve the marriage relation.

I am of the judgment of the former. For,

First, this divorce *a mensa et thoro* only is no true divorce, but a mere fiction of a divorce, of no use in this case, nor lawful to be made use of, neither by the law of nature, nor the law of God. For,

1. It is, as stated, but a late invention of no use in the world, nor known in more ancient times. For those of the Roman church, who assert it, do grant that divorces by the law of nature were *a vinculo*;[3] and that so they were also under the Old Testament: and this fiction they would impose on the grace and state of the gospel; which yet makes indeed no alteration in moral relations, or duties, but only directs their performance.

2. It is deduced from a fiction, namely, that marriage among Christians is a sacrament of that signification, as renders it indissolvable. And therefore they would have it to take place only among believers, the rest of mankind being left to their natural right and privilege. But this is a fiction, and as such in sundry cases they make use of it.

Secondly, a divorce perpetual *a mensa et thoro* only, is no way useful to mankind, but hurtful and noxious. For,

1 Lat. "of the bond of matrimony."
2 Lat. "from board and bed," an expression used to describe a marital separation rather than a formal dissolution of the bond.
3 Lat. "from the bond."

1. It would constitute a new condition, or state of life, wherein it is not possible that a man should either have a wife, or not have a wife, lawfully. In one of which estates yet really every man, capable of the state of wedlock, is and must be, whether he will or no. For a man may, as things may be circumstantiated, be absolutely bound in conscience not to receive her again, who was justly repudiated for adultery. Nor can he take another on this divorce. But into this estate God calls no man.

2. It may, and probably will cast a man under a necessity of sinning. For suppose he has not the gift of continency,[4] it is the express will of God, that he should marry for his relief. Yet on this supposition he sins, if he does so; and in that, he sins if he does not so.

Thirdly, it is unlawful. For if the bond of marriage abides, the relation still continues. This relation is the foundation of all mutual duties. And while all that continues, none can dispense with, or prohibit from the performance of those duties. If a woman does continue in the relation of a wife to a man, she may claim the duties of marriage from him. Separation there may be by consent for a season, or upon other occasions, that may hinder the actual discharge of conjugal duties; but to make an obligation unto such duties void, while the relation does continue, is against the law of nature, and the law of God. This divorce therefore, supposing the relation of man and wife between any, and no mutual duty thence to arise, is unlawful.

Fourthly, the light of nature never directed to this kind of divorce. Marriage is an ordinance of the law of nature; but in the light and reason thereof, there is no intimation of any such practice. It still directed, that they who might justly put away their wives, might marry others. Hence some, as the ancient Grecians, and the Romans afterward, allowed the husband to kill the adulteress. This among the Romans was changed *lege Julia*,[5] but the offense still made capital. In the room hereof afterward divorce took place, purposely to give the innocent person liberty of marriage. So that this kind of divorce is but a fiction.

The first opinion therefore is according to truth. For,

First, that which dissolves the form of marriage, and destroys all the forms of marriage, does dissolve the bond of marriage. For take away the form and end of any moral relation, and the relation itself ceases. But this is done by adultery, and a divorce ensuing thereon. For the form of marriage consists in this, that two become "one flesh" (Gen. 2:24; Matt. 19:6). But this is dissolved

---

4   I.e., the ability to exercise sexual self-constraint.
5   This is a reference to Caesar Augustus's *Lex Julia de adulteriis coercendis*. This law made adultery a public crime when it had previously been dealt with privately, as the offended party saw fit.

by adultery: for the adulteress becomes one flesh with the adulterer (1 Cor. 6:16), and so no longer one flesh in individual society with her husband. And it absolutely breaks the bond or covenant of marriage. And how can men contend that is a bond which is absolutely broken? Or fancy a *vinculum*[6] that does not bind? And, that it absolutely destroys all the forms of marriage, will be granted. It therefore dissolves the bond of marriage itself.

Secondly, if the innocent party upon a divorce be not set at liberty, then

1. He is deprived of his right by the sins of another, which is against the law of nature; and so every wicked woman has it in her power to deprive her husband of his natural right.

2. The divorce in case of adultery, pointed by our Savior to the innocent person to make use of, is, as all confess, for his liberty, advantage, and relief. But on sup-position, that he may not marry, it would prove a snare, and a yoke unto him. For if hereon he has not the gift of continency, he is exposed to sin and judgment.

Thirdly, our blessed Savior gives express direction in the case, "Whosoever shall put away his wife, except it be for fornication, and shall marry another, committeth adultery" (Matt. 19:9). Hence it is evident, and is the plain sense of the words, that he who puts away his wife for fornication, and marries an-other, does not commit adultery. Therefore the bond of marriage in that case is dissolved, and the person that put away his wife, is at liberty to marry. While he denies putting away and marrying again for every cause, the exception of fornication allows both putting away, and marrying again in that case. For an exception always affirms the contrary unto what is denied in the rule, where-unto it is an exception; or, denies what is affirmed in it, in the case comprised in the exception. For every exception is a particular proposition contradictory to the general rule: so that when the one is affirmative, the other is negative; and on the contrary. The rule here in general is affirmative: he that puts away his wife, and marries another, commits adultery. The exception is negative: but he that puts away his wife for fornication, and marries another, does not commit adultery. Or, they may be otherwise conceived, so that the general rule shall be negative, and the exception affirmative: it is not lawful to put away a wife, and marry another, it is adultery. Then the exception is: it is lawful for a man to put away his wife for fornication, and marry another. And this is the nature of all such exceptions, as I could manifest in instances of all sorts.

It is to no purpose to except, that the other evangelists (Mark 10; Luke 16)[7] do not express the exception insisted on. For,

---

6 Lat. "a means of binding."
7 Owen is referring to Mark 10:11–12 and Luke 16:18.

1. It is twice used by Matthew and therefore was assuredly used by our Savior (5:32 and 19:9).

2. It is a rule owned by all, that where the same thing is reported by several evangelists, the briefer, short, more imperfect expressions, are to be measured and interpreted by the fuller and larger. And every general rule in any place, is to be limited by an exception annexed unto it in any one place whatever. And there is scarce any general rule, but admits of an exception.

It is more vain to answer, that our Savior speaks with respect unto the Jews only, and what was, or was not allowed among them. For,

1. In this answer he reduces things to the law of creation, and their primitive institution. He declares what was the law of marriage, and the nature of that relation antecedent to the law and institution of Moses; and so reducing things to the law of nature, gives a rule directive to all mankind in this matter.

2. The Pharisees inquired of our Savior about such a divorce as was absolute, and gave liberty of marriage after it. For they never heard of any other. The pretended separation *a mensa et thoro* only, was never heard of in the Old Testament. Now if our Savior does not answer concerning the same divorce about which they inquired, but another which they knew nothing of; he does not answer them, but delude them. They ask after one thing, and he answers another in nothing to their purpose. But this is not to be admitted: it were blasphemy to imagine it. Wherefore denying the causes of divorce which they allowed, and asserting fornication to be a just cause thereof, he allows in that case of that divorce which they inquired about, which was absolute, and from the bond of marriage.

Again the apostle Paul expressly sets the party at liberty to marry, who is maliciously and obstinately deserted, affirming that the Christian religion does not prejudice the natural right and privilege of men in such cases. "If the unbelieving depart, let him depart; a brother, or a sister, is not under bondage in such cases" (1 Cor. 7:15). If a person obstinately departs, on pretense of religion or otherwise, and will no more cohabit with a husband or wife, it is known that by the law of nature, and the usage of all nations, the deserted party, because, without his or her default all the ends of marriage are frustrated, is at liberty to marry. But it may be, it is not so among Christians. What shall a brother, or a sister, that is a Christian, do in this case, who is so departed from? Says the apostle: they are not in bondage, they are free, at liberty to marry again.

This is the constant doctrine of all Protestant churches in the world. And it has had place in the government of these nations: for Queen Elizabeth was born during the life of Queen Katharine, from whom her father was divorced.

General Index

Aaron, 389–90

Aaron ben Moses ben Asher, 86, 166, 171, 245, 248, 252

Abel, offering of, 470

abiding with Christ, 38, 386, 443–45, 465
  in acts of faith, 456–57
  in love, 457
  permanency against opposition, 447–48

Abraham
  justified by faith, 390–91
  servant of, 307

Abraham ibn David, 211

Abraham ibn Ezra, 27, 174, 229, 231, 237–40

Abrahamic covenant, 42, 588, 590–91

abstinence, in worship from all things Christ has not appointed, 310

abuse
  of God's patience, 491
  in the administration of the Lord's Supper, 313–14

acceptance with God, 320

adjuvant efficient cause, 35, 290, 291

adultery, as just cause of divorce, 603

affections
  and abiding in Christ, 466, 468
  kindled by the love of Christ, 36

aged Christians, contemplation of Christ, 466–67

agony of Christ, 358

Ainsworth, Henry, 247

Akiva ben Yosef, 204

Alexandrian Jews, 265

Alsted, Johann Heinrich, 58

Amama, Sixtinus, 58, 70, 173n55

Ames, William, 57

ancient Judaical coins, 226

Andrade, Diogo de Paiva de, 55, 199

angels
  knowledge of, 406
  not redeemed but confirmed, 406

anger of God, 490

Answer unto Two Questions, 40–41, 437, 557–71

antichrist, 502

Antioch, gave account of troubles and differences to church in Jerusalem, 542

Antiochus IV Epiphanes, 86, 163n9

"antiquarianization" of biblical scholarship, 22

Antoninus Pius, Emperor, 208, 209n95

Antwerp Polyglot Bible, 175–76, 177n80

apocryphal books, 129

apostasy, 455–56

Appendix to the *Biblia polyglotta*, 77, 151–52, 158, 180n9, 248, 251, 270
  New Testament lections contained in, 182–83

approaching judgments, 498

approaching the Table, 34-37, 347–49

approving the way of salvation by Christ, 449

Aquila, 168n30, 169, 208, 249

Arabic translation, 28, 154, 256–58

Aramaic Targums, 220n140

Arians, 554

Arias Montanus, Benedictus, 15, 55, 58, 70, 167n26, 175n62, 177, 182, 198, 244–45, 263

Aristobulus II, 211

Aristotle, 165

Scripture Index